THE MECHANISMS
OF GOVERNANCE

THE MECHANISMS
OF GOVERNANCE

Oliver E. Williamson

New York   Oxford
OXFORD UNIVERSITY PRESS
1996

Oxford University Press

Oxford   New York
Athens   Auckland   Bangkok   Bombay
Calcutta   Cape Town   Dar es Salaam   Delhi
Florence   Hong Kong   Istanbul   Karachi
Kuala Lumpur   Madras   Madrid   Melbourne
Mexico City   Nairobi   Paris   Singapore
Taipei   Tokyo   Toronto

and associated companies in
Berlin   Ibadan

Published by Oxford University Press, Inc.,
198 Madison Avenue, New York, New York 10016

Oxford is a registered trademark of Oxford University Press

Library of Congress Cataloging-in-Publication Data
Williamson, Oliver E.
The mechanisms of governance / Oliver E. Williamson,
p.   cm.
Includes bibliographic references (p.   ) and index.
ISBN 0-19-507824-1
1. Industrial organization (Economic theory)   2. Corporate
governance.   3. Transaction costs.   I. Title.
HD2326.W494   1996
658.4—dc20   95-6839

1 3 5 7 9 8 6 4 2

Printed in the United States of America
on acid-free paper

Permission to reprint selections from the following sources is gratefully acknowledged:

Chapter 1: "Transaction Cost Economics and the Carnegie Connection," forthcoming in the *Journal of Economic Behavior and Organization,* reprinted by permission of Elsevier Science, B.V. Amsterdam, the Netherlands.

Chapter 2: "Chester Barnard and the Incipient Science of Organization" in Oliver E. Williamson, ed., *Organization Theory: From Chester Barnard to the Present and Beyond* (1990), reprinted by permission of Oxford University Press.

Chapter 3: "Transaction Cost Economics" in Richard Schmalensee and Robert Willig, eds., *Handbook of Industrial Organization* (1989), vol. 1, pp. 136–82, reprinted by permission of Elsevier Science, B.V. Amsterdam, the Netherlands.

Chapter 4: "Comparative Economic Organization: The Analysis of Discrete Structural Alternatives," *Administrative Science Quarterly* 36 (June 1991), reprinted by permission of *Administrative Science Quarterly.*

Chapter 5: "Credible Commitments: Using Hostages to Support Exchange," *American Economic Review* 73 (September 1983), reprinted by permission of the American Economic Association.

Chapter 6: "Economic Institutions: Spontaneous and Intentional Governance," *Journal of Law, Economics, and Organization* 7 (special issue) (1991), reprinted by permission of Oxford University Press.

Chapter 7: "Corporate Finance and Corporate Governance," *Journal of Finance* 43 (July 1988), reprinted by permission of the *Journal of Finance.*

Chapter 8: "The Politics and Economics of Redistribution and Inefficiency," *Greek Economic Review* (1995), reprinted by permission of the *Greek Economic Review.*

Chapter 9: "Transaction Cost Economics and Organization Theory," *Industrial and Corporate Change* 2, 2 (1993), reprinted by permission of Oxford University Press.

Chapter 10: "Calculativeness, Trust, and Economic Organization," *Journal of Law and Economics* 36 (April 1993), reprinted by permission of the *Journal of Law and Economics.*

Chapter 11: "Delimiting Antitrust," *Georgetown Law Journal* 76 (December 1987), reprinted by permission of the Georgetown Law Journal Association.

Chapter 12: "Strategizing, Economizing, and Economic Organization," *Strategic Management Journal* 12 (special issue) (1991), reprinted by permission of John Wiley and Sons.

Chapter 13: "The Institutions and Governance of Economic Development and Reform," *Annual Bank Conference on Development Economics* (1994), reprinted by permission of the World Bank.

Chapter 14: "Transaction Cost Economics and the Evolving Science of Organization," in Arnold Heertje, ed., *Makers of Modern Economics II* (1995), reprinted by permission of Edward Elgar Publishing Ltd.

To my students, who have been both patient
and perceptive as we have struggled with
and through the problems of
complex economic organization.

Preface

My first concerted effort to study the economics of organization from a comparative institutional perspective in which economizing was featured and the analytical action was concentrated in the details of contracting was in my paper "The Vertical Integration of Production: Market Failure Considerations" (1971b). That approach turned out to have considerable generality and led to follow-on research. In combination with other, related papers, what has come to be known as *transaction cost economics* began to take shape.

The highways and byways of transaction cost economics are many and varied, and I have met many interesting and stimulating travelers along the way. Many of them were students who encountered transaction cost economics under the guise of organization theory, the economics of organization, the economics of institutions, or bureaucracy. Although not all of them were able to relate productively to the transaction cost economics enterprise from the outset, some did. Among those who were initially discouraged by "nonstandard analysis," many subsequently discovered that it provided a useful entré, even a framework, for their research.

Indeed, I think of the New Institutional Economics (NIE), of which transaction cost economics (TCE) is a part, as young people's economics. Not only are students more apt to be open to these ideas, but the New Institutional Economics requires that many disparate strands of new knowledge be joined. Students are often well positioned to do this.

By this, I do not mean to suggest that established scholars are not, have not been, and will not continue to be, vital to the exercise. Indeed, as demonstrated here and elsewhere, the NIE/TCE has been the beneficiary of many distinguished antecedents. The NIE also is the product of a movement whose time has come: The 1980s witnessed a revival of interest in institutions throughout the social sciences. Likewise, the issues with which TCE has been concerned and the manner in which it examines them resonate with much that is going on in economics.

The Mechanisms of Governance can be thought of as a good-news, bad-news story. The bad news is that economic organization is made vastly more complicated by the numerous hazards that accrue to the combination of uncertainty with bounded rationality and opportunism. Part of the good news is that the study of economic organization has become much more interesting as a result. The even better news is that human actors are often perceptive about these hazards and are rather good, even creative, in fashioning institutions that can mitigate them. Indeed, one answer to why we observe so many kinds of organization is that hazards come in many forms, for which nuanced governance structures are devised and chosen and/or selected.

Colleagues and students who have read and commented on the various papers on which this book is based and to whom I express my appreciation include Erin Anderson, Masahiko Aoki, Kenneth Arrow, James Baron, Dennis Carlton, Glenn Carroll, Richard Craswell, Paul DiMaggio, Frank Easterbrook, Melvin Eisenberg, Albert Fishlow, Herbert Gintis, Gillian Hadfield, Henry Hansmann, Bengt Holmstrom, Paul Joskow, Sanford Kadish, Benjamin Klein, David Kreps, David Levine, James March, Scott Masten, Claude Menard, Richard Nelson, Dan Ostas, Matthew Rabin, Michael Riordan, Roberta Romano, David Sappington, Neil Smelser, Pablo Spiller, Richard Stewart, Lars Stole, Richard Swedberg, David Teece, Lester Telser, Jean Tirole, Birger Wernerfelt, Robert Willig, and Brian Wright.

I would also like to express my appreciation to the Alexander von Humboldt-Stiftung and to Rudolf Richter and the Center for the New Institutional Economics for a satisfying visit to Saarbrücken; to the Sloan Foundation for Workshop and graduate student support while I was at Yale; to the Institute of Management, Innovation, and Organization at Berkeley for Workshop and other support; to the Olin Foundation and the Bradley Foundation for graduate student support at Berkeley; and to the Institute for Policy Research and the World Bank for research support.

Finally, I express my appreciation to two women who have been staunch supporters. My wife Dolores has been a good and loyal friend and companion in adventure. My secretary, Gwen Cheeseburg, has turned around endless numbers of revisions of my manuscripts with remarkable energy and good cheer.

My thanks to each and all of these people and to the students to whom this book is dedicated.

Berkeley, Calif.   O.E.W.
March 1995

Contents

IV. Public Policy

V. Controversy and Perspectives

THE MECHANISMS
OF GOVERNANCE

Prologue: The Mechanisms
of Governance

Institutions. What are they? How do they differ? To what purpose and effect? Where does the action reside? What are the mechanisms? What are the refutable implications? What are the public-policy ramifications? What do the data support? In contrast to both the main tradition in economics, which held that institutions figure negligibly in economic performance,[1] and the older institutional economics, which was hostile to orthodoxy and proposed substituting a more sociological approach to economic organization, the New Institutional Economics (1) holds that institutions matter and are susceptible to analysis (Matthews, 1986, p. 903), (2) is different from but not hostile to orthodoxy, and (3) is an interdisciplinary combination of law, economics, and organization in which economics is the first among equals.

This book develops the argument that many puzzles of economic organization turn on an examination and explication of the mechanisms of ex post governance. It operates at a more microanalytic level than is customary in economics, and it appeals to law (especially contract law) and organization (which is broadly construed to include organization theory, sociology, and political science) as well as to economics. Contrary to once-prevailing economic views that nonstandard and unfamiliar business practices and organizational forms operate in the service of price discrimination, barriers to entry, and/or risk aversion, I contend that the main purpose and effect of nonstandard forms are to economize on transaction costs. The identification, explication, and mitigation of contractual hazards—which take many forms, many of which long went unremarked—are central to the exercise.

As I shall show in this book, the analytical action resides in the details of transactions and governance. I propose a logic of organization in which the discriminating alignment of transactions with governance structures is the source of refutable implications. A wide variety of phenomena turn out to be

---

1. Believing institutions to be unimportant, orthodoxy aspired to work out of what Vernon Smith once referred to (in conversation) as an "institution-free core." Real successes with that project notwithstanding, it is a needlessly self-limiting exercise.

variations on a few key themes—in which farsighted contracting, credible commitments, and hazard mitigation figure prominently—in response to which a large and growing empirical literature has taken shape. This last is especially noteworthy. Awaiting a demonstration that institutional economics could generate new insights that are susceptible to empirical testing, the proposition that institutions matter was understandably dismissed as an obscurant to economic orthodoxy.

Although the New Institutional Economics, which has now been in progress for a quarter of a century,[2] does not have instant answers for all the interesting issues that can be raised, it does have answers to some and has promise for others. Legitimate skepticism notwithstanding, there is growing agreement that the institutional environment (laws, polity, etc.) and the institutions of governance (markets, hierarchies, etc.) matter a lot and in ways that are pertinent to industrial organization and much else, such as economic history, comparative economic systems, labor economics, economic development and reform, health care, business strategy, multinational business, and even aspects of corporate finance. Applications outside of economics to law and the other social sciences are numerous and growing.

1.   Institutions

Institutions have been variously defined. According to Douglass North, Institutions are "the humanly devised constraints that structure political, economic, and social interactions. They consist of both informal constraints (sanctions, taboos, customs, traditions, and codes of conduct), and formal rules (constitutions, laws, property rights)" (1991, p. 97). Elsewhere he argues that "institutions consist of a set of constraints on behavior in the form of rules and regulations; and, finally, a set of moral, ethical, behavioral norms which define the contours and that constrain the way in which the rules and regulations are specified and enforcement is carried out" (North, 1984, p. 8). Allan Schmid defines institutions as "sets of ordered relationships among people which define their rights, exposures to the rights of others, privileges, and responsibilities" (1972, p. 893); Daniel Bromley contends that institutions fall into two classes: conventions, and rules or entitlements (1989, p. 41); and Andrew Schotter views institutions as "regularities in behavior which are agreed to by all members of a society and which specify behavior in specific recurrent situations" (1981, p. 9). According to Eirik Furubotn and Rudolf Richter, "Modern institutional economics focuses on the institution of property, and on the system of norms governing the acquisition or transfer of property rights" (1991, p. 3).

These definitions of institutions mainly operate at the level of the institutional environment, the so-called rules of the game. The second, more microanalytic, level at which institutional economics works is at the level of the

2. For a sketch of antecedents to and early developments in the New Institutional Economics, see Williamson, 1975, chap. 1; 1985b, prologue.

institutions of governance. This book is principally concerned with the institutions of governance (markets, hybrids, hierarchies, bureaus).

One of the salient differences between the institutional environment and the institutions of governance is that the former mainly defines—can be thought of as constraints on—the environment of the latter. Focusing as I do on the institutions of governance, I mainly take the institutional environment as a given. A second difference is that the level of analysis is very different. The institutions of governance operate at the level of individual transactions, whereas the institutional environment is more concerned with composite levels of activity. (Mundane questions of whether to make or buy a component to be used in the manufacture of an automobile or whether to expand the hospital into outpatient and home health services are ones that arise at the level of governance. By contrast, composite economic growth and income distribution are more apt to be the objects of interest in an inquiry into the institutional environment.) A third difference is that the two operate differently with respect to intentionality.

Although both the institutional environment and the institutions of governance have evolutionary origins, the ramifications of each are different. The immense difficulties of changing the institutional environment in order to promote economizing outcomes in the aggregate helps explain North's conclusion that "economic history is overwhelmingly a story of economies that failed" (1991, p. 98). By contrast, the transaction cost economics story contemplates success: Taking the institutional environment as given, economic agents purportedly align transactions with governance structures to effect economizing outcomes. Not only is that the source of numerous refutable implications, but the data are largely corroborative.

As they are conceived here, institutions are the mechanisms of governance. Jon Elster's dictum that "explanations in the social sciences should be organized around (partial) *mechanisms* rather than (general) *theories*" (1994, p. 75; emphasis in original) is one to which I subscribe.

Kenneth Arrow defined transaction costs as the "costs of running the economic system" (1969, p. 48). Viewing the economic system from the standpoint of contract, transaction costs can be thought of as the costs of contracting.

Although the concept of transaction cost has widespread appeal, the measurement of transaction costs poses formidable difficulties. These difficulties are significantly relieved by looking at the issue of governance comparatively, so that the costs of one mode of governance are always examined in relation to alternative feasible modes. Differential transaction costs thus become the cutting edge. Chief among these costs are the costs of maladaptation. If a contract becomes maladapted by reason of an unanticipated disturbance, is it easy for the parties to get relief by turning elsewhere, or do they need to work through the problems together? If it is the latter, do the governance structure supports inspire confidence, or do they carry a large hazard premium? Prescribing governance structures in order to provide cost-effective relief against maladaptation hazards is a recurrent theme. More generally, the study of governance is concerned with the *identification, explication, and mitigation of all forms of contractual hazards.*

2.   Law, Economics, and Organization

The ways that transaction cost economics joins law, economics, and organization are sketched here. Inasmuch as this sketch is little more than a checklist of concepts and moves that are developed in succeeding chapters, unfamiliar readers may question whether all these concepts and moves are really necessary. Parsimony, after all, is what science is after.

As with most things, there are trade-offs. Simple theories that finesse or obfuscate core issues are unhelpful at best and can be misleading, even bankrupt, at worse. If, as I contend, the action is in the details of transactions and governance, we need to meet the problems on terms that are responsive to the needs.

2.1.   Economics

Transaction cost economics differs from orthodoxy—or at least a stereotypical, perhaps even a straw-man, version of orthodoxy—in numerous ways. Straw man or not, the attributes that I ascribe to orthodoxy will be recognized as those that appear in most microeconomic textbooks (although that is beginning to change). These differences include (1) the behavioral assumptions, (2) the transaction as the basic unit of analysis, (3) the description of the firm as a governance structure, (4) the insistence that property rights and contract are problematic, (5) the reliance on discrete structural analysis, and (6) the remediableness criterion. Let us consider each.

2.1.1.   Behavioral assumptions

The cognitive and self-interestedness assumptions from which transaction cost economics works are bounded rationality, defined as behavior that is *"intendedly* rational, but only *limitedly* so" (Simon, 1961, p. xxiv, emphasis in original), and opportunism, defined as self-interest seeking with guile, respectively. All complex contracts are unavoidably incomplete by reason of bounded rationality, and the convenient concept of contract as promise (unsupported by credible commitments) is vitiated by opportunism.

Orthodoxy invokes stronger rationality assumptions (often hyperrationality) and often suppresses the hazards of opportunism.

2.1.2.   Unit of analysis

The transaction is the basic unit of analysis, whereas orthodoxy is concerned with composite goods and services. Pin making, how to organize (more generally, how to govern) the "eighteen distinct operations" (transactions) made famous by Adam Smith (1776), rather than how many pins to make and at what price, becomes the object of the analysis.

2.1.3. Governance structure

Whereas the neoclassical firm is defined as a production function (a technological construction), transaction cost economics describes the firm as a governance structure (an organizational construction). According to the first definition, the firm is a technological black box in which inputs are transformed into outputs without reference to organization. According to the second definition, firms and markets are *alternative* modes of governance (Coase, 1937), and the allocation of activity between firms and markets is not taken as given but is something to be derived.

2.1.4. Problematic property rights and contracts

Problematic property rights and contracts are developed in the discussion of the law in Section 2.2. Suffice it to observe here that orthodoxy frequently assumes (often implicitly) that property rights are easy to define and that the courts knowledgeably enforce property rights and contracts at a negligible cost. Transaction cost economics treats property rights and contract as problematic.

2.1.5. Discrete structural analysis

Transaction cost economics describes alternative modes of governance—markets, hybrids, hierarchies, bureaus—as syndromes of related attributes, on which account governance structures differ from one another in discrete structural ways. Discrete structural rather than marginal modes of analysis are therefore employed (Simon, 1978). First-order economizing (getting the basic alignments right) rather than second-order refinements (adjusting the margins) is therefore featured.

2.1.6. Remediableness

Transaction cost economics eschews hypothetical ideals and insists that the relevant comparisons are with feasible alternatives, all of which are flawed (Coase, 1964). The relevant criterion is thus that of remediableness, according to which an outcome for which no superior alternative can be described and implemented with net gains is presumed to be efficient. (Not surprisingly, public-policy intervention to correct market failures is much more circumspect when the remediableness test is applied.)

Transaction cost economics clearly differs from orthodoxy in numerous and significant ways. How, then, can it be said that economics is the first among equals in the combined law, economics, and organization enterprise?

There are several reasons, the first of which is that transaction cost economics holds that the main purpose and effect of economic organization is economizing on transaction costs. Considerations of power (organization theory) and justice (law) thus give way to or are subsumed under the economizing calculus.[3]

Second, transaction cost economics is concerned with many of the same phenomena that are of interest to orthodoxy, such as vertical and lateral integration, nonstandard contracting, labor organization, regulation (and deregulation), corporate governance, and the uses of debt and equity. More generally, any problem that arises as or can be posed as a contracting problem can be examined to advantage in transaction cost economics terms. (Oligopoly is an example. Although this is often thought of as a market structure problem, it becomes a contracting problem when it is phrased in terms of the comparative efficacy of cartel agreements.)

But third, and most important, transaction cost economics subscribes to and works out of what I see to be the core commitments of orthodoxy, namely, the combination of a "rational spirit" with a "systems" perspective. Taken together, these lead to a relentlessly calculative and comparative approach to economic organization. Assuming that the excesses of calculativeness to which organization theorists have called our attention (March and Simon, 1958, chap. 3; see also chap. 10 of this book) can be avoided, a calculative approach to economic organization in which a rational spirit and a systems perspective are combined turns out to be a powerful lens.

Although all the social sciences have a stake in rationality analysis (Homans, 1958; Simon, 1978), what distinguishes economists is that they push the approach further and more persistently. As Arrow put it: "An economist by training thinks of himself as the guardian of rationality, the ascriber of rationality to others, and the prescriber of rationality to the social world. It is this role that I will play" (1974, p. 16). History records that that has been a productive role—for Arrow as well as more generally. Rationality is a deep and pervasive condition that is manifested in many subtle ways.

The many accomplishments of hyperrationality analysis notwithstanding,[4] the rational spirit approach is not coterminous with hyperrationality. Strong form, semistrong form, and weak form rational spirits are usefully distinguished. Whereas the strong form subscribes to hyperrationality, the latter two work out of bounded rationality. Semistrong form analysis joins bounded

3. There are two caveats. First, firms are not concerned with transaction costs to the exclusion of revenues and production costs. (For a model in which revenues, production costs, and transaction costs all are included, see Chapter 3 of this book.) A great deal of action nevertheless turns on transaction cost economizing, the importance of which is ignored or finessed by most constructions. Second, excesses of calculativeness are a legitimate concern (see especially Chapter 10 of this book).

4. The outer limits of hyperrationality reasoning are reached by the Arrow–Debreu model of comprehensive contracting, according to which contracts for all goods and services across all future contingencies are made among all agents at the outset. Although the Coase theorem, according to which the assignment of liability one way rather than another has no allocative efficiency consequences, is a partial rather than a general equilibrium construction, it similarly assumes zero transaction costs (Coase, 1960). Analyses of both kinds make patently unrealistic assumptions about the cognitive ability of human actors to receive, store, retrieve, and process information.

rationality with farsighted contracting, and the weak form joins bounded rationality with myopic contracting.

Transaction cost economics is a semistrong form construction. It concedes that comprehensive contracting is not a feasible option (by reason of bounded rationality), yet it maintains that many economic agents have the capacities both to learn and to look ahead, perceive hazards, and factor these back into the contractual relation, thereafter to devise responsive institutions.[5] In effect, limited but intended rationality is translated into incomplete but farsighted contracting. The concept of contract from which transaction cost economics works is therefore that of "incomplete contracting in its entirety," which has the appearance of a contradiction in terms. In fact, such a concept of contract presents healthy tensions to which both economics and organization theory can productively relate, and systems considerations are raised.

One of the advantages that Ronald Coase ascribes to economics, as compared with the other social sciences, is that economics adopts a systems conception of the issues:

> The success of economists in moving into the other social sciences is a sign that they possess certain advantages in handling the problems of those disciplines. One is, I believe, that they study the economic system as a unified interdependent system and, therefore, are more likely to uncover the basic interrelationships within a social system than is someone less accustomed to looking at the working of a system as a whole.... [The] study of economics makes it difficult to ignore factors which are clearly important and which play a role in all social systems. (1978, pp. 209–10).

Farsighted, as against myopic, contracting is, I submit, the principal systems move that distinguishes economics from the other social sciences. It is also what the other social sciences have most to learn from economics. The "handing on" of benefits—from producers to consumers as the competitive process unfolds (Schumpeter, 1947, p. 155)—and the remediableness criterion for assessing "failures" are related systems concepts to which economics appeals.

This is quite different from the more familiar claim that "what economics has to export ... is ... a very particular and special form of [rationality]—that of the utility maximizer" (Simon, 1978, p. 2). Other social scientists have been understandably chary of such trade. But what was once a yawning abyss between economics and the other social sciences has begun to close as non-

---

Counterfactuals are often illuminating, however, and there is no disputing that the fictions of comprehensive contracting/zero transaction costs have been productive. One instructive way to proceed is to use the counterfactuals to display what an "ideal" system would accomplish and thereafter to inquire into what factors are responsible for missing markets, in response to which nonmarket forms of organization often arise (Arrow, 1963b), and where and why positive transaction costs arise, whereupon assignments of property rights one way rather than another do have efficiency consequences.

5. This is not, however, done at the behest of or as a concession to orthodoxy. It is done because the idea of "incomplete contracting in its entirety" is a productive research orientation. That orthodoxy has been so successful, as compared with rival approaches, is in no small measure because farsighted contracting is an extraordinarily powerful analytic concept.

economists (especially political scientists) have begun to recognize merit in a systems conception of farsighted (but incomplete) contracting and as economists have gotten beyond the idea that bounded rationality implies "satisficing" (which has intuitive appeal but has not yet to prove itself as a productive research program in economics; Aumann, 1985) and have begun to relate instead to the idea that bounded rationality implies incomplete contracting. In addition, many economists have come to terms with the idea that "organization matters" (Kreps, 1992).

2.2.   Law

Contract law and the limits of court ordering play important roles in transaction cost economics, in two different ways. First, transaction cost economics holds that each generic mode of governance (market, hybrid, hierarchy, etc.) is supported by and in significant ways is defined by a distinctive form of contract law. The idea of contract laws (plural) rather than of a single, all-purpose law of contract thus plays an active role in transaction cost economics (Summers, 1969; Macneil, 1974, 1978).

Second, transaction cost economics subscribes to Karl Llewellyn's notion of contract as framework. According to this, a contract between two parties "almost never accurately indicates real working relations, but ... affords a rough indication around which such relations vary, an occasional guide in cases of doubt, and a norm of ultimate appeal when the relations cease in fact to work" (Llewellyn, 1931, p. 737). The main contractual action thus takes place between the parties in the context of private ordering, and court ordering appears late, if at all.[6]

That reverses the "legal centralism" tradition, which holds that "disputes require 'access' to a forum external to the original social setting of the dispute [and that] remedies will be provided as prescribed in some body of authoritative learning and dispensed by experts who operate under the auspices of the state" (Galanter, 1981, p. 1). The facts, however, reveal something else. Most disputes, including many that under current rules could be brought to a court, are resolved by avoidance, self-help, and the like (Galanter, 1981, p. 2). That is because in "many instances the participants can devise more satisfactory solutions to their disputes than can professionals constrained to apply general rules on the basis of limited knowledge of the dispute" (Galanter, 1981, p. 4). Private ordering through ex post governance is therefore where the main action resides.

2.3.   Organization

As indicated, transaction cost economics owes its behavioral assumptions to organization theory. These are truly important, in that all interesting problems of complex economic organization would vanish were it not for the twin

---

6. Access to the courts for purposes of ultimate appeal nevertheless delimits threat positions and thereby promotes more effective private ordering.

conditions of bounded rationality and opportunism. Herbert Simon's remarks are apposite: "Nothing is more fundamental in setting our research agenda and informing our research methods than our view of the nature of the human beings whose behavior we are studying" (1985, p. 303). The reasons for this should become apparent in this book.

The second significant way in which transaction cost economics relates to organization theory is in regard to intertemporal process transformations. Because organization theory has been much more alert than economics to some of the main intertemporal features and because intertemporal process transformations play a central role in transaction cost economics, transaction cost economics owes a special debt to organization theory.

Developing this is beyond the scope of a prologue, but I nonetheless put the reader on notice that the following list of process transformations (which will be discussed later) are pertinent: (1) the Fundamental Transformation; (2) the impossibility of selective intervention; the (3) costs (bureaucratization) and (4) benefits (which often take the form of tacit knowledge) that predictably accrue to internal organization and are a manifestation of the proposition that "organization has a life of its own"; (5) the limits of calculativeness, especially piecemeal excesses of calculativeness that have adverse systems consequences; (6) the differential efficacy of reputation effect mechanisms; and (7) the limits of natural selection (in general and as these apply to different forms of organization, such as for-profits, nonprofits, and bureaus). Of these seven process features, the first two are actually transaction cost economics constructions (but appeal to organization theory nonetheless), and the last two are seriously underdeveloped (here and elsewhere in the literature).

3. Governance

Not only does the study of governance pose distinctive challenges, but also much of the predictive content and most of the empirical research in institutional economics has been at the level of governance (Matthews, 1986, p. 907).

3.1. Antecedents

As explained elsewhere, there are many antecedents to the governance arguments developed here (Williamson, 1975, chap. 1, 1985b, prologue). My purpose here is to make special note of two.

Lon Fuller's definition of *eunomics* as "the science, theory or study of good order and workable arrangements" (1954, p. 477) is very much in the spirit of what I refer to as *governance.* As Fuller later observed, "the primary concern of eunomics is with the means aspect of the means–end relation" (1954, p. 478). Governance is also an exercise in assessing the efficacy of alternative modes (means) of organization. The object is to effect good order through the mechanisms of governance. A governance structure is thus usefully thought of as an institutional framework in which the integrity of a transaction, or related set of transactions, is decided.

John R. Commons also anticipated much of the conceptual argument in his insisitence that "the ultimate unit of activity ... must contain in itself the three principles of conflict, mutuality, and order. This unit is a transaction" (1932, p. 4). Not only does transaction cost economics agree that the transaction is the basic unit of analysis but also that governance is the means by which *order* is accomplished in a relation in which potential *conflict* threatens to undo or upset opportunities to realize *mutual* gains.

After making the transaction the basic unit of analysis, the question that then needs to be resolved is what the principal dimensions are on which transactions differ. Furthermore, because order is accomplished through governance, similar efforts need to be made to identify the principal dimensions on which governance structures differ. A predictive theory of economic organization will, moreover, indicate which transactions will be organized how. The discriminating alignment hypothesis, to which transaction cost economics owes much of its predictive content, is this: Transactions, which differ in their attributes, are aligned with governance structures, which differ in their cost and competence, so as to effect a discriminating—mainly a transaction cost–economizing—result.

3.2. A Sketch of the Core Argument

As indicated, transaction cost economics is an effort to identify, explicate, and mitigate contractual hazards. In general, all hazards can be attributed to the twin behavioral assumptions from which transaction cost economics works: bounded rationality and opportunism. Although that does not get us very far—in that the resulting theory of organization reduces mainly to ex post rationalization—it nonetheless constitutes progress. First, theories of organization that ignore or suppress either of these behavioral conditions will never reach the hazard conditions with which transaction cost economics is chiefly concerned.[7] Accordingly, bounded rationality and opportunism are crucial first steps. Second, the microanalytic attributes for describing transactions need to be delimited. Those attributes that create hazards, by reason of bounds on rationality and opportunism, are the subset of relevance. Third, the feasibility and efficacy with which governance structures serve to mitigate hazards relate directly to bounded rationality and opportunism.

Intuition tells us that simple governance structures should mediate simple transactions and that complex governance structures should be reserved for complex transactions. Using a complex structure to govern a simple transaction incurs unneeded costs, and using a simple structure to govern a complex transaction invites strain. But what is simple and complex in transactional and governance respects?

---

7. I attended a workshop in the mid-1980s at which formal work on incomplete contracting was being presented. One of the economists in the audience protested that the idea of noncontractibility was ad hoc and would have been denounced by the authors of the paper two years earlier. The authors did not disagree that the idea of incomplete contracting would earlier have concerned them. Methodological rectitude was not, however, their research criterion. Rather, making headway in understanding complex organization was the purpose of the exercise.

Technology is an obvious candidate, but anomalies quickly appear. Some high-technology transactions (e.g., the procurement of semiconductors) are contractually very simple, and some low-technology transactions (e.g., the supply of molten pig iron from a blast furnace to a rolling mill) may create serious contractual hazards. In addition, although hierarchies have the appearance of being more complex governance structures than markets are, that can be disputed. As Friedrich Hayek observed, "The price system is just one of those formations which man has learned to use . . . after he stumbled upon it without understanding it" (1945, p. 528). If the "natural" way to manage transactions is through authority (hierarchy), then the presumption that "in the beginning there were markets" must be reversed. Authority is something with which we have direct experience (in managing households and more generally) and think that we understand. By comparison, markets are where the subtleties reside.

Transaction cost economics (1) eschews intuitive notions of complexity and asks what the dimensions are on which transactions differ that present differential hazards. It further (2) asks what the attributes are on which governance structures differ that have hazard mitigation consequences. And it (3) asks what main purposes are served by economic organization. Because, moreover, contracting takes place over time, transaction cost economics (4) inquiries into the intertemporal transformations that contracts and organizations undergo. Also, in order to establish better why governance structures differ in discrete structural ways, it (5) asks why one form of organization (e.g., hierarchy) is unable to replicate the mechanisms found to be efficacious in another (e.g., the market). The object is to implement this microanalytic program, this interdisciplinary joinder of law, economics, and organization,[8] in a "modest, slow, molecular, definitive" way.[9]

---

8. By way of illustration, transaction cost economics attributes many of the problems of complex contracting to a hitherto little remarked but, in fact, widespread condition of "asset specificity" (which is a measure of asset redeployability and gives rise to the hazard of bilateral dependency). It also observes that one of the principal reasons that governance structures differ is because they work out of different contract law regimes. It furthermore holds that the central problem of economic organization is that of adaptation (Barnard, 1938; Hayek, 1945), of which autonomous and cooperative kinds are distinguished. One of the intertemporal transformations that transaction cost economics calls to attention is the so-called Fundamental Transformation, according to which a large numbers condition at the outset is sometimes transformed into a small numbers–exchange relation thereafter. Upon posing and explicating the "impossibility of selective intervention," a deeper understanding why mechanisms cannot be replicated across governance structures obtains. Although much of this is opaque to the uninitiated reader, I should point out that all five of these moves take transaction cost economics into the details of transactions and governance in an interdisciplinary way. All five are elaborated in subsequent pages.

9. The full quotation (source unknown) reads:

"The longer I live, citizen . . ."—this is the way the great passage in Peguy begins, words I once loved to say (I had them almost memorized)—"The longer I live, citizen, the less I believe in the efficiency of sudden illuminations that are not accompanied or supported by serious work, the less I believe in the efficiency of conversion, extraordinary, sudden and serious, in the efficiency of sudden passions, and the more I believe in the efficiency of modest, slow, molecular, definitive work. The longer I live the less I believe in the efficiency of an extraordinary sudden social revolution, improvised,

3.3.   Hazards

The fact that hazards can take many forms has been recognized only gradually as transaction cost economics has moved beyond from its initial preoccupation with vertical integration (Coase, 1937; Williamson, 1971b) to consider related contractual transactions (labor, finance, vertical market restraints, and other forms of nonstandard contracting, regulation, trust, and the like) and to push beyond governance (markets, hybrids, hierarchies, bureaus) to consider the influence of the institutional environment (the political, legal, and social rules of the game).

Among the hazards with which transaction cost economics is concerned are (1) the aforementioned hazards of bilateral dependency, (2) hazards that accrue to weak property rights,[10] (3) measurement hazards (especially in conjunction with multiple tasks) (Holmstrom and Milgrom, 1991) and/or over-searching (Barzel, 1982; Kenney and Klein, 1983), and (4) intertemporal hazards, which can take the form of disequilibrium contracting, real-time responsiveness, long latency, and strategic abuse. Also, (5) the hazards that accrue to weaknesses in the institutional environment (North and Weingast, 1989; Levy and Spiller, 1994; Weingast, 1995) are important, need to be explicated, and are beginning to be factored in.

Variety notwithstanding, all these hazards entail variations on the following themes: (1) All the hazards would vanish but for the twin conditions of bounded rationality and opportunism; (2) the action resides in the details of transactions and the mechanisms of governance; and (3) superior performance is realized by working out of a farsighted but incomplete contracting setup in which the object is to use institutions as (cost-effective) instruments for hazard mitigation. To repeat, the identification, explication, and mitigation of hazards through governance are what transaction cost economics is.

3.4.   Some Examples

3.4.1.   Insurance

Insurance issues are not a matter of great concern to transaction cost economics, as they turn on considerations of risk aversion (which transaction cost economics typically eschews) (Williamson, 1985b, pp. 388–89; Goldberg, 1990). However, insurance also raises governance issues.

It is not controversial that risk pooling through insurance is often an efficient hazard-mitigating response to stochastic events that, if realized, would cause severe individual burdens, examples being flood, fire, earthquake, per-

---

marvelous, with or without guns and impersonal dictatorship—and the more I believe in the efficiency of modest, slow, molecular, definitive work."

10. Weak property rights pose contractual hazards for which "convoluted" forms of organization are sometimes the cost-effective response. For examples of "inefficiency by design," see Benjamin Klein and Keith Leffler, 1981; David Teece, 1986; Jan Heide and George John, 1988; and Terry Moe, 1990a, 1990b.

sonal accidents, and disease. But insurance must also come to terms with recalcitrant problems that have their origins in human nature. The most familiar of these problems take the forms of adverse selection and moral hazard, which arise because individuals will not candidly disclose their objective risk attributes (adverse selection) and individuals who are covered by insurance will not exercise the same degree of due care (moral hazard).

Note that both these problems have behavioral origins. Adverse selection would vanish if individuals candidly disclosed their true attributes (the absence of opportunism), and moral hazard would vanish if ex post behavior were costlessly known to all parties (a strong variety of unbounded rationality).

The first response to an added hazard of any kind is to price it out. Farsighted insurers recognize hazards of both kinds and factor them into the terms on which insurance is made available. Good and poor risks respond to such a hazard premium differently, however, and the market may unravel. The second response is to "tune up" the incentive alignment. For example, a menu of contracts (e.g., different deductibles) sometimes supports a separating equilibrium between high-risk and low-risk types (Rothschild and Stiglitz, 1976), whereupon market viability is restored. But there may also be a third response, which goes beyond the ex ante incentive alignment. Enter ex post governance.

In the context of insurance, the use of experience rating (a type of reputation effect mechanism, which sometimes works well and sometimes poorly, depending on the particulars) is an obvious possibility. The requirements that insurance claims be documented, possibly supported by multiple, independent estimates, and subject to review by insurance adjusters are further ex post safeguards. It can also be stipulated that contested claims be presented to a particular forum (e.g., arbitration). And the insurance company, lest it be a fly-by-night firm that collects premiums up front and thereafter vanishes (or declares bankruptcy), may also be placed under regulatory oversight by the state.

But the more general argument is this: Insurance is merely the tip of the hazard mitigation iceberg. Not only are there many other hazards for which insurance is not the appropriate response, but many of these added hazards may create much more complicated hazard mitigation problems. Inasmuch as the efficacy of ex ante incentive alignment for hazard mitigation purposes becomes even more problematic outside the insurance arena, ex post governance becomes all the more important.

3.4.2. Bilateral dependency

The paradigm problem out of which transaction cost economics works is that of vertical integration. This is the mundane make-or-buy decision in intermediate product markets.

Working out of the firm-as-production function construction, Joe Bain held that "physical or technical aspects" were responsible for vertical integration. The unified ownership of a blast furnace and a rolling mill was thus explained by the thermal economies that result by locating these two stages in close proximity. Moreover, vertical integration that lacked this physical or technical aspect purportedly had an anticompetitive purpose and effect (Bain, 1968, p. 381).

Transaction cost economics views the firm not in technological but in comparative organizational terms and takes issue with both parts of Bain's argument. Not only is it unnecessary for a single firm to own both the blast furnace and the rolling mill in order for thermal economies to be realized, but many of the problematic uses of vertical integration to which Bain referred—integration into distribution by manufacturers, and the ownership of specialized transport facilities by a processor of iron ore and petroleum—often serve economizing purposes (of a transactional rather than a technological kind). Thus the thermal economies to which Bain refers can be realized by locating the blast furnace and the rolling mill on a common site and mediating by contract the exchange between the autonomous owners of each stage. If the unified ownership of both stages is somehow more efficient, it must be because the contract between collocated stages is mediated more effectively by hierarchy than by market.

The generic transaction cost economics interpretation of this and related conditions of bilateral dependency is this: (1) Although large numbers of parties may compete (say, to deliver molten ingot) at the outset, transactions that are supported by significant investments in durable transaction-specific assets undergo a Fundamental Transformation, in that what was a large numbers–supply condition at the outset is transformed into a small numbers–exchange relation thereafter, as a consequence of which the parties become bilaterally dependent; (2) because all complex contracts are unavoidably incomplete and because adaptation is the central problem of economic organization, autonomous contracts in bilaterally dependent circumstances are fraught with maladaptation hazard; and (3) although the unified ownership of both stages incurs bureaucratic costs of its own, hierarchy (vertical integration) becomes the cost-effective governance structure as asset specificity progressively deepens.

Or recall the pin-making example to which I referred earlier. One way to proceed is to treat the pin factory as a production function that transforms wire into finished pins. Because organization is not problematic, the economic problem is deciding how much to produce. Assuming that price is a parameter, marginal analysis reveals that output should be set so that marginal cost equals price.

But one could also take the pin factory in a different direction. Assuming that there are eighteen distinct operations (transactions) to be organized, one could ask what the ramifications are of different forms of ownership (each stage could be independently owned, or all could be collectively owned, or ownership could be concentrated in a single capitalist) and what the ramifications are of different decision-making mechanisms (consensus, autonomy, hierarchy, etc.). Indeed, one could even ask whether the pin-making factory should integrate backward into wire making or forward into distribution. One could also examine the possibility of subcontracting out some of the manufacturing operations.

The neoclassical apparatus clearly enjoys the advantage for studying the price and output decision. This same apparatus is distinctly limited, however, when issues of ownership/decision making/boundaries of the firm are raised. This latter group of issues becomes grist for the transaction cost economics mill.

3.4.3. Bureaucracy

In comparison with the study of market failure, the study of hierarchical failure is seriously underdeveloped. If, however, each generic mode of governance enjoys distinctive strengths and weaknesses, then that disparity should be redressed. Chief among the issues that warrant study in this connection is that of bureaucracy.

On the one hand, we all know that bureaucracy is beset with costs, many of which appear to be mindless and some of which appear to be insidious. Almost surely, the added costs of bureaucracy are responsible for limitations in firm size.

Explicating that intuition turns out to be elusive if the problem of organization is faced, as it should be, in a genuinely comparative–institutional way. The first thing to observe in this connection is that all firms, both large and small, are bureaucracies. The second thing is that all comparative assessments need to hold constant the composition of activity to be organized. Subject to that provision, the relevant question is whether the aggregate costs of bureaucracy will be larger or smaller if the output in question is produced by two or more smaller firms or by one combined entity.

To keep things simple, suppose that there are two successive stages of production. One stage supplies the intermediate product to the second stage, and the second stage produces the final product. How will the aggregate costs of bureaucracy compare if these two stages are independent or unified?

Answering that turns on how the two stages are organized under a unified ownership. Assume for this purpose that the acquisition proceeds according to the following rules for "selective intervention": (1) Each stage continues its business as usual except when the acquiring division exercises authority over the acquired division; (2a) the acquired division agrees to accede to the authority of the owner without resistance whenever asked; and (2b) the acquiring division intervenes always but only when expected net gains from adaptation can be projected.

If selective intervention could be implemented in this way, unified ownership would always be superior to autonomy. The reason is that the unified firm could never do worse (through replication) and would sometimes do better (when implementing unprogrammed adaptations to unanticipated disturbances). Thus, whereas the unified firm can implement adaptations to unprogrammed disturbances by fiat, the autonomous stages would need to bargain these through to agreement, which entails haggling costs and causes delays. The result is that a unified ownership that observes the strictures of selective intervention can always beat autonomy.

That, however, assumes that selective intervention can in fact be implemented. Because repeated application of this reasoning leads to a counterfactual prediction—namely, that everything will be organized in one large firm—presumably something is wrong. Since the action purportedly resides in the details, then the mechanisms for implementing selective intervention must be the culprit.

Although the arguments here become rather involved (Williamson, 1985b, chap. 6), they are essentially the following: All three parts of this described "agreement" are defective. Not only are the incentives unavoidably degraded when transactions are moved from market to hierarchy, on which account replication is not a feasible option, but also mere words, without more, are not self-enforcing. This applies both to the assent agreement and, even more, to the agreement to intervene only for good cause. Because incentives are degraded and because neither assent nor selective intervention agreements can be costlessly enforced, acquisition gains are always attended by added bureaucratic costs.

The argument helps explain why the puzzle of limits to firm size persisted for so long, from Frank Knight's early reference to this puzzle (in 1921 and 1933; see Knight, 1965) through Ronald Coase's restatement of the problem in 1937 through my purported "solution" to the puzzle in 1967. The puzzle persisted because the issues were never correctly articulated in the appropriate comparative institutional terms, and so a microanalytic assessment of the relevant comparative contracting features was never attempted.

4.   A Sketch of This Book

Judging from my experience and that of some of my students and colleagues, the transaction cost economics approach to the study of economic organization can be infectious. What for me started out as the study of vertical integration (Williamson, 1971b) evolved into *Markets and Hierarchies* (1975). That in turn was followed by *The Economic Institutions of Capitalism* (1985b). This book converts the enterprise into a trilogy.

Although there have been false starts and frustrations along the way, doing institutional economics has been challenging and rewarding. Also, as I tell my students, institutional economics is good for your health: Witness that so many institutional economists have long lives. But ever wary of malpractice suits, I quickly add that institutional economics is not for everyone. I nevertheless take satisfaction in the fact that there is increasing agreement with the twin propositions to which I referred at the outset: Institutions matter, and institutions are susceptible to analysis.

Markets and Hierarchies was the product of two key ideas. First, as a result of my Carnegie background, I was persuaded that the combined study of economics and organization was a fruitful undertaking. (This is developed in chapter 1.) Second, Coase (1937, 1960) and Arrow (1963a, 1963b, 1969) persuaded me that transaction cost economizing was a coherent explanation for many nonstandard and purportedly problematic organization and contracting practices. Although both the interdisciplinary joinder of economics with organization theory and the study of transaction cost economizing have substantial merit and can stand alone, the combination has turned out—for many (Kreps, 1992) if not all of us (Posner, 1993a)—to be especially productive.

Moving beyond *Markets and Hierarchies,* my continuing study of economic organization convinced me that the regularities were even more pronounced and the applications more numerous than I had previously imagined. *The Economic Institutions of Capitalism* was an effort to make a more prominent place for the law and to extend, refine, and, especially, further operationalize key transaction cost economics concepts.[11]

If Coase's classic 1937 article, "The Nature of the Firm," is interpreted as an informal statement of the transaction cost economics project, then *Markets and Hierarchies* can be regarded as a preformal effort and *Institutions* as a semiformal effort to implement the program. Fully formal work of this genre is illustrated by the evolving theory of incomplete contracting (Grossman and Hart, 1986; Holmstrom and Tirole, 1989; Hart and Moore, 1990; Riordan (1990); Kreps, 1990b; Aghion and Tirole, 1994), which is a forbiddingly difficult undertaking.[12]

Taken together, *Markets and Hierarchies* and *Institutions* set out the general approach and basic framework from which transaction cost economics works. There is not, I think, the same need to tell a coherent story today, and I do not attempt to do so in *The Mechanisms of Governance.* Rather, my purpose is to extend the analysis of comparative economic organization and to display the wide array of interesting applications that can be and remain to be made by studying complex economic organization from a combined law, economics, and organizations perspective in which hazard mitigation through the mechanisms of governance is featured.

That transaction cost economics has had better success[13] than earlier efforts to craft an economics of institutions is explained by (1) a series of significant interim developments—in law (Coase, 1960; Macneil, 1974, 1978), economics (Alchian, 1950; Muth, 1961; Arrow, 1963b, 1969), organization theory (March and Simon, 1958; Cyert and March, 1963), and combinations

11. Although a number of basic issues of economics and organization were reconceptualized in *Markets and Hierarchies,* a sustained research program required more. Papers that helped accomplish operationalization included "Franchise Bidding for Natural Monopoly—in General and with Respect to CATV" (Williamson, 1976), "Vertical Integration, Appropriable Rents, and the Competitive Contracting Process" (Klein, Crawford, and Alchian, 1978), "Transaction Cost Economics: The Governance of Contractual Relations" (Williamson, 1979b), "The Role of Market Forces in Assuring Contractual Performance" (Klein and Leffler, 1981), and "Credible Commitments: Using Hostages to Support Exchange" (Williamson, 1983). *The Economic Institutions of Capitalism* (1985b) pulled these and other materials together, and an empirical research program has progressively taken shape (see n. 14).

12. The book by Paul Milgrom and John Roberts (1992) works partly out of a transaction cost economics setup and is also in the more fully formal modeling tradition.

13. Concurring views include those of Matthews (1986), Arrow (1987, p. 734), Eirik Furubotn and Rudolf Richter (1991), Coase (1992), and Gerald Davis and Walter Powel (1992). Skeptics include Geoffrey Hodgson (1988), Richard Posner (1993a), and (sometimes) Milgrom and Roberts (1988). I respond to Posner in Williamson (1993d).

thereof (Chandler, 1962; Arrow, 1974)—and (2) an insistence on refutable implications coupled with an ambitious program of empirical research. But for its predictive content, transaction cost economics would be met with a shrug. Without an empirical research program demonstrating that the data line up, the exercise would remain a curiosity. As it is, transaction cost economics is an empirical success story.[14]

Like both *Markets and Hierarchies* and *Institutions,* this book is based on a collection of my recently published papers. With the exception of this prologue and the prefactory remarks that introduce each of the five parts, all the chapters have appeared elsewhere. Although I was not consciously working on "the mechanisms of governance" over the past decade, the central message and recurring theme are that the mechanisms of ex post governance are where the main action of economic organization resides.

The Mechanisms of Governance is organized in five parts, of which Part I is an overview. Concepts and applications are developed in Part II. The complementary relations between transaction cost economics and organization theory are the focus of Part III. Public-policy applications are developed in Part IV, and Part V deals with recent controversy and perspectives.

14. For recent empirical surveys, see Paul Joskow, 1988, and Peter Klein and Howard Shelanski, 1995. Some of the more important empirical papers are reprinted in volume 2 of Oliver Williamson and Scott Masten, eds., *Transaction Cost Economics* (1995).

I

OVERVIEW

This volume begins, as it should, with some recollections about my years in the Ph.D. program at the Graduate School of Industrial Administration at Carnegie-Mellon (then Carnegie Tech). Those were exciting days. Orchestrating cutting-edge interdisciplinary research and teaching are never easy; the number of failed efforts speak to that. But in the late 1950s and early 1960s, Carnegie was the place to be. Chapter 1 recalls those events and describes how transaction cost economics relates to them.

Although the study of organization goes back to antiquity (to include Aristotle), the modern classic is Chester Barnard's book *The Functions of the Executive* (1938). Barnard was a businessman with an unusually keen economic intuition about what was central to the study of organization. Not only did the prevailing approach to management, which featured abstract "principles" of organization, fail to engage the relevant issues as Barnard had experienced them, but even worse, the social sciences paid little heed to the formal and purposeful features of organization to which Barnard ascribed special importance: "There was lacking much recognition of formal organization as a most important characteristic of social life" (Barnard, 1938, p. ix).

Having sensed that formal organizations possessed a common conceptual core and finding little in the literature that helped explicate that condition, Barnard set about to provide the requisite framework himself. A remarkable transformation of the study of organization resulted. As Thomas Kuhn and others have observed, new paradigms are often associated with those who are young or new to a crisis-ridden field (Kuhn, 1970, p. 144). Barnard's relation to and impact on organization theory is an illustration.

Chapter 2 argues that a new science of organization is in progress, of which transaction cost economics is a part. Although we have come a long way since Barnard first commented on the unmet (and even unrecognized) need for a science of organization (1938, p. 290), that project still has a long

21

way to go and is better described as an aspiration rather than a realization. I nevertheless predict that the 1990s will be remembered as the decade when the New Science came of age.[1]

The rudiments of transaction cost economics are developed in Chapter 3, "Transaction Cost Economics." This chapter is a survey and was written for the *Handbook of Industrial Organization* (Schmalensee and Willig, 1989). In it, I sketch the general approach, set out some of the apparatus and main applications, and examine public-policy ramifications, mainly of antitrust and regulation/deregulation. Because any issue that arises or can be posed as a contracting problem can be examined to advantage in transaction cost–economizing terms, transaction cost economics can be and has been brought to bear on many and varied issues. Indeed, the practical applications and research opportunities are unending.

---

1. That a science of organization is in progress can be inferred from the new journals that have appeared since 1980 in support of this project. These include (years of first publication in parentheses): *Managerial and Decision Economics* (1980), *Journal of Economic Behavior and Organization* (1980), *Journal of Law, Economics, and Organization* (1985), *Organization Science* (1988), *Rational Choice* (1990), *Industrial and Corporate Change* (1991), *Journal of Economics and Management Strategy* (1992), *Journal of Business Economics* (1994), *Economic Design* (1994), and *Journal of Corporate Finance: Contracting, Governance, and Organization* (1994). Many other journals, moreover, have begun to feature the study of economic organization more prominently. New books, of which *Economics, Organization, and Management* (Milgrom and Roberts, 1992) is an example, likewise speak to these developments.

1

Transaction Cost Economics and the Carnegie Connection

This chapter tracks my remarks at the September 1993 conference honoring Richard M. Cyert. It begins with some recollections of my years as a graduate student at the Graduate School of Industrial Administration (GSIA) in the early 1960s. I then shift to transaction cost economics and how this project relates to what I learned from Dick Cyert and others at Carnegie.

1. Carnegie in the 1960s

Dick Cyert deserves great credit for many things. One of those things is that he helped open up the world of economics to organization theory.

Thus whereas the other social sciences—political science, organization theory, aspects of sociology and social psychology, parts of the law—have regularly availed themselves of economics, economics was always special: It was self-contained; it was the queen of the social sciences; it played hardball.

Dick Cyert did not think that any of the social sciences (economics included) were self-contained, and he and others at Carnegie were determined to correct this misconception. The Cyert and March book, *A Behavioral Theory of the Firm* (1963), joined economics and organization theory to pry open what had been a black box, in order to examine the business firm in more operationally engaging ways.

Those who lived through the 1960s will recall that the world of economics was not overjoyed with these intrusions. But a beachhead was established from which further excursions could be launched.

To be sure, the idea that firms are production functions to which an assumption of profit maximization is appropriately ascribed is still useful for many purposes. But there are many other purposes for which a richer conception of firm and market organization—in the spirit of the behavioral theory, of evolutionary theory, of transaction cost economics, or of still other variants—is needed. Dick Cyert, Jim March, Herbert Simon, and others at Carnegie opened the door to these developments.

Carnegie has always been an incredible place at which to be a student. That was obvious to me in the 1960s and has become even more evident to me since then. The faculty at GSIA was small but extraordinarily able, highly motivated, mainly accessible, and very serious about research. It was an infectious place.

The astonishing thing about Carnegie is that it joined two fundamental and seemingly incompatible strands of research. One dealt with bounded rationality, organization theory, and behavioral economics. The leading members of that group were Herbert Simon, Richard Cyert, and James March. The second strand dealt with rational expectations and efficient markets. Members of that group include Franco Modigliani (who, unfortunately, left Carnegie just as I arrived), John Muth, Merton Miller, and Allan Meltzer, to be joined later by Robert Lucas (who arrived as I was graduating), Thomas Sargent (who was my first research assistant), and Edward Prescott.

I worked mainly with the behavioral economics group at Carnegie. Bounded rationality—which Simon (1957a) defined as behavior that was intendedly rational but only limitedly so—seemed to me, then and since, as the most useful way to go. March's course in organization theory demonstrated that one did not need to think about organizations in classical (machine model) or fanciful (hyperrationality or nonrationality) terms but could address these matters in a behaviorally informed and scientific way. I learned about the behavioral theory of the firm (BTOF) from the horse's mouth, Richard Cyert, in 1961 when the famous Cyert and March book of that title was in the late stages of completion. I cotaught the BTOF course with Dick during my last semester at Carnegie, by which time Cyert had become dean.

My dissertation had its origins in Jim March's class, when he playfully remarked that "managers maximize slack" and lightbulbs in my mind began to blink and beckon. I shortly thereafter set about to examine managerial discretion issues in terms of constrained utility maximization (in which several measures of slack as well as profits were entered into the managerial utility function). That was only partly in the behavioral theory tradition. Thus although the objective function of the firm was reformulated in favor of realism in motivation, I worked out of a maximization rather than a satisficing setup. My dissertation therefore reflected some of the tensions between behavioral economics and orthodoxy to which I referred earlier.

Allan Meltzer was on my dissertation committee and was comfortable with the maximizing setup. I also discussed the issues with Jack Muth, who emphasized the importance of thinking problems through "in their entirety." Although I did not grasp all the ramifications (Jack, in my experience, is always one step ahead of everyone else), I was persuaded of the need to avoid myopic formulations.

Because Carnegie was a permissive place—the test being not methodological rectitude but whether a formulation deepens our understanding of complex issues—I was comfortable operating between the two extremes of behavioral economics on the one hand and rational expectations on the other.

In a nutshell, the research approach as I learned it at Carnegie was this: Have an active mind; be disciplined; be interdisciplinary, to which there was an additional lesson, which I associate also with Kenneth Arrow (1969, 1974): Research problems that do not fit into orthodox boxes should be addressed on their own terms. It would have been unthinkable at Carnegie, for example, to declare that bureaucratization was a more serious problem for economic organization than was resource allocation yet to restrict attention to the latter because bureaucracy, as Oskar Lange put it, "belongs to the field of sociology rather than to economic theory and must therefore be dispensed with here" (1938, p. 109). Such discipline-based property rights were alien to Carnegie. The fact that I have found the alliance of law, economics, and organization so productive is partly because, as a student of Carnegie, it could hardly be otherwise.

2. Transaction Cost Economics

In addition to being an interdisciplinary alliance of law, economics, and organization, I would describe transaction cost economics as (1) relentlessly comparative (organization forms are always examined in relation to alternative feasible forms), (2) microanalytic (the action resides in the details), (3) discrete structural (alternative forms of governance differ in kind, and so it is impossible to replicate markets by hierarchies or the reverse), and (4) preoccupied with economizing, principally with reference to organization rather than technology. Moreover, rather than being preoccupied with the imperative "This is the law here," the enterprise is inspired mainly by the question: "What's going on here?"

In contrast with the firm-as-production function approach, which treats technology (economies of scale, nonseparabilities) as the main determinants of the "natural" boundaries of the firm, transaction cost economic approaches firm and market organization from an efficient contracting/comparative organizational perspective. As Ronald Coase (1937) so perceptively observed, firms and markets are alternative forms of organization for managing the *very same transactions*. Whether a firm makes or buys—that is, produces for its own needs or procures a good or service from an outside supplier—turns largely on the transaction costs of managing the transaction in the firm, as compared with mediating the transaction through the market. Which transactions go where depends on the attributes of transactions, on the one hand, and the costs and competence of alternative modes of governance, on the other.

The production function or the precontractual view of vertical integration was that without special "physical or technical aspects"—the standard example being that of a blast furnace and a rolling mill, for which integration purportedly avoided the need to reheat ingots and hence realized thermal economies—vertical integration was deeply problematic and probably anticompetitive. As discussed in the Prologue, however, the thermal economies to which Joe Bain (1968, p. 381) referred to supply a physical–technical rationale for vertical integration did not withstand comparative institutional scrutiny. Holding constant the technology, including the location, the unrecognized need was to assess the comparative efficacy of alternative modes of governance.

To be sure, technology does matter, in that if the transportation expenses of locating at a distance are negligible, if reheating expenses are trivial, and if the economies of scale in blast furnaces are not great, then rolling mills can procure ingots from large numbers of parity suppliers. Markets, both currently and prospectively, can then be presumed to work well. The really interesting problems of managing transactions across successive stages of production show up when bilateral dependency conditions appear.

Because a preexisting bilateral monopoly is a rare event, bilateral dependency was held to be a special and unusual condition. Bilateral dependency need not, however, have preexisting (technological) origins. And there is the rub: Bilateral dependency can also have intertemporal, contractual origins. The reason is that what begins as a large numbers supply condition frequently is transformed into a small numbers exchange relation during contract execution and at contract renewal intervals. That had been missed by the "prevailing thinking," which slighted organization in favor of technology, was a myopic construction, and led to public-policy mistakes.

Transaction cost economics adopts John R. Commons's (1934) proposal that the transaction be made the unit of analysis and moves the argument forward by asking what the critical dimensions are on which transactions differ. As it turns out, the condition of asset specificity, which refers to the redeployability of assets and is implicated in the aforementioned bilateral (or, sometimes, multilateral) dependency condition, is the most important of these.

Adaptation is taken to be the central problem of economic organization, of which two types are distinguished: autonomous or Hayekian adaptation (in which markets enjoy the advantage) and cooperative or Barnardian adaptation (in which the advantage accrues to hierarchy). What is distinctive about the study of governance is that it provides for both spontaneous and intentional forms of organization, the Hayekian markets and the Barnardian hierarchies to which I just referred. More generally, the study of "incomplete contracting in its entirety" implicates both ex ante incentive alignment and ex post administration (which is what governance is).

Of special relevance in this connection is the concept of credible commitment. Recall that Machiavelli advised his prince to breach contracts with impunity, "when by doing so would be against his interest, and when the reasons which made him bind himself no longer exist" (1952, p. 92). This myopic approach to contract should be contrasted with a more farsighted (but nonetheless incomplete) approach to contract, according to which the prince is advised to mitigate ex post opportunism by crafting ex ante safeguards. Rather than reply to opportunism in kind, the wise prince is one who seeks both to give and to receive "credible commitments" (Williamson, 1983). Partly that entails incentive realignment, but mainly the need is to craft governance structures with superior adaptive properties.

Whereas the behavioral theory of the firm has been described as the intersection of economics and organization theory, transaction cost economics works out of the intersection of law, economics, and organization. Contract law plays an integral role in the exercise, the argument being that each generic mode of governance—market, hybrid, and hierarchy—is supported by a distinctive form of contract law. Following Ian Macneil (1974, 1978), the market mode is supported by an exacting application of legal rules (classical contract law), and hybrid modes are supported by more elastic contracting relations (neoclassical contract law). But whereas prior treatments describe the contract law of internal organization as that of the employment relation, transaction cost economics maintains that the implicit contract law of hierarchy is that of forbearance (Williamson, 1991a). Thus whereas the courts routinely hear disputes over prices, delivery, quality, and the like in transactions between firms, these same courts refuse to be drawn into identical disputes between divisions within a single firm. In effect, hierarchy becomes its own court of ultimate appeal. It is largely because of forbearance law that firms are able to exercise fiat, whereas markets cannot, to manage transactions. That has pervasive comparative institutional ramifications.

Although some social scientists appear to hold otherwise, my reading of the literature is that transaction cost economics is an empirical success story, there being in the neighborhood of two hundred published empirical studies and more in progress. Empirical work is always demanding, and those who have pioneered in this area deserve enormous credit. Unable to work from census reports and data tapes, because these do not record the relevant observations and/or are too aggregative, empirical transaction cost economics has had to develop primary, microanalytical data. But this cost has been more than repaid by the analytical benefits. As Thomas Kuhn (1970) remarked, a new science collects its own, rather than working from extant, data.

To be sure, transaction cost economics (like everything else) needs more and better empirical research. I agree, however, with Paul Joskow that "this empirical work is in much better shape than much of the empirical work in industrial organization generally" (1991, p. 81). Empirical transaction cost economics is a success story that we should celebrate.

I have not spoken of the public-policy applications, but transaction cost economics has numerous ramifications for, and has even had some influence on, antitrust and regulation. Also, as James Robinson is in the process of demonstrating (1993a, 1993b), it helps engage the relevant institutional issues that are pertinent to the study of health care. Likewise and more generally, transaction cost economics is pertinent to a comparative assessment of public, nonprofit, and private bureaus in both developed and reform economies. It furthermore has a bearing on the ideas of "core competence" and "corporate capabilities," which David Teece (1988) and others are addressing. Finally, transaction cost economics has helped promote an interdisciplinary dialogue among law, economics, and organization that is richer and more respectful of what each has to offer than was the case ten and twenty years ago.

3.   Conclusion

This last brings me back to my opening remarks. Maybe a productive dialogue would have gotten under way without Carnegie, but it is clear that Carnegie took the lead and made it respectable for others to follow. The participation of economists in this exercise was vital, and someone needed to make the first move. Dick Cyert is the Carnegie economist who took the lead, for which those of us who were his students and are his followers are forever grateful. That others have similar recollections of Carnegie is evident from the following statement by Jacques Dreze: "Never since then have I experienced such intellectual excitement" (1995, p. 123).

2

Chester Barnard and the Incipient Science of Organization

This chapter argues that an incipient science of organization has been taking shape over the past ten and fifteen years and that it is inspired, directly and indirectly, by Chester Barnard's classic book, *The Functions of the Executive.* Interestingly, Barnard observed in the last chapter of that book that there was a need for, but that we did not have, a "science of organization" (1938, p. 290).[1] Although that unrealized need remains today, we have nonetheless made recent progress.

The incipient science of organization to which I refer involves an interdisciplinary joinder of law, economics, and organization theory. Barnard is everywhere recognized for his path-breaking contributions to the field of organization theory,[2] and this is the main use I make of Barnard here. Barnard's intuitions, however, were very much those of an economist. Thus, although he expressed dismay that economic theory and thought had not helped him in the least—indeed, had gotten in the way of his understanding of the problems of organization (pp. x–xi)—Barnard approached the study of organization very much in a rational spirit, which is to say, "in the spirit of an economist" (Arrow, 1974, p. 16).

As discussed later, economics and organization theory form the main axis of the incipient science of organization. I argue that each needs to inform and be informed by the other. Law, however, also plays a role—albeit of a background or supporting kind.[3]

---

1. References to Barnard with page numbers only are to his 1938 book, *The Functions of the Executive.*

2. Even those who take vigorous exception with Barnard conceded his vast influence (Perrow, 1986). Not only did Barnard's work influence the human relations approaches to organization, but the work of two giants in the study of organization—Philip Selznick's institutionalist views and Herbert Simon's theory of decision making—drew inspiration from Barnard. For a discussion, see W. Richard Scott (1987, pp. 61–68).

3. The New Institutional Economics distinction between institutional environment (political, social, and legal ground rules) and institutional arrangements (governance) is pertinent in this connection (Davis and North 1971, pp. 6–7). The incipient science of organization encompasses

The first two sections of this chapter examine leading developments in organization theory, with special emphasis on Barnard. The third section indicates how transaction cost economics draws on parts of these, rejects others, and combines economics with organization theory to effect a joinder. Concluding remarks follow.

1.   Barnard

Barnard came to the study of organization as a deeply perceptive practitioner. It was his experience that executives in large organizations could communicate easily about "essential problems of organization, provided that the questions are stated without dependence upon the technologies of their respective fields" (p. viii). Presumably there were underlying regularities and a common conceptual core to which individuals experienced in and skilled at organization could and did relate. What were these?

Barnard's first and insistent point was that formal organization was important. What was obvious to him, however, was evidently not so obvious to others, since the study of formal organization had been neglected by social scientists.[4] Believing this to be a remediable condition, he set about to correct it. This required that a new conceptual framework be fashioned, out of which a theory of formal organization could be developed.

1.1.   Spontaneous Versus Induced Cooperation

The invisible hand of Adam Smith and the marvel of the market to which Friedrich Hayek referred have spontaneous origins: "The price system is . . . one of those formations which man has learned to use . . . after he stumbled on it without understanding it" (Hayek, 1945, p. 528). Karl Menger's approach to economics was similar. He averred that the most noteworthy problem in the social sciences was to ascertain how "institutions which serve the common welfare and are extremely significant for its development came into being without a *common will* directed toward establishing them" (Menger, 1963, p. 147).

What interested Barnard, however, was not spontaneous cooperation but induced cooperation. He simply asserted that in his experience formal organization was important and undervalued, where formal organization was defined

---

both but puts principal emphasis on governance structures (which mainly implicates economics and organization) rather than on the institutional environment (where the law is more salient).

   4. Barnard observed that while social scientists had studied "mores, folkways, political structures, institutions, attitudes, motives, propensities, [and] instincts . . . *in extenso,*" there was a general failure among social scientists "to sense the processes of coordination and decision that underlie a large part at least of the phenomena they described. More important, there was lacking much recognition of formal organization as the most important characteristic of social life, and as being the principal structural aspect of society itself" (p. ix).

as "that kind of cooperation among men that is conscious, deliberate, purposeful" (p. 4).

The self-conscious, intentional cooperation with which Barnard was concerned was widely believed to be of lesser importance than cooperation that results from organic evolution. Thus Hayek observed that "If social phenomena showed no order except insofar as they were consciously designed, there would be . . . only problems of psychology. It is only insofar as some sort of order arises as a result of individual action but without being designed by any individual that a problem is raised which demands theoretical exploration" (1955, p. 39). The plain meaning of this is that if "the task of social science is to explain planned behavior or consciously planned social institutions, then all that remains to be studied are the preferences of the planner" (Schotter, 1981, p. 21).

The long tradition within economics of treating firms as production possibility sets (Kreps, 1990a, p. 96) contributed to this condition. Inasmuch as individual agents were described by utility functions and consumption sets, profit functions and production possibility sets were arguably the appropriate terms with which to describe firms. The neoclassical scheme of things simply made no place for "conscious, deliberate, purposeful" efforts to craft formal structures in support of internal organization.

Barnard's experience told him otherwise. Since there was little theory to which he could appeal, he set out to supply it.

1.2. Adaptation as the Central Problem

Barnard observed that the main concern of organization was that of adaptation to changing circumstances, the reason being that problems of organization in a steady state are comparatively trivial.

The remarkable adaptive properties of markets were ignored by Barnard. What concerned him was internal organization. Confronted with a continuously fluctuating environment, the "survival of an organization depends upon the maintenance of an equilibrium of complex character. . . . [This] calls for readjustment of processes internal to the organization . . . , [whence] the *center of our interest* is the processes by which [adaptation] is accomplished" p. 6, emphasis added).

Moreover, adjustments of cooperative systems are not piecemeal but require "balance of the various types of organizational activities. The capacity for making these adjustments is a limiting factor . . . ; for if cooperation cannot adjust to attack new limitations in the environment, it must fail. The adjustment processes become management processes, and the specialized organs are executives and executive organization. . . . Barring extraordinary cataclysms, . . . [such processes and organs] are in fact the most important limitations in most, and especially in complex, cooperative systems" (p. 35).

Efficacious adaptations to changing circumstances were thus the central concern of Barnard. Interestingly, despite his emphasis on intentionality, he fully appreciated that most cooperative efforts fail: "successful cooperation in or by formal organizations is the abnormal, not the normal, condition" (p. 5). One possibility, albeit unmentioned by Barnard, is that those who craft cooperative systems often err for lack of a (more or less correct) conceptual framework. Whether for that reason or otherwise, Barnard decided to supply one.

1.3. The Framework

Instead of technology, Barnard examined the human attributes of organization. Instead of focusing on markets, Barnard focused entirely on internal organization. Of special importance were the following: (1) a theory of authority, (2) the employment relation, (3) informal organization, and (4) an economizing orientation. We consider these each in turn.

1.3.1. Authority

The natural and usual approach to the origin and nature of authority—in both the theory of the state and the theory of internal organization—is to regard authority as originating at the top. Sometimes this top-down imposition of authority is believed to have societal benefits—as in Thomas Hobbes's theory of state, in which the law is a means by which to "compel men equally to perform their covenants" (1928, p. 94). More often, authority is believed to be a means by which one group (e.g., bosses) exploits another (e.g., workers) (Marglin, 1974).

Barnard argued that authority is a solution to a complex problem of coordination/adaptation and that it arises out of mutual consent. He was influenced in this by his study of Eugen Ehrlich's book on the *Fundamental Principles of the Sociology of Law* (1936). In Ehrlich's view, "the center of gravity of legal development lies not in legislation, nor in juristic science, nor in judicial decision, but in society itself" (1936, p. xv). Barnard held the thesis of this study to be "that all law arises from the formal and especially informal understandings of the people as socially organized." Such was "broadly consistent with the facts" of organization as he had experienced them (p. x).

Barnard thus viewed authority as an instrumental solution to the problems of cooperation/coordination that were posed by the adaptive needs of complex organization. Moreover, Barnard insisted that rather than being top down, authority rested on the acceptance or consent of subordinates (p. 164). It was his experience that orders are commonly disobeyed (p. 162), which is unsurprising if the "decision as to whether an order has authority . . . lies with the person to whom it is addressed" (p. 163). If authority implies compliance, then lower-level consent is needed.

To be sure, long-run versus short-run distinctions may be pertinent. Thus orders that are refused in the long run (possibly by reallocating resources) may be binding in the short run. Given the added degrees of freedom that the long run affords, attempts to impose law on unwilling participants—be they individuals or organizations—are apt to be fatuous (pp. 181–82).

Although one could complain that this concept of authority can be pushed too far and is contradicted by authoritarian states and the like,[5] the consensual view of authority—more generally, the consensual view of contract—has been enormously influential for reconceptualizing the study of economic organization. Barnard's novel theory of the employment relation works out of this consensual orientation.

1.3.2. The employment relation

Barnard maintained that both the decision of an individual to join an organization and the decision to continue reflected a comparative net benefit assessment. Presented with different employment scenarios, persons consciously "choose whether or not they will enter into a specific cooperative system" (p. 17). Continuation thereafter depends on whether or not net gains can be projected (p. 85).

The need was to craft a contractual relation that would facilitate adaptability. The distinguishing feature of the employment relation, according to Barnard, is that employees (implicitly and explicitly) agree to accede to authority within a "zone of acceptance."[6] The size and nature of this zone of acceptance, moreover, is priced out: the zone "will be wider or narrower depending upon the degree to which the inducements exceed the burdens and sacrifices which determine the individual's adhesion to the organization" (p. 169). At the outset, therefore, expanding a zone to include greater (potential) burdens or sacrifices must be attended by greater inducements.

To be sure, things can get complicated once an employment relation has been agreed to. Although workers will not thereafter have the same degree of choice, they are not without resources. If an order is "believed to involve a burden that destroys the net advantage of connection with the organization, . . . [the] net inducement, [which] is the only reason for accepting *any* order as having authority," vanishes (p. 166). In the extreme, the individual will quit. But there are many other ways to deflect, defeat, or otherwise frustrate orders:

5. Even this might be questioned. Authoritarian states, such as Nazi Germany, and other controlled societies, such as prisons, are never totally controlled from the top in the manner that is often ascribed to them.

6. Mark Granovetter observes that Barnard originally described the zone as one of "indifference" and that Simon had substituted the term "acceptance" without explanation (1985, p. 495, n. 5). Granovetter objects to this substitution because it undercuts "Barnard's emphasis on the problematic nature of obedience" (1985, p. 495, n. 5). The reason for the substitution is this: several degrees of indifference are included within the zone of acceptance. Usually, only a very small subset of orders place an individual at the margin of indifference between staying and leaving.

One of Simon's main purposes was to develop a more scientific vocabulary for describing organizations (1957a, p. xiv). The substitution of acceptance for indifference in the context of the employment relation accomplishes that purpose.

"Malingering and intentional lack of dependability are the more usual methods" (p. 166). Also, as described later, informal organization is pertinent.

In effect, Barnard examined the employment relation from something akin to a rational expectations point of view—with all the burdens and benefits that accrue thereto. This contrasts with myopic contracting, according to which participants approach contract noncomparatively and incur commitments (make investments in human assets) the future ramifications of which are not worked out. Instead, Barnard treats the ex-ante bargain and the ex-post contractual relation in a unified way—a much more sophisticated conception of contracting.

1.3.3.   Informal organization

Barnard argued that formal and informal organization always and everywhere coexist (p. 20) and that informal organization contributes to the viability of formal organization in three significant respects: "One of the indispensable functions of informal organizations in formal organizations . . . [is] that of communication. . . . Another function is that of maintaining the cohesiveness in formal organizations through regulating the willingness to serve and the stability of objective authority. A third function is the maintenance of the feeling of personal integrity, of self-respect, and independent choice" (p. 122).

These effects occur spontaneously, as a consequence of or in conjunction with formal organization. Presumably firm and market organization differ in informal organization respects—which differences should be taken into account in the decision to use one or the other. The comparison of markets and hierarchies was not, however, a concern of Barnard's. Also, arguably, informal organization could be supported or suppressed. Although this latter is closer to Barnard's concerns, he was silent on that aspect as well.

The communication benefits of informal organization include coding, rumors, and the like. These effects are familiar and widely conceded. More subtle is the claim that informal organization serves to stabilize authority:

> Since the efficiency of organization is affected by the degree to which individuals assent to orders, denying the authority of an organization communication is a threat to the interests of all individuals who derive a net advantage from their connection with the organization, unless the orders are unacceptable to them also. Accordingly, at any given time there is among most of the contributors an active personal interest in the maintenance of the authority of all orders which to them are within the zone of [acceptance]. The maintenance of this interest is largely a function of informal organization. (p. 169)

Inasmuch as the third function of informal organization—that of protecting personal integrity and self-respect—affords "opportunities for reinforcement of personal attitudes," this function is often "deemed destructive of formal organization" (p. 122). That, however, construes things too narrowly if such protections are "a means of maintaining the personality of the individual against certain effects of formal organizations which tend to disintegrate the personality" (p. 122).

Not only can informal organization give succor to individuals that are devalued or demeaned by formal organization, but informal organization may be a means by which collective dissent from authority is supported. Thus, just as contributors have the aforementioned "active personal interest in the maintenance of the authority of all orders which to them are within the zone of indifference" (p. 169), so likewise do they have an interest in resisting or securing clarification on problematic claims of authority. Albeit unmentioned by Barnard, this too can play a useful role.

A fourth effect of informal organization that may, in fact, undercut the efficacy of internal organization also goes unmentioned by Barnard. This is that informal organization can lead to resource misallocation distortions—including on-the-job leisure, waste, investment distortions, and other forms of subgoal pursuit. Barnard's frequent references to moral codes, moral factors, moral elements, and so forth—in the context of executive responsibility—are, perhaps, his way of dealing with (finessing) concerns over subgoal pursuit (chap. 17).

1.3.4. The economy of incentives

Barnard disputed the efficacy of material incentives, which he associated with the prevailing economic approach to organization (pp. x, 143), and asserted that "Inducements of a personal, non-materialistic character are of great importance to secure cooperative effort above the minimum material rewards essential to subsistence. The opportunities for distinction, prestige, personal power, and the attainment of dominating position are much more important than material rewards in the development of . . . commercial organizations" (p. 145).

Although Barnard advanced these and related arguments in a chapter titled "The Economy of Incentives," and might have developed the argument that nonmaterial incentives are substitutes for material incentives and that this has comparative institutional significance, he pulled up short in both respects. There is at least a hint of such broader significance, however, in his expansive treatment of incentive issues.

2.   Simon and Others

2.1.   The Science of Administration

One could conclude that a splendid start had been made toward the development of a new science of organization. That Herbert Simon's book, *Administrative Behavior,* which relies on Barnard and is expressly designed to advance the science of administration, was published in 1947 must be counted as an auspicious development. In Simon's judgment, the study of organization suffered for lack of "adequate linguistic and conceptual tools for realistically and significantly describing even a simple administrative organization—describing it, that is, in a way that will provide the basis for scientific analysis of the effectiveness of its structure and operation" (1957a, p. xiv). Using Barnard's earlier work as framework, Simon set out to develop more relevant concepts and a more precise vocabulary (1957a, p. xiv): "Before we can establish any immutable 'principles' of administration, we must be able to describe, in words, exactly how an administrative organization looks and exactly how it works. . . . I have attempted to construct a vocabulary which will permit such description."

Of Simon's numerous and important contributions to the science of administration, I focus on five features: bounded rationality, microanalytics, the employment relation, hierarchy, and subgoal pursuit.

2.1.1. Bounded rationality

Although the term *bounded rationality* was not coined until 1957, Simon's approach to the study of organization has consistently been of a bounded rationality kind. Albeit sometimes confused with irrationality, nonrationality, and the like, bounded rationality refers to behavior that is "*intendedly* rational, but only *limitedly* so" (Simon 1957a, p. xxiv).

Bounded rationality is important to the study of economic organization in several respects. For one thing, it is "only because individual human beings are limited in knowledge, foresight, skill, and time that organizations are useful instruments for the achievement of human purpose" (Simon 1957b, p. 199). But for bounded rationality, all issues of organization collapse in favor of comprehensive contracting of either Arrow–Debreu or mechanism design kinds.

A second (related) way in which bounded rationality is relevant is that mind now becomes a scarce resource (Simon, 1978). The study of organization as a means by which to economize on mind as the scarce resource is thus suggested. Simon, however, chose to emphasize a different lesson. He insistently argued that social scientists (especially economists) should give up maximizing in favor of "satisficing."

Simon defined the principle of bounded rationality as follows: "The capacity of the human mind for formulating and solving complex problems is very small compared with the size of the problems whose solution is required for objectively rational behavior in the real world" (Simon 1957b, p. 198; emphasis omitted). He averred that the "key to the simplification of the choice process . . . is the replacement of the goal of *maximizing* with the goal of *satisficing*, of finding a course of action that is good enough . . . [T]his substitution is an essential step in the application of the principle of bounded rationality" (Simon 1957b, pp. 204–5; emphasis in original).

This turned out to be a fateful choice. Rather than encourage economizing reasoning, to which economists could easily relate and usefully contribute, bounded rationality became identified with aspiration level mechanics instead—which has wide appeal but is more closely associated with psychology. Simon's repeated insistence that satisficing was the way to go (1959, 1962b, 1972) and some specific economic applications (especially Cyert and March, 1963) notwithstanding, a cumulative research tradition within economics did not develop. It is now generally agreed that the satisficing approach has not been broadly applicable (Aumann, 1985, p. 35).

As discussed later, economics could have (and, more recently, has) gleaned another and, as it turns out, less controversial lesson from bounded rationality: *all complex contracts are unavoidably incomplete.* That is the transaction cost economics story.

2.1.2. Microanalytics

Simon's contrast between the physical sciences and economics in microanalytic respects is instructive. As he observes, "In the physical sciences, when errors of measurement and other noise are found to be of the same order of magnitude as the phenomena under study, the response is not to try to squeeze more information out of the data by statistical means; it is instead to find techniques for observing the phenomena at a higher level of resolution. The corresponding strategy for economics is obvious: to secure new kinds of data at the micro level" (1984, p. 40).

But this immediately poses the questions: What particulars of organization are pertinent? What is the basic unit of analysis? As Simon had earlier remarked, "It is not possible to build an adequate theory of human behavior unless we have an appropriate unit of analysis," to which he responded that the "decision *premise* is . . . the appropriate unit for the study of human behavior" (1957a, p. xxxii). Although Simon and others have used very microanalytic methods to study human problem solving to good advantage (Newell and Simon, 1972), the use of the decision premise as the unit of analysis for studying organization has never been shown to have general application.

2.1.3. The employment relation

Simon specifically adopted and refined Barnard's concept of authority and of the employment relation. Of special importance was his 1951 article, "A Formal Theory of the Employment Relation." In it he described the zone of acceptance to which an employee could be induced to agree and compared sales contracts, in which actions are stipulated in advance, with employment contracts, in which actions can be decided later, depending on state realizations. Unsurprisingly, the employment relation is favored as uncertainty increases. Simon also makes the sophisticated point that worker and firm are faced with a complex incentive problem: "If the worker had confidence that the employer would take account of his preferences [once the wage had been agreed to], the former would . . . be willing to work for a smaller wage than if he thought these satisfactions were going to be ignored in the employer's exercise of authority and only profitability to the employer taken into account"

(1957b, p. 192). This has been a recurrent theme in much of the subsequent labor economics literature.

2.1.4. Hierarchy

Simon regards hierarchy as an instrument and observes that complex biological, physical, and social systems are all characterized by hierarchy: "The central theme that runs through my remarks is that complexity frequently takes the form of hierarchy, and that hierarchic systems have some common properties that are independent of their specific content. Hierarchy ... is one of the central structural schemes that the architect of complexity uses" (1962a, p. 468).

Simon notes that a condition of "near-decomposability" is commonly associated with hierarchy and serves to distinguish interactions between subsystems from interactions within subsystems (Simon, 1962a, p. 473). In hierarchical systems with near-decomposability, not only are "intracomponent linkages ... generally stronger than intercomponent linkages" but the short-run or "higher frequency dynamics are associated with the subsystems" and the longer-run or "lower frequency dynamics with the larger systems" (Simon, 1962a, p. 477). W. Ross Ashby's (1960) analysis of adaptive systems that employ double feedback—one of a frequent and short-run kind; the other of a less frequent but longer-run kind—can be interpreted in precisely these terms. In organizational terms, operating and strategic levels of decision making correspond to the higher and lower frequency dynamics, respectively. These are natural outcomes of an unconvoluted, evolutionary kind (Simon, 1962a)—although, to be sure, design distortions can be and sometimes are introduced into hierarchies as well. It is nonetheless vital to understand that hierarchy is a basic organizing principle for all complex social systems—which is a message that some students of economic organization resist or deny (Marglin, 1974).

2.1.5. Subgoal pursuit

Subgoal pursuit makes its appearance in March and Simon (1958) but is not a subject with which Simon (before or since) has been greatly concerned. As indicated, factoring complex problems into manageable parts is something that has been of continuous interest to Simon. Such factoring can lead to subgoal pursuit of both instrumental and strategic kinds.

The general argument is that "members of an organizational unit [tend] to evaluate action only in terms of subgoals, even when these are in conflict with the goals of the larger organization" (March and Simon, 1958, p. 152). Selective perceptions are partly responsible. Within-group reinforcement is another factor. Selective exposure to problems is a third (March and Simon, 1958, pp. 152–53). Goal distortions, bargaining, and coalition formation result (March and Simon, 1958, p. 156). Strategic subgoal pursuit gets little attention and possible remedies go unremarked.

2.2.   Subsequent Developments

As this and other chapters in this book make clear, organization theory is an enormously rich field. Only a few subsequent developments are treated here. These are: (1) posterior rationality, (2) resource dependency, and (3) disciplinary borrowing.

2.2.1.   Posterior rationality

The behavior of individuals who engage in satisficing will be stabilized if these same individuals are given to ex-post rationalization. A substantial literature on "posterior rationality" (Weick, 1969; March, 1973) developed along these lines. As James March puts it, "Posterior rationality models maintain the idea that action should be consistent with preferences, but they conceive action as being antecedent to goals" (1988, pp. 273–74). Though this is instructive, one of the consequences of work along these lines is that it discouraged the analysis of what I refer to as "incomplete contracting in its entirety." A disjunction between organization theory and economics developed as a consequence.

2.2.2.   Resource dependency

Jay Barney and William Ouchi remark that throughout "the 1960s and 1970s, the dominant theoretical frameworks in organization theory were drawn from sociology and social psychology and relied heavily on the concept of power" (1986, p. 12). Specifically, the resource dependency approach to organization works out of a power perspective. The argument is that "The need to acquire resources creates dependencies between organizations and outside units. How important and how scarce these resources are determine the nature and extent of organizational dependency. Dependency is the obverse of power (Emerson, 1962). Economic dependencies give rise to political problems and may succumb to political solutions" (Scott, 1987, p. 111).

As discussed later, many dependency issues can be addressed in efficiency terms, whereupon power considerations largely vanish. It suffices for my purpose here merely to remark that power, for a long time, has been the congenial organization theory perspective—March's early conclusion that "power is a disappointing concept" (1966, p. 70) notwithstanding.

2.2.3.   Borrowing

Research in organization theory has a history of borrowing from other disciplines:

> This borrowing began ... early ... [with borrowing] from psychology and social psychology to establish what became known as the human relations school. Later, concepts and a way of thinking were borrowed from sociology and political science to develop the contingency and resource dependence theories. More recently, concepts from biology have been borrowed in the

development of the population ecology model, and anthropology has been a source of concepts and a way of thinking for those studying organizational cultures. (Barney and Ouchi, 1986, p. xi)

The latest discipline from which organization theory has begun to borrow is economics (Barney and Ouchi, 1986, pp. xi–xii). Although this is often described as a one-way street, whereby economics informs organization theory (Jensen, 1983), economics and organization theory ought to inform each other.

One of the distinctive things that economics brings to organization the- ory—and to the study of the "contiguous disciplines" more generally—is a systems orientation. According to Coase, cited previously, this is what explains the success of economics in moving into the other social sciences: economists "study the economic system as a unified interdependent system and, therefore, are more likely to uncover the basic interrelationships within a social system than is someone less accustomed to looking at the working of a system as a whole," one consequence of which is that "economics makes it more difficult to ignore factors which are clearly important and which play a part in all social systems" (1978, pp. 290–91). These views are pertinent to my discussion of transaction cost economics, which follows.

3. Transaction Cost Economics: Concepts

Kenneth Arrow queries "Why . . . has the work of Herbert Simon, which meant so much to all of us, . . . had so little direct consequence? Why did the older institutional school fail so miserably, though it contained such able analysts as Thorstein Veblen, J. R. Commons, and W. C. Mitchell?" (1987, p. 734). He ventures two answers, one of which is that the issues are intrinsically difficult. But he further remarks that the New Institutional Economics move- ment, of which transaction cost economics is a part, has made more headway. He attributes this headway to the fact that the New Institutional Economics "does not consist primarily of giving new answers to the traditional questions of economics—resource allocation and degree of utilization. Rather it consists of answering new questions, why economic institutions have emerged the way they did and not otherwise; it merges into economic history, but brings sharper nanoeconomic . . . ('nano' is an extreme version of 'micro') reasoning to bear than has been customary" (1987, p. 734). R. C. O. Matthews similarly concludes that whereas institutional economics had until recently been relegated to the pages of the history of thought, the economics of institutions has, over the past decade, "become one of the liveliest areas in our discipline" (Matthews, 1986, p. 903).

My purpose in this section is to examine the transaction cost economics branch of the New Institutional Economics movement, mainly in relation to the organization theory literature referred to earlier. The uses that are made of earlier organization theory work are discussed first, after which some of the significant differences are treated.

3.1. Uses

3.1.1. Barnard

Transaction cost economics concurs with Barnard's assessment that formal organization is important and that the study of induced cooperation deserves a prominent place on the research agenda. The firm is therefore not described as a technological unit to which a profit maximization purpose is ascribed but is described instead as an organizational unit, the efficacy of which is to be examined in comparative institutional (mainly, transaction cost economizing) terms.

Barnard's view that the central problem of organization is that of adaptation is likewise embraced. Of special interest in this connection is how parties engaged in a long-term contract can adapt effectively to disturbances. The need to craft contractual structures in which they have mutual confidence in support of cooperative adaptation is plainly posed.

The zone of acceptance within the employment relation was Barnard's way of introducing an adaptive capacity. His view of contract and, more generally, of the law as being farsighted and consensual are both noteworthy. Transaction cost economics relates constructively to both "incomplete contracting in its entirety" and the importance of private ordering (as opposed to legal centralism).

As discussed in chapter 3 of this book, the implementation of an incomplete contract viewed in its entirety requires that price, technology, and contractual safeguards all be addressed simultaneously. Not only will wider zones of acceptance be priced out, as Barnard indicated, but they will also be embedded in protective governance structures. Much more concerted attention to the design of governance in this latter respect is needed.

Also, real differences between the employment relation and all other forms of contracting notwithstanding, our understanding of contract and of economic organization more generally will benefit from a realization that very strong similarities recur across markets of all kinds—labor, intermediate product, and capital included. Transaction cost economics emphasizes and works out the ramifications of these commonalities, as a consequence of which it supports a broader approach to economic organization than exclusive focus on the employment relation yields. Indeed, the canonical transaction, for the purposes of transaction cost economics, is not the employment relation but vertical integration.

Focusing on the make-or-buy decision has advantages of two kinds. For one thing, intermediate product market contracting is easier to address in instrumental terms than is labor market contracting.[7] For another, the study

7. Compared with the study of the employment relation, which implicates complicated emotive and dignitarian features, decisions to make or buy an intermediate good or service are much more instrumental.

I once attended a conference several years ago at which the participants were advised that the analysis of work organization should be informed by "unabashed rooting for the workers." Those are understandable sentiments, but it is not obvious that better analysis is promoted in this way.

of vertical integration invites the query, what is responsible for limitations to firm size? This is a central query to which the economics of organization should be expected to speak[8] but which does not arise—as easily or at all—in conjunction with the study of the employment relation.

Like Barnard, transaction cost economics works out of a private ordering rather than legal centralism approach to contract law. The legal centralism approach to contract law assumed that efficacious rules of law regarding contract disputes were in place and were applied by the courts in an informed, sophisticated, and low-cost way. Purportedly, "disputes require 'access' to a forum external to the original social setting of the dispute [from which] remedies will be provided as prescribed in some body of authoritative learning and dispensed by experts who operate under the auspices of the state" (Galanter, 1981, p. 1). But the facts disclose otherwise: most disputes, including many that under current rules could be brought to a court, are resolved by avoidance, self-help, and the like (Galanter, 1981, p. 2).

To be sure, a private ordering approach to contract requires support. For one thing, good intentions or mere agreements are prone to breakdown. This invites precisely the type of analysis of credible commitments with which transaction cost economics is concerned. Also, as discussed later in the subsection on Incomplete Contracting in Its Entirety, private ordering benefits from having the law available for purposes of ultimate appeal.

Barnard's notion of "informal organization" is useful to transaction cost economics in two respects. First, informal organization arguably helps to safeguard the security and integrity needs of employees. This is a governance structure feature, the ramifications of which need to be taken into account. For another, informal organization may be a manifestation of a more general condition of "atmosphere," the effects of which serve to distinguish market and hierarchical modes of organization. Such distinctions support comparative analysis of a discrete structural rather than (as is more customary) of a marginal analysis kind.

Finally, although the economy of incentives to which Barnard refers is a narrow use of economizing reasoning, an economizing approach, broadly conceived, is what transaction cost economics holds to be the main case (to which alternative main case scenarios should be compared). The issues here are discussed further in the next section on Differences.

3.1.2. Simon

Simon's concept of bounded rationality is specifically embraced by transaction cost economics. Moreover, both parts of the definition—*intended* but *limited* rationality—are accorded respect. Intentionally rational agents are attempting to cope effectively. This is plainly in the "rational spirit" tradition. But their limitations also need to be admitted. The principal lessons of bounded rational-

---

8. Indeed, there is a long literature. For a summary and discussion, see Williamson, 1985b, chap. 6.

ity for transaction cost purposes are these: (1) all complex contracts are unavoidably incomplete, on which account the hitherto neglected study of ex-post governance is placed at the very center of the research agenda;[9] and (2) economizing on bounded rationality is a leading purpose of economic organization.

Microanalytics is likewise a matter of special concern to transaction cost economics.[10] This is partly tied up with the choice of a unit of analysis (see Differences, next). But the study of process considerations is also implicated. Transaction cost economics maintains that there are no shortcuts and that economic organization needs to be examined in a "modest, slow, molecular, definitive" way.[11]

If the details matter in assessing the efficacy of alternative forms of organization, then whether franchise bidding is an effective way of dealing with natural monopoly cannot rest entirely on an imaginative formulation of the issues (Demsetz, 1968b; Stigler, 1968; Posner, 1972). Instead, both the attributes of transactions (with special attention to the assets) and the details of the contracting process need to be carefully examined. There is no other way adequately to deal with the franchise bidding hypothesis except by moving beyond the general description to assess the underlying attributes and contractual microanalytics (Williamson, 1985b, chap. 13).

The same is true in assessing the assertion that transactions can be moved out of markets and into firms without loss of incentive intensity (Grossman and Hart, 1986). Convenient though this assumption is, a microanalytic examination of the effort to preserve high-powered incentives within firms discloses that such an effort elicits adverse cost consequences (Williamson, 1985b, 1988d). *Incentive differences,* rather than unchanged incentive intensity, *thus characterize firm and market organization.*

More generally, the argument is this: although several different trade-off scenarios may yield similar crude, qualitative predictions, that is not the only test. A second test is whether the trade-offs postulated are plausible. Assessing this normally requires that the underlying microanalytics be examined—tiresome and troublesome as such an effort may be. Nonetheless, "study the microanalytics" is the unchanging message of transaction cost economics. Or, as Stephen Jay Gould puts it, "God dwells in the details" (1987, p. 32).

Understanding the employment relation and the differences between sales and employment contracts are of central interest to transaction cost economics.[12] Also, hierarchy, especially the differences between markets and hierarchies, is prominently featured in the transaction cost economics scheme of things. Like Simon, hierarchy is treated instrumentally—principally with reference to its transaction cost economizing properties. This is pertinent both in

9. Theories of comprehensive contracting, with and without private information, concentrate all of the contracting action on the ex-ante incentive alignment.

10. Recall that Arrow ascribed the differential success of the New Institutional Economics to its nanoeconomic orientation (1987, p. 734).

11. The quote is from Peguy (source unknown).

12. Note, however, that whereas the crucial feature for Simon is uncertainty, I focus mainly on the condition of asset specificity.

assessing the decision to take a transaction out of the market (or not) and, for those transactions that are organized internally, for purposes of choosing between alternative hierarchical designs. (In fact, of course, these two decisions are related.)

Finally, transaction cost economics subscribes to subgoal pursuit. Indeed, it goes beyond the March and Simon formulation and argues that "opportunism" is a behavioral assumption of such pervasive reach and importance that it deserves coequal status with bounded rationality in any concerted effort to assess the comparative efficacy of alternative modes of contracting. Thus, just as the absence of bounded rationality would vitiate the need for internal organization, since all of the relevant contracting action could be concentrated in a comprehensive ex-ante agreement, so likewise would the absence of opportunism vitiate the need for added safeguards, since "contract as promise" could be used to annihilate ex-post defections from even incomplete contracts.[13]

3.2.   Differences

That transaction cost economics relies very substantially on the "science of administration" of Barnard and Simon is apparent from the foregoing. But transaction cost economics aspires to move beyond administration to deal symmetrically with all forms of organization. The eventual object is to realize a science of organization. Work toward that purpose is in progress.

The numerous and important dependencies of transaction cost economics on organization theory notwithstanding, there are also real differences, which are the matters of concern here. With reference to Simon, these are (1) the rejection of the decision premise as the unit of analysis in favor of the transaction and (2) the rejection of satisficing in favor of economizing. Also (3) a myopic treatment of contracting (the power perspective) is rejected in favor of incomplete contracting in its entirety. Moreover, an economic theory of organization poses further needs. Of special importance are the needs to (4) explicate opportunism, (5) make selective appeal to contract law, (6) work through crucial process-related particulars of a firm and market kind, and (7) develop the applications. The core features and recurrent variations are captured in (8) the simple contractual schema and (9) the generic trade-off. These last two are treated in chapter 3.

3.2.1.   Unit of analysis

Simon proposed that the decision premise be made the basic unit of analysis. This is a highly microanalytic unit of analysis—arguably more microanalytic than is needed to examine issues of economic organization that are of interest even to institutional economists. In any event, that question is moot: the decision premise as a unit of analysis has never been operationalized in such a way as to give it broad and general application.

13. The argument is elaborated in Williamson, 1985b, pp. 64–67.

An alternative unit, proposed earlier by John R. Commons, has proved more promising. Thus, Commons saw the problem of economic organization as that of dealing simultaneously with conflict, mutual dependence, and order. The transaction, in his view, was responsive to these principles and he proposed that it be made the basic unit of analysis (Commons, 1925, p. 4; 1934, pp. 4–8). But neither Commons nor his followers took the obvious next step: if the transaction is the basic unit of analysis, then what are the principal dimensions with respect to which transactions differ?

The transaction is a semimicroanalytic unit of analysis—more microanalytic than economics has characteristically been concerned with but a larger unit than the decision premise. It is also a unit that lends itself to dimensionalization. This permits the study of economic organization to be developed in a more operational way than had been hitherto feasible.

Transaction cost economics maintains that the key dimensions for describing transactions are (1) asset specificity, (2) uncertainty, and (3) frequency. Of the three, asset specificity is the most important and most distinctive. Investments in durable, specialized assets that cannot be redeployed from existing uses and users except at a significant loss of productive value are transaction specific. Contracting for goods and services that are produced with the support of transaction specific assets poses serious problems. Classical market contracting gives way to bilateral trading (or, more generally, hybrid modes of organization), which in turn gives way to unified ownership (hierarchies) as the condition of asset specificity builds up.[14]

The usual way in which the organization theory literature deals with asset specificity is in conjunction with "resource dependency." The general argument here is that exchanges of important and scarce resources "create dependencies." A power orientation is adopted, such dependencies being the obverse of power (Scott, 1987, p. 111).

Albeit very much concerned with bilateral dependency conditions, transaction cost economics assumes that parties *anticipate such conditions and organize with respect to them.* Resource dependency therefore does not come as a "surprise" to unwitting victims. To the contrary, parties explore alternative supply scenarios. Each alternative node in the general contracting schema described in chapter 3 is characterized by (1) the supply technology, (2) the

14. Interestingly, the organization theory literature deals expressly, albeit in a somewhat different way, with both asset specificity and uncertainty. Cyert and March contend that the main way of dealing with uncertainty is by avoidance. One way of doing this is by focusing on the short run: rather than plan for an uncertain future, managers use short-run reactions to deal with current disturbances. It may also, however, be possible to mitigate uncertainty "by arranging a negotiated environment: [managers] impose plans, standard operating procedures, industry tradition, and uncertainty-absorbing contracts" (Cyert and March, 1963, p. 119).

Mitigating uncertainty, especially "behavioral uncertainty," by supplanting interfirm by intrafirm organization is emphasized by transaction cost economics (Williamson, 1985b; Helfat and Teece, 1987). The use of "excuse doctrine" in contract law also serves to limit uncertainty (Williamson, 1985b). More generally, the comparative efficacy of alternative forms of organization for dealing with uncertainty through adaptive, sequential decision making is a recurrent concern in the transaction cost economics literature (Williamson, 1975, 1985b; Wiggins, 1990). The degree to which transaction specific assets are implicated has an important bearing on such comparative assessments.

price at which product is traded, and (3) the governance structure (including safeguards) in which the contract is embedded. These three features—asset specificity, price, and governance—are determined simultaneously in an internally consistent way. Therefore, rather than interpret dependency in ex-post power terms, transaction cost economics examines ex-ante and ex-post contractual features simultaneously within an efficiency framework.

Put differently, whereas much of the resource dependency literature works out of a *myopic* incomplete contracting set-up, whereupon dependency is an unwanted surprise, transaction costs economics examines incomplete contracts in their *entirety*—hence the absence of surprise, victims, and the like. This is not to say that all outcomes are equally good. Often, however, contrived breach, expropriation, holdups, and so forth can be and are mitigated.

3.2.2. Economizing and discriminating alignment

Upon supplanting hyperrationality with bounded rationality, Simon argued that the key analytical consequence was that maximizing be supplanted by satisficing. That placed Simon on a collision course with economics. Although it is perhaps still in doubt, most economists have concluded that satisficing never developed a cumulative and compelling research product and lost out to the economics mainstream in the contest that ensued.

Transaction cost economics embraces bounded rationality but urges that the principal ramification of bounded rationality for studying economic organization is that all complex contracts are unavoidably incomplete. If, moreover, mind is a scarce resource, then an economizing orientation, broadly construed to include organization, brings economics and organization theory together (rather than placing them in opposition or locating them on different domains). Frank Knight's views of economics are pertinent: "Men in general, and within limits, wish to behave economically, to make their activities *and their organization* 'efficient' rather than wasteful. This fact does deserve the utmost emphasis; and an adequate definition of the science of economics ... might well make it explicit that the main relevance of the discussion is found in its relation to social policy, assumed to be directed toward the end indicated, of increasing economic efficiency, of reducing waste" (1941, p. 252, emphasis added).

Transaction cost economics maintains that the economic institutions of capitalism have the main purpose and effect of economizing on transaction costs. To be sure, economic organization is very complex and a variety of economic and noneconomic purposes are normally at work. If, however, all are not equally important, our understanding of the weight to be ascribed to each will be promoted by examining economic organization from several well-focused perspectives. Qualifications, extensions, refinements, and so forth can then be introduced into each main case which, in such a contest, qualifies as a finalist. But the incipient science of organization needs to start somewhere. That is what the choice of a main case is all about.

The main case hypothesis out of which transaction cost economics works is this: align transactions (which differ in their attributes) with governance structures (which differ in their costs and competencies) in a discriminating (mainly transaction cost economizing) way. This discriminating alignment hypothesis predicts a large number of organizational regularities. The preliminary data are broadly corroborative (Williamson, 1985b; Joskow, 1988; Klein and Shelanski, 1995).

3.2.3. Incomplete contracting in its entirety

Not every transaction poses defection hazards, and it may not be possible to safeguard all that do. However, where the potential hazards that beset contracts are evident to the parties from the beginning—possibly because they have previously had bad experience, possibly by noting the experience of others, possibly by consciously working the contracting ramifications through—studies of contract and of contracting institutions should start at the beginning.

That contracts are incomplete does not, therefore, imply myopia. Instead, alternative contracting scenarios are described and their ramifications compared. Manifestly bad games, of which the prisoners' dilemma is one, will be avoided or reorganized in a larger contracting context in which the incentives to defect are attenuated As developed in Chapter 6, the use of reciprocity to equilibrate hazards is an example.

3.2.4. Opportunism and credible commitments

Most organization theorists subscribe to bounded rationality and count it a distinct gain that bounded rationality has made inroads into economics. To be sure, many might emphasize different aspects from those to which I refer here. But the argument that both markets and hierarchies need to come to terms with bounded rationality is uncontroversial.

By contrast, most organization theorists avoid making express reference to, much less relying on, the assumption of opportunism. Instead, assumptions of opportunism, moral hazard, agency costs and the like are regarded as demeaning variations on the familiar assumption of self-interest seeking, on which economics has long relied.

I submit, however, that organization theorists were familiar with and had an extensive literature dealing with opportunism long before economists got around to it. And I further submit that the assumption is less jaundiced than it first appears.

To be sure, there were (and are) language differences between economics and organization theory. The terms *unofficial rewards, managerial discretion,* and *subgoal pursuit* are the organization theory counterparts for opportunism, moral hazard, shirking, agency costs, and the like.[15] Whereas economists were

15. The following remarks of Simon are pertinent: "Organization theory is centrally concerned with identifying and studying those limits to the achievement of goals that are, in fact, limits on the flexibility and adaptability of the goal-striving individuals and groups of individuals themselves. . . . The fact that these limits . . . are largely determined by social and even organizational forces creates problems of theory construction of great subtlety" (1957b, p. 199). Although the goal-striving "limits" to which Simon refers are not specifically identified, I submit that the absence of opportunism greatly relieves goal-striving strains.

reluctant to grant these conditions, preferring instead to work out of a profit-maximization set-up, organization theorists came to terms easily with these conditions.

Economists are thus late comers to the opportunism scene. When they arrived, however, they pulled in new paraphernalia and wrung out different implications. Rather than regard opportunism in myopic terms, they instead viewed it from the aforementioned standpoint of incomplete contracting in its entirety.

The contrast between the Machiavellian treatment of promise and that of transaction cost economics is instructive. Machiavelli advised his prince that "a prudent ruler ought not to keep faith when by so doing it would be against his interest, and when the reasons which made him bind himself no longer exist. . . . [L]egitimate grounds [have never] failed a prince who wished to show colourable excuse for the promise" (Gauss, 1952, pp. 92–93). But reciprocal or preemptive opportunism is not the only lesson to be gleaned from an awareness that human agents are not fully trustworthy. Indeed, that is a very primitive response.

The more important lesson, for the purposes of studying economic organization, is this: Transactions that are subject to ex-post opportunism will benefit if appropriate safeguards can be devised ex ante. Rather than reply to opportunism in kind, therefore, the wise prince is one who seeks both to give and to receive "credible commitments." Incentives may be realigned, or superior governance structures within which to organize transactions may be devised.

So regarded, the transaction cost economics assumption of opportunism is less offensive than it at first appears. To assume, moreover, that human agents are opportunistic does not mean that all are continually given to opportunism. Rather, the assumption is that *some* individuals are opportunistic *some* of the time and that it is costly to ascertain differential trustworthiness ex ante. H. L. A. Hart's remarks help to put the issues into perspective: "Neither understanding of long-term interest, nor the strength of goodness of will . . . are shared by all men alike. All are tempted at times to prefer their own immediate interests. . . . 'Sanctions' are . . . required not as the normal motive for obedience, but as a *guarantee* that those who would voluntarily obey shall not be sacrificed by those who would not" (1961, p. 193, emphasis in original). Lest the world be reorganized to the advantage of the more opportunistic agents, checks against opportunism are needed.

Taken together, the overall import of bounded rationality and opportunism for transaction cost economics is this: organize transactions so as to economize on bounded rationality while simultaneously safeguarding the transactions in question against the hazards of opportunism. That is a message to which both economists and organization theorists can relate.

3.2.5. *Contract law*

Although transaction cost economics emphasizes private ordering over legal centralism, and thus pushes contract law into the institutional background, contract law nonetheless has three important roles to play. One of these is to serve as ultimate appeal, thereby delimiting threat positions.

Additionally relevant in this connection is the important role played by "excuse doctrine." Thus, parties that are able to enforce the terms of the contract in court might do this not only for good but also for poor cause. If, for example, a party asked that the letter of a contract be enforced for state realizations of a very low probability kind for which literal enforcement would impose egregious hardship on the other, then contract would be made to serve a purpose for which it was not originally intended. The use of contract, compared with internal organization, would suffer relatively if such punitive uses of contract were permitted.

Contract excuse doctrine is arguably intended to relieve such contractual "abuses." More generally, the "less than total commitment to the keeping of promises" by the legal system to which Ian Macneil refers is pertinent:

> Contract remedies are generally among the weakest of those the legal system can deliver. But a host of doctrines and techniques lies in the way of even those remedies: impossibility, frustration, mistake, manipulative interpretation, jury discretion, consideration, illegality, duress, undue influence, unconscionability, capacity, forfeiture and penalty rules, doctrines of substantial performance, severability, bankruptcy laws, statutes of fraud, to name a few; almost any contract doctrine can and does serve to make the commitment of the legal system to promise keeping less than complete. (1974, p. 730)

To be sure, there are trade-offs. One way of examining these is to assume that the object is to encourage the use of contracting (as opposed to internal organization). Both "too lax" and "too strict" contract enforcement are then to be avoided. Assessing the balance is a matter to which transaction cost reasoning can be and, to a degree, has been applied (Williamson, 1985a).

As developed in Chapter 4, contract law also has a third role to play: Each generic mode of organization is supported by a distinctive form of contract law. There is a need, therefore, to study contract laws (plural) rather than contract law (singular).

3.2.6. Process particulars

Two processes of special relevance to an understanding of economic organization are the Fundamental Transformation and the impossibility of selective intervention. The first of these deals with the transformation of what had been a large numbers bidding competition at the outset into one of bilateral exchange during contract execution and at contract renewal intervals. The second explains why internal organization is not able to beat markets everywhere by combining replication (where markets work well) with selective intervention (where markets do poorly).

Both the Fundamental Transformation and the impossibility of selective intervention are tedious process arguments and are developed at length elsewhere (Williamson, 1975, 1985b). Suffice it to observe here that process analysis (1) goes to the very core of economic organization, (2) is needed to evaluate the plausibility of alternative trade-off scenarios, and (3) invites further application—to life cycle and reputation effect features of organization (Fama, 1980; Weizisäcker, 1980; Kreps, 1990), among other things.

Examples of issues to which the new economics of organization can be or has been applied include the following:

The Theory of Economic Organization

1. If the firm is a governance structure, then the boundary of the firm ought to be set with reference to the capacity of the firm (compared with the market) to provide useful organizational functions. Accordingly, an organizational theory of the firm needs to take its place alongside a technological theory of the firm. That has been occurring.

2. If the benefits of supplying contractual safeguards against breakdown and premature breach vary systematically with the attributes of transactions, then an economic theory of contract will prescribe significant safeguards for some transactions and fewer safeguards for others. It does and the data line up (see especially Joskow, 1985, 1987, 1988, and references therein).

3. If the preceding theory of contract has general application, it should apply—with variation—to labor, intermediate product, and capital market transactions alike. It does.
   a. Labor. The collective organization of labor (unions) and the governance structures within internal labor markets should vary systematically with the attributes of labor. The preliminary evidence suggests that they do.
   b. Intermediate product. Make or buy decisions should vary systematically with the attributes of transactions. The evidence is abundant. They do. (Much of this is summarized in Williamson, 1985b, chap. 5.)

4. Leakage. The need to seal off some technologies or protect some investments against loss of appropriability will predictably elicit leakage attenuation of a discriminating kind. It does (see Teece, 1986; Heide and John, 1988).

5. The limits of internal organization. Lest internal organization be overused, with adverse increases in cost, internal organization needs to be used in a discriminating way. The powers and limits of both markets and hierarchies need to be worked out. The basic trade-offs need to be displayed. The data need to be worked up. Nuances need to be discovered. More generally, market failure and organizational failure need to be put on a parity. Work of this kind is in progress but will take a decade and more to work out.

6. Integrity. The relentless emphasis on efficiency should not obscure the needs of individuals—especially for personal integrity. The integrity-respecting (or demeaning) attributes of markets and hierarchies of different kinds need to be worked out. Albeit enormously difficult problems, they nevertheless need to be addressed.

Applications to Functional Areas

7. Finance. Debt and equity can be described as financial instruments. But it is misleading to think of debt and equity only in financial terms if the critical economic differences between these two instruments turn equally on their governance structure differences. A combined theory of corporate finance and corporate governance is needed. Alliance capitalism issues are implicated. Work on these matters has been progressing (see Gerlach, 1987; Williamson, 1988c; Berglof, 1989).

8. Marketing. A contractual approach to marketing should lead to a discriminating theory of forward integration into distribution, the use of franchising, the use of agents, and so on. Work of this kind and evidence that pertains thereto are coming along (see Anderson and Schmittlein, 1984; John and Weitz, 1988).

9. Comparative systems. A variety of approaches to the study of comparative economic systems have been employed, with varying degrees of success. An assessment of the incentive and bureaucratic features of capitalism and socialism—the powers, limits, contradictions—of each is sorely needed. The logic of economic organization to which I refer is germane and should be developed along these lines.

10. Business strategy. Strategic thinking is always appealing. But a lot of strategizing is mistaken and can be costly. A discriminating theory of strategy—when it pays, when it does not, what the instruments are, how they work—is needed. The contractual approach supplies some of the needed framework.

11. Business history. Business history ought both to inform and to be informed by the combined study of economics and organization. Business history is a field that appears to be experiencing a new life.

Applications to Contiguous Disciplines

12. Politics. Contractual theories of how to organize regulatory agencies and how federalism should be structured would add greatly to our understanding of politics. Work of both kinds is in progress (see Weingast and Marshall, 1988; North and Weingast, 1989).

13. Reconceptualizing the modern corporation in governance structure/organizational terms has ramifications for the way in which the multinational corporation is interpreted. The selective use of the multinational corporation to facilitate technology transfer is one example. More generally, the multinational corporation is usefully thought of in transnational terms—which has ramifications for the theory of the nation state (see Yarborough and Yarborough, 1987; Keoshane, 1984).

14. Sociology. The new economics of organization has brought economics and sociology into active contact with one another whereas they used to operate at a distance. A rich dialogue is needed and is in progress (see Chapter 9).

15. The law. In addition to antitrust and regulation, the new economics of organization has an important bearing on corporate governance

and on contract law. Among other things, new interpretations of "excuse doctrine," the rationale for which has been an ancient contract law puzzle, have been proposed.

Public Policy

16. Public policy toward business needs to be informed and reformed accordingly. That too has been going on. Antitrust has already been reshaped (especially with respect to vertical integration and vertical contracting practices) and more is in prospect—joint research ventures being an example (see Jorde and Teece, 1988).

17. If contracts work well in some circumstances but predictably break down in others, then the merits of deregulation (moving out of regulation into autonomous contracting) ought to be susceptible to analysis. It is. Deregulation—including mistaken deregulation—has been examined along these lines (see Joskow and Schmalensee, 1983; Williamson, 1985b, chap. 13).

18. Policy implementation—in general but specifically with reference to developing countries—needs to be reexamined from an institutional point of view. The time has come and the apparatus is at hand to examine policy implementation in a disciplined, microanalytic way. Older theories—of neoclassical, rent seeking, and property rights kinds—simply fail to address pertinent institutional issues. . . .

4.   Conclusions

Significant interim accomplishments notwithstanding, all would agree that the "science of organization" to which Barnard referred fifty years ago has not been realized. The past ten and fifteen years have nonetheless witnessed a combined law, economics, and organizations assault on the issues—the effect of which has been to push the incipient science of organization across a threshold from which there is no returning. Economics and organization theory form the axis off of which this new work operates—to which contract law provides added support.

Although much of what is in progress differs from Barnard in many ways, Barnard's imprint throughout these fifty years remains highly visible. Plainly, this was a man with great knowledge and a deep understanding of organization.

The incipient new science of organization is not a separate discipline. As indicated, it works off of and integrates the underlying disciplines of law, economics, and organization. Note, moreover, that I refer to this new science not as the "science of administration," which is the organization theory way of describing things, but as the "science of organization." The latter subsumes the former as a special case.

The aspect of the new science of organization with which I have been especially concerned (in this chapter and elsewhere) is that of transaction cost economics. This approach is distinguished by the fact that it examines economic organization in a way that is simultaneously microanalytic, comparative institutional, and economizing in its orientation. The first of these has long been resisted by economics,[16] the last by organization theory.[17] I argue that the two go together and that the prospects for a science of organization are improved as a consequence.

16. Compared with earlier economic approaches (see Prologue and Chapter 3), transaction cost economics (1) is more microanalytic, (2) is more self-conscious about its behavioral assumptions, (3) introduces and develops the economic importance of asset specificity, (4) relies more on comparative institutional analysis, (5) regards the business firm as a governance structure, (6) places greater weight on the ex-post institutions of contract, with special emphasis on private ordering (compared with court ordering), (7) works out of a combined law, economics, and organization perspective, and (8) asserts that economizing on transaction costs is the main case.

17. Compared with a standard organization theory set-up, transaction cost economics (1) eschews satisficing in favor of economizing; (2) works out of a systems framework, whereupon myopia and/or posterior rationality are eschewed in favor of "incomplete contracting in its entirety"; (3) regards the transaction as the basic unit of analysis, the dimensionalization of which is thereafter pertinent; (4) repeatedly appeals to the hypothesis that transactions will be aligned with governance structures in a discriminating (mainly, transaction cost economizing) way; (5) regards opportunism as a behavioral assumption of coequal importance with bounded rationality; (6) maintains that any issue that can be posed directly or indirectly as a contracting issue can be examined to advantage in transaction cost economizing terms; and (7) examines the process ramifications of alternative modes of contracting in microanalytic detail.

3

Transaction Cost Economics

1. Introduction

Recent and continuing headway notwithstanding, transaction cost economics maintains that our understanding of the economic institutions of capitalism—firms, markets, hybrids, bureaus—is very primitive. It subscribes to the following modest research objective: "to organize our necessarily incomplete perceptions about the economy, to see connections that the untutored eye would miss, to tell plausible . . . causal stories with the help of a few central principles, and to make rough quantitative judgments about the consequences of economic policy and other exogenous events" (Solow, 1985, p. 329).

Transaction cost economics adopts a contractual approach to the study of economic organization. Questions such as the following are germane: Why are there so many forms of organization? What main purpose is served by alternative modes of economic organization and best informs the study of these matters? Striking differences among labor markets, capital markets, intermediate product markets, corporate governance, regulation, and family organization notwithstanding, is it the case that a common theory of contract informs all? What core features—in human, technology, and process respects—does such a common theory of contract rely on? These queries go to the heart of the transaction cost economics research agenda.

The background out of which transaction cost economics works is sketched in Section 2. The operationalization of transaction cost economics is discussed in Section 3. Vertical integration, an understanding of what serves as a paradigm for helping to unpack the puzzles of complex economic organization more generally, is the subject of Section 4. Other applications of the transaction cost approach are examined in Section 5. Some empirical tests of the transaction cost hypotheses are briefly summarized in Section 6. Public policy ramifications are developed in Section 7. Concluding remarks follow.

2. Background

2.1. Main Case

Economic organization services many purposes. Among those that have been ascribed by economists are monopoly and efficient risk bearing. Power and associational gains are sometimes held to be the main purposes of economic organization, especially by noneconomists. And some hold that "social institutions and arrangement . . . [are] the adventitious result of legal, historical, or political forces" (Granovetter, 1985, p. 488).

The study of complex systems is facilitated by distinguishing core purposes from auxiliary purposes. Transaction cost economics subscribes to and develops the view that economizing is the core problem of economic organization.

Main case frameworks do not purport to be exhaustive but are designed to go to the fundamentals.[1] Especially in an area where opinions proliferate, of which the economics of organization is one, insistence upon refutable implications is needed to sort the wheat from the chaff. This is the touchstone function to which Georgescu-Roegan refers (1971, p. 37).

2.2. Behavioral Assumptions

Many economists treat behavioral assumptions as unimportant. This reflects a widely held opinion that the realism of the assumptions is unimportant and that the fruitfulness of a theory turns on its implications (Friedman, 1953). But whereas transaction cost economics is prepared to be judged (comparatively) by the refutable implications which this approach uniquely affords, it also maintains that the behavioral assumptions are important—not least of all because they serve to delimit the study of contract to the feasible subset.

Knight insisted that the study of economic organization needed to be informed by an appreciation for "human nature as we know it" (1965, p. 270), with special reference to the condition of "moral hazard" (1965, p. 260). And Bridgeman reminded social scientists that "the principal problem in understanding the actions of men is to understand how they think—how their minds work" (1955, p. 450). Coase more recently remarked that "modern institutional economics should start with real institutions. Let us also start with man as he is" (1984, p. 231). Coase urges in this connection that the view of man as a "rational utility maximizer" should be abandoned (1984, p. 231), but the salient attributes of "man as he is" otherwise remain undescribed.

I have previously argued that contracting man is distinguished from the orthodox conception of maximizing man in two respects. The first of these is the condition of bounded rationality. Second, contracting man is given to self-

---

1. Agreement on the main case does not imply that extensions to the main case, to make allowance, for example, for monopoly purposes (where the appropriate preconditions hold), cannot be made. But this is very different from making monopoly the main case—to which economizing is an added wrinkle

interest seeking of a deeper and more troublesome kind than his economic man predecessor.

Although it is sometimes believed that Herbert Simon's notion of bounded rationality is alien to the rationality tradition in economics, Simon actually enlarges rather than reduces the scope for rationality analysis. Thus, the economic actors with whom Simon is concerned are *"intendedly* rational, but only *limitedly* so" (Simon, 1961, p. xxiv). Both parts of the definition warrant respect. An economizing orientation is elicited by the intended rationality part of the definition, while the study of institutions is encouraged by acknowledging that cognitive competence is limited: "It is only because individual human beings are limited in knowledge, foresight, skill, and time that organizations are useful investments for the achievement of human purpose" (Simon, 1957b, p. 199).

Transaction cost economics pairs the assumption of bounded rationality with a self-interest-seeking assumption that makes allowance for guile. Specifically, economic agents are permitted to disclose information in a selective and distorted manner. Calculated efforts to mislead, disguise, obfuscate, and confuse are thus admitted. This self-interest-seeking attribute is variously described as opportunism, moral hazard, and agency.[2]

Bounded rationality and opportunism serve both to refocus attention and help to distinguish between feasible and infeasible modes of contracting. Both impossibly complex and hopelessly naive modes of contracting are properly excluded from the feasible set. Thus:

1. Incomplete contracting. Although it is instructive and a great analytical convenience to assume that agents have the capacity to engage in comprehensive ex ante contracting (with or without private information), the condition of bounded rationality precludes this. All contracts within the feasible set are incomplete. Accordingly, the ex post side of a contract takes on special economic importance. The study of structures that facilitate gapfilling, dispute settlement, adaptation, and the like thus become part of the problem of economic organization. Whereas such institutions play a central role in the transaction cost economics scheme of things, they are ignored (indeed, suppressed) by the fiction of comprehensive ex ante contracting.[3]

2. Critics of transaction cost economics sometimes characterize it as "neo-Hobbesian" because it assumes that economic agents are given to opportunism (in varying degrees). See, for example, Bowles and Gintis (1986, p. 201). Note, however, that the bilateral design of credible commitments (as well as other forms of private ordering) is a very non-Hobbesian response.

3. Note, moreover, that impossibly complex contracting processes cannot be saved by invoking economic natural selection arguments. Natural selection applies only to the set of viable practices and cannot be used to extend the domain. Alchian's claim that "the economist, using the present analytical tools developed in the analysis of the firm under certainty, can predict the more adoptable or viable types of economic interrelationships that will be induced by environmental change even if individuals themselves are unable to ascertain them" (1950, p. 218) is both prescient and provocative. But the argument needs to be invoked with care (Nelson and Winter, 1982). Thus, whereas it is plausible to invoke natural selection to support an efficient factor proportions outcome in a competitively organized industry (Becker, 1962), since the choice of efficient proportions—by accident, insight, or otherwise—by some subset of firms is entirely feasible, to invoke natural selection to support a vaguely described process of "ex post settling

2. Contract as promise. Another convenient concept of contract is to assume that economic agents will reliably fulfill their promises. Such stewardship behavior will not obtain, however, if economic agents are given to opportunism. Ex ante efforts to screen economic agents in terms of reliability and, even more, ex post safeguards to deter opportunism take on different economic significance as soon as the hazards of opportunism are granted. Institutional practices that were hitherto regarded as problematic are thus often seen to perform valued economizing purposes when their transaction cost features are assessed.

Inasmuch as alternative theories of contract with different behavioral assumptions support different definitions of the feasible set, rival theories of contact can, in principle, be evaluated by ascertaining which of the implied feasible sets is borne out in the data.

2.3. Legal Centralism Versus Private Ordering

It is often assumed, sometimes tacitly, that property rights are well defined and that the courts dispense justice costlessly. The mechanism design literature expressly appeals to the efficacy of court ordering (Baiman, 1982, p. 168). Much of the legal literature likewise assumes that the appropriate legal rules are in place and that the courts are the forum to which to present and resolve contract disputes.

The attractions of legal centralism notwithstanding, this orientation was disputed by Llewellyn (1931). He took exception to prevailing contract law doctrine, which emphasized legal rules, and argued that more attention should be given to the purposes served. Less concern with form and more with substance was thus indicated—especially since being legalistic could stand in the way of getting the job done. A rival conception of "contract as framework" was advanced.

If, as Galanter has subsequently argued, the participants to a contract can often "devise more satisfactory solutions to their disputes than can professionals constrained to apply general rules on the basis of limited knowledge of the dispute" (1981, p. 4), then court ordering is better regarded as a background factor rather than the central forum for dispute resolution. Albeit useful for purposes of ultimate appeal, legal centralism (court ordering) gives way to private ordering. This is intimately connected to the incomplete contracting/ex post governance approach to which I refer above.

---

up," whereby managers are purportedly paid their individual marginal products (Fama, 1980), is highly problematic. Unless and until *feasible process mechanics* are described, ex post settling up, at least in its stronger forms, looks like and performs the functions of a deus ex machina.

This is not, however, to say that natural selection plays no role in the study of contract. To the contrary, transaction cost economics maintains that those forms of organization that serve to economize on bounded rationality and safeguard transactions against the hazards of opportunism will be favored and will tend to displace inferior modes in these respects. But transaction cost economics insistently deals only with feasible modes. Within this subset it focuses analytic attention on those properties of organization that have economizing and safeguarding features.

3. Operationalizing Transaction Cost Economics

As elaborated elsewhere (Williamson, 1985b, pp. 2–7), the decade of the 1930s recorded striking insights—in law, economics, and organization—on which transaction cost economics has subsequently built. A thirty-five year interval elapsed, however, during which time the transaction cost approach to economic organization languished and the applied price theory approach to Industrial Organization ruled the day (Coase, 1972, pp. 63–64). The significant accomplishments of the firm-as-production-function approach notwithstanding, orthodox analysis ignored both the internal organization of the firm and the private ordering purposes of contract. As a consequence, "very little [was known] about the cost of conducting transactions on the market or what they depend on; we know next to nothing about the effect on costs of different groupings of activities within firms" (Coase, 1972, p. 64).

Lack of progress with transaction cost economics notwithstanding, the intuition that the leading institutions of economic organization had transaction cost origins was widely shared. As Arrow observed, "market failure is not absolute, it is better to consider a broader category, that of transaction costs, which in general impede and in particular cases completely block the formation of markets" (1969, p. 48). It was not, however, obvious how to operationalize this insight.

3.1. The Technology of Transacting

Adopting Commons' proposal that the transaction be made the basic unit of analysis, attention is focused on economizing efforts that attend the organization of transactions—where a transaction occurs when a good or service is transferred across a technologically separable interface. One stage of activity terminates and another begins. With a well-working interface, as with a well-working machine, these transfers occur smoothly. In mechanical systems we look for frictions: do the gears mesh, are the parts lubricated, is there needless slippage or other loss of energy? The economic counterpart of friction is transaction cost: for that subset of transactions where it is important to elicit cooperation,[4] do the parties to the exchange operate harmoniously, or are there frequent misunderstandings and conflicts that lead to delays, breakdowns, and other malfunctions? Transaction cost analysis entails an examination of the comparative costs of planning, adapting, and monitoring task completion under alternative governance structures.

---

4. The genius of neoclassical economics is that there are large numbers of transactions where conscious cooperation between traders is not necessary. The invisible hand works well if each party can go its own way—the buyer can secure product easily from alternative sources; the supplier can redeploy his assets without loss of productive value—with little cost to the other. Transaction cost economics is concerned with the frictions that obtain when contractual hazards arise by reason of bilateral dependency, leakage, strategizing, or the like.

Assessing the technology of transacting is facilitated by making the transaction the basic unit of analysis. The central question then becomes: What are the principal dimensions with respect to which transactions differ? Refutable implications are derived from the hypothesis that transactions, which differ in their attributes, are assigned to governance structures, which differ in their costs and competencies, in a discriminating—mainly transaction cost economizing—way.

The principal dimensions on which transaction cost economics presently relies for purposes of describing transactions are (1) the frequency with which they recur, (2) the degree and type of uncertainty to which they are subject, and (3) the condition of asset specificity. Although all are important, many of the refutable implications of transaction cost economics turn critically on this last.

3.1.1.   Asset specificity

Asset specificity has reference to the degree to which an asset can be redeployed to alternative uses and by alternative users without sacrifice of productive value. This has a relation to the notion of sunk cost. But the full ramifications of asset specificity become evident only in the context of incomplete contracting and went unrecognized in the pre-transaction cost era (Williamson, 1975, 1979a); Klein, Crawford, and Alchian, 1978).

Interestingly, Marshall recognized that idiosyncratic human capital could sometimes accrue during the course of employment (1948, p. 626). Becker (1962), moreover, made express provision for human capital in his examination of labor market incentive schemes. Marschak expressly took exception with the readiness with which economists accept and employ assumptions of fungibility. As he put it, "There exist almost unique, irreplaceable research workers, teachers, administrations; just as there exist unique choice locations for plants and harbors. The problem of unique or imperfectly standardized goods ... has indeed been neglected in the textbooks" (1968, p. 14). Polanyi's (1962) remarkable discussion of "personal knowledge" further illustrates the importance of idiosyncratic knowledge and working relations.

Transaction cost economics accepts all of the foregoing and moves the argument forward in three respects: (1) asset specificity can take many forms, of which human asset specificity is only one; (2) asset specificity not only elicits complex ex ante incentive responses but, even more important, it gives rise to complex ex post governance structure responses; and (3) the study of economic organization in all of its forms—industrial organization, labor, international trade, economic development, family organization, comparative systems, and even finance—becomes grist for the transaction cost economics mill.

Without purporting to be exhaustive, asset specificity distinctions of six kinds have been made: (1) site specificity, as where successive stations are located in a cheek-by-jowl relation to each other so as to economize on inventory and transportation expenses; (2) physical asset specificity, such as specialized dies that are required to produce a component; (3) human asset specificity that arises in a learning-by-doing fashion; (4) dedicated assets, which are discrete investments in general purpose plant that are made at the behest of a particular customer; to which (5) brand name capital and (6) temporal specificity have been added. As discussed in Sections 4 and 5, the organizational ramifications of each type of specificity differ. Additional predictive content arises in this way.

3.1.2.   Uncertainty

Koopmans described the core problem of the economic organization of society as that of facing and dealing with uncertainty (1957, p. 147). He distinguished between primary and secondary uncertainty in this connection, the distinction being that whereas primary uncertainty is of a state-contingent kind, secondary uncertainty arises "from lack of communication, that is from one decision maker having no way of finding out the concurrent decisions and plans made by others"—which he judges to be "quantitatively at least as important as the primary uncertainty arising from random acts of nature and unpredictable changes in consumer's preferences" (pp. 162–63).

Note, however, that the secondary uncertainty to which Koopmans refers is of a rather innocent or nonstrategic kind. There is a lack of timely communication, but no reference is made to strategic nondisclosure, disguise, or distortion of information. Such strategic features are unavoidably presented, however, when parties are joined in a condition of bilateral dependency. A third class of uncertainty—namely, behavioral (or binary) uncertainty—is thus usefully recognized.[5]

The distinction between *statistical risks* and *idiosyncratic trading hazards* is pertinent in this connection. This is akin to, but nonetheless different from, Knight's (1965) distinction between risk and uncertainty. Hazards are due to the behavioral uncertainties that arise when incomplete contracting and asset specificity are joined. Of special importance to the economics of organization is that the mitigation of hazards can be the source of mutual gain. The language of governance, rather than statistical decision theory, applies.

3.1.3.   The fundamental transformation

Economists of all persuasions recognize that the terms upon which an initial bargain will be struck depend on whether noncollusive bids can be elicited from more than one qualified supplier. Monopolistic terms will obtain if there is only a single highly qualified supplier, while competitive terms will result if there are many. Transaction cost economics fully accepts this description of ex ante bidding competition but insists that the study of contracting be extended to include ex post features. Thus, initial bidding merely sets the contracting process in motion. A full assessment requires that both contract

---

5. The recent paper by Helfat and Teece (1987) examines vertical integration with reference to this condition.

execution and ex post competition at the contract renewal interval come under scrutiny.

Contrary to earlier practice, transaction cost economics holds that a condition of large numbers bidding at the outset does not necessarily imply that a large numbers bidding condition will obtain thereafter. Whether ex post competition is fully effacious or not depends on whether the good or service in question is supported by durable investments in transaction specific human or physical assets. Where no such specialized investments are incurred, the initial winning bidder realizes no advantage over nonwinners. Although it may continue to supply for a long period of time, this is only because, in effect, it is continuously meeting competitive bids from qualified rivals. Rivals cannot be presumed to operate on a parity, however, once substantial investments in transaction specific assets are put in place. Winners in these circumstances enjoy advantages over nonwinners, which is to say that parity at the renewal interval is upset. Accordingly, what was a large numbers bidding condition at the outset is effectively transformed into one of bilateral supply thereafter. The reason why significant reliance investments in durable, transaction specific assets introduce contractual asymmetry between the winning bidder on the one hand and nonwinners on the other is because economic values would be sacrificed if the ongoing supply relation were to be terminated.

Faceless contracting is thereby supplanted by contracting in which the pairwise identity of the parties matters. Not only is the supplier unable to realize equivalent value were the specialized assets to be redeployed to other uses, but the buyer must induce potential suppliers to make similar specialized investments were he to seek least-cost supply from an outsider. The incentives of the parties to work things out rather than terminate are thus apparent. This has pervasive ramifications for the organization of economic activity.

3.2. A Simple Contractual Schema

3.2.1. The general approach

Assume that a good or service can be supplied by either of two alternative technologies. One is a general purpose technology, the other a special purpose technology. The special purpose technology requires greater investment in transaction-specific durable assets and is more efficient for servicing steady-state demands.

Using k as a measure of transaction-specific assets, transactions that use the general purpose technology are ones for which $k = 0$. When transactions use the special purpose technology, by contrast, a $k > 0$ condition exists. Assets here are specialized to the particular needs of the parties. Productive values would therefore be sacrificed if transactions of this kind were to be prematurely terminated. The bilateral monopoly condition described above and elaborated below applies to such transactions.

Whereas classical market contracting—"sharp in by clear agreement; sharp out by clear performance" (Macneil, 1974, p. 738)—suffices for transactions of the $k = 0$ kind, unassisted market governance poses hazards whenever nontrivial transaction-specific assets are placed at risk. Parties have an incentive to devise safeguards to protect investments in transactions of the latter kind. Let s denote the magnitude of any such safeguards. An $s = 0$ condition is one in which no safeguards are provided; a decision to provide safeguards is reflected by an $s > 0$ result.

Figure 3.1 displays the three contracting outcomes corresponding to such a description. Associated with each node is a price. So as to facilitate comparisons between nodes, assume that suppliers (1) are risk neutral, (2) are prepared to supply under either technology, and (3) will accept any safeguard condition whatsoever so long as an expected breakeven result can be projected. Thus, node A is the general purpose technology ($k = 0$) supply relation for which a breakeven price of p_1 is projected. The node B contract is supported by transaction-specific assets ($k > 0$) for which no safeguard is offered ($s = 0$). The expected breakeven price here is $\bar{p}$. The node C contract also employs the special purpose technology. But since the buyer at this node provides the supplier with a safeguard, ($s > 0$), the breakeven price, $\hat{p}$, at node C is less than $\bar{p}$.[6]

The protective safeguards to which I refer normally take on one or more of three forms. The first is to realign incentives, which commonly involves some type of severance payment or penalty for premature termination. Albeit important and the central focus of much of the formal contracting literature, this is a very limited response. A second is to supplant court ordering by private ordering. Allowance is expressly made for contractual incompleteness; and a different forum for dispute resolution (of which arbitration is an example) is commonly provided (see Joskow, 1985, 1987; Williamson, 1985b, pp. 164–66). Third, the transaction may be embedded in a more complex trading network. The object here is to better assure continuity purposes and facilitate adaptations. Expanding a trading relation from unilateral to bilateral exchange—through the concerted use, for example, of reciprocity—thereby to effect an equilibration of trading hazards is one illustration. Recourse to collective decision-making under some form of combined ownership is another.

This simple contracting schema applies to a wide variety of contracting issues. It facilitates comparative institutional analysis by emphasizing that technology (k), contractual governance/safeguards (s) and price (p) are fully interactive and are determined simultaneously. It is furthermore gratifying that so many applications turn out to be variations on a theme.

By way of summary, the nodes A, B, and C in the contractual schema set out in Figure 3.1 have the following properties:

1. Transactions that are efficiently supported by general purpose assets ($k = 0$) are located at node A and do not need protective governance structures. Discrete market contracting suffices. The world of competition obtains.

---

6. Specialized production technologies commonly afford steady-state cost savings over general purpose production technologies. But since the former are less redeployable than the latter, stochastic disturbances may reverse the cost advantage (whether p_1 is greater than or less than $\hat{p}$ requires that stochastic factors be taken into account). See Williamson, 1985b, pp. 169–75.

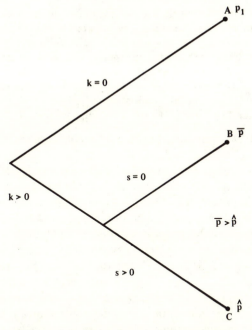

Figure 3.1. A simple contracting schema.

2. Transactions that involve significant investments of a transaction-specific kind ($k > 0$) are ones for which the parties are effectively engaged in bilateral trade.

3. Transactions located at node *B* enjoy no safeguards ($s = 0$), on which account the projected breakeven supply price is great ($\bar{p} > \hat{p}$). Such transactions are apt to be unstable contractually. They may revert to node *A* [in which event the special purpose technology would be replaced by the general purpose ($k = 0$) technology] or be relocated to node *C* (by introducing contractual safeguards that would encourage use of the $k > 0$ technology).

4. Transactions located at node *C* incorporate safeguards ($s > 0$) and thus are protected against expropriation hazards.

·5. Inasmuch as price and governance are linked, parties to a contract should not expect to have their cake (low price) and eat it too (no safeguard). More generally, it is important to study *contracting in its entirety*. Both the ex ante terms and the manner in which contracts are thereafter executed vary with the investment characteristics and the associated governance structures within which transactions are embedded.

3.2.2.   *An illustration*

Klein and Leffler (1981) argue that franchisees may be required to make investments in transaction-specific capital as a way by which to safeguard the franchise system against quality shading. As Klein puts it, franchisers can better assure quality by requiring franchisee investments in specific . . . assets that upon termination imply a capital loss penalty larger than can be obtained by the franchisee if he cheats. For example, the franchiser may require franchisees to rent from them short term (rather than own) the land upon which their outlet is located. This lease arrangement creates a situation where termination can require the franchisee to move and thereby impose a capital loss on him up to the amount of his initial nonsalvageable investment. Hence a form of collateral to deter franchisee cheating is created. (1980, p. 359)

The arrangement is tantamount to the creation of hostages to restore integrity to an exchange.

That logic notwithstanding, the use of hostages to deter franchisees from exploiting the demand externalities that inhere in brand name capital is often regarded as an imposed (top down) solution. Franchisees are "powerless"; they accept hostage terms because no others are available. Such power arguments are often based on ex post reasoning. That the use of hostages to support exchange can be and often is an efficient systems solution, hence is independent of who originates the proposal, can be seen from the following revised sequence.

Suppose that an entrepreneur develops a distinctive, patentable idea that he sells outright to a variety of independent, geographically dispersed suppliers, each of which is assigned an exclusive territory. Each supplier expects to sell only to the population within its territory, but all find to their surprise (and initially to their delight) that sales are also made to a mobile population. Purchases by the mobile population are based not on the reputation of individual franchisees but on customers' perceptions of the reputation of the system. A demand externality arises in this way.

Thus, were sales made only to the local population, each supplier would fully appropriate the benefits of its promotional and quality enhancement efforts. Population mobility upsets this: because the cost savings that result from local quality debasement accrue to the local operator while the adverse demand effects are diffused throughout the system, suppliers now have an incentive to free ride off of the reputation of the system. Having sold the exclusive territory rights outright, the entrepreneur who originated the program is indifferent to these unanticipated demand developments. It thus remains for the collection of independent franchisees to devise a correction themselves, lest the value of the system deteriorate to their individual and collective disadvantage.

The franchisees, under the revised scenario, thus create an agent to police quality or otherwise devise penalties that deter quality deterioration. One possibility is to return to the entrepreneur and hire him to provide such services. Serving now as the agent of the franchisees, the entrepreneur may undertake a program of quality checks (certain purchasing restraints are introduced, whereby franchisees are required to buy only from qualified suppliers; periodic inspections are performed). The incentive to exploit demand externalities may further be discouraged by requiring each franchisee to post a hostage and by making franchises terminable.

This indirect scenario serves to demonstrate that it is the *system* that benefits from the control of externalities. But this merely confirms that the normal scenario in which the franchiser controls the contractual terms is not an arbitrary exercise of power. Indeed, if franchisees recognize that the demand externality exists from the outset, if the franchiser refuses to make provision for the externality in the original contract, and if it is very costly to reform the franchise system once initial contracts are set, franchisees will bid less for the right to a territory than they otherwise would. It should not therefore be concluded that perceptive franchisers, who recognize the demand externality in advance and make provision for it, are imposing objectionable ex ante terms on unwilling franchisees. They are merely taking steps to realize the full value of the franchise. Here, as elsewhere, contracts must be examined in their entirety.

3.3.   The Measurement Branch

Most of the foregoing and most of this chapter deal with the governance issues that arise in conjunction with asset specificity. There is, however, another branch that focuses on problems of measurement. The treatment of team organization by Alchian and Demsetz (1972) in the context of technological nonseparabilities is one example. Barzel's (1982) concerns with product quality is another.

All measurement problems are traceable to a condition of information impactedness—which is to say that either (1) information is asymmetrically distributed between buyer and seller and can be equalized only at great cost or (2) it is costly to apprise an arbiter of the true information condition should a dispute arise between opportunistic parties who have identical knowledge of the underlying circumstances (Williamson, 1975, pp. 31–37). Interestingly, measurement problems with different origins give rise to different organizational responses. Thus, whereas team organization problems give rise to supervision, the classical agency problem elicits an incentive alignment response. Reputation effect mechanisms are responses to quality uncertainty, and common ownership is often the device by which concerns over asset dissipation are mitigated. Plainly, an integrated treatment of governance and measurement is ultimately needed.[7]

4.   The Paradigm Problem: Vertical Integration

The leading studies of firm and market organization—in 1937 and over the next thirty-five years—typically held that the "natural" or efficient boundaries

---

7. Alchian joins the two as follows: "One might . . . define the firm in terms of two features: the detectability of *input* performance *and* the expropriability of quasi-rents of [transaction specific] resources" (1984, p. 39). See also Milgrom and Roberts (1992).

of the firm were defined by technology and could be taken as given. Boundary extension was thus thought to have monopoly origins.[8]

Coase (1937) took exception with this view in his classic article on "The Nature of the Firm." He not only posed the fundamental question: When do firms choose to procure in the market and when do they produce to their own requirements?, but he argued that comparative transaction cost differences explain the result. Wherein, however, do these transaction cost differences reside?

The proposition that asset specificity had significant implications for vertical integration was first advanced in 1971. A comparative institutional orientation was employed to assess when and for what reasons market procurement gives way to internal organization. Given the impossibility of comprehensive contracting (by reason of bounded rationality) and the need to adapt a supply relation through time (in response to disturbances), the main comparative institutional alternatives to be evaluated were between incomplete short-term contracts and vertical integration. Problems with short-term contracts were projected "if either (1) efficient supply requires investment in special-purpose, long-life equipment, or (2) the winner of the original contract acquires a cost advantage, say by reason of 'first mover' advantages (such as unique location or learning, including the acquisition of undisclosed or proprietary technical and managerial procedures and task-specific labor skills)" (Williamson, 1971b, p. 116).

4.1. A Heuristic Model

The main differences between market and internal organization are these: (1) markets promote high-powered incentives and restrain bureaucratic distortions more effectively than internal organization; (2) markets can sometimes aggregate demands to advantage, thereby to realize economies of scale and scope; and (3) internal organization has access to distinctive governance instruments.

Consider the decision of a firm to make or buy a particular good or service. Suppose that it is a component that is to be joined to the mainframe and assume that it is used in fixed proportion. Assume, furthermore, that economies of scale and scope are negligible. Accordingly, the critical factors that are determinative in the decision to make or buy are production cost control and the ease of effecting intertemporal adaptations.

Although the high-powered incentives of markets favor tighter production cost control, they impede the ease of adaptation as the bilateral dependency of the relation between the parties builds up. The latter effect is a consequence of the fundamental transformation that occurs as a condition of asset specificity

---

8. The main monopoly emphasis was on the use of boundary extension to exercise economic muscle (Stigler, 1951, 1955; Bain, 1968). McKenzie (1951) and others have noted, however, that vertical integration may also be used to correct against monopoly-induced factor distortions. Arguments of both kinds work out of the firm-as-production-function tradition. For a much more complete treatment of vertical integration, see Martin Perry, 1989.

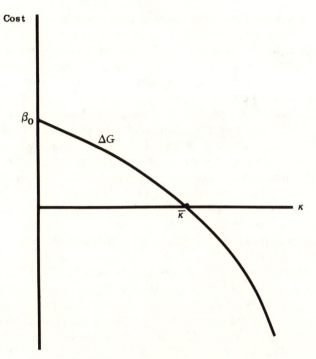

Figure 3.2. Comparative governance cost.

deepens. For a fixed level of output (say $X = \bar{X}$), let $B(k)$ be the bureaucratic costs of internal governance and $M(k)$ the corresponding governance costs of markets, where k is an index of asset specificity. Assume that $B(0) > M(0)$, by reason of the above-described incentive and bureaucratic effects. Assume further, however, that $M' > B'$ evaluated at every k. This second condition is a consequence of the comparative disability of markets in adaptability respects. Letting $\Delta G = B(k) - M(k)$, the relation shown in Figure 3.2 obtains.

Thus, market procurement is the preferred supply mode where asset specificity is slight—because $\Delta G > 0$ under these circumstances. But internal organization is favored where asset specificity is great, because the high-powered incentives of markets impair the comparative ease with which adaptive, sequential adjustments to disturbances are accomplished. As shown, the switchover value, where the choice between firm and market is a matter of indifference, occurs at $\bar{k}$.

The foregoing assumes that economies of scale and scope are negligible, so that the choice between firm and market rests entirely on the governance cost differences. Plainly that oversimplifies. Markets are often able to aggregate diverse demands, thereby to realize economies of scale and scope. Accordingly, production cost differences also need to be taken into account.[9]

9. The argument assumes that the firm produces exclusively to its own needs. If diseconomies of scale or scope are large, therefore, technological features will deter all but very large firms from supplying to their own needs.

Again it will be convenient to hold output unchanged. Let ΔC be the steady-state production cost difference between producing to one's own requirements and the steady-state cost of procuring the same item in the market. (The steady-state device avoids the need for adaptation.) Expressing ΔC as a function of asset specificity, it is plausible to assume that ΔC will be positive throughout but will be a decreasing function of k.

The production cost penalty of using internal organization is large for standardized transactions for which market aggregation economies are great, whence ΔC is large where k is low. The cost disadvantage decreases but remains positive for intermediate degrees of asset specificity. Thus, although dissimilarities among orders begin to appear, outside suppliers are nevertheless able to aggregate the diverse demands of many buyers and produce at lower costs than can a firm that produces to its own needs. As goods and services become very close to unique (k is high), however, aggregation economies of outside supply can no longer be realized, whence ΔC asymptotically approaches zero. Contracting out affords neither scale nor scope economies in those circumstances. The firm can produce without penalty to its own needs.

This ΔC relation is shown in Figure 3.3. The object, of course, is not to minimize ΔC or ΔG taken separately but, given the optimal or specified level of asset specificity, to minimize the sum of production and governance cost differences. The vertical sum $\Delta G + \Delta C$ is also displayed. The crossover value of k for which the sum ($\Delta G + \Delta C$) becomes negative is shown by $\hat{k}$, which value exceeds $\bar{k}$. Economies of scale and scope thus favor market organization over a wider range of asset specificity values than would be observed if steady state production cost economies were absent.

More generally, if $k*$ is the optimal degree of asset specificity,[10] Figure 3.3 discloses:

1. Market procurement has advantages in both scale economy and governance respects where optimal asset specificity is slight ($k* \ll \hat{k}$).

Plausible though this appears, neither economies of scale nor scope are, by themselves, responsible for decisions to buy rather than make. Thus, suppose that economies of scale are large in relation to a firm's own needs. Absent prospective contracting problems, the firm could construct a plant of size sufficient to exhaust economies of scale and sell excess product to rivals and other interested buyers. Or suppose that economies of scope are realized by selling the final good in conjunction with a variety of related items. The firm could integrate forward into marketing and offer to sell its product together with related items on a parity basis—rival and complementary items being displayed, sold, and serviced without reference to strategic purposes.

That other firms, especially rivals, would be willing to proceed on this basis, is surely doubtful. Rather than submit to the strategic hazards, some will decline to participate in such a scheme (Williamson, 1975, pp. 16–19; 1979a, pp. 979–80). The upshot is that *all* cost differences between internal and market procurement ultimately rest on transaction cost considerations. Inasmuch, however, as the needs of empirical research on economic organization are better served by making the assumption that firms which procure internally supply exclusively to their own needs, whence technological economies of scale and scope are accorded independent importance, I employ this assumption here.

10. Reference to a single "optimal" level of k is an expository convenience: the optimal level actually varies with organization form. This is further developed in Subsection 4.2.

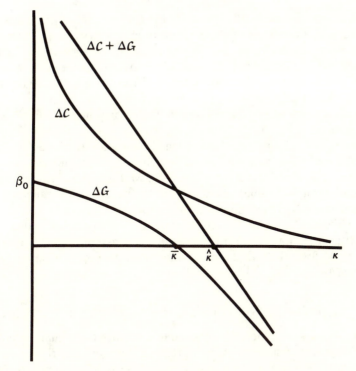

Figure 3.3. Comparative production and governance costs.

2. Internal organization enjoys the advantage where optimal asset specificity is substantial ($k^* \gg \hat{k}$). Not only does the market realize little aggregation economy benefits, but market governance, because of maladaptation problems that arise when assets are highly specific, is hazardous.

3. Only small cost differences appear for intermediate degrees of optimal asset specificity. Mixed governance, in which some firms will be observed to buy, others to make, and all express "dissatisfaction" with their procurement solution, are apt to arise for k^* in the neighborhood of $\hat{k}$. Accidents of history may be determinative. Nonstandard contracts of the types discussed briefly above and developed more fully in Subsection 4.2 may arise to serve these.

4. More generally, it is noteworthy that, inasmuch as the firm is everywhere at a disadvantage to the market in production cost respects ($\Delta C < 0$ everywhere), the firm will never integrate for production cost reasons alone. Only when contracting difficulties intrude does the firm and market comparison support vertical integration—and then only for values of k^* that significantly exceed $\hat{k}$.

Additional implications may be gleaned by introducing quantity (or firm size) and organization form effects. Thus, consider firm size (output). The basic proposition here is that diseconomies associated with own production will be everywhere reduced as the quantity of the component to be supplied increases. The firm is simply better able to realize economies of scale as its own requirements become larger in relation to the size of the market. The curve ΔC thus everywhere falls as quantity increases. The question then is: What happens to the curve ΔG? If this twists about $\bar{k}$, which is a plausible construction,[11] then the vertical sum $\Delta G + \Delta C$ will intersect the axis at a value of k that progressively moves to the left as the quantity to be supplied increases. Accordingly:

5. Larger firms will be more integrated into components than will smaller, ceteris paribus.

Finally, for reasons that have been developed elsewhere (Williamson, 1970), the bureaucratic disabilities to which internal organization is subject vary with the internal structure of the firm. Multidivisionalization, assuming that the M-form is feasible, serves as a check against the bureaucratic distortions that appear in the unitary form (U-form) of enterprise. Expressed in terms of Figure 3.3, the curve ΔG falls under multidivisionalization as compared with the unitary form organization. Thus, assuming ΔC is unchanged:

6. An M-form firm will be more integrated than its U-form counterpart, ceteris paribus.

4.2. A Combined Neoclassical–Transaction Cost Treatment

A unified framework is herein employed to formalize the arguments advanced above.[12] It is in the spirit of Arrow's remark that new theories of economic organization takes on greater "analytic usefulness when these are founded on more directly neoclassical lines" (1985b, p. 303). The spirit of the analysis is consonant with that of economics quite generally: use more general modes of analysis as a check on the limitations that inform more specialized types of reasoning.

The heuristic model assumes that both firm and market modes of supply produce the same level of output and that the optimal level of asset specificity is the same in each. These are arbitrary constraints, however. What happens when both are relaxed? This is examined below in the context of a combined production and transaction cost model that is itself highly simplified—in that it (1) deals only with polar firm or market alternatives, (2) examines only one transaction at a time, and (3) employs a reduced form type of analysis, in that it ascribes rather than derives the basic production and governance cost competencies of firms and markets. (See, however, Chapter 4.)

It will facilitate the argument to assume initially that firm and market employ the identical production cost technology. This assumption is subsequently relaxed.

---

11. Assume that $I(k, X) = I(k)X$ where $I(0) > 0$ and $I(k)$ is the internal governance cost per unit of effecting adaptations. Assume, furthermore, that $M(k, X) = M(k)X$ where $M(0) = 0$ and $M(k)$ is the corresponding governance cost per unit of effecting market adaptations. Then $\Delta G = [I(k) - M(k)]X$, and the value at which ΔG goes to zero will be independent of X. The effect of increasing X is to twist ΔG clockwise about the value of k at which it goes to zero.

12. The argument is based on Riordan and Williamson, 1985. See also Masten, 1982.

4.2.1. Common production technology

Revenue is given by $R = R(X)$, and production costs of market and internal procurement are assumed to be given by the relation:

$$C = C(X, k; \alpha); \quad C_X > 0; C_k < 0; C_{Xk} < 0,$$

where the parameter α is a shift parameter, a higher value of α yielding greater cost reducing consequences to asset specificity:

$$C_{k\alpha} < 0; \quad C_{X\alpha} < 0.$$

Asset specificity is assumed to be available at the constant per unit cost of γ. The neoclassical profit expression corresponding to this statement of revenue and production costs is given by

$$\pi^*(X, k; \alpha) = R(X) - C(X, k; \alpha) - \gamma k.$$

Governance costs are conspicuously omitted from this profit relation, there being no provision for such costs in the neoclassical statement of the problem.

Assume that this function is globally concave. At an interior maximum the decision variables X^* and k^* are determined from the zero marginal profit conditions:

$$\pi_X^*(X, k; \alpha) = 0; \quad \pi_k^*(X, k; \alpha) = 0.$$

Consider now the governance costs of internal and market organization. Let the superscripts i denote internal and m denote market organization. Governance cost expressions congruent with the cost differences described above are given by

$$G^i = \beta + V(k); \quad \beta > 0; V_k > = 0,$$
$$G^m = W(k); \quad W_k > 0,$$

where $W_k > V_k$, evaluated at common k.

The corresponding profit expressions for internal market procurement in the face of positive governance costs are

$$\pi^i = R(X) - C(X, k; \alpha) - \gamma k - (\beta + V(k)),$$
$$\pi^m = R(X) - C(X, k; \alpha) - \gamma k - W(k).$$

The zero marginal profit conditions for internal procurement are

$$\pi^i_X = R_X - C_X = 0,$$

$$\pi^i_k = -C_k - \gamma - V_k = 0.$$

Those for market procurement are

$$\pi^m_k = R_X - C_X = 0,$$

$$\pi^m_k = -C_k - \gamma - W_k = 0.$$

In each instance, therefore, optimal output, given asset specificity, is obtained by setting marginal revenue equal to the marginal costs of production, while optimal asset specificity, given output, is chosen to minimize the sum of production and governance costs.

Given that $\pi^*_{Xk} = -C_{Xk} > 0$, the neoclassical locus of optimal output given asset specificity and the corresponding locus of optimal asset specificity given output will bear the relations shown by $\pi^*_X = 0$ and $\pi^*_k = 0$ in Figure 3.4. The corresponding loci for internal and market organization are also shown. Inasmuch as the zero marginal profit expressions for output for all three statements of the maximand are identical, the loci $\pi^i_X = 0$ and $\pi^m_X = 0$ track $\pi^*_X = 0$ exactly. The zero marginal profit expressions for asset specificity, however, differ. Given that $W_k > V_k > 0$, the locus $\pi^m_k = 0$ is everywhere below $\pi^i_k =$

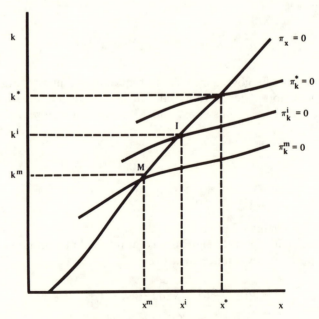

Figure 3.4. Marginal profit loci.

0, which in turn is below $\pi_k^* = 0$. Accordingly, profit maximizing values of X and k for these three statements of the optimization problem bear the following relation to each other: $X^* > X^i > X^m$ and $k^* > k^i > k^m$. The output effects are indirect or induced effects, attributable to shifts in the zero marginal profit asset specificity loci.

Of course, the X^* and k^* choices are purely hypothetical since, in reality, a zero transaction cost condition is not a member of the feasible set. The relevant choices thus reduce to using input combinations I under internal procurement or M under market procurement. An immediate implication is that if the firm were operating in two identical markets and was constrained to buy in one and to make in the other, it would sell more goods of a more distinctive kind in the region where it produced to its own needs.

Ordinarily, however, the firm will not be so constrained but will choose to make or buy according to which mode offers the greatest profit in each region. Figure 3.5 shows profit as a function of asset specificity, the choice of output assumed to be optimal for each value of k. Whereas there is a family of π^i curves, one for each value of the bureaucratic cost parameter β, there in only a single π^m curve. Which mode is favored depends on which has the highest peak. This is the internal mode for $\beta = \beta_0$ but the market mode for $\beta = \beta_1$, where $\beta_1 > \beta_0$. The optimal values of k and X depend only on the mode selected and not on β, however, since β does not influence the marginal conditions.

The comparative statics ramifications of the production cost parameter α are more central. Applications of the envelope theorem reveal that

$$\pi_\alpha^m = -C_\alpha(X^m, k^m; \alpha),$$

$$\pi_\alpha^i = -C_\alpha(X^i, k^i; \alpha).$$

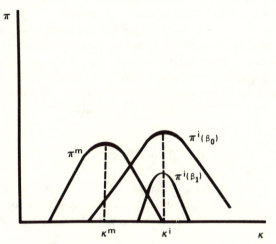

Figure 3.5. Bureaucratic cost effects.

Inasmuch as $X^i > X^m$ and $k^i > k^m$, it follows from our earlier production cost assumptions that $\pi_a^i > \pi_a^m$. In other words, as asset specificity has greater cost reducing impact, internal organization is progressively favored.

4.2.2. Production cost differences

Consider now the case, to which earlier reference was made and is arguably the more realistic, where the firm is unable to aggregate demands and sell product that exceeds its own demands without penalty. Let $H(X,k)$ denote the production cost disadvantage per unit of output associated with internal organization. The production costs of the two modes then are

$$C^m = C(X, k; \alpha),$$

$$C^i = C(X, k; \alpha) + H(X, k)X.$$

Assume that $H_X < 0$ and $H_k < 0$ but that $H(X, k)X$ is positive and asymptotically approaches zero as X and k approach infinity. Denote the marginal production cost disadvantage by $M(X, k) = H_X(X, k)X + H(X, k)$.

The analysis depends on the way in which the total production cost disadvantage experienced by internal organization changes for outputs within the relevant range. At low levels of output, decreasing unit cost disadvantages will normally be attended by an increasing total cost, whence $M(X, k) > 0$. Beyond some threshold level of output, however, the total production cost disadvantage of internal organization will begin to decline. Indeed, as the firm progressively increases in relation to the size of the market, the production cost disadvantage presumably approaches zero—since firm and market have access to identical economies of scale as a monopoly condition evolves. Accordingly, $M(X, k) < 0$ once this threshold is crossed.

The main results are strengthened within the (large output) range where $M(X, k) < 0$: $X^m < X^i$, $k^m < k^i$; and $\pi_a^i < \pi_a^m$. Within the (small output) range, however, where $M_x > 0$, the marginal production cost disadvantage of internal organization and the marginal governance cost disadvantage of market procurement operate in opposite directions. An unambiguous ordering of optimal output and asset specificity is not possible in terms of the above-described qualitative features of the problem in this instance. An anomaly thus arises that was not evident in the heuristic presentation above.

5.   Other Applications

The underlying transaction cost economizing theme repeats itself, with variation, almost endlessly. Three applications are sketched here: to nonstandard commercial contracting, career marriages, and corporate finance.[13] The sys-

---

13. Applications to labor market organization and comparative economic systems are developed in Williamson, 1985b, chaps. 9 and 10.

tems' ramifications of organizational innovation are also noteworthy. These are examined with reference to "Full Functionalism" (Elster, 1983).

5.1. Nonstandard Commercial Contracting

Many nonstandard contracting phenomena are explained with the aid of one of two models: the hostage model and the oversearching model.

5.1.1. The hostage model

The hostage model developed in Chapter 5 is a member of the family of models dealing with credible commitments (Klein and Leffler, 1981; Telser, 1981; Williamson, 1983). Although the particulars differ, all of these models feature intertemporal contracting, uncertainty, and investments in transaction specific assets. The application to reciprocal trading is sketched here.

Reciprocity is believed to be a troublesome practice. Reciprocity transforms a unilateral supply relation—whereby A sells X to B—into a bilateral one, whereby A agrees to buy Y from B as a condition for making the sale of X and both parties understand that the transaction will be continued only if reciprocity is observed. Although reciprocal selling is widely held to be anticompetitive (Stocking and Mueller, 1957; Blake, 1973), others regard it more favorably. Stigler offers the following affirmative rationale for reciprocity.

> The case for reciprocity arises when prices cannot be freely varied to meet supply and demand conditions. Suppose that a firm is dealing with a colluding industry which is fixing prices. A firm in this collusive industry would be willing to sell at less that the cartel price if it can escape detection. Its price can be reduced in effect by buying from the customer-seller at an inflated price. Here reciprocity restores flexibility of prices.[14]

Inasmuch, however, as many industries do not satisfy the prerequisites for oligopolistic price collusion (Posner, 1969b; Williamson, 1975, chap. 12) and as reciprocity is sometimes observed among these, reciprocity presumably has other origins as well. Tie breaking is one of these. A second is that reciprocity can have advantageous governance structure benefits. These two can be distinguished by the type of product being sold.

The tie-breaker explanation applies where firm B, which is buying specialized product from A, asks that A buy standardized product from B on the condition that B meets market terms. Other things being equal, procurement agents at A are apt to accede. Scherer notes that "Most of the 163 corporation executives responding to a 1963 survey state that their firms' purchases were awarded on the basis of reciprocity only when the price, quality, and delivery conditions were equal" (1980, p. 344).

14. President's Task Force Report on Productivity and Competition, reprinted in Commerce Clearing House *Trade Regulation Reporter*, June 24, 1969, p. 39.

The more interesting case is where reciprocity involves the sale of special-ized product to B conditioned on the procurement of specialized product from B. The argument here is that reciprocity can serve to equalize the exposure of the parties, thereby reducing the incentive of the buyer to defect from the exchange—leaving the supplier to redeploy specialized assets at greatly reduced alternative value. Absent a hostage (or other assurance that the buyer will not defect), the sale by A of specialized product to B may never materialize. The buyer's commitment to the exchange is more assuredly signaled by his willingness to accept reciprocal exposure of specialized assets. Defection haz-ards are thereby mitigated.

Lest the argument be uncritically considered to be a defense for reciprocal trading quite generally, note that it applies only where specialized assets are placed at hazard by both parties. Where only one or neither invests in special-ized assets, the practice of reciprocity plainly has other origins.

Shepard (1986) has recently developed another interesting application of transaction cost reasoning that involves not the creation but the release of a hostage. The puzzle to be explained is the insistence by buyers that semicon-ductor producers license their design of chips to others. One explanation is that this averts delivery failures attributable to idiosyncratic disruptive events at the parent company (earthquakes, labor strife, and the like). If, however, exposure to geographic hazards and supply interruptions due to company-wide bargaining were the only concerns, then subcontracting would afford adequate relief. Since the parent company could retain full control over total production via subcontracting, and since such control offers the prospect of added monopoly gains, licensing is evidently a poorly calibrated—indeed, in relation to the above described economic purposes, it is an excessive—response.

The possibility that the demand for licensing has other origins is thus suggested. The transaction cost rationale for insistence upon licensing is that buyers are reluctant to specialize their product and production to a particular chip without assurance of "competitive" supply. The concern is that a monop-oly seller will expropriate the buyer when follow-on orders are placed—which is after the buyer has made durable investments that cannot be redeployed without sacrifice of productive value. The insistence on licensing is thus ex-plained by the fact that access to several *independent* sources of supply relieves these expropriation hazards.[15]

5.1.2. Oversearching

Most of the applications of transaction cost economics have dealt with gover-nance issues. Transaction cost economics also deals, however, with measure-ment problems (Barzel, 1982). One manifestation of this is oversearching.

15. This is akin to, though slightly different from, Shepard's (1986) explanation.

Kenney and Klein (1983) address themselves to several such cases. One is a reinterpretation of the *Loew's* case,[16] where Kenney and Klein take exception to Stigler's interpretation of block-booking as an effort to effect price discrimination. They argue instead that block-booking economizes on measurement costs for motion picture films the box-office receipts of which are difficult to estimate ex ante.

A more interesting case is their interpretation of the market for gem-quality uncut diamonds. Despite classification into more than two thousand categories, significant quality variation in the stones evidently remains. How can such a market be organized so that oversearching expenses are not incurred and each party to the transaction has confidence in the other? The "solution" that the market evolved and which Kenney and Klein interpret entailed the assembly of groups of diamonds—or "sights"—and imposing all-or-none and in-or-out trading rules. Thus, buyers who refuse to accept a sight are thereafter denied access to this market.

These two trading rules may appear to "disadvantage" buyers. Viewed in systems terms, however, they put a severe burden on de Beers to respect the legitimate expectations of buyers. Thus, suppose that only an all-or-none trading rule were to be imposed. Although buyers would thereby be denied the opportunity to pick the better diamonds from each category, they would nonetheless have the incentive to inspect each sight very carefully. Refusal to accept would signal that a sight was over-priced—but no more.

Suppose now that an in-or-out trading rule is added. The decision to refuse a sight now has much more serious ramifications. To be sure, a refusal could indicate that a particular sight is egregiously over-priced. More likely, however, it reflects a succession of bad experiences. It is a public declaration that de Beers is not to be trusted. In effect, a disaffected buyer announces that the expected net profits of dealing with de Beers under these constrained trading rules is negative.

Such an announcement has a chilling effect on the market. Buyers who were earlier prepared to make casual sight inspections are now advised that there are added trading hazards. Everyone is put on notice that a confidence has been violated and to inspect more carefully.

Put differently, the in-or-out trading rule is a way of encouraging buyers to regard the procurement of diamonds not as a series of independent trading events but as a long-term trading relation. If, overall, things can be expected to "average out," then it is not essential that an exact correspondence between payment made and value received be realized on each sight. In the face of systematic underrealizations of value, however, buyers will be induced to quit. If, as a consequence, the system is moved from a high to a low trust trading culture, then the costs of marketing diamonds increase. de Beers has strong incentives to avoid such an adverse outcome—whence, in a regime which combines all-or-none with in-or-out trading rules, will take care to present

---

16. *United States* v. *Loew's Inc.*, 371 U.S. 38 (1962).

sights such that legitimate expectations will be achieved. The combined rules thus infuse greater integrity of trade.

5.2. Economics of the Family

Transaction cost economics has been brought to bear on the economics of family organization in two respects: the one deals with family firms and productive relations; the other deals with "career marriages."

5.2.1. Family firms

Pollak's (1985) recent examination of families and households actually addresses a broader subject than family firms. I nevertheless focus these remarks on the family firm issue.

Pollak introduces his article with the following overview of the literature:

> The traditional economic theory of the household focuses exclusively on observable market behavior (i.e., demand for goods, supply of labor) treating the household as a "black box" identified only by its preference ordering. The "new home economics" takes a broader view, including not only market behavior but also such nonmarket phenomena as fertility, the education of children, and the allocation of time. The major analytic tool of the new home economics is Becker's household production model, which depicts the household as combining the time of household members with market goods to produce the outputs or "commodities" it ultimately desires.
>
> The new home economics ignores the internal organization and structure of families and households. Although this may surprise noneconomists who tend to believe that the internal organization and structure of an institution are likely to affect its behavior, economists find it natural. For the economist the most economical way to exploit the fundamental insight that production takes place within the household is to apply to households techniques developed for studying firms. Since neoclassical economics identifies firms with their technologies and assumes that firms operate efficiently and frictionlessly, it precludes any serious interest in the economizing properties of the internal structure and organization of firms. The new home economics, by carrying over this narrow neoclassical view from firms to households, thus fails to exploit fully the insight of the household production approach. . . . [By contrast,] the transaction cost approach which recognizes the significance of internal structure provides a broader and more useful view of the economic activity and behavior of the family. (1985, pp. 581–82)

Pollak then goes on to examine the strengths and limitations of the family in governance structure and technological respects and identifies the circumstances where family firms can be expected to enjoy a comparative advantage. The advantages of the firm are developed under four headings: incentives, monitoring, altruism, and loyalty. The main disadvantages of the family as a production unit are conflict spillover from nonproduction into production activities, a propensity to forgive inefficient or slack behavior, access to a restricted range of talents, and possible diseconomies of small scale. He concludes that the strongest case for the family firm is "in low-trust environments (that is, in societies in which nonfamily members are not expected to perform honestly or reliably) and in sectors using relatively simple technologies" (1985, p. 593).

5.2.2. Career marriages

Career marriages of two kinds can be distinguished. One of these involves the marriage of a manager with a firm. The other involves cohabitation by two people, usually but not always of the opposite sex. The analysis here deals with the latter, but much of the argument carries over to marriages of manager and firm with minor changes.

I examine career marriages in the context of the contracting schema set out in Figure 3.1. Career being the entire focus, the parties are assumed to contract for marriage in a wholly calculative way.

Recall that node A corresponds to the condition where $k = 0$. Neither party in these circumstances makes career sacrifices in support of, or at the behest of, the other. This is strictly a marriage of convenience. Each party looks exclusively to his/her own career in deciding on whether to continue the marriage or split. If, for example, a promotion is offered in a distant city to one but not both, the marriage is severed and each goes his/her own way. Or if one job demands late hours or weekends and this interferes with the leisure time plans of the other, each seeks a more compatible mate. A wholly careerist orientation is thus determinative. Nothing being asked or given, there are no regrets upon termination.

The case where $k > 0$ is obviously the more interesting. Nodes B and C here describe the relevant outcomes.

A $k > 0$ condition is one in which one of the parties to the marriage is assumed to make career sacrifices in support of the other. Let X and Y be the parties, and assume that X subordinates his/her career for Y. Thus, X may help Y pay for his/her education by accepting a menial job that pays well but represents a distinctly inferior promotion track. Or X may agree to specialize in nonmarket transactions called "homemaking." Or X may agree to be available to Y as a companion. Not only are career sacrifices incurred, but X's homemaking and companionship skills may be imperfectly transferable if Y has idiosyncratic tastes.

Whatever the particulars, the salient fact is that X's future employment prospects are worsened by reason of career sacrifices made on behalf of Y.[17] The interesting question is: How will the life styles of such career marriages differ depending on whether Y offers a marriage safeguard to X or refuses one?

A node B outcome obtains if Y refuses (or is unable) to provide a safeguard to X. Under the assumption that contracts are struck in full awareness of the

17. This ignores the possibility that Y is a "celebrity" and that having been married to Y carries cachet. X then realizes an immediate status gain upon marriage. Career sacrifices by X can then be interpreted as "payment" for the status gain. But Y, under these circumstances, is the vulnerable party.

hazards, X will demand up-front pay for such circumstances. This is the condition to which Carol Channing had reference in the line "diamonds are a girl's best friend."

If, however, Y is willing and able to offer a safeguard, a node C outcome can be realized. Since X has better assurance under these circumstances that Y will not terminate the relation except for compelling reasons (because Y must pay a termination penalty), X's demands for current rewards (diamonds, dinner, travel, etc.) will be reduced.

This raises the question, however, of what form these safeguards can or do take. There are several possibilities, some of which are dependent on the prevailing legal rules.

Children provide a safeguard if the prevailing legal rules award custody to X and severely limit Y's visitation rights (place these rights under X's control). The award of other assets that Y is known to value also perform this function.

Dividing the property accumulated in the marriage and making alimony conditional on the magnitude of X's career sacrifice is another type of safeguard. In effect, such legal rules deny node B outcomes. If X is awarded wealth and income protection under the law, then Y will be deterred from terminating.

As with most deterrents, however, there are side-effects. Thus, Y can squander assets in contemplation of termination. And Y may refuse to work or flee if alimony payments are thought to be punitive.

A third possibility is to develop a reciprocal career dependency. This may not be easy, but it may be done (at some sacrifice, usually) in certain complementary career circumstances. A pair of dancers with a highly idiosyncratic style is one illustration. Lawyers with complementary specialties and idiosyncratic knowledge of a particular class of transactions (say, of a particular corporation) is another. An artist and his/her agent is a third possibility.

5.3. Corporate Finance

The Modigliani–Miller theorem that the cost of capital in a firm was independent of the proportion of debt and equity revolutionized modern corporate finance. It gave rise to an extensive literature in which a special rationale for debt in an otherwise equity-financed firm was sought. The first of these, unsurprisingly, was that debt had tax advantages over equity. But this was scarcely adequate. Further and more subtle reasons why debt would be used in preference to equity even in a tax-neutral world were also advanced. The leading rationales were: (1) debt could be used as a signal of differential business prospects (Ross, 1977); (2) debt could be used by entrepreneurs with limited resources who were faced with new investment opportunities and did not want to dilute their equity position, thereby to avoid sacrifice of incentive intensity (Jensen and Meckling, 1976); and (3) debt could serve as an incentive bonding device (Grossman and Hart, 1982).

The Modigliani–Miller theorem and each of the debt rationales referred to above treats capital as a composite and regards the firm as a production

Table 3.1.

Governance Feature	Financial Instrument	
	Debt	Equity
Contractual constraints	Numerous	Nil
Security	Pre-emptive	Residual claimant
Intrusion	Nil	Extensive

function. By contrast, transaction cost economics maintains that the asset characteristics of investment projects matter and furthermore distinguishes between debt and equity in terms of their governance structure attributes. The basic argument is this: the investment attributes of projects and the governance structure features of debt and equity need to be aligned in a discriminating way. The key governance structure differences between debt and equity are shown in Table 3.1.

The transaction cost approach maintains that some projects are easy to finance by debt and *ought to be financed by debt.* These are projects for which physical asset specificity is low to moderate. As asset specificity becomes great, however, the pre-emptive claims of the bondholders against the investment afford limited protection—because the assets in question have limited redeployability. Not only does the cost of debt financing therefore increase, but the benefits of closer oversight also grow. The upshot is that equity finance, which affords more intrusive oversight and involvement through the board of directors (and, in publicly held firms, permits share ownership to be concentrated), is the preferred financial instrument for projects where asset specificity is great. The argument is developed in Chapter 7.

5.4. The Modern Corporation

Transaction cost economics appeals to the business history literature for the record and description of organizational innovations.[18] The work of Alfred Chandler, Jr. (1962, 1977) has been especially instructive. Among the more notable developments have been the invention of the line and staff structure by the railroads in the mid-nineteenth century, the *selective* appearance of vertical integration (especially forward integration out of manufacturing into distribution) at the turn of the century, and the appearance in the 1920s and subsequent diffusion of the multidivisional structure.

Transaction cost economics maintains that these innovations are central to an understanding of the modern corporation. The study of such organizational innovations requires, however, that the details of internal organization be

18. Arrow observes that "truly among man's innovations, the use of organization to accomplish his ends is among both his greatest and earliest" (1971, p. 224). And Cole asserts that "if changes in business procedures and practices were patentable, the contributions of business change to the economic growth of the nation would be as widely recognized as the influence of mechanical innovations or the inflow of capital from abroad" (1968, pp. 61–62).

examined. That technological and monopoly conceptions of the corporation ruled in an earlier era is precisely because the details of internal organization were passed off as economically irrelevant.

From a transaction cost point of view, the main purpose of studying internal organization is to better understand the comparative efficacy of internal governance processes. What are the ramifications—for economizing on bounded rationality; for attenuating opportunism; for implementing a program of adaptive, sequential decisionmaking—of organizing the firm this way rather than that? The shift from the functionally organized (U-form) structure by large corporations that began in the 1920s is especially noteworthy.

The M-form innovation began as an effort to cope. Chandler's statement of the defects of the large U-form enterprise is pertinent:

> The inherent weakness in the centralized, functionally departmentalized operating company . . . became critical only when the administrative load on the senior executives increased to such an extent that they were unable to handle their entrepreneurial responsibilities efficiently. This situation arose when the operations of the enterprise became too complex and the problems of coordination, appraisal, and policy formulation too intricate for a small number of top officers to handle both long-run, entrepreneurial, and short-run operational administrative activities. (Chandler, 1962, pp. 382–83)

Bounds on rationality were evidently reached as the U-form structure labored under a communication overload. Moving to a decentralized structure relieved some of these strains.

But there was more to it than this. The M-form structure served not only to economize on bounded rationality, but it further served (in comparison with the U-form structure which it supplanted) to attenuate subgoal pursuit (reduce opportunism). This is because, as Chandler puts it, the M-form structure "clearly removed the executives responsible for the destiny of the entire enterprise from the more routine operational activities, and so gave them the time, information, and even psychological commitment for long-term planning and appraisal" (1966, p. 382).

The upshot is that the M-form innovation (X), which had mainly bounded rationality origins, also had unanticipated effects on corporate purpose (Y) by attenuating subgoal pursuit. Benefits of two kinds were thereby realized in the process.

There were still further unexpected consequences in store, moreover. Once the M-form organization had been perfected and extended from specialized lines of commerce (automobiles; chemicals) to manage diversified activities, it became clear that this structure could be used to support takeover of firms in which managerial discretion excesses were occurring (Z). A transfer of resources to higher valued purposes arguably obtains (Williamson, 1985b, pp. 319–22).

The spread of multidivisionalization through takeover thus yields the *reproductive link* that Elster notes is normally missing in most functional arguments in social science (1983, p. 58). The requisites of full functionalism are evidently satisfied.

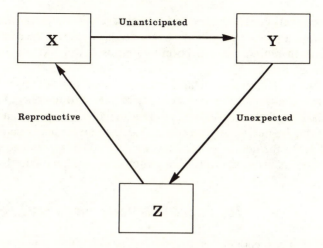

X : M-form innovation
Y : Attenuated subgoal pursuit
Z : Takeover

Figure 3.6. Full functionalism.

Indeed, there is an additional process of spreading the M-form that ought also to be mentioned: mitosis. The large and diversified M-form structure may discover that the benefits associated with new activities or acquisitions do not continue indefinitely. Acquired components or diversified parts may therefore be divested. To the extent that these are spun-off or otherwise divested as discrete multidivisional units themselves, propagation through cell division may be said to exist. This quasi-biological process would also presumably qualify as a reproductive link and thereby contribute to successful functional explanation. Figure 3.6 summarizes the argument.

6.   The Evidence

Transaction cost economics operates at a more microanalytic level of analysis than does orthodoxy. Whereas prices and quantities were thought to be the main if not the only relevant data in the orthodox scheme of things (Arrow, 1971, p. 180), transaction cost economics looks at the attributes of transactions and maintains that the details of organization matter. Additional data thus come under review.

Although the costs of such data collection can be great, resolution gains are frequently realized. Recent microanalytic studies in which transaction costs are featured are surveyed in Joskow, 1988 and Klein and Shelanski, 1995. To be sure, many empirical studies and tests of transaction cost economics are crude, yet the main implications are borne out and/or fare well in comparison with the leading alternatives. The crudeness to which I refer has two sources.

First, transaction cost theory and models are still very primitive. Only gross predictions are usually available. Secondly, severe measurement problems are posed. Both limitations will be mitigated as better models and better data become available.

Albeit real, current data limitations ought not to be exaggerated. Empirical researchers in transaction cost economics have had to collect their own data. They have resolved the trade-off of breadth (census reports; financial statistics) for depth (the microanalytics of contract and investment) mainly in favor of the latter. In the degree to which a subject becomes a science when it begins to develop its own data, this data switch is a commendable response.

7.   Public Policy Ramifications

Transaction cost economics can be brought to bear on a wide variety of public policy issues. Although most of the applications have dealt with matters of microeconomic policy, the transaction cost economics perspective can also help to inform public policy toward stagflation.

7.1.   Microeconomics

Microeconomic applications include regulation and antitrust. Consumer protection is another possibility.

7.1.1.   Regulation/deregulation

Monopoly supply is efficient where economies of scale are large in relation to the size of the market. But, as Friedman laments, "There is unfortunately no good solution for technical monopoly. There is only a choice among three evils: private unregulated monopoly, private monopoly regulated by the state, and government operation" (1962, p. 128).

Friedman characterized private unregulated monopoly as an evil because he assumed that private monopoly ownership implied pricing on monopoly terms. As subsequently argued by Demsetz (1968b), Stigler (1968), and Posner (1972), however, a monopoly price outcome can be avoided by using ex ante bidding to award the monopoly franchise to the firm that offers to supply product on the best terms. Demsetz advances the franchise bidding for natural monopoly argument by stripping away "irrelevant complications"—such as equipment durability and uncertainty (1968b, p. 57). Stigler contends that "customers can auction off the right to sell electricity, using the state as an instrument to conduct the auction. . . . The auction . . . consists of [franchise bids] to sell cheaply" (1968, p. 19). Posner agrees and furthermore holds that franchise bidding is an efficacious way by which to award and operate cable TV franchises.

Transaction cost economics recognizes merit in the argument but insists that both ex ante and ex post contracting features be examined. Only if competition is efficacious at *both* stages does the franchise bidding argument go through. The attributes of the good or service to be franchised are crucial to the assessment. Specifically, if the good or service is to be supplied under conditions of uncertainty and if nontrivial investments in specific assets are involved, the efficacy of franchise bidding is highly problematic. Indeed, the implementation of a franchise bidding scheme under those circumstances essentially requires the progressive elaboration of an administrative apparatus that differs mainly in name rather than in kind from the sort associated with rate of return regulation.

This is not, however, to suggest that franchise bidding for goods or services supplied under decreasing cost conditions is never feasible or to imply that extant regulation or public ownership can never be supplanted by franchise bidding with net gains. Examples where gains are in prospect include local service airlines and, possibly, postal delivery. The winning bidder for each can be displaced without posing serious asset valuation problems, since the base plant (terminals, post office, warehouses, and so on) can be owned by the government, and other assets (planes, trucks, and the like) will have an active second-hand market. It is not, therefore, that franchise bidding is totally lacking in merit. On the contrary, it is a very imaginative proposal. Transaction cost economics maintains, however, that all contracting schemes—of which franchise bidding for natural monopoly is one—need to be examined micro-analytically and assessed in a comparative institutional manner. The recent examination of alternative modes for organizing electricity generation by Joskow and Schmalensee (1983) is illustrative.

7.1.2. Antitrust

The inhospitality tradition maintains the rebuttable presumption that nonstandard forms of contracting have monopoly purpose and effect. The firm-as-production function theory of economic organization likewise regards vertical integration skeptically. Integration that lacks technological purpose purportedly has monopoly origins [Bain, 1968, p. 381]. The argument that "vertical integration loses its innocence if there is an appreciable degree of market power at even one stage of the production process" (Stigler, 1955, p. 183)—a 20 percent market share being the threshold above which market power is to be inferred (Stigler, 1955, p. 183)—is in this same spirit.

Transaction cost economics views integration differently. It maintains the rebuttable presumption that nonstandard forms of contracting, of which vertical integration is an extreme form, have the purpose and effect of economizing on transaction costs. It thus focuses on whether the transactions in question are supported by investments in specific assets. It furthermore examines monopoly purpose in the context of strategic behavior.[19]

19. Strategic behavior has reference to efforts by established firms to take up advance positions in relation to actual or potential rivals, to introduce contrived cost disparities, and/or respond punitively to new rivalry. Suffice it to observe here that strategic behavior is interesting only in an intertemporal context in which uncertainty and specific assets are featured.

Consider, in this connection, two stages of supply—which will be referred to generically as stages I and II (but for concreteness can be thought of as production and distribution). If the leading firms in a highly concentrated stage I were to integrate into an otherwise competitive stage II activity, the nonintegrated sector of the market may be so reduced that only a few firms of efficient size can service the stage II market. Then, entry would be deterred by the potential entrant's having to engage in small-numbers bargaining with those few nonintegrated stage II firms. Furthermore, the alternative of integrated entry will be less attractive because prospective stage I entrants that lack experience in stage II activity would incur higher capital and start-up costs were they to enter both stages themselves. If, instead, stages I and II were of low or moderate concentration, a firm entering either stage can expect to strike competitive bargains with either integrated or nonintegrated firms in the other stage, because no single integrated firm can enjoy a strategic advantage in such transactions, and because it is difficult for the integrated firms to collude. Except, therefore, where strategic considerations intrude— namely, in highly concentrated industries where entry is impeded—vertical integration will rarely pose an antitrust issue.

Whereas the original 1968 Guidelines reflected pre-transaction cost thinking and imposed severe limits on vertical integration (the vertical acquisition of a 6 percent firm by a 10 percent firm was above threshold), the revised Guidelines are much more permissive. The 1982 Guidelines are congruent with the policy implications of transaction cost economics in three respects. First, the 1982 Guidelines express concern over the competitive consequences of a vertical merger only if the acquired firm is operating in an industry in which the HHI exceeds 1800. The presumption is that nonintegrated stage I firms can satisfy their stage II requirements by negotiating competitive terms with stage II firms where the HHI is below 1800. The Guidelines thus focus exclusively on the monopolistic subset, which is congruent with transaction cost reasoning. Second, the anticompetitive concerns in the Guidelines regarding costs of capital, (contrived) scale diseconomies, and the use of vertical integration to evade rate regulation are all consonant with transaction cost reasoning. Finally, the Guidelines make express reference to the importance of asset specificity, although the analysis is less fully developed than it might be. Also, whereas the 1982 Guidelines make no provision for an economies defense, the 1984 Guidelines take this further step—which provision is especially important where asset specificity is demonstrably great.

7.2. Macroeconomics: Stagflation

Martin Weitzman's notable treatment of stagflation in his influential book *The Share Economy* mainly works out of a monopolistic competition framework. Weitzman augments the standard monopolistic competition apparatus, however, by distinguishing between redeployable and nonredeployable assets. Thus, he regards labor as redeployable while intermediate product is not: a "coalminer and a fruitpicker are infinitely closer substitutes than the products they handle. Rolled sheet and I-beams . . . are virtually inconvertible in use" (Weitzman, 1984, p. 28). Unfortunately, this is a technological rather than a transactional distinction.

Such a technological view leads to a much different assessment of the contracting process than does a contractual view. Thus, whereas Weitzman regards labor market contracting as unique and flawed by rigidities, transaction cost economics maintains that labor markets and intermediate product markets are very similar and puts a different construction on rigidities. In particular, an examination of the governance needs of contract discloses that the full flexibility of wages and prices advocated by Weitzman would pose a serious threat to the integrity of contracts that are supported by durable investments in firm-specific assets. The lesson is that macroeconomics needs to come to terms with the study of contracting of a more microanalytic kind (Wachter and Williamson, 1978).

8. Conclusions

Friction, the economic counterpart for which is transaction costs, is pervasive in both physical and economic systems. Our understanding of complex economic organization awaits more concerted study of the sources and mitigation of friction. What is referred to herein as transaction cost economics merely records the beginnings of a response.

Refinements of several kinds are in prospect. One is that many of the insights of the transaction cost approach will be absorbed within the corpus of "extended" neoclassical analysis. The capacity of neoclassical economics to expand its boundaries is quite remarkable in this respect. Second, transaction cost arguments will be qualified to make allowance for process values such as fairness that now appear in a rather ad hoc way. (As Michelman [1967] has demonstrated, however, fairness and efficiency considerations converge when an extended view of contracting in its entirety is adopted. This insight is important and needs further development.) Third, numerous phenomena have yet to be brought under the lens of transaction cost reasoning. Recent experience suggests that new insights and new models are both in prospect. Fourth, a more carefully and fully developed theory of bureaucracy is greatly needed. Among other things, the powers and limits of alternative forms of internal organization with respect to reputation effects, internal due process, complex contingent rewards, auditing, and life cycle features need to be assessed. Finally, empirical research on transaction cost issues has been growing exponentially.

II

CONCEPTS AND APPLICATIONS

Chapter 4 is entitled "Comparative Economic Organization: The Analysis of Discrete Structural Alternatives." This chapter is, for me, an ambitious effort to operationalize transaction cost economics. Among its purposes are (1) to dimensionalize governance structures and display their properties as discrete structural alternatives; (2) to develop the view that adaptation is the central problem of economic organization, of which two kinds—autonomous adaptations through markets (Hayek, 1945) and cooperative adaptations within hierarchies (Barnard, 1938)—need to be distinguished; (3) to describe the (implicit) contract law of internal organization as that of forbearance, which has the effect of supporting fiat within firms and thereby distinguishing markets from hierarchies; and (4) to treat the institutional environment as a set of shift parameters, which change the relative costs of alternative modes of governance. This chapter, invites follow-on research. Empirical research opportunities are the most obvious of these, but the stochastic model in the chapter could be developed further and utilized more generally. The concepts of disequilibrium contracting and real-time responsiveness also warrant further development. Applications to other modes of governance, such as nonprofits, regulation, and public bureaus, can and should be attempted.

Chapter 5, "Credible Commitments: Using Hostages to Support Exchange," is the only chapter in this volume that is based on a paper published before 1987. It is included because an understanding of credibility and the mechanisms through which it works are so crucial to the institutions of governance (this chapter) and the institutional environment (Chapter 13). My interest in these issues goes back to a puzzle that I first encountered in the early 1970s and to a discussion that I had with Macneil in the late 1970s.

The puzzle was over why petroleum firms engaged in bilateral exchanges. The standard response was that exchanges were efficient because they relieved the need for inefficient cross hauling. Thus if firm A had a surplus of production in relation to its distribution needs in region I and a deficit in region II, and if firm B had a deficit of production in relation to its distribution needs in region I but a surplus in region II, then it would be efficient for firm A and firm B to engage in exchange. That argument was fine as far as it went, but it did not address yet another possibility: Why not report surpluses and deficits to a central market and operate in a market-clearing fashion rather than through bilateral exchanges? The petroleum industry people—engineers, lawyers, economists, managers—with whom I discussed this "obvious" alternative were discomfited by it and so preferred to ignore it. But the possibility that exchanges were a nonstandard practice with anticompetitive purpose and effect had to be seriously entertained.

My discussion with Macneil had to do with the distribution of transactions across modes. What was the frequency distribution of transactions such as between markets (spot contracts), hybrids (various forms of long-term contracting), and hierarchies? Macneil argued that the distribution of transactions was bell shaped, which meant that there were few transactions at the two polar extremes. Because, however, it seemed to me difficult to stabilize transactions in the middle range and because it was obvious that there were many spot and many hierarchical transactions, I argued that the distribution of transactions was bimodal, with spot markets and hierarchies predominating.

I had set these questions aside and was working on other problems when an eight-volume study, *The State of Competition in the Canadian Petroleum Industry,* arrived on my desk. Volume 5, *The Refining Sector,* included an extensive discussion of exchanges.

The study included a lot of detail, including memoranda from the files of petroleum firms that the Canadian antitrust authorities interpreted as evidence of anticompetitive purpose and effect. One of the memoranda from the Gulf Oil Company files reported: "We do believe that the oil industry generally, although grudgingly, will allow a participant who has paid his ante to play the game; the ante in this game being the capital for refining, distributing, and selling products." Another memorandum recorded that an exchange agreement between Imperial and Shell would be renewed only if Shell did not exceed "normal growth rates" in expanding its markets and did not obtain additional product from third parties.

Examining these memoranda and interpreting the references to antes, games, and restraints on growth and trade through a neoclassical lens easily led to an anticompetitive conclusion. Viewed, however, through the spectacles of comparative contracting, if suggested an altogether different interpretation. Exchange agreements could (as well or instead) be a device by which to infuse confidence into trade. They were a means by which to give and receive "credible commitments."

Not only did these memoranda suggest to me a rationale for exchanges that had hitherto been neglected, but it also indicated that the devices for stabilizing hybrid contracts were more numerous and subtle than I had previously imagined. To be sure, there were still many transactions located near the poles. But it evidently was possible to support transactions in the intermediate range as well.

This chapter works out of a farsighted contracting setup and demonstrates the importance of private ordering. Contrary to the Machiavellian advice to break contracts with impunity (get them before they get us), the message is that the offer and acceptance of credible commitments will infuse confidence into contracts that would otherwise be fraught with hazard.[1] More durable and specialized investments will be made and superior trading terms will be realized if contracts are supported by credible commitments, of which the offer and acceptance of a hostage is an early example.[2]

In Chapter 6, "Economic Institutions: Spontaneous and Intentional Governance," I take issue with the disproportionate attention paid by economists to spontaneous (especially market) mechanisms, to the neglect of intentional (hierarchical) mechanisms. If adaptation is the central problem of economic organization and if both autonomous and cooperative forms of adaptation are needed, then it is necessary to make provision for spontaneous, intentional, and mixed modes of organization. This chapter asks and attempts to answer the question "What's going on here?" both in general and with reference to the price mechanism, reputation effect mechanisms, sequential short-term contracting, and socialist economic organization.

Chapter 7, "Corporate Governance and Corporate Finance," utilizes the transaction cost economics approach to take exception with the Modigliani–

---

1. I am therefore surprised by advice that "our textbooks . . . should be saying that decision-makers will strike an optimal *balance* between . . . the way of production with mutually advantageous exchange, and the dark-side way of confiscation, exploitation, and conflict" (Hirshleifer, 1994, p. 3, emphasis added). The appropriate balance, in my judgment, is one part Machiavelli to nine parts Coase.

2. A still earlier example of an effort to craft a credible commitment was recently unearthed in Mesopotamia. Tablets dated around 1750 B.C. show that curses were used to deter the breach of treaties. One of these reads as follows:

When you ask us for troops, we will not withhold our best forces, we will not answer you with evasions, we shall brandish our maces and strike down your enemy. . . .

As wasted seeds do not sprout, may my seed never rise, may someone else marry my wife under my very eyes, and may someone else rule my country. (*China Daily*, March 22, 1988, p. 1)

Miller theorem and advances the argument that debt and equity are not merely instruments of finance but are also instruments of governance. Of the two, debt relies more on rules governance, is akin to a market form, and is better suited to finance generic assets, whereas equity is a more discretionary form of governance, is more akin to hierarchy, and is reserved for financing firm-specific assets. The argument leads to a number of empirical implications, in relation to which the data appear to be corroborative. Extensions to the basic model (which works out of project financing) to deal with composite finance would be useful.

Chapter 8, "The Politics and Economics of Redistribution and Ineffi-ciency," is probably the most controversial essay in the book. In the spirit of those who have taken issue with "Nirvana Economics" (Robinson, 1934; Coase, 1964; Demsetz, 1969; Stigler, 1992), I eschew reference to or reliance on frictionless ideals—benign government, costless regulation, omniscient courts, and the like—especially for purposes of public-policy analysis. Inasmuch as all feasible forms of organization are flawed, I argue that the relevant standard is that of remediableness, according to which extant forms of organization for which no superior feasible alternative can be described and implemented with net gains are declared to be efficient. This argument applies to economics and politics alike.[3] Breakdowns of both organizational and political kinds are discussed.

---

3. Indeed, the argument applies more generally. Consider the following exchange between Countess Olenska and Newland Archer in Edith Wharton's *Age of Innocence*:

> "Is it your idea, then, that I should live with you as your mistress—since I can't be your wife?" she asked.
> The crudeness of the question startled him . . . and he floundered.
> "I want—I want somehow to get away with you into a world where words like that—categories like that—won't exist. Where we shall be simply two human beings who love each other, who are the whole of life to each other; and nothing else on earth will matter."
> She drew a deep sigh that ended in another laugh. "Oh, my dear—where is that country? Have you ever been there?" (1986, p. 290)

Madame Olenska, in this exchange, insists that the comparisons be made among feasible alterna-tive forms of organization, whereas Archer operates out of hypothetical ideals. Transaction cost economics is relentlessly comparative and, like Madame Olenska, eschews hypotheticals.

4

Comparative Economic Organization: The Analysis of Discrete Structural Alternatives

Although microeconomic organization is formidably complex and has long resisted systematic analysis, that has been changing as new modes of analysis have become available, as recognition of the importance of institutions to economic performance has grown, and as the limits of earlier modes of analysis have become evident. Information economics, game theory, agency theory, and population ecology have all made significant advances.

This chapter approaches the study of economic organization from a comparative institutional point of view in which transaction-cost economizing is featured. Comparative economic organization never examines organization forms separately but always in relation to alternatives. Transaction-cost economics places the principal burden of analysis on comparisons of transaction costs—which, broadly, are the "costs of running the economic system" (Arrow, 1969, p. 48).

My purpose in this chapter is to extend and refine the apparatus out of which transaction-cost economics works, thereby to respond to some of the leading criticisms. Four objections to prior work in this area are especially pertinent. One objection is that the two stages of the new institutional economics research agenda—the institutional environment and the institutions of governance—have developed in disjunct ways. The first of these paints on a very large historical canvas and emphasizes the institutional rules of the game: customs, laws, politics (North, 1986). The latter is much more microanalytic and focuses on the comparative efficacy with which alternative generic forms of governance—markets, hybrids, hierarchies—economize on transaction costs. Can this disjunction problem be overcome? Second, transaction-cost economics has been criticized because it deals with polar forms—markets and hierarchies—to the neglect of intermediate or hybrid forms. Although that objection has begun to be addressed by recent treatments of long-term contracting in which bilateral dependency conditions are supported by a variety of specialized governance features (hostages, arbitration, take-or-pay procurement clauses, tied sales, reciprocity, regulation, etc.), the abstract attributes that characterize alternative modes of governance have remained obscure. What are the key attributes and how do they vary among forms? This is responsive to the third objection, namely, that efforts to operationalize transaction-cost economics have given disproportionate attention to the abstract description of transactions as compared with the abstract description of governance. The dimensionalization of both is needed. Finally, there is the embeddedness problem: Transaction-cost economics purports to have general application but has been developed almost entirely with reference to Western capitalist economies (Hamilton and Biggart, 1988). Is a unified treatment of Western and non-Western, capitalist and noncapitalist economies really feasible? This paper attempts to address these objections by posing the problem of organization as one of discrete structural analysis.

1.   Discrete Structural Analysis

The term discrete structural analysis was introduced into the study of comparative economic organization by Simon, who observed that

> As economics expands beyond its central core of price theory, and its central concern with quantities of commodities and money, we observe in it . . . [a] shift from a highly quantitative analysis, in which equilibration at the margin plays a central role, to a much more qualitative institutional analysis, in which discrete structural alternatives are compared. . . .
>
> [S]uch analyses can often be carried out without elaborate mathematical apparatus or marginal calculation. In general, much cruder and simpler arguments will suffice to demonstrate an inequality between two quantities than are required to show the conditions under which these quantities are equated at the margin. (1978, pp. 6–7).

But what exactly is discrete structural analysis? Is it employed only because "there is at present no [satisfactory] way of characterizing organizations in terms of continuous variation over a spectrum" (Ward, 1967, p. 38)? Or is there a deeper rationale?

Of the variety of factors that support discrete structural analysis, I focus here on the following: (1) firms are not merely extensions of markets but employ different means, (2) discrete contract law differences provide crucial support for and serve to define each generic form of governance, and (3) marginal analysis is typically concerned with second-order refinements to the neglect of first-order economizing.

1.1.   Different Means

Although the study of economic organization deals principally with markets and market mechanisms, it is haunted by a troublesome fact: a great deal of economic activity takes place within firms (Barnard, 1938; Chandler, 1962,

1977). Conceivably, however, no novel economizing issues are posed within firms, because technology is largely determinative—the firm is mainly defined by economies of scale and scope and is merely an instrument for transforming inputs into outputs according to the laws of technology—and because market mechanisms carry over into firms. I have taken exception with the technology view elsewhere (Williamson, 1975). Consider, therefore, the latter.

In parallel with von Clausewitz's (1980) views on war, I maintain that hierarchy is not merely a contractual act but is also a contractual instrument, a continuation of market relations by other means. The challenge to comparative contractual analysis is to discern and explicate the different means. As developed below, each viable form of governance—market, hybrid, and hierarchy—is defined by a syndrome of attributes that bear a supporting relation to one another. Many hypothetical forms of organization never arise, or quickly die out, because they combine inconsistent features.

1.2.   Contract Law

The mapping of contract law onto economic organization has been examined elsewhere (Williamson, 1979b, 1985a). Although some of that is repeated here, there are two significant differences. First, I advance the hypothesis that each generic form of governance—market, hybrid, and hierarchy—needs to be supported by a different form of contract law. Second, the form of contract law that supports hierarchy is that of forbearance.

1.2.1.   Classical contract law

Classical contract law applies to the ideal transaction in law and economics in which the identity of the parties is irrelevant. "Thick" markets are ones in which individual buyers and sellers bear no dependency relation to each other. Instead, each party can go its own way at negligible cost to another. If contracts are renewed period by period, that is only because current suppliers are continuously meeting bids in the spot market. Such transactions are monetized in extreme degree; contract law is interpreted in a very legalistic way: more formal terms supersede less formal should disputes arise between formal and less formal features (e.g., written agreements versus oral amendments), and hard bargaining, to which the rules of contract law are strictly applied, characterizes these transactions. Classical contract law is congruent with and supports the autonomous market form of organization (Macneil, 1974, 1978).

1.2.2.   Neoclassical contract law and excuse doctrine

Neoclassical contract law and excuse doctrine, which relieves parties from strict enforcement, apply to contracts in which the parties to the transaction maintain autonomy but are bilaterally dependent to a nontrivial degree. Identity plainly matters if premature termination or persistent maladaptation would place burdens on one or both parties. Perceptive parties reject classical contract law and move into a neoclassical contracting regime because this better facilitates continuity and promotes efficient adaptation.

As developed below, hybrid modes of contracting are supported by neoclassical contract law. The parties to such contracts maintain autonomy, but the contract is mediated by an elastic contracting mechanism. Public utility regulation, in which the relations between public utility firms and their customers are mediated by a regulatory agency, is one example (Goldberg, 1976a; Williamson, 1976). Exchange agreements or reciprocal trading in which the parties experience (and respond similarly to) similar disturbances is another illustration (Williamson, 1983). Franchising is another way of preserving semi-autonomy, but added supports are needed (Klein, 1980; Hadfield, 1990). More generally, long-term, incomplete contracts require special adaptive mechanisms to effect realignment and restore efficiency when beset by unanticipated disturbances.

Disturbances are of three kinds: inconsequential, consequential, and highly consequential. Inconsequential disturbances are ones for which the deviation from efficiency is too small to recover the costs of adjustment. The net gains from realignment are negative for minor disturbances because (as discussed below) requests for adjustments need to be justified and are subject to review, the costs of which exceed the prospective gains.

Middle-range or consequential disturbances are ones to which neoclassical contract law applies. These are transactions for which Karl Llewellyn's concept of "contract as framework" is pertinent (1931, p. 737). The thirty-two-year coal supply agreement between the Nevada Power Company and the Northwest Trading Company illustrates the elastic mechanisms employed by a neoclassical contract. That contract reads in part as follows:

> In the event an inequitable condition occurs which adversely affects one Party, it shall then be the joint and equal responsibility of both Parties to act promptly and in good faith to determine the action required to cure or adjust for the inequity and effectively to implement such action. Upon written claim of inequity served by one Party upon the other, the Parties shall act jointly to reach an agreement concerning the claimed inequity within sixty (60) days of the date of such written claim. An adjusted base coal price that differs from market price by more than ten percent (10%) shall constitute a hardship. The Party claiming inequity shall include in its claim such information and data as may be reasonably necessary to substantiate the claim and shall freely and without delay furnish such other information and data as the other Party reasonably may deem relevant and necessary. If the Parties cannot reach agreement within sixty (60) days the matter shall be submitted to arbitration.

By contrast with a classical contract, this contract (1) contemplates unanticipated disturbances for which adaptation is needed, (2) provides a tolerance zone (of $\pm$ 10%) within which misalignments will be absorbed, (3) requires information disclosure and substantiation if adaptation is proposed, and (4) provides for arbitration in the event voluntary agreement fails.

The forum to which this neoclassical contract refers disputes is (initially at least) that of arbitration rather than the courts. Fuller described the procedural differences between arbitration and litigation:

[T]here are open to the arbitrator ... quick methods of education not open to the courts. An arbitrator will frequently interrupt the examination of witnesses with a request that the parties educate him to the point where he can understand the testimony being received. This education can proceed informally, with frequent interruptions by the arbitrator, and by informed persons on either side, when a point needs clarification. Sometimes there will be arguments across the table, occasionally even within each of the separate camps. The end result will usually be a clarification that will enable everyone to proceed more intelligently with the case. (1963, pp. 11–12)

Such adaptability notwithstanding, neoclassical contracts are not indefinitely elastic. As disturbances become highly consequential, neoclassical contracts experience real strain, because the autonomous ownership status of the parties continuously poses an incentive to defect. The general proposition here is that when the "lawful" gains to be had by insistence upon literal enforcement exceed the discounted value of continuing the exchange relationship, defection from the spirit of the contract can be anticipated.

When, in effect, arbitration gives way to litigation, accommodation can no longer be presumed. Instead, the contract reverts to a much more legalistic regime—although, even here, neoclassical contract law averts truly punitive consequences by permitting appeal to exceptions that qualify under some form of excuse doctrine. The legal system's commitment to the keeping of promises under neoclassical contract law is modest (Macneil, 1974, p. 731).

From an economic point of view, the tradeoff that needs to be faced in excusing contract performance is between stronger incentives and reduced opportunism. If the state realization in question was unforeseen and unforeseeable (different in degree and/or especially in kind from the range of normal business experience), if strict enforcement would have truly punitive consequences, and especially if the resulting "injustice" is supported by (lawful) opportunism, then excuse can be seen mainly as a way of mitigating opportunism, ideally without adverse impact on incentives. If, however, excuse is granted routinely whenever adversity occurs, then incentives to think through contracts, choose technologies judiciously, share risks efficiently, and avert adversity will be impaired. Excuse doctrine should therefore be used sparingly—which it evidently is (Farnsworth, 1968, p. 885; Buxbaum, 1985).

The relief afforded by excuse doctrine notwithstanding, neoclassical contracts deal with consequential disturbances only at great cost: arbitration is costly to administer and its adaptive range is limited. As consequential disturbances and, especially, as highly consequential disturbances become more frequent, the hybrid mode supported by arbitration and excuse doctrine incurs added costs and comes under added strain. Even more elastic and adaptive arrangements warrant consideration.

1.2.3. Forbearance

Internal organization, hierarchy, qualifies as a still more elastic and adaptive mode of organization. What type of contract law applies to internal organization? How does this have a bearing on contract performance?

Describing the firm as a "nexus of contracts" (Alchian and Demsetz, 1972; Jensen and Meckling, 1976; Fama, 1980) suggests that the firm is no different from the market in contractual respects. Alchian and Demsetz originally took the position that the relation between a shopper and his grocer and that between an employer and employee was identical in contractual respects:

> The single consumer can assign his grocer to the task of obtaining whatever the customer can induce the grocer to provide at a price acceptable to both parties. That is precisely all that an employer can do to an employee. To speak of managing, directing, or assigning workers to various tasks is a deceptive way of noting that the employer continually is involved in renegotiation of contracts on terms that must be acceptable to both parties. . . . Long-term contracts between employer and employee are not the essence of the organization we call a firm. (1972, p. 777)

That it has been instructive to view the firm as a nexus of contracts is evident from the numerous insights that this literature has generated. But to regard the corporation only as a nexus of contracts misses much of what is truly distinctive about this mode of governance. As developed below, bilateral adaptation effected through fiat is a distinguishing feature of internal organization. But wherein do the fiat differences between market and hierarchy arise? If, moreover, hierarchy enjoys an "advantage" with respect to fiat, why can't the market replicate this?

One explanation is that fiat has its origins in the employment contract (Coase, 1937; Barnard, 1938; Simon, 1951; Masten, 1988). Although there is a good deal to be said for that explanation, I propose a separate and complementary explanation: The implicit contract law of internal organization is that of forbearance. Thus, whereas courts routinely grant standing to firms should there be disputes over prices, the damages to be ascribed to delays, failures of quality, and the like, courts will refuse to hear disputes between one internal division and another over identical technical issues. Access to the courts being denied, the parties must resolve their differences internally. Accordingly, hierarchy is its own court of ultimate appeal.

What is known as the "business judgment rule" holds that "absent bad faith or some other corrupt motive, directors are normally not liable to the corporation for mistakes of judgment, whether those mistakes are classified as mistakes of fact or mistakes of law" (Gilson, 1986, p. 741). Not only does that rule serve as "a quasi-jurisdictional barrier to prevent courts from exercising regulatory powers over the activities of corporate managers" (Manne, 1967, p. 271), but "The courts' abdication of regulatory authority through the business judgment rule may well be the most significant common law contribution to corporate governance" (Gilson, 1986, p. 741). The business judgment rule, which applies to the relation between shareholders and directors, can be interpreted as a particular manifestation of forbearance doctrine, which applies to the management of the firm more generally. To review alleged mistakes of judgment or to adjudicate internal disputes would sorely test the competence of courts and would undermine the efficacy of hierarchy.

Accordingly, the reason why the market is unable to replicate the firm with respect to fiat is that market transactions are defined by contract law of an altogether different kind. There is a logic to classical market contracting and there is a logic for forbearance law, and the choice of one regime precludes the other. Whether a transaction is organized as make or buy—internal procurement or market procurement, respectively—thus matters greatly in dispute-resolution respects: the courts will hear disputes of the one kind and will refuse to be drawn into the resolution of disputes of the other. Internal disputes between one division and another regarding the appropriate transfer prices, the damages to be ascribed to delays, failures of quality, and the like, are thus denied a court hearing.

To be sure, not all disputes within firms are technical. Personnel disputes are more complicated. Issues of worker safety, dignity, the limits of the "zone of acceptance," and the like sometimes pose societal spillover costs that are undervalued in the firm's private net benefit calculus. Underprovision of human and worker rights could ensue if the courts refused to consider issues of these kinds. Also, executive compensation agreements can sometimes be written in ways that make it difficult to draw a sharp line between personnel and technical issues. Even with personnel disputes, however, there is a presumption that such differences will be resolved internally. For example, unions may refuse to bring individual grievances to arbitration:

> [G]iving the union control over all claims arising under the collective agreement comports so much better with the functional nature of a collective bargaining agreement. . . . Allowing an individual to carry a claim to arbitration whenever he is dissatisfied with the adjustment worked out by the company and the union . . . discourages the kind of day-to-day cooperation between company and union which is normally the mark of sound industrial relations—a relationship in which grievances are treated as problems to be solved and contracts are only guideposts in a dynamic human relationship. When . . . the individual's claim endangers group interests, the union's function is to resolve the competition by reaching an accommodation or striking a balance. (Cox, 1958, p. 24)

As compared with markets, internal incentives in hierarchies are flat or low-powered, which is to say that changes in effort expended have little or no immediate effect on compensation. This is mainly because the high-powered incentives of markets are unavoidably compromised by internal organization (Williamson, 1985b, chap. 6; 1988d). Also, however, hierarchy uses flat incentives because these elicit greater cooperation and because unwanted side effects are checked by added internal controls (see Williamson, 1988d; Holmstrom, 1989). Not only, therefore, will workers and managers be more willing to accommodate, because their compensation is the same whether they "do this" or "do that," but an unwillingness to accommodate is interpreted not as an excess of zeal but as a predilection to behave in a noncooperative way. Long-term promotion prospects are damaged as a consequence. Defection from the spirit of the agreement in favor of litigiousness is quite perverse if neither immediate nor long-term gains are thereby realized. The combination of fiat with low-powered incentives is a manifestation of the syndrome condition of economic organization to which I referred earlier (and develop more fully below).

The underlying rationale for forbearance law is twofold: (1) parties to an internal dispute have deep knowledge—both about the circumstances surrounding a dispute as well as the efficiency properties of alternative solutions—that can be communicated to the court only at great cost, and (2) permitting the internal disputes to be appealed to the court would undermine the efficacy and integrity of hierarchy. If fiat were merely advisory, in that internal disputes over net receipts could be pursued in the courts, the firm would be little more than an "inside contracting" system (Williamson, 1985b, pp. 218–22). The application of forbearance doctrine to internal organization means that parties to an internal exchange can work out their differences themselves or appeal unresolved disputes to the hierarchy for a decision. But this exhausts their alternatives. When push comes to shove, "legalistic" arguments fail. Greater reliance on instrumental reasoning and mutual accommodation result. This argument contradicts Alchian and Demsetz's claim that the firm "has no power of fiat, no authority, no disciplinary action any different in the slightest degree from ordinary market contracting" (1972, p. 777). That is exactly wrong: firms can and do exercise fiat that markets cannot. Prior neglect of contract law differences and their ramifications explain the disparity.

1.3. First-Order Economizing

Although the need to get priorities straight is unarguable, first-order economizing—effective adaptation and the elimination of waste—has been neglected. Adaptation is especially crucial. As developed below, it is the central economic problem. But as Frank Knight insisted, the elimination of waste is also important (1941, p. 252).

Relatedly, but independently, Oskar Lange held that "the real danger of socialism is that of the bureaucratization of economic life, and not the impossibility of coping with the problem of allocation of resources" (1938, p. 109). Inasmuch, however, as Lange believed that this argument belonged "in the field of sociology" he concluded that it "must be dispensed with here" (1938, p. 109). Subsequent informed observers of socialism followed this lead, whereupon the problems of bureaucracy were, until recently, given scant attention. Instead, the study of socialism was preoccupied with technical features—marginal cost pricing, activity analysis, and the like—with respect to which a broadly sanguine consensus took shape (Bergson, 1948; Montias, 1976; Koopmans, 1977).

The natural interpretation of the organizational concerns expressed by Knight and Lange—or, at least, the interpretation that I propose here—is that economics was too preoccupied with issues of allocative efficiency, in which marginal analysis was featured, to the neglect of organizational efficiency, in which discrete structural alternatives were brought under scrutiny. Partly that is because the mathematics for dealing with clusters of attributes is only now beginning to be developed (Topkis, 1978; Milgrom and Roberts, 1990b; Holmstrom and Milgrom, 1991). Even more basic, however, is the propensity to focus exclusively on market mechanisms to the neglect of discrete structural alternatives. The argument, for example, that all systems of honest trade are variants on the reputation-effect mechanisms of markets (Milgrom, North, and Weingast, 1990, p. 16) ignores the possibility that some ways of infusing contractual integrity (e.g., hierarchy) employ altogether different means. Market-favoring predispositions need to be disputed, lest the study of economic organization in all of its forms be needlessly and harmfully truncated.

2. Dimensionalizing Governance

What are the key attributes with respect to which governance structures differ? The discriminating alignment hypothesis to which transaction-cost economics owes much of its predictive content holds that transactions, which differ in their attributes, are aligned with governance structures, which differ in their costs and competencies, in a discriminating (mainly, transaction-cost-economizing) way. But whereas the dimensionalization of transactions received early and explicit attention, the dimensionalization of governance structures has been relatively slighted. What are the factors that are responsible for the aforementioned differential costs and competencies?

One of those key differences has been already indicated: market, hybrid, and hierarchy differ in contract law respects. Indeed, were it the case that the very same type of contract law were to be uniformly applied to all forms of governance, important distinctions between these three generic forms would be vitiated. But there is more to governance than contract law. Crucial differences in adaptability and in the use of incentive and control instruments are also germane.

2.1. Adaptation as the Central Economic Problem

Hayek insistently argued that "economic problems arise always and only in consequence of change" and that this truth was obscured by those who held that "technological knowledge" is of foremost importance (1945, p. 523). He disputed the latter and urged that "the economic problem of society is mainly one of rapid adaptation in the particular circumstances of time and place" (1945, p. 524). Of special importance to Hayek was the proposition that the price system, as compared with central planning, is an extraordinarily efficient mechanism for communicating information and inducing change (1945, pp. 524–27).

Interestingly, Barnard (1938) also held that the main concern of organization was that of adaptation to changing circumstances, but this concern was with adaptation within internal organization. Confronted with a continuously fluctuating environment, the "survival of an organization depends upon the maintenance of an equilibrium of complex character. . . . [This] calls for readjustment of processes internal to the organization ... , [whence] the center of our interest is the processes by which [adaptation] is accomplished" (Barnard, 1938, p. 6).

That is very curious. Both Hayek and Barnard hold that the central problem of economic organization is adaptation. But whereas Hayek locates this adaptive capacity in the market, it was the adaptive capacity of internal organization on which Barnard focused attention. If the "marvel of the market" (Hayek) is matched by the "marvel of internal organization" (Barnard), then wherein does one outperform the other?

The marvel to which Hayek referred had spontaneous origins: "The price system is ... one of those formations which man has learned to use ... after he stumbled on it without understanding it" (1945, p. 528). The importance of such spontaneous cooperation notwithstanding, it was Barnard's experience that intended cooperation was important and undervalued. The latter was defined as "that kind of cooperation among men that is conscious, deliberate, purposeful" (Barnard, 1938, p. 4) and was realized through formal organization, especially hierarchy.

I submit that adaptability is the central problem of economic organization and that both Hayek and Barnard are correct, because they are referring to adaptations of different kinds, both of which are needed in a high-performance system. The adaptations to which Hayek refers are those for which prices serve as sufficient statistics. Changes in the demand or supply of a commodity are reflected in price changes, in response to which "individual participants ... [are] able to take the right action" (Hayek, 1945, p. 527). I will refer to adaptations of this kind as adaptation (A), where (A) denotes autonomy. This is the neoclassical ideal in which consumers and producers respond independently to parametric price changes so as to maximize their utility and profits, respectively.

That would entirely suffice if all disturbances were of this kind. Some disturbances, however, require coordinated responses, lest the individual parts operate at cross-purposes or otherwise suboptimize. Failures of coordination may arise because autonomous parties read and react to signals differently, even though their purpose is to achieve a timely and compatible combined response. The "nonconvergent expectations" to which Malmgren (1961) referred is an illustration. Although, in principle, convergent expectations could be realized by asking one party to read and interpret the signals for all, the lead party may behave strategically—by distorting information or disclosing it in an incomplete and selective fashion.

More generally, parties that bear a long-term bilateral dependency relation to one another must recognize that incomplete contracts require gapfilling and sometimes get out of alignment. Although it is always in the collective interest of autonomous parties to fill gaps, correct errors, and effect efficient realignments, it is also the case that the distribution of the resulting gains is indeterminate. Self-interested bargaining predictably obtains. Such bargaining is itself costly. The main costs, however, are that transactions are maladapted to the environment during the bargaining interval. Also, the prospect of ex post bargaining invites ex ante prepositioning of an inefficient kind (Grossman and Hart, 1986).

Recourse to a different mechanism is suggested as the needs for coordinated investments and for uncontested (or less contested) coordinated realignments increase in frequency and consequentiality. Adaptations of these coordinated kinds will be referred to as adaptation (C), where (C) denotes cooperation. The conscious, deliberate, and purposeful efforts to craft adaptive internal coordinating mechanisms were those on which Barnard focused. Independent adaptations here would at best realize imperfect realignments and could operate at cross-purposes. Lest the aforementioned costs and delays associated with strategic bargaining be incurred, the relation is reconfigured by supplanting autonomy by hierarchy. The authority relation (fiat) has adaptive advantages over autonomy for transactions of a bilaterally (or multilaterally) dependent kind.

2.2.   Instruments

Vertical and lateral integration are usefully thought of as organization forms of last resort, to be employed when all else fails. That is because markets are a "marvel" in adaptation (A) respects. Given a disturbance for which prices serve as sufficient statistics, individual buyers and suppliers can reposition autonomously. Appropriating, as they do, individual streams of net receipts, each party has a strong incentive to reduce costs and adapt efficiently. What I have referred to as high-powered incentives result when consequences are tightly linked to actions in this way (Williamson, 1988a). Other autonomous traders have neither legitimate claims against the gains nor can they be held accountable for the losses. Accounting systems cannot be manipulated to share gains or subsidize losses.

Matters get more complicated when bilateral dependency intrudes. As discussed above, bilateral dependency introduces an opportunity to realize gains through hierarchy. As compared with the market, the use of formal organization to orchestrate coordinated adaptation to unanticipated disturbances enjoys adaptive advantages as the condition of bilateral dependency progressively builds up. But these adaptation (C) gains come at a cost. Not only can related divisions within the firm make plausible claims that they are causally responsible for the gains (in indeterminate degree), but divisions that report losses can make plausible claims that others are culpable. There are many ways, moreover, in which the headquarters can use the accounting system to effect strategic redistributions (through transfer pricing changes, overhead assignments, inventory conventions, etc.), whatever the preferences of the parties. The upshot is that internal organization degrades incentive intensity, and added bureaucratic costs result (Williamson, 1985b, chap. 6; 1988d).

These three features—adaptability of type A, adaptability of type C, and differential incentive intensity—do not exhaust the important differences between market and hierarchy. Also important are the differential reliance on administrative controls and, as developed above, the different contract law regimes to which each is subject. Suffice it to observe here that (1) hierarchy is buttressed by the differential efficacy of administrative controls within firms, as compared with between firms, and (2) incentive intensity within firms is sometimes deliberately suppressed. Incentive intensity is not an objective but is merely an instrument. If added incentive intensity gets in the way of bilateral adaptability, then weaker incentive intensity supported by added administrative controls (monitoring and career rewards and penalties) can be optimal.

Markets and hierarchies are polar modes. As indicated at the outset, however, a major purpose of this chapter is to locate hybrid modes—various forms of long-term contracting, reciprocal trading, regulation, franchising, and the like—in relation to these polar modes. Plainly, the neoclassical contract law of hybrid governance differs from both the classical contract law of markets and the forbearance contract law of hierarchies, being more elastic than the former but more legalistic than the latter. The added question is How do hybrids compare with respect to adaptability (types A and C), incentive intensity, and administrative control?

The hybrid mode displays intermediate values in all four features. It preserves ownership autonomy, which elicits strong incentives and encourages adaptation to type A disturbances (those to which one party can respond efficiently without consulting the other). Because there is bilateral dependency, however, long-term contracts are supported by added contractual safeguards and administrative apparatus (information disclosure, dispute-settlement machinery). These facilitate adaptations of type C but come at the cost of incentive attenuation. Concerns for "equity" intrude. Thus the Nevada Power Company–Northwest Trading Company coal contract, whose adaptation mechanics were set out above, begins with the following: "It is the intent of the Parties hereto that this agreement, as a whole and in all of its parts, shall be equitable to both Parties throughout its term." Such efforts unavoidably dampen incentive-intensity features.

One advantage of hierarchy over the hybrid with respect to bilateral adaptation is that internal contracts can be more incomplete. More importantly, adaptations to consequential disturbances are less costly within firms because (1) proposals to adapt require less documentation, (2) resolving internal disputes by fiat rather than arbitration saves resources and facilitates timely adaptation, (3) information that is deeply impacted can more easily be accessed and more accurately assessed, (4) internal dispute resolution enjoys the support of informal organization (Barnard, 1938; Scott, 1987), and (5) internal organization has access to additional incentive instruments—including especially career reward and joint profit sharing—that promote a team orientation. Furthermore, highly consequential disturbances that would occasion breakdown or costly litigation under the hybrid mode can be accommodated more easily. The advantages of hierarchy over hybrid in adaptation C respects are not, however, realized without cost. Weaker incentive intensity (greater bureaucratic costs) attend the move from hybrid to hierarchy, ceteris paribus.

Table 4.1. Distinguishing Attributes of Market, Hybrid, and Hierarchy Governance Structures[a]

Attributes	Governance Structure		
	Market	Hybrid	Hierarchy
Instruments			
Incentive intensity	++	+	0
Administrative controls	0	+	++
Performance attributes			
Adaptation (A)	++	+	0
Adaptation (C)	0	+	++
Contract law	++	+	0

[a]++ = strong; + = semi-strong; 0 = weak.

Summarizing, the hybrid mode is characterized by semistrong incentives, an intermediate degree of administrative apparatus, displays semi-strong adaptations of both kinds, and works out of a semi-legalistic contract law regime. As compared with market and hierarchy, which are polar opposites, the hybrid mode is located between the two of these in all five attribute respects. Based on the foregoing, and denoting strong, semi-strong, and weak by ++, +, and 0, respectively, the instruments, adaptive attributes, and contract law features that distinguish markets, hybrids, and hierarchies are shown in Table 4.1.

3. Discriminating Alignment

Transaction-cost economics subscribes to Commons' view (1924, 1934) that the transaction is the basic unit of analysis. That important insight takes on operational significance upon identifying the critical dimensions with respect to which transactions differ. As heretofore indicated, these include the frequency with which transactions recur, the uncertainty to which transactions are subject, and the type and degree of asset specificity involved in supplying the good or service in question (Williamson, 1979b). Although all are important, transaction-cost economics attaches special significance to this last (Williamson, 1975, 1979b; Klein, Crawford, and Alchian, 1978; Grossman and Hart, 1986).

Asset specificity has reference to the degree to which an asset can be redeployed to alternative uses and by alternative users without sacrifice of productive value. Asset-specificity distinctions of six kinds have been made: (1) site specificity, as where successive stations are located in a cheek-by-jowl relation to each other so as to economize on inventory and transportation expenses; (2) physical asset specificity, such as specialized dies that are required to produce a component; (3) human-asset specificity that arises in learning by doing; (4) brand name capital; (5) dedicated assets, which are discrete investments in general purpose plant that are made at the behest of a particular customer; to which (6) temporal specificity, which is akin to technological nonseparability and can be thought of as a type of site specificity in which timely responsiveness by on-site human assets is vital has been added (Masten, Meehan, and Snyder, 1991). Asset specificity, especially in its first five forms, creates bilateral dependency and poses added contracting hazards. It has played a central role in the conceptual and empirical work in transaction-cost economics.

The analysis here focuses entirely on transaction costs: neither the revenue consequences nor the production-cost savings that result from asset specialization are included. Although that simplifies the analysis, note that asset specificity increases the transaction costs of all forms of governance. Such added specificity is warranted only if these added governance costs are more than offset by production-cost savings and/or increased revenues. A full analysis will necessarily make allowance for effects of all three kinds (Riordan and Williamson, 1985). Only a truncated analysis appears here.

3.1. Reduced-Form Analysis

The governance-cost expressions set out herein are akin to reduced forms, in that governance costs are expressed as a function of asset specificity and a set of exogenous variables. The structural equations from which these reduced forms are derived are not set out. The key features that are responsible for cost differences among governance structures are nonetheless evident in the matrix version of the models set out below.[1]

Although asset specificity can take a variety of forms, the common consequence is this: a condition of bilateral dependency builds up as asset specificity deepens. The ideal transaction in law and economics—whereby the identities of buyers and sellers is irrelevant—obtains when asset specificity is zero. Identity matters as investments in transaction-specific assets increase, since such specialized assets lose productive value when redeployed to best alternative uses and by best alternative users.

Assume, for simplicity, that asset specificity differences are entirely due to physical or site specificity features. I begin with the situation in which classical market contracting works well: autonomous actors adapt effectively to exogenous disturbances. Internal organization is at a disadvantage for transactions of this kind, since hierarchy incurs added bureaucratic costs to which no added benefits can be ascribed. That, however, changes as bilateral dependency sets in. Disturbances for which coordinated responses are required become more numerous and consequential as investments in asset specificity deepen. The high-powered incentives of markets here impede adaptability, since each party to an autonomous exchange that has gotten out of alignment and for which mutual consent is needed to effect an adjustment will want to

---

1. Developing the deeper structure that supports the reduced forms—by explicating contractual incompleteness and its consequences in a more microanalytic way and by developing the bureaucratic cost consequences of internal organization more explicitly—is an ambitious but important undertaking.

appropriate as much as possible (ideally, all but epsilon) of the adaptive gains to be realized. When bilaterally dependent parties are unable to respond quickly and easily, because of disagreements and self-interested bargaining, maladaptation costs are incurred. Although the transfer of such transactions from market to hierarchy creates added bureaucratic costs, those costs may be more than offset by the bilateral adaptive gains that result.

Let $M = M(k; \theta)$ and $H = H(k; \theta)$ be reduced-form expressions that denotes market and hierarchy governance costs as a function of asset specificity (k) and a vector of shift parameters (θ). Assuming that each mode is constrained to choose the same level of asset specificity, the following comparative-cost relations obtain: $M(0) < H(0)$ and $M' > H' > 0$.[2] The first of these two inequalities reflect the fact that the bureaucratic costs of internal organization exceed those of the market because the latter is superior in adaptation (A) respects—which is the only kind that matters if asset specificity is negligible. The intercept for market governance is thus lower than is the intercept for hierarchy. The second inequality reflects the marginal disability of markets as compared with hierarchies in adaptation (C) respects as asset specificity, hence bilateral dependency, becomes more consequential.

As described above, the hybrid mode is located between market and hierarchy with respect to incentives, adaptability, and bureaucratic costs. As compared with the market, the hybrid sacrifices incentives in favor of superior coordination among the parts. As compared with the hierarchy, the hybrid sacrifices cooperativeness in favor of greater incentive intensity. The distribution of branded product from retail outlets by market, hierarchy, and hybrid, where franchising is an example of this last, illustrates the argument.

Forward integration out of manufacturing into distribution would be implied by hierarchy. That would sacrifice incentive intensity but would (better) assure that the parts do not operate at cross-purposes with one another. The market solution would be to sell the good or service outright. Incentive intensity is thereby harnessed, but suboptimization (free riding on promotional efforts, dissipation of the brand name, etc.) may also result. Franchising awards greater autonomy than hierarchy but places franchisees under added rules and surveillance as compared with markets. Costs control and local adaptations are stronger under franchising than hierarchy, and suboptimization is reduced under franchising as compared with the market. The added autonomy (as compared with hierarchy) and the added restraints (as compared with the market) under which franchisees operate nevertheless come at a cost. If, for example, quality assurance is realized by constraining the franchisee to use materials supplied by the franchisor, and if exceptions to that practice are not permitted because of the potential for abuse that would result, then local opportunities to make "apparently" cost-effective procurements will be prohibited. Similarly, the added local autonomy enjoyed by franchisees may get in the way of some global adjustments.

---

2. A more general optimizing treatment in which the level of asset specificity varies with organization form is set out in Riordan and Williamson, 1985; a shorter version of which appears in Chapter 3.

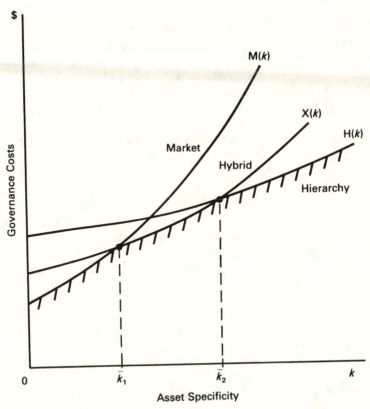

Figure 4.1. Governance costs as a function of asset specificity.

Transactions for which the requisite adaptations to disturbances are neither predominantly autonomous nor bilateral, but require a mixture of each, are candidates to be organized under the hybrid mode. Over some intermediate range of k, the mixed adaptation (A/C) that hybrids afford could well be superior to the A-favoring or C-favoring adaptations supported by markets and hierarchies, respectively.

Letting $X = X(k; \theta)$ denote the governance costs of the hybrid mode as a function of asset specificity, the argument is that $M(0) < X(0) < H(0)$ and that $M' > X' > H' > 0$.[3] The relations shown in Figure 4.1 then obtain. Efficient supply implies operating on the envelope, whence, if k^* is the optimal value of k, the rule for efficient supply is as follows: I, use markets for $k^* < \bar{k}_1$; II, use hybrids for $\bar{k}_1 < k^* < \bar{k}_2$; and III, use hierarchy for $k^* > \bar{k}_2$.

In a very heuristic way, moreover, one can think of moving along one of these generic curves as moving toward more intrusive controls. Thus, consider two forms of franchising, one of which involves less control than the other.

3. This assumes that $X(0)$ is less than $H(0)$ to a nontrivial degree, since otherwise the hybrid mode could be dominated throughout by the least-cost choice of either market or hierarchy, which may occur for certain classes of transactions, as discussed below.

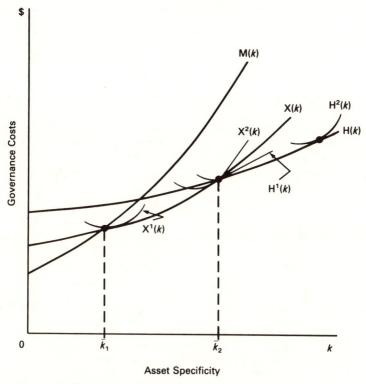

Figure 4.2. Governance differences within discrete structural forms.

If $X^1(k)$ and $X^2(k)$ refer to franchising with little and much control, respectively, then $X^2(k)$ will be located to the right of $X^1(k)$ in Figure 4.2. Or consider the M-form (multidivisional) and U-form (unitary or functionally organized) corporation. Because the former provides more market-like divisionalization than does the latter, the M-form is given by $H^1(k)$ and is located closer to $\bar{k}_2$ in Figure 4.2.

3.2.   A Stochastic Representation

Suppose that disturbances are distinguished in terms of the type of response—autonomous or bilateral—that is needed to effect an adaptation. Suppose further that the type of adaptation depends on the degree of asset specificity. Let asset specificity be denoted by k_j and suppose that it can take on any of three values: $k_1 = 0$ (generic investment), $k_2 > 0$ (semi-specific investment), or $k_3 \gg 0$ (highly specific investment). Assume that adjustments to disturbances can be any of four kinds: I, strictly autonomous; II, mainly autonomous; III, mainly coordinated; or IV, strictly coordinated. Let p_{ij} be the probability that an adaptation of type $i =$ I, II, ..., IV will be required if asset-specificity condition k_j ($j = 1, 2, 3$) obtains and let the matrix $[p_{ij}]$ be given by

		k_1	k_2	k_3
	I	1.00	.25	.10
	II	.00	.25	.10
$[p_{ij}]$:	III	.00	.25	.40
	IV	.00	.25	.40

Note that, the k_1 column excepted, positive probability is associated with every element in the matrix. What added asset specificity does is shift the distribution of required responses in favor of greater cooperativeness.

Assume that each adaptation, if costlessly and successfully implemented, would yield identical expected cost savings. For the reasons given above, however, the efficacy with which different modes adapt to disturbances of different kinds varies. Let e_{im} be the efficacy with which mode m ($m = M, X, H$) is able to implement adaptations of type i ($i = I, II, \ldots, IV$) and assume that the matrix e_{im} is given by

		M	X	H
	I	1.0	0.9	0.7
	II	0.7	0.9	0.4
$[e_{im}]$:	III	0.2	0.5	0.5
	IV	-0.2	0.0	0.5

where 1.0 is the ideal degree of adaptiveness and 0.0 is equivalent (in terms of efficacy) to no adaptation.

The efficacy assumptions embedded in this last matrix warrant remark: (1) Only the entry e_{IM} has a value of 1.0. This condition—market adaptations to a disturbance for which strictly autonomous adaptation is appropriate—corresponds to the ideal transaction in law and economics (classical market contracting); (2) The efficacy of the market falls off as bilateral dependency builds up, becoming negative (worse than no adaptation at all) for the strictly cooperative case (IV). This last reflects the conflictual nature of market exchange for transactions of the bilaterally dependent kind; (3) The hybrid mode is almost as good as the market for strictly autonomous adaptations, is better than the market in all other adaptation categories, and is as good or better than hierarchy in all categories save that for which strict coordination is indicated; (4) Hierarchy is burdened by bureaucracy and never scores high in efficacy for any category of adaptation.[4] What matters, however, is comparative efficacy. The hierarchy comes into its own (comparatively) where adaptations of a strictly cooperative kind are needed; and (5) The efficacy of hierarchy is lowest for disturbances requiring a mainly autonomous adaptation. As compared with strictly autonomous disturbances, where bureaucratic costs are

---

4. Hierarchy is able to deal with type I (strictly autonomous) disturbances reasonably well by instructing the operating parts to respond to local disturbances on their own motion and by using the market as an alternate source of supply and/or standard.

held in check by an objective market standard, ready recourse to the market is compromised by the need for some coordination. Because, however, the gains from coordination are not great, efforts to coordinate are problematic. If efforts to adapt autonomously are protested (my costs are greater because you moved without consulting me) while failures to adapt quickly are costly, the hierarchy is caught between the proverbial rock and a hard place.

Let C_{jm} be the expected maladaptation costs of using mode m to effect adaptations if asset specificity is of type k_j. Since inefficacy is given by $1 - e_{im}$, the expected maladaptation costs are $C_{jm} = \Sigma_i\, p_{ij}\, (1 - e_{im})$. That matrix is given by

		M	X	H
	k_1	**.000**	.100	.300
$[C_{jm}]$:	k_2	.575	**.425**	.475
	k_3	.830	.620	**.490**

The lowest values in each row are realized by matching market, hybrid, and hierarchy with asset specificity conditions k_1, k_2, k_3, respectively. These costs are consonant with the reduced-form relations shown in Figure 4.1. Thus if $\beta \geq 0$ is the irreducible setup costs of economic participation, then the bureaucratic cost intercepts associated with zero asset specificity (k_1) for market, hybrid, and hierarchy will be given by β plus .000, .100, and .300, respectively. Also, the relation between the implied slopes associated with each mode in the matrix (expressed as a function of asset specificity) is that $M' > X' > H'$, which corresponds exactly to the relations shown in Figure 4.1.

4. Comparative Statics

Transaction-cost economics maintains that (1) transaction-cost economizing is the "main case," which is not to be confused with the only case (Williamson, 1985b, pp. 22–23; 1989c, pp. 137–38), and (2) transaction costs vary with governance structures in the manner described above. Assuming that the institutional environment is unchanging, transactions should be clustered under governance structures as indicated. Variance will be observed, but the main case should be as described.

The purpose of this section is to consider how equilibrium distributions of transactions will change in response to disturbances in the institutional environment. That is a comparative static exercise. Both parts of the new institutional economics—the institutional environment and the institutions of governance—are implicated. The crucial distinctions are these:

> The *institutional environment* is the set of fundamental political, social and legal ground rules that establishes the basis for production, exchange and

distribution. Rules governing elections, property rights, and the right of contract are examples. . . .

An *institutional arrangement* is an arrangement between economic units that governs the ways in which these units can cooperate and/or compete. It . . . [can] provide a structure within which its members can cooperate . . . or [it can] provide a mechanism that can effect a change in laws or property rights. (Davis and North, 1971, pp. 6–7)

The way that I propose to join these two is to treat the institutional environment as a set of parameters, changes in which elicit shifts in the comparative costs of governance. An advantage of a three-way setup—market, hybrid, and hierarchy (as compared with just market and hierarchy)—is that much larger parameter changes are required to induce a shift from market to hierarchy (or the reverse) than are required to induce a shift from market to hybrid or from hybrid to hierarchy. Indeed, as developed below, much of the comparative static action turns on differential shifts in the intercept and/or slope of the hybrid mode. The critical predictive action is that which is located in the neighborhood of $\bar{k}_1$ (M to X) and $\bar{k}_2$ (X to H) in Figure 4.1. Parameter changes of four kinds are examined: property rights, contract law, reputation effects, and uncertainty.

Among the limitations of the discrete structural approach is that parameter changes need to be introduced in a special way. Rather than investigate the effects of increases (or decreases) in a parameter (a wage rate, a tax, a shift in demand), as is customary with the usual maximizing setup, the comparative governance cost setup needs to characterize parameter changes as improvements (or not). It is furthermore limited by the need for those improvements to be concentrated disproportionately on one generic mode of governance. Those limitations notwithstanding, it is informative to examine comparative static effects.

4.1. Property Rights

What has come to be known as the economics of property rights holds that economic performance is largely determined by the way in which property rights are defined. Ownership of assets is especially pertinent to the definition of property rights, where this "consists of three elements: (a) the right to use the asset [and delimitations that apply thereto] . . ., (b) the right to appropriate returns from the asset . . ., (c) the right to change the asset's form and/or substance" (Furubotn and Pejovich, 1974, p. 4).

Most discussions of property rights focus on definitional issues. As is generally conceded, property rights can be costly to define and enforce and hence arise only when the expected benefits exceed the expected costs (Demsetz, 1967). That is not my concern here. Rather, I focus on the degree to which property rights, once assigned, have good security features. Security hazards of two types are pertinent: expropriation by the government and expropriation by commerce (rivals, suppliers, customers).

4.1.1. Governing expropriation

Issues of "credible commitments" (see Chapter 5) and "security of expectations" (Michelman, 1967) are pertinent to expropriation by the government. If property rights could be efficiently assigned once and for all, so that assignments, once made, would not subsequently be undone—especially strategically undone—governmental expropriation concerns would not arise. Firms and individuals would confidently invest in productive assets without concern that they would thereafter be deprived of their just deserts.

If, however, property rights are subject to occasional reassignment, and if compensation is not paid on each occasion (possibly because it is prohibitively costly), then strategic considerations enter the investment calculus. Wealth will be reallocated (disguised, deflected, consumed) rather than invested in potentially expropriable assets if expropriation is perceived to be a serious hazard. More generally, individuals or groups who either experience or observe expropriation and can reasonably anticipate that they will be similarly disadvantaged in the future have incentives to adapt.

Michelman (1967) focused on cost-effective compensation. He argued that if compensation is costly and if the "demoralization costs" experienced by disadvantaged individuals and interested observers are slight, then compensation is not needed. If, however, demoralization costs can be expected to be great and losses can be easily ascertained, compensation is warranted. Michelman proposed a series of criteria by which to judge how this calculus works out. Suppose that the government is advised of these concerns and "promises" to respect the proposed criteria. Will such promises be believed? This brings us to the problem of credible commitments.

Promises are easy to make, but credible promises are another thing. Kornai's observation that craftsmen and small shopkeepers fear expropriation in Hungary despite "repeated official declarations that their activity is regarded as a permanent feature of Hungarian socialism" (1986, pp. 1705–6) is pertinent. That "many of them are myopic profit maximizers, not much interested in building up lasting goodwill ... or by investing in long-lived fixed assets" (1986, p. 1706) is partly explained by the fact that "These individuals or their parents lived through the era of confiscations in the forties" (Kornai, 1986, p. 1705).

But there is more to it than that. Not only is there a history of expropriation, but, as of 1986, the structure of the government had not changed in such a way as to assuredly forestall subsequent expropriations. Official declarations will be more credible only with long experience or if accompanied by a credible (not easily reversible) reorganization of politics. As one Polish entrepreneur recently remarked, "I don't want expensive machines. If the situation changes, "I'll get stuck with them" (Newman, 1989, p. A10). Note, in this connection, that the objectivity of law is placed in jeopardy if the law and its enforcement are under the control of a one-party state (Berman, 1983, p. 37). Credibility will be enhanced if a monarch who has made the law "may not make it arbitrarily, and until he has remade it—lawfully—he is bound by it" (Berman,

1983, p. 9). Self-denying ordinances and, even more, inertia that has been crafted into the political process have commitment benefits (North and Weingast, 1989).

That this has not fully registered on Eastern Europe and the Soviet Union is suggested by the following remarks of Mikhail Gorbachev (advising U.S. firms to invest quickly in the Soviet Union rather than wait): "Those [companies] who are with us now have good prospects of participating in our great country ... [whereas those who wait] will remain observers for years to come—*we will see to it*" (*International Herald Tribune*, 1990, p. 5, italics added). That the leadership of the Soviet Union "will see to it" that early and late movers will be rewarded and punished, respectively, reflects conventional carrot-and-stick incentive reasoning. What it misses is that ready access to administrative discretion is the source of contractual hazard. The paradox is that fewer degrees of freedom (rules) can have advantages over more (discretion) because added credible commitments can obtain in this way. Effective economic reform thus requires that reneging options be foreclosed if investor confidence is to be realized.

Lack of credible commitment on the part of the government poses hazards for durable, immobile investments of all kinds—specialized and unspecialized alike—in the private sector. If durability and immobility are uncorrelated with asset specificity, then the transaction costs of all forms of private-sector governance increase together as expropriation hazards increase. In that event, the values of $\bar{k}_1$ and $\bar{k}_2$ might then change little or not at all. What can be said with assurance is that the government sector will have to bear a larger durable investment burden in a regime in which expropriation risks are perceived to be great. Also, private-sector durable investments will favor assets that can be smuggled or are otherwise mobile—such as general-purpose human assets (skilled machinists, physicians) that can be used productively if emigration is permitted to other countries.

4.1.2. Leakage

Not only may property rights be devalued by governments, but the value of specialized knowledge and information may be appropriated and/or dissipated by suppliers, buyers, and rivals. The issues here have recently been addressed by Teece (1986) in conjunction with "weak regimes of appropriability" and are related to earlier discussions by Arrow (1962) regarding property rights in information. If investments in knowledge cannot lawfully be protected or if nominal protection (e.g., a patent) is ineffective, then (1) the ex ante incentives to make such investments are impaired and (2) the incentives to embed such investments in protective ex post governance structures are increased. As Teece (1986) discussed, vertical or lateral integration into related stages of production where the hazards of leakage are greatest is sometimes undertaken for precisely these protective purposes. Trade secret protection is an example.

Interpreted in terms of the comparative governance cost apparatus employed here, weaker appropriability (increased risk of leakage) increases the cost of hybrid contracting as compared with hierarchy. The market and hybrid curves in Figure 4.1 are both shifted up by increased leakage, so that $\bar{k}_1$ remains approximately unchanged and the main effects are concentrated at $\bar{k}_2$. The value of $\bar{k}_2$ thus shifts to the left as leakage hazards increase, so that the distribution of transactions favors greater reliance on hierarchy.

4.2.   Contract Law

Improvements or not in a contract law regime can be judged by how the relevant governance-cost curve shifts. An improvement in excuse doctrine, for example, would shift the cost of hybrid governance down. The idea here is that excuse doctrine can be either too lax or too strict. If too strict, then parties will be reluctant to make specialized investments in support of one another because of the added risk of truly punitive outcomes should unanticipated events materialize and the opposite party insist that the letter of the contract be observed. If too lax, then incentives to think through contracts, choose technologies judiciously, share risks efficiently, and avert adversity will be impaired.

Whether a change in excuse doctrine is an improvement or not depends on the initial conditions and on how these trade-offs play out. Assuming that an improvement is introduced, the effect will be to lower the cost of hybrid contracting—especially at higher values of asset specificity, where a defection from the spirit of the contract is more consequential. The effect of such improvements would be to increase the use of hybrid contracting, especially as compared with hierarchy.

Hadfield has recently examined franchise law and has interpreted the prevailing tendency by the courts to fill in the gaps of an incomplete contract "by according the franchisor unfettered discretion, much as it would enjoy if it [the franchisor] were a vertically integrated corporation" as a mistaken application of forbearance reasoning from hierarchy (where the logic holds) to neoclassical contracting (where the logic fails) (1990, pp. 981–82). Such a failure of franchise law would increase the cost of franchising in relation to forward integration into distribution (Hadfield, 1990, p. 954). This would imply a shift in the value of $\bar{k}_2$ in Figure 4.1 to the left.

A change in forbearance doctrine would be reflected in the governance cost of hierarchy. Thus, mistaken forbearance doctrine—for example, a willingness by the courts to litigate intrafirm technical disputes—would have the effect of shifting the costs of hierarchical governance up. This would disadvantage hierarchy in relation to hybrid modes of contracting ($\bar{k}_2$ would shift to the right).

4.3.   Reputation Effects

One way of interpreting a network is as a nonhierarchical contracting relation in which reputation effects are quickly and accurately communicated. Parties to a transaction to which reputation effects apply can consult not only their own experience but can benefit from the experience of others. To be sure, the efficacy of reputation effects is easily overstated (Williamson, 1991b), but comparative efficacy is all that concerns us here and changes in comparative efficacy can often be established.

Thus, assume that it is possible to identify a community of traders in which reputation effects work better (or worse). Improved reputation effects attenuate incentives to behave opportunistically in interfirm trade—since the immediate gains from opportunism in a regime where reputation counts must be traded off against future costs. The hazards of opportunism in interfirm trading are greatest for hybrid transactions—especially those in the neighborhood of $\bar{k}_2$. Since an improvement in interfirm reputation effects will reduce the cost of hybrid contracting, the value of $\bar{k}_2$ will shift to the right. Hybrid contracting will therefore increase, in relation to hierarchy, in regimes where interfirm reputation effects are more highly perfected, ceteris paribus. Reputation effects are pertinent within firms as well. If internal reputation effects improve, then managerial opportunism will be reduced and the costs of hierarchical governance will fall.

Ethnic communities that display solidarity often enjoy advantages of a hybrid contracting kind. Reputations spread quickly within such communities and added sanctions are available to the membership (Light, 1972). Such ethnic communities will predictably displace nonethnic communities for activities for which interfirm reputation effects are important. Nonethnic communities, to be viable, will resort to market or hierarchy (in a lower or higher k niche, respectively).

4.4.   Uncertainty

Greater uncertainty could take either of two forms. One is that the probability distribution of disturbances remains unchanged but that more numerous disturbances occur. A second is that disturbances become more consequential (due, for example, to an increase in the variance).

One way of interpreting changes of either kind is through the efficacy matrix, above. I conjecture that the effects of more frequent disturbances are especially pertinent for those disturbances for which mainly coordinated or strictly coordinated responses are required. Although the efficacy of all forms of governance may deteriorate in the face of more frequent disturbances, the hybrid mode is arguably the most susceptible. That is because hybrid adaptations cannot be made unilaterally (as with market governance) or by fiat (as with hierarchy) but require mutual consent. Consent, however, takes time. If a hybrid mode is negotiating an adjustment to one disturbance only to be hit by another, failures of adaptation predictably obtain (Ashby, 1960). An increase in market and hierarchy and a decrease in hybrid will thus be associated with an (above threshold) increase in the frequency of disturbances. As shown in Figure 4.3, the hybrid mode could well become nonviable when the frequency of disturbances reaches high levels.[5]

5. The range of asset specificity is from zero (purely generic) to complete (purely firm-specific). The range of frequency is from "low" (a positive lower bound in a nearly unchanging environment) to "very high."

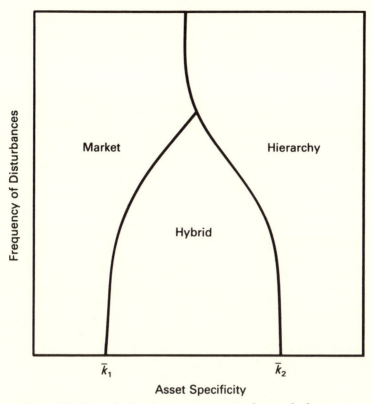

Figure 4.3. Organization form responses to changes in frequency.

If an increase in the variance of the disturbances uniformly increases the benefits to be associated with each successful adaptation, then the effect of increasing the consequentiality of disturbances can again be assessed through the effects on efficacy. Since outliers induce greater defection on the spirit of the agreement for hybrid modes, the efficacy of the hybrid is adversely affected by added variance. Unless similar disabilities can be ascribed to market or hierarchy, the hybrid is disfavored by greater variance, ceteris paribus.

5. Discussion

The foregoing is concerned with the organization of transactions for mature goods and services and introduces parameter shifts one at a time. Added complications arise when innovation is introduced and when a series of parameter shifts occur together.

5.1. Innovation

Some of the added problems posed by innovation take the form of weak property rights. These are discussed above in conjunction with leakage. A second class of problems that confront innovation is that of timeliness. Non-standard forms of organization, such as parallel R&D (Nelson, 1961) and joint ventures, are sometimes employed because these facilitate timely entry.

Timing can be crucial if a party expects to be a "player" when events are fast-moving or if learning-by-doing is essential. Although transaction-cost economics can relate to some of the pertinent issues, such as those posed by tacit knowledge (Polanyi, 1962) and the limits of imitation (Williamson, 1975, pp. 31–32, 203–7), added apparatus is needed to deal with the full set of issues that arise when responsiveness in real time, rather than equilibrium contracting, is the central concern. Awaiting such developments, the apparatus developed here should not be applied uncritically. For example, joint ventures are sometimes described as hybrids. If, however, joint ventures are temporary forms of organization that support quick responsiveness, and if that is their primary purpose, then both successful and unsuccessful joint ventures will commonly be terminated when contracts expire. Successful joint ventures will be terminated because success will often mean that each of the parties, who chose not to merge but, instead, decided to combine their respective strengths in a selective and timely way, will have learned enough to go it alone. Unsuccessful joint ventures will be terminated because the opportunity to participate will have passed them by. Joint ventures that are designed to give a respite should be distinguished from the types of hybrid modes analyzed here, which are of an equilibrium kind.

The need to distinguish continuing from temporary supply does not, however, mean that transaction-cost economizing principles do not apply to each. To the contrary, although the particulars differ, I would urge that the same general transaction-cost economizing framework has application (Williamson, 1985b). The quasi-firms described by Eccles (1981), for example, can be interpreted as the efficient solution to a particular type of recurrent contracting problem. But the details do matter.

5.2. Simultaneous Parameter Shifts

The comparative static analysis set out above treats each generic form of organization as a syndrome of attributes and introduces parameter shifts one at a time. Suppose, instead, that a series of shifts were to occur together. Could these be processed as a sequence of independent changes? If such changes were in fact independent, that is precisely what I would propose. If, however, a related set of changes is made simultaneously, it will not do to treat these independently. If strong interaction effects exist, these must be treated as a cluster.

Relying extensively on the recent work of Aoki (1988, 1990), I interpret the Japanese corporation as follows: (1) three key factors—employment, subcontracting, and banking—are fundamentally responsible for the success of the Japanese firm; (2) the efficacy of each of these rests on distinctive institutional supports; and (3) the three factors bear a complementary relation to each other (see Chapter 12).

The search for key factors and their institutional supports is wholly consistent with the spirit of this chapter. Because employment, subcontracting, and banking changes are linked, however, the American corporation cannot expect to replicate the Japanese corporation by making changes in only one of these practices and not in the others. That is not to say that American firms cannot learn by observing subcontracting practices in Japanese firms. Exact replication of individual practices will be suboptimal, however, if linkages are important.

Similar considerations apply to economic reforms in China and Eastern Europe. If, for example, the efficacy of privatization turns crucially on the manner in which banking is organized and on the security of property rights, then piecemeal proposals that ignore the support institutions are fraught with hazard. The study of viable clusters of organization is a combined law, economics, and organizations undertaking. Although the apparatus in this paper is pertinent, applications to economic reform need to make express provision for contextual differences between alternative forms of capitalism (Hamilton and Biggart, 1988).

6.   Conclusion

This chapter advances the transaction-cost economics research agenda in the following five respects: (1) the economic problem of society is described as that of adaptation, of which autonomous and coordinated kinds are distinguished; (2) each generic form of governance is shown to rest on a distinctive form of contract law, of which the contract law of forbearance, which applies to internal organization and supports fiat, is especially noteworthy; (3) the hybrid form of organization is not a loose amalgam of market and hierarchy but possesses its own disciplined rationale; (4) more generally, the logic of each generic form of governance—market, hybrid, and hierarchy—is revealed by the dimensionalization and explication of governance herein developed; and (5) the obviously related but hitherto disjunct stages of institutional economics—the institutional environment and the institutions of governance—are joined by interpreting the institutional environment as a locus of shift parameters, changes in which parameters induce shifts in the comparative costs of governance. A large number of refutable implications are derived from the equilibrium and comparative static analyses of governance that result. The growing empirical literature, moreover, is broadly corroborative (for summaries, see Williamson, 1985b, chap. 5; Joskow, 1988; Klein and Shelanski, 1995).

Further developments of conceptual, theoretical, and empirical kinds are needed. Taken together with related developments in information economics, agency theory, and population ecology, there is reason to be optimistic that a "new science of organization" will take shape by the turn of the century (see Chapter 2). Whether that materializes or not, organization theory is being renewed in law, economics, and organizational respects. These are exciting times for interdisciplinary social theory.

5

Credible Commitments: Using Hostages to Support Exchange

Credible commitments and credible threats share the following common attribute: both appear mainly in conjunction with irreversible, specialized investments. But whereas credible commitments are undertaken in support of alliances and to promote exchange, credible threats appear in the context of conflict and rivalry.[1] The former involve reciprocal acts designed to safeguard a relationship, while the latter are unilateral efforts to preempt an advantage. Efforts to support exchange generally operate in the service of efficiency; preemptive investments, by contrast, are commonly antisocial. Both are plainly important to politics and economics, but the study of credible commitments is arguably the more fundamental of the two.

Interest in credible threats is much more widespread and the credible threat literature is more fully developed,[2] however, than is the interest and economic literature dealing with credible commitments. This disparity is consistent with the treatment accorded to each in Thomas Schelling's classic essay (1956) on bargaining, where the main emphasis is placed on tactics by which one party can realize an advantage in relation to a rival by credibly "tying one's hands." But Schelling also, albeit briefly, addresses the matter of promise. He

1. It should be noted that I use the terms threat and commitment differently than do Curtis Eaton and Richard Lipsey (1981). They distinguish between empty and credible threats and use the term commitment to refer to the latter. I submit that the language of rivalry is well serviced by reference to threats; and I suggest that the term commitment be reserved to describe exchange. Thus both credible and noncredible threats would be distinguished in assessing rivalry. Similarly, credible and noncredible commitments are distinguished in evaluating exchange. Alliances complicate matters in that these are organized in relation to another party. This could be wholly beneficial, but it need not be. Thus suppliers could form an alliance in relation to buyers, with possible antisocial results. Credible commitments which simultaneously support exchange and promote alliances thus sometimes pose tradeoffs.

2. Recent applications within economics involve investments in specific capital undertaken for the purpose of impending new entry (Dixit, 1979, 1982; Eaton and Lipsey, 1981; Schmalensee, 1981). For a discussion of reputation effects and quasi credibility in the economics literature, see David Kreps and Robert Wilson, 1982; Paul Milgrom and John Roberts, 1982; and Williamson, 1982a.

observes in this connection that "Bargaining may have to concern itself with an 'incentive' system as well as the division of gains" (p. 300) and adds in a footnote that the exchange of hostages served incentive purposes in an earlier age (p. 300, n. 17).

That the study of credible commitments has been relatively neglected is explained by the assumption, common to both law and economics, that the legal system enforces promises in a knowledgeable, sophisticated, and low-cost way. Albeit instructive, this convenient assumption is commonly contradicted by the facts—on which account additional or alternative modes of governance have arisen. Bilateral efforts to create and offer hostages are an interesting and, as it turns out, economically important illustration. Absent a recognition and appreciation for the merits of "private ordering," the suggestion that hostages are used to support contemporary exchange is apt to be dismissed as fanciful. I submit, however, that not only are the economic equivalents of hostages widely used to effect credible commitments, but failure to recognize the economic purposes served by hostages has been responsible for repeated policy error.

The private ordering approach to the study of contract is sketched in Section 1. A simple model for assessing the efficiency ramifications of alternative contracts, one of which involves hostages, is developed in Section 2. The model demonstrates that the investments made by suppliers are influenced by the incentives experienced by buyers. Incentive complications that reach beyond the model are discussed in Section 3. Applications of the argument to unilateral and to bilateral exchange are set out in Sections 4 and 5. Some evidence bearing on petroleum exchanges and public policy attitudes that relate thereto are examined in Section 6.

1. Private Ordering

1.1. Contracting Traditions

Most studies of exchange assume that efficacious rules of law regarding contract disputes are in place and that these are applied by the courts in an informed, sophisticated, and low-cost way. These assumptions are convenient, in that lawyers and economists are relieved of the need to examine the variety of ways by which individual parties to exchange "contract out of or away from" the governance structures of the state by devising private orderings. A division of effort thus arises whereby economists are preoccupied with the economic benefits that accrue to specialization and exchange, while legal specialists focus on the technicalities of contract law.[3] My concern with this

3. Lawyers do not have a monopoly on refining contractual rules. For two contributions by economists, see Peter Diamond and Eric Maskin, 1979 and Steven Shavell, 1980. Such an economic approach to contract focuses on the technicalities of legal rules. The approach taken here holds that even refined rules of law are costly to implement, whence private ordering is widely employed.

tradition is that the law and economics of private ordering have been pushed into the background as a consequence.[4]

Four distinct, albeit related, literatures within economics[5] have developed since the early 1970s, in which private ordering is expressly or implicitly featured: the incentive compatibility literature (Hurwicz, 1972); the literature on the economics of internal organization (Coase, 1937; Arrow, 1963b, 1974; Williamson, 1971b, 1975, 1979b; Klein, Crawford, and Alchian, 1978; Teece, 1982a; Fama and Jensen, 1983); the financial economics literature dealing with bonding (Stiglitz, 1974; Jensen and Meckling, 1976; Grossman and Hart, 1982); and the study of self-enforcing agreements (Telser, 1981; Klein and Leffler, 1981). The first two of these have been reviewed elsewhere (Hurwicz, 1973; Williamson, 1981b, 1982a). The third takes issue with the Modigliani–Miller theorem that the firm's production plan is independent of its financial structure.[6] The fourth deals with contracting in intermediate product markets and expressly relies on private ordering.

Telser characterizes a self-enforcing agreement as one which, if "one party violates the terms the only recourse of the other is to terminate the agreement" (1981, p. 27). Contrary to legal centralism, the courts and other third parties are assumed away. Klein and Leffler are explicit on this: "we assume throughout . . . that contracts are not enforceable by the government or any third party" (1981, p. 616). Commercial contract law in late nineteenth-century Taiwan evidently approximated this condition (Brockman, 1980). Stewart Macaulay's remarks about the informality of contract in business are likewise in this spirit: "Often businessmen do not feel they have 'a contract'—rather they have 'an order.' They speak of 'cancelling the order' rather than 'breaching our contract'" (1963, p. 61).

To be sure, pure private ordering is extreme. As Robert Mnookin and Lewis Kornhauser state, private ordering invariably operates in "the shadow of the law" (1979).[7] It suffices for my purposes to argue that the incentives

4. For a discussion, see Chapters 2 and 3 in this book; see also Marc Galanter, 1981.

5. There is also a long legal tradition in which contract as legal rule is disputed. Karl Llewellyn's views regarding "contract as framework" (1931) are especially important. Recent significant contributions include Steward Macaulay, 1963 and Ian Macneil, 1974. For a discussion, see Williamson, 1979b.

6. Grossman and Hart make the interesting distinction between a bonding and a signaling equilibrium: in the former, agents communicate "their endogenous intentions, while the latter involves agents communicating their exogenous characteristics" (1982, p. 110). Put differently, bonding has reference to the incentives of agents at the contract execution stage (an ex post condition), whereas signaling involves inferring the directly unobservable ex ante attributes of agents, which are fully prespecified. Thus whereas Stephen Ross (1977) uses the debt–equity ratio to signal objective (exogenous) differences in the quality of management, Grossman and Hart use debt to precommit managers to a course of action whereby closer ex post adherence to profit maximization is induced. Specifically, debt becomes an instrument by which managers place themselves at hazard, in recognition of which the financial market places a higher value on the firm (Grossman and Hart, 1982, p. 130). Since managers are assumed to benefit from this higher market valuation (Grossman and Hart, 1982, p. 109), they self-consciously accept the hazards of bankruptcy which debt financing poses.

7. Galanter suggests that a better way to characterize the study of contract is "law in the shadow of indigenous ordering" (1981, p. 23). There is a good deal to be said for this. The main point is that a place for law is properly provided in any comprehensive study of contract.

of private parties to devise bilateral contractual safeguards is a function of the efficacy of court adjudication, and that this varies with the attributes of transactions. Specifically the courts experience serious disabilities with respect to the transactions of the kinds herein described.

1.2. Some Attributes of This Chapter

This chapter examines self-enforcing agreements in transaction cost terms. Contracting agents are thus assumed to be subject to bounded rationality and, where circumstances permit, are given to opportunism.[8]

Although hostages can have both *ex ante* (screening) and *ex post* (bonding) effects, the *ex post* contract execution consequences are of principal interest here.[9] This is also the focus of the self-enforcing agreement literature. Additionally, like both Telser and Klein–Leffler, the intertemporal contracts of concern here feature both uncertainty and transaction-specific capital. But in other respects there are important differences.

Thus, whereas Telser deals with "a sequence of transactions over time such that the ending date is unknown and uncertain" (1981, p. 30), because any finite sequence of transactions using his model will unravel (p. 29), the transactions that I consider can be (indeed, normally are) finite. Furthermore, the role of transaction specific capital is more explicit and fully developed in this chapter than in Telser's.

The self-enforcing contracts studied by Klein and Leffler (1981) are likewise of indefinite rather than finite duration. The hostage model is further distinguishable from Klein–Leffler in that (1) they deal with quality uncertainty in final goods markets, whereas I assume that quality is known and focus on stochastic demand in intermediate product markets;[10] (2) their "fundamental theoretical result" involves the assurance of quality through the sacrifice of "minimum-cost production techniques" (1981, p. 618, 628–29), while the hostage model involves no such sacrifice (indeed, the use of hostages to support exchange encourages investment in specific asset technologies which have *lower* expected costs);[11] and (3) suppliers in their model are confronted neither

8. Whereas previously I have emphasized firm versus market governance, here I focus strictly on market-mediated exchange. The governance issue of interest thus involves choice among alternative interfirm contracts.

9. *Ex ante* screening attributes are briefly examined in an earlier version of this chapter (1982b, pp. 6–9). The assessment of a screening equilibrium is complex, however, and is not central to the main argument. See Michael Rothschild and Stiglitz, 1976; and John Riley, 1979a, 1979b, for a discussion of screening equilibrium issues.

10. My discussion of franchising in Section 4.3 parallels Klein–Leffler and assumes that quality uncertainty is responsible for a demand externality. The hostage model developed in Section 2 does not apply directly to this case, but the spirit carries over in three respects: (1) franchisees, like buyers, are given a choice among alternative contracts; (2) the decision to expose specific assets is deliberately taken because this has superior incentive effects; and (3) the sunk cost technology is *more* efficient, which vitiates the inefficiency tradeoff that is central to the Klein–Leffler paper.

11. Contrary to the argument advanced by Klein and Leffler, total costs need not increase in a quality assurance model because investments are shifted from a reversible (fixed cost) to an irreversible (sunk cost) technology. Thus instead of a general purpose building of nondescript

with expropriation nor adaptation hazards, while these are both of concern to me. More generally, the hostage model and imagery have application to a quite different set of contractual circumstances than the analysis of quality assurance contemplates.

2. The Hostage Model

The simple hostage model serves to illuminate both unilateral and bilateral exchange, permits the concept of specific capital to be extended beyond earlier uses, and clarifies how costs should be described in assessing exchange. While it is primitive and suggestive, rather than refined and definitive, it serves as a paradigmatic wedge by which the importance of private ordering is exposed and is easily made the vehicle for further analysis.

2.1. Technologies and Costs

The assessment of alternative contracts will be facilitated by assuming that the product in question can be produced by either of two technologies. One is a general purpose technology; the second is a special purpose technology. The special purpose technology requires greater investment in transaction specific durable assets and, as described below, is more efficient for servicing steady-state demands.

Costs that are highly specific to a transaction have two attributes: they are incurred in advance of the contemplated exchange; and their value in alternative uses, or by alternative users, is greatly reduced.[12] As Klein and Leffler put it, the irreversible, nonsalvageable part of an advance commitment is sunk (1981, p. 619). It is common to think of this as applying to physical plant or accounting costs that are reported as fixed, but this is not the critical distinction. Thus investments in labor (transaction specific human capital) can be highly specific. And many costs that for accounting purposes are reported to be fixed are in fact nonspecific, hence can be recovered (salvaged) by redeployment. Durable but mobile assets such as general purpose trucks or airplanes are illustrations.

The two technologies in question will thus be described in value realization terms. The value that can be realized by redeploying variable and fixed costs

---

design, the producer could construct a building with a distinctive "signature." The durable investments could be the same, but the alternative value that can be realized from the second building might be much lower. The long-term commitments that are signaled by this second design relieve customers of quality shading hazards, which is the central issue with which Klein and Leffler are concerned.

12. Klein et al. use the term "appropriable quasi rent" to describe this condition. Use vs. user distinctions are relevant in this connection: "The quasi-rent value of the asset is the excess of its value over its salvage value, that is, its value in its next best *use* to another renter. The potentially appropriable specialized portion of the quasi-rent is the portion, if any, in excess of its value to the second highest-valuing *user*" (1978, p. 298).

will be given by v. The nonsalvageable value of advance commitments will be denoted by k. The two technologies can thus be described as T_1: the general purpose technology, all advance commitments of which are salvageable, the redeployable unit operating costs of which are v_1; and T_2: the special purpose technology, the nonsalvageable value of advance commitments of which are k and the redeployable unit operating costs of which are v_2.

2.2. Contracting

There are two periods. Orders are placed in the first, and production if any occurs in the second. Buyers can either take delivery or refuse it. Demand is stochastic. The gross value to buyers is assumed to be uniformly distributed over the interval $[0, 1]$, and the quantity demanded at every price will be assumed to be constant, which it will be convenient to set equal to unity. Sunk costs, if any, are incurred in the first period. Inasmuch as sunk costs are incurred for certain while the decision to incur redeployable costs is contingent on the buyer's decision to confirm or cancel an order, a choice between technologies is interesting only if $k + v_2 < v_1$. The demand and cost relations are set out in Figure 5.1.

2.2.1. Net benefits

The criterion by which decisions to take or refuse delivery will be evaluated is that of joint profit maximization. Feasibility and/or bureaucratic disabilities aside, vertical integration assuredly accomplishes the joint profit-maximization result. Thus the reference condition for evaluating contracts will be an integrated firm with two divisions, a producing division and a marketing division. The producing division has access to the same two technologies described above, one of which involves specific assets, the other of which does not. Whichever technology is employed, product is transferred between divisions at marginal cost.

That $k + v_2 < v_1$ does not establish that the special purpose technology (T_2) is the more efficient. Whether it is or not depends on a net benefit calculation. The expected net benefits of using the general purpose technology (T_1) are given by the product of the probability that the integrated firm will decide to produce and the average net benefits that are realized when product is supplied. The integrated firm will decide to produce only if the realized demand price exceeds marginal costs, whence the probability of produc-

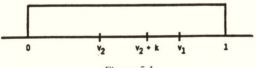

Figure 5.1

tion under T_1 is $1 - v_1$. The mean net benefits during production periods are $(1 - v_1)/2$, whence the expected net benefits for technology T_1 are

$$b_1 = (1 - v_1)(1 - v_1)/2 = (1 - v_1)^2/2. \tag{5.1}$$

The expected net benefits for the specific asset technology (T_2) are found similarly. Again, the integrated firm will produce whenever realized demand price exceeds marginal costs. Expected net receipts, however, must be reduced by the amount of the earlier investment in specific assets, k, in computing expected net benefits. Thus we have

$$b_2 = (1 - v_2)(1 - v_2)/2 - k = (1 - v_2)^2/2 - k, \tag{5.2}$$

where the first term is the expected excess of revenue over out-of-pocket costs.

The specific asset technology will be selected only if $b_2 > b_1$, which requires that

$$k < (1 - v_2)^2/2 - (1 - v_1)^2/2. \tag{5.3}$$

2.2.2. Autonomous contracting

Assume that the inequality in 5.3 holds and consider the case of autonomous contracting between a buyer, who services final demand, and a producer, who manufactures the product. Assume that demand and production technologies are as described above. Efficient contracting relations are those that replicate the vertical integration result,[13] namely, (1) select the specific asset technology, and (2) produce and sell product whenever realized demand price exceeds v_2. Assume that both parties are risk neutral and that the production side of the industry is competitively organized. Whatever contracting relation is described, producers will be willing to supply if a break-even condition (expressed in expected value terms) can be projected.[14]

Recall that orders are placed in the first period. Specific assets, if any, are committed in the first period in anticipation of second-period supply. Whether second-period production actually occurs, however, is contingent on demand

13. Here and throughout the remainder of this chapter I assume that exchange is governed by contract rather than by vertical integration. Vertical integration is thus used merely as a reference condition. That manufacturers do not integrate forward or distributors integrate backward can be explained on a number of grounds—one of which is that there are economies of scope at both stages, but that very different product mixes are needed to realize these scope economies at each stage.

14. There is no problem in principle in allowing suppliers to extract positive profits as a condition of supply. The salient features of the hostage model are all preserved if, instead of an expected break-even condition, the supplier was assumed to realize expected profits of $\bar{\pi} > 0$ on each contract. Although final demands will be choked off as a consequence, the main features of the contractual argument survive.

realizations. Buyers have the option of confirming or cancelling orders in the second period. Consider three contracting alternatives:

I. The buyer purchases specific assets and assigns them to whichever seller submits the lowest bid, p;

II. The producer makes the specific asset investment himself and receives a payment of $\bar{p}$ in the second period if the buyer confirms the order but nothing otherwise; and

III. The producer makes the specific asset investment himself and receives $\hat{p}$ from the buyer if the buyer confirms the order, is paid αh, $0 \leq \alpha \leq 1$, if the order is cancelled while the buyer pays $\hat{p}$ upon taking delivery and experiences a reduction in wealth of h if second-period delivery is cancelled.

The third scenario can be thought of as one where the buyer posts a hostage that he values in amount h, which hostage is delivered to the producer, who values it in amount αh if the order is cancelled.

The producer will break even under contracting relation I if he is compensated in amount v_2, which is his out of pocket cost, for each unit demanded. The low bidder will thus offer to supply product for $p = v_2$. Since the buyer's net benefits are maximized if he invests in the specific assets, and since product is transferred on marginal cost terms, this contract replicates the vertical integration relation. Contracts of type I are feasible, however, only if the specialized assets are mobile and the specificity is attributable to physical features (for example, specialized dies). Market procurement can then service the needs of the parties without posing hold-up problems by concentrating the ownership of the specific assets on the buyer (who then assigns them to the low bidder). Inasmuch as the buyer can reclaim the dies and, without cost, solicit new bids should contractual difficulties develop, type I contracts yield an efficient result.[15]

Attention hereafter will be focused on contracts II and III, the assumption being that asset specificity is of the human or dedicated asset kinds (see Section 2.3). The autonomous buyer will confirm an order under contract II whenever realized demand price exceeds $\bar{p}$ but not otherwise. The producer will thus break even if $(1 - \bar{p})\bar{p} - [(1 - \bar{p})v_2 + k] = 0$, whence

$$\bar{p} = v_2 + k/(1 - \bar{p}). \tag{5.4}$$

Product will thus be exchanged at a price that exceeds marginal cost under this contracting scenario.[16] Plainly if $\bar{p} \geq v_1$, the buyer is better off to scuttle

15. This ignores the possibility that suppliers will abuse the dies if ownership resides with the buyer.

16. Conceivably $\bar{p}$ will exceed v_1, in which event the buyer who is contemplating contract II will prefer instead to purchase from sellers who use the general purpose technology. The comparison in the text implicitly assumes that $\bar{p} < v_1$. Also note that a standby technology that can be costlessly switched into and out of the product in question could effectively truncate demand at v_1. This would be true if potential middlemen could place orders to take product at v_1 from general purpose manufacturers, which orders could be costlessly cancelled (and general purpose assets redeployed) if demands fell below this value. I will arbitrarily assume that this is not feasible. The problem could, however, be reformulated by describing demand as uniformly distributed over the interval 0 to v_1, with v_1 having measure $1 - v_1$.

contract II and purchase instead from producers who utilize the (inferior) variable cost technology T_1 (and will break even by supplying product on demand for a price of v_1).

The buyer will confirm an order under contract III whenever the realized demand price exceeds $\hat{p} - h$. Let $\hat{p} - h$ be denoted by m. The seller will then break even when $(1 - m)\hat{p} + m\alpha h - [(1 - m)v_2 + k] = 0$, whence

$$\hat{p} = v_2 + (k - m\alpha h)/(1 - m). \tag{5.5}$$

The case where $h = k$ and $\alpha = 1$ is one where the buyer gives up wealth in amount of the investment in specific assets in cancellation states and this is delivered to the producer who values it in amount k. Under these circumstances, (5.5) becomes

$$\hat{p} = v_2 + k. \tag{5.5'}$$

Since the buyer places an order whenever demand exceeds $m = \hat{p} - h$, this yields the result that $m = v_2$, whence orders will be placed whenever demand exceeds v_2, which is the efficient (marginal cost) supply criterion.

The buyer's net benefits under contracting scheme III are

$$b_3 = (1 - m)\left[\left(m + \frac{1 - m}{2}\right) - \hat{p}\right] - mh, \tag{5.6}$$

where $(1 - m)$ is the probability of placing an order, $m + (1 - m)/2$ is the expected demand price for all orders that are placed, $\hat{p}$ is the payment in demand confirmation states to the producer, and h is the wealth sacrifice in cancellation states (which occur with probability m). Under the assumptions that $h = k$ and $\alpha = 1$, this reduces to

$$b_3 = (1 - v_2)^2/2 - k, \tag{5.6'}$$

which is identical to the net benefit calculation for technology T_2 under the vertical integration reference condition (see Equation 5.2).

Accordingly, contracting scheme III accompanied by the stipulations that $h = k$ and $\alpha = 1$ replicates the efficient investment and supply conditions of vertical integration. Problems arise, however, if $h < k$ or $\alpha < 1$. The disadvantage, moreover, accrues entirely to the buyer—since the seller, by assumption, breaks even whatever contracting relation obtains. Thus although *after* the contract has been made, the buyer would prefer to offer a lesser-valued hostage and cares not whether the hostage is valued by the producer, at the time of the contract he will wish to assure the producer that a hostage of k for which the producer realizes full value ($\alpha = 1$) will be transferred in nonexchange states. Failure to make this commitment will result in an increase in the contract price. Thus, whereas producers who are concerned only with *ex ante* screening can tolerate values of α less than one—see the discussion of ugly princesses in Section 3.1—this is not the case at all when *ex post* opportunism is the concern. If the producer is not indifferent, as between two princesses, each of whom is valued identically by the buyer, the producer's preferences now need to be taken into account.[17]

To summarize, therefore, it can be observed that contract I mimics vertical integration, but only under special asset specificity conditions; contract II is inferior; and contract III yields the vertical integration result if $h = k$ and $\alpha = 1$. Furthermore, note that an important feature of contract III is that the buyer takes delivery in all demand states for which realized demand exceeds $m = \hat{p} - h$. Since the supplier is always paid $\hat{p}$ upon execution, the buyer sometimes takes delivery when his realized receipts (upon resale of the product) are less than $\hat{p}$. This does not, however, signal inefficiency, since orders are never confirmed when realized demand price falls below marginal cost (v_2). Indeed, it is precisely because of the hostage feature that efficiency is realized and contract III is superior to contract II.

2.3. Dedicated Assets

Dedicated assets[18] represent a discrete investment in plant. Although these assets add to the firm's generalized (as contrasted with special purpose) production capability, the investment would not be undertaken but for the prospect of selling a significant amount of product to a specific customer. As with other types of asset specificity, dedicated assets lose value if employed in alternative uses (or by or to service alternative users). Dedicated assets thus are those that are put in place contingent upon particular supply agreements and, should such contracts be prematurely terminated, would result in significant excess capacity.

3. Engaging the Supplier

Suppliers are passive instruments in this model. They are indifferent among contracts, since their expected profits are the same (zero) whichever choice the buyer makes. What drives the argument is that buyers can secure better terms only by relieving producers of demand cancellation penalties. Buyers cannot have their cake (product supplied by the efficient technology at a price of $\hat{p}$) and eat it too (cancel without cost).

Inasmuch as optimality is realized if $h = k$ and $\alpha = 1$, the ideal hostage would appear to be an offer of generalized purchasing power: money. A security bond in amount $h = k$ would serve this purpose. That the argument does not terminate here is because such an arrangement does not assuredly

17. Placing an upper bound of unity on α precludes the possibility that the supplier values the hostages more than does the buyer. Potential gains from trade would exist for all hostages for which α exceeds unity. A case for negatively valued hostages could be made in the context of ugly princesses (see Section 3.1).

18. See Chapters 3 and 4 in this book for more expansive discussions of asset specificity and its various forms.

engage the interests and cooperation of the supplier. Three reasons can be adduced for this condition: contrived cancellation, uncertain valuation, and incomplete contracting. All are a consequence of joining bounded rationality with opportunism.

3.1. Supplier Opportunism

3.1.1. Contrived cancellation

The issue of contrived cancellation has been addressed by Kenneth Clarkson, Roger Miller, and Timothy Muris in their discussion of refusal of the courts to enforce stipulated damage clauses where breach has been deliberately induced (1978, pp. 366–72). Induced breach could arise where a party intentionally withholds relevant information, yet complies with the letter of the contract. Or it might involve perfunctory fulfillment of obligations where more resourceful cooperation is needed (pp. 371–72). In either case, induced breach is costly to detect and/or prove (p. 371).

This explanation for selective enforcement of liquidated damage clauses has troubled other legal scholars (Posner, 1979, p. 290), but a more satisfactory explanation has yet to be advanced. At the very least, the Clarkson et al. treatment reflects a sensitivity to the subtleties of opportunism—on which account private ordering is more complicated than the bare bones hostage model would suggest. Among other things, the expropriation hazard to which they refer may explain the use of ugly princesses.

Thus suppose that demand uncertainties are negligible, whence order cancellation hazards can be disregarded. Suppose further, however, that buyers differ in credit risk respects, and that producers would, if they could, refuse sales to poor risks. Assuming that the difference between good and poor risks is sufficiently great that a separating equilibrium is feasible,[19] producers could demand hostages (or, put differently, good risks could offer hostages) as a way by which to screen. Given, moreover, that the only use to which hostages are put is as a screen, a value of $\alpha = 0$ would accomplish this purpose without exposing the buyer to an expropriation hazard (based, say, on a legal technicality). Specifically, a king who is known to cherish two daughters equally and is asked, for screening purposes, to post a hostage is better advised to offer the ugly one.

3.1.2. Uncertain valuation

The model assumes that the value of the specific investment (k) is well specified. This need not be the case. Indeed, it may be difficult for buyers to ascertain whether the investments made in response to first-period orders are of the amount or of the kind that producers claim. This is not a serious problem if the production side of the market is competitively organized and fly-by-night concerns can be disregarded. Where, however, this cannot be presumed, the possibility that buyers will be expropriated arises. Producers may feign

19. See n. 9.

delivery competence (claim to have invested in specific assets in amount k but only committed $k' < k$) and expropriate bonds for which $h = k$ by contriving breach or invoking a technicality.

This hazard is especially great if the producer, who retains possession of the assets for which specificity is claimed, can preserve asset values by integrating forward into the buyer's market upon taking possession of the hostage. Even though the producer is poorly suited to perform successor stage functions, the possession of specialized stage I assets effectively reduces the costs that would otherwise attend de novo stage II entry.

To be sure, the buyer who offers a hostage and recognizes a risk of contrived expropriation will adjust the original terms to reflect this. Specifically, contracts supported by hostages for which expropriation risks are believed to be great will command less than those where these same hazards are believed to be lower. But this is to concede that, absent additional safeguards, neither the transfer of product on marginal cost terms nor the efficient level and kind of investment will assuredly attend contracts of type III. Deeper governance issues than those contemplated by the simple model are evidently posed.

3.1.3. Incomplete contracts/haggling

For the reasons given above and described elsewhere (see my 1975 study, pp. 20–36, 91–94), complex contracts are invariably incomplete and many are maladaptive. The reasons are two: many contingencies are unforeseen (and even unforeseeable); and the adaptations to those contingencies that have been recognized and for which adjustments have been agreed to are often mistaken—possibly because the parties acquire deeper knowledge of production and demand during contract execution than they possessed at the outset (Nelson and Winter, 1982, pp. 96–136). Instrumental gap filling, thus, is an important part of contract execution. Whether this is done easily and effectively, or if instead reaching successive agreements on adaptations and their implementation is costly, makes a huge difference in evaluating the efficacy of contracts.

Thus even if contrived breach hazards could be disregarded, producers who are entirely open and candid about contract execution may nevertheless be in a position to haggle—thereby to expropriate sellers—because contracts are incomplete or maladaptive. Specialized governance structures that have the purpose and effect of promoting harmonious adaptations and preserving the continuity of exchange relations arise in response to this condition. Knowledgeable third parties and reciprocal exposure of specialized assets are two possibilities.

3.2. Protective Governance Structures

3.2.1. Arbitration

Institutions that have the capacity to evaluate disputes in a more knowledgeable way than the courts may arise in this way. The parties, for example, may agree to submit disputes over contract execution to arbitrators who have specialized knowledge of the industry. Lon Fuller's remarks concerning procedural differences between arbitration and litigation bear repeating:

> there are open to the arbitrator . . . quick methods of education not open to the courts. An arbitrator will frequently interrupt the examination of witnesses with a request that the parties educate him to the point where he can understand the testimony being received. The education can proceed informally, with frequent interruptions by the arbitrator, and by informed persons on either side, when a point needs clarification. Sometimes there will be arguments across the table, occasionally even within each of the separate camps. The end result will usually be a clarification that will enable everyone to proceed more intelligently with the case. (1963, pp. 11–12)

Many agreements which, were it not for arbitration, would be regarded as excessively hazardous can, in this way, be reached and implemented.[20]

3.2.2.   Reciprocal exposure

An alternative way by which to protect contracts against expropriation is to expand the contractual relation. One way of accomplishing this is for buyer and seller to devise a *mutual reliance relation*. Thus suppose that the buyer does not post a hostage as such, but himself invests in specific capital that has value only in conjunction with servicing final demands for the product in question. Assume that these are valued in amount k''. The buyer then has the incentive to take delivery as long as realized demand exceeds $\hat{p} - k''$. If $k'' = k$, this yields the marginal cost supply result,[21] and the producer will be satisfied with the buyer's incentives. Or suppose that producer and buyer engage in reciprocal trade. Specifically, suppose that the producer contracts to procure product from the buyer, the supply of which requires the buyer to invest in specific assets in amount k'''. Each party to this reciprocal trade will experience appropriate incentives if (1) $k''' = k$, (2) demand variation in the two markets is perfectly correlated, and (3) each party has the option to cancel an order if a cancellation notice is received from his opposite.[22] As discussed in Section 5, bilateral trades (reciprocity; swaps) can sometimes be made to approximate these conditions.

20. Labor unions can help to assure integrity in contractual relations where workers are asked to accept assignments that involve considerable investments in human capital. Not only can the union intercede on behalf of the worker(s) where an expropriation effort is suspected, but it provides an institutional memory whereby reputation effects can be communicated to successor generations of workers. For both of these reasons, the firm is deterred from attempting expropriation. Setting aside the possibility that unions will attempt to negotiate monopoly wages, perceptive firms will prefer and actively assist in the creation of unions if these serve to attenuate expropriation risks—since otherwise workers may refuse to make (or will need to be bribed to make) mutually beneficial investments in human capital.

21. The buyer must, of course recover his full costs if he is to place specialized marketing assets at hazard. This will obtain if final demand is uniformly distributed over the interval k'' to $1 + k''$ and derived demand is as described earlier.

22. This last condition protects each against a prisoner's dilemma result.

4. Unilateral Trading

The argument that buyers can affect the terms and manner of supply by offering (or refusing to offer) hostages has ramifications for Robinson–Patman price discrimination and to an understanding of franchising and two-part pricing.

4.1. Robinson–Patman

The Robinson–Patman Act has been interpreted as an effort "to deprive a large buyer of [discounts] except to the extent that a lower price could be justified by reason of a seller's diminished costs due to *quantity* manufacture, delivery, or sale, or by reason of the seller's good faith effort to meet a competitor's equally low price."[23] Plainly, that $\hat{p}$ is less than $\bar{p}$ in the hostage model has neither quantity nor meeting competition origins. Neither is it contrary to the public interest. Indeed, it would be inefficient and unwarranted for a producer to charge the same price to two customers who order an identical amount of product, but only one of which offers a hostage, if (1) investments in specialized assets are required to support the transactions in question, or (2) if, because of a refusal to make a credible commitment, transactions of the second kind are produced with a general purpose (but high cost) technology.

The missing ingredients, plainly, are the differential commitment to buy (as reflected by the willingness to offer hostages) and the differential incentives to breach once hostages have been posted. The confusion is explained by the propensity to employ conventional (steady state) microtheory to the neglect of transaction cost aspects. Rectifying this involves examination of the microanalytics of transactions, with special reference to asset specificity and the hazards thereby posed, and evaluating alternative contracts with respect to a *common reference condition*—prospective break even being a useful standard. Once this is done, a different understanding of many nonstandard or unfamiliar contracting practices, many of which are held to be presumptively unlawful, frequently emerges.[24]

4.2. Franchising

Klein and Leffler (1981) argue that franchisees may be required to make investments in transaction specific capital as a way by which to safeguard the franchise system against quality shading. The arrangement is tantamount to the creation of hostages to restore integrity to an exchange.

23. *FTC* v. *Morton Salt Co.,* 334 U.S. 37 (1948); emphasis added.

24. Note that the argument applies only to $\hat{p}$ vs. $\bar{p}$ comparisons in trades where specific assets are involved. The efficiency properties of customer price differentials that do have these origins are not reached by the argument in this paper.

The application of hostage logic to franchising is set out in Chapter 3, Section 3.2.2. Suffice it to observe here that the use of hostages to support franchising would be unneeded if reputation effects worked costlessly.

4.3. Two-Part Pricing

Victor Goldberg and John Erickson describe an interesting two-part pricing scheme that they observed in the sale of coke. The producer both sold coke to the calciner, and owned and leased the land upon which the plant of the calciner was built. Inasmuch as the coke was sold for "about one-quarter the current market price of equivalent quality coke" (1982, p. 25), Goldberg and Erickson conjecture that "the rental rate was above the fair market rate and that the contract was designed to ensure that [the calciner] would continue to perform" (p. 25). Assuming that marginal costs are much less than average, such an arrangement can be interpreted as one by which the parties are attempting to strike efficient pricing terms that approximate those of the hostage model.

The pricing of utility services, whereby *ex ante* installation fees are paid by subscribers, also have interesting two-part pricing attributes.[25] The risk that sellers will expropriate buyers upon receipt of advance payment can be mitigated by creating a specialized third party, which for convenience may be referred to as a regulatory commission (Goldberg, 1976a). Utilization of utility services can then be priced so as to more nearly approximate marginal cost.

More generally, Goldberg and Erickson conjecture that nonlinear pricing schemes are much more widespread than is commonly believed. They further point out that such arrangements are often very subtle and will require detailed knowledge of contracts to investigate (1982, pp. 56–57).

5. Bilateral Applications

As indicated, the offer of hostages poses a hazard of expropriation. One way to deter this is to expand the contracting relationship from one of unilateral to bilateral exchange. Credible commitments are signaled without exposing assets to expropriation hazards. Reciprocal trades, especially those that involve product exchanges (swaps), sometimes come about in this way.

5.1. Reciprocity, General

Reciprocity transforms a unilateral supply relation—whereby A sells X to B—into a bilateral one, whereby A agrees to buy Y from B as a condition for making the sale of X and both parties understand that the transaction will be continued only if reciprocity is observed. Although reciprocal selling is widely held to be anticompetitive (Stocking and Mueller, 1957; Blake, 1973),

25. This possibility was suggested to me by Alvin Klevorick.

reciprocity can serve to equalize the exposure of the parties, thereby reducing the incentive of the buyer to defect from the exchange—leaving the supplier to redeploy specialized assets at greatly reduced alternative value. Absent a hostage (or other assurance that the buyer will not defect), the sale by A of specialized product to B may never materialize. The buyer's commitment to the exchange is more assuredly signaled by his willingness to accept reciprocal exposure of specialized assets. Defection hazards are thereby mitigated.

Lest the argument be uncritically considered to be a defense for reciprocal trading quite generally, note that it applies only where specialized assets are placed at hazard by *both* parties. Where only one or neither invests in specialized assets, the practice of reciprocity plainly has other origins.[26]

5.2. Exchanges

Although reciprocal trading among nonrivals may occasionally be justified, the exchange of product among nominal rivals is surely more puzzling and troublesome. Firms that are presumed to be in head-to-head competition ought to be selling product against one another rather than to one another. What explains the reverse?

Several distinctions are useful in considering exchanges. First, trade among rivals—short term or long term, unilateral or bilateral—is feasible only if product is fungible. This is not true for many differentiated goods and services, whence the issue of trade among rivals never arises for these. Second, short-term supply agreements are usefully distinguished from long term. The former may be explained as an "occasional exception," whereby one rival will sell product to another on a short-term, gap-filling basis so as to provide temporary relief against unanticipated product shortfalls (occasioned by either demand or supply changes). Recognizing that the shoe may be on the other foot next time, otherwise rivalrous firms may assist one another for stop-gap purposes. Public policy can presumably recognize merit in such trades and, so long as they lack a pattern, hence do not give rise to a "web of interdependence," will regard these as unobjectionable. Long-term trading among rivals is, however, much less consistent with the notion of effective head-to-head rivalry. At the very least, such arrangements warrant scrutiny.

Whether there are efficiency incentives for rivals to supply product to one another on a long-term basis turns initially on prospective realization of production cost savings. The realization of production cost savings through long-term trade between rivals requires that economies of scale be large in relation to the size of geographic markets and, if they are, that firm-specific reputation effects extend across geographic market boundaries. The former is obvious since, absent economies of scale, every firm would presumably supply everywhere to its own long-term needs. Where, however, scale econo-

---

26. Possible trading objections are discussed by Scherer (1980, pp. 344–45). Another objection is that reciprocity becomes a bureaucratic habit that salesmen and purchasing agents find convenient and that outsiders are thereby disadvantaged in attempting to secure sales. See my 1975 study, pp. 163–64.

mies are significant, each market will support only a limited number of plants of minimum efficient size.

But fungibility and scale economies do not establish that gains from trade will be realized from such sales. This will obtain only if the value of (identical) product sold by rivals exceeds that sold by the local supplier. The issue here is whether valued reputation effects will go unrealized if rivals are unable to secure local product on favorable terms. Firms that possess valued reputations that extend beyond their local market to include distant markets are thus the ones for which long-term supply by rivals will be attractive.[27]

Even supposing that fungibility, scale economy, and reputation effect conditions are satisfied, this merely establishes that *unilateral* long-term trade among rivals can yield economies. A justification for *bilateral* (exchange) agreements is not reached by these arguments. Indeed, the usual defense for exchanges—that inefficient cross-hauling will occur if every firm is required to supply everywhere to its own needs—conveniently suppresses the obvious alternative, which is not zero trade, but rather unilateral long-term trade. Failure to address these matters directly and demonstrate wherein exchanges enjoy comparative institutional advantages over more standard and familiar forms of unilateral trade presumably explains the suspect or hostile attitude with which exchanges are typically regarded. The argument that emerges from this chapter is that bilateral exchanges offer prospective advantages over unilateral trade *if* the resulting exposure of transaction specific assets effects a credible commitment without simultaneously posing expropriation hazards.

The type of specific asset that is placed at hazard by unilateral long-term trade, but which a reciprocal long-term exchange agreement serves to protect, is that of a dedicated asset. Recall that dedicated assets were described as discrete additions to generalized capacity that would not be put in place but for the prospect of selling a large amount of product to a particular customer. Premature termination of the contract by the buyer would leave the supplier with a large excess of capacity that could be disposed of only at distress prices. Requiring buyers to post a bond would mitigate this hazard, but only by posing another: the supplier may contrive to expropriate the bond. More generally, the interests of the supplier in adapting efficiently to new circumstances are not fully engaged. Reciprocal trading supported by separate but concurrent investments in specific assets provides a mutual safeguard against this second class of hazards. The hostages that are thereby created have the interesting property, moreover, that they are *never exchanged.* Instead, each party retains possession of its dedicated assets should the contract be prematurely terminated.

The usual argument that exchanges are justified because they avoid costly cross-hauling does not get to these issues and, by itself, is not an adequate justification for widespread use of exchanges. Were it only that transportation cost savings were realized, unilateral trading would suffice. Indeed, petroleum firms should be expected to create a central exchange in which supplies and

27. Reputation effect valuations may be illusory or real. Those that are real take the form of customer convenience (billing, contracting) or assured knowledge of product characteristics.

demands were brought into correspondence by an auctioneer. Firms would end up selling to each other only by accident in these circumstances. Where dedicated assets are exposed, however, *the identity of the parties clearly matters*. Trades of this kind will not go through an auction market but will be carefully negotiated between the parties. Reciprocity in these circumstances is thus a device by which the continuity of a specific trading relation is promoted with risk attenuation effects.

6. Petroleum Exchanges

The phenomenon of petroleum exchanges has puzzled economists for a long time. It routinely comes up in antitrust cases and investigations. The 1973 case brought by the United States Federal Trade Commission against the major petroleum firms maintained the view that exchanges were instrumental in maintaining a web of interdependencies among these firms, thereby helping to effect an oligopolistic outcome in an industry that was relatively unconcentrated on normal market structure criteria.[28] The more recent study on *The State of Competition in the Canadian Petroleum Industry* likewise regards exchanges as objectionable.[29] The Canadian Study, moreover, produces documents—contracts, internal company memoranda, letters, and the like—as well as deposition testimony to support its views that exchanges are devices for extending and perfecting monopoly among the leading petroleum firms. Such evidence on the details and purposes of contracting is usually confidential and hence unavailable. But detailed knowledge is clearly germane—and sometimes essential—to a microanalytic assessment of the transaction cost features of contract.

6.1. The Evidence from the Canadian Study

Volume 5 of the Canadian Study deals with the refining sector. Arguments are advanced and supporting evidence is developed that interfirm supply arrangements permit the major refiners to perfect oligopolistic restrictions in the following four respects.[30] (1) valuable knowledge about investment and marketing plans of rivals are disclosed by such agreements (p. 56); (2) leading firms are able to control lesser firms by exercising discretionary power through the terms of exchange (pp. 49–50); (3) competition is impaired by conditioning

28. *FTC* v. *Exxon et al.,* Docket No. 8934 (1963).

29. Robert J. Bertrand, Q. C., Director of Investigation and Research, Combines Investigation Act, coordinated the eight-volume study, *The State of Competition in the Canadian Petroleum Industry* (Quebec, 1981). All references in this paper are to vol. 5, *The Refining Sector.* This study will hereinafter be referred to as the Canadian Study.

30. The Canadian Study contends that "a close examination of the interest of the [major refiners] and their actions shows that refining arrangements were meant to restrict competition. The collection of information, the intent to control lesser firms, the imposition of an 'entry fee,' the use of restrictions on downstream growth are not characteristics that would be expected normally from a competitive market" (vol. 5, p. 76).

supply on the payment of an "entry fee" (pp. 53–54); and (4) exchange agreements impose limits on growth and supplementary supply (pp. 51–52).

The first two of these fail to pass scrutiny of the most rudimentary comparative institutional kind. Thus assuming that trade between rivals is efficient and that unilateral supply agreements (if not exchange) will be permitted, the objectionable information disclosures attributed to exchanges would presumably continue—since investment and marketing plans will be unavoidably disclosed in the process. Accordingly, evaluated in comparative institutional terms, the information disclosure objection is properly regarded as an objection to long term trade of any kind. Exchanges are not uniquely culpable.

The suggestion that exchanges are anticompetitive because they permit firms to realize bargaining advantages is similarly misplaced. The correct view is that firms should always be expected to realize such bargaining advantages as their positions lawfully permit. Absent a showing that exchanges are different from unilateral trades in bargaining respects, this objection is properly disregarded also.

The entry fee and marketing restraint objections are more substantial, however, and warrant elaboration.

6.1.1. Entry fees

The entry fee objection to exchanges is that this has foreclosure consequences. That such fees are required as a precondition for trade, or at least the sale of product at favorable prices, is set out in the Canadian Study as follows:

> Evidence of an understanding that a fee relating to investment was required for acceptance into the industry can be found in the following quotation from Gulf: "We do believe that the oil industry generally, although grudgingly, will allow a participant who has paid his ante, to play the game; the ante in this game being the capital for refining, distributing and selling products" (Document #71248, undated, Gulf). The significance of the quotation lies equally in the notion that an "entry fee" was required and in the notion that the industry set the rules of the "game." The meaning of the "entry fee" as well as the rules of the "game" as understood by the industry can be found in the actual dealings between companies where the explicit mention of an "entry fee" arises. These cases demonstrate the rules that were being applied—the rules to which Gulf was referring. Companies which had not paid an "entry fee", that is, companies which had not made a sufficient investment in refining capacity or in marketing distribution facilities would *either not be supplied or would be penalized in the terms of the supply agreement.* (pp. 53–54, emphasis added)

6.1.2. Marketing restraints

The Canadian Study notes that exchanges were made conditional on growth and territorial restraints and regards both as objectionable. The Imperial–Shell exchange agreement, under which Imperial supplied product to Shell in the Maritimes and received product in Montreal, is cited in both connections.

> The agreement between Imperial and Shell, originally signed in 1963, was renegotiated in 1967. In July 1972, Imperial did this because Shell had been growing too rapidly in the Maritimes. In 1971/72, Imperial had expressed its dissatisfaction with the agreement because of Shell's marketing policies. Shell noted:
> "There [*sic*] [Imperial's] present attitude is that we have built a market with their facilities, we are aggressive and threatening them all the time, and they are not going to help and in fact get as tough as possible with us" (Document #23633, updated, Shell). (Vol. 5, p. 51)

Imperial renewed the agreement with Shell only after imposing a price penalty if expansion were to exceed "normal growth rates" and furthermore stipulated that "Shell would not generally be allowed to obtain product from third party sources" to service the Maritimes (p. 52).

Gulf Oil likewise took the position that rivals receiving product under exchange agreements should be restrained to normal growth: "Processing agreements (and exchange agreements) should be entered into only after considering the overall economics of the Corporation and should be geared to providing competitors with volumes required for the normal growth only."[31] If furthermore sought and secured assurances that product supplied by Gulf would be used only by the recipient and would not be diverted to other regions or made available to other parties (p. 59).

6.2. Interpretations

These practices are subject to several interpretations. One is that the entry fees and marketing restraints are both anticompetitive. A second is that efficiency purposes are arguably served, especially by the former. A third is that there are mixed effects.

6.2.1. The inhospitality tradition

The two polar contracting traditions for evaluating nonstandard or unfamiliar contracting practices are the common law tradition, and the antitrust or inhospitality tradition. Donald Turner makes reference to both of them in expressing his views about vertical market restrictions: "I approach territorial and customer restrictions not hospitably in the common law tradition, but inhospitably in the tradition of antitrust law."[32] Thus whereas contractual irregularities are presumed to serve affirmative economic purposes under the common law tradition, a deep suspicion of anticompetitive purposes is maintained by the antitrust (or inhospitality) tradition.

---

31. The Canadian Study (p. 59) identifies the source as Document #73814, January 1972, Gulf.

32. The quotation is attributed to Turner by Stanley Robinson, 1968, N.Y. State Bar Association, Antitrust Symposium, p. 29.

The inhospitality tradition is supported by the widespread view that economic organization is technologically determined. Economies of scale and technological nonseparabilities explain the organization of economic activity within firms. All other activity is appropriately organized by market exchanges. Legitimate market transactions will be mediated entirely by price; restrictive contractual relations signal anticompetitive intent.

The authors of the Canadian Study are evidently persuaded of the merits of this tradition. Long-term trade among rivals of any kind is suspect. And exchanges, which represent an irregular if not unnatural contracting form, are especially objectionable. Not only do exchanges facilitate information disclosure and permit bargaining strength, but they are used punitively against nonintegrated independents who, because they have not paid an entry fee, are denied product on parity terms. Furthermore, the marketing restraints that are associated with exchanges are patently offensive.

6.2.2. An efficiency assessment

Unlike the inhospitality tradition, the transaction cost approach is in the common law tradition. A comparative institutional orientation (Coase, 1964) is maintained. "Defects" are thus objectionable only where superior feasible alternatives can be described. Inasmuch as the information disclosure and bargaining concerns raised by the authors of the Canadian Study continue under unilateral trading, these are set aside and attention is focused on other matters.

Entry fees. The entry fee issue is a matter of special interest to this chapter. Long-term exchange agreements permit firms to secure product in geographic markets where own-production is not feasible because economies of scale are large in relation to their own needs. The amount of product in question may nevertheless be substantial. Firms with whom exchange agreements are reached will thus construct and maintain larger plants than they otherwise would. Specific investments in dedicated assets are made as a consequence of such agreements.

Were it that supply agreements were of a unilateral kind and the buyer was unable or unwilling to offer a hostage, contracts of type II would presumably be negotiated—whence the trading price would be $\bar{p}, = v_2 + k/(1 - \bar{p})$. If, instead, the contract is extended to include bilateral rather than unilateral trade, the contract is converted to one of type III. Although exchange agreements stipulate the physical flows of product, the effective price is $\hat{p} = v_2 + k$, which is less than $\bar{p}$. Moreover, the parties have the incentive to exchange product so long as realized demand price in both regions exceeds v_2,[33] which is the marginal cost supply criterion. Assuming that demands in the two regions are highly correlated, the parties will normally reach common decisions on the desirability of trade.[34]

33. This assumes common costs, which condition will normally be approximated in exchanges of product between firms within a single country where factor prices are very similar.

34. The possibility that the contract will drift out of alignment nevertheless needs to be

Marketing restraints. The supply and growth restraints discussed by the Canadian Study can be looked at in three ways. First, these can be viewed as a means by which to protect the exchange agreement against unilateral defection. Second, such restraints may serve strategic market division purposes. Third, restraints may serve to regularize markets. These are not mutually exclusive.

Only the first of these purposes is consonant with an efficiency interpretation. The argument here is that marketing restraints help to preserve symmetrical incentives. Such symmetry could be upset if one of the firms were to receive product in its deficit region from third parties. Such a firm might then be in a position to play one supplier off against the other. Or symmetry could be placed under strain if one party were to receive product from the other such that it began to grow "in excess of normal"—in which event it might be prepared to construct its own plant and scuttle the exchange agreement. Marketing restraints which help to forestall such outcomes encourage parties to participate in exchanges that might otherwise be unacceptable.

6.2.3. A mixed view

Monopoly explanations are commonly advanced when economists, lawyers, or other interested observers come across contractual practices that they do not understand (Coase, 1972, p. 67). A rebuttable presumption that nonstandard contracting practices are serving affirmative economic purposes, rather than monopoly purpose, would arguably serve antitrust law and economics better than the inhospitality presumption which, until recently, has prevailed.[35]

The presumption that exchanges have efficiency purposes could be challenged on any or all of three grounds. First, it might be argued that exchanges are merely a clever device by which to deny product to nonintegrated rivals. Refusals to sell to nonintegrated firms on $\bar{p}$ terms would support this contention. (It is plainly unrealistic, however, for buyers that have not made credible commitments to expect to receive product at $\hat{p}$.) Second, the market

---

recognized. Should one of the firms in an exchange agreement operate much closer to its capacity limits than the other, the latter party would incur much higher costs of termination than would the former. Recognition of this may explain why "during the renegotiation of a reciprocal purchase/sale agreement covering Montreal and the Maritimes," Shell noted that Imperial advised them that "they were not satisfied with the extent of Shell's investment in the Maritimes" (p. 54). In addition to the investment in refining in Montreal, which Shell interpreted as an investment "by exchange" in the Maritimes, Imperial wanted Shall to make direct investment in a Maritime distribution network (p. 54). Shell observed in this connection that although it had made no significant investment of its own in the Maritimes, "we have invested in Montreal and by exchange invested in the Maritimes so we have paid an entrance fee, although we have not paid for distribution network." The Canadian Study (p. 54) identifies the source as Document #23633, updated, Shell.

35. To be sure, this is an oversimplification. Antitrust, has been loath to declare contractual constraints to be per se illegal. It came perilously close to taking this step in *U.S.* v. *Arnold Schwinn & Co.*, 388 U.S. 365 (1967), however. The prevailing enforcement view toward contractual restraints in the 1960's is accurately characterized as inhospitable.

in question could be shown to have troublesome structural properties. The issue here is whether the requisite preconditions for market power—mainly high concentration coupled with high barriers to entry[36]—are satisfied. A third would be that the preconditions for efficiency are not satisfied. Factors favorable to the efficiency interpretation are the following: the exchange should be of a long-term kind; the amount of product exchanged should represent a significant fraction of plant capacity; and economies of plant scale should be large in relation to the amount of product traded. Exchanges for a small quantity of product where economies of scale are insubstantial are much more problematic.

To be sure, exchanges might simultaneously service efficiency and anti-competitive purposes. Here as elsewhere, where tradeoffs are posed, they need to be evaluated.

7. Concluding Remarks

The study of contract in both law and economics has mainly emphasized legal rules and technicalities. Such an orientation is supported by the implicit assumption that the courts "work well." Whether they work well or poorly, however, requires a comparative institutional assessment. There is growing awareness that the (comparative) limitations of the courts are more severe than the legal centralism tradition admits.

The severity of these limitations is not uniform but varies with the circumstances. A discriminating approach to the study of contract will necessarily make provision for this. Specifically, if different transactions have different governance needs, these will be expressly recognized. Accordingly, the study of contract is appropriately extended from legal rules to include an assessment of alternative governance structures, of which the courts are only one. Of special interest in this connection is the use of bilateral governance structures (private ordering) to implement nonstandard contracts where the adaptation and continuity needs of the parties are especially great.

This chapter is an effort to deepen the understanding of private ordering. The central points are these:

1. Hostages: Contrary to the prevailing view that hostages are a quaint concept with little or no practical importance to contemporary contracting, the use of hostages to support exchange is widespread and economically important. But hostage creation is only part of the story. Expropriation hazards and prospective maladaptation conditions also need to be considered. Complex governance structures, of which reciprocal trading is one, arise in response to such conditions.

36. There is growing agreement that the structural preconditions that must be satisfied before claims of strategic anticompetitive behavior are seriously entertained are very high concentration coupled with barriers to entry (Williamson, 1977b, pp. 292–93; Joskow and Klevorick, 1979, pp. 225–31; Ordover and Willig, 1981, pp. 307–8).

. 2. Asset specificity: The organization of economic activity is massively influenced by the degree to which the transactions under examination are supported by assets that are specific to the parties. This chapter (1) reaffirms the basic proposition that governance structures need to be matched to the underlying attributes of transactions in a discriminating way if the efficiency purposes of economic organization are to be realized, (2) extends the scope of asset specificity to include dedicated assets, and (3) establishes that, as between two buyers, one of whom posts a hostage in support of specific asset investments by suppliers while the other does not, suppliers will offer better terms to the former, *ceteris paribus*.

3. Microanalytics: The relevant unit of analysis for studying exchange relations of the kinds discussed in this article is the transaction. Assessing transactions and assigning them to governance structures in a discriminating (mainly transaction cost economizing) way requires much more microanalytic knowledge of economic activity and organization than is customary within economics. Empirical work will necessarily reflect this.[37] Price and quantity of course remain relevant, but the contractual devices by which prices are made to track costs, the manner in which adaptations are effected, and the safeguards that are provided are not only germane but are sometimes decisive.

4. Contracting in its entirety: Not every transaction poses defection hazards, and it may not be possible to safeguard all that do. Where the potential hazards that beset contracts are evident to the parties from the outset, however, studies of contracts and of contracting institutions arguably start "at the beginning." This has ramifications for assessing the importance of the prisoners' dilemma and for understanding the administration of justice.

a. Prisoners' dilemma: The benefits of cooperation notwithstanding, the achievement of cooperation is widely thought to be frustrated by the relentless logic of the prisoners' dilemma. To be sure, it has always been evident that defection can be deterred if payoffs are appropriately altered. But this stratagem is held to be infeasible or is otherwise dismissed—on which account the dilemma persists or appeal is made to "exogenous norms of cooperative behavior [that are] adhered to by the actors" (Hirschman, 1982, p. 1470). I submit that the feasibility of crafting superior *ex ante* incentive structures warrants more attention. A leading reason for its neglect is because the study of the institutions of contract has occupied such a low place on the research agenda. Subtle incentive features that are incorporated in nonstandard contracting practices have gone undetected as a consequence of this nonchalance—on which account the practical significance of the prisoners' dilemma to the study of exchange has been vastly exaggerated.

b. Justice: The notion that hostages are demanded as a condition for supplying product on favorable terms has the appearance of an arbitrary exercise of power: the stronger party "demands" a hostage from the weaker, who accedes it because it has no other choice. In fact, a comparative institu-

37. See Peter Klein and Howard Shelanski, 1995, for a survey of the evidence.

tional assessment of contractual alternatives discloses that efficiency purposes are often served by hostages and that it is in the mutual interest of the parties to achieve this result. Not only can producers be induced to invest in the most efficient technology, but buyers can be induced to take delivery whenever demand realizations exceed marginal cost. More generally, contracts need to be examined *in their entirety,* with special attention to their governance features. Principles of justice or competition that look at the relation between the parties at the execution stage without examining the *ex ante* bargaining relation are at best incomplete and are frequently mistaken.[38] Parties to a contract should not expect to have their cake (low price) and eat it too (no hostage).

38. Robert Nozick's views on justice are apposite: "whether a distribution is just depends upon how it came about. In contrast, *current-time-slice* principles of justice hold that the justice of a distribution is determined by how things are distributed (who has what)" (1974, p. 153). What he refers to as the current-time-slice approach to justice neglects *ex ante* bargaining and evaluates justice in terms of outcomes alone. Upon realization that justice is administered in this way, initial bargains will be struck on different terms than they would if the parties were given assurance that the complete contract would be subject to review in evaluating the merits of a contracting relation. Two difficult issues nevertheless remain if the comprehensive bargain orientation to justice is adopted: the initial distribution of resources; and the competence of the parties to evaluate complex contracts. The relative importance of these varies with the circumstances.

6

Economic Institutions: Spontaneous and Intentional Governance

Spontaneous governance has been the prevailing economic approach to economic organization since Adam Smith made perceptive reference to, and briefly described, the "invisible hand," according to which each businessman "by pursuing his own interest . . . frequently promotes that of society more effectively than when he really intends to promote it" (Smith, 1922, p. 423). That formulation is properly regarded as a watershed event and has had a massive and continuing influence on economics. One of the most praiseworthy intellectual activities with which an economist can become engaged is to identify and explicate spontaneous control mechanisms through which hands-off governance operates.

Not only does it take a powerful mind—or, usually, the combined efforts of many powerful minds—to discover and model the mechanisms of spontaneous governance, but the benefits are stupendous. The need to become knowledgeable about, much less engrossed in the study of, institutional details is relieved if not vitiated if spontaneous mechanisms are the main arena. That we appear to be subject to intentional governance structures everywhere we turn is thus misleading: the real action is largely invisible.[1]

As discussed below, our understanding of spontaneous governance has improved steadily over the past 50 years. Unfortunately, however, and arguably as a consequence of the disproportionate attention given to spontaneous governance, the importance of intentional governance has been undervalued (Simon, 1991). Not only does a surefooted treatment of economic organization need to make express provision for both spontaneous and intentional forms

1. The "confusion" of the mythical Martian described by Herbert Simon (1991) is illustrative. The Martian is approaching the Earth equipped with a telescope that reveals social structures. Boundaries of firms show up as green contours and market transactions show up as red lines. Simon then avers that "A message sent back home, describing the scene [of economic organization], would speak of 'large areas bounded in green connected by a web of red lines.' It would not likely speak of 'a network of red lines connecting green spots'" (1991, p. 27). Alas, if spontaneous market mechanisms, rather than intentional administration, are where crucial economic activity resides, the Martian would be mistaken.

of governance, but it needs to explain which forms of governance apply where and why. At present, the study of economic organization suffers from a limp.

1. A Preview

Writing in 1945 in the context of the "socialist controversy," Friedrich Hayek lamented the *under*valuation of spontaneous governance and averred that the core task of the science of economic organization

> is precisely how to extend the span of our utilization of resources beyond the span of control of any one mind; and, therefore, *how to dispense with the need of conscious control* and how to provide inducements which will make the individuals do the desirable things without anyone having to tell them what to do. . . .
>
> [This describes] the really central theoretical problem of all social science. As Alfred Whitehead has said in another connection, "It is a profoundly erroneous truism, repeated by all copy-books and by eminent people when they are making speeches, that we should cultivate the habit of thinking what we are doing. The precise opposite is the case. Civilization advances by extending the number of important operations which we can perform without thinking about them. . . ."
>
> The price system is just one of those formulations which man has learned to use . . . after he stumbled on it without understanding it. (1945, pp. 527–28, emphasis added)

But if intentionality was overvalued and spontaneous governance under-valued in 1945, that is no longer the case today. As John Ferejohn remarks, "Theorists regard thin rational accounts, when available, as more fundamental than thick rational accounts" (1990, p. 6, n. 10). Given its privileged status and the fact that the availability of thin rational accounts has been growing steadily, spontaneous governance carries the day.

How robust, however, is Ferejohn's statement to the replacement of "available" by "plausible"? Put differently, are most of the available thin rational accounts also plausible? I submit that (1) availability is a very weak test, in that many thin accounts exist and the number is limited only by imagination; (2) many thin accounts are infeasible, in that they place impos-sible demands on bounded rationality; and (3) even feasibility is a weak test, in that many feasible mechanisms make negligible contact with the phenomena of interest. Whether thin feasible accounts that make limited contact are superior to thicker feasible accounts that make significant contact is surely problematic. Plausible accounts, those that are both feasible and make signifi-cant contact with the phenomena, are what the positive theory of economic organization is all about.

Whereas thin rational accounts work out of the imperative "This is the law here," plausibility purposes are better served by posing the question "What's going on here?" (see D'Andrade, 1986; McCloskey, 1986). Unbiased consideration of both spontaneous and intentional forms of governance is better assured under the latter formulation. If, as I believe, the New Science of Organization is neither one nor the other but implicates both spontaneous and intentional mechanisms (in discriminating ways), then a symmetrical treatment of both is needed.

A standard spontaneous governance ploy is to neuter both law and organization. A key, usually implicit, assumption is that disputes are resolved quickly and costlessly by the courts. Upon presenting the relevant information, the appropriate legal rules are applied and verdicts are announced and enforced. Inasmuch as the rules are known by, and outcomes can be inferred by, the parties, the parties never actually appear in court. Instead, they simply project the consequences and resolve the issues privately. Unsurprisingly, the legal enforcement of contracts receives little or no mention in the usual microeconomics text. The possibility that there are many pertinent laws of contract (Macneil, 1974, 1978) goes unremarked.

The usual ploy for neutering organization theory has been to describe firms as production functions. If technology is determinative, then what purpose is served by examining the anatomy? The powers and limits of hierarchy (and of hybrid forms of economic organization) are simply not engaged by this formulation. More recently, as a common contractual approach to firm and market organization has taken shape, the neutering assumption is that of contractual hyperrationality. To be sure, this is rarely invoked in an explicit way. Implicitly, however, hyperrationality can often be detected behind the scenes.

Even if bounds on rationality are admitted, neutering can be effected through the assumed absence of opportunism. One-sided opportunism, according to which only one of the two parties to a transaction needs to be candid and honest, is one such device. Leonid Hurwicz employs this device to examine private contracting. The economics of market socialism routinely assumes that the central government behaves in a benign way (Nuti, 1989).

Finally, intentionality can be minified by denial. One of the troublesome conditions with which spontaneous governance needs eventually to come to terms is the fact that a great deal of economic activity takes place within firms (Barnard, 1938; Chandler, 1962, 1977).[2] Conceivably, however, internal organization can be explained in technological terms: economies of scale or scope or technological nonseparabilities are responsible for that condition. Express attention to intentionality is unneeded because the crucial mechanisms through which internal organization operates are merely extensions of spontaneous governance mechanisms from the market into the firm.

I submit that hierarchy is much more than a continuation of market mechanisms. In very much the same way as "War is not merely a political

2. It is sometimes argued that intentional forms of organization have been progressively displacing spontaneous forms. Hierarchies purportedly supplanted markets in the late nineteenth century (Chandler, 1977, pp. 1, 286, 455) and this has accelerated more recently (Coleman, p. xv). I do not have a position on this. My sense is that the volume of transactions of both market and hierarchical kinds has increased, and it is unclear to me which way the ratio goes. It suffices for my purposes that both forms co-exist and are quantitatively important.

act, but also a political instrument, a continuation of political relations . . . *by other means*" (von Clausewitz, 1980, p. 13, emphasis added), so likewise is hierarchy not merely a contractual act, but also a contractual instrument, a continuation of market relations *by other means*. The comparative contractual challenge is to discern and explicate the *different* means.

Awaiting a theoretical proof of the impossibility of all-purpose hands-off governance, I proceed by examining the principal spontaneous governance mechanisms for which expansive claims have been made. I deal with each by first describing the way in which the mechanism in question purportedly works, next assess the efficacy, and then ask the question "What's going on here?"

The limits of franchise bidding (Williamson, 1976), pecuniary bonding (Williamson, 1985, pp. 176–79), and property rights (Williamson, 1990b) approaches having been addressed elsewhere, I focus here on four other mechanisms. The first of these is the price mechanism. The use of reputation effects to support autonomous contracting is examined in Section 3. The use of sequential short-term contracting as an answer to problems of contractual incompleteness, and the implied shift out of a transaction cost framework into a bargaining cost framework, is treated in Section 4. The best, however, is saved for last: the argument that hands-off socialism is and always has been feasible is disputed in Section 5. Concluding remarks follow.

2.   The Price Mechanism

2.1.   Spontaneous Adaptation

Writing in the context of the "socialist controversy" (see Section 5.1.1 below), Hayek took exception with the prevailing view that efficient resource allocation, to be realized by applying the principles of welfare economics (mainly, marginal cost pricing), was the key need. Hayek insisted instead that "the economic problem of society is *mainly one of rapid adaptation* to changes in the particular circumstances of time and place" (1945, p. 524, emphasis added). Observing, interpreting, and reacting to changes in information are crucial for these purposes. Because much of the relevant information was idiosyncratic, and hence could not be communicated quickly and cheaply to a center, those with *local knowledge* needed to be empowered to decide upon and make the adaptations. Hayek's solution to the economic problem of society was to use the price system to signal opportunities, whereupon decentralized decision-makers, who possessed the requisite local knowledge, would adapt. Mechanistic arguments about the efficacy of socialism failed because they neither recognized the real needs of economic organization (for rapid adaptation) nor appreciated that the marvel of the market serviced these needs in subtle, spontaneous ways.

2.2.   An Assessment

I am persuaded that Hayek was substantially correct in his critique of socialism. As Michael Jensen and William Meckling point out, however, Hayek's solution to the economic problem of society posed a puzzle: "Pushed to its logical extreme, Hayek's focus on knowledge of particular circumstances implies more or less complete atomization of the economy. There is no room for the firm" (Jensen and Meckling, 1990, p. 9).

To be sure, Hayek did discuss the firm as an instrument of cost control and expressly took exception with the prevailing firm-as-production function tradition. Thus, in response to the query "Is it true that, once a plant has been built, the rest is all more or less mechanical?" he answered as follows:

> The fairly widespread belief in the affirmative is not, so far as I can ascertain, borne out by the experience of the businessman. . . . How easy it is for an inefficient manager to dissipate the differentials on which profitability rests, and that it is possible, with the same technical facilities, to produce with a great variety of costs, are among the commonplaces of business experience which do not seem to be equally familiar in the study of the economist. (1945, p. 523)

But whereas Hayek plainly respected the importance of management in cost-control respects, he did not regard the firm as an instrument of adaptation. That crucial role was reserved for the market.

2.3. What's Going on Here?

Interestingly, Chester Barnard also subscribed to the view that adaptation was the central problem of economic organization. But whereas Hayek lamented the neglect of markets, Barnard lamented the neglect of "formal organization as the most important characteristic of social life" (1938, p. ix). And whereas Hayek imputed an adaptive advantage to markets, the adaptations that interested Barnard were those of internal organization.

As developed in Chapter 4, both Hayek and Barnard are correct. That both are correct is because they are referring to adaptations of different kinds, both of which are needed in a high-performance system. The adaptations to which Hayek referred could be implemented autonomously: each party examined prices in relation to his own opportunities and responded autonomously. Accordingly, such adaptations will be referred to as adaptations A, where A denotes autonomous. By contrast, the adaptations with which Barnard was concerned involved "that kind of cooperation among men that is conscious, deliberate, purposeful" (Barnard, 1938, p. 4) and were realized through formal organization—especially hierarchy. Adaptations of a consciously coordinated kind will be referred to as adaptations C, where C denotes cooperative. Recourse to fiat provides better assurance that adaptations of the latter kind will be performed in a coordinated way. Contrary opinions notwithstanding, markets and hierarchies are not indistinguishable in fiat respects. Hierarchy is superior to the market in bilateral adaptability respects—precisely because of its differential access to fiat.

This, however, poses deeper questions: Wherein does fiat arise? And why does the firm not judiciously combine autonomy and fiat, thereby to dominate either of these polar alternatives? And if it cannot, what are the trade-offs?

I have addressed these questions elsewhere (Williamson, 1985a, 1988d, 1991a) and focus here on two features: contract law differences that distinguish markets and hierarchies and the impossibility of selective intervention. Pertinent to the former is the hypothesis that each generic form of governance is supported by a distinctive form of contract law.

2.3.1. The contract law of internal organization

As developed in Chapter 4, the contract law of internal organization is that of forbearance. Access to the courts being denied, the parties *must* resolve their differences internally. Accordingly, hierarchy is its own court of ultimate appeal.

The underlying rationale for forbearance is twofold: (1) parties to an internal dispute have deep knowledge—both about the circumstances surrounding a dispute as well as the efficiency properties of alternative solutions—that can be communicated to the court only at great cost; and (2) permitting internal disputes to be appealed to the court would undermine the efficacy and integrity of hierarchy. Relevant to the latter is the proposition that market and hierarchy differ in nontrivial respects, of which fiat is one and informal organization is another. Were it that managers could always pursue claims against net receipts in the courts, the firm would be reduced to an "inside contracting system" (Buttrick, 1952; Williamson, 1975, pp. 96–98; 1985b, pp. 218–31). The efficacy of fiat would be seriously compromised as a consequence, whereupon the main advantages of internal organization as a governance structure through which to orchestrate bilateral adaptations would be lost.

2.3.2. Selective intervention

The puzzle of selective intervention is a variant on the theme, "Why aren't more degrees of freedom always better than less?" In the context of firm and market organization, the puzzle is, "Why can't a large firm do everything that a collection of small firms can do and more?" By merely replicating the market, the firm can do no worse than the market. And if the firm can intervene selectively (namely, intervene always but only when expected net gains can be projected), then the firm will sometimes do better. Taken together, the firm will do at least as well as, and will sometimes do better than, the market. A troublesome implication of this result is that firms will grow without limit (Coase, 1937).

As developed in Chapters 1 and 4, *selective intervention is impossible.* Not only do asset dissipation losses obtain if transactions are taken out of markets and organized internally (if, simultaneously, market-like incentives are kept in place), but the high-powered incentives of markets are unavoidably degraded by any effort to exercise selective intervention. The latter obtains because the option to intervene can be exercised both for good cause (to support expected net gains) and for bad (to support the subgoals of the intervenor) (see Grossman and Hart, 1986, for a formal model). Unable to disallow *strategic* intervention, claims over net receipts in firms are weaker than in markets, ceteris paribus.

Since, moreover, the contract law of markets—which offers legal recourse for purposes of ultimate appeal—precludes parity access to fiat in market-mediated transactions, markets are unable to replicate firms. The upshot is that the spontaneous mechanisms of markets and the intentional mechanisms of hierarchy are both nonreplicable, whence economizing requires that each generic form of governance (including hybrids) be used in a discriminating way. Specifically, if the mix of adaptive needs of transactions (of type *A* and type *C* kinds) varies with the attributes of the transactions, then the objective is to align transactions with the differential competencies of governance structures to effect an economizing result.

2.3.3. The trade-offs

The main market and hierarchy trade-offs involve comparative assessments of adaptability, incentive intensity, and bureaucracy. Markets are superior in autonomous adaptability respects, employ high-powered incentives, and are less subject to bureaucratic distortions. Hierarchies enjoy the advantage in bilateral and multilateral adaptability respects, work out of lower-powered incentives, and are beset by intertemporal bureaucratic distortions. Hybrids are located in between. As set out in Chapter 4, the least cost made of governance varies systematically with the attributes of transactions.

3.   Reputation Effect Mechanisms

Complete contingent claims contracting is widely conceded to be cognitively impossible (Radner, 1968), whence "markets for most future commodities do not exist" (Arrow, 1983, p. 123). Might, however, the limitations of fully comprehensive contracting be relieved by devising contract supports that permit nearly comprehensive contracting, thereby to preclude the need for hierarchical governance?

I deal in this section with successive refinements to the reputation effect mechanism. I begin with a sketch of how the mechanism operates, next examine some of the limits to which reputation effects are subject, and then inquire into "What's going on here?"

3.1.   Successive Refinements

David Kreps's article on "Corporate Culture and Economic Theory" deals so much with reputation effects that I originally thought that the article should have been titled "Reputation Effects and Economic Theory—With Afterthoughts on Corporate Culture." I will come back to this in Section 3.3, but begin with a brief sketch of the reputation effect argument.

The thrust of the reputation effect literature is that spontaneous or nearly spontaneous governance will do the job. Kreps develops the argument in three stages: repeated contracting between an unchanging buyer and seller; repeated contracting between a series of buyers and an unchanging seller; and repeated contracting between a series of buyers and a succession of sellers.

The basic setup is a one-sided version of the Prisoners' Dilemma game, in which there is a sequence of two moves on every play of the game. First, Party A decides whether to put himself at hazard ("trust B") or not ("do not trust B"). If Party A accepts the hazard, then Party B decides whether to take advantage of A ("abuse A's trust") or not ("honor A's trust"). The payoffs are such that the joint gain is maximized by the trust/honor outcome. But since B's immediate gains are maximized if he abuses A's trust, the no trust/no trust result will obtain if played as a one-shot game.

Kreps, however, postulates a repeated game in which there is a high probability that each round will be followed by another. This changes the analysis "dramatically" (Kreps, 1990a, p. 102). If, for example, A says to B, "I will begin by trusting you, hoping that you will honor that trust. Indeed, I will continue to trust you as long as you do not abuse that trust. But if ever you abuse that trust, I will never again trust you," if B hears and believes that statement, and if the game is played repeatedly (with high probability), then the honor-trust arrangement is self-enforcing (Kreps, 1990a, p. 103).

The argument can be extended, moreover, to a sequence of A's who must decide whether or not to trust a single trading partner B. Assuming that the experience of the most recent trade is known to all potential A's on the next round and that all A's follow the rule that none will trade if trust is ever abused, the argument generalizes to include this possibility. Indeed, a further extension is possible by creating a succession of B's in which each successor B buys the reputation of his predecessors. If all have honored trust, then the capitalized value of the firm will reflect this high trust reputation. This gives each successive owner the incentive to continue to honor trust, since to do otherwise would be to destroy the reputation and the capitalized value of the firm would reflect this loss at the next sale.

Milgrom, North, and Weingast (1990) push beyond the Kreps formulation to consider many A's and many B's in many periods. They accomplish this by creating a court that serves as a central repository for reputation and metes out penalties in the event that a party defects from the cooperative outcome. Milgrom et al. interpret the institution of the medieval law merchant as having these purposes.

As Milgrom et al. describe it, "the role of the judges in the system, far from being substitutes for the reputation mechanism, is to make the reputation system more effective as a means of promoting honest trade" (1990, p. 3). They argue that, because it is too costly to keep everyone informed in a large community of traders, "the system of private judges is designed to promote private resolution of disputes and otherwise to transmit *just enough* information to the right people in the right circumstances to enable the reputation mechanism to function effectively for enforcement" (Milgrom et al., 1990,

p. 3; emphasis in original). They furthermore aver that "the *kind* of costs incurred by the [Law Merchant] system are inevitable if Honest trade is to be sustained in the face of self-interested behavior and that the system seems well designed to keep those costs as low as possible" (1990, p. 16; emphasis in original).

3.2. An Assessment

Kreps recognizes that his is a very simple setup and offers a number of qualifications. For one thing, he concedes that there are many possible equilibria. More importantly, the argument assumes that A knows what action B has taken. If instead A only observes his own payoff, and if this payoff is not deterministic but is probabilistic, then A has to decide whether a bad outcome is due to B's defection or is explained by an unlucky draw. Faced with "noisy, indirect observations, the problem of finding self-enforcing arrangements is vastly more complicated" (Kreps, 1990a, p. 105). Moreover, unforeseeability further compounds the difficulties: "by definition, it cannot be clear ex ante precisely what is called for in a contingency that ex ante has not been foreseen" (Kreps, 1990a, p. 124).

Bernard Williams also expresses reservations over game theoretic treatments of trust. The most important of these take the form of cognitive limitations. Not only are people (1) "imperfectly informed, both about other people's preferences and about their assessment of probabilities," but (2) this limitation may itself be imperfectly understood, (3) "the acquisition of such knowledge may be variously impossible [or] expensive . . . [and could] raise more questions, and generally confuse the issue," and (4) there is a "very significant limit, for social as well as cognitive reasons, on the recursive complexity of possible calculation" (Williams, 1988, p. 4).

Yet additional reasons to be skeptical of the purported efficacy of reputation effect mechanisms—even in simple situations of the repeated game kind, a fortiori in more complicated circumstances—include the following.

1. *Communication.* That A may know he was cheated is one thing. But if A cannot communicate this condition accurately and without cost to other members of the population of which he is a part, then the reputation effect mechanism is degraded. The limits of languages are real.
2. *Hubris.* Hubris can further complicate the problem. If A_n imagines himself to be more clever than A_{n-1}, and if A_{n-1} reports that he has been cheated, then A_n may discount that experience and explain it as "contributory negligence." If, upon projecting that he is more clever, A_n contracts with B, that compromises the mechanism whereby B is assuredly penalized.
3. *Forgiveness.* Successor B's, moreover, may plead for mercy: They should not be held responsible for the sins of their fathers, especially if they are prepared to denounce their forebears and "promise" not

to repeat the deceit. The reputation effect mechanism is weakened if forgiveness results.

4. *Complexity*

  a. How is a reputation to be assigned when many individual and composite decisions are being made by many different managers in each of the trading entities in question? How does self-enforcement carry over to these?

  b. Also, which relates to but goes beyond Kreps's concern with probabilistic outcomes, what is to be done if performance is multidimensional and, period by period, goods and services are changing rather than identical?

5. *Scaling up.* Unlike the owner-operator succession of *B*'s that Kreps describes, most firms are not owner-operated. What is the basis for scaling up the powerful incentive effects of the reputation effect mechanism in the owner-operator context to apply to the large, diffusely owned, hierarchical enterprise?

6. *Strategic concerns*

  a. Additional complications intrude if the *A*'s are rivals and an *A* chooses to reveal his experience with *B* in an incomplete or distorted manner, thereby to disadvantage his rivals (Williamson, 1975, p. 36).

  b. What is to be done if reputation is strategically built up in contemplation of "milking" the reputation over a long trading interval (Shapiro, 1982)?

7. *Penalties*

  a. The reputation effect argument would be made more credible if it were supported by penalties. Thus, although it is rational for *A* to assert that once he has been cheated by *B* that he will never again deal with *B*, might an individual *A* waver in his resolve? Such weakness of will by *A* would be deterred if immediate and automatic penalties were applied to *A* should he ever respond to being cheated by subsequently offering trust.

  b. Inasmuch as successor *A*'s are subject to hubris and may be even more susceptible to forgiveness or weakness of will, the use of penalties to deter successor *A*'s from dealing with a cheating *B* is even more important.

  c. Penalizing *A*'s for offenses by *B* is convoluted. Surely it is easier and comports more with "justice" to prohibit a cheating *B* from ever doing business again than to police the entire population of *A*'s. (All mechanisms that eschew the obvious are suspect.)

Additional concerns are posed by the Milgrom et al. setup. Most importantly, there is no demonstrated correspondence between the Theoretical Law Merchant (TLM) system that they describe and any Actual Law Merchant (ALM) system in the historical record. But even their TLM system is deeply problematic.

8. Milgrom et al. describe the Law Merchant and the Law Merchant *system* interchangeably. The Law Merchant system is evidently the collection of geographically dispersed Law Merchants. How the *system* is apprised of the contents of each of the *parts* is never mentioned, much less developed. Scaling up from the individual Law Merchant, who is in possession of the totality of the historical record and has full recall of all of the nuances, to a geographically dispersed set of Law Merchants, who are in imperfect correspondence with one another, is an ambitious move.

9. The subset of products and organizations that satisfy the parameter values for which the Law Merchant System strategy is a sequential equilibrium strategy is never described. In the absence of indications to the contrary, the TLM is presumably meant to apply quite generally. But then issues 1 through 6 above need to be addressed.

10. One of the attributes of the TLM is that the Law Merchant is never called upon to settle a dispute in equilibrium (Milgrom et al., 1990, p. 15). Like the Maytag repairman, the TLM merely reports period-by-period that there have been no breakdowns. The record, however, shows that Actual Law Merchants were presented with disputes and did give decisions. What were the characteristics of these transactions and what explains the breakdowns?[3]

To be sure, none of this poses difficulties for what Milgrom et al. characterize as their "core contention"—namely, that "institutions sometimes arise to make reputation effect mechanisms more effective by communicating information" (1990, p. 19). If, however, the nearly spontaneous institutional response described by Milgrom et al. is very limited in its efficacy, what other mechanisms are available and how do they work?

3.3. What's Going on Here?

Reputation effect mechanisms are no exception to the general proposition that all theories of economic organization must eventually be confronted by the realities.[4] Among the more intrusive realities of the organizational land-

---

3. If an examination of the record does not support the conclusion that "both players play cheat" (Milgrom et al., 1990, p. 11) after a query discloses that one of the players has an outstanding judgment, then what is to be concluded about the design and operation of ALM? Why do the ALM and TLM differ?

4. Herbert Simon used to ask his students in mathematical social science to disengage from the model periodically and engage in "reality testing." In a similar spirit, Tjalling Koopmans has urged that "we have to exploit all of the evidence that we can secure, direct and indirect . . . [including] opportunities for direct introspection by, and direct observation of, individual decision makers" (1957, p. 140).

Anecdotal evidence regarding reputation effects is pertinent to, although hardly dispositive of, the purported efficacy of reputation effects. Consider Carl Shapiro's experience in Franklin Fisher's econometrics class at MIT

scape is that a very large fraction of economic activity is organized in large, diffusely owned, hierarchical forms of organization. What explains this?

One possibility is that firms are reputation effect mechanisms—no more and no less. The Kreps argument that successor B's buy the capitalized value of the reputation of their predecessors interprets the firm in this way. But that works only for small firms and concentrated ownership. What's going on in the large, diffusely owned corporation?

Kreps is sensitive to this last query and introduces "focal points" and "corporate culture" to explain how reputation effects infuse confidence in trades within and between large, hierarchical, diffusely owned organizations in the face of unforeseeable contingencies. The creation and inculcation of a corporate culture is viewed as a defining attribute of a corporation, which

---

When I was a graduate student at M.I.T., the required econometrics course had a reputation of truly testing—and surely frightening—all aspiring economists at M.I.T. Along with the associated econometrics project, it was rightly viewed as a centerpiece of the graduate program. At the helm in this econometrics class was the more-than-slightly intimidating Professor Franklin Fisher.

If you know fear, you can imagine the mood of the class as we shifted in our seats while Professor Fisher prepared to return our graded midterm exams to us. This mood was hardly lightened as Professor Fisher proceeded to explain the intricacies hidden in the exam questions, which the bulk of us had failed to fathom. Apparently, our collective performance was the weakest he had seen in his many years teaching econometrics at M.I.T.

The effort exerted by the class in the wake of this midterm disaster was truly impressive. And by the time the final arrived, we really had learned a lot about econometrics. Only later did we learn that every class was treated to the same performance after the midterm. (Shapiro, 1989, p. 131)

If, however, MIT graduate students, who are in direct personal contact with one another and have keen interests in sharing relevant educational experiences, are unable to communicate such traumatic events from one year to the next, what reputation effects did they share? Is there a lesson for reputation effects more generally?

Or consider the embezzler who was able to move from one embezzled job to another, sometimes because the new employer did not do a background check, but sometimes because previous employers would help the embezzler to secure new employment, thereby to improve his prospects of paying off the outstanding judgments that they had against him.

To my astonishment, one faculty member (not Franklin Fisher) reacted to the MIT anecdote by asserting that the conditions described were "optimal." For that to be true, the participants in the education game (Franklin Fisher, other MIT faculty, first-year MIT graduate students, advanced MIT graduate students) must understand that (1) Fisher's course warrants a disproportionate share of graduate student effort, (2) this can be most efficiently realized by recourse to midterm terror, (3) it is in the interests of all to support this result by maintaining a wall of silence, and (4) anyone who breaks the wall of silence will be sanctioned.

One implication of this scenario is that the Spring 1989 issue of the *Rand Journal* has been banned to first-year students at MIT (and incoming students who know of the anecdote somehow wash it from their minds). If, however, public knowledge has irretrievably resulted, then presumably the terror to which Franklin Fisher had access is no longer effective and Carl Shapiro has been severely sanctioned (as a warning to others).

The above is so tortured that I offered to sell the Brooklyn Bridge to the faculty member who advanced it. My purpose in relating this, however, is different: since economists can always invent ways to resuscitate spontaneous rationality, it is important to add one proviso: only plausible accounts get a hearing.

attribute influences both the terms and the types of intrafirm and of interfirm trade. Among the properties that Kreps ascribes to corporate culture are (1) "consistency and simplicity being virtues, the culture/principle will reign even when it is not first best"; (2) culture should be aligned "with the sorts of contingencies that are likely to arise"; and (3) culture evolves through "evolutionary adaptation" (Kreps, 1990a, pp. 127–29).

Kreps's reference to simple rules is a concession to the limits of ascribing nuanced reputation effects to individual managers in large corporations.[5] The discriminating alignment to which Kreps refers is also a major concession and moves the argument in the direction of transaction cost economics—which urges that transactions be aligned with governance structures (of which reputation effects are one) in a discriminating way.[6] Also, Kreps's remarks about the creation and preservation of corporate culture opens up a role for the careful screening and social conditioning of the membership (or at least the reputation-relevant subset thereof). This moves further in the direction of hands-on governance. The main thrust of the Kreps argument, however, is that the large, diffusely owned corporation works through reputation effect mechanisms.

I do not disagree that reputation effects are operative in large corporations. It would be a mistake, however, to conclude that reputation effect mechanisms explain *most* of economic organization. By this I do not mean to disparage the considerable intellectual feat whereby reputation effect mechanisms are successfully extended from simple repeated games between unchanging A and B, to many A's with unchanging B, to many A's and a sequence of B's, to many A's and B's in many periods, to hierarchy defined by corporate culture. But the plausibility test that I proposed at the outset asks that we inquire into (1) the feasibility and (2) the applicability of thin rational constructions.

As discussed in Section 3.2, many reputation effect mechanisms are wanting in feasibility respects. Furthermore, reputation effect mechanisms make little or no contract with the contract law and trade-off issues discussed in Section 2.3. (Game theoretic treatments do not, at present at least, invite attention to these matters.)

Thus, Milgrom et al. claim that their model is applicable to *any* system of organization that attempts to promote "Honest trade . . . in the face of self-interested behavior" (1990, p. 16). But that is mistaken. Their claim implicitly assumes that exchanges take place between *autonomous traders*. But why should the examination of economic organization be so constrained? Why the preoccupation with markets to the exclusion of hierarchy? And when hierarchy is introduced, as it is in the later stages of Kreps's article, why treat hierarchy as merely another form of reputation effect mechanism?

5. By contrast, Eugene Fama's treatment of "ex post settling up" within the large corporation projects highly nuanced internal reputation effect mechanisms (Fama, 1980).

6. As I interpret the work of Masahiko Aoki (1988, 1990) in Chapter 12, the relation among Japanese banks that own, finance, and control Japanese business enterprises appears to be one in which reputation effects are very strong. Failure of a "main bank" to assume its burdens in the context of this banking relation would elicit strong reputation effect penalties.

Because spontaneous governance analysis rarely asks the question "What's going on here?"—or, if it is raised, answers it in attenuated ways—hierarchy is neglected and/or delimited. Intentionality gets short shrift when the mechanisms drive the phenomena rather than the reverse.[7]

4. Sequential Short-Term Contracting

The sequential short-term contracting argument begins by "solving" the problem of economic organization by postulating the efficacy of sequential short-term contracts, next concedes that this is costly, and finally reverts to hands-on governance as a remedy. This is an interesting exercise both on its own merits and because it purports to correct a "defect" in earlier transaction cost economics arguments.

4.1. The Hands-Off Theory

The argument that a succession of short-term contracts can implement the first best for a complete long-term contract turns on six assumptions: (1) public outcomes are costlessly known to principal, agent, and arbiter; (2) the contracting horizon is finite; (3) agents can borrow and save at a secure bank; (4) there is common knowledge of technology; (5) there is common knowledge of preferences over action-payment streams; and (6) the utility frontier is decreasing (Fudenberg, Holmstrom, and Milgrom, 1990). Subject to those conditions, Fudenberg et al. show that *"If there is an optimal long-term contract, then there is a sequentially optimal contract, which can be implemented via a sequence of short-term contracts"* (1990, p. 21, emphasis in original).[8]

7. As set out above, I concur with Hayek's view that the central problem of economic organization is that of efficient adaptation. Although reputation effects are supporting mechanisms for effective adaptation for both markets and hierarchies under such a conception, they play minor roles in comparison with autonomy and fiat (supported by classical and forbearance contract laws, respectively). That at least is my contention. The proof is in the refutable implications to which alternative "main case" theories of economic organization lead and in their correspondence with the data.

8. The argument works off of the Optimality Principle of Dynamic Programming. Kreps provides a succinct summary as follows:

> In the final stage of any transaction, the assumptions guarantee that an efficient arrangement will be reached. Move back to the penultimate stage. Because the two parties are farsighted, they know what arrangements will arise in the final period, and they know those arrangements will be efficient. Because they are risk neutral, any redistribution of wealth that will take place in the final round of arrangements can be "undone" at the current stage. Applying the no-bargaining-costs assumption again, they achieve an efficient arrangement concerning the penultimate round of actions, and so on. They can work back to the start of the transaction, and their short-term agreements will guarantee efficient actions all the way along.
>
>   All of Milgrom and Roberts' assumptions play a role in this argument, but two deserve special highlighting. The assumption that the two parties are rational (in particular, farsighted) is crucial, and it reinforces the importance Williamson attaches to human factors. The assumption that enforceable short-term contracts can be reached is crucial. (1990b, p. 760)

The infeasibility of complete long-term contracting is widely conceded. The Fudenberg et al. conditions being very stringent, one might conclude that a complete sequence of short-term contracts is infeasible also. That is not, however, the Milgrom and Roberts position. They contend that complete sequential short-term contracting is feasible and illustrate the way in which sequential short-term contracting would work by describing the supply relation between Fisher Body and General Motors as follows:

> In the first period, the parties reach an agreement about plant size and design (investments in specialized assets . . .). . . . In the second period, the parties negotiate prices, possibly a fixed transfer payment, quality standards, and a delivery schedule . . . in *full knowledge* of the circumstances then prevailing (e.g., current model year body designs, demands for various models, the costs and availabilities of steel and substitute materials, and so on . . .). (1990a, p. 68, emphasis added)

Feasibility having been asserted, if not established (see below), Milgrom and Roberts contend that transaction cost economics errs in its claim that transactions are removed from markets and organized internally because of the hazards associated with *incomplete* contracts of a bilaterally dependent (asset-specific) kind. The real reason for internal organization is that a *feasibly complete sequence of short-term contracts is prohibitively costly.*

4.2. An Assessment

Although the Fudenberg et al. article is an intellectual tour de force, the main lesson, I submit, is that sequential short-term contracting is a very ambitious process and that the incompleteness with which long-term contracts are beset is rarely saved by reverting to a series of complete short-term contracts. As indicated, however, Milgrom and Roberts contend otherwise.

Milgrom and Roberts develop the ramifications of Fudenberg et al. by contrasting sequential short-term contracting with transaction cost economics. The basic transaction cost economics argument, as they see it, is that "opportunistic behavior, imperfect long-term contracting, specialized assets, and uncertainty about the future . . . are sufficient to prevent a market arrangement based on a series of short-term contracts from yielding an efficient outcome" (Milgrom and Roberts, 1990a, p. 66).

That is a truncated characterization of transaction cost economics. Conspicuously omitted from the list of features on which transaction cost economics relies is any mention of *bounded rationality*. Since bounded rationality and opportunism are the two key behavioral assumptions to which transaction cost economics repeatedly refers, that could be—and is—a serious omission.

Note in this connection that bounded rationality does not imply myopia. To the contrary, transaction cost economics assumes that parties to a contract are farsighted. The lesson of bounded rationality, for the purposes of contracting, is that "*all* forms of comprehensive contracting (with and without private information) . . . [are relegated] to the infeasible set" (Williamson, 1988d, p. 68, emphasis added). As my discussion of franchise bidding for natural monopoly indicates, that applies to recurrent short-term contracts as well as to incomplete long-term contracts (Williamson, 1976, pp. 79–91). Indeed, it is precisely because all complex contracts are unavoidably incomplete that "The study of structures that facilitate gapfilling, dispute settlement, adaptation, and the like . . . become part of the problem of economic organization" (Williamson, 1989c, pp. 139–40).[9]

The obvious answer to the query as to whether the Fudenberg et al. assumptions are reasonable is to admit that common knowledge is a very expansive assumption. Absent that, costless enforcement cannot be presumed. But suppose that third-party enforcement issues are set aside. Is common knowledge reasonable even between the immediate parties? And how short is short in their scheme of things?

Common knowledge of the full set of circumstances relevant to complex trade is, I submit, a rarity (if not the null set). Even with respect to technology, which has the appearance of being well-defined and intrinsically knowable, Michael Polanyi reports that

> The attempt to analyze scientifically the established industrial arts has everywhere led to similar results. Indeed even in the modern industries the indefinable knowledge is still an essential part of technology. I have myself watched in Hungary a new, imported machine for blowing electric lamp bulbs, the exact counterpart of which was operating successfully in Germany, failing for a whole year to produce a single flawless bulb. (1962, p. 52)

The Milgrom and Roberts discussion of technology in the GM–Fisher Body context admits to no such deficiencies. Firm-specific investments can be precisely described and will be implemented exactly as stipulated. Not only is there faithful execution (suppliers do not say one thing and do another), but there is no learning-by-doing—or, if there is, the contracting interval is collapsed appropriately. More generally, the details that would implement *full* knowledge of even the listed characteristics in the Milgrom and Roberts contract are truly stupendous. Milgrom and Roberts' short list of full knowledge attributes conveniently ends with the encapsulating phrase "and so on." Such elastic language will not, however, serve the full knowledge needs of General Motors and Fisher Body—which firms would need to be concerned with detail after endless detail. Furthermore, the interval over which the GM–Fisher Body short-term contract would operate is obscure not merely because specialized investments typically have indefinable qualities (see above), but also in adaptation respects. Possibly the reference to "the first period" and to "current model year body designs" implies that the interval is for a year. To suggest, however, that actions and transfers can be stipulated for such an interval—whereupon no gaps, omissions, errors, and the like would arise, hence no unprogrammed bilateral adaptations would be required—is implausible.

---

9. Albeit without making express reference to contracting, Simon makes the following related point: "It is only because individual human beings are limited in knowledge, foresight, skill, and time that organizations are useful investments for the achievement of human purpose" (Simon, 1957b, p. 199).

4.3.   What's Going on Here?

As Joan Robinson once remarked, it is unsurprising when a rabbit is pulled out of a hat into which it has just been placed. If the feasibility claim on which Milgrom and Roberts rely is a rabbit, in that the real lesson of Fudenberg et al. is that the strong assumptions of their model are tantamount to infeasibility,[10] then complete, sequential short-term contracting is not a feasible contender.

Suppose, however, that the feasibility of complete, sequential short-term contracting is granted. What then? Milgrom and Roberts advise that the key to understanding economic organization is not to be discovered in the behavioral assumptions, the attributes of transactions, the focus on adaptations (of types A and C), the contract law supports on which governance structures rely, and related transaction cost economizing arguments. Instead, "bargaining costs" are the key to understanding economic organization, where bargaining costs are defined very expansively "to include the opportunity costs of bargainers' time $[B_1]$, the costs of monitoring $[B_2]$ and enforcing $[B_3]$ the agreement, and any costly delays $[B_4]$ and failures $[B_5]$ to reach agreement when efficiency requires that parties cooperate" (Milgrom and Roberts, 1990a, p. 72).

To be sure, they argue—as transaction cost economics has recognized from its inception (Coase, 1937)—that the limits of internal organization as well as the limits of markets need to be established. Milgrom and Roberts argue in this connection that hierarchies differ from markets in that they rely on authority and they trace the limits of authority to the impossibility of selective intervention and related "influence costs." They further remark that "received transaction-cost theory leaves unclear why market transactions are *ever* to be preferred to nonmarket ones" (1990a, p. 70, emphasis in original). Finally, they explain that bilateral dependencies "*cause* bargaining costs." That purportedly explains why transaction cost economics, which emphasizes that bilateral dependency is a result of asset specificity, has had good predictive success (1990a, p. 74, emphasis in original).

My own sense is that bargaining costs are a subset of transaction costs. Arrow's characterization of transaction costs as the "costs of running the economic system" (1969, p. 48) is, I think, a more useful and natural way to proceed. Bargaining costs, measurement costs, and maladaptation costs are all subsumed in this definition.[11]

Unless, moreover, "received transaction-cost theory" refers to pre-1985 work, for which there is no indication, the Milgrom and Roberts claim that transaction cost economics has never explained why market transactions are ever preferred to nonmarket ones is mistaken. As I have explained elsewhere (Williamson, 1985b, chap. 6) and in Section 2.3 above, the *impossibility of selective intervention* is responsible for limits on firm size and precludes firms

10. See the list of six assumptions in the text accompanying n. 7 as well as Kreps's assessment in n. 8. See also Hadfield, 1991.

11. Recall that Arrow described market failure as a more general category than externality and that transaction cost is a still broader concept (Arrow, 1969, p. 48).

from replicating the high-powered incentives of markets. Also, the fact that bilateral dependencies are responsible for transaction costs (including bargaining costs) is not adventitious. This condition and its origins in asset specificity have been *featured* in the transaction cost literature for many years (Williamson, 1971, 1975, 1979b, 1985b, 1988d; Klein, Crawford, and Alchian, 1978; Grossman and Hart, 1986).

Note, moreover, that Milgrom and Roberts fail to mention the important role of contract law differences as these relate to the efficacy of alternative generic forms of governance. As discussed in Chapter 4, contract law differences play a vital role in supporting the discrete structural differences between market and hierarchy. Also, Milgrom and Roberts never identify the unit of analysis. That the transaction is the appropriate unit of analysis, that the unit of analysis needs to be dimensionalized, and that a discriminating alignment between transactions and governance structures plays a central role in the economics of organization are all omitted from their construction.

Lest I be misunderstood, I hereby concede—indeed, insist—that it can be useful to suspend bounds on rationality for theoretical purposes (witness the Arrow–Debreu model). Express provision for bounded rationality nevertheless needs to be made when theory gives way to a comparative institutional assessment of alternative *feasible* forms of governance.[12] Organization forms that make impossible demands on limited cognitive competence are properly excluded from the latter exercise because they do not satisfy the feasibility stipulation. Upon recognizing that all complex contracts are unavoidably incomplete (because of bounded rationality), that contract as promise is fraught with hazard (because of opportunism), and if the central problem of economic organization is that of adaptation, then the object of economic organization reduces to the following: adapt to disturbances (of both autonomous and bilateral kinds) in ways that economize on bounded rationality while simultaneously safeguarding the transactions in question against the hazards of opportunism. Greater degrees of intentional governance appear as the need for bilateral adaptability increases, ceteris paribus.

5.   Socialist Economic Organization

5.1.   The Hands-Off Tradition and Critique

Most efforts by economists to understand socialist economic organization have been normative and have operated out of a hands-off governance orientation. Two such efforts are considered here: the early socialist controversy and more recent proposals for financial reform

5.1.1.   *The socialist controversy*

The socialist controversy of the 1930s pitted the critics of socialism (Ludwig von Mises and Friedrich Hayek) against its proponents (Oskar Lange and

12. See n. 8.

Abba Lerner). Abram Bergson reviewed that controversy and concluded that von Mises, who disputed the logic of socialism, was mistaken: the necessary logic was already present in the theoretical work of Pareto and Barone (Bergson, 1948, p. 446). Hayek's more limited challenge to the practicability of socialism was likewise disputed:

> there can hardly be any room for debate: of course, socialism can work. On this, Lange certainly is convincing. . . . [Moreover], the Soviet planned economy has been operating for thirty years. Whatever else may be said of it, it has not broken down. (Bergson, 1948, p. 447)

Indeed, Joseph Schumpeter had advanced similar views previously. His response to the question "Can socialism work?" was emphatic: "Of course it can" (Schumpeter, 1942, p. 167). Not only did the success of the Soviet planned economy speak to this—"I have been over into the future and it works" (Steffens)—but "There is nothing wrong with the pure theory of socialism" (Schumpeter, 1942, p. 172).

Working out of welfare economics premises, the optimum conditions for socialist economic organization to realize efficiency were summarized as follows: "The total cost incurred in the production of the optimum output would be at a minimum and, in the optimum, price must equal marginal cost" (Bergson, 1948, p. 424). Moreover, there was widespread confidence that this formulation could be implemented (Schumpeter, 1942, chap. 16–17). Abba Lerner is reported to have gone to Mexico to see Trotsky "to persuade him that all would be well in a communist state if only it reproduced the result of a competitive system and prices were set equal to marginal cost" (Coase, 1988a, p. 8).

To be sure, there were nagging problems—such as incentives, controls, and bureaucracy. Although these repeatedly surfaced, they were never systematically addressed. Mainly, they were assumed away. Thus, Bergson observed with respect to incentives that "Provided the question of controls could be disposed of satisfactorily, our impression is that the question of managerial incentives would not present any serious difficulties" (Bergson, 1948, p. 435). But inasmuch as "control plays no role in the socialist controversy" (Ward, 1967, p. 37), the control proviso was never assessed. That is an egregious lapse—since managerial incentives in large enterprises are assuredly ineffective unless supported by effective controls.

Even more telling is Lange's treatment of bureaucracy:

> There is also the argument which might be raised against socialism with regard to the efficiency of public officials as compared with private entrepreneurs as managers of production. Strictly speaking, these public officials must be compared with corporation officials under capitalism, and not with private small-scale entrepreneurs. The argument thus loses much of its force. The discussion of this argument belongs to the field of sociology rather than of economic theory and must therefore be dispensed with here. By doing so we do not mean, however, to deny its great importance. It seems to us, indeed, that *the real danger of socialism is that of a bureaucratization of economic life,* and not the impossibility of coping with the problem of allocation of

resources. Unfortunately, we do not see how the same, or even greater, danger can be averted under monopolistic capitalism. Officials subject to democratic control seem preferable to private corporation executives who practically *are responsible to nobody.* (1938, pp. 109–10)

Thus, although Lange avers that the key problem of socialism is not that of efficient resource allocation but of bureaucracy, bureaucracy is dismissed because (1) it is beyond the competence of economists to deal with bureaucracy, and (2) a comparison of capitalism and socialism in bureaucratization respects reveals that bureaucratization is of equal or greater danger under capitalism. How the latter conclusion was reached is not disclosed. Subsequent work on socialist economic organization followed Lange's lead—whence problems of bureaucracy were thereafter ignored.[13] With the benefit of hindsight, that was a fateful fork in the road.

5.1.2. Feasible financial reform

An extensive hands-off literature on socialist economic organization has developed since Bergson summarized the status of the debate in 1948. Indeed, hands-off socialism has remained the main tradition. I focus here on one of the most recent contributions: D. M. Nuti's proposal for financial reform.

One of the remarkable and little remarked differences between capitalism and socialism is that capitalist economic organization is subject to discipline from competition in the capital market. To be sure, the efficacy of these competitive forces has long been questioned (Berle and Means, Greenwald and Stiglitz). Capitalism is nonetheless judged to have the advantage over socialism in capital market respects—in that spontaneous controls from this sector do operate while socialism relies preponderantly on hands-on planning. Nuti observes in this connection that "the role of financial markets and their possible features under a socialist system have been conspicuously neglected from the time of Enrico Barone (1908) through such modern treatises as Alex Nove (1984)" (Nuti, 1989, p. 87). His article on "Feasible Financial Innovation under Market Socialism" (1989) proposes to relieve this disparity.

Nuti advances a three-part program of financial innovation. Stage I is designed to revalue assets to reflect true economic values. Stage II introduces "a kind of 'slow motion' stock market" in which state agencies, but not individuals, can buy and trade shares (Nuti, 1989, p. 98). An options market

---

13. Moreover, while bureaucratization may have been the "real danger," Lange contends that the "real issue in the discussion of socialism . . . is *whether the further maintenance of the capitalist system is compatible with economic progress*" (Lange, 1938, p. 110, emphasis in original). The remarkable innovative performance of the past two centuries notwithstanding (Lange, 1938, p. 111), capitalist energies were purportedly spent. Having reached the monopoly stage of capitalism, the absence of competition allows the capitalist to forsake innovation in favor of a more conservative purpose: avoid innovation because it reduces the value of existing investment (Lange, 1938, pp. 112–15). Small-scale industry and farming aside (where "real competition still prevails"), socialism is declared to be the "only solution available" (Lange, 1938, pp. 120–21). Interestingly, this last conclusion is a comparative one and presumably rests, in part at least, on the sanguine assessment of bureaucracy that Lange had reached earlier. For a related critique, see Richter, 1990.

is created in Stage III, the object being to permit individuals "to benefit from their ability to identify above- or below-average performing enterprises in spite of being excluded from ownership and control" (Nuti, 1989, p. 102).

Interestingly, the efficacy of these financial innovations rests on what Nuti refers to as a "successfully reformed" socialist economy, the entire discussion of which is covered in two sentences of text

> [E]nterprises are engaged in production and trade through contractual rela-
> tions with other state agencies, while planning is confined to macroeconomic
> policies and *truly parametric* (that is, non-enterprise specific) instruments for
> the *central manipulation* of market signals. Sectoral policies can be undertaken
> by the government, but sector-specific subsidy on tax differentials must be
> applied by the government *consistently and predictably.* (Nuti, 1989, pp. 94–95,
> emphasis added)

My discussion of the Nuti program focuses on Stage I and on the above-described conditions for successful reform. Consider the latter.

Two things are noteworthy about the successfully reformed socialist economy described by Nuti: (1) the description is very brief, and (2) Nuti is evidently very sanguine as to its efficacy. Lacking institutional supports, the prescription appears to assume the abolition of opportunism by agencies of the state. That simplifies the organizational design problem enormously (Hurwicz, 1973).

The key features on which Nuti relies are parametric instruments that are manipulated by a central authority in a consistent and predictable way. That is tantamount to *credible selective intervention.* Unless, however, the absence of opportunism can be credibly ascribed to central authorities, that is implausible: the same impossibility of selective intervention that applies within firms applies likewise to governments.[14] Accordingly, the Nuti setup is utopian.

But assume otherwise, since to introduce feasible financial innovations into an infeasible system is without purpose. Suppose, *arguendo,* that the central authority behaves as Nuti prescribes, whence opportunism is concentrated entirely in the enterprise sector. Will Nuti's asset revaluation scheme work even in these idealized circumstances?

The capital revaluation scheme proposed by Nuti has the purpose of bidding assets up to their full valuations. It invites the managers of a state enterprise or interested outsiders (mainly other state enterprises) to announce a valuation of the assets of the enterprise different from book value. The

14. It could be argued that central authorities have less incentive to a manipulate strategically because they cannot participate as directly as can managers of firms in the disposition of net
receipts. As the history of central controls records, however, indirect ways for central authorities to
participate are numerous, convoluted, and important.

Suppose, for example, that the strategic manipulation of price signals by planners could
somehow be annihilated. There are many other ways to favor and disfavor clients. For example,
unless the government sector is very small in relation to the economy, planners can influence
outcomes through their procurement decisions. Also, the administration of justice—in disputes
between firms or disputes between firms and the government—can be tilted. And the administration of controls—priorities, quotas, exemptions, audits, etc.—is subject to manipulation.

announcement of a higher value by an outside enterprise must either be met by a revaluation by the incumbent management or the assets must be sold to the high bidder. In either event, the added value is treated as a profit and is taxed at a rate that exceeds that on operating profit. "Alternatively, or at the same time, any profit-linked bonus for managers and staff is calculated at a lower rate for that part of the enterprise profit which is due to the revaluation of existing assets" (Nuti, 1989, p. 95). Nuti contends that Stage I provides both "a continuous, nonbureaucratic, decentralized, and automatic evaluation of enterprise capital" and "an incentive for enterprises to use their capital equipment in the way that maximizes their valuation" (Nuti, 1989, p. 96).

But is it really so? Thus, suppose that assets have been revalued in the manner described and that managers discover that the revaluation is excessive. What will happen? One possibility is that managers will be held to these values by the state and current profits will suffer. But that is not the only possibility. For one thing, current profits could be restored if some expenses—maintenance, research, product promotion—could be deferred without detection.[15] The problems of excess valuation could thereby be pushed onto a later generation of managers. Or accounting relief could be effected (e.g., through a change in inventory accounting). Also, middle managers and workers whose bonuses are adversely affected could complain, with cause, that they ought not to be penalized for the valuation excesses of their superiors. Turn the leaders out and start anew with a more objective valuation of the assets. And if that appeal does not succeed, then declare bankruptcy and let the state liquidate the assets for whatever they will bring. The problem is that if mistakes can be externalized, by pushing them off onto others, or socialized, by pushing them onto the state, then Nuti's valuation mechanism is seriously lacking in credibility respects—even with a benign state.

A related (nonbenign state) problem with the mechanism is that tax payments are made at the outset while the benefits (in the form of added future net receipts) are delayed. How does the state convince asset valuators that it will not tax now and tax later?

If, moreover, enterprises are subject to "mutual recrimination"—I respond to your bid for my assets by bidding for your assets—and if that is obvious to the parties, then why would tacit collusion not set in? But then if bids are fanciful or hazardous (for the reasons given above) and/or if threats are responded to in kind, why bother?

5.2. What's Going on Here?

An emphasis on actual, as opposed to ideal, systems of socialist economic organization has become more prevalent as problems of *actual economic*

---

15. It might be objected that managers have incentives to defer expenses in the pre-revaluation regime. That is true. If, however, deferred expenses that yield greater current profits invite the *ratcheting* up of profit targets in the pre-revaluation regime, then incentives to defer will be weaker. (To be sure, ratcheting would violate Nuti's strictures against nonparametric adjustments. But even if the strictures are assumed to hold, the equity and bankruptcy arguments in the text still apply.)

reform in Eastern Europe and the Soviet Union have presented themselves. Both Jan Winiecki and John Litwack address problems of reform not in terms of abstract resource allocation mechanisms but as problems of de facto property rights and ineffective (or noncredible) commitments.

5.2.1. De facto ownership

Possible social cost distortions aside, the ideal capitalist firm is relentlessly engaged in profit maximization. That is a useful construction, especially as it provides the micro foundations for industry analysis. But the profit maximization hypothesis assumes away problems of managerial discretion. That is because ideal (de jure) and effective (de facto) ownership converge under the profit maximization construction: both in principle and in fact, control and all rights to residual claims are concentrated on the suppliers of equity finance.

The managerial discretion hypothesis holds differently. It ascribes de facto control to those who are knowledgeable, strategically situated, and disposed to be active (Williamson, 1964, p. 25). Upon examination of the groups that potentially qualify under this triple, the management in the large, diffusely owned corporation enjoys a nontrivial degree of discretion. A similar assessment of effective property rights is needed under socialism.

Ideally, property rights under socialism belong to the people. Even, however, if the leadership is originally committed to that prescription, the Iron Law of Oligarchy shortly thereafter applies: "It is organization which gives birth to the dominion of the elected over the electors, of the mandatories over the mandators, of the delegates over the delegators. Who says organization, says oligarchy" (Michels, 1962, p. 365). The questions for socialism are (1) which groups are knowledgeable, strategically situated, and disposed to be active, (2) with what degree of latitude, and (3) what are their predilections?

Winiecki ascribes effective control over property rights in Soviet-type economies to the communist party *apparatchiks* and economic bureaucrats (Winiecki, 1990, pp. 198–200). Under the principle of *nomenklatura,* according to which appointments to managerial positions of all kinds are made upon the recommendation and approval of the communist party, party officials primarily appoint their friends. The principal appointment criterion is that "of loyalty rather than managerial competence" (Winiecki, 1990, p. 198). Rent extraction, through a system of side payments or kickbacks, proliferates.

Understandably, the party *apparatchiks* and economic bureaucrats have strong incentives to resist reform in favor of the status quo (Winiecki, 1990, p. 200). Moreover, strategically positioned as they are, party and bureaucracy are able frequently to defeat reforms (Winiecki, 1990, p. 207). This can be done through delay, obfuscation, selective application of rules, and the like. But the guise of "further perfectioning" is also employed to undermine reform (Winiecki, 1990, p. 209). "Ironically, counterreformers use the perverse results arising from their interference as evidence of the failure of the reforms" (Winiecki, 1990, p. 213).

Note that the language for assessing socialism and its reform has changed. Considerations of managerial discretion predominate. Rather than the anti-

septic language of efficient resource allocation, which is in the hands-off tradition, the relevant issues are those of subgoal pursuit, strategic behavior, waste,
bureaucracy, and the like. Managerial discretion invites students of socialism
to deal first and insistently with hands-on considerations. If the positive theory
of socialism implicates anything, it implicates *hands-on administration.*

5.2.2. Noncredible commitments

Litwack observes that the most common critique of Soviet reform is "the
reluctance of the leadership to decree large-scale nongovernment property
rights" (1991, p. 255). He urges, however, that the inability of the Soviet
leadership to infuse reform proposals with credible commitments is the more
serious lapse: "Soviet leaders in the USSR today would be well advised to
reallocate their energies somewhat away from the question of what to commit
to and toward the question of how to lay the institutional groundwork for
enforcing commitments" (1991, p. 274). Lacking confidence that rule changes
will persist, parties will respond to rule changes in a tentative or myopic
way: get all that you can immediately, because long-run investments will be
expropriated. The reluctance of peasants to accept long-term lease arrangements in agriculture, for example, is explained by the fact that "there is a
widespread belief that one fine day the attitude [of the leadership] toward
leasing will move 180 degrees, and then it is goodbye to everything that was
earned through blood and guts" (Litwack, 1991, p 260).

   Litwack examines reneging on incentive reforms both at the level of the
individual firm (1991, p. 262) and at a systemwide level (1991, p. 263). The
recent 1988 Law on Cooperation is an example. As Litwack describes it, "This
law begins with a declaration of cooperative property rights, giving cooperative
property the same legal status as state property. Furthermore, according to
this law, the taxation of cooperatives must be based on stable rates that cannot
be changed for at least a five-year period" (1991, p. 267). The new law elicited
a strong response: the number of cooperatives in the USSR increased by 5.6
times in 1988 alone (Litwack, 1991, p. 267). Problems—some in the form of
"unanticipated consequences"—quickly thereafter set in.

   One unanticipated consequence was that several cooperatives recognized
that repressed inflation in the market for consumers' goods presented large
arbitrage opportunities (Litwack, 1991, p. 267).[16] Arbitrage gains became the
source of popular and political resentment, however; cooperatives were ac-
cused of "'speculating' at the expense of society" (Litwack, 1991, p. 267).
Restraints on speculation were therefore introduced. Also, tax increases, which
expressly violated the new law, were approved—although these were subsequently repealed in the face of protest. But there is more than one way to
skin/tax/expropriate a cooperative. Strategic price setting is one possibility:
"the prices at which cooperatives . . . purchase inputs in the government sector

---

16. Interestingly, arbitrage is one of the functions ascribed to firms by early Austrian theories
of the firm. Arguably, this is a very basic role for the firm to play in a primitive market economy.

have been officially raised significantly above those for government enterprises" (Litwack, 1991, p. 268).

So unused is the Soviet leadership to the importance of credibility that
it "invites" investment by issuing threats.[17] The paradox is that fewer degrees
of freedom can have advantages over more because added credible commitments can obtain by substituting rules for discretion. A key lesson of hands-on
governance is to give and receive credible commitments. Effective economic
reform requires that reneging options be foreclosed if investor confidence is
to be realized.

5.2.3. *A combined assessment*

Winiecki is surely correct in giving prominent attention to property rights in
his examination of socialism. Not only does a focus on de facto property rights
help to explain economic practices and the distribution of favors in a centrally
planned economy, but such a focus also helps to identify crucial impediments
to reform. Lest reform be frustrated, *apparatchiks* and bureaucrats need to
be accommodated if they are to be removed. Generous retirement bonuses,
even in the amount of the discounted value of their projected future rents,
warrant sympathetic consideration.

Furthermore, the privatization efforts to which Winiecki refers need to
be accompanied by contractual assurances of credible commitment, thereby
to preclude subsequent expropriation. Otherwise, parties will be reluctant to
pay full value for extant assets, to maintain and improve those assets, and to
put durable, nonredeployable assets in place.[18] The pressing need to buttress
privatization with credible commitments appears not to be well understood,
however. That is perhaps partly because the contractual approach to economic
organization has only recently taken hold.

6.   Conclusions

Economists have done well by thin constructions. That economics is the queen
of the social sciences is largely because subtle, spontaneous, thin governance
mechanisms have been recognized and explicated by successive generations
of economists. That extraordinary intellectual achievement is by no means
played out, moreover. Considering the intellectual power and economic importance of spontaneous governance, economists can be expected to continue to
invest heavily in the study of "nearly" hands-off mechanisms.

There is a real tension nonetheless between thin rational accounts and
the world of organization: there are not nearly enough markets (Arrow, 1983,
p. 123); there is too much administrative organization. Sooner or later the
question must be asked, "What's going on here?"

17. Recall the Gorbachev quotation in Chapter 4.
18. For a Yugoslav example, see Horvat, 1982, p. 256. For a Hungarian example, see Kornai,
1986, pp. 1705–6.

To be sure, the world of organization gets complicated when intentional mechanisms of a "conscious, deliberate, purposeful" kind intrude. A comparison of any leading organization theory text (e.g., Scott, 1987) with any leading microeconomics text (e.g., Kreps, 1990b) quickly confirms that. If, moreover, the chief advantage that economics enjoys over the other social sciences is that it works out of a systems orientation (Coase, 1978), might that advantage be sacrificed by moving to a combined treatment of spontaneous and intentional governance?

There are, however, offsetting considerations. For one thing, an understanding of each generic form of governance is useful not merely in its own right but also because it helps to understand other generic forms. Thus, thin rational accounts are useful not merely because they uncover subtleties of organization but because, by being explicit, they help to make clear exactly which assumptions fail (Tirole, 1986; Kreps, 1990a; Fudenberg et al., 1990). If intentional governance arises where spontaneous governance fails, then it is important to know both where and why. Also, as the foregoing makes evident, subtle market mechanisms (e.g., reputation effects) do cross corporate boundaries and manifest themselves within firms. And there is also a reverse flow, in that relations found useful within firms can also be partly replicated by markets (e.g., cost-plus contracting supported by audits).

Added complications of internal organization notwithstanding, it is not the case that every microanalytic feature of intentional organization is consequential. The main factors that distinguish markets and hierarchies (in transaction cost economizing respects) involve only a few key features. Of special importance are (1) adaptability differences, (2) contract law differences, (3) incentive intensity differences, and (4) bureaucratic cost consequences. Inasmuch, moreover, as these differences are systematic—being in the nature of a syndrome (Williamson, 1988d, 1991a)—the logic of economic organization becomes more evident when markets, hybrids, and hierarchies are studied together.

Based on the foregoing, the key features of economic organization are discovered by appealing to law, economics, and organization. To be sure, that does not preclude more specialized orientations. The New Science of Organization is at a pre-unified state of development and will benefit from many lenses. I merely urge that a combined law, economics, and organizations approach to the issues has merit. Although organization theory and the law (especially contract law) are not accorded co-equal status with economics under this combined conception, both play very significant roles nonetheless.

7

Corporate Finance and Corporate Governance

This chapter examines corporate finance through the lens of transaction-cost economics. A fundamental tenet of this approach is that the supply of a good or service and its governance need be examined simultaneously. Corporate finance is no exception—whence the combined reference to corporate finance *and* corporate governance in the title.

Agency theory provides an alternative lens to which transaction-cost economics is sometimes compared. The leading similarities and differences between these two approaches are examined in Section 1. The core of the chapter, Section 2, deals with "project financing." Extensions, qualifications and applications are treated in Section 3. Concluding remarks follow.

1. Agency Theory and Transaction-Cost Economics Comparisons

Terminology aside, in what ways do agency theory and transaction-cost economics differ? Although this question has been posed repeatedly in oral discussions and sometimes in writing,[1] only piecemeal responses have hitherto been attempted. A more systematic reply is sketched here. If my answer appears to favor one of these approaches over the other, it will not go unnoticed that I am not a disinterested participant. Be that as it may, my "objective" view is that these two perspectives are mainly complementary. Both have helped and will continue to inform our understanding of economic organization.

---

1. Thus Gilson and Mnookin observe that "it is somewhat difficult to understand the relationship between the positive theory of agency, identified with Jensen and Meckling, and transaction cost economics, identified with Oliver Williamson" (1985, p. 333, n. 32). Ross more recently remarks that "many of our theories [of the firm] are now indistinguishable from the transactional approach ... Agency theory ... is now the central approach to the theory of managerial behavior" (1987, p. 33).

Any effort to answer the above question is complicated by the fact that both agency theory and transaction-cost economics come in two forms. Thus Jensen distinguishes between formal and less formal branches of agency theory. Much of the more formal agency literature is concerned with issues of efficient risk bearing and works out of a "mechanism design" setup. The less formal literature is referred to by Jensen as the "positive theory of agency." This is concerned with "the technology of monitoring and bonding on the form of . . . contracts and organizations" (Jensen, 1983, p. 334).

One branch of transaction-cost economics is mainly concerned with issues of measurement while the other emphasizes the governance of contractual relations (Williamson, 1985b, pp. 26–29). Although measurement and governance are not unrelated (Alchian, 1984), I am principally concerned here with the latter. The positive theory of agency and the governance branch of transaction-cost economics are what I compare.

The different origins of transaction-cost economics (hereafter, often abbreviated as TCE) and positive agency theory (hereafter, often abbreviated as AT) explain some of the differences between them. The classic transaction-cost problem was posed by Ronald Coase in 1937: When do firms produce to their own needs (integrate backward, forward, or laterally) and when do they procure in the market? He argued that transaction-cost differences between markets and hierarchies were principally responsible for the decision to use markets for some transactions and hierarchical forms of organization for others.

The classical agency-theory problem was posed by Adolf Berle and Gardiner Means in 1932. They observed that ownership and control in the large corporation were often separated and inquired whether this had organizational and public-policy ramifications.

Although both the Coase problem (vertical integration) and the Berle and Means problem (the separation of ownership and control) were subject to repeated public-policy scrutiny during the ensuing 35 years, there was very little conceptual headway. More microanalytic and operational approaches to each awaited developments in the 1970s.

A transaction-cost approach to the economic organization of technologically separable stages of production was successively worked by Williamson (1964, 1971b, 1975) and by Klein, Crawford, and Alchian (1978). The appearance of the "classic capitalist firm" and its financing was explicated by Alchian and Demsetz (1972) and Jensen and Meckling (1976). The Jensen and Meckling paper was expressly concerned with the separation of ownership from control and is widely regarded as the entering wedge out of which the positive theory of agency has since developed. Applications of TCE and AT to related contractual issues have been made since and both now deal with many common issues. That TCE traces its origins to vertical integration while AT was originally concerned with corporate control has nevertheless had continuing influence over each and helps to explain some of the differences between them.

I sketch what I consider to be the main commonalities and leading differences between these two. Real differences notwithstanding, these have been shrinking as each approach has come to work on issues previously dealt with by the other.

It will facilitate the comparison of TCE and AT to identify the core references. For the purposes of this chapter, I will take agency theory to be defined by Jensen and Meckling (1976, 1979), Fama (1980), Fama and Jensen (1983, 1985), and Jensen (1983, 1986). Transaction-cost economics is defined by Williamson (1975, 1979b, 1985b, 1988c), Klein, Crawford, and Alchian (1978), Klein (1980, 1988), Klein and Leffler (1981), Teece (1980), Alchian (1984), and Joskow (1985, 1988).

1.1. Commonalities

TCE and AT are very similar in that both work out of a managerial-discretion setup. They also adopt an efficient-contracting orientation to economic organization. And both argue that the board of directors in the corporation arises endogenously. Consider these seriatim.

1.1.1. Managerial discretion

Both TCE and AT take exception with the neoclassical theory of the firm whereby the firm is regarded as a production function to which a profit-maximization objective has been ascribed. Rather, TCE regards the firm as a governance structure and AT considers it a nexus of contracts. A more microanalytic study of contracts has resulted.[2] The behavioral assumptions out of which the theory of the firm (more generally, the theory of contract) works have been restated in the process.

TCE expressly assumes that human agents are subject to bounded rationality and are given to opportunism. Incomplete contracting is a consequence of the first of these. Added contractual hazards result from the second.

Although many economists, including those who work out of AT, are reluctant to use the term bounded rationality (which, in the past, has been thought to imply irrationality or satisficing), bounded rationality has gradually become the operative rationality assumption.[3] Also, AT refers to "moral hazard" and "agency costs" rather than opportunism. But the concerns are the same, whence these are merely terminological differences.

AT and TCE both normally assume risk neutrality rather than impute differential risk aversion to the contracting parties (the latter being associated with the formal agency literature). The upshot is that both TCE and AT work

---

2. This is not to suggest that the firm-as-production-function, agency, and governance approaches are opposed. It is more useful to think of them as complements. Thus the "value of the firm" construction in Jensen and Meckling (1976) works out of a production-function setup. Also, transaction costs and production costs have been brought together in a combined "neoclassical" framework by Riordan and Williamson (1985).

3. Fama's argument that managerial discretion is effectively held in check by "ex post settling up" (1980) is closer in spirit to the unbounded-rationality tradition. Weaker forms of ex post settling up (Fama and Jensen, 1983) are consonant with bounded rationality.

out of substantially identical behavioral assumptions. The opportunity sets to which each refers are substantially identical also.[4]

1.1.2. Efficient contracting

TCE examines alternative forms of economic organization with reference to their capacity to economize on bounded rationality while simultaneously safeguarding the transactions in question against the hazards of opportunism. Although AT is more concerned with the latter, an "incomplete contracting in its entirety" orientation is employed by both.

Incomplete contracting in its entirety may appear to be a contradiction in terms. It is not. The first part (incomplete contracting) merely vitiates a mechanism design setup (Grossman and Hart, 1982; Hart, 1988). The second part (contracting in its entirety) means that parties to a contract will be cognizant of prospective distortions and of the needs to (1) realign incentives and (2) craft governance structures that fill gaps, correct errors, and adapt more effectively to unanticipated disturbances. Prospective incentive and governance needs will thus be anticipated and thereafter "folded in."[5]

Although both AT and TCE are cognizant of both of these contractual design needs, AT examines contract predominantly from an *ex ante* incentive-alignment point of view while TCE is more concerned with crafting *ex post* governance structures within which the integrity of contract is decided. Differences between AT and TCE with respect to their choice of the basic unit of analysis and with reference to organization form are largely responsible for these incentive/governance differences (see Section 1.2).[6]

1.1.3. Endogenous board of directors

Both AT and TCE maintain that the board of directors arises endogenously as a control instrument. As originally described by Fama, the board is princi-

---

4. This was not always so. Thus whereas TCE has always maintained that discretionary distortions will be a function of competition in product, capital, and factor markets, Jensen and Meckling originally maintained that product- and factor-market competition were unrelated to managerial discretion, since "owners of a firm with monopoly power have the same incentives to limit divergences of the manager from value maximization . . . as do the owners of competitive firms" (1976, p. 329). Jensen now holds that the opportunity set to which managers have access is a function of product- and factor-market competition (1986, p. 123).

5. Among other things, folding in implies that projected future effects will be priced out. This is the central focus of the original Jensen and Meckling (1976) argument. What I have referred to as the "simple contractual schema" in Chapter 3, is a TCE illustration of the argument. Note that different governance structures that have different assurance properties and adaptive capacities for dealing with potentially disruptive events (the general nature, but not the particulars, of which are anticipated) will be priced out differently. This is a key feature of incomplete contracting in its entirety.

6. The aforementioned difference in their origins is also a contributing factor. AT works out of a financial economics tradition that has continuously invoked incentive-alignment arguments to great advantage. TCE, by contrast, is more concerned with firm and market-structure issues of an industrial organization kind. Governance issues are more congenial to this latter perspective.

pally an instrument by which managers control other managers: "If there is competition among the top managers themselves . . . , then perhaps they are the best ones to control the board of directors" (1980, p. 393). Although a board with such a composition and purpose approximates an executive committee, Fama and Jensen (1983) subsequently distinguish between decision management and decision control and argue that the latter function is appropriately assigned to the board of directors. Such a board is really different from an executive committee. It is an instrument of the residual claimants.

As discussed elsewhere (Williamson, 1985b, chap. 12) and developed in Section 2, TCE also regards the board of directors in a manufacturing corporation principally as an instrument for safeguarding equity finance. But it goes further and links equity finance to the characteristics of the assets.[7]

1.2.   Leading Differences

That there are differences between AT and TCE is already apparent from the above. The most important differences is in the choice of the basic unit of analysis. But there are also differences with respect to the cost concern and the main organizational concern of each.

1.2.1.   Unit of analysis/dimensionalizing

TCE follows Commons (1934) and regards the transaction as the basic unit of analysis. By contrast, "the individual agent is the elementary unit of analysis" (Jensen, 1983, p. 327) for AT. Both of these are microanalytic units and both implicate the study of contracting. But whereas identifying the transaction as the basic unit of analysis leads naturally to an examination of the principal dimensions with respect to which transactions differ, use of the individual agent as the elementary unit has given rise to no similar follow-on effort in AT.

Many of the refutable implications of TCE are derived from the following organizational imperative: align transactions (which differ in their attributes) with governance structures (the costs and competencies of which differ) in a discriminating (mainly, transaction-cost economizing) way. Of the several dimensions with respect to which transactions differ, the most important is the condition of asset specificity. This has a relation to the notion of sunk cost, but the organizational ramifications become evident only in an intertemporal, incomplete-context. As discussed in Section 1.3 below, a condition of bilateral dependency arises when incomplete contracting and asset specificity are joined.

The joining of incomplete contracting with asset specificity is distinctively associated with TCE. This joinder has contractual ramifications both in general[8] and specifically with reference to corporate financing.

7. Another (but minor) difference is that Fama and Jensen argue that "outside directors have incentives to develop reputations as experts in decision control" (1983, p. 315). I do not disagree, but would argue that outside directors often have stronger incentives to "go along."

8. With variation, the very same attributes recur across intermediate product markets, labor

1.2.2. Agency costs/transactions costs

Jensen and Meckling define agency costs as the sum of "(1) the monitoring expenditures of the principal, (2) the bonding expenditures by the agent, and (3) the residual loss" (1976, p. 308). This last is the key feature, since the other two are incurred only in the degree to which they yield cost-effective reductions in the residual loss.

Residual loss is the reduction in the value of the firm that obtains when the entrepreneur dilutes his ownership. The shift out of profits and into managerial discretion induced by the dilution of ownership is responsible for this loss. Monitoring expenditures and bonding expenditures can help to restore performance toward pre-dilution levels. The irreducible agency cost is the minimum of the sum of these three factors.

Since all of these features are evident to prospective buyers, those who purchase equity will pay only for the projected performance of the firm after agency costs of these three kinds have been taken into account. Accordingly, "the [entrepreneur] will bear the entire wealth effects of these expected costs so long as the equity market anticipates these effects" (Jensen and Meckling, 1976, p. 314). The full set of repositioning effects is thus reflected in the *ex ante* incentive alignments.

By contrast, TCE emphasizes *ex post* costs. These include (1) the maladaptation costs incurred when transactions drift out of alignment in relation to what Masahiko Aoki refers to as the 'shifting contract curve,' (2) the haggling costs incurred if bilateral efforts are made to correct *ex post* misalignments, (3) the setup and running costs associated with the governance structures (often not the courts) to which disputes are referred, and (4) the bonding costs of effecting secure commitments (Williamson, 1985b, p. 21). Of these, the maladaptation costs are the key feature. Such costs occur only in an intertemporal, incomplete-contracting context. Reducing these costs through judicious choice of governance structure (market, hierarchy, or hybrid), rather than merely realigning incentives and pricing them out, is the distinctive TCE orientation.

1.2.3. Organizational concern

The aforementioned *ex ante* and *ex post* differences show up in the relative importance that AT and TCE ascribe to private ordering and in the way that each deals with organization form.

Whereas AT is little concerned with dispute resolution (which lack of concern is characteristic of all *ex ante* approaches to contract) (see Baiman, 1982, p. 168), dispute avoidance and the machinery for processing disputes are central to TCE. Rather than assume that disputes are routinely submitted to and efficaciously settled by the courts, TCE maintains that court ordering

---

markets, regulation, career marriages, and, as discussed later, in financial markets. The "solutions," moreover, displaying striking regularities. This is consonant with Hayek (1967, p. 50) and Friedman (1953).

is a very crude instrument[9] and that most disputes, including many that under current rules could be brought to a court, and resolved by avoidance, self help, and the like (Galanter, 1981, p. 2). Private ordering rather than court ordering is thus the principal arena. How are gaps to be filled, contractual errors to be corrected, and disputes to be settled when the contract drifts out of alignment? Assessing the comparative efficacy of alternative governance structures for harmonizing *ex post* contractual relations (Commons, 1934; Williamson, 1985b), is the distinctive focus and contribution of TCE. (The availability of the courts to serve as a forum of ultimate appeal nonetheless serves to delimit the range of indeterminancy within which private ordering bargains must be reached. Put differently, access to the courts delimits threat positions.)

Fama and Jensen maintain that "organization forms are distinguished by the characteristics of their residual claims" (Fama and Jensen, 1983, p. 101). This leads them to separate decision management (which is located in the firm) and decision control (the board of directors). But the details of internal organization otherwise go unremarked. TCE, by contrast, treats hierarchical decomposition and control as part of the organization-form issue. Unitary versus multidivisional structures are thus distinguished and their comparative properties in bounded-rationality and managerial-discretion (goal pursuit) respects are assessed.

1.3. Other Differences

Two other differences, both of which are related to the above discussion, are the way that each deals with process and with the neutral nexus of contract.

1.3.1. Process distinctions

Both AT and TCE invoke economic natural selection. Although AT assumes that natural selection processes are reliably efficacious (Fama, 1980), referring even to "survival of the fittest" (Jensen, 1983, p. 331), TCE is somewhat more cautious—subscribing, as it does, to weak-form rather than strong-form selection, the distinction being that "in a relative sense, the *fitter* survive, but there is no reason to suppose that they are fittest in any absolute sense" (Simon, 1983, p. 69; emphasis in original). Rarely, however, does AT or TCE give an account of how the selection process works in particular cases.[10] Both are frequently criticized for this reason, but critics almost never offer alternative hypotheses and rely on vague "existence" arguments in claiming selection-process breakdowns.[11]

---

9. As Lawrence Friedman observes, relationships are effectively fractured if a dispute reaches litigation (1965, p. 205). Since continuity is thereafter rarely intended, the parties are merely seeking damages.

10. For an exception, see the TCE account of takeover.

11. The issues are elaborated in exchanges between Granovetter (1985) and myself (1988c) and between Dow (1987) and myself (1987b).

A related process argument on which AT once relied is that "ex post settling up" (Fama, 1980) will reliably discipline managers. Assessing this requires an examination of when reputation effects work well and when poorly. Awaiting on explication of the detailed mechanisms out of which this process works, ex post settling up plays a less prominent role in AT presently.

TCE invokes two quite different process arguments. The first of these is the Fundamental Transformation; the second deals with the impossibility of "selective intervention." Both require that *ex post* contractual features be examined in detail.

The Fundamental Transformation has reference to a situation where, by reason of asset specificity, an *ex ante* large-numbers bidding competition is transformed into what, in effect, is a bilateral trading relation thereafter. The details are set out elsewhere (Williamson, 1975, 1985b and Chapter 3). Suffice it to observe here that the governance of *ex post* contractual relations is greatly complicated for all transactions that undergo a transformation of this kind. AT makes no express reference to any corresponding process transformation.

The impossibility of selective intervention arises in conjunction with efforts to replicate incentives found to be effective in one contractual/ownership mode upon transferring transactions to another. Such problems would not arise but for contractual incompleteness, since, if contracts were complete, then, asymmetric information notwithstanding, "each party's obligation [will be] fully specified in all eventualities; and hence it will be possible [to replicate] any rights" associated with one contracting mode in another (Hart, 1988, p. 121).

TCE maintains that the high-powered incentives found to be effective in market organization give rise to dysfunctional consequences if introduced into the firm. It also argues that control instruments found to be effective within firms are often less effective in the market (between firms). The upshot is that whereas market organization is associated with higher powered incentives and lesser controls, internal organization joins lower powered incentives with greater controls (Williamson, 1985b, 1988c). The assignment of transactions to one mode or another necessarily must make allowance for these respective incentive-and-control syndromes. Again, AT makes no provision for these effects.

1.3.2. Neutral nexus

Although the nexus of contract conception of the firm was originally introduced by Alchian and Demsetz (1972), the approach has been more fully developed by Jensen and Meckling. As they put it, "Viewing the firm as a nexus of a set of contracting relationships ... serves to make clear that the ... *firm is not an individual* ... [but] is a legal fiction which serves as a focus for a complete process in which the conflicting objectives of individuals (some of which may 'represent' other organizations) are brought into equilibrium within a framework of contractual relations" (Jensen and Meckling, 1976, pp. 311–12, emphasis added). That this has been a productive way to think about contractual behavior in the firm is plain from the record. The firm, according to this conception, is a neutral nexus within which equilibrium relations are worked out.

The neutral-nexus conception is also employed by TCE. As discussed elsewhere, each constituency is processed through the very same "simple contractual schema" in working out its equilibrium contracting relationship—which entails the simultaneous determination of asset specificity, price, and contractual safeguards—with the firm (Williamson, 1985b, chap. 12). Albeit instructive, this approach to contracts can be disputed in two respects.

First, the contract made with one constituency may affect others. Contractual interdependencies therefore need to be dealt with. So long, however, as the firm is a neutral nexus, this is merely a refinement. The second and more important objection disputes the neutrality of the nexus.

Thus, suppose that some constituencies bear a strategic relation to the firm and can disclose information pertinent to other constituencies selectively. The management of the firm is the obvious constituency to which to ascribe such a strategic informational advantage. Given its centrality in the contracting process (the neutral nexus needs someone to contract on its behalf), the management will sometimes be in a position to realize advantages by striking mutually "inconsistent" contracts with other constituencies. Undisclosed contractual hazards can arise in this way (Williamson, 1985b, pp. 318–19).

To be sure, this last is merely an existence argument. Reputation effects, if they work well, plainly deter such abuses. TCE nevertheless makes express allowance for the possibility that the neutral nexus breaks down. Added contractual safeguards may be warranted as a consequence.[12]

1.4.   Recapitulation

Significant commonalities notwithstanding, AT and TCE also differ. The leading differences are these:

	AT	TCE
unit of analysis	individual	transaction
focal dimension	?	asset specificity
focal cost concern	residual loss	maladaptation
contractual focus	*ex ante*	*ex post*
	alignment	governance

2.   Project Financing[13]

The TCE approach to economic organization examines the contractual relation between the firm and each of its constituencies (labor, intermediate

12. For example, placing suppliers or workers on the board of directors so as better to assure information disclosure (but not necessarily voting participation) may be warranted.

13. The material in this section was originally prepared for and presented at the 50th

product, customers, etc.) mainly with reference to transaction-cost economizing. Assessing contractual needs requires that the attributes of differing transactions be examined. Discriminating matches result.

This same approach is herein applied to corporate finance. Whereas most prior studies of corporate finance have worked out of a composite-capital setup, I argue that investment attributes of different projects need to be distinguished. I furthermore argue that rather than regard debt and equity as "financial instruments," they are better regarded as different governance structures.[14] This is consonant with a unified approach to the study of contract referred to above. The discriminating use of debt and equity thus turns out to be yet another illustration of the proposition that many apparently disparate phenomena are variations on the very same underlying transaction-cost economizing theme.

As developed below, the parallels between corporate finance and vertical integration are especially striking. Thus the (corporate finance) decision to use debt or equity to support individual investment projects is closely akin to the (vertical integration) decision to make or buy individual components or subassemblies. Not only is the "market mode" (debt; outside procurement) favored if asset specificity is slight, but the costs of the market mode go up relatively as the contractual hazards increase. Also, the disabilities of internal organization (equity; internal supply) turn critically in both instances on the impossibility of "selective intervention."

I begin with a brief sketch of earlier explanations for the combined use of debt and equity before setting out the rudimentary TCE model of project financing. The proposed model is a reduced form and solves one problem only to pose another: why not invent a new governance structure—called dequity—that combines the best properties of debt and equity, thereby to dominate both? Only upon posing and working through the puzzle of dequity—which entails comparative institutional analysis of an incomplete contracting kind—does the rationale for the discriminating use of debt and equity fully emerge.

2.1. Earlier Treatments

Whereas corporate finance had once been the domain of those with practical knowledge of investment banking, the Modigliani and Miller paper in 1958 changed all of that. Upon applying the standard tools of economic analysis

---

Anniversary Celebration of the Norwegian School of Economics and Business Administration. The celebration was held in September 1986 in Bergen, Norway.

14. Some contend that they have been so regarded all along. So what else is new? I submit, however, that the governance-structure attributes of debt and equity have been underdeveloped and undervalued. As discussed below, prior attention has focused on the tax, signalling, incentive, and bonding differences between debt and equity. Only this last comes close to a governance-structure treatment, and even here the governance-structure differences are obscured by (1) working out of a composite-capital setup and (2) failure to treat the differential bureaucratic costs of these two forms of finance.

to study corporate finance, they demonstrated that the conventional wisdom on the uses of debt and equity in the corporate capital structure was fallacious. The main ingredients of the new learning were these: the firm was characterized as a production function; investments were distinguished with respect to risk class but were otherwise treated as undifferentiated (composite) capital; and equilibrium arguments were brought effectively to bear. The main Modiagliani–Miller theorem, which revolutionized corporate finance, was this: *"the average cost of capital to any firm is completely independent of its capital structure and is equal to the capitalization rate of a pure equity stream of its class"* (Modigliani and Miller, 1958, pp. 268–69, emphasis in original).[15]

Financial economists have since developed a series of qualifications to this basic result, the leading ones being (1) taxes and bankruptcy, (2) signaling, (3) resource constraints, and (4) bonding. The tax argument is the most obvious and will hereafter be suppressed by assuming that debt and equity are taxed identically. The early bankruptcy argument was also a rather narrow, technical construction.[16] Information asymmetries between managers and investors play a major role in the signaling, resource constraints, and bonding arguments.

2.1.1. Signaling

Ross (1977) used a signaling model to explain the use of debt. Thus assume that two firms have objectively different prospects and that these are known by the management but are not discerned by investors. Debt, in these circumstances, can be used to signal differential prospects. Specifically, the firm with better prospects can issue more debt than the firm with lesser prospects. This signaling equilibrium comes about because the issue of debt by the firm whose prospects are poor will result in a high probability of bankruptcy, which is assumed to be a costly outcome to the management.

2.1.2. Resource constraints

Stiglitz (1974) and Jensen and Meckling (1976) begin with a firm that is wholly owned by an entrepreneur. An investment opportunity then arises which, if it is to be realized, requires an investment of funds that exceeds the entrepreneur's resources. How should it be financed?

15. Upon examining the opportunities for investors to adjust portfolios by borrowing on personal account, Modigliani and Miller showed that the market value of levered and unlevered firms that had identical expected returns could not differ. "It is this possibility of undoing leverage which prevents the value of levered firms from being consistently less than those of unlevered firms, or more generally prevents the average cost of capital . . . from being systematically higher for levered than for nonlevered companies in the same class" (Modigliani and Miller, 1958, p. 270).

It is now widely believed that "there is no difference between debt and equity claims from an economic perspective" (Easterbrook and Fischel, 1986, p. 274, n. 8).

16. Grossman and Hart summarize the original bankruptcy rationale for debt as follows: "if the probability of bankruptcy is positive, then, as long as investors cannot borrow on the same terms as the firm, i.e., go bankrupt in the same states of the world, then, by issuing debt, the firm is issuing a new security, and this will increase its market value" (1982, p. 130).

One possibility is to sell equity. This, however, will dilute the entrepreneur's incentives. Inasmuch as monitoring is costly, the entrepreneur whose incentives have been diluted can and will partake of greater on-the-job consumption. An obvious way to avoid this sacrifice of incentive intensity is to use debt rather than equity to finance the expansion.

But then why not finance the firm with debt up to the hilt—say one hundred percent less epsilon? Jensen and Meckling contend that the answer to this question turns on "(1) the incentive effects associated with highly levered firms, (2) the monitoring costs these incentive effects engender, and (3) bankruptcy costs" (1976, p. 334). Thus large debt could induce equity to take very large *ex post* risks—knowing that the penalties would accrue to debtholders in the event of failure and would be captured by equity should the project succeed. Since perceptive lenders will see through this risk and demand a premium (Jensen and Meckling, 1976, pp. 336–37), debt will become available on progressively worse terms. The optimal mix of debt and equity (in entrepreneurial firms where the resources of the entrepreneur are limited) will obtain when the effects of incentive dilution (from issuing new equity) and risk distortions (from issuing debt) are equalized at the margin.[17]

Inasmuch as the entrepreneurial firms to which the argument applies are rather special, additional analysis is evidently needed to deal with the modern corporation in which there is no single owner-manager and where the equity ownership of management in the aggregate is small. The bonding approach is responsive.[18]

2.1.3. Bonding

Grossman and Hart (1982) and Jensen (1986) treat debt as a means by which to bond the management. The main Grossman and Hart model assumes that

17. Debt will "be utilized if the ability to exploit potentially profitable investment opportunities is limited by the resources of the owner ... [and] the marginal wealth increments from the new investment projects are greater than the marginal agency costs of debt, and these agency costs are in turn less than those caused by the sale of additional equity" (Jensen and Meckling, 1976, p. 343).

18. Jensen and Smith summarize the current agency view on the use of equity in terms of bonding and risk aversion:

> Activities of large, open, nonfinancial corporations are typically complicated. They involve contractually specified payoffs to many agents in the production process. Contracting costs with these agents increase if there is significant variation through time in the probability of contract default. ... Concentrating much of this risk on a specific group of claimants can create efficiencies. ... However, specialized risk bearing by common stockholders is effective only if they bond their contractual risk-bearing obligation. This is accomplished by having the stockholders put up wealth used to purchase assets to bond payments promised to other agents. ...
>
> In addition, the common stock of open corporations allows more efficient risk sharing. ... Since employees and managers develop firm-specific human capital, risk aversion generally causes them to charge more for the risk they bear compared to that charged by common shareholders. (1985, pp. 99–100)

A curiosity with this formulation is that while risk sharing and bonding roles are ascribed to equity, there is no apparent reason to use debt in the modern corporation where equity ownership is very diffuse.

management has negligible ownership of equity, whence "a switch from debt finance to equity finance does not change management's marginal benefit from an increase in profit directly" (1982, p. 131). Instead, the incentive effect in their main model comes from the desire to avoid bankruptcy (Grossman and Hart, 1982, pp. 116, 127, 131).[19]

Whereas the managers in Ross's model are given to profit maximization and differ with respect to their objective opportunities, the Grossman and Hart model assumes that managers are given to managerial discretion. Debt serves both as a signal and as a check against managerial discretion. Thus if issuing debt (which is easy to observe) will permit the market to make inferences about the quality of the firm's investments (which is difficult to observe), which inferences are thereafter reflected in market-valuation differences, then debt may be used so as to persuade the market that the management "will pursue profits rather than perquisites" (Grossman and Hart, 1982, p. 109). By issuing debt the "management (the agent) deliberately changes its incentives in such a way as to bring them into line with those of the shareholders (the principal)—because of the resulting effect on market value. In other words, . . . the management bonds itself to act in the shareholders' interests" (1982, p. 109).

Note with respect to each of these arguments that debt is used only for special purposes. It signals better opportunities (Ross); it avoids dilution (Stiglitz, Jensen and Meckling); it compels managers to behave in a fashion more consonant with the stockholders' interests (Grossman and Hart, Jensen). Capital being of an undifferentiated (composite) kind, there is no suggestion that debt is better suited for some projects and equity for others.

2.2. The TCE Rationale

The TCE approach to corporate finance examines individual investment projects and distinguishes among them in terms of their asset-specificity characteristics. It also regards debt and equity principally as governance structures rather than as financial instruments. Earlier approaches, by contrast, work out of a more aggregative, composite-capital setup in which the differential governance features of debt and equity are underdeveloped (or treated not at all).[20]

19. They subsequently argue that debt can also be used for bonding purposes to deter takeover (Grossman and Hart, 1982, pp. 128–29).

20. Myers' interesting treatment of corporate uses of debt financing begins with the observation that the theory should not merely explain why the tax advantages of debt "do not lead firms to borrow as much as possible . . . [but it] should explain why some firms borrow more than others, why some borrow with short-, and others with long-maturity instruments, and so on" (1977, p. 147). He further observes that "the most fundamental distinction is . . . between (1) assets that can be regarded as call options, in the sense that their ultimate values depend, at least in part, on further discretionary investment by the firm and (2) assets whose ultimate value does not depend on further discretionary investment" (1977, p. 155)—where discretionary investment takes the form of maintenance, marketing, and, more generally "all variable costs" (1977, p. 155). But rather than focus on the ways by which "lenders often protect themselves by obtaining security in the form of specific assets for which secondary markets exist," he regards that as "an attempt to avoid the problems analyzed in this paper. . . . The heart of the matter is

It will simplify the argument to assume that there are only two forms of finance and that projects must be financed entirely by debt or by equity but not both. To motivate the argument, assume initially that there is only one form of finance, debt, and that projects are arrayed, from least to most, in terms of their asset specificity. Thus suppose that a firm is seeking to finance the following: general-purpose, mobile equipment; a general-purpose office building located in a population center; a general-purpose plant located in a manufacturing center; distribution facilities located somewhat more remotely; special-purpose equipment; market and product development expenses; and the like.

Suppose further that debt is a governance structure that works almost entirely out of rules. Specifically, assume that debt financing requires the debtor to observe the following: (1) stipulated interest payments will be made at regular intervals, (2) the business will continuously meet certain liquidity tests, (3) sinking funds will be set up and principal repaid at the loan-expiration date, and (4), in the event of default, the debt-holders will exercise pre-emptive claims against the assets in question. If everything goes well, interest and principal will be paid on schedule. But debt is unforgiving if things go poorly. Failure to make scheduled payments thus results in liquidation.[21] The various debt-holders will then realize differential recovery in the degree to which the assets in question are redeployable.

Since the value of a pre-emptive claim declines as the degree of asset specificity deepens, the terms of debt financing will be adjusted adversely. Confronted with the prospect that specialized investments will be financed on adverse terms, the firm might respond by sacrificing some of the specialized investment features in favor of greater redeployability. But this entails trade-offs: production costs may increase or quality decrease as a result. Might it be possible to avoid these by inventing a new governance structure to which suppliers of finance would attach added confidence? In the degree to which this is feasible, value-enhancing investments in specific assets could thereby be preserved.

Suppose arguendo, that a financial instrument called equity is invented and assume that equity has the following governance properties: (1) it bears a residual-claimant status to the firm in both earnings and asset-liquidation respects; (2) it contracts for the duration of the life of the firm; and (3) a board of directors is created and awarded to equity that (a) is elected by the pro-rata votes of those who hold tradeable shares, (b) has the power to replace the management, (c) decides on management compensation, (d) has access to internal performance measures on a timely basis, (e) can authorize audits in depth for special follow-up purposes, (f) is apprised of important investment and operating proposals before they are implemented, and (g) in other respects

---

that the existence of debt" sets up *ex post* strain between stockholders and debtholders. This *ex post* strain between debt and equity occupies much of the finance literature of the past decade. It is *not* my interest here.

21. More generally, such failures place limits on discretion in favor of rule-bound behavior.

bears a decision-review and monitoring relation to the firm's management (Fama and Jensen, 1983).

The board of directors thus "evolves" as a way by which to reduce the cost of capital for projects that involve limited redeployability. Not only do the added controls to which equity has access have better assurance properties, but equity is more forgiving than debt. Efforts are therefore made to work things out and preserve the values of a going concern when maladaptation occurs. Thus whereas the governance structure associated with debt is of a very market-like kind, that associated with equity is much more intrusive and is akin to administration. The correspondence to which I referred earlier between outside procurement/debt and vertical integration/equity therefore obtains.

Let k be an index of asset specificity and let the cost of debt and equity capital, expressed as a function of asset specificity, be $D(k)$ and $E(k)$, respectively. A switchover will obtain as asset specificity increases if $D(0) < E(0)$ but $D' > E' > 0$.

That $D(0) < E(0)$ is because debt is a comparatively simple governance structure. Being a rule-governed relation, the setup costs of debt are relatively low. By contrast, equity finance, which is a much more complex governance relation that contemplates intrusive involvement in the oversight of a project, has higher setup costs. Allowing, as it does, greater discretion, it compromises incentive intensity and invites politicking.[22]

Although the costs of both debt and equity finance increase as asset specificity deepens, debt financing rises more rapidly. This is because a rule-governed regime will sometimes force liquidation or otherwise cause the firm to compromise value-enhancing decisions that a more adaptable regime (into which added controls have been introduced), of which equity governance is one, could implement. Accordingly, $D' > E' > 0$.

The upshot is that whereas highly deployable assets will be financed with debt, equity is favored as assets become highly nonredeployable. Let $\bar{k}$ be the value of k for which $E(k)$ 5 $D(k)$. The optimal choice of all-or-none finance thus is to use debt finance for all projects for which $k < \bar{k}$ and equity finance for all $k > \bar{k}$. Equity finance is thus reserved for projects where the needs for nuanced governance are great.

By contrasting with the earlier literature, which began with an equity-financed firm and sought a special rationale for debt, the TCE approach postulates that debt (the market form) is the natural financial instrument. Equity (the administrative form) appears as the financial instrument of *last resort*.

2.3. Dequity

The discriminating use of debt and equity is thus predicted by the foregoing. Debt is a governance structure that works out of rules and is well-suited to

---

22. For a related discussion in the context of vertical integration, see Williamson, 1985b, (chap. 5; 1988d). Also see Section 2.3.

projects where the assets are highly redeployable. Equity is a governance structure that allows discretion and is used for projects where assets are less redeployable.

A chronic puzzle is nevertheless posed in *all* systems for which rules versus discretion are being compared: Why doesn't discretion strictly dominate rules? Thus suppose that the discretionary system is advised to replicate rules across all activities for which rules work well and intervene only on those occasions where expected net gains can be projected. The discretionary system will then everywhere do as well as and will sometimes do better than rules. I have discussed this issue elsewhere as the puzzle of "selective intervention" (Williamson, 1985b, chap. 6; 1988d).

Expressed in terms of debt and equity, the puzzle can be examined by creating a new financial instrument/governance structure called dequity. Let this instrument include all of the constraining features of debt to which benefits (on average) are ascribed. When, however, these constraints get in the way of value-maximizing activities, the board of directors (or some similar high-level oversight unit) can temporarily suspend the constraints, thereby to permit the corporation to implement a value-maximizing plan. The constraints are thus the norm from which selective relief is permitted.

Let the cost of dequity capital be given by $\delta(k)$. If dequity operates as described then it will have the property that $\delta(0) = D(0)$ and $\delta' = E'$. The first of these reflects the fact that dequity is not burdened by the bureaucratic costs of equity, and since selective relief from the rules is permitted, dequity mimics equity in facilitating adjustment to unanticipated disturbances. Combining, as it does, the best properties of each, dequity supplants both debt and equity.[23]

Whether or not dequity will operate as described turns on the feasibility of selective intervention. If selective intervention is a fiction—in that it predictably breaks down—then this condition must be acknowledged and the added cost consequences factored in.

The central problem with all promises to "behave responsibly" during contract execution and at project-renewal intervals is that such promises, without more, lack credibility. Here as elsewhere, those who enjoy discretion can be expected to exercise it in their favor.

Thus although sometimes management's decision to waive the rules, thereby to implement an adaptive response to unanticipated disturbances, will serve value-enhancing purposes, at other times (especially in conjunction with project extension and renewals) managerial subgoal pursuit[24] will intrude. Such subgoal pursuit arises because the circumstances under which the rules can be waived are manipulable (if the criteria were clearly defined and if state

23. Although it oversimplifies, dequity, if it works as described, mimics debt at project-approval and project-renewal intervals, when partisan political input for equity-financed projects is especially severe, and it reverts to equity during the project-execution interval whenever the exacting observance of debt convenants prospectively leads to suboptimization.

24. Subgoals include growth, easy-life preferences, perquisites, and the like. Logrolling and internal politicking among members are commonly involved.

realizations were common knowledge, then the appropriate waivers could and presumably would be incorporated in the debt agreement). Accordingly, selective intervention will be subject to errors of both commission (discretion will sometimes be exercised when it suits the purpose of the management) and of omission (the rules will sometimes be observed when they should not).[25] The hypothesized gain without cost that results from introducing judgment into a rules regime will not therefore obtain. Dequity should therefore be regarded as an intermediate form of financing (akin to preferred stock) rather than as a superior form that dominates both debt and equity over the full range of parameter values.

Put differently, the admonition to "follow the rules with discretion" is too facile. Since to combine rules with discretion will never realize the hypothetical ideal but will always entail compromise, dequity can be expected to have the following properties: $D(0) < \delta(0) < E(0)$; and $D' > \delta' > E' > 0$.

3.   Extensions, Qualifications, Applications

3.1.   The Modern Corporation

Project financing simplifies and thereby helps to disclose key features of the finance decision. But does it inform the study of finance in the modern corporation—which, after all, is the real object of the exercise?

There are two main research strategies for studying the modern corporation. One is to posit that the firm is large, complex, and diffusely owned and inquire into the consequences.[26] The second is to work out of microfoundations. Although the latter has obvious appeal, and is employed here, does the argument scale up? Put differently, is it the case that the corporation is merely the sum of its individual projects?

Transaction-cost economics is not uniquely culpable in its use of a simple model to investigate what is plainly a very complex phenomenon. To the contrary, this is a time-honored research tradition. Consider the following: (1) the neoclassical theory of the firm works out of a firm-as-production-function setup. Although the hierarchical features of the firm and a comparison of transaction costs (between firms and markets) are both suppressed by this construction, public policy toward business was nevertheless long informed by this "applied price theory" approach (Coase, 1972, p. 61). (2) The Alchian and Demsetz (1972) treatment of the classical capitalist firm turns critically on the existence of technological nonseparabilities. Although such nonseparabilities explain recourse to unified ownership and hierarchical controls in relatively small units, both Alchian and Demsetz and others nevertheless

25. One of the reasons why rules will sometimes be observed when they should not is that holders of dequity will suspect managers of waiving the rules opportunistically. If, therefore, an occasion for legitimate rule relief arises that, if exercised, has the appearance of opportunism, managers may forego discretion.

26. The earlier managerial-discretion literature (Baumol, 1959; Marris, 1964; Williamson, 1964, and recent variants thereof (Fama, 1980; Grossman and Hart, 1982; Jensen, 1986) take it as a given that the modern corporation is a large and diffusely owned entity.

treated the modern corporation "as if" the nonseparabilities observed among small groups of workers (such as those engaged in manual freight loading) apply equally to enterprise sizes of 10,000 and even 100,000 workers (to include even firms that are diversified and divisionalized).[27] (3) The Jensen and Meckling (1976) treatment examines the consequences of diluting a one hundred percent equity position in an entrepreneurial firm. Their real interest is in the diffusely owned modern corporation, but the basis for moving from the one to the other is not described.[28] (4) The Grossman and Hart treatment (1986) of vertical integration assumes that the manager of each stage is also the owner. This is a simplification, one consequence of which is that incentive intensity is assumed to be unaffected by vertical integration. The application of the argument to the case where the manager of each stage has a negligible ownership position is not developed. More generally, the logic that connects tractable micro models and the composite uses to which they are put is often asserted but is rarely fully worked out.

Although it is possible, perhaps even plausible, to think of the modern corporation as a series of separately financed investment projects, such a conception can be disputed in at least five respects. First, the approach set out here misses interaction effects among projects. Second, the all-or-none finance assumption—either debt or equity, but not both—ought to be relaxed. Third, the corporation as a going concern sometimes possesses important team features, on which account the whole is more than the sum of the parts. Fourth, only a few large and discrete projects are apt to be financed individually. And finally, additional financing instruments—leasing, preferred stocks, etc.—need to be introduced.[29]

Leasing is briefly discussed in Section 3.2.1, below, and preliminary headway has been made with combining debt and equity for single projects.[30] But project aggregation issues have not been addressed. Also, the influence of uncertainty ought to be made more explicit.

An important question, with respect to this last, is how does the value of $\bar{k}$ vary as uncertainty changes. If, as seems plausible, $D(k)$ and $E(k)$ are both twisted up by a parametric increase in uncertainty, $D(k)$ more than $E(k)$, then the value of $\bar{k}$ will be reduced. The reasons for the differential shift are

27. Note that Alchian and Demsetz specifically eschewed appeal to contractual considerations in their initial explanation for the firm (1972, pp. 777–78). Both have since qualified this position (Alchian, 1984; Demsetz, 1988).

The possibility that very large administrative entities arise in support of contractual relations between technologically separable, *but bilaterally dependent,* trading entities is the TCE way of motivating the large corporation.

28. They expressly acknowledge this condition: "One of the most serious limitations of this analysis is that as it stands we have not worked out in this paper its application to the very large modern corporation whose managers own little or no equity. We believe our approach can be applied to this case but . . . [these issues] remain to be worked out in detail and will be included in a future paper" (Jensen and Meckling, 1976, p. 356).

29. The discussion of dequity in Section 2.3 can be thought of as a move in the direction of preferred-stock financing.

30. Thomas Hartmann-Wendels and I have made preliminary headway with this.

that (1) added uncertainty pushes the firm into a maladapted state more often and/or more consequentially, and (2) rule-governed systems, as compared with discretionary systems, are placed under greater stress by such circumstances. Accordingly, the differential shift described above obtains and greater use of equity financing is favored, *ceteris paribus*. (Explicating the decision process that lies behind each of the reduced-form expressions is needed, however, to prove this conjecture. An even more microanalytic level of analysis is therefore implicated.)

3.2. Applications

The foregoing limitations notwithstanding, applications of three kinds are sketched here: leasing; the pecking-order theory of finance; and leveraged buyouts.

3.2.1. Leasing

Assume that standby access to an asset is required and that market procurement of the services supplied by this asset is believed to be defective. Does it follow that the firm should own the asset in question?

Consider, in particular, durable, general-purpose assets on wheels and assume that such assets are resistant to user abuse (and/or that the costs of inspection and attributing abuse are low). The possibility of procuring the services of these assets by leasing deserves consideration.

General-purpose assets on wheels satisfy the $k = 0$ condition in superlative degree. Given, moreover, that measurement problems are assumed to be negligible, there is no need to combine owner and user for user-cost reasons. Since an outside owner that is specialized to this type of equipment (e.g., truck leasing; airplane leasing) can repossess and productively redeploy these assets more effectively than could a more specialized debt-holder, leasing is arguably the least-cost form of finance for such assets. Recourse to leasing to finance assets on wheels is thus merely a special case of the general TCE asset-based approach to project finance set out earlier.

3.2.2. Pecking-order finance

Myers attributes the "pecking-order" theory of finance to Donaldson (1981) and summarizes it as follows: "(1) firms prefer internal finance. (2) They adapt their target dividend payment ratios to their investment requirements.... (3) If external finance is required, firms issue the safest security first. That is, they start with debt, then possibly hybrid securities such as convertible bonds, then equity" (Myers, 1985, pp. 348–49). Myers goes on to observe that while he used to ignore pecking-order theory, "recent work based on asymmetric information, problems of adverse selection, moral hazard, and signaling" gives him more confidence (1985, p. 349).

The approach to project financing set out here is similar in some respects but different in others. For one thing, the pecking-order theory makes no reference to the characteristics of the assets. Also, the use of retained earnings in preference to debt lacks a TCE justification. If such projects are appropriately financed by debt in the comparison of debt with equity, then the use of retained earnings to support such projects (because it is a "safer security") reflects behavioral rather than transaction-cost economizing purposes. It is nonetheless interesting that both the behavioral approach (Donaldson) and the comparative governance approach employed here conclude that equity is the financial instrument of last resort, albeit for different reasons.

3.2.3. Leveraged buyouts

Leveraged buyouts are a relatively recent development. Jensen (1986) advances what he calls a "free cash flow" explanation for this condition. Free cash flow is essentially a managerial-discretion argument: unless somehow constrained, managers will dissipate free cash flows to support growth and related activities that favor managerial objectives.[31] Jensen concludes that the data are broadly corroborative.

I am also concerned with the possibility that leveraged buyouts are used as a way by which to curb managerial discretion. But I examine the problem from the standpoint of assets rather than cash flows. In fact, these two explanations are not mutually exclusive.

Suppose, as an evolutionary matter, that a firm is originally financed along lines that are consistent with the debt and equity financing principles set out above. Suppose further that the firm is successful and grows through retained earnings. The initial debt-equity ratio thus progressively falls. And suppose finally that many of the assets in this now-expanded enterprise are of a kind that could have been financed by debt.

Added value, in such a firm, can be realized by substituting debt for equity. This argument applies, however, selectively. It only applies to firms where the efficient mix of debt and equity has gotten seriously out of alignment. These will be firms that combine (1) a very high ratio of equity to debt with (2) a very high ratio of redeployable to nonredeployable assets.

Interestingly, many of the large leveraged buyouts in the 1980s displayed precisely these qualities.[32] Thus Colman's examination of leveraged buyouts

---

31. Free cash flow is defined as "cash flow in excess of that required to fund all projects that have positive net present values when discounted at the relevant cost of capital" (Jensen, 1986, p. 323).

32. One that does not is the Mushroom King leveraged buyout for which Citicorp was the principal source of funds. That Mushroom King was a poor candidate is suggested by the following: "In a leveraged buyout, investors buy a company almost entirely with borrowed money, using the company's cash flow and sales of the company's assets, to reduce the debt. The best candidates, therefore, are companies that have a predictable stream of earnings and hard assets that can be sold for good prices. Investors also look for companies in low-tech fields, so that a venture is not overly dependent on any one or two managers. . . . Mushroom King broke all the rules, and its collapse illustrates what can happen when a good idea is yanked so far that it snaps" (Cowan, 1987, p. 1)

disclosed that "only an existing firm with a small amount of debt is able to support" a leveraged buyout and that a "frequent characteristic of the leveraged buyout company is that the firm has a high proportion of its total assets in tangible property" (1981, p. 531). Although the tangible-intangible distinction is not identical to the redeployability test that I employ, there is plainly a correlation. Lowenstein's observation that many of these firms are in "prosaic businesses—retailing, textiles and soft drink bottling" (1985, p. 749) and related observations about "mundane product lines" by Wallner and Greve (1982, pp. 78–79) are also consonant with the view that many of the assets in question have a stable, long-term value and hence would afford redeployable security.

Colman furthermore observes that leveraged buyouts are put together with a view toward providing managers with added incentives. This may or may not involve equity investment by the management, but it always involves a significant contingent-compensation, arrangement (Colman, 1981, pp. 532, 537, 539). The management, moreover, is usually on a tight leash. It ordinarily owns a minority (often less than fifteen percent) of the equity, the remainder being concentrated in the hands of the banks, insurance companies, and the investment bankers who package the deal (Mason, 1984). According to Wallner, "The management never gets more than 50 percent of the equity unless the second lenders are the only other participants in the deal" (1980, p. 20), in which event those outsiders who supply finance are little concerned over inept management because their pre-emptive claims against redeployable assets provide them with adequate protection.

As earlier remarked, the most interesting feature of leveraged buyouts is the substitution of debt for equity. The following points are pertinent:

1. The major lenders are finance companies and banks and insurance companies. The finance companies specialize in shorter term inventory and receivable financing, where they have an advantage over the banks in policing the collateral, and will lend up to eighty-five percent of the liquidation value. Banks and insurance companies specialize in intermediate and longer term financing, usually at a lower lending percentage of liquidation value (Colman, 1981, p. 539).

2. The cash flow and asset-based financing approaches are distinguished by the fact that under "the conventional approach, the lender wanted protection primarily via cash flow" whereas under "the asset-based approach ... the lender ties all or at least part of his loan to the liquid value of the borrower's assets ... , [and realizes protection by] taking a security interest in the assets ... , [establishing] a lending formula on the basis of the liquid value, and ... [obtaining] periodic information on the nature and size of those assets." (Colman, 1981, p. 542)

Plainly, the shift from cash flow to asset-based financing lines up rather closely with the transaction-cost economics rationale for secure transactions.

Note, moreover, that there is no necessary inconsistency in initially taking a corporation private (in the above-described way) and subsequently going public. Two factors support such a two-stage program.

For one thing, those who take the corporation private can be presumed to have deep knowledge of the merits of the transaction. Outsiders, by contrast, may need to have a performance record to be convinced of the merits. Public ownership, on terms that reflect full valuation, thus awaits an examination of the data.

Secondly, the prospect that added rewards will be realized at the going public stage if the company performs well in the period between going private and its return to (albeit reconfigured) public status is a source of added incentive to the management. Harnessing incentive intensity is a leading purpose of the transaction.[33]

The transaction-cost approach to economic organization also has ramifications for whether the incumbent management will participate extensively in a buyout refinancing (thereafter to hold a substantial equity position in the restructured organization) or should be displaced instead. The argument is this: since employment continuity is the source of added value wherever firm-specific human capital is great, a management buyout is favored by high human-asset specificity, *ceteris paribus*. Thus whereas a substitution of debt for equity is warranted in any firm where redeployable physical assets are equity financed, an informed choice between continuing and removing incumbent managers requires that the human assets of the managers be assessed. The buyout transaction is therefore influenced by the condition of *both* physical and human-asset specificity.[34]

3.3.   Institutional Finance

Financial economics, like general equilibrium theory more generally, is essentially noninstitutional (or, as Tjalling Koopmans once put it, "preinstitutional"). The scientific aspiration was to work out of an "institution-free core."[35] The substantial accomplishments of this research tradition notwithstanding, there is growing agreement that institutions matter in ways not hitherto acknowledged or even imagined. A "New Institutional Economics" has been appearing in response.

Financial economics has not been immune to these developments. The possibility of supplanting composite capital by a richer theory of investment is an obvious candidate. The recent Long and Malitz, (1985) distinction between tangible and intangible investments (advertising and R & D) is an illustration.

---

33. The foregoing is not meant to suggest that all leveraged buyouts are unproblematic. Rather, the argument is that neither unremitting hostility to nor unqualified support for leveraged buyouts is warranted. Sorting the wheat from the chaff requires that the underlying logic be worked out.

34. It should not go unnoticed that the argument is not working entirely out of a project-financing framework. If the object is to find assets that have good redeployability in the aggregate, then firms that are operating in mature (but not declining), competitively organized industries would appear to be good candidates. Something akin to composite-asset considerations thus appears.

35. The phrase originates with Vernon Smith.

My treatment of project financing in terms of asset specificity also breaks with the composite-capital tradition. Albeit similar to Long and Malitz, their tangible/intangible breakdown is a very incomplete measure of asset specificity. Thus although intangible investments in R & D and advertising have poor redeployability properties, this is also true of many tangible assets. If differential redeployability goes to core issues, then a general theory that features this (rather than an ad hoc approach that employs proxy measures that can be gleaned from accounting statements) is really needed.

Also note that whereas earlier treatments of the corporation begin with stock financing and inquire whether a justification for debt can be discovered, TCE reverses this order. It therefore posits that debt (rule-based governance) is the original form of finance and introduces equity (discretionary governance) only when the cost of debt financing becomes prohibitive. Regarding debt and equity as alternative governance structures, rather than merely financial instruments with different tax implications, is central to the TCE exercise.

Finally, the TCE approach to corporate finance and corporate governance has numerous empirical ramifications. These include the study of leasing, rank-order finance, and the use of leveraged buyouts—all from an asset-specificity point of view.

Corporate finance being an enormously complicated subject, TCE brings another (different but nonetheless complementary) lens to bear.

4.   Concluding Remarks

The transaction-cost approach to economic organization focuses on the governance needs of exchange relations. Governance structures that mitigate hazards and facilitate adaptation plainly have much to commend them. A compelling economic rationale for a large number of otherwise anomalous institutional structures is "revealed" only when these hitherto neglected contractual purposes become the object of analysis.

The transaction is made the basic unit of analysis, the most important dimension of which is asset specificity. Aligning transactions—be they for intermediate product, labor, finance, final product, etc.—with governance structures in a discriminating way is the central TCE exercise. Transactions differ in their attributes; governance structures differ in their costs and competencies. The object is to effect an economizing match.

In general, simple governance structures (often rule based, such as debt) are able to cope effectively with the needs of simple transactions. Simple governance structures experience stress, however, as the contractual hazards ramify. A switch to more complex and costly governance structures that supplant rules in favor of discretion can be and often is the source of added value in such circumstances.

The TCE approach maintains that some projects are easy to finance by debt and *ought to be financed by debt*. These are projects for which physical asset specificity is low to moderate. As asset specificity becomes great, however, the preemptive claims of the bondholders against the investment afford limited protection—because the assets in question have limited redeployability. Not only does the cost of debt financing therefore increase, but the benefits of closer oversight also grow. The upshot is that equity finance, which affords more intrusive oversight and involvement through the board of directors (and, in publicly held firms, permits share ownership to be concentrated), is the preferred financial instrument for projects where asset specificity is great.

By contrast with the formal modeling apparatus associated with much of the financial economics literature, the transaction-cost economics approach to corporate governance and corporate finance is of a relatively preformal kind. Inasmuch as subsequent formalization would appear to be feasible, that condition is not necessarily objectionable. Indeed, since the relevant reduced forms are unlikely to be discerned without first explicating the underlying microanalytics, omitting this step is to proceed parlously. Some problems, of which corporate finance is arguably one, are so complex that they first need to be dealt with "on their own terms." Focus is nevertheless required. Transaction-cost economics offers one focused perspective.

8

The Politics and Economics of Redistribution and Inefficiency

It is customary to evaluate efficiency by comparing an actual form of organization with a hypothetical ideal. Albeit instructive, that can be a misleading or defective test in three respects. For one thing, because all feasible forms of organization are flawed, the relevant operational comparison is between alternative feasible forms. Also, if one of the alternatives under comparison is an extant form, then allowance needs to be made for incumbency advantages. Thus, even if mode A is judged to be inefficient in relation to mode B on a simple side-by-side comparison, if mode A is in place and mode B incurs setup costs, then mode A may prevail. Finally, and related to this, it may not be possible to implement mode B for lack of political support.

Accordingly, the appropriate test of "failures" of all kinds—markets, bureaucracies, redistribution—is that of remediableness: *An outcome for which no feasible superior alternative can be described and implemented with net gains is presumed to be efficient.* That is a comparative institutional test and, the market failure area excepted, is widely resisted.

I begin, therefore, with a brief examination of the market failure literature. Although similar lessons carry over to an assessment of redistribution, redistribution continues to be assessed predominantly with respect to a hypothetical ideal. A contributing factor is that redistribution is saturated with politics.

The orthodox (apolitical) approach to redistribution is contrasted with the more permissive "test of time" criterion proposed by George Stigler (1992) in Section 2. The paradox of "inefficiency by design," in which the inefficiencies in question have the purpose and effect of buttressing weak property rights, is examined in Section 3. Grounds for rebutting the presumption that redistribution is efficient, both in general and with respect to the U.S. sugar program, are developed in Section 4. Concluding remarks follow.

1.   Market Failure

It was once customary to establish market failure by comparing an actual market with a hypothetical ideal. Since actual markets could never do better (and would usually do worse) in the comparison with an ideal, market failure was held to be a widespread condition. Ronald Coase took exception and proposed that a comparative institutional approach to market failure be adopted instead:

> Contemplation of an optimal system may provide techniques of analysis that would otherwise have been missed and, in certain special cases, it may go far to providing a solution. But in general its influence has been pernicious. It has directed economists' attention away from the main question, which is *how alternative arrangements will actually work in practice.* It has led economists to derive conclusions for economic policy from a study of an abstract of a market situation. It is no accident that in the literature . . . we find a category "market failure" but no category "government failure." Until we realize that we are choosing between social arrangements which are all more or less failures, we are not likely to make much headway. (1964, p. 195; emphasis added)

Although this symmetrical approach to the matter of market failure now enjoys widespread assent (Stiglitz, 1989, pp. 38–39), it took a long time to register. The propensity to regard the "government as a benevolent guardian, hampered only by ignorance of proper economic policy as it seeks disinterestedly to maximize a Benthamite social welfare function" (Krueger, 1990, p. 172), was a deterrent factor.

One justification for ascribing benevolent properties to the government is that it is analytically convenient. Another is that some people really believe that "the most intractable problems [will] give way before the resolute assault of intelligent, committed people" (Morris, 1980, p. 23). Analytical convenience is a poor excuse for bad public policy, however, and so is hubris. It is elementary that intelligent people need to come to terms with their cognitive limitations and that committed people are rarely disinterested, which is to say that most have an agenda. If all feasible forms of organization are flawed, then references to benign government, costless regulation, omniscient courts, and the like are operationally irrelevant. Comparative institutional economics is always and everywhere beset with trade-offs.

Lapses into ideal but operationally irrelevant reasoning can be avoided by (1) recognizing that it is impossible to do better than one's best, (2) insisting that all the finalists in an organization form competition meet the test of feasibility, (3) symmetrically exposing the weaknesses as well as the strengths of all proposed feasible forms, and (4) describing and costing out the mechanisms of any proposed reorganization. To this list, there is yet another consideration: (5) making a place for and being respectful of politics. This last item has been the most difficult for public-policy analysts to concede.

2.   Redistribution: Rival Conceptions

Although some redistribution programs are the product of a broad political consensus, many are more focused and are regarded as problematic. That is because redistribution is frequently a means by which winning politicians discharge obligations and award favors (Moe, 1990b; Moe and Caldwell, 1994). Redistribution is especially troublesome when it takes convoluted forms that appear to be inefficient. It is particularly frustrating when demonstrably inefficient programs are beyond reach. Joseph Stiglitz spoke to all three of these concerns:

> [R]edistributions ... are the consequences of special interest groups using the powers of the state to reap private gains at the expense of the general public. These redistributions are not only inequitable, but also inefficient. They are not only inefficient because of the rent-seeking expenditures that the special interest groups make in the quest for the special treatment; they are also inefficient because the equity constraint results in government programs that are ill-suited to any "rational" objective.
>
> There is, alas, no way in a democratic society to proscribe such activities. There is no obvious way to distinguish these activities from more "legitimate" activities, e.g., providing information, remedying market failures. (1989, p. 61)

An oft-cited example is the U.S. sugar program, which was described by George Stigler as follows:

> The United States wastes (in ordinary language) perhaps $3 billion per year producing sugar and sugar substitutes at a price two to three times the cost of importing the sugar. Yet that is the tested way in which the domestic sugar-beet, cane, and high-fructose-corn producers can increase their incomes by perhaps a quarter of the $3 billion—the other three quarters being deadweight loss. The deadweight loss is the margin by which the domestic costs of sugar production exceed import prices. (1992, p. 459)

The usual interpretation is that such deadweight losses represent inefficiency: "The Posnerian theory would say that the sugar program is grotesquely inefficient because it fails to maximize national income" (p. 459). A contributing factor, according to efficiency of the law scholarship, is that the sugar program is based on statutes rather than common law.

Stigler took exception with the efficiency of the law approach in general and with the conclusion that the sugar program is inefficient in particular. The problem with the former is that it works from a truncated logic (pp. 460–61). A problem with the latter is that it fails to respect the political process: "Maximum national income ... is not the only goal of our nation as judged by policies adopted by our government—and government's goals as revealed by actual practice are more authoritative than those pronounced by professors of law or economics" (p. 459).

In opposition to Posnerian theory, Stigler declared that the "sugar program is efficient. This program is more than fifty years old—it has met the test of time" (p. 459). By contrast with those who regard redistribution as problematic and even illegitimate, Stigler clearly interpreted redistribution as a manifestation of the legitimate purposes of government.

A somewhat backhanded way of ascribing legitimacy to redistribution is to view this as an unavoidable cost of democratic government. We may not like what we get, but it is part of the package. Thus although less redistribution would be preferable to what we observe, we need to become reconciled to the political realities. This, as I understand it, is Stiglitz's position.

A more favorable construction is that redistribution is a central and foreseeable architectural feature of democratic politics. To be sure, that could be disputed: Voters, after all, are poorly informed, and many fail to participate. That, however, is scarcely dispositive if the key players are politicians and interest groups (Moe, 1990b, p. 121). Because both groups are well informed and deeply strategic, we should expect to find that redistribution is the product of a strategic political calculus, which is consistent with many of the data.

But what, then, is to be made of redistribution that is accomplished in tortured ways, as compared with less costly and feasible alternatives? Surely that is inefficient and ought to be reformed?

Maybe, but then again, maybe not. Two issues are raised. First, it is much easier to postulate more efficient alternatives—lump-sum transfers being an example—than it is to describe the enabling mechanisms. The latter is a much more demanding microanalytic exercise. Second, apparent inefficiencies sometimes serve intended purposes, which is to say that they should be described as inefficiencies by design.

3. Inefficiency by Design

Consider two private-sector regimes, one in which property rights are well defined and easy to protect under the law and the other in which property rights are poorly defined and costly to protect. Parties that organize economic activities in the first regime examine the adaptive properties and associated costs of each feasible mode and choose the least-cost form (Williamson, 1991a). Components that can be produced more cheaply by outside suppliers thus are bought rather than made.

Matters become more complicated when private-sector property rights are poorly defined and costly to enforce. Firms in these circumstances may decide to make rather than buy because outside procurement runs the risk that valued know-how will leak out (Teece, 1986). Also, manufacturers' agents sometimes incur added expenses, over and above those needed to develop the market, because these added expenses strengthen customer bonds in a cost-effective way, thereby deterring manufacturers from entering into the distribution stage and expropriating market development investments (Heide and John, 1988). Similarly, franchisors sometimes impose costly bonding on franchisees as a means by which to deter franchisees from violating quality norms (Klein and Leffler, 1981).

The common thread that runs through all these examples is that insecure but legitimate property rights are supported by added expenses to the degree that these are perceived to be the most cost-effective way to protect against the loss of value. Whether such added costs are inefficient cannot be established by reference to a hypothetical ideal.

To be sure, if it were always and everywhere the case that we could rely on "a [costless] legal system to define property rights and arbitrate disputes," then anyone "wishing to use a resource has to pay the owner to obtain it" (Coase, 1959, p. 14). If, however, it is costly to define and enforce property rights through the courts, then court ordering needs to be evaluated in relation to alternative, feasible private-ordering forms of organization. If the most cost-effective way to protect property rights is to incur private-ordering expenses of the kinds just described, then—awaiting a superior measurement technology or other device by which property rights can be better protected—the resulting "inefficiency by design" is not inefficient in any remediable sense whatsoever.[1]

Terry Moe (1990b) contended that political property rights are especially insecure in democratic regimes in which programs that are put in place by one generation of politicians are subsequently subject to reversal when incumbent politicians are voted out of office. If efficiently designed bureaus and programs are more responsive but easier to reverse than are those that are encumbered, then politicians face an intertemporal trade-off: Inefficiency (nonrespon-siveness, inertia) that has been crafted into the design of bureaus is the price of ensuring that original purposes are not quickly reversed. To be sure, the originators would prefer to have programs that are both efficient and responsive now and are resistant to redirection by successors who would use them for other purposes. Not having that choice, however, inefficiency (both now and later) is intentionally introduced as the means by which to achieve program persistence.

Politics, moreover, is responsible for yet another design complication: Because politics is the art of compromise, losers are sometimes included in the design process. The design of the Occupational Safety and Health Administration (OSHA) is an example of inefficiency due to compromise:

> If business firms were allowed to help design OSHA, they would structure it in a way that it could not do its job. They would try to cripple it.
>
> This is not a hypothetical case. Interest groups representing business actually did participate in the design of OSHA, . . . [and] OSHA is an administrative nightmare, in large measure because some of its influential designers fully intended to endow it with structures that would not work. (Moe, 1990b, p. 126).

What we find, therefore, is that inefficiencies are intentionally created in the public sector as a means by which to protect weak political property rights and/or to obtain approval for programs that would otherwise be defeated (half a loaf is judged to be better than none at all). This is akin to the inefficiencies by design that we found earlier in the private sector, only more so. Although such inefficiencies show up as deadweight losses and are regularly

1. This assumes away second-best considerations.

condemned, that reflects a political disconnect or analytical myopia. Without egregious defects of the kinds discussed in Section 4, inefficiencies that arise by design may not be inefficiencies at all.

In order to examine this issue more closely and carefully, assume that the democratic process in question is widely conceded to possess merit. (Among other things, everyone in the system who "ought to" be awarded the franchise to vote is able to vote.) Assume further that redistribution is recognized from the outset as one of the legitimate purposes to which government may be put. And assume, too, that both interest groups and politicians are farsighted players in that they look ahead and perceive how different configurations of activity affect their interests.

The government will thus proceed not merely to supply various services— such as law and order, common defense, and foreign relations—but it will also redistribute income. And although some of these redistributions may be the product of a broad consensus and take the form of simple income transfers, others will be much more convoluted. What should we make of the latter?

Specifically, suppose that a particular interest group enjoys the support of the current winning coalition and asks politicians to redistribute income in their favor. Suppose that there are three programs, A, B, and C, through which this can be done. Program A is a direct payment and is the least-cost way to redistribute, but it is also the most easily reversed. Neither the interest group nor the politicians will favor this. Programs B and C deliver identical expected net benefits to the interest group, but politicians perceive that Program C, which incurs larger deadweight losses, provides a stronger tie between the interest group and the incumbent politicians, thereby better ensuring their reelection. Understandably, Program C will often be the variant that is approved.

Evaluated in conventional deadweight loss terms, Program A is preferred to Program B is preferred to Program C. The apolitical pronouncement is that Program C should give way to the more efficient Program B and that Program A is superior still. It is widely recommended, for example, that the redistributional purposes of the sugar program (which are now accomplished through import quotas and incur large deadweight losses) could be realized much more efficiently through deficiency payments. Consider the mechanisms.

One possibility is to make monthly or annual payments equal to the current and projected benefits received by current and future beneficiaries. This requires that the current benefits for each be determined, which, since these are not unambiguous, is costly and immediately invites controversy. More troublesome is the payment of future benefits. What is the formula by which these vary? Will the mechanism be respected? What to do about disputes? Are the benefits transferable across generations? Do they attach to the property, independent of the usage? What should be done if the attributes of successor claimants differ from those under the current program? Because, moreover, periodic deficiency payments may be easily reduced or terminated if incumbents are voted out of office, both the interest group and the present dominant coalition will ascribe hazards to this means of effecting redistribution.

Consider, therefore, another form of monetary payment that prospectively overcomes the political hazards and is easier to administer: making a onetime payment to current beneficiaries. The stream of future net benefits is thus discounted back to the present and paid out. Does that overcome the difficulties?

Not really. For one thing, the beneficiaries may accept their lump-sum payment only to repeat their political request for help. If they had the political clout once, then why not again? The issue reduces to one of credible commitment. Recalling the definition of an honest politician, the question is whether beneficiaries that are once bought will stay bought. (Any answer in the affirmative needs to be accompanied by a statement of the mechanism through which such credibility will be realized.) Moreover, politicians will oppose once-and-for-all payment schemes that effectively disconnect them from the interest groups with which they have struck deals and on which they have come to rely for support and votes. This is not to say that beneficiaries are ingrates and that the delivery of past benefits will have no lingering effects. Programs, however, that deliver current and (contingent) future benefits will be regarded as a more reliable basis on which to project continuing political support.[2]

Interestingly, there are numerous parallels between this discussion and one that took place thirty years earlier in the antitrust arena. Just as the use of a hypothetical ideal form of contracting led antitrust authorities (see Williamson, 1985b, pp. 183–89) to declare that nonstandard and unfamiliar contracting practices were inefficient and unlawful,[3] so does the use of a hypothetical ideal form of redistribution permit professors of law and economics to declare that nonstandard and convoluted forms of redistribution are inefficient and grotesque. But that is where the parallels end: Although antitrust has since been reformed, the critics of redistribution persist.

Whereas antitrust now concedes that nonstandard and unfamiliar contracting practices can and sometimes do serve to protect weak but legitimate property rights[4] (as well as or instead of monopoly purposes), orthodox critics of redistribution make no such concessions. And whereas remediableness has, in effect, become the operative test criterion for market failure, political failures are still examined in relation to a hypothetical ideal.

Possibly these differences are explained by unfamiliarity with the political terrain. Or perhaps economists, as the guardians of rationality (Arrow, 1974, p. 16), have the responsibility and right to prescribe what is efficient to others. If the implicit weights of politics and economics differ, economics will trump politics rather than the reverse.

Stigler objected to this last and declared that redistribution programs that have passed the test of time are efficient. Albeit a useful concession to realpolitik, the test of time is also very nearly tautological. My proposal for unpacking the puzzles of redistribution is to recognize that the action resides in the details. The mechanisms of redistribution thus need to be examined in

2. This assumes that incumbents enjoy advantages over challengers in delivering contingent future benefits.

3. The Supreme Court agreed. *United States* v. *Arnold, Schwinn & Co.,* 388 U.S. 365 (1967).

4. The Supreme Court reversed itself in *Continental T.V. Inc. et al.* v. *GTE Sylvania Inc.* 433 U.S. 36 (1977).

order to ascertain (1) whether or not a proposed alternative mode for accomplishing redistribution is even feasible, (2) whether apparent inefficiencies have the deeper purpose and effect of buttressing weak (yet possibly legitimate) political property rights, and (3) whether organizational or political failures are properly described as egregious and hence, remediable or not, are denied efficiency status. All three entail an examination of the microanalytics.

4.   Possible Exceptions

Suppose that it were agreed that (1) the relevant comparisons are between alternative feasible forms (in which event hypothetical ideals are introduced only as they facilitate the comparison of alternative feasible forms), (2) extant forms are privileged in the degree to which rival forms incur setup costs, and (3) weak property rights are sometimes buttressed by (value-preserving) inefficiencies by design. All three propositions apply to both private- and public-sector activity, but politics differs in the degree to which it is a purposeful effort to award favors. Although the benign tradition holds that politicians balance the interests and deliver value to "all of the people, all of the time," realpolitik advises that the winners get to use public authority at the expense of others (Moe and Caldwell, 1994, p. 173).

As discussed earlier, inefficiency is introduced into the design of public bureaus and public programs because political property rights are insecure and/or because of the need for compromise. Although such inefficiencies would be reduced (in the limit, would vanish) as these insecurities and the need for compromise are lessened, political insecurity and compromise are themselves the product of a larger architectural exercise, namely, the design of what is intended to be a well-functioning democratic system.

I will assume, for the purposes of this discussion, that the democracy in question satisfies threshold standards for merit, which is to say that there is no case for general reform[5] and that politicians and interest groups make structural choices in an informed and farsighted way. Given these assumptions, which give rise to a presumption of efficiency, the issue that concerns me in this section is this: If we treat efficiency as a rebuttable presumption, what are the grounds for rebuttal? I examine this issue first in general and then with reference to the sugar program.

---

5. This is a very important assumption. If a polity is declared to exceed threshold standards for merit, then there are no general grounds for objecting to a particular outcome (or even to a class of outcomes, e.g., all pork-barrel programs). Instead, all challenges to the presumed efficiency of successively renewed political programs must be made in program-specific terms. I will turn to this shortly.

Note that to declare that a polity exceeds threshold standards for merit does not imply that every polity is regarded on a parity. One might argue that the French polity has superior properties to the English (or the reverse), or that some combination of both systems is superior to either. Were it that we were organizing a polity de novo, these superior structural features would be displayed and (hopefully) adopted. However, because we are not starting de novo, and since both systems are judged to exceed threshold (hence a case for general reform that has any chance of implementation cannot be made), we must work with what we have.

4.1.   General

Possible bases for rebutting the efficiency of a redistributional program include a showing that (1) the deadweight losses are vastly greater than had previously been recognized; (2) the program has taken on a life of its own, of which capture is an especially troublesome example; (3) rival programs are unfairly disadvantaged in other organizational respects; and (4) the political process was (or is) locally defective. Let us consider each.

4.1.1.   Deadweight loss burdens

Programs (such as the sugar program) that are known to carry a large deadweight loss burden are naturally suspect. At the very least, a periodic display of these burdens requires that supporters come to their defense. Such periodic reexamination is especially important to programs that are front-end loaded, which because of the political uncertainties, many evidently are (Moe, 1990b, p. 136). Lest the political net benefits turn negative yet go undetected because of inertia in the political process, a periodic review and the display of large deadweight losses by economists or other social scientists may have salutary effects.

An assessment of deadweight loss may also be warranted because the costs of some programs are uncritically assumed to be negligible, possibly because the case to the contrary has never been made. The presumption of efficiency is carried too far if all time-tested programs are, in effect, exempt from review. The state of antitrust enforcement with respect to mergers in the 1960s is an example.[6]

The then prevailing state of affairs is reflected by the Federal Trade Commission's opinion in *Foremost Dairies,* in which the commission ventured the view that necessary proof of violation of Section 7 "consists of types of evidence showing that the acquiring firm possesses significant power in some markets or that its over-all organization gives it a decisive advantage in efficiency over its smaller rivals."[7] Although Donald Turner, among others, was quick to label that as bad law and bad economics (1965, p. 1324), in that it protects competitors rather than promotes the welfare benefits of competition, the commission carried forward its reasoning in *Procter & Gamble* and linked it with barriers to entry in the following way:

> In stressing as we have the importance of advantages of scale as a factor heightening the barriers to new entry into the liquid bleach industry, we reject, as specious in law and unfounded in fact, the argument that the Commission ought not, for the sake of protecting the "inefficient" small firms in the industry, proscribe a merger so productive of "efficiencies." The short answer to this argument is that, in a proceeding under Section 7, economic efficiency or any other social benefit resulting from a merger is pertinent only

6. The remainder of this subsection is based on Williamson, 1985b, pp. 366–67, 369.
7. In re *Foremost Dairies, Inc.,* 60 F.T.C., 944, 1084 (1962), emphasis added.

insofar as it may tend to promote or retard the vigor of competition. (Bork, 1978, p. 254)

The emphasis on entry barriers and the low regard accorded to economies also appear in the Supreme Court's opinion. Thus the Court observed that Procter & Gamble's acquisition of Clorox may

> have the tendency of raising the barriers to new entry. The major competitive weapon in the successful marketing of bleach is advertising. Clorox was limited in this area by its relatively small budget and its inability to obtain substantial discounts. By contrast, Procter's budget was much larger, and although it would not devote its entire budget to advertising Clorox, it could divert a large portion to meet the short-term threat of a new entrant. Procter would be able to use its volume discounts to advantage in advertising Clorox. Thus, a new entrant would be much more reluctant to face the giant Procter than it would have been to face the smaller Clorox.
>
> Possible economies cannot be used as a defense to illegality.[8]

The low opinion and perverse regard for economies went so far that beleaguered respondents disclaimed efficiency gains. Thus Procter & Gamble insisted that its acquisition of Clorox was not objectionable because the government was unable definitively to establish that any efficiencies would result:

> [The government is unable to prove] any advantages in the procurement or price of raw materials or in the acquisition or use of needed manufacturing facilities or in the purchase of bottles or in freight costs. . . . [T]here is no proof of any savings in any aspect of manufacturing. There is no proof that any additional manufacturing facilities would be usable for the production of Clorox. There is no proof that any combination of manufacturing facilities would be usable for the production of Clorox. There is no proof that any combination of manufacturing facilities would effect any savings, even if such combination were feasible.[9]

The fact that efficiency benefits were held in such low regard in the 1960s is partly explained by the widespread opinion that between two structural alternatives—one of which simultaneously presents greater market power and greater efficiency than the other—the more competitive structure is invariably preferred. That view was supported by the implicit assumption that even small anticompetitive effects would surely swamp efficiency benefits in arriving at a net valuation. The FTC's opinion that "economic efficiency or any other social benefit [is] pertinent only insofar as it may tend to promote or retard the vigor of competition" (in which *competition* is defined in structural terms) is a clear indication of such thinking.

An application of the basic partial equilibrium welfare economics model to an assessment of market power versus economies disclosed that the unrelieved hostility to economies came at a high cost (Williamson, 1968b). Faced with

---

8. *Federal Trade Commission* v. *Procter & Gamble Co.*, 386 U.S. 568, 574 (1967).

9. The disclaimer of efficiencies appeared in Procter & Gamble's brief as respondent in the Clorox litigation. See Alan Fisher and Robert Lande, 1983, p. 1582, n. 5.

the mounting criticism[10] and with growing international competition (from foreign firms that were not burdened by the protectionist propensities of U.S. antitrust), the antitrust policy toward economies was eventually reformed. The display of deadweight losses in this instance arguably had a salutary effect.

4.1.2. Intertemporal transformations/capture

Organizations, like the law, have a life of their own. Sometimes the transformations are understood and foreseeable and should have been (arguably were) folded into the design calculus at the outset. But some transformations are wholly unanticipated: The complexity of the systems are simply beyond our limited understanding.

Limits on understanding are not, however, immutable. Robert Michaels's Iron Law of Oligarchy is an example of a transformation that, although once unanticipated, has since been explicated: "It is organization which gives birth to the dominion of the elected over the electors, of the mandatories over the mandators, of the delegates over the delegators. Who says organization, says oligarchy" (1962, p. 365). Good intentions to the contrary notwithstanding, the behavioral propensities of human actors eventually take hold, with the result that the initial leadership (or its successors) develop attachments to the office. Being strategically situated, the leadership entrenches itself by controlling information, manipulating rewards and punishments, and mobilizing resources to defeat rivals. Even worse, the entrenched leadership uses the organization to promote its own agenda at the expense of the membership.

One response would be to eschew all proposals to organize in favor of anarchy, but that is extreme. The better and deeper lesson is to take into account at the outset all predictable regularities, at which time it may be possible to mitigate foreseeable oligarchical excesses at the initial design stage. Thus although the oligarchical propensities of organization may have been poorly understood by everybody until Michels clarified the issue, oligarchical outcomes should not surprise serious practitioners and students of organization once the Iron Law of Oligarchy becomes common knowledge. Today's organizational designers presumably take this into account in the design calculus.

Inasmuch, however, as our knowledge of the intertemporal transformations to which organizations are given is still primitive, some outcomes will still come as a surprise. What efficiency properties are to be ascribed to these?

One response is to accept all with resignation as the best that can be done. That has a lot to recommend it, but another is to object when an egregiously inefficient result materializes. That is my recommendation, subject

10. Although the merits of that framework have been disputed (Posner, 1975b, p. 821), the general approach, if not the framework itself, has since been employed by others. Joe Bain was among the first to acknowledge the merits of an economies defense in assessing mergers (1968, p. 658). Wesley Liebeler (1978), Robert Bork (1978), and Timothy Muris (1979) all made extensive use of the partial equilibrium trade-off model in their insistence that antitrust enforcement that proceeds heedless of trade-offs is uninformed and contrary to the social interest. The *Merger Guidelines* now treat economies in a favorable way.

to the following qualification: Because some degree of ex post inefficiency is unavoidable and because claims of inefficiency are made strategically, the threshold for egregious inefficiency should be set very high. Capture is a specific case in point.

Marver Bernstein (1955) described the transformation of the independent regulatory commissions that had been created during the New Deal. Good intentions were ascribed to these commissions at the outset, and many have served and do serve useful purposes.[11]

Realizations, however, often differ from declared intentions.[12] A systematic factor contributing to this disparity is that the continuing relations between the industries to be regulated and the regulatory agencies are so close, the exchange of personnel so common, and the comparative disadvantage of unorganized consumers to influence outcomes so great that the inevitable happened: In varying degrees, the commissions have become captive to the industries.

Although capture may not have been foreseeable in the 1930s,[13] such errors should not be repeated twenty and forty years later. What once was unforeseeable has become fully anticipated. Indeed, Stigler (1971) took the argument a step further: Industries that expect to capture the process and become net beneficiaries will actively seek to be regulated—under the guise, to be sure, of the public interest. Assuming, moreover, that all the interests eventually come to understand the nature of the game that is being played, we will end up with an unimprovable (hence efficient) result (Becker, 1983).[14]

11. This is an empirical question and should be decided by examining the data. Consider Stigler's interesting assessment of the impact of the Securities and Exchange Commission. He describes the basic test as "simplicity itself. . . . We take all the new issues of industrial stocks with a value exceeding $2.5 million in 1923–28, and exceeding $5 million in 1949–55, and measure the values of these issues . . . in five subsequent years . . . relative to the market average" (1964a, p. 120). The pre-SEC versus post-SEC performance of new issues in relation to the market at one-year intervals is as follows (in which the first figure is the pre-SEC mean and the second is post-SEC after one year): 81.9 versus 81.6; after two years 65.1 versus 73.3; after three years, 56.2 versus 72.6; after four years 52.8 versus 71.9; and after five years, 58.5 versus 69.6.

Stigler declares that since these differences are statistically significant only in the third and fourth years, the SEC had no effect. Inasmuch, however, as tests of statistical significance are unneeded when, as in Stigler's case, the attributes of entire populations, rather than samples thereof, are measured, the data can be interpreted very differently: Except for the first year, the SEC had a beneficial effect in all years.

12. A recent example of what was thought initially to be a good idea that turned out otherwise is the "Pioneer Policy" adopted by the FCC with the endorsement of its general counsel, Henry Geller. The Pioneer Policy has had the effect of awarding free licenses valued at $250 million to high-technology start-ups. Unsurprisingly, this has led to "indefatigable lobbying," and Geller now says he "made a mistake." See Peter Passell, "F.C.C. 'Pioneer' Policy Under Attack," *New York Times,* January 31, 1994, p. C1.

13. That may be a naive assessment. Regulated industries always have a hand in the design of agencies and should be presumed to be farsighted players. (Clinton's reform of health care raised precisely these issues.)

14. Assuming that a producer interest group has the incentive and ability to organize collectively, the question is not whether it will organize, but how. One way to organize would be to create an association or cartel. A second way would be through a regulatory commission. Capture notwithstanding, the interests of consumers (as well as the producer interest group) could well converge on the regulatory solution.

Accordingly, those who protest capture are merely poor losers: Having lost the ex ante political competition, they are seeking ex post relief by claiming that a fully foreseeable result (capture) could not reasonably have been anticipated—the rhetoric of "good intentions" from the *Congressional Record* being offered as evidence.

Although the rationality logic out of which Stigler and Becker operate is very strong, the proposition that politics is played knowledgeably by strategic actors has a great deal to recommend it. Even, however, if we grant that foreseeable capture is the main case, some realizations may be so offensive—beyond even the worst imagined scenario—as to be declared unacceptable. For example, an underground industry may emerge that operates side by side with the regulated industry but is run by criminals. And there may be other outcomes that are deemed to be the unacceptable consequences of an evolved and entrenched structure, corruption in law enforcement being an example. Bureaucracy being what it is, however, some entrenchment and some corruption (later, if not sooner) should be expected. Corruption that cannot be rectified with net gains is, by definition, irremediable.[15]

4.1.3. Setup costs

Although it could be argued that redistribution will cease as soon as its political support wanes, this assumes that potential rivals and established programs are on a parity. Clearly, however, established programs enjoy the benefits of an infrastructure that is in place and working, and bureaucrats whose job it is to administer programs rarely have a neutral view about abolishing their jobs. Would-be rival programs incur setup costs: Rivals need to organize, which entails finding out who their supporters and potential leaders are; they need to assemble resources and work out routines, which requires learning; and they need to persuade political "investors" that there is not only merit in the project but also net gains.

The problem is instantly recognized as the public-sector counterpart of the "first-mover advantages" that arise in private-sector competition. As it is in the private sector, so it is in the public sector: Some of these advantages accrue naturally and are not objectionable, but others are due to strategic

---

In any event, the choice is between feasible alternatives, of which benign alternatives are not included. All perceived cost-effective deals will be made.

15. Note in this connection that feasible superior alternatives that are blocked by the political process—hence cannot be implemented—are irremediable. In that event, only a political reform can accomplish structural change. Experience teaches that genuine reform is a rare event.

Awaiting political reform, demands to "clean up corruption" can frequently be defused and defeated by creating "investigative commissions" that look into wrongdoing in a deliberative way. Wily politicians and their benefactors ascribe worthy purposes to these efforts, and the fact that this strategy works repeatedly suggests that intergenerational learning across voters and journalists is very limited. A few years and a few conspicuous prosecutions later, the structure survives and business as usual (corruption) continues. See James Lardner's examination of recurrent corruption in the New York City Police Department in "The Whistle-Blower-Part II," *The New Yorker,* July 12, 1993, pp. 39–58.

behavior. Efforts to raise political barriers to entry well above those that would obtain in the normal course of events are especially reprehensible.

The question then is whether meaningful criteria can be devised by which to recognize when current beneficiaries of redistribution have become entrenched by egregiously manipulating the political process to the disadvantage of later generations. That is a difficult and, as yet, unanswered question. Except for the political defects mentioned later, I am not hopeful.

4.1.4. Initial conditions

Intertemporal disadvantages that can be attributed not to historical accident (e.g., who happened to be there first and therefore got a head start) but to unacceptable initial conditions are the concern here. Specifically, what is to be done if those who are made to pay were excluded from parity participation at the time that a redistribution program was first approved? Given the aforementioned first-mover advantages of established programs, such programs are resistant to subsequent undoing when renewal is considered, even though those who were previously excluded (or otherwise disadvantaged) may not possess a political voice.

The prior restriction of voting rights (de jure or de facto) to women and minorities are obvious cases for which redress might be warranted. Again, however, the right to redress needs to be restricted. The right would be much more compelling if those who were previously denied participation in politics were observed to bear a disproportionate share of the burdens.

An especially troublesome case is that of future generations (Brennan and Buchanan, 1985). Minors are always denied the franchise yet, under pay-as-you-go systems (as opposed to insurance systems), are expected to pay the retirement benefits created by their elders. When does an intergenerational "deal" exceed the bounds of reason and become abuse?

4.2. The Sugar Program

Recall that Stigler used the time-tested sugar program to critique the orthodox conclusion that the deadweight losses of redistribution imply inefficiency. Conceivably, however, his cryptic description of the sugar program missed serious defects. Anne Krueger's more detailed review (1990) of the political economy of sugar controls is therefore pertinent.

A recurrent theme in Krueger's examination of the sugar program is that complex programs designed to benefit economic interests through price and quantity controls take on a "life of their own" (1990, p. 212). They evolve in unimaginable ways in which parties err, learn, and strategize and outcomes are partly the adventitious product of political happenstance. Among her salient observations are these:

1. "[O]nce created, a policy instrument will: (a) be seized upon by groups who perceive themselves to benefit (regardless of whether they had anything to do with initiating the programme or not); (b) induce economic market

reactions which will minimize the costs of the programme; (c) lead to political responses to (b) by the groups formed under (a) to attempt to offset these economic market reactions, which in turn will lead to (d) increasingly complex policy instruments designed both to deal with the competing interest groups that form around the policy instrument and simultaneously to subvert the sorts of market responses perceived to be detrimental" (pp. 209–10).

2. The complexities of the sugar program were great and conferred benefits on those who "learned the intricacies" and whose "human capital would have depreciated sharply had the programme been greatly simplified or eliminated" (p. 208).

3. Outsiders were disadvantaged by both their lack of nuanced understanding of the program and the "technocratic element" by which "people moved back and forth between administering the programme and lobbying for it" (p. 190).

4. The sugar program was institutionally "unusual" in several respects. For one thing, "there is the anomaly (for the American Congress) that sugar legislation was handled by the Senate Finance Committee (because it is an import) and the House Agriculture Committee (by historical accident). Moreover, because it was an import and thus had revenue implications, only the House had the power to initiate legislation. This gave the House Agriculture Committee considerably more power over sugar than it would have had the counterpart body been the Senate Agriculture Committee, and the House Agriculture Committee had considerably more ability to focus its attention on sugar than would the House Ways and Means Committee" (p. 208). The fact, moreover, that sugar was used as an instrument of foreign policy (especially in relation to Cuba) was a further complication (p. 209).

5. Although deficiency payments would have accomplished the redistribution at far less cost, the sugar growers were opposed, possibly because they were concerned "that a ceiling would be placed on the size of the payment that might be made to any individual farm" (Krueger, 1990, p. 204).

Given this history, should one conclude that the sugar program was so egregiously flawed that the Stigler's efficiency verdict is incorrect? I would be reluctant to reach that result, but others might not. After all, the deadweight losses as a fraction of the total are especially large; the program evolved in an unusually convoluted way; and the congressional oversights are unique and arguably defective.

This last is an especially troublesome point, but it is not, in my judgment, dispositive. Lacking more, I would describe the sugar program as a close call. Although that may be too timid and/or permissive, to register a close call is not without purpose. For one thing, programs that are judged to be close calls will presumably be operated more circumspectly thereafter. Also, if many programs are of a close-call kind, then the case for general reform will become more compelling.

Setting the latter aside, the lesson for particular reform is that the action resides in the details. Deadweight losses notwithstanding, if a program of redistribution is regularly renewed, then opponents should support their claims of inefficiency by displays of organizational or political failures. In a reasonably well working system—one that may warrant particular but not general reform—that is an exercise in microanalytics.

5. Conclusions

The concept of remediableness has a long history. Both E. A. G. Robinson (1934) and Harold Demsetz (1969) made perceptive reference to the analytical poverty of "nirvana economics," which entailed comparisons of actual forms of organization with ideals. As observed earlier, hypothetical ideals are operationally irrelevant. Within the feasible subset, the relevant test is whether (1) an alternative can be described that (2) can be implemented with (3) expected net gains. This is the remediableness criterion.

Robinson used the concept of remediableness to critique the concept of the ideal firm advanced by Nicholas Kaldor (1934). Coase and Demsetz used remediableness to critique noncomparative assessments of market failure. More recent examples in which inefficiency claims are made without reference to a remediableness test are the purported advantages of worker-managed firms[16] and the purported inefficiencies that accrue to path dependency.[17] This chapter examines yet another source of inefficiency, namely, inefficiencies ascribed to politics, as revealed by the deadweight losses of redistribution.

16. John Bonin and Louis Putterman ascribe benefits to the worker-managed form of organization by assuming that the worker-managed firm can replicate the private enterprise in all relevant respects and experiences no cost of capital disadvantage (1987, p. 2). For a critique, see Williamson, 1993e, pp. 144–46. D. M. Nuti (1989) also described financial reforms under market socialism by appealing to benign governance. See Williamson, 1991b, for a critique.

17. Brian Arthur (1989) illustrated path dependency with a numerical example in which the payoffs to individual firms on adopting either of two technologies (A or B) depend on the number of prior adoptions of each. Technology A has a higher payoff than B does if there are few prior adoptions, but the advantage switches to technology B if there have been many prior adoptions. The "problem" is that if each potential adopter consults only its own immediate net gain, then each will select A, and there will be a "lock-in" to an inferior technology. A tyranny of micromotives thereby obtains (Schelling, 1978).

As S. J. Liebowitz and Stephen Margolis observed in regard to this argument, however, whether or not the choice of technology A is inefficient depends on what assumptions are made about the state of knowledge (1992, p. 15). Also, even if one could assume that individual parties know that technology B would become the more efficient choice after thirty or fifty adoptions, the added costs of collective action to deter individuals from choosing technology A would need to be taken into account. If it is unrealistic to assume that individuals possess the relevant knowledge that a switchover (from A to B) will occur after thirty or fifty adoptions or if, given that knowledge, the costs of orchestrating collective action are prohibitive, then the inefficiency in question is effectively irremediable through private ordering.

Similar considerations apply to politics. Thus even in the fullness of time, if it becomes "obvious" that redistributional program B would have been superior to redistributional program A, that may have been anything but obvious ex ante. Rather, politicians should be assumed to choose as best they can. Claims of inefficiency that can be recognized only after the fact and/or that cannot be implemented with net gains have no operational importance.

Although the relentless application of marginal analysis and, more generally, of calculativeness is sometimes excessive (Simon, 1978; Williamson, 1993a), applications of the economic approach—a "rational spirit" in combination with "systems analysis"—do usefully inform a wide variety of noneconomic phenomena. Contrary to widespread opinion, moreover, the result is not always one of economic imperialism.

Stigler's application of economic reasoning to politics is an illustration. According to Stigler, politically approved projects that carry large deadweight losses should be regarded as unobjectionable if they have passed the "test of time." This crude criterion could be contested both in general and as it applies to particular cases.

The general objection to this criterion is that economics trumps politics: Economics is scientific and objective, whereas politics is haphazard and myopic. If, however, the game of politics is commonly played by well-informed and deeply strategic actors (special interests, politicians and their staffs) who perceive and intend most realized effects, then politics is intentional. If, moreover, economics is the servant of politics, then politics trumps economics when these two are in apparent conflict.

Without a general case for reforming the political system (because it lacks egregious defects),[18] the focus shifts to defects associated with particular outcomes. Objections of either organizational or political kinds can be presented. As it turns out, convincing displays of organizational or political defects of a program-specific kind are hard to make. If, however, neither egregious organizational nor political breakdowns can be ascribed to a political program, then programs that have passed the test of time should be presumed to be the product of a system that is doing what it was designed to do. The result is that while awaiting a more successful demonstration that the defects are more numerous and more serious than I have been able to show, the test of time turns out to be a robust criterion, more robust than I had initially projected.

The widely denounced Proposition 13, which is held to be responsible for much of what ails state and local government in California, is an example. Because vastly different taxes are imposed on side-by-side properties that are substantially identical, a lawsuit was brought that challenged the constitutionality of Proposition 13. Not only did blatant inequities result, but older home owners had incentives to make massive but inefficient home improvements rather than purchase new properties. The U.S. Supreme Court ruled against the suit, and Justice Harry Blackmun observed that the proposition was serving the purposes for which it was intended.[19] That is an unhappy decision for

18. Things change when we turn from developed to less-developed economies. The World Bank, AID, and other development agencies may be able to strike deals in which political reform is made the price of receiving assistance. Assuming that the reform is well conceived, that is altogether felicitous. This chapter applies entirely to developed economies, for which such bargains are normally out of reach.

19. *Nordlinger* v. *Hahn,* 112 S. Ct. 2326 (1992) 2333–36.

those who have recently purchased homes in California. But it is a principled decision and is respectful of politics.

The core arguments of this chapter are the following:

1. To show that redistribution experiences deadweight losses in relation to a hypothetical ideal is, without more, operationally irrelevant.

2. Even, moreover, to show that an extant redistribution program experiences economic losses in relation to a feasible alternative is not dispositive. The possibility that extant programs service valued political purposes that are not picked up by the economic calculus is the missing element and needs to be factored in.

3. More generally, economics needs to make express provision for both organization and politics. The market failure and antitrust literatures have come to terms with the proposition that organization matters. Redistribution needs to come to terms with politics. The study of redistribution, like the study of economic organization more generally, is an exercise in comparative institutional analysis in which the action resides in the microanalytics.[20]

A Postscript

As developed in the text, there are many parallels between the transaction cost economics treatment of private sector contracting and public sector contracting. For one thing, practices of both kinds are evaluated not with reference to a hypothetical ideal but in terms of feasible alternatives. Also, because of intertemporal contracting hazards, apparent "inefficiencies by design" can arise in each. And the display of large deadweight losses poses a challenge to public policy as it applies to both (private sector) antitrust enforcement and (public sector) redistribution. A reader of this chapter has nevertheless correctly observed that my analysis of political programs differs from that of private programs in that the feasible alternatives for implementing redistribution programs are less fully developed.

One way of redressing this is to think about the three redistribution mechanisms schemes that I briefly describe in Section 3—mode A (direct redistribution), mode B (indirect redistribution with weak ties), and mode C (indirect redistribution with strong ties)—as roughly corresponding to market, hybrid, and hierarchical mechanisms of private sector governance, respectively. Moreover, just as movements from simpler private sector governance to more complex are attended by added costs and must be justified by added (economic) benefits, correspondingly the movement from simpler redistributional programs to more complex programs is attended by added costs for which added (political) benefits should obtain. Accordingly, mode C redistribution becomes the redistributional mode of last resort—which recalls the parallel private sector argument in Chapter 4: Try markets, try hybrids, and employ hierarchy only as a matter of last resort.

20. For a related transaction cost economics treatment of politics that concludes similarly, see Arinash Dixit (1995).

To be sure, these correspondences are imperfect. They nevertheless suggest a follow-on research program, the object of which is to identify and explicate the attributes that distinguish alternative modes of redistribution. Such an effort would be akin to the dimensionalization of private sector governance set out in Chapter 4.

Note, moreover, that indirect redistributional mechanisms with strong ties (mode C) signal highly politicized forms of redistribution. That may be politics as usual, but those who are monitoring and reporting on the political process should be alert to the possibility that these are problematic programs of redistribution.

III

ORGANIZATIONS

The two chapters in Part III concern issues in which economics and organization are joined. Chapter 9 relates transaction cost economics to organization theory; and Chapter 10 deals with the elusive notion of trust.

Having benefited from organization theory since my years as a Ph.D. candidate at Carnegie, I knew that transaction cost economics owes a huge debt to organization theory. But the relation between transaction cost economics and organization theory has also generated controversy.[1] My initial inclination, when I started working on Chapter 9, was to emphasize the contested terrain. The first draft was thus entitled "Transaction Cost Economics *Meets* Organization Theory."

The revised title is less adversarial: "Transaction Cost Economics and Organization Theory." As the chapter shows, transaction cost economics has been the beneficiary of and offers value to organization theory. But there are still occasional (and arguably productive) collisions on this two-way street.

Because opportunism is such a controversial behavior assumption and is responsible for many of the tensions between transaction cost economics and organization theory, I take the opportunity here to add a few clarifying remarks. As I see it, the choice between alternative statements of self-interest seeking—in particular, the choice between the "frailties of motive," to which Herbert Simon referred (1985, p. 303), and opportunism, defined as self-interest seeking with guile—need not be addressed in mutually exclusive terms. Rather, the issue is which description best applies to which circumstances.

---

1. See the exchange among Charles Perrow and myself and William Ouchi in Andrew Van de Ven and William Joyce, 1981. Also see the volume edited by Arthur Francis, Jeremy Turk and Paul Willman (1983). Mark Granovetter's 1985 prize-winning essay is especially notable.

If the question is which of these two best describes day-to-day activity most of the time, I believe that frailty of motive is descriptively more accurate. Most people do what they say (and some do more) without self-consciously asking whether the effort is justified by expected discounted net gains. If they slip, it is a normal friction and often a matter of bemusement.

Suppose, however, that we ask another question: Which assumption better takes us into the deep structure of economic organization? Specifically, if our concern is not with day-to-day affairs but with long-term contractual relations, how should we proceed?

The object now is to look ahead, perceive hazards, and fold these back into the organizational design, in all significant contractual contexts whatsoever (intermediate product market, labor market, capital market, etc.). Robert Michels's concluding remarks about oligarchy are pertinent: "Nothing but a serene and frank examination of the oligarchical dangers of democracy will enable us to minimize these dangers" (1962, p. 370). If a serene and frank reference to opportunism alerts us to avoidable dangers that the more benign reference to frailties of motive would not do, then there are real hazards in the more benevolent construction.

This same general concern carries over to the use by social scientists of other user-friendly terms, of which trust is one. The growing tendency to use trust to describe probabilistic events from which the expected net gains from cooperation are perceived to be positive seems to me to be inadvisable. Not only does the use of familiar terms (like trust) invite us to draw mistaken parallels between personal and commercial experience, but user-friendly terms do not encourage us to examine the deep structure of organization. Rather, we need to understand when credible commitments add value and how to create them, when reputation effects work well, when poorly, and why. Trust glosses over, rather than helps unpack, the relevant microanalytic features and mechanisms. As developed in Chapter 10, "Calculativeness, Trust, and Economic Organization," a calculative approach to economic organization helps unpack these and other issues.

To be sure, this could be contested. One response is that social scientists (especially economists) are too cynical and should use softer concepts, thereby enlarging their understanding of complex organization. Less, rather than more, calculativeness is needed. Put differently, calculativeness is the problem rather than the solution.

For example, some economists have been heard to say—partly in jest but not entirely—that "the only reliable human motive is avarice." I would agree that this takes calculativeness to excess. I further agree that we need to provide for all significant regularities, formal and informal, direct and indirect, hard and soft. The calculative approach need not, however, be myopic or dysfunctional. Adopting a farsighted, calculative approach to commercial contracting is what we need if we are to build up the scientific vocabulary for organizations to which Simon made early reference (1957a, p. xiv).

9

Transaction Cost Economics and Organization Theory

1. Introduction

Economic and sociological approaches to economic organization have reached a state of healthy tension. That is to be contrasted with an earlier state of affairs in which the two approaches were largely disjunct, hence ignored one another, or described each other's research agendas and research accomplishments with disdain (Swedberg, 1990, p. 4). Healthy tension involves genuine give-and-take. Neither the obsolescence of organization theory, to which Charles Perrow has recently alluded (1992, p. 162), nor the capitulation of economics, to which James March (tongue-in-cheek) remarks,[1] is implied.

A more respectful relation, perhaps even a sense that economics and organization are engaged in a joint venture, is evident in W. Richard Scott's remark that "while important areas of disagreement remain, more consensus exists than is at first apparent" (1992, p. 3), in game theorist David Kreps's contention that "almost any theory of organization which is addressed by game theory will do more for game theory than game theory will do for it" (1992, p. 1), and in my argument that a science of organization is in progress in which law, economics, and organization are joined.[2]

Joint ventures sometimes evolve into mergers and sometimes unravel. I do not expect that either will happen here. That merger is not in prospect is because economics, organization theory, and law have separate as well as combined agendas. A full-blown merger, moreover, would impoverish the evolving science of organization—which has benefitted from the variety of insights that are revealed by the use of different lenses. I expect that the joint venture will hold until one of the parties has learned enough from the others

---

1. James March advised the Fourth International Conference of the Society for the Advancement of Socio-Economics that economics had been so fully reformed that the audience should 'declare victory and go home' (Coughlin, 1992, p. 23).

2. Richard Posner comes out differently. He argues that "organization-theory ... [adds] nothing to economics that the literature on information economics had not added years earlier" (1993a, p. 84).

to go it alone. Progress attended by controversy is what I project for the remainder of the decade.

This chapter focuses on connections between transaction cost economics and organization theory and argues that a three-part relation is taking shape. The first and most important of these is that transaction cost economics has been (and will continue to be) massively influenced by concepts and empirical regularities that have their origins in organization theory. Secondly, I sketch the key concepts out of which transaction cost economics works to which organization theorists can (and many do) productively relate. But thirdly, healthy tension survives—as revealed by an examination of phenomena for which rival interpretations have been advanced, remain unsolved, and provoke controversy.

I begin this paper with some background on institutional economics, both old and new. A three-level schema for studying economic organization is proposed in Section 3. Some of the more important ways in which transaction cost economics has benefitted from organization theory are examined in Section 4. The key concepts in transaction cost economics are sketched in Section 5. Empirical regularities, as discerned through the lens of transaction cost economics, that are pertinent to organization theory are discussed in Section 6. Contested terrain is surveyed in Section 7. Concluding remarks follow.

2. Institutional Economics

2.1. Older Traditions

Leading figures in the older institutional economics movement in the United States were Wesley Mitchell, Thorstein Veblen, and John R. Commons. Although many sociologists appear to be sympathetic with the older tradition, there is growing agreement that the approach was "largely descriptive and historically specific" (DiMaggio and Powell, 1991, p. 2) and was not cumulative (Granovetter, 1988, p. 8). Criticisms of the old institutional economics by economists have been scathing (Stigler, 1983, p. 170; Coase, 1984, p. 230; Matthews, 1986, p. 903).

My general agreement with these assessments notwithstanding, I would make an exception for John R. Commons. Not only is the institutional economics tradition at Wisconsin still very much alive (Bromley, 1989), but also the enormous public policy influence of Commons and his students and colleagues deserves to be credited. Andrew Van de Ven's summary of Commons's intellectual contributions is pertinent to the first of these:

> Especially worthy of emphasis [about Commons] are his (a) dynamic views
> of institutions as a response to scarcity and conflicts of interest, (b) original
> formulation of the transaction as the basic unit of analysis, (c) part-whole
> analysis of how collective action constrains, liberates, and expands individual
> action in countless numbers of routine and complementary transactions on
> the one hand, and how individual wills and power to gain control over limiting
> or contested factors provide the generative mechanisms for institutional
> change on the other, and (d) historical appreciation of how customs, legal

precedents, and laws of a society evolve to construct a collective standard of prudent reasonable behavior for resolving disputes between conflicting parties in pragmatic and ethical ways. (1993, p. 148).

Albeit in varying degree, transaction cost economics is responsive to Commons in *all four of these respects.*[3]

Commons and his colleagues and students were very influential in politics during and after the Great Depression—in shaping social security, labor legislation, public utility regulation, and, more generally, public policy toward business. Possibly because of its public policy successes, the Wisconsin School was remiss in developing its intellectual foundations. The successive operationalization—from informal into preformal, semiformal, and fully formal modes of analysis—that I associate with transaction cost economics (Williamson, 1993e) never materialized. Instead, the institutional economics of Commons progressed very little beyond the informal stage.

There is also an older institutional economics tradition in Europe. Of special importance was the German Historical School. (Interested readers are advised to consult Terrence Hutchison, 1984, and Richard Swedberg, 1991, for assessments.) And, of course, there were the great works of Karl Marx.

A later German School, the Ordoliberal or Freiburg School, also warrants remark. As discussed by Heinz Grossekettler (1989), this School was inspired by the work of Walter Eucken, whose student Ludwig Erhard was the German Minister of Economics from 1949 to 1963, Chancellor from 1963 to 1966, and is widely credited with being the political father of the "economic miracle" in West Germany. Grossekettler describes numerous parallels between the Ordoliberal program and those of Property Rights Theory, Transaction Cost Economics, and especially Constitutional Economics (1989, pp. 39, 64–67).

The Ordoliberal program proceeded at a very high level of generality (Grossekettler, 1989, p. 47) and featured the application of lawful principles to the entire economy (Grossekettler, 1989, pp. 46–57). Its great impact on postwar German economic policy notwithstanding, the influence of the School declined after the mid-1960s. Although Grossekettler attributes the decline to the "wide scale of acceptance of the Keynesian theory . . . [among] young German intellectuals" (1989, pp. 69–70), an additional problem is that the principles of Ordoliberal economics were never given operational content. Specific models were never developed; key trade-offs were never identified; the mechanisms remained very abstract. The parallels with the Wisconsin School—great public policy impact, underdeveloped conceptual framework, loss of intellectual influence—are striking.

---

3. Briefly, the transaction cost economics responses are: (i) institutions respond to scarcity as economizing devices, (ii) the transaction is expressly adopted as the basic unit of analysis, (iii) conflicts are recognized and relieved by the creation of credible commitments/*ex post* governance apparatus, and (iv) the institutional environment is treated as a set of shift parameters that change the comparative costs of governance. Although these may be incomplete responses, the spirit of the transaction cost economics enterprise nevertheless makes serious contact with Commons's prescription.

2.2. The New Institutional Economics

The new institutional economics comes in a variety of flavors and has been variously defined. The economics of property rights—as developed especially by Coase (1959, 1960), Armen Alchian (1961), and Harold Demsetz (1967)—was an early and influential dissent from orthodoxy. An evolutionary as opposed to a technological approach to economic organization was advanced, according to which new property rights were created and enforced as the economic needs arose, if and as these were cost effective.

The definition of ownership rights advanced by Eirik Furubotn and Svetozar Pejovich is broadly pertinent: "By general agreement, the right of ownership of an asset consists of three elements: (a) the right to use the asset ... , (b) the right to appropriate the returns from the asset ... , and (c) the right to change the asset's form and/or substance" (1974, p. 4). Strong claims on behalf of the property rights approach to economic organization were set out by Coase as follows:

> A private enterprise system cannot function unless property rights are created
> in resources, and when this is done, someone wishing to use a resource has
> to pay the owner to obtain it. Chaos disappears; and so does the government
> except that a legal system to define property rights and to arbitrate disputes
> is, of course, necessary. (1959, p. 14)

As it turns out, these claims overstate the case for the property rights approach. Not only is the definition of property rights sometimes costly—consider the difficult problems of defining intellectual property rights—but also court ordering can be a costly way to proceed. A comparative contractual approach rather than a pure property rights approach, therefore has a great deal to recommend it.

Although the earlier property rights approach and the more recent comparative contractual approach appear to be rival theories of organization, much of that tension is relieved by recognizing that the new institutional economics has actually developed in two complementary parts. One of these parts deal predominantly with background conditions (expanded beyond property rights to include contract laws, norms, customs, conventions, and the like) while the second branch deals with the mechanisms of governance.

What the economics of organization is predominantly concerned with is this: holding these background conditions constant, why organize economic activity one way (e.g., procure from the market) rather than another (e.g., produce to your own needs: hierarchy)?

3.   A Three-Level Schema

Transaction cost economics is mainly concerned with the governance of contractual relations. Governance does not, however, operate in isolation. The comparative efficacy of alternative modes of governance varies with the institutional environment on the one hand and the attributes of economic actors on the other. A three-level schema is therefore proposed, according to which the object of analysis, governance, is bracketed by more macro features (the institutional environment) and more micro features (the individual). Feedbacks aside (which are underdeveloped in the transaction cost economics set-up), the institutional environment is treated as the locus of shift parameters, changes in which shift the comparative costs of governance, and the individual is where the behavioral assumptions originate.

Roger Friedland and Robert Alford also propose a three-level schema in which environment, governance, and individual are distinguished, but their emphasis is very different. They focus on the individual and argue that the three levels of analysis are "nested, where organization and institution specify progressively higher levels of constraint and opportunity for individual action" (1991, p. 242).

The causal model proposed here is akin to and was suggested by, but is different from, the causal model recently proposed by W. Richard Scott (1992, p. 45), who is also predominantly concerned with governance. There are three main effects in my schema (see Figure 9.1). These are shown by the solid arrows. Secondary effects are drawn as dashed arrows. As indicated, the institutional environment defines the rules of the game. If changes in property rights, contract laws, norms, customs, and the like induce changes in the comparative costs of governance, then a reconfiguration of economic organization is usually implied.

The solid arrow from the individual to governance carries the behavioral assumptions within which transaction cost economics operates, and the circular arrow within the governance sector reflects the proposition that organization, like the law, has a life of its own. The latter is the subject of Section 3.

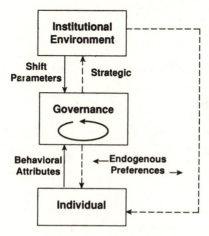

Figure 9.1. A layer schema.

Although behavioral assumptions are frequently scanted in economics, transaction cost economics subscribes to the proposition that economic actors should be described in workably realistic terms (Simon, 1978; Coase, 1984). Interestingly, "outsiders," especially physicists, have long been insistent that a better understanding of the actions of human agents requires more self-conscious attention to the study of how men's minds work (Bridgeman, 1955, p. 450; Waldrop, 1992, p. 142). Herbert Simon concurs:

> Nothing is more fundamental in setting our research agenda and informing our research methods than our view of the nature of the human beings whose behavior we are studying. It makes a difference, a very large difference, to our research strategy whether we are studying the nearly omniscient *Homo economicus* of rational choice theory or the boundedly rational *Homo psychologicus* of cognitive psychology. It makes a difference to research, but it also makes a difference for the proper design of political institutions. James Madison was well aware of that, and in the pages of the *Federalist Papers* he opted for this view of the human condition (*Federalist,* No. 55):
>
>> As there is a degree of depravity in mankind which requires a certain degree of circumspection and distrust, so there are other qualities in human nature which justify a certain portion of esteem and confidence.
>
> —a balanced and realistic view, we may concede, of bounded human rationality and its accompanying frailties of motive and reason. (1985, p. 303)

Transaction cost economics expressly adopts the proposition that human cognition is subject to bounded rationality—where this is defined as behavior that is "intendedly rational, but only limitedly so" (Simon, 1957a, p. xxiv)—but differs from Simon in its interpretation of the "degree of depravity" to which Madison refers.

Whereas Simon regards the depravity in question as "frailties of motive and reason," transaction cost economics describes it instead as opportunism—to include self-interest seeking with guile. The former is a much more benign interpretation, and many social scientists understandably prefer it. Consider, however, Robert Michels's concluding remarks about oligarchy: "nothing but a serene and frank examination of the oligarchical dangers of democracy will enable us to minimize these dangers" (1962, p. 370). If a serene and frank reference to opportunism alerts us to avoidable dangers which the more benign reference to frailties of motive and reason would not, then there are real hazards in adopting the more benevolent construction. As discussed in Section 5, below, the mitigation of opportunism plays a central role in transaction cost economics.

Opportunism can take blatant, subtle, and natural forms. The blatant form is associated with Niccolò Machiavelli. Because he perceived that the economic agents with whom the Prince was dealing were opportunistic, the Prince was advised to engage in reciprocal and even pre-emptive opportunism—to breach contracts with impugnity whenever "the reasons which made him bind himself no longer exist" (1952, p. 92). The subtle form is strategic and has been described elsewhere as "self-interest seeking with guile" (Williamson, 1975b, pp. 26–37; 1985b, pp. 46–52, 64–67). The natural form involves tilting the system at the margin. The so-called "dollar-a-year" men in the Office of Production Management, of which there were 250 at the beginning of World War II, were of concern to the Senate Special Committee to Investigate the National Defense Program because

> Such corporate executives in high official roles were too inclined to make decisions for the benefit of their corporations. "They have their own business at heart," [Senator] Truman remarked. The report called them lobbyists "in a very real sense," because their presence inevitably meant favoritism, "human nature being what it is" (McCullough, 1992, p. 265)

Michel Crozier's treatment of bureaucracy makes prominent provision for all forms of opportunism, which he describes as "the active tendency of the human agent to take advantage, in any circumstances, of all available means to further his own privileges" (1964, p. 194).

Feedback effects from governance to the institutional environment can be either instrumental or strategic. An example of the former would be an improvement in contract law, brought about at the request of parties who find that extant law is poorly suited to support the integrity of contract. Strategic changes could take the form of protectionist trade barriers against domestic and/or foreign competition. Feedback from governance to the level of the individual can be interpreted as "endogenous preference" formation (Bowles and Gintis, 1993), due to advertising or other forms of "education." The individual is also influenced by the environment, in that endogenous preferences are the product of social conditioning. Although transaction cost economics can often relate to these secondary effects, other modes of analysis are often more pertinent.

More generally, the Friedland and Alford scheme, the Scott scheme, and the variant that I offer are not mutually exclusive. Which to use when depends on the questions being asked. To repeat, the main case approach to economic organization that I have proposed works out of the heavy line causal relations shown in Figure 9.1, to which the dashed lines represent refinements.

4. The Value Added of Organization Theory

Richard Swedberg (1987, 1990), Robert Frank (1992), and others have described numerous respects in which economics has been influenced by sociology and organization theory. The value added to which I refer here deals only with those aspects where transaction cost economics has been a direct and significant beneficiary.

The behavioral assumptions to which I refer in Section 3 above—bounded rationality and opportunism—are perhaps the most obvious examples of how transaction cost economics has been shaped by organization theory. But the proposition that organization has a life of its own (the circular arrow in the governance box in Figure 9.1) is also important. And there are yet additional influences as well.

4.1. Intertemporal Process Transformations

Describing the firm as a production function invites an engineering approach to organization. The resulting "machine model" of organization emphasizes intended effects to the neglect of unintended effects (March and Simon, 1958, chap. 3). But if organizations have a life of their own, and if the usual economic approach is unable to relate to the intertemporal realities of organization, then—for some purposes at least—an extra-economic approach may be needed.

Note that I do not propose that the economic approach be abandoned. Rather, the "usual" or orthodox economic approach gives way to an augmented or extended economic approach. That is very different from adopting an altogether different approach—as, for example, that of neural networks.

As it turns out, the economic approach is both very elastic and very powerful. Because it is elastic and because increasing numbers of economists have become persuaded of the need to deal with economic organization" as it is," warts and all, all significant regularities whatsoever—intended and unintended alike—come within the ambit. Because it is very powerful, economics brings added value. Specifically, the "farsighted propensity" or "rational spirit" that economics ascribes to economic actors permits the analysis of previously neglected regularities to be taken a step further. Once the unanticipated consequences are understood, those effects will thereafter be anticipated and the ramifications can be folded back into the organizational design. Unwanted costs will then be mitigated and unanticipated benefits will be enhanced. Better economic performance will ordinarily result.

Unintended effects are frequently delayed and are often subtle. Deep knowledge of the details and intertemporal process transformations that attend organization is therefore needed. Because organization theorists have wider and deeper knowledge of these conditions, economists have much to learn and ought to be deferential. Four specific illustrations are sketched here.

4.1.1. Demands for control

A natural response to perceived failures of performance is to introduce added controls. Such efforts can have both intended and unintended consequences (Merton, 1936; Gouldner, 1954).

One illustration is the employment relation, where an increased emphasis on the reliability of behavior gives rise to added rules (March and Simon, 1958, pp. 38–40). Rules, however, serve not merely as controls but also define minimally acceptable behavior (Cyert and March, 1963). Managers who apply rules to subordinates in a legalistic and mechanical way invite "working to rules," which frustrates effective performance.

These unintended consequences are picked up by the wider peripheral vision of organization theorists. In the spirit of farsighted contracting, however, the argument can be taken yet a step further. Once apprised of the added consequences, the farsighted economist will make allowance for them by factoring these into the original organizational design. (Some organization theorists might respond that this last is fanciful and unrealistic. That can be decided by examining the data.)

4.1.2. Oligarchy

The Iron Law of Oligarchy holds that "It is organization which gives birth to the dominion of the elected over the electors, of the mandatories over the mandators, of the delegates over the delegators. Who says organization, says oligarchy" (Michels, 1962, p. 365). Accordingly, good intentions notwithstanding, the initial leadership (or its successors) will inevitably develop attachments for the office.

One response would be to eschew organization in favor of anarchy, but that is extreme. The better and deeper lesson is to take all predictable regularities into account at the outset, whereupon it may be possible to mitigate foreseeable oligarchical excesses at the initial design stage.[4]

4.1.3. Identity/capability

The proposition that identity matters has been featured in transaction cost economics from the outset. As developed in Section 6, below, identity is usually explained by some form of "asset specificity." The "capabilities" view of the firm (Penrose, 1959; Selznick, 1957; Wernerfelt, 1984; Teece et al., 1992) raises related but additional issues.

One way to unpack the "capabilities" view of the firm is to ask what—in addition to an inventory of its physical assets, an accounting for its financial assets, and a census of its workforce—is needed to describe the capabilities of a firm. Features of organization that are arguably important include the following: (i) the communication codes that the firm has developed (Arrow, 1974); (ii) the routines that it employs (Cyert and March, 1963; Nelson and

---

4. Oligarchy is usually applied to composite organization, but it applies to subdivisions as well. Whether a firm should make or buy is thus a matter for which oligarchy has a bearing. If the decision to take a transaction out of the market and organize it internally is attended by subsequent information distortions and subgoal pursuit, then that should be taken into account at the outset (Williamson, 1975, chap. 7; 1985b, chap. 6). Not only do operating costs rise but also a constituency develops that favors the renewal of internal facilities. An obvious response is to demand high hurdle rates for new projects, thereby to protect against the unremarked but predictable distortions (added costs; advocacy efforts) to which internal (as compared with market) procurement is differentially subject.

The argument applies to public sector projects as well. Because of the deferred and undisclosed but nevertheless predictable distortions to which "organization" is subject, new projects and regulatory proposals should be required to display large (apparent) net gains.

Winter, 1982); (iii) the corporate culture that has taken shape (Kreps, 1990b). What do we make of these?

One response is to regard these as spontaneous features of economic organization. As interpreted by institutional theory in sociology, "organizational structures, procedures, and decisions are *largely ritualistic and symbolic,* especially so when it is difficult or impossible to assess the efficacy of organizational decisions on the basis of their tangible outcomes" (Baron and Hannan, 1992, p. 57, emphasis added).

If, of course, efficiency consequences are impossible to ascertain, then intentionality has nothing to add. Increasingly, however, some of the subtle efficiency consequences of organization are coming to be better understood, whereupon they are (at least partly) subject to strategic determination. If the benefits of capabilities vary with the attributes of transactions, which arguably they do, then the cost effective thing to do is to *shape* culture, *develop* communication codes, and *manage* routines in a deliberative (transaction specific) way. Implementing the intentionality view will require that the microanalytic attributes that define culture, communication codes, and routines be uncovered, which is an ambitious exercise.

4.1.4. Bureaucratization

As compared with the study of market failure, the study of bureaucratic failure is underdeveloped. It is elementary that a well-considered theory of organization will make provision for failures of all kinds.

Albeit underdeveloped, the bureaucratic failure literature is vast, partly because purported failures are described in absolute rather than comparative terms. Unless, however, a superior and feasible form of organization to which to assign a transaction (or related set of transactions) can be identified, the failure in question is effectively irremediable. One of the tasks of transaction cost economics is to assess purported bureaucratic failures in comparative institutional terms.

The basic argument is this: it is easy to show that a particular hierarchical structure is beset with costs, but that is neither here nor there if all feasible forms of organization are beset with the same or equivalent costs. Efforts to ascertain bureaucratic costs that survive comparative institutional scrutiny are reported elsewhere (Williamson, 1975, chap. 7; 1985b, chap. 6), but these are very provisional and preliminary. Although intertemporal transformations and complexity are recurrent themes in the study of bureaucratic failure, much more concerted attention to these matters is needed.

4.2. Adaptation

As described in earlier chapters, the economist Friedrich Hayek maintained that the main problem of economic organization was that of adaptation and argued that this was realized spontaneously through the price system. The organization theorist Chester Barnard also held that adaptation was the central problem of organization. But whereas Hayek emphasized autonomous adaptation of a spontaneous kind, Barnard was concerned with cooperative adaptation of an intentional kind.

Transaction cost economics (i) concurs that adaptation is the central problem of economic organization; (ii) regards adaptations of both autonomous and cooperative kinds as important; (iii) maintains that whether adaptations to disturbances ought to be predominantly autonomous, cooperative, or a mixture thereof varies with the attributes of the transactions (especially on the degree to which the investments associated with successive stages of activity are bilaterally or multilaterally dependent); and (iv) argues that each generic form of governance—market, hybrid, and hierarchy—differs systematically in its capacity to adapt in autonomous and cooperative ways. A series of predicted (transaction cost economizing) alignments between transactions and governance structures thereby obtain (Williamson, 1991a), which predictions invite and have been subjected to empirical testing (Joskow, 1988; Klein and Shelanski, 1995; Masten, 1992).

4.3. Politics

Terry Moe (1990b) makes a compelling case for the proposition that public bureaucracies are different. Partly that is because the transactions that are assigned to the public sector are different, but Moe argues additionally that public sector bureaucracies are shaped by politics. Democratic politics requires compromises that are different in kind from those posed in the private sector and poses novel expropriation hazards. Added "inefficiencies" arise in the design of public agencies on both accounts.[5]

The inefficiencies that result from compromise and from political prepositioning are as described in Chapter 8.

4.4. Embeddedness and Networks

Gary Hamilton and Nicole Biggart take exception with the transaction cost economics interpretation of economic organization because it implicitly assumes that the institutional environment is everywhere the same; namely, that of Western democracies, and most especially that of the United States. They observe that large firms in East Asia differ from United States corporations

---

5. Politics really is different. But it is not as though there is no private sector counterpart. The more general argument is this: weak property rights regimes—both public and private—invite farsighted parties to provide added protection. The issues are discussed further in conjunction with remediableness (see Section 5.5 below).

Note, as a comparative institutional matter, that secure totalitarian regimes can, according to this logic, be expected to design more efficient public agencies. That is neither here nor there if democratic values are held to be paramount—in which event the apparent inefficiencies of agencies under a democracy are simply a cost of this form of governance.

in significant respects and explain that "organizational practices . . . are fashioned out of preexisting interactional patterns, which in many cases date to preindustrial times. Hence, industrial enterprise is a complex modern adaptation of pre-existing patterns of domination to economic situations in which profit, efficiency, and control usually form the very conditions of existence" (1988, p. S54).

The evidence that East Asian corporations differ is compelling. The argument, however, that transaction cost economics does not have application to East Asian economies goes too far.

The correct argument is that the institutional environment matters and that transaction cost economics, in its preoccupation with governance, has been neglectful of that. Treating the institutional environment as a set of shift parameters—changes in which induce shifts in the comparative costs of governance—is, to a first approximation at least, the obvious response (Williamson, 1991a). That is the interpretation advanced above and shown in Figure 9.1.

The objection could nevertheless be made that this is fine as far as it goes, but that comparative statics—which is a once-for-all exercise—does not go far enough. As Mark Granovetter observes, "More sophisticated . . . analyses of cultural influences . . . make it clear that culture is not a once-for-all influence but an *ongoing process,* continuously constructed and reconstructed during interaction. It not only shapes its members but is also shaped by them, in part for their own strategic reasons" (1985, p. 486).

I do not disagree, but I would observe that "more sophisticated analyses" must be judged by their value added. What are the deeper insights? What are the added implications? Are the effects in question really beyond the reach of economizing reasoning?

Consider, with reference to this last; the embeddedness argument that "concrete relations and structures" generate trust and discourage malfeasance of non-economic or extra-economic kinds:

> Better than a statement that someone is known to be reliable is information from a trusted informant that he has dealt with that individual and found him so. Even better is information from one's own past dealings with that person. This is better information for four reasons: (1) it is cheap; (2) one trust one's own information best—it is richer, more detailed, and known to be accurate; (3) individuals with whom one has a continuing relation have an economic motivation to be trustworthy, so as not to discourage future transactions; and (4) departing from pure economic motives, continuing economic relations often become overlaid with social content that carries strong expectations of trust and abstention from opportunism. (Granovetter, 1985, p. 490)

This last point aside, the entire argument is consistent with, and much of it has been anticipated by, transaction cost reasoning. Transaction cost economics and embeddedness reasoning are evidently complementary in many respects.

A related argument is that transaction cost economics is preoccupied with dyadic relations, whereupon network relations are given short shrift. The former is correct,[6] but the suggestion that network analysis is beyond the reach of transaction cost economics is too strong. For one thing, many of the network effects described by Ray Miles and Charles Snow (1992) correspond very closely to the transaction cost economics treatment of the hybrid form of economic organization (Williamson, 1983, 1991a). For another, as the discussion of Japanese economic organization (see Section 6.4, below) reveals, transaction cost economics can be and has been extended to deal with a richer set of network effects.

4.5. Discrete Structural Analysis

One possible objection to the use of maximization/marginal analysis is that "Parsimony recommends that we prefer the postulate that men are reasonable to the postulate that they are supremely rational when either of the two assumptions will do our work of inference as well as the other" (Simon, 1978, p. 8). But while one might agree with Simon that satisficing is more reasonable than maximizing, the analytical toolbox out of which satisficing works is, as compared with maximizing apparatus, incomplete and very cumbersome. Thus if one reaches the same outcome through the satisfying postulate as through maximizing, and if the latter is much easier to implement, then economists can be thought of as analytical satisficers: they use a short-cut form of analysis that is simple to implement. Albeit at the expense of realism in assumptions, maximization gets the job done.

A different criticism of marginal analysis is that this glosses over first-order effects of a discrete structural kind. Capitalism and socialism, for example, can be compared in both discrete structural (bureaucratization) and marginal analysis (efficient resource allocation) respects. Recall Oskar Lange's conjectured that, as between the two, bureaucratization posed a much more severe danger to socialism than did inefficient resource allocation (1938, p. 109).

That he was sanguine with respect to the latter was because he had derived the rules for efficient resource allocation (mainly of a marginal cost pricing kind) and was confident that socialist planners and managers could implement them. Joseph Schumpeter (1942) and Abram Bergson (1948) concurred. The study of comparative economic systems over the next fifty years was predominantly an allocative efficiency exercise.

Bureaucracy, by contrast, was mainly ignored. Partly that is because the study of bureaucracy was believed to be beyond the purview of economics and belonged to sociology (Lange, 1938, p. 109). Also, Lange held that "monopolistic capitalism" was beset by even more serious bureaucracy problems (p. 110). If, however, the recent collapse of the former Soviet Union is attribut-

---

6. Interdependencies among dyadic contracting relations and the possible manipulation thereof have, however, been examined (Williamson, 1985b, pp. 318–19). Also see the discussion of appropriability in Section 5.

able more to conditions of waste (operating inside the frontier) than to ineffi-cient resource allocation (operating at the wrong place on the frontier), then it was cumulative burdens of bureaucracy—goal distortions, slack, maladapta-tion, technological stagnation—that spelt its demise.

The lesson here is this: always study first-order (discrete structural) effects before examining second-order (marginalist) refinements. Arguably, more-over, that should be obvious: waste is easily a more serious source of welfare losses than are price induced distortions (cf. Harberger, 1954, with William-son, 1968b).

Simon advises similarly. Thus he contends that the main questions are

> Not "how much flood insurance will a man buy?" but "what are the structural conditions that make buying insurance rational or attractive?"
> Not "at what levels will wages be fixed" but "when will work be per-formed under an employment contract rather than a sales contract?" (1978, p. 6)

Friedland and Alford's recent treatment of institutions is also of a discrete structural kind. They contend that "Each of the most important institutional orders of contemporary Western societies has a central logic—a set of material practices and symbolic constructions—which constitutes its organizing princi-ples and which is available to organizations and individuals to elaborate" (1991, p. 248). Transaction cost economics concurs. But whereas Friedland and Alford are concerned with discrete structural logics between institutional orders—capitalism, the state, democracy, the family, etc.—transaction cost economics maintains that distinctive logics within institutional orders also need to be distinguished. Within the institutional order of capitalism, for example, each generic mode of governance—market, hybrid, and hierar-chy—possesses its own logic and distinctive cluster of attributes. Of special importance is the proposition that each generic mode of governance is sup-ported by a distinctive form of contract law (see Chapter 4).

5. Transaction Cost Economics, the Strategy

The transaction cost economics program for studying economic organization has been described elsewhere (Williamson, 1975, 1981a, 1985b, 1988d, 1991a; Klein, Crawford, and Alchian, 1978; Alchian and Woodward, 1987; Davis and Powell, 1992). My purpose here is to sketch the general strategy that is em-ployed by transaction cost economics, with the suggestion that organization theorists could adopt (some already have adopted) parts of it.

The five-part strategy that I describe entails (i) a main case orientation (transaction cost economizing), (ii) choice and explication of the unit of analy-sis, (iii) a systems view of contracting, (iv) rudimentary trade-off apparatus, and (v) a remediableness test for assessing "failures."

5.1. The Main Case

Economic organization being very complex and our understanding being primitive, there is a need to sort the wheat from the chaff. I propose for this purpose that each rival theory of organization should declare the *main case* out of which it works and develop the *refutable implications* that accrue thereto.

Transaction cost economics holds that economizing on transaction costs is mainly responsible for the choice of one form of capitalist organization over another. It thereupon applies this hypothesis to a wide range of phenomena—vertical integration, vertical market restrictions, labor organization, corporate governance, finance, regulation (and deregulation), conglomerate organization, technology transfer, and, more generally, to any issue that can be posed directly or indirectly as a contracting problem. As it turns out, large numbers of problems which on first examination do not appear to be of a contracting kind turn out to have an underlying contracting structure—the oligopoly problem (Williamson, 1975, chap. 12) and the organization of the company town (Williamson, 1985b, pp. 35–38) being examples. Comparisons with other—rival or complementary—main case alternatives are invited.

Three of the older main case alternatives are that economic organization is mainly explained by (i) technology, (ii) monopolization, and (iii) efficient risk bearing. More recent main case candidates are (iv) contested exchange between labor and capital, (v) other types of power arguments (e.g., resource dependency), and (vi) path dependency. My brief responses to the first three are that (i) technological non-separabilities and indivisibilities explain only small groups and, at most, large plants, but explain neither multiplant organization nor the organization of technologically separable groups/activities (which should remain autonomous and which should be joined), (ii) monopoly explanations require that monopoly preconditions be satisfied, but most markets are competitively organized, and (iii) although differential risk aversion may apply to many employment relationships, it has much less applicability to trade between firms (where portfolio diversification is more easily accomplished and where smaller firms ([for incentive intensity and economizing, but not risk bearing, reasons] are often observed to bear inordinate risk). Responses to the last three are developed more fully below. My brief responses are these: (iv) the failures to which contested exchange refers are often irremediable, (v) resource dependency is a truncated theory of contract, and (vi) although path dependency is an important phenomenon, remediable inefficiency is rarely established.

To be sure, transaction cost economizing does not always operate smoothly or quickly. Thus we should "expect [transaction cost economizing] to be most clearly exhibited in industries where entry is [easy] and where the struggle for survival is [keen]" (Koopmans, 1957, p. 141).[7] Transaction cost economics

7. The statement is a weakened variant on Tjalling Koopmans. Where he refers to "profit maximization," "easiest," and "keenest." I have substituted transaction cost economizing, easy, and keen.

nevertheless maintains that later, if not sooner, inefficiency in the commercial sector invites its own demise—all the more so as international competition has become more vigorous. Politically imposed impediments (tariffs, quotas, subsidies, rules) can and have, however, delayed the reckoning[8] and disadvantaged parties (railroad workers, longshoremen, managers) may also be able to delay changes unless compensated by buyouts.

The economizing to which I refer operates through weak-form selection (Simon, 1983, p. 69)[9] and works through a private net benefit calculus. That suits the needs of positive economics—What's going on out there?—rather well, but public policy needs to be more circumspect. As discussed below, the relevant test of whether public policy intervention is warranted is that of remediableness.

These important qualifications notwithstanding, transaction cost economics maintains that economizing is mainly determinative of private sector economic organization and, as indicated, invites comparison with rival main case hypotheses.

5.2.   Unit of Analysis

A variety of units of analysis have been proposed to study economic organization. Simon has proposed that the *decision premise* is the appropriate unit of analysis (1957a, pp. xxx–xxxii). *"Ownership"* is the unit of analysis for the economics of property rights. The *industry* is the unit of analysis in the structure–conduct–performance approach to industrial organization (Bain, 1956; Scherer, 1970). The *individual* has been nominated as the unit of analysis by positive agency theory (Jensen, 1983). Transaction cost economics follows John R. Commons (1924, 1934) and takes the *transaction* to be the basic unit of analysis.

Whatever unit of analysis is selected, the critical dimensions with respect to which that unit of analysis differs need to be identified. Otherwise the unit

8. Joel Mokyr observes that resistance to innovation "occurred in many periods and places but seems to have been neglected by most historians" (1990, p. 178). He nevertheless gives a number of examples in which established interests, often with the use of the political process, set out to defeat new technologies. In the end, however, the effect was not to defeat but to delay machines that pressed pinheads, an improved slide rest lathe, the ribbon loom, the flying shuttle, the use of arabic numerals, and the use of the printing press (Mokyr, 1990, pp. 178–79). That, of course, is not dispositive. There may be many cases in which superior technologies were in fact defeated—of which the typewriter keyboard (see Section 7, below) is purportedly an example. Assuming, however, that the appropriate criterion for judging superiority is that of remediableness (see below), I register grave doubts that significance technological or organizational efficiencies can be delayed indefinitely.

9. The Schumpeterian process of "handing on"—which entails "a fall in the price of the product to the new level of costs" (Schumpeter, 1947, p. 155) and purportedly works whenever rivals are alert to new opportunities and are not prevented by purposive restrictions from adopting them—is pertinent. The efficacy of handing on varies with the circumstances. When are rivals *more* alert? What are the underlying information assumptions? Are there other capital market and/or organizational concerns?

will remain non-operational. Also, a paradigm problem to which the unit of analysis applies needs to be described. Table 9.1 sets out the relevant comparisons.

As shown, the representative problem with which transaction cost economics deals is that of vertical integration—when should a firm make rather than buy a good or service? The focal dimension on which much of the predictive content of transaction cost economics relies, moreover, is asset specificity, which (as discussed in Section 6, below) is a measure of bilateral dependency. More generally, transaction cost economics is concerned with the governance of contractual relations (which bears a resemblance to the "going concerns" to which Commons referred). As it turns out, economic organization—in intermediate products markets, labor markets, capital markets, regulation, and even the family—involves variations on a few key transaction cost economizing themes. The predictive action turns on the hypothesis of discriminating alignment.

The arguments are familiar and are developed above. Suffice it to observe here that empirical research in organization theory has long suffered from the lack of an appropriate unit of analysis and the operationalization, which is to say, dimensionalization, thereof.

5.3. Farsighted Contracting

The preoccupation of economists with direct and intended effects to the neglect of indirect and (often delayed) unintended effects is widely interpreted as a condition of myopia. In fact, however, most economists are actually farsighted. The problem is one of limited peripheral vision.

Tunnel vision is both a strength and a weakness. The strength is that a focused lens, provided that it focuses on core issues, can be very powerful. The limitation is that irregularities which are none the less important will be missed and/or, even worse, dismissed.

Transaction cost economics relates to these limitations by drawing on organization theory. Because organization has a life of its own, transaction cost economics (i) asks to be apprised of the more important indirect effects,

Table 9.1. Comparison of Units of Analysis

Unit of Analysis	Critical Dimensions	Focal Problem
Decision premise	Role; information; idiosyncratic[a]	Human problem solving[b]
Ownership	'Eleven characteristics'[c]	Externality
Industry	Concentration; barriers to entry	Price–cost margins
Individual	Undeclared	Incentive alignment
Transaction	Frequency; uncertainty; asset specificity	Vertical integration

[a]Simon 1957a, pp. xxx–xxxi.

[b]Newell and Simon, 1972.

[c]Bromley, 1989, pp. 187–190.

whereupon (ii) it asks what, given these prospective effects, are the ramifications for efficient governance. A joinder of unanticipated effects (from organization theory) with farsighted contracting (from economics) thereby obtains.

Lest claims of farsightedness be taken to hyper-rationality extremes, transaction cost economics concedes that all complex contracts are unavoidably incomplete. That has both practical and theoretical significance. The practical lesson is this: all of the relevant contracting action cannot be concentrated in the *ex ante* incentive alignment but some spills over into *ex post* governance. The theoretical lesson is that differences among organization forms lose economic significance under a comprehensive contracting set-up because any form of organization can then replicate any other (Hart, 1990).

Transaction cost economics combines incompleteness with the farsighted contracting by describing the contracting process as one of "incomplete contracting in its entirety." But for incompleteness, the above-described significance of *ex post* governance would vanish. But for farsightedness, transaction cost economics would be denied access to one of the most important "tricks" in the economist's bag, namely the assumption that economic actors have the ability to look ahead, discern problems and prospects, and factor these back into the organizational/contractual design. "Plausible farsightedness," as against hyper-rationality, will often suffice.

Consider, for example, the issue of threats. Threats are easy to make, but which threats are to be believed? If *A* says that it will do *X* if *B* does *Y*, but if after *B* does *Y*, *A*'s best response is to do *Z*, then the threat will not be perceived to be credible to a farsighted *B*. Credible threats are thus those for which a farsighted *B* perceives that *A*'s *ex post* incentives comport with its claims, because, for example, *A* has made the requisite kind and amount of investment to support its threats (Dixit, 1980).

Or consider the matter of opportunism. As described above, Machiavelli worked out of a myopic logic, whereupon he advised his Prince to reply to opportunism in kind (get them before they get you). By contrast, the farsighted Prince is advised to look ahead and, if he discerns potential hazards, to take the hazards into account by redesigning the contractual relation—often by devising *ex ante* safeguards that will deter *ex post* opportunism. Accordingly, the wise Prince is advised to give and receive "credible commitments."

To be sure, it is more complicated to think about contract as a triple—*p*, *k*, *s*—where *p* refers to the price at which the trade takes place, *k* refers to the hazards that are associated with the exchange, *s* denotes the safeguards within which the exchange is embedded, and price, hazards, and safeguards are determined simultaneously—than as a scalar, where price alone is determinative. The simple schema shown in Chapter 3 nevertheless captures much of the relevant action (also see the discussion of trust in Chapter 10).

5.4. Trade-Offs

The ideal organization adapts quickly and efficaciously to disturbances of all kinds, but actual organizations experience trade-offs. Thus whereas more decentralized forms of organization (e.g., markets) support high-powered incentives and display outstanding adaptive properties to disturbances of an autonomous kind, they are poorly suited in cooperative adaptation respects. Hierarchy, by contrast, has weaker incentives and is comparatively worse at autonomous adaptation but is comparatively better in cooperative adaptation respects.

Simple transactions (for which $k = 0$)—in intermediate product markets, labor, finance, regulation, and the like—are easy to organize. The requisite adaptations here are preponderantly of an autonomous kind and the market-like option is efficacious (so firms buy rather than make, use spot contracts for labor, use debt rather than equity, eschew regulation, etc.). Problems with markets arise as bilateral dependencies, and the need for cooperative adaptations, build up. Markets give way to hybrids which in turn give way to hierarchies (which is the organization form of last resort) as the needs for cooperative adaptations ($k > 0$) build up.

More generally, the point is this: informed choice among alternative forms of organization entails trade-offs. Identifying and explicating trade-offs is the key to the study of comparative economic organization. Social scientists—economists and organization theorists alike—as well as legal specialists, need to come to terms with that proposition.

5.5. Remediableness

As developed in Chapter 8, the concept of remediableness has special relevances to politics. But it applies quite generally.

Note in this connection that "inefficiency" is unavoidably associated with contractual hazards. The basic market and hierarchy trade-off that is incurred upon taking transactions out of markets and organizing them internally substitutes one form of inefficiency (bureaucracy) for another (maladaptation). Other examples where one form of inefficiency is used to patch up another are (i) decisions by firms to integrate into adjacent stages of production (or distribution) in a weak intellectual property rights regime, thereby to mitigate the leakage of valued know-how (Teece, 1986), (ii) decisions by manufacturers' agents to incur added expenses, over and above those needed to develop the market, if these added expenses strengthen customer bonds in a cost-effective way, thereby to deter manufacturers from entering and expropriating market development investments (Heide and John, 1988), and (iii) the use of costly bonding to deter franchisees from violating quality norms (Klein and Leffler, 1981). Organization also has a bearing on the distribution of rents as well as asset protection. Concern over rent dissipation influenced the decision by the United States automobile industry firms to integrate into parts (Helper and Levine, 1992) and also helps to explain the resistance by oligopolies to industrial unions.

To be sure, any sacrifice of organizational efficiency, for oligopolistic rent protection reasons or otherwise, poses troublesome public policy issues.[10] A

---

10. This has public policy ramifications. As between two oligopolies, one of which engages in rent-protective measures while the other does not, and assuming that they are identical in other respects, the dissolution of the rent-protective oligopoly will yield larger welfare gains.

remediability test is none the less required to ascertain whether public policy should attempt to upset the oligopoly power in question. The issues are discussed further in relation to path dependency in Section 7.

6.   Added Regularities

It is evident from the foregoing that the comparative contractual approach out of which transaction cost economics works can be and needs to be informed by organization theory. Transaction cost economics, however, is more than a mere user. It pushes the logic of self-interest seeking to deeper levels, of which the concept of credible commitment is one example. More generally, it responds to prospective dysfunctional consequences by proposing improved *ex ante* designs and/or alternative forms of governance. Also, and what concerns me here, transaction cost has helped to discover added regularities that are pertinent to the study of organization. These include (i) the Fundamental Transformation (see Chapter 3), (ii) the impossibility of selective intervention (see Chapter 6), (iii) the economics of atmosphere (see Chapter 10), and (iv) an interpretation of Japanese economic organization (see Chapter 12).

These will not be repeated here (see, however, Williamson, 1993a, pp. 133–37, for a summary). All are important to an understanding of economic organization.

7.   Unresolved Tensions

The healthy tension to which I referred at the outset has contributed to better and deeper understandings of a variety of phenomena. The matters that concern me here—power, path dependence, the labor managed enterprise, trust, and tosh—are ones for which differences between transaction cost economics and organization theory are great.

7.1.   Power/Resource Dependence

That efficiency plays such a large role in the economic analysis of organization is because parties are assumed to consent to a contract and do this in a relatively farsighted way. Such voluntarism is widely disputed by sociologists, who "tend to regard systems of exchange as embedded within systems of power and domination (usually regarded as grounded in a class structure in the Marxian tradition) or systems of norms and values" (Baron and Hannan, 1992, p. 14).

The concept of power is very diffuse. Unable to define power, some specialists report that they know it when they see it. That has led others to conclude that power is a "disappointing concept. It tends to become a tautological label for the unexplained variance" (March, 1988, p. 6).

Among the ways in which the term power is used are the following: the power of capital over labor (Bowles and Gintis, 1993); strategic power exercised by established firms in relation to extant and prospective rivals (Shapiro, 1989); special interest power over the political process (Moe, 1990a); and resource dependency. Although all are relevant to economic organization, the last is distinctive to organization theory.[11] I examine it.

Two versions of resource dependency can be distinguished. The weak version is that parties who are subject to dependency will try to mitigate it. That is unexceptionable and is akin to the safeguard argument advanced in Section 5, above. There are two significant differences, however: (i) resource dependency nowhere recognizes that price, hazards, and safeguards are determined simultaneously; (ii) resource dependency nowhere remarks that asset specificity (which is the source of contractual hazard) is intentionally chosen because it is the source of productive benefits.

The strong version of resource dependency assumes myopia. The argument here is that myopic parties to contracts are victims of unanticipated and unwanted dependency. Because myopic parties do not perceive the hazards, safeguards will not be provided and the hazards will not be priced out.

Evidence pertinent to the myopic versus farsighted view of contract includes the following. (i) Are suppliers indifferent between two technologies that involve identical investments and have identical (steady state) operating costs, but one of which technologies is much less redeployable than the other? (ii) Is the degree of non-redeployability evident *ex ante* or is it revealed only after an adverse state realization (which includes defection from the spirit of the agreement) has materialized? (iii) Do added *ex ante* safeguards appear as added specificity builds up? (iv) Does contract law doctrine and enforcement reflect one or the other of these concepts of contract? Transaction cost economics answers these queries as follows: (i) the more generic (redeployable) technology will always be used whenever the cetera are paria; (ii) non-redeployability can be discerned *ex ante* and is recognized as such (Masten, 1984; Palay, 1984, 1985; Shelanski, 1993); (iii) added *ex ante* safeguards do appear as asset specificity builds up (Joskow, 1985, 1988); (iv) because truly unusual events are unforeseeable and can have punitive consequences if contracts are enforced literally, various forms of "excuse" are recognized by the law, but excuse is granted sparingly.[12]

---

11. Friedland and Alford identify resource dependency as one of the two dominant theories of organization (the other being population ecology) (1991, p. 235).

12. Because contracts are incomplete and contain gaps, errors, omissions, and the like, and because the immediate parties may not be able to reconcile their differences when an unanticipated disturbance arises, parties to a contract will sometimes ask courts to be excused from performance. Because, moreover, literal enforcement can pose unacceptably severe contractual hazards—the effects of which are to discourage contracting (in favor of vertical integration) and/or to discourage potentially cost-effective investments in specialized assets—some relief from strict enforcement recommends itself. How much relief is then the question. Were excuse to be granted routinely whenever adversity occurred, then incentives to think through contracts, choose technologies judiciously, share risks efficiently, and avert adversity would be impaired. Accordingly, transaction cost economics recommends that (i) provision be made for excuse but (ii) excuse should be awarded sparingly—which it evidently is (Farnsworth, 1968, p. 885; Buxbaum, 1985).

7.2. Path Dependency

Transaction cost economics not only subscribes to the proposition that history matters but relies on that proposition to explain the differential strengths and weaknesses of alternative forms of governance. The Fundamental Transformation, for example, is a specific manifestation of the proposition that history matters. (Transactions that are not subject to the Fundamental Transformation are much easier to manage contractually.) The bureaucracy problems that afflict internal organization (entrenchment; coalitions) are also the product of experience and illustrate the proposition that history matters. Were it not that systems drifted away from their initial conditions, efforts to replicate markets within hierarchies (or the reverse) and selectively intervene would be much easier—in which event differences between organization forms would diminish.

The benefits that accrue to experience are also testimony to the proposition that history matters. Tacit knowledge and its consequences (Polanyi, 1962; Marschak, 1968; Arrow, 1974) attest to that. More generally, firm-specific human assets of both spontaneous (e.g. coding economies) and intentional (e.g. learning) kinds are the product of idiosyncratic experience. The entire institutional environment (laws, rules, conventions, norms, etc.) within which the institutions of governance are embedded is the product of history. And although the social conditioning that operates within governance structures (e.g. corporate culture; Kreps, 1990a) is reflexive and often intentional, this too has accidental and temporal features.

That history matters does not, however, imply that only history matters. Intentionality and economizing explain a lot of what is going on out there. Also, most of the path dependency literature emphasizes technology (e.g. the QWERTY typewriter keyboard) rather than the organizational consequences referred to above, Paul David's recent paper (1992) being an exception. I am not persuaded that technological, as against organizational, path dependency is as important as much of that literature suggests. Many of the "inefficiencies" to which the technological path dependency literature refers are of an irremediable kind.

7.2.1. Remediable inefficiencies

As described in Chapter 8, transaction cost economics emphasizes remediable inefficiencies; that is, those conditions for which a feasible alternative can be described which, if introduced, would yield net gains. That is to be distinguished from hypothetical net gains, where the inefficiency in question is judged by comparing an actual alternative with a hypothetical ideal.

To be sure, big disparities between actual and hypothetical sometimes signal opportunities for net gains. The need, however, is to realize real gains. Both public and private ordering are pertinent.

Whether public ordering can do better depends on whether (i) the public sector is better informed about externalities, (ii) the requisite collective action is easier to orchestrate through the public sector (possibly by fiat), and/or (iii) the social net benefit calculus differs from the private in sufficient degree to warrant a different result. Absent *plausible* assumptions that would support a prospective net gain (in either private or social respects), the purported inefficiency is effectively irremediable.

That is regrettable, in that society would have done better if it had better knowledge or if a reorganization could have been accomplished more easily. Hypothetical regrets are neither here nor there. Real costs in relation to real choices is what comparative institutional economics is all about.

7.2.2. *Quantitative significance*

Path dependency, remediable or not, poses a greater challenge if the effects in question are large and lasting rather than small and temporary. It is not easy to document the quantitative significance of path dependency. Arthur provides a series of examples and emphasizes especially the video cassette recorder (where VHS prevailed over the Beta technology [1990, p. 92]) and nuclear power (where light water reactors prevailed over high-temperature, gas-cooled reactors [1990, p. 99]). But while both are interesting examples of path dependency, it is not obvious that the "winning" technology is significantly inferior to the loser, or even, for that matter, whether the winner is inferior at all.

Much the most widely cited case study is that of the typewriter keyboard. The QWERTY keyboard story has been set out by Paul David (1985, 1986). It illustrates "why the study of economic history is a necessity in the making of good economists" (David, 1986, p. 30).

QWERTY refers to the first six letters on the top row of the standard typewriter keyboard. Today's keyboard layout is the same as that which was devised when the typewriter was first invented in 1870. The early mechanical technology was beset by typebar clashes, which clashes were mitigated by the QWERTY keyboard design.

Subsequent developments in typewriter technology relieved problems with typebar clashes, but the QWERTY keyboard persisted in the face of large (reported) discrepancies in typing speed between it and later keyboard designs. Thus the Dvorak Simplified Keyboard (DSK), which was patented in 1932, was so much faster than the standard keyboard that, according to United States Navy experiments, the "increased efficiency obtained with DSK would amortize the cost of retraining a group of typists within the first ten days of their subsequent full-time employment" (David, 1986, p. 33). More recently, the Apple IIC computer comes with a built-in switch which instantly converts its keyboard from QWERTY to DSK: "If as Apple advertising copy says, DSK 'lets you type 20–40% faster,' why did this superior design meet essentially the same resistance . . . ?" (David, 1986, p. 34).

There are several possibilities. These include non-rational behavior, conspiracy among typewriter firms, and path dependency (David, 1986, pp. 34–46). David makes a strong case for the last, but there is a fourth possibility, subsequently raised and examined by Liebowitz and Margolis (1990): neither the Navy study nor Apple advertising copy can support the astonishing claims made on their behalf. Upon going back to the archives and examining the data, Liebowitz and Margolis conclude that "the standard history of QWERTY versus Dvorak is flawed and incomplete. . . . [The] claims of superiority of the Dvorak keyboard are suspect. The most dramatic claims are traceable to Dvorak himself, and the best documented experiments, as well as recent ergonomic studies, suggest little or no advantage for the Dvorak keyboard" (1990, p. 21). If that assessment stands up, then path dependence has had only modest efficiency effects in the QWERTY keyboard case. Such effects could easily fall below the threshold of remediable inefficiency.

Recent studies of the evolution of particular industries by sociologists also display path dependency. Population ecologists have used the ecological model of density-dependent legitimation and competition to examine the evolutionary process—both in particular industries (e.g. the telephone industry [Barnett and Carroll, 1993]) and in computer simulations. Glenn Carroll and Richard Harrison conclude from the latter that "chance can play a major role in organizational evolution" (1992, p. 26).

Although their simulations do suggest that path dependency has large and lasting effects, Carroll and Harrison do not address the matter of remediableness. Until a feasible reorganization of the decision process for choosing technologies can be described, the effect of which is to yield expected net private or social gains, it seems premature to describe their experiments as a test of the "relative roles of chance and rationality" (Carroll and Harrison, 1992, p. 12). Large but irremediable inefficiencies nevertheless do raise serious issues for modelling economic organization.[13]

7.2.3. Perspectives

David contends and I am persuaded that "there are many more QWERTY worlds lying out there" (1986, p. 47). An unchanged keyboard layout does not, however, strike me as the most important economic attribute of typewriter development from 1870 to the present. What about improvements in the mechanical technology? What about the electric typewriter? What about personal computers and laser printers? Why did these prevail in the face of path dependency? Were other "structurally superior" technologies (as defined by Carroll and Harrison) bypassed? If, with lags and hitches, the more efficient

---

13. I have argued that dominant firm industries in which chance plays a role do warrant public policy intervention (Williamson, 1975, chap. 11), but whether net gains would really be realized by implementing that proposal (especially as international competition becomes more intensive) is problematic.

technologies have regularly supplanted less efficient technologies, should not that be featured? Possibly the response is that "everyone knows" that economizing is the main case: "It goes without saying that economizing is the main case to which path dependency, monopolizing, efficient risk bearing, etc. are qualifications."

The persistent neglect of economizing reasoning suggests otherwise. Thus the "inhospitability tradition" in antitrust proceeded with sublime confidence that non-standard and unfamiliar business practices had little or no efficiency rationale but mainly had monopoly purpose and effect. Similarly, the vast inefficiencies that brought down the economies of the Soviet Union and Eastern Europe may now be obvious, but that could never have been gleaned from the postwar literature on comparative economic systems or from CIA intelligence estimates. The preoccupation in the area of business strategy with clever "plans, ploys, and positioning" to the neglect of economizing is likewise testimony to the widespread tendency to disregard efficiency (Williamson, 1991b). And the view that the "effective organization is (1) *garrulous,* (2) *clumsy,* (3) *superstitious,* (4) *hypocritical,* (5) *monstrous,* (6) *octopoid,* (7) *wandering,* and (8) *grouchy*" (Weick, 19777, pp. 193–94, emphasis in original) is reconciled with economizing only with effort. More recent "social construction of industry" arguments reduce economizing to insignificance.[14]

If economizing really does get at the fundamentals, then that condition ought to be continuously featured. Some progress has been made (Zald, 1987), but there is little reason to be complacent.

---

14. The "new sociology of organization" holds that "even in identical economic and technical conditions, outcomes may differ dramatically if social structures are different" (Granovetter, 1992, p. 9). The "social construction of industry" argument is developed in a major book by Patrick McGuire, Mark Granovetter, and Michael Schwartz on the origins of the American electric power industry. That book has been described as follows:

> Building on detailed historical research, . . . this book treats the origins of the electrical utility industry from a sociological perspective. The idea that industries, like other economic institutions, are 'socially constructed,' derives from Granovetter's work on 'embeddedness' (1985) and presents an alternative to the new institutional economics, which contends that economic institutions should be understood as the efficient solutions to economic problems. . . .
>
> We believe that the way the utility industry developed from its inception in the 1880s was not the only technologically practical one, nor the most efficient. It arose because a set of powerful actors accessed certain techniques and applied them in a highly visible and profitable way. Those techniques resulted from the shared personal understandings, social connections, organizational conditions, and historical opportunities available to these actors. This success, in turn, triggered pressures for uniformity across regions, even when this excluded viable and possibly more efficient alternative technologies and organizational forms.
>
> Our argument resembles that made by economists Paul David and Brian Arthur on the 'lock-in' of inefficient technologies (such as the QWERTY keyboard . . .), but draws on the sociology of knowledge and of social structure. (McGuire, Granovetter, and Schwartz, 1992, pp. 1–2)

7.3.   Worker-Managed Enterprises

John Bonin and Louis Putterman define a worker-managed firm as

> a productive enterprise the ultimate decision-making rights over which are
> held by member-workers, on the basis of equality of those rights regardless
> of job, skill grade, or capital contribution. A full definition would state that
> no non-workers have a direct say in enterprising decisions, and that no workers
> are denied an equal say in those decisions. This definition does not imply
> that any particular set of decisions must be made by the full working group,
> nor does it imply a particular choice rule, such as majority voting. It says
> nothing about financing structures other than that financiers are not accorded
> direct decision-making powers in the enterprise by virtue of their non-labor
> contributions, and it does not say anything about how income is distributed
> among workers. On all of these matters, all that is implied is that ultimate
> decision-making rights are vested in the workers, and only in the workers.
> Thus, the basic definition centers on an allocation of governance rights, and
> is simultaneously economic and political. (1987, p. 2)

This definition does not preclude hierarchical structure, specialized decision-
making, a leadership élite, or marginal product payment schemes. It merely
stipulates that finance can have no decision rights in the labor-managed enterprise. The question is whether these financial restrictions come at a cost.
Putterman evidently believes that they do not, since he elsewhere endorses
Roger McCain's proposal that the labor-managed enterprise be financed in
part by "risk participation bonds," where these purportedly differ from "ordinary equity" only in that "its owner can have no voting control over enterprise
decisions, or over the election of enterprise management" (Putterman, 1984,
p. 1989). Since "the labor-managed firm whose objective is to maximize profit-
per-worker, having both ordinary and 'risk participation' bonds at its disposal,
would 'attain the same allocation of resources as would a capitalist corporation, under comparable circumstances and informationally efficient markets'"
(1984, p. 189), Putterman concludes that the labor-managed firm is on a parity.

The argument illustrates the hazards of addressing issues of economic
organization within a framework that ignores, hence effectively suppresses,
the role of governance. Operating, as he does, out of a firm-as-production-
function framework, McCain (1977) is only concerned with examining the
marginal conditions that obtain under two different set-ups, under both of
which the firm is described as a production function.

Governance issues never arise and hence are not amenable to analysis
within this orthodox framework. If, however, a critical—indeed, I would say,
the critical—attribute of equity is the ability to exercise contingent control
by concentrating votes and taking over the board of directors, then McCain's
demonstration that allocative efficiency is identical under standard equity and
risk participation bonds is simply inapposite.

Indeed, if risk participation finance is available on more adverse terms
than standard equity because holders are provided with less security against

mismanagement and expropriation, then the constraints that Bonin and Putterman have built into the worker-managed firm come at a cost. To be sure, the worker-managed firm may be able to offset financial disabilities by offering compensating advantages. If those advantages are not uniform but vary among firms and industries, then the net gains of the worker-managed firm will vary accordingly.

I submit that firms that can be mainly financed with debt are the obvious candidates for worker-management. Thus, if there is little equity-like capital at stake, then there is little reason for equity to ask or expect that preemptive control over the board of directors will be awarded to equity as a contractual safeguard. The question then is what types of firms best qualify for a preponderance of debt financing?

As discussed elsewhere, peer group forms of organization can and do operate we in small enterprises where the membership has been carefully screened and is committed to democratic ideals (Williamson, 1975, chap. 3). Also, the partnership form of organization works well in professional organizations, such as law and accounting firms, where the need for firm-specific physical capital is small (Hansmann, 1988). There being little need for equity capital to support investment in such firms, the control of these firms naturally accrues to those who supply specialized human assets (Williamson, 1989b, pp. 24–26). These exceptions aside, "third forms" experience serious incentive disabilities.[15]

7.4. Trust

There is a growing tendency, among economists and sociologists alike, to describe trust in calculative terms: both rational choice sociologists (Coleman, 1990) and game theorists (Dasgupta, 1988) treat trust as a subclass of risk. I concur with Granovetter that to craft credible commitments (through the use of bonds, hostages, information disclosure rules, specialized dispute settlement mechanisms, and the like) is to create functional substitutes for trust (Granovetter, 1985, p. 487). Albeit vitally important to economic organization, such substitutes should not be confused with (real) trust.[16]

15. The limits of third forms for organizing *large* enterprises with *variegated* membership are severe in both theory and fact. To be sure, some students of economic organization remain sanguine (Horvat, 1991). The evidence from Eastern Europe has not, however, been supportive. Maciej Iwanek (1991, p. 12) remarks of the Polish experience that "except [among] advocates of workers' management, nobody believes that the . . . governance scheme of state-owned enterprises [by workers' management] creates strong incentives"; Manuel Hinds (1990, p. 28) concludes that "absenteeism, shirking, and lack of initiative are pervasive in the self-managed firm"; Janos Kornai (1990, p. 144) counsels that "it would be intellectually dishonest to hide the evidence concerning the weakness of third forms."

16. Note that the trust that Granovetter ascribes to ongoing relations can go either way—frequent suggestions to the contrary notwithstanding. That is because experience can be either good (more confidence) or bad (less confidence), which, if contracts of both kinds are renewed, will show up in differential contracting (Crocker and Reynolds, 1993).

That calculativeness plays a larger role in economics than in the other social sciences is evident from my discussion of farsighted contracting. But calculativeness can also be taken to excesses. The issues as they bear on both the economics of atmosphere and personal trust relations are developed in Chapter 10.

7.5. Tosh

The legal philosopher, Lon Fuller, distinguished between "essentials" and "tosh," where the former involves an examination of the "rational core" (1978, pp. 359–62) and tosh is preoccupied with "superfluous rituals, rules of procedure without clear purpose, [and] needless precautions preserved through habit" (1978, p. 356). According to Fuller, to focus on the latter would "abandon any hope of fruitful analysis" (1978, p. 360).

I think that this last goes too far: a place should be made for tosh, but tosh should be kept in its place.[17] Consider in this connection the Friedland and Alford interpretation of Clifford Geertz's description of Balinese cockfights:

> Enormous sums of money can change hands at each match, sums that are *irrational* from an individualistic, utilitarian perspective. The higher the sums, the more *evenly matched* the cocks are arranged to be, and the more likely the odds on which the bet is made are even. The greater the sum of money at stake, the more the decision to bet is not individualistic and utilitarian, but collective—one bets with one's kin or village—and status-oriented. (1991, pp. 247–48, emphasis added)

That there are social pressures to support one's kin or village is a sociological argument. Absent these pressures, the concentration of bets on evenly matched cocks would be difficult to explain. It does not, however, follow that it is "irrational" to bet enormous sums on evenly matched cocks. Given the social context, it has become non-viable, as a betting matter, to fight unevenly matched cocks.

Thus suppose that the objective odds for a proposed match are 4:1. Considerations of local pride may reduce the effective odds to 3:2. Such a match will not attract much betting because those from the village with the lesser cock who view it from an individualistic, acquisitive perspective will make only perfunctory bets. Accordingly, the only interesting matches are those *where social pressures are relieved by the even odds*.[18] The "symbolic construction of

---

17. The evolution of cooperation between opposed armies or gangs that are purportedly engaged in 'deadly combat' is illustrated by Robert Axelrod's examination of "The Live-and-Let-Live System in Trench Warfare in World War I" (1984, pp. 73–87). Interestingly and important as the live-and-let-live rituals were, these non-violent practices should not be mistaken for the main case. Rather, these rituals were the exception to the main case, which was that British and German troops were at war.

18. Richard M. Coughlin contends that the "essence" of the socio-economic approach proposed by Amitai Etzioni is that

reality" to which Friedland and Alford refer thus has real consequences. It delimits the feasible set within which rationality operates; but rationality is fully operative thereafter.

One interpretation of this is that tosh has discrete structural effects and that rationality, operating through the marginal calculus, applies thereafter. Indeed, that seems to fit the Balinese cockfight rather well. Whether the social construction of reality has such important consequences more generally is then the question. My sense is that it varies with the circumstances.

Tosh is arguably more important in non-commercial circumstances—state, family, religion—than in the commercial sector, although the Hamilton and Biggart (1988) examination of differences in corporate forms in Far East Asia might be offered as a contradiction. Hamilton and Biggart, however, go well beyond tosh (as described by Fuller) to implicate the institutional environment—to include property rights, contract law, politics, and the like.

Thus although both tosh (superfluous rituals) and the institutional environment refer to background conditions, the one should not be confused with the other. Tosh is a source of interesting variety and adds spice to life. Core features of the institutional environment, as defined by North (1986, 1991) and others (Sundaram and Black, 1992), are arguably more important, however, to the study of comparative economic organization.[19]

8.   Conclusions

The science of organization to which Barnard made reference (1938, p. 290) over fifty years ago has made major strides in the past ten and twenty years. All of the social sciences have a stake in this, but none more than economics and organization theory.

If the schematic set out in Figure 9.1 is an accurate way to characterize much of what is going on, then the economics of governance needs to be informed both from the level of the institutional environment (where sociology has a lot to contribute) and from the level of th individual (where psychology is implicated). The intertemporal process transformations that take place

---

human behavior must be understood in terms of the fusion of individually-based and communally-based forces, which Etzioni labels the *I and We*. The *I* represents the individual acting in pursuit of his or her own pleasure; the *We* stands for the obligations and restraints imposed by the collectivity. (1992, p. 3)

That is close to the interpretation that I advance here to interpret the Balinese cock fights.

19. This is pertinent, among other things, to the study of the multinational enterprise. As Anant Sundaram and J. Stewart Black observe, MNEs "pursue different entry/involvement strategies in different markets and for different products at any given time" (1992, p. 740). Their argument, that transaction cost economics "is inadequate for explaining simultaneously different entry modes because . . . asset specificity . . . [is] largely the same the world over" (1992, p. 740) assumes that the governance level operates independently of the institutional environment under a transaction cost set-up. This is mistaken.

within the institutions of governance (with respect to which organization theory has a lot to say) are also pertinent. The overall schema works out of the rational spirit approach that is associated with economics.[20]

This multilevel approach relieves some, perhaps much, of the strain to which Baron and Hannan refer: "we think it important to understand the different assumptions and forms of reasoning used in contemporary sociology versus economics. . . . These disciplinary differences . . . represent major barriers to intellectual trade between economics and sociology" (1992, p. 13). If, however, deep knowledge at several levels is needed and is beyond the competence of any one discipline, and if a systems conception can be devised in which intellectual trade among levels can be accomplished, then some of the worst misunderstandings of the past can be put behind us.

I summarize here what I see to be some of the principal respects in which the healthy tension to which I referred at the outset has supported intellectual trade, of which more is in prospect.

Organization Theory Supports for Transaction Cost Economics

Behavioral assumptions. Organization theory's insistence on workably realistic, as opposed to analytically convenient, behavioral assumptions is a healthy antidote. Transaction cost economics responds by describing economic actors in terms of bounded rationality and opportunism.

Adaptation. The cooperative adaptation emphasized by Barnard is joined with the autonomous adaptation of Hayek, with the result that transaction cost economics makes an appropriate place for both market and hierarchy.

Unanticipated consequences. The subtle and unintended consequences of control and organization need to be uncovered, whereupon provision can be made for these in the *ex ante* organizational design.

Politics. Because property rights in the public arena are shaped by democratic politics, provision needs to be made for these in the *ex ante* organizational design of public sector bureaus.

Embeddedness. The first-order response to the proposition that embeddedness matters is to regard the institutional environment as a locus of shift parameters, changes in which change the comparative costs of governance.

Discrete structural analysis. Each generic form of organization is described as a syndrome of attributes and possesses its own logic. These discreteness features need to be discovered and explicated both within and between sectors.

20. I borrow the term "rational spirit" from Kenneth Arrow (1974, p. 16). The rational spirit approach holds that there is a *logic* to organization and that this logic is mainly discerned by the relentless application of economic reasoning (subject, however, to cognitive constraints). The rational spirit approach is akin to but somewhat weaker (in that it eschews stronger forms of utility maximization) than the 'rational choice' approach associated with James Coleman (1990).

Transaction Cost Economics Supports for Organization Theory

Unit of analysis.   Any theory of organization that fails to name the unit of analysis out of which it works and thereafter identify the critical dimensions with respect to which that unit of analysis varies is non-operational at best and could be bankrupt.

The main case.   All rival theories of organization are asked to nominate the main case, develop the refutable implications that accrue thereto, and examine the data. Economizing on transaction costs is the transaction cost economics candidate.

Farsighted contracting.   Looking ahead, recognizing hazards, and folding these back into the design of governance is often feasible and explains a very considerable amount of organizational variety.

Trade-offs.   Because each mode of governance is a syndrome of attributes, the move from one mode to another involves trade-offs. The key trade-offs need to be stated and explicated.

Remediableness.   Relevant choices among feasible forms of organization are what the analysis of comparative economic organization is all about.

10

Calculativeness, Trust, and Economic Organization

My main purpose in this chapter is to explicate what Diego Gambetta has referred to as "the elusive notion of trust" (1988, p. ix). As the literature on trust reveals, and as developed here, "trust" is a term with many meanings. The relentless application of calculative economic reasoning is the principal device that I employ to define and delimit the elusive notion of trust.

The calculative approach to economic organization is sketched in Section 1. The concept of "calculative trust," which enjoys widespread and growing acceptance but with which I take exception, is examined in Section 2. Societal trust, which works through the institutional environment and takes a series of hyphenated forms, is briefly treated in Section 3. Nearly noncalculative uses of trust of a personal kind are developed in Section 4. Concluding remarks follow in Section 5.

1. Calculativeness

As compared with the other social sciences, the economic approach to economic organization is decidedly more calculative. That is widely regarded as both the distinctive strength and the Achilles' heel of economics. A failure to appreciate the limits of calculativeness purportedly gives rise to excesses, as a consequence of which economists are prone to make mistaken assessments of many economic phenomena.

I do not disagree, but I contend that the excesses to which calculativeness is sometimes given are usually remediable. I furthermore contend that the analytical reach of the calculative approach to economic organization is *extended rather than diminished by admitting to these limitations*. Once the excesses to which calculativeness is given are displayed and understood, the distortions can be anticipated and can thereafter be folded in at the design stage. A (more farsighted) calculative response to the (myopic) excesses of calculativeness thereby obtains. Provided that bounds on rationality are respected, calculativeness opens the door to a deeper understanding of economic organization.

1.1. Economics and the Contiguous Disciplines[1]

Applications of economic analysis and economic reasoning to the contiguous social sciences—principally law, political science, and sociology—have increased considerably in the past thirty years. To be sure, John R. Commons deserves credit for his early recognition that "law and economics" was a combined enterprise (Commons, 1924, 1925). The institutional economics program with which he was involved enjoyed only limited success,[2] however, and the first concerted applications of economics to the law were mainly concentrated on antitrust (Posner, 1979). That quickly changed after 1960 with the publication of Ronald Coase's "Social Cost" article (1960) and Guido Calabresi's related work on torts (1961). Economics has since made its way into virtually every field of legal scholarship (Posner, 1977).

The joinder of economics and political science has also undergone a significant transformation. Kenneth Arrow's work (1951) on social choice, Anthony Downs's treatment (1957) of an economic theory of democracy, Mancur Olson's logic of collection action (1965) and James Buchanan and Gordon Tullock's work on constitutions (1964) were all implicated in this transformation. As recent conference volumes in the *Journal of Law, Economics, and Organization* make clear,[3] the use of economic reasoning to examine politics and political institutions has become widespread and, for some issues, even essential.

Economics and sociology bear a more distant relation to each other,[4] although this too has been changing, especially as the "rational choice" approach to sociology has been taking shape (see Hechter, 1987; Coleman, 1990; Lindenberg, 1990). A wide gulf between them nevertheless needed to be bridged. Thus, Paul Samuelson (1947) distinguished economics and sociology in terms of their rationality orientations, with rationality being the domain of economics and nonrationality being relegated to sociology. James Duesenberry subsequently quipped (1960) that economics was preoccupied with how individuals made choices, whereas sociology maintained that individuals did not have any

1. The heading is borrowed from Coase (1978).

2. The most significant contribution to law and economics stemming from the Commons's tradition is his book *Legal Foundations of Capitalism* (1924). Albeit important, older-style institutional economics became embroiled in methodological controversy and failed to develop a research agenda to rival orthodoxy (see George Stigler's remarks appearing in Kitch, 1963). Some concluded, too harshly I think, that the work of American institutionalists "led to nothing . . . [since] without a theory, they had nothing to pass on" (Coase, 1984, pp. 229–30).

3. The 1990 conference volume is entitled "The Organization of Political Institutions," while the 1992 conference volume deals with "The Economics and Politics of Administrative Law and Procedures."

4. Much of the distance between economics and sociology appears to be attributable to the need for sociology, as a new discipline, to define itself in such a way as to avoid confrontation with economics, from which it had been spun off. See Swedberg, 1987.

choices to make. Both George Homans (1958) and Herbert Simon (1978) protested that sociology had a stake in rationality analysis and could not accept this division of labor, but such a division persisted.

What, it might be asked, is behind the successes of economics in moving into law, political science, and sociology? Coase observes that what binds a group of scholars together is "one or more of the following: common techniques of analysis, a common theory or approach to a subject, or a common subject matter" (Coase, 1978, p. 204). Although, in the short run, the use of certain techniques or a distinctive approach may provide the means by which economists are able to move successfully into another field, Coase argues that the subject matter is decisive in the long run: "What economists study is the working of the social institutions which bind together the economic system: firms, markets for goods and services, labor markets, capital markets, the banking system, international trade, and so on. It is the common interest in these social institutions which distinguishes the economics profession" (1978, pp. 206–7). He subsequently remarks, however, that it is because economists "study the economic system as a unified whole, . . . [that they] are more likely to uncover the basic interrelationships within a social system than is someone less accustomed to looking at the working of a system as a whole. . . . [Also, the] study of economics makes it difficult to ignore factors which are clearly important and which play a part in all social systems [such as relative prices]" (1978, pp. 209–10).

These last remarks seem to me to be more an endorsement of the economic approach than of the economic subject matter. Be that as it may, the economic approach, rather than the subject matter, is what I emphasize here. Calculativeness is the general condition that I associate with the economic approach and with the progressive extension of economics into the related social sciences. (I view it as the strategy that Gary Becker [1976] has applied so widely and effectively.)[5] Note in this connection that calculative economic reasoning can take several forms—of which price theory, property rights theory, agency theory, and transaction cost economics are all variants.[6]

5. Note that there are real differences between the incomplete contracting approach out of which transaction cost economics works, in which bounded rationality is featured, and the optimality setup out of which Becker works. Herbert Simon, however, takes exception with both. Becker is scored for excesses of hyperrationality (Simon, 1978, p. 2), while I am scored for using an incomplete contracting setup for which empirical support is purportedly lacking (Simon, 1991, pp. 25–27). Becker is his own best agent. As for myself, I would observe that empirical work in transaction cost economics is much greater than Simon indicates (see Williamson, 1985b, chap. 5; Joskow, 1988, 1991; Klein and Shelanski, 1985) and is growing exponentially. Joskow concludes that the empirical research in transaction cost economics "is in much better shape than much of the empirical work in industrial organization generally" (1991, p. 81)—to which, however, he quickly adds that more and better theoretical and empirical work is needed: "[T]here is no rest for the weary" (1991, p. 82). I concur.

6. Note in this connection that the massive expansion of economic reasoning out of antitrust law into the law more generally had transaction cost economics origins (Coase, 1960). Many of the initial applications of economic reasoning to economic organization also rely, directly and indirectly, on transaction cost arguments (Arrow, 1951, 1969; Alchian and Demsetz, 1972; Williamson, 1975; Jensen and Meckling, 1976).

1.2.   Transaction Cost Economics

1.2.1.   Institutional economics

As developed in in Chapters 4 and 9, institutional economics works at two levels of analysis. The macro variant, which is especially associated with the work of Douglass North (1991) deals with the institutional environment. The micro variant deals with the institutions of governance.

These two levels are joined in Chapter 4 by treating the institutional environment in which a transaction (or a related set of transactions) is embedded as a set of shift parameters, changes in which elicit shifts in the comparative costs of governance. These issues are developed further in Section 3 below. Consider here the rudiments of governance.

1.2.2.   Governance

Although hyperrationality has been responsible for some of the truly deep insights of economics, there is a need, at some stage, to describe "man as he is, acting within the constraints imposed by real institutions" (Coase, 1984, p. 231). What are the key attributes of economic actors?

Opportunism and bounded rationality are the key behavioral assumptions on which transaction cost economics relies.[7] An immediate ramification of bounded rationality is that impossibly complex forms of economic organization (such as complete contingent-claims contracting) (Radner, 1968) are infeasible. Standing alone, that is a negative result. But there is more to it than that. If mind is a scarce resource (Simon, 1978, p. 12), then economizing on bounded rationality is warranted. This expands, rather than reduces, the range of issues to which the economic approach can be applied. Among other things, the "conscious, deliberate, purposeful" use of organization as a means by which to economize on bounded rationality is made endogenous (Barnard, 1938).

Opportunism is a self-interest-seeking assumption. By contrast with simple self-interest seeking, according to which economic agents will continuously consult their own preferences but will candidly disclose all pertinent information on inquiry and will reliably discharge all covenants, opportunistic agents are given to self-interest seeking with guile. Whether economic agents will tell the truth, the whole truth, and nothing but the truth and will reliably self-enforce covenants to behave "responsibly" are therefore problematic. Note, however, that Machiavellian grabbing is not implied if economic agents have a farsighted understanding of the economic relation of which they are a part.

---

7. The aspect of bounded rationality that is most frequently emphasized is that of limited cognitive competence, on which account irrationality or satisficing are often thought to be implied. Intended (but limited) rationality, however, is a broader concept. Not only are intendedly rational agents attempting effectively to cope, whence irrationality (except, perhaps, for certain pathological cases) is not implied, but satisficing is merely one manifestation of coping. The satisficing approach, which appeals to psychology and works out of an aspiration level mechanics, has not found wide application within economics (Aumann, 1985; Arrow, 1987).

Note also that the idea of credible commitments is a thoroughly hard-headed one. Contracts that have no need for added support (the "ideal" contracts of both law and economics) (Macneil, 1974, p. 738) will not be provided with them. More generally, contracts will be provided with added supports only in the degree to which these are cost-effective.[8] Calculativeness is thus pervasive.

Taken together, the lessons of bounded rationality and opportunism lead to the following combined result: organize transactions so as to economize on bounded rationality while simultaneously safeguarding them against the hazards of opportunism. Not only do credible commitments arise when incomplete contracts are examined in their entirety, but complaints over obsessive calculativeness, truncated calculativeness, and anticalculativeness are mitigated as well.

1.3. Purported Excesses of Calculativeness

1.3.1. Obsessive calculativeness

A calculative approach to economic organization can and sometimes does result in obsessive demands for control. One of the prescient lessons of sociology is that demands for control can have both intended and unintended effects and that unintended effects often have dysfunctional consequences (see Merton, 1936; March and Simon, 1958).

One possible response to this finding is to argue that the economic approach is flawed because of its preoccupation with intended effects to the neglect of unintended effects. But that assumes that the economic approach is unable or unwilling to take into account all relevant regularities whatsoever. If the deeper lesson is to design control systems with reference to all consequences—both those that are intended and those that were (originally) unanticipated—and if economics can implement this deeper lesson, then the claim that the economic approach is mindlessly given to obsessive calculativeness is overdrawn. The correct view is that a naive application of calculativeness can be and sometimes is given to excesses but that this is often remediable. On being informed about added consequences, these will be factored into the design exercise from the outset. (A calculative response to the excesses of calculativeness thereby obtains.)

---

8. See Chapter 5. The remarks of Richard Dawkins about conscious foresight, expressed in the context of selfish genes, are pertinent:

> One unique feature of man ... [is] his capacity for conscious foresight. Selfish genes ... have no foresight.
>
> [Thus] even if we look on the dark side and assume that individual man is fundamentally selfish, our conscious foresight ... could save us from the worst selfish excesses of the blind replicators. We have at least the mental equipment to foster our long-term selfish interests rather than merely our short-term selfish interests. We can see the long-term benefits of participating.... and we can sit down to discuss ways of making ... [agreements] work. (1976, p. 215)

1.3.2. Truncated calculativeness

Many models of economic organization work out of truncated logic, according to which economic actors are assumed to be myopic. Aspects of the Keynesian macro model work out of a myopic logic. The same is true of the cobweb cycle (Coase and Fowler, 1935), barriers to entry arguments (Stigler, 1968), and the resource dependency approach to economic organization (Pfeffer and Salancik, 1978; Pfeffer, 1981).

Transaction cost economics responds to all of these conditions identically: although complex contracts are unavoidably incomplete, a farsighted approach to contract is often feasible. Many of the problems associated with truncated contracting are relieved in the process. As developed in Chapter 9, the resource dependency and credible commitment approaches to economic organization are illustrative of myopia and farsightedness, respectively.

1.3.3. Anticalculativeness: voice

Yet another view is that the calculative approach to economic organization emphasizes exit (the traditional economic means by which to express dissatisfaction) to the neglect of voice (which is associated with politics and is purportedly less calculative) (Hirschman, 1970). Transaction cost economics is sometimes held to be especially reprehensible (see Granovetter, 1985, 1988).

My response is twofold. First, if voice in the absence of an exit option is relatively ineffective, which evidently it is (Hirschman, 1970), then voice really does have a calculative aspect. Second, voice works through mechanisms, and those mechanisms are often carefully designed.

Karl Llewellyn's view of contract as framework, as against contract as legal rules, is pertinent: "[T]he major importance of legal contract is to provide a framework for well-nigh every type of group organization and for well-nigh every type of passing or permanent relation between individuals and groups . . . a *framework highly adjustable,* a framework which almost never accurately indicates real working relations, but which affords a rough indication around which such relations vary, an occasional guide in cases of doubt, and a norm of *ultimate appeal* when the relations cease in fact to work" (1931, pp. 736–37, emphasis added).

Plainly, Llewellyn provides for voice: parties to a (bilaterally dependent) contract will try to work things out when confronted by unanticipated disturbances. Within a broad range, the contract serves as framework. Llewellyn nevertheless observes that the contract serves also as a norm of ultimate appeal if the parties are unable to reconcile their differences. An exit option is thereby preserved, but court ordering of the contract serves to delimit threat positions. Bargaining through voice is thus greatly influenced by knowledge that the terms of exit are defined by the contract.

But there is more to it than that. The voice mechanics are often defined by the terms of the contract. Recall the provisions in the thirty-two-year coal supply agreement between the Nevada Power Company and the Northwest Trading Company (see Chapter 4):

> In the event an inequitable condition occurs which adversely affects one Party, it shall be the joint and equal responsibility of both Parties to act promptly and in good faith to determine the action required to cure or adjust for the inequity and effectively to implement such action. Upon written claim of inequity served by one Party upon the other, the Parties shall act jointly to reach an agreement concerning the claimed inequity within sixty (60) days of the date of such written claim. An adjusted base coal price that differs from market price by more than ten percent (10%) shall constitute a hardship. The Party claiming inequity shall include in its claim such information and data as may be reasonably necessary to substantiate the claim and shall freely and without delay furnish such other information and data as the other Party reasonably may deem relevant and necessary. If the Parties cannot reach agreement within sixty (60) days the matter shall be submitted to arbitration.

Plainly, the procedures through which voice is expected to work are laid out in advance. Again, therefore, calculativeness is implicated in the design of ex post governance (voice).

As previously remarked, moreover, transaction cost economics maintains that ex post governance is aligned with the needs of transactions in a discriminating way. Some, but not all, transactions are provided with voice mechanisms. Specifically, classical transactions in which each party can go its own way without cost to the other will not be supported with voice.

The upshot is that calculativeness, albeit of a much richer and more varied kind that the orthodox exit-without-voice approach contemplates, applies throughout. The importance of voice is not in the least discredited. Instead, voice is encompassed within the extended calculative perspective.

2.　Calculative Trust

My purpose in this and the next two sections is to examine the aforementioned "elusive notion of trust" (Gambetta, 1988, p. ix). That will be facilitated by examining a series of examples in which the terms trust and risk are used interchangeably—which has come to be standard practice in the social science literature—after which the simple contractual schema out of which transaction cost economics works is sketched. As set out there, transaction cost economics refers to contractual safeguards, or their absence, rather than trust, or its absence. I argue that it is redundant at best and can be misleading to use the term "trust" to describe commercial exchange for which cost-effective safeguards have been devised in support of more efficient exchange. Calculative trust is a contradiction in terms.[9]

9. There is an enormous literature on trust. Some of that will be apparent from the discussion. For a more expansive survey, see Thomas, 1991.

2.1. Trust as Risk

"Trust" is a good word. So is "risk." Social scientists have begun to describe situations of trust as "a subclass of those involving risk. They are situations in which the risk one takes depends on the performance of another actor" (Coleman, 1990, p. 91). According to this formulation, trust is warranted when the expected gain from placing oneself at risk to another is positive, but not otherwise. Indeed, the decision to accept such a risk is taken to imply trust (Coleman, 1990, p. 105).

This theme is repeated throughout the influential seminar series organized by Gambetta and published under the title *Trust: Making and Breaking Cooperative Relations*. That volume closes with the following unifying observation. "[T]here is a degree of convergence in the definition of trust which can be summarized as follows: trust . . . is a particular level of the subjective probability with which an agent assesses that another agent or group of agents will perform a particular action. . . . When we say we trust someone or that someone is trustworthy, we implicitly mean that the probability that he will perform an action that is beneficial or at least not detrimental to us is high enough for us to consider engaging in some form of cooperation with him" (Gambetta, 1988, p. 217). Jeffrey Bradach and Robert Eccles expressly embrace this view in their recent (1989) treatment of "Price, Authority, and Trust" in the *Annual Review of Sociology*. As discussed below, David Kreps (1990a) and Partha Dasgupta (1988, p. 49) employ similar notions in their game theoretic treatments of trust. The upshot is that trust is purportedly made more transparent and operational by treating calculated trust as a subset of calculated risk.

James Coleman's chapter on "Relations of Trust" (1990) develops the rational choice approach to trust through three examples. The first involves a Norwegian shipowner who is urgently seeking a £200,000 loan, thereby to release a ship of his that had undergone repairs in Amsterdam. The second involves the arrival of a farmer to a new area and the unexpected breakdown of his equipment. The third is that of an immigrant high school girl who lacked companionship in her new surroundings.

Confronted by the unwillingness of the Amsterdam shipyard to release his ship, the Norwegian shipowner telephoned his merchant banker, Hambros, in the City of London to arrange a loan. Within three minutes, the Hambros banker had arranged for an Amsterdam bank to deliver the money, whereupon the shipowner was told that his ship would be released. Coleman summarizes this case as follows:

> This case clearly involves trust. The manager of the Norwegian department at Hambros placed trust in the Norwegian shipowner who telephoned him—trust to the extent of £200,000 of Hambros's money. There was no contract signed, no paper involved in the transaction, nothing more substantial than the shipowner's intention to repay the money and the Hambros man's belief in both the shipowner's honesty and his ability to repay. Similarly, the bank in Amsterdam trusted Hambros to the extent of £200,000, again merely on

the basis of a verbal request over the telephone. It committed £200,000 of its money on the assumption that Hambros would, on Monday morning, repay the sum (1990, p. 92)

The farmer example involves the breakdown of a hay baler and the prospect that the crop would be ruined by rain. This was avoided by a neighbor's offer to use his baler and to help bale the hay without charge. When the farmer who had received assistance asked what was needed in return, he was told "all he wants is the gasoline it took to bale the hay." Coleman interprets this as the "placement of trust by the second farmer in the first—trust that in a situation of need or time of trouble, when he might call on the first farmer, that farmer would provide help, as he had in this case" (1990, p. 93).

The third example begins with the assent by a high school girl to be walked home by a boy. She further assented, at his request, to take a shortcut through the woods. He then made a sexual advance, which she resisted. She was thereupon roughed up and sexually assaulted. Coleman interprets this as "a special case of a special circumstance involving trust" in which weaker women place themselves at hazard where "[s]ometimes, as in this episode, that trust is misplaced" (1990, p. 94).

Another example that is widely believed to reflect trust is that of diamond dealers in New York City. Yoram Ben-Porath (1980) describes the relationship as one in which major deals are "sealed by a handshake." Such deals would not be possible were it not for the prevalence of trust within the Jewish community. Interestingly, those conditions of trust are said to be undergoing a change. An elderly Israeli diamond dealer has described the changes as follows: "[W]hen I first entered the business, the conception was that truth and trust were simply the way to do business, and nobody decent would consider doing it differently. Although many transactions are still consummated on the basis of trust and truthfulness, this is done because these qualities are viewed as good for business, a way to make a profit" (Bernstein, 1990, p. 38).

James Henlin's account of the decisions by cab drivers to pick up a fare or not is used by Craig Thomas to illustrate "characteristic-based trust": "Since cabbies do not know anything specific about the prospective passenger based through past experiences with that person, they must make their decision to stop based on what they can infer from the setting, the physical appearance of the person, and the manner in which the person presents himself. Henlin . . . argues that trust consists of an actor offering a definition of herself, and an audience choosing either to interact with (trust) or not to interact with (distrust)" (1991, p. 45).

Recent game theoretic treatments of economic organization routinely refer to trust, usually in the context of parties engaged in sequential, repeated games. David Kreps's description of the game is typical. The basic setup is a one-sided version of the Prisoner's Dilemma game in which there is a sequence of two moves on every play of the game. First, Party X decides whether to put himself at hazard ("trust Y") or not ("do not trust Y"). If Party X accepts the hazard, then Party Y decides whether to take advantage of X ("abuse X's trust") or not ("honor X's trust"). The payoffs are such that the joint gain is maximized by the trust/honor outcome. But since Y's immediate gains are maximized if he abuses X's trust, the no-trust/no-play result will obtain if presented as a one-shot game.

Kreps thereupon converts the relation to a repeated game in which there is a high probability that each round will be followed by another. This changes the analysis "dramatically" (1990a, p. 102). Say, for example, X tells Y, "I will begin by trusting you, hoping that you will honor that trust. Indeed, I will continue to trust you as long as you do not abuse that trust. But if ever you abuse that trust, I will never again trust you." If Y hears and believes that statement, and if the game is played repeatedly (with high probability), then the honor-trust arrangement is self-enforcing (Kreps, 1990a, p. 103). The commercial context notwithstanding, trust and honor are evidently what this game is all about.

Probably the most expansive treatment of trust in a gaming context is Partha Dasgupta's chapter on "Trust as a Commodity." He begins with the claim that "[t]rust is central to all transactions and yet economists rarely discuss the notion" (1988, p. 49). He elaborates as follows: "For trust to be developed between individuals they must have repeated encounters, and they must have some memory of previous experiences. Moreover, for honesty to have potency as a concept there must be some *cost* involved in honest behavior. And finally, trust is linked with reputation, and reputation has to be acquired" (1988, p. 59). Dasgupta further remarks that "[i]f the incentives are 'right,' even a trustworthy person can be relied upon to be untrustworthy" (1988, p. 54).

2.2. The Simple Contractual Schema

Risk entails exposure to probabilistic outcomes. If a gamble has two outcomes, good and bad, the utility valuation of each is G and B, respectively, and if the probability of a good outcome is q, then the expected utility of the gamble can be expressed as $V = qG + (1 - q)B$.

Actions can sometimes be taken to mitigate bad outcomes and/or enhance good outcomes. I will define competent calculativeness as a situation in which the affected parties (1) are aware of the range of possible outcomes and their associated probabilities, (2) take cost-effective actions to mitigate hazards and enhance benefits, (3) proceed with the transaction only if expected net gains can be projected, and, (4) if X can complete the transaction with any of several Ys, the transaction is assigned to that Y for which the largest net gain can be projected.[10]

---

10. This may appear to be indistinguishable from maximizing—at least if due allowance is made for (1) the incompleteness of contracting. (2) the crude quality of information, and (3) discrete choices. For a discussion of satisficing versus maximizing, see Chapter 9.

Parties to such transactions understand a great deal about the contractual relation of which they are a part and manage it in a calculative way.[11] The simple contractual schema in Chapter 3 describes exchange as a triple (p, k, s), where p refers to the price at which the trade takes place, k refers to the hazards that are associated with the exchange, and s denotes the safeguards within which the exchange is embedded. The argument is that price, hazards, and safeguards are determined simultaneously.

The schematic and the values that each element in the vector take on are reproduced in Figure 10.1. As shown. Node A involves no hazards. The good or service in question is completely generic. Goods or services are exchanged now for prices paid now. This is the classical market exchange (Macneil, 1974, p. 738) for which competition provides a safeguard.[12]

Node B is more interesting. The contractual hazard here is $\bar{k}$. If the buyer is unable or unwilling to provide a safeguard, then $s = 0$. The corresponding break-even price is $\bar{p}$.

Node C poses the same contractual hazard, namely, $\bar{k}$. In this case, however, a safeguard in amount $\hat{s}$ is provided. The break-even price that is projected under these conditions is $\hat{p}$. It is elementary that $\hat{p} < \bar{p}$.

In the language of Section 2.1 above, Node A poses no risk, hence trust us unneeded. Nodes B and C, by contrast, do pose a risk. In the language of trust, Node B is the low-trust and Node C is the high-trust outcome.

Note that Bradach and Eccles contend that "mutual dependence [i.e., $k > 0$] between exchange partners ... [promotes] trust, [which] contrasts sharply with the argument central to the transaction cost economics that ... dependence ... fosters opportunistic behavior" (1989, p. 111). What transaction cost economics says, however, is that because opportunistic agents will not self-enforce open-ended promises to behave responsibly, efficient exchange will be realized only if dependencies are supported by credible commitments. Wherein is trust implicated if parties to an exchange are farsighted and reflect the relevant hazards in the terms of the exchange? (A better price $(\hat{p} < \bar{p})$ will be offered if the hazards $(k > 0)$ are mitigated by cost-effective contractual safeguards $(s > 0)$.) Indeed, I maintain that trust is irrelevant to commercial exchange and that reference to trust in this connection promotes confusion.

Note further that while credible commitments deter breach and support more efficient exchange, breach is not wholly precluded. On the contrary, it is inefficient to supply under some state realizations, then an optimal contract will project breach for those states. Whereas *efficient breach* of commercial contract is easy to reconcile with a calculative approach to contract, the notion

11. Pervasive calculativeness notwithstanding, the rhetoric of exchange often employs the language of promises, trust, favors, and cooperativeness. That is understandable, in that the artful use of language can produce deals that would be scuttled by abrasive calculativeness. If, however, the basic deal is shaped by objective factors, then calculativeness (credibility, hazard, safeguards, net benefits) is where the crucial action resides.

12. Another way of putting it is that (transition problems aside) each party can go its own way without cost to the other.

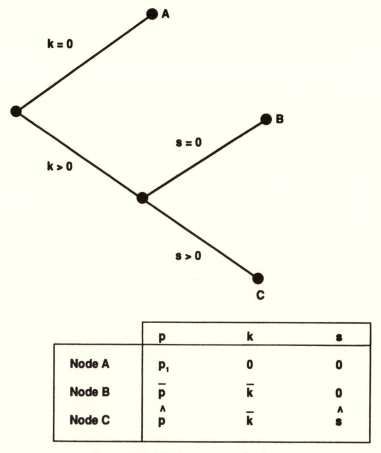

Figure 10.1. Simple contractual schema.

that trust can be efficiently breached experiences considerable strain. Much of the contract law literature would be clarified if trust were consistently used in a delimited way.

2.3. Applications

If calculative relations are best described in calculative terms, then diffuse terms, of which trust is one, that have mixed meanings should be avoided when possible. As discussed below, all of the above examples save one can be interpreted in terms of efficiency and credibility. (The exception is the assaulted girl, but that, I contend, is not properly described as a condition of trust either.) Were my arguments to prevail, the word "trust" would hereafter be used much more cautiously—at least among social scientists, if not more generally.

2.3.1. The Norwegian Shipowner

The Norwegian shipowner required a loan. Let q_1, q_2, and q_3 be the probabilities of a good outcome (timely loan repayment and profitable future business) that are projected by the shipyard, the Amsterdam bank, and the London merchant banker (Hambros), respectively. Let G_1, G_2, and G_3 be the corresponding gains and B_1, B_2, and B_3 be the corresponding losses that each associates with dealing with the Norwegian shipowner directly. The expected net gains are then given by $V_i = q_iG_i + (1 - q_i)B_i$. As I interpret Coleman, the reason why the Hambros deal went through, while the other two did not, is because $V_3 > 0$ (the merchant banker trusts) and $V_1 < 0$, $V_2 < 0$ (the shipyard and Amsterdam bank distrust). But that is not necessary. As a matter of good business practice, the Hambros deal should go through if $V_3 > 0$ and $V_3 > V_1$ and V_2.

On my interpretation, (1) all parties were calculative, (2) the loan was made by the party that projected the largest expected net gain, and (3) no trust is implied. That the merchant banker was best suited to bear the risk is, I conjecture, because it had the most knowledge of the shipowner and the best prospect of future business. Indeed, the Amsterdam shipbuilder may have the policy of never releasing ships without payment. That is not because he always projects a net negative outcome. Instead, his policy is one of efficient decision making in the context of the *system* of which shipbuilding is a part.[13] Shipbuilders know shipbuilding but have much less experience with and knowledge of clients' financial conditions, have less assurance of repeat business, and have less competence to pursue their claims for unpaid debts in court. Since the merchant banker is more well-suited in all of these respects, the shipbuilder adopts a policy whereby production is specialized to one party and financial risk is specialized to another.

Even assuming, arguendo, that the merchant banker in London was better suited than the Amsterdam bank or the shipbuilder to bear the risk, might not trust come in through knowledge possessed by the London banker of the personal integrity of the Norwegian shipowner? That is, in addition to the objective features mentioned above, might idiosyncratic knowledge of personal integrity also favor running the transaction through London? Is trust then implicated after all?

I would argue that the London banker's deep knowledge of the personal integrity of the Norwegian shipowner merely permitted him to improve his estimate of integrity. That the London banker has a better estimate, in this sense, does not imply that he has a more favorable estimate of the Norwegian shipowner's integrity. (Indeed, the London banker may refuse the loan because

---

13. The main systems argument is in the text. But there is another possibility. Shipbuilders (or, more general, businessmen—as opposed to bankers) are optimistic fellows, on which account they project subjective probabilities for good outcomes that exceed the objective conditions. Refusing to release ships may be a good policy for bringing such excesses of optimism under control. An important but little remarked purpose of having "firm but arbitrary" policies is to protect parties against idiosyncratic appeals.

he knows the Norwegian shipowner to be a crook.) More generally, if N shipowners approach Hambros with the same request and only $M < N$ are approved, what are we to infer? I submit that calculativeness is determinative throughout and that invoking trust merely muddies the (clear) waters of calculativeness.

2.3.2. The hay baler

The hay baler case is one where issues of informal organization are posed. If accidents occur with stochastic regularity and if there is a great deal of indeterminacy in setting the price for emergency aid, then there are advantages to embedding these transactions in an institutional form in which quick responsiveness on nonexploitative terms will obtain. An informal, reciprocal aid mechanism is one possible institutional response.

Cheating is nevertheless a hazard. Sanctions are needed lest opportunistic farmers abuse informal supports. Thus, although almost all requests for emergency aid elicit quick and favorable responses, failures to reciprocate are not forgotten or forgiven and, if they persist, will elicit moral suasion and, eventually, sanctions—such as ostracism and refusals of assistance. The efficacy of informal organization thus turns on calculative supports. If almost-automatic and unpriced assistance is the most efficient response, provided that the practice in question is supported by sanctions and is ultimately made contingent on reciprocity, then calculativeness obtains and appeal to trust adds nothing.

The proviso that "the practice in question is supported by sanctions" is, however, crucial. In regions where informal organization delivers very weak sanctions, deferred payment schemes that rely on a reciprocal sense of responsibility will be less viable. Less "spontaneous" cooperation will therefore be observed and/or immediate payment will be expected (demanded) on providing emergency assistance.

2.3.3. Diamond dealers

The appearance of trust among diamond dealers is deceptive. As Mark Granovetter observes, these transactions are "embedded in a close-knit community of diamond merchants who monitor one another's behavior closely" (1985, p. 492). Lisa Bernstein elaborates:

> What is unique about the diamond industry is not the importance of trust and reputation in commercial transactions, but rather the extent to which the industry is able to use reputation/social bonds at a cost low enough to be able to create a system of private law which enables most transactions to be consummated and most contracts enforced completely outside of the legal system. . . . This is accomplished in two main ways: (1) through the use of reputation bonds; (2) through a private arbitration system whose damage awards are not bounded by expectancy damages, and whose judgments are enforced by both reputation bonds and social pressure. (1990, pp. 35–36)

Put differently, Node C "trust relations" do not obtain because the diamond industry had the good luck to be organized by an ethnic community in which trust is pervasive. On the contrary, the Jewish ethnic community that organized this market succeeded because it was able to provide cost-effective sanctions more efficiently than rivals. Until recently, moreover, the efficacy of those sanctions (Bernstein, 1990, p. 41) depended on restrictive entry: In the past, Jews formed a cohesive geographically concentrated social group in the countries in which they lived. Jewish law provided detailed substantive rules of commercial behavior, and the Jewish community provided an array of extralegal dispute resolution institutions. Non-Jews to whom the sanctions for rule violation were weak—hence, would follow the rules only if that suited their convenience—could not be admitted without jeopardy to the Node C condition.[14]

The organization of this industry has nevertheless been changing in response to new information and monitoring technologies. (Conceivably, the efficacy of ethnic sanctions may be weakening, too.) Despite resistance by "older dealers accustomed to dealing primarily with friends and long standing business acquaintances" (Bernstein, 1990, p. 42), new governance structures Bernstein, 1990, p. 43) are making headway: "Among the proposals currently being considered by the World Federation of Diamond Bourses are: setting up an international computer database with reports of arbitration judgments from all member bourses in an attempt to foster international uniformity in trade customs, and a rule requiring that every bourse be equipped with a fax machine for rapid transmission of credit worthiness information. Also under consideration, although staunchly opposed by many dealers, is the creation of an international computer database describing goods available for sale worldwide."

14. The question of endgames sometimes arises. If Jews do not defect on the last play, does that imply that trust is operative after all? I would respond negatively if retired Jews remain in their community (in which event they would be subject to sanctions) or have active religious consciences. The contrast between a retiring Jew who remains within the community and the illicit deal related by Dostoyevsky in *The Brothers Karamazov* is instructive. Hardin retells that event as follows:

[A] lieutenant colonel . . . managed substantial sums of money on behalf of the army. Immediately after each periodic audit of his books, he took the available funds to the merchant Trifonov, who soon returned them with interest and a gift. In effect, both the lieutenant colonel and Trifonov benefited from funds that would otherwise have lain idle, producing no benefit for anyone. Because it was highly irregular, theirs was a secret exchange that depended wholly on personal trust not backed by the law of contracts. When the day came that the lieutenant colonel was to be abruptly replaced in his command, he asked Trifonov to return the last sum, 4,500 rubles, entrusted to him.

Trifonov replied, "I've never received any money from you, and couldn't possibly have received any." (1990, p. 185)

Although Hardin describes the relation between the lieutenant colonel and Trifonov as "personal trust," I submit that Trifonov did view (and the lieutenant colonel should have viewed) the relation calculatively—as a self-enforcing contract to which no legal or social sanctions apply (Telser, 1981, p. 27).

The change is akin to a new technology, where the need for learning-by-doing is reduced by the appearance of a standardized machine. In the diamonds case, a new information technology makes it possible to support greater dealer diversity. To be sure, ethnic identity within markets may still have value. But ethnic disparity between markets is now easier to support. To describe the earlier arrangement as a high-trust condition and the emerging arrangement as a low-trust condition confuses rather than illuminates. Both reflect calculativeness.

Put differently, it is a mistake to suppose that commercial trust has supplanted real trust. Rather, the basis for commercial trust has become more transparently calculative as new communication technologies have made inroads into this small trading community by making it possible to track commercial reputation effects in larger trading networks. As a consequence, the diamond market has become larger and more faceless.[15]

2.3.4. Cab drivers

Cab drivers need to decide whether to pick up a fare or not. Although the probability assessment out of which they work is highly subjective (it reflects risk attitudes, knowledge of particular circumstances, and prior own—and indirect—experience), this is an altogether calculative exercise. There is no obvious value added by describing a decision to accept a risk (pick up a fare) as one of trust.

2.3.5. Game theory

The "dramatic" change in the games described by Kreps comes about on moving from a one-shot game (where refusal to play was the rational choice) to a game that is repeated with high probability. Given the behavioral rules stipulated by Kreps, reputation effects relentlessly track those who breach contracts. Trading hazards are thus mitigated by embedding trades in networks in which reputation effects are known to work well.

Again, that can be interpreted as a Node C outcome. The parties have examined alternative trading scenarios and have opted for one in which the immediate gains of breach are deterred by the prospective loss of future business. To be sure, some markets are better able to support reputation effects than others. Reputation effects can and sometimes do break down and are not therefore a trading panacea (see Williams, 1988; Kreps, 1990a; Chapter 6, above). Calculative assessments of the efficacy of reputation effects are, however, properly included within the efficient contracting exercise. Reference to trust adds nothing.

Kreps might agree, but he could argue that this misconstrues his enterprise. What Kreps is really concerned with is the evolution of trading relationships—

---

15. Ethnic groups that greatly prefer continued trading within an identifiable membership, but whose costs are great in comparison with the new alternative, may need to accept lower compensation to be competitively viable, ceteris paribus.

these being the product of learning, social conditioning, corporate culture, and the like. His use of the word "trust" is merely incidental. The intertemporal mechanisms are the key.

I am not only sympathetic with this line of argument, but I would call attention to the fact that the static schema in Figure 10.1 oversimplifies, in that it takes these types of intertemporal effects as given. I submit, however, that Kreps's use of the term "trust," especially as stated in the behavioral rules that he employs, obscures rather than illuminates these mechanisms. More microanalytic attention to the *processes* through which trading relationships evolve is indeed a rewarding research enterprise (see Arrow, 1963b; Kreps, 1990a; Orbell and Davies, 1991).

2.3.6.   The assaulted girl

Consider finally the case of the assaulted girl and suppose that the matter is put to her in the abstract: should she take shortcuts through the woods with ostensibly friendly boys of slight acquaintance? I submit that the girl in question would assign a nontrivial probability to a bad outcome $(1 - q)$, and a large negative value to B. Even for large values of $G,$ the expected net gain from such walks would commonly be negative. Posed therefore as an abstract policy decision, the rational choice results is this: do not walk in the woods with strangers.

People, however, often cross bridges when they come to them rather than develop an abstract policy in advance. Still, why did she make the "wrong" decision when faced with the particulars?

One possibility is that she did not have the time to work out the calculus. Another possibility is that she had the time but got rattled. Still another possibility is that there is a dynamics to the situation which complicated matters. She cannot simply say no but needs a reason, otherwise her negative response to a "friendly" invitation will appear to be antisocial. Lacking a previously prepared response such as "I am sorry but I cannot walk in the woods because my hay fever is bothering me," and not wanting to appear unfriendly, she takes a chance.

This last involves a two-stage net benefit calculus. The first stage is as described earlier and, if the expected net gain comes out positive, the person assents and events thereafter unfold. If, however, the first stage comes out net negative, then the issue of tactful refusal must be faced. If a tactful refusal quickly presents itself, then the first stage calculus rules. But if a tactful refusal cannot be devised, then a choice between two net negatives needs to be made. Is a blunt refusal, which gives offense and/or results in a reputation for unfriendliness, more or less negative than the projected net loss from accepting the invitation (taking the risk)? Expressed in this way, the assaulted girl was caught up in a coercive situation. She was confronted with a contingency for which she was not prepared, and the social forces coerced her into taking a risky choice.

Situations that are mainly explained by bounded rationality—the risk was taken because the girl did not get the calculus right or because she was not clever enough to devise a contrived but polite refusal on the spot—are not illuminated by appealing to trust.[16]

3. Hyphenated Trust

Opportunism and bounded rationality are the key behavioral assumptions on which transaction cost economics relies. That parsimonious description is suitable for some purposes. But if man, after all, is a "social animal," then socialization and social approvals and sanctions are also pertinent. How can these be accommodated?

My response is suggested, if not evident, from my discussions of embeddedness and the institutional environment above. The Norwegian shipowner was part of a network, the farmer and diamond dealers are part of a community, and the assaulted high school girl is presented with a coercive situation. More generally, the argument is that trading hazards vary not only with the attributes of transaction but also with the trading environment of which they are a part.

Although the environment is mainly taken as exogenous, calculativeness is not suspended but remains operative. That is because the need for transaction-specific safeguards (governance) varies systematically with the institutional environment within which transactions are located. Changes in the condition of the environment are therefore factored in—by adjusting transaction-specific governance in cost-effective ways. In effect, institutional environments that provide general purpose safeguards relieve the need for added transaction-specific supports. Accordingly, transactions that are viable in an institutional environment that provides strong safeguards may be nonviable in institutional environments that are weak—because it is not cost-effective for the parties to craft transaction-specific governance in the latter circumstances.

One should not, however, conclude that stronger environmental safeguards are always better than weaker. Not only can added environmental sanctions be pushed to dysfunctional extremes in purely commercial terms, but the environment can be oppressive more generally. My purpose here is merely to describe some of the contextual features with respect to which transaction-specific governance is crafted, rather than to prescribe an optimal institutional environment. Embeddedness attributes of six kinds are distinguished: societal culture, politics, regulation, professionalization, networks,

---

16. To be sure, individuals trapped in coercive situations are attempting to cope. Is it really useful, however, to interpret a bad outcome from a coercive event as a bad draw? It is more instructive, I submit, to regard coercive events as a special class of problems that "invite" people to make risky choices from which they should be shielded (for example, by protecting them against exposure to coercive situations—possibly through training, possibly through draconian penalties against those who contrive coercion). Becker's recent treatment of addiction (1991) affords a somewhat different perspective.

and corporate culture.[17] Each can be thought of as institutional trust of a hyphenated kind: "societal-trust," "political-trust," and so forth.

3.1. Societal Culture

Culture applies to very large groups, sometimes an entire society, and involves very low levels of intentionality. The degree of trading trust in Japan, for example, is said to be much higher than in Great Britain (Dore, 1983). By contrast, the villages in southern Italy described by Edward Banfield (1958) are characterized by very low trading trust outside of the family.

The main import of culture, for purposes of economic organization, is that it serves as a check on opportunism. Social conditioning into a culture that condones lying and hypocrisy limits the efficacy of contract in three respects. First, social sanctions against strategic behavior (such as contrived breach) are weak. Second, court enforcement is problematic—since bribery is widespread. Third, individuals feel slight remorse when they behave in opportunistic ways. Given the added hazards, transactions will tend to be of a more generic (Node A, spot market) kind in societies where cultural checks on opportunism are weak, ceteris paribus.

3.2. Politics

Legislative and judicial autonomy serve credibility purposes. As Harold Berman observes, credibility will be enhanced if a monarch who has made the law "may not make it arbitrarily, and until he has remade it—lawfully—he is bound by it" (1983, p. 9). Self-denying ordinances and, even more, inertia that have been crafted into the political process have commitment benefits (North and Weingast, 1989). As discussed in Chapters 6 and 13, fewer degrees of freedom (rules) can have advantages over more (discretion) because added credible commitments can obtain in this way. Effective economic reform thus requires that political reneging options be foreclosed if investor confidence is to be realized.

3.3. Regulation

As Victor Goldberg (1976a) and Lynne Zucker (1986) have explained, regulation can serve to infuse trading confidence into otherwise problematic trading relations. The creation and administration of a regulatory agency are both very intentional acts—although that is not to say that regulation does not have a (spontaneous) life of its own (Bernstein, 1955). Provided that the regulation in question is "appropriate," both parties to the transaction—the regulated firm and its customers—will be prepared to make investments in specialized assets on better terms than they would in the absence of such regulation.

17. For more expansive discussions of the institutional environment, see Zucker 1986; Shapiro, 1987; Thomas, 1991.

3.4. Professionalization

The obligation to fulfill the definition of a role is especially important for professionals—physicians, lawyers, teachers, and so on. Although these roles generally arise in a spontaneous (evolutionary) manner, they are thereafter supported by entry limitations (such as licensing), specific ethical codes, added fiduciary obligations,[18] and professional sanctions. Such support features are highly intentional. They can have the effect of infusing trading confidence into transactions that are characterized by costly information asymmetries, although sometimes the (intentionality) purposes served are strategic (Arrow, 1963b).

3.5. Networks

The diamond dealers described above are an example of a trading network. So are the network forms of organization that have recently appeared in northern Italy (Mariotti and Cainara, 1986). Other ethnic trading groups also qualify (Landa, 1981). Although many of these networks have spontaneous origins, the maintenance of these networks depends on the perfection of intentional trading rules, the enforcement of sanctions, and the like. Credibility turns on whether these reputation effects work well or poorly.

3.6. Corporate Culture

The above-described features of the institutional environment are population-level effects, mainly of a spontaneous kind. Corporate culture displays both spontaneous and intentional features and works mainly within particular organizations. Informal organization (Barnard, 1938) is one example; the use of focal points (Kreps, 1990a) is another.

Barnard argued that formal and informal organization always and everywhere coexist (1938, p. 20) and that informal organization contributes to the viability of formal organization in three significant respects: "One of the indispensable functions of informal organizations in formal organizations . . . [is] that of communication. . . . Another function is that of maintaining the cohesiveness in formal organizations through regulating the willingness to serve and the stability of objective authority. A third function is the maintenance of the feeling of personal integrity, of self-respect, and independent choice" (1938, p. 122). That has turned out to be a productive formulation. Economic activity will be better organized where there is an appreciation for and intentional use of informal organization.

Internal effects spill over, moreover, onto external trade if firms take on distinctive trading reputations by reason of the corporate culture through which they come to be known and evaluated (Kreps, 1990a). Whether added corpo-

---

18. Fiduciary obligations arise in the context of information asymmetries where the less informed party is exposed to serious losses by failures of "due care."

rate culture is warranted, however, varies with the circumstance: "In general, it will be crucially important to align culture with the sorts of contingencies that are likely to arise" (Kreps, 1990a, p. 128). Accordingly, calculativeness characterizes even such apparently "soft" notions as corporate culture, of which Japanese economic organization is an example (see Chapter 12).

4.   Nearly Noncalculative Trust

Just as it is mind-boggling to contemplate hyperrationality of a comprehensive contracting kind, so is it mind-boggling to contemplate the absence of calculativeness. That is not to say that calculativeness cannot be suppressed or to deny that some actions or individuals are more spontaneous than others. Indeed, I shall argue that it is sometimes desirable to suppress calculativeness. If, however, the decision to suppress calculativeness is itself purposive and calculative, then the true absence of calculativeness is rare if not nonexistent.[19]

Unable to foreclose some shred of calculativeness in the personal trust relations described here, I describe personal trust as nearly noncalculative. The argument proceeds in two stages. Discrete structural analysis, with special reference to the economics of atmosphere, is discussed first. Personal trust is then examined.

4.1.   Discrete Structural Analysis

A colleague noted that the economics of atmosphere plays a larger role in *Markets and Hierarchies* (Williamson, 1975) than in *The Economic Institutions of Capitalism* (Williamson, 1985b) and asked about the de-emphasis. I replied that I thought atmosphere at least as important to an understanding of economic organization in 1985 as I had in 1975. Not having made more headway, however, I had little to add.

One of the lessons of the economics of atmosphere is that calculativeness can be taken to dysfunctional extremes. That can show up within governance structures as well as between them. The employment relation is one such context.

Suppose that a job can be split into a series of separable functions. Suppose further than differential metering at the margin is attempted with reference to each. What are the consequences?

If functional separability does not imply attitudinal separability, then piecemeal calculativeness can easily be dysfunctional. The risk is that pushing metering at the margin everywhere to the limit will have spillover effects from easy-to-meter onto hard-to-meter activities. If cooperative attitudes are impaired, then transactions that can be metered only with difficulty, but for which consummate cooperation is important, will be discharged in a more

---

19. Conceivably, some situations are so complicated that we decide to throw darts or examine entrails. But we are attempting to cope nonetheless. My discussion assumes that noncontingently selfless behavior of a Good Samaritan kind is the exception.

perfunctory manner. The neglect of such interaction effects is encouraged by piecemeal calculativeness, which is to say by an insensitivity to atmosphere.

A related issue is the matter of externalities. The question may be put as follows: ought all externalities to be metered that, taken separately, can be metered with net gains? Presumably, this turns partly on whether secondary effects obtain when an externality is accorded legitimacy. All kinds of grievances may be "felt," and demands for compensation made accordingly, if what had hitherto been considered to be harmless byproducts of normal social intercourse are suddenly declared to be compensable injuries. The transformation of relationships that will ensue can easily lead to a lower level of felt satisfaction among the parties than prevailed previously—at least transitionally and possibly permanently.

Part of the explanation is that filing claims for petty injuries influences attitudes toward other transactions. My insistence on compensation for A leads you to file claims for B, C, and D, which induces me to seek compensation for E and F, and so on. Although an efficiency gain might be realized were it possible to isolate transaction A, the overall impact can easily be negative. Realizing this to be the case, some individuals would be prepared to overlook such injuries. But everyone is not similarly constituted. Society is rearranged to the advantage of those who demand more exacting correspondences between rewards and deeds if metering at the margin is everywhere attempted. Were the issue of compensation to be taken up as a constitutional matter, rather than on a case-by-case basis, a greater tolerance for spillover would commonly obtain (Schelling, 1978).

Also pertinent is that individuals keep informal social accounts and find the exchange of reciprocal favors among parties with whom uncompensated spillovers exist to be satisfying (Goulder, 1954). Transforming these casual social accounts into exact and legal obligations may well be destructive of atmosphere and lead to a net loss of satisfaction between the parties. Put differently, pervasive pecuniary relations impair the quality of "contracting"—even if the metering of the transactions in question were costless.[20]

The argument that emerges from the above is not that metering ought to be prohibited but that the calculative approach to organization that is associated with economics can be taken to extremes. An awareness of attitudinal spillovers and nonpecuniary satisfactions serves to check such excesses of calculativeness. Consider now a more extreme possibility: there are some transactions for which the optimal level of *conscious* metering is zero.[21]

20. The buying of "rounds" in English pubs is an example. Would a costless meter lead to a superior result? Suppose that everyone privately disclosed a willingness to pay and that successive bids were solicited until a break-even result was projected. Suppose that the results of the final solicitation are either kept secret or posted, depending on preferences, and that rounds are thereafter delivered to the table on request. Monthly bills are sent out in accordance with the break-even condition. How is camaraderie affected?

21. Unconscious or subconscious metering is another problem. Observations that are not consciously processed may be processed by the subconscious nonetheless, and their ramifications may insistently intrude on consciousness.

The idea here is that conscious monitoring, even of a low-grade kind, introduces unwanted calculativeness that is contrary to the spirit of certain very special relations and poses intertemporal threats to their viability. Not only can intendedly noncalculative relations can be upset by Type I error, according to which a true relation is incorrectly classified as false, but calculativeness may be subject to (involuntary) positive feedback. Intendedly noncalculative relations that are continuously subject to being reclassified as calculative are, in effect, calculative.

Issues akin to those examined by Robert Nozick in his discussion of "Love's Bond" (1988) are implicated. Nozick contends that the idea of "trading up" is inimical to a loving relationship: "The intention in love is to form a *we* and to identify with it as an extended self, to identify one's fortunes in large part with its fortunes. A willingness to trade up, to destroy the *we* you largely identify with, would then be a willingness to destroy yourself in the form of your own extended self" (1988, p. 78, emphasis in original). If entertaining the possibility of trading up devalues the relation, a discrete structural shift that disallows trading up, which is a variety of calculativeness, is needed.

4.2. Personal Trust

John Dunn's recent treatment of "Trust and Political Agency" raises many of the pertinent issues (1988, p. 73). Thus, Dunn distinguishes between trust as a "human passion" and trust as a "modality of human action," where the latter is "a more or less consciously chosen policy for handling the freedom of other human agents or agencies" (1988, p. 73). He subsequently remarks that "trust as a passion is the confident expectation of benign intentions by another agent," but as a "modality of action, . . . trust is ineluctably strategic" (1988, p. 74). He also contends that "the twin of trust is betrayal" (1988, p. 81) and avers that "human beings need, as far as they can, to economize on trust in persons and confide instead in well-designed political, social, and economic institutions" (1988, p. 85).

Trust as a passion versus trust as a modality corresponds in my treatment to personal trust and calculative trust, respectfully. Moreover, Dunn's characterization of calculative trust as strategic, whereas personal trust is not, is exactly right. But whereas Dunn contends that the twin of trust is betrayal, I would reserve betrayal for personal trust and would use breach of contract to describe calculative relations. As hitherto remarked, breach of contract is sometimes efficient, even in a commercial contract that is supported by perfect safeguards (see Chapter 5). By contrast, betrayal of a personal trust can never be efficient. Betrayal is demoralizing.

Also, although I subscribe to the notion of economizing on trust, I would put the issue somewhat differently. Trust, I submit, should be concentrated on those personal relations in which it really matters, which will be facilitated by the use of "political, social, and economic institutions" to govern calculative relations.[22]

22. Dennis Robertson's remark is pertinent: "[I]f we economists mind our own business, and do that business well, we can, I believe, contribute mightily to the economizing, that is to

If calculativeness is inimical to personal trust, in that a deep and abiding trust relation cannot be created in the face of calculativeness, and if preexisting personal trust is devalued by calculativeness, then the question is how to segregate and preserve relations of personal trust.[23] I will take it that X reposes personal trust in Y if X (1) consciously refuses to monitor Y, (2) is predisposed to ascribe good intentions to Y when things go wrong, and (3) treats Y in a discrete structural way. Conditions 1 and 3 limit calculativeness. Under condition 2, "bad outcomes" are given a favorable construction: they are interpreted by X as stochastic events, or as complexity (Y didn't fully understand the situation), or as peccadillos (Y was inebriated).

To be sure, there are limits. An event where Y unambiguously violates the trust that X reposes in him threatens the relationship. Also (and here is where calculativeness creeps back in), a succession of minor violations may jeopardize the condition of trust. What further distinguishes personal trust, however, is that X insists that Y "reform" rather than merely "do better." That is because experience rating with continuous updating of the trustworthiness of Y places X in a calculative relation to Y. That degrades the relationship. Rather than do that, X elevates the relationship by placing it on all-or-none terms. Should Y refuse to make a discrete structural break with his past, then X will no longer trust him.[24] If instead Y agrees to reform, then trust will be renewed.

Personal trust is therefore characterized by (1) the absence of monitoring, (2) favorable or forgiving predilections, and (3) discreteness. Such relations are clearly very special. Although some individuals may have the natural instincts to behave noncalculatively, others will need to figure it out—to look ahead and recognize that calculativeness will devalue the relation, which is a farsighted view of contract. It does not, moreover, suffice merely to figure it out, in that some of those who do may be unable to shed calculativeness—because calculativeness (or fear) is so deeply etched by their experience.[25] Be that as it may, trust, if it obtains at all, is reserved for very special relations between family, friends, and lovers. Such trust is also the stuff of which tragedy is made. It goes to the essence of the human condition.[26]

---

the full but thrifty utilization, of that scarce resource Love—which *we* know, just as well as anybody else, to be the most precious thing in the world" (1976, p. 154).

23. There is nonetheless a sense in which incomplete contracts are continuously calculative, and that is in relation to reputation effects. If one party cannot make significant commercial moves without notice of the other—even moves that have no direct bearing on the immediate contract but involve different contracts with different trading partners—then continuous Bayesian updating may "ineluctably" obtain. In that event, reputation effects are pervasive (Kreps, 1990a).

24. That does not mean that X will no longer have anything to do with Y. If, however, the relation continues, X will thereafter treat Y in a calculative way.

Note in this connection that any shred of calculativeness does not imply that the relation is calculative. Rather, calculativeness needs to cross some (rather low) threshold before the relation is classified as calculative. The line is drawn—that is, a discrete structural break occurs—where X asks Y to reform.

25. Joseph Raz makes a related argument: some people "fail to see that personal relations cannot be valued in terms of commodities" (1986, p. 353).

26. See Nozick, 1988. Note that to repose trust in someone does not imply confidence in their judgment. Rather, as Dunn (1988) has put it, to trust is to ascribe benign intent. Selective

5.   Concluding Remarks

5.1.   Linguistic and Conceptual Tools

A case can be made, and I will assume here, that a science of organization is in progress (see Chapter 2). The development of "specialized vocabularies" and "new languages" commonly attend such a project (Kuhn, 1970).

The development of a science of administration,[27] which was Simon's objective in *Administrative Behavior* (1957a, pp. 248–53) posed exactly those needs. Given the deep insights afforded by Chester Barnard's path-breaking book *The Functions of the Executive* (1938), how could that project be advanced? Simon observed in this connection that "we do not yet have, in this field, adequate linguistic and conceptual tools for realistically and significantly describing even a simple administrative organization—describing it, that is, in a way that will provide the basis for scientific analysis of the effectiveness of its structure and operation" (1957a, p. xiv). The need, as he saw it, was to "be able to describe, in words, exactly how an administrative organization looks and how it works. . . . I have attempted to construct a vocabulary which will permit such a description" (1957a, p. xiv).

5.2.   Calculativeness

The way in which human actors are described and the processes through which contracting is perceived to work are both crucial to the development of a science of organization. Human actors are described here as boundedly rational and opportunistic, while the contracting process entails "incomplete contracting in its entirety." This last views the governance of contractual relations broadly, including an examination of the systems context within which contracts are embedded. A very calculative orientation to commercial contracting is the result.

Such a farsighted approach to contract (in which credible commitments, or the lack thereof, play a key role) collides with sociological views on power and trust. The recent tendency for sociologists and economists alike to use the terms "trust" and "risk" interchangeably is, on the arguments advanced here, ill-advised.

Not only is "calculated trust" a contradiction in terms, but user-friendly terms, of which "trust" is one, have an additional cost. The world of commerce is reorganized in favor of the cynics, as against the innocents, when social scientists employ user-friendly language that is not descriptively accurate— since only the innocents are taken in. Commercial contracting will be better served if parties are cognizant of the embeddedness conditions of which they

---

delegation is consistent with trust if the judgment of the trusted delegate is believed to be better in some contexts than in others.

27. A science of organization deals with markets, hybrids, hierarchies, bureaucracies, and the like, whereas the science of administration is preoccupied with internal organization.

are a part and recognize, mitigate, and price out contractual hazards in a discriminating way.[28]

5.3.   Categories of Trust

Without purporting to be exhaustive, trust differences of three types are distinguished: calculative trust, personal trust, and institutional (or hyphenated) trust. For the reasons given above, calculative relations should be described in calculative terms, to which the language of risk is exactly suited. The practice of using "trust" and "risk" interchangeably should therefore be discontinued.

Personal trust is made nearly noncalculative by switching out of a regime in which the marginal calculus applies into one of a discrete structural kind. That often requires added effort and is warranted only for very special personal relations that would be seriously degraded if a calculative orientation were "permitted." Commercial relations do not qualify.[29]

Institutional trust refers to the social and organizational context within which contracts are embedded. In the degree to which the relevant institutional features are exogenous, institutional trust has the appearance of being noncalculative. In fact, however, transactions are always organized (governed) with reference to the institutional context (environment) of which they are a part. Calculativeness thus always reappears.[30]

Should these arguments prevail, trust will hereafter be reserved for noncalculative personal relations (and, possibly, in a hyphenated form, to describe differences in the institutional environment). Although this is a long article to reach such a modest result, the literature on trust is truly enormous, and the confusions associated with calculativeness are growing. The incipient science of organization needs common concepts and language as the productive dialogue between law, economics, and organization takes shape. The irony is that the limits of calculativeness are realized by examining user-friendly terms—of which "trust" is one—in a thoroughly calculative way.

28. This is not to deny the excesses of calculativeness that sociologists (for example, Merton, 1936) and contract law specialists (for example, Macauley, 1963) have forcefully called to our attention. Transaction cost economics takes a farsighted view of contract in which "feasible" calculativeness is featured.

29. I subscribe to the proposition that "[t]he core idea of trust is that it is not based on an expectation of its justification. When trust is justified by expectations of positive reciprocal consequences, it is simply another version of economic exchange" (March and Olsen, 1989).

30. Also, the parties to a transaction sometimes influence the context, the capture (Bernstein, 1955) or precapture (Stigler, 1971) of regulation being examples.

IV

PUBLIC POLICY

The first two chapters in Part IV have the same general message: Respect the limits of good arguments. Indeed, this is an old message in Industrial Organization. As Ronald Coase (1972) observed many years ago, describing the firm as a production function predisposed Industrial Organization to ascribe monopoly purpose and effect to every nonstandard and unfamiliar business practice. As a consequence, barriers to entry and price discrimination arguments were overused, and so public policy was, at best, skeptical of, and frequently inhospitable toward, complex forms of contract and organization.

Transaction cost economics describes the firm instead as a governance structure, in which complex firm and market forms of organization are presumed to have economizing purpose and effect. That, however, is a rebuttable presumption, because transaction cost economics also expressly makes an allowance for strategic behavior in circumstances in which preexisting monopoly power is substantial.

Although many strategic arguments fail because the requisite preconditions are not satisfied, I argue in Chapter 11, "Delimiting Antitrust," that Frank Easterbrook's "five-filter" approach to antitrust makes insufficient allowance for strategic behavior. The same is true, moreover, of the U.S. Supreme Court (in *Matsushita*), the Federal Trade Commission (in *White*), and the Antitrust Division (in *Montfort*): All have been too sanguine in passing off monopoly purposes. Antitrust does not overcome the excesses of earlier monopoly reasoning by swinging to the opposite extreme.

Chapter 12, "Strategizing, Economizing, and Economic Organization," nevertheless counsels that excesses of monopoly reasoning are a continuing hazard. Thus although the new literature on strategic behavior (sometimes referred to as the New Industrial Organization) is much more rigorous and avoids some of the logical pitfalls that beset the entry barrier arguments of the 1960s, there is still a tendency to overreach when these models—of raising rivals' costs, of vertical integration, of networks, and the like—are applied to public policy. Especially in the long run, when Schumpeterian "handing on" can be presumed to apply, economizing is a very robust policy. By contrast, clever plans, ploys, positioning, and the like are often ephemeral.

Chapter 13, "The Institutions and Governance of Economic Development and Reform," is an effort to bring institutional economics to bear on the enormously difficult problems posed by economic development and reform. Although there is growing agreement that institutions have a major impact on the prospects for reform, institutional economists still can offer little specific advice (Coase, 1992; North, 1994). The approach recommended in this chapter is to work at these problems in a bottom–up way, emphasizing the mechanisms of governance rather than "general theories" of economic reform. This repeats a now-familiar theme, that much of the relevant analytic action resides in the details.

11

Delimiting Antitrust

Both the law and economics of antitrust have undergone significant change in the past twenty years. The expansive antitrust attitudes and enforcement practices of the 1960s have been delimited. Greater respect for economies and the subtleties of market processes and competition have developed. Efforts to focus antitrust policy and further delimit antitrust enforcement are in progress. Although I am sympathetic with these general purposes, I am also concerned with overshooting.

Section 1 of this chapter examines the changing attitudes toward antitrust and distinguishes between inflexible legal rule and more flexible legal process bases for delimiting enforcement. Section 2 assesses the "filters" approach to antitrust proposed by Frank Easterbrook (1984), parts of which have been embraced by the enforcement agencies and the courts. Section 3 sketches the scope of strategic behavior. Several recent cases in which filter and strategic behavior issues arise are discussed in Section 4.

1. The Logic of Antitrust

Antitrust is a complicated subject and is usefully informed by several points of view. In the following paragraphs I discuss and distinguish economic and legal logic and argue that antitrust is best analyzed by regarding "economizing" as the "main case"—where, in the context of antitrust, the main case is that factor that is held to be primarily responsible for shaping and changing the organization of economic activity. I hold that economizing on production costs but, even more, on transactions costs qualifies for main case standing.

Once alternative main case hypotheses have been stated and their ramifications displayed, qualifications of both legal and economic kinds can thereafter be introduced. Some, however, who ask that their antitrust voices be heard fail or refuse to state the main case out of which they work. This is a dereliction (or worse). A pressing need in antitrust is that alternative main case hypotheses be clearly stated and their ramifications exposed.

1.1. The Economic Logic

1.1.1. Main case reasoning

"Monopolizing" and "economizing" are the two leading economic purposes that are used to interpret business behavior. These factors are not mutually exclusive. If, however, one predominates, then it should be regarded as the main case and the other treated as the exception (rather than on parity and certainly not as the rule). Deeper understanding will be realized and needless confusion will be avoided by keeping the main case clearly in mind and introducing qualifications as and where they are needed.

During the 1960s, monopolizing was thought to be mainly responsible for nonstandard or unfamiliar business practices. Ronald Coase captured the prevailing spirit by remarking:

> [i]f an economist finds something—a business practice of one sort or another—that he does not understand, he looks for a monopoly explanation. And as in this field we are very ignorant, the number of ununderstandable practices tends to be very large, and the reliance on a monopoly explanation frequent. (1972, p. 67)

One factor responsible for this monopoly predisposition was the prevailing practice of describing the firm as a production function whose natural boundaries were defined by technology. Economic inputs were thus transformed by the production technology into economic outputs; organizational considerations were effectively suppressed. Efforts to extend the reach of the firm by merger or by complex contracting practices (vertical restraints, reciprocity, joint ventures, etc.) were thus presumed to be anticompetitive (see Williamson, 1985b, pp. 15–42, 365–84).

Lawyers were willing accomplices. What has come to be referred to as "creative lawyering"[1] enjoyed unusual latitude during the 1960s. The standards for judging an antitrust offense fell so low that respondents not only made no affirmative case for economies as an antitrust defense but even *disclaimed* economies that were ascribed to a merger by the government.[2] The role of

---

1. John Shenefield represented that "creative lawyering" could be employed to bring antitrust suits against conglomerate mergers that did not obviously fall within the scope of the merger statutes. Given the vague language of the statutes and the wide latitude of the case law, imaginative lawyers would "find a way" to bring such suits (Hearings, 1978).

2. *Federal Trade Commission* v. *Proctor & Gamble Corp.,* 386 U.S. 568 (1967). Thus Proctor & Gamble insisted that its acquisition of Clorox was unobjectionable because the government was unable to establish definitively that any efficiencies would result:

> [The government is unable to prove] any advantages in the procurement or price of raw materials or in the acquisition or use of needed manufacturing facilities or in the purchase of bottles or in freight costs.... [T]here is no proof of any savings in any aspect of manufacturing. There is no proof that any additional manufacturing facilities would be usable for the production of Clorox. There is no proof that any combination of manufacturing facilities would effect any savings, even if such combination were feasible. (Fisher and Lande, 1983, pp. 1580–82)

the economist in the Antitrust Division was compromised. A nadir in antitrust enforcement was reached. The "inhospitality tradition" flourished.[3]

This unsatisfactory state of affairs was increasingly criticized during the 1970s. First, the social benefits of efficient resource allocation—to include the importance of economies as an antitrust defense[4]—became much more widely appreciated. More importantly, the nature of the business firm was reconceptualized. The older theory of the firm as production function gradually made way (or gave way) to a theory of the firm in which express allowance was made for transaction costs. Accordingly, the firm was thereafter described as a governance structure. Factors that contributed to the comparative integrity of contract were thus introduced. Technology was no longer determinative, and the boundaries of the firm (what to make, what to buy, how to trade, etc.) now needed to be derived.

This reconceptualization of the business firm together with a demonstration that economies constituted a meaningful (if not dispositive) antitrust defense across a wide range of pertinent economic circumstances (parameter values) placed antitrust enforcement under severe strain. Although some commentators argued that the influence of economic reasoning on antitrust enforcement was slight (see Stigler, 1982), there is growing agreement that antitrust would not have been reformed but for the development of new theory. The differences between the 1968 and the 1982 merger guidelines of the United States Department of Justice evidence some of the changes that resulted from the paradigm shift away from market power (monopolizing) in favor of efficiency (economizing).

To be sure, antitrust is not innocent of politics (see Section 4); however, ideas matter more in antitrust than in most regulated areas. As one observer noted, "a genuine scientific revolution has occurred . . . [and] has led to a more thoughtful and rational approach to antitrust" (Frech, 1987, p. 263). Indeed, William Baxter's forcefulness notwithstanding, "it would have been politically impossible for . . . Baxter to have done what he did [as Assistant Attorney General for Antitrust], had there not been an intellectual shift in the underpinnings of antitrust" (Bork, 1985, pp. 21, 25).

3. Frank Easterbrook characterizes the inhospitality tradition as one in which "judges view each business practice with suspicion" (1984, p. 4). This characterization is much too narrow. The entire 1960s enforcement process worked out of this orientation with only minor exceptions. The prevailing applied price theory orientation within industrial organization, whereby firms were regarded as production functions and nonstandard contracting was interpreted as an effort to extend the reach of the firm beyond its natural boundaries, gave succor to the inhospitality tradition (Coase, 1972, p. 62).

4. Thus suppose one ascribes adverse economic effects to a merger with both market power and efficiency consequences. One can assess the plausibility of adverse effects by asking (1) what range of price effects are reasonably attributed to the merger, (2) what range of cost savings are reasonably attributed to the merger, (3) what is the relevant range of demand elasticities, and (4) what is the preexisting degree of market power. If for all reasonable parameter values the net allocative efficiency effects are judged positive by applying partial equilibrium welfare apparatus, then the claims of adverse effect must fail on grounds of implausibility (Williamson, 1968b, 1977a; Harberger, 1971).

1.1.2.   Strategic behavior

Strategic behavior can take either defensive or offensive forms. The former involve efforts to protect ill-defined property rights against loss of appropriability. Lest the benefits of an investment or innovation be appropriated by other participants in the vertical chain of supply, firms that originate an investment or innovation may be induced to make "linking investments" (Heide and John, 1988) or to integrate (backward, forward, or laterally) into other stages (Teece, 1986, p. 285). The object of these investments is defensive, in that, were it not for the hazard of leakage, they would not be undertaken. Albeit sometimes complicated, defensive strategic moves that are designed to deter leakage rarely pose antitrust problems (Klein, 1980).

By contrast, offensive strategic behavior is concerned not with leakage in the vertical contracting process but rather is directed at actual and potential rivals. It entails efforts by established firms to take up advance positions and/or respond punitively toward rivals. As discussed below, such behavior (1) can take a wide variety of forms, some of which are very subtle, and (2) is often problematic in antitrust respects, especially when the strategies in question are focused on a particular rival (or well-defined subset of rivals) or are exercised in a disciplinary (contingent) fashion. My concern hereafter is with strategic behavior of this second kind.

A new logic of strategic behavior progressively took shape in the 1980s. Although much of this work bears on entry barrier arguments that constituted the centerpiece of the inhospitality tradition, recent work is careful and does not indicate that monopoly will again be accepted as the main case. First, while the mere existence of entry barriers was previously thought both objectionable and unlawful, this noncomparative approach has been supplanted by one in which (as an enforcement matter) the relevant test is not whether entry impediments *exist* but whether a *remedy* can be effected with net social gains. As a result, arguments regarding the mere existence of entry barriers no longer carry the day. Second, the logic of strategic models is much more carefully developed with credibility features given special attention.[5] Third, the structural preconditions—mainly high concentration coupled with severe hurdles to entry—necessary for support of exclusionary or other anticompetitive effects now are meticulously respected. Because these conditions are the exception rather than the rule, economizing remains the main case to which appropriate strategic qualifications are added.

1.2.   The Legal Logic

Kenneth Arrow has described the economist as "the guardian of rationality, the ascriber of rationality to others, and the prescriber of rationality to the social world."[6] The law, however, has needs of its own that are sometimes

---

5. Credibility issues are discussed in Williamson, 1985b, pp. 373–77.

6. Arrow, 1974, p. 17. To be sure, noneconomists also engage in the rationality dialogue (Simon, 1978). That the economist is the preeminent user and spokesman of rationality analysis, however, is conceded generally.

thought to be poorly served by rationality analysis. If the economist is the guardian of rationality, many regard the lawyer as the guardian of administrability. Judge Stephen Breyer when on the First Circuit observed:

> While technical economic discussion helps to inform the antitrust laws, those cannot precisely replicate the economists' (sometimes conflicting) views. For, unlike economics, law is an administrative system the effects of which depend upon the content of rules and precedents only as they are applied by judges and juries in courts and by lawyers advising their clients. Rules that seek to embody every economic complexity and qualification ... [thus sometimes give way to] the administrative virtues of simplicity.[7]

This language is favorably cited by Frank Easterbrook in conjunction with his proposal to screen out highly problematic antitrust cases by employing a series of antitrust filters (1984, pp. 16–17).

There are two different approaches to administrability. I refer to the first of these as the "legal process" approach and the second as the "legal rules" approach. The main distinction is that the latter works out of economic certitudes—usually, that the relevant economic models are in place and are correctly understood by the antitrust authorities—while the former is much more tentative. Rather than assert false certitude, the legal process approach urges that complicated issues of economic organization that are poorly understood by accorded respect. The object is to move toward a progressively more informed disposition of the issues as the relevant theory is refined and implemented, due allowance having been made for the infirmities of the courts. The immediate object is to discover the relevant tradeoffs implied by the theory, thereafter to develop an operational framework whereby these tradeoffs can be assessed.

1.2.1. Legal process

The legal process approach counsels gradualism. Antitrust responsiveness to new developments in economic theory only occurs with a lag. After all, economics is subject to fads and fashions,[8] which are best sorted out through sustained academic critique. Moreover, even those developments that survive such criticism must be operationalized. Consequently, crude approximating devices may have to be developed. Derek Bok's discussion of the enforcement of merger law illustrates these concerns:

> Although truth is the preeminent aim of economic study it can only be one of several goals in law. Lawyers have perhaps not always been explicit enough in articulating the peculiar qualifications which their institutions place upon the unbridled pursuit of truth, and this failure may in some measure explain the irritation with which their handiwork is so often greeted by even thoughtful economists. This problem cannot be solved, nor can the economist-critic be placated, by embracing more and more of the niceties of economic theory

---

7. *Barry Wright Corp.* v. *ITT Grinnell Corp.*, 724 F.2d 227, 234 (1st Cir. 1983).

8. The widespread use of differential risk aversion to explain contractual anomalies in the 1970s is an illustration.

into our antitrust proceedings. Unless we can be certain of the capacity of our legal system to absorb new doctrine, our attempts to introduce it will only be made ludicrous in failure and more costly in execution. (1960, pp. 227–28)

That antitrust enforcement was not ready in 1968 to absorb economies as an antitrust defense is probably consonant with Bok's views. That economies arguments influenced the enforcement process during the 1970s and today play an even larger role is a gradualist outcome which many consider beneficial.[9] Arguably, this is the way antitrust enforcement should work.

1.2.2. Legal rules

The legal rules approach to antitrust enforcement assumes that the relevant economic theory is already in hand and is adequately understood by the antitrust authorities.[10] It further holds that the courts have limited ability to deal with tradeoffs or more sophisticated economic reasoning and that these conditions are unchanging. A predilection to pronounce simple legal rules *now* is characteristic of legal scholars who work out of the legal rules framework.

For example, several leading legal scholars have advised against an examination of economies as an antitrust defense or an assessment of the condition of entry, and have instead favored inelastic legal rules. Consider the following:

1. [C]laims of economic efficiency will not justify a course of conduct conferring excessive market power. The objective of maintaining a system of self-policing markets requires that all such claims be rejected.[11]

2. Rebuttal based on ease of entry, economies of scale, or managerial efficiencies should not be allowed, because these factors, although clearly relevant to a correct evaluation of the competitive significance of a merger, are intractable subjects for litigation. (Posner, 1975a, pp. 282, 313)

As it turns out, however, the question of what market power is excessive must be assessed in relation to any benefits (economies) simultaneously conferred by the objectionable practice or structure in question. Similarly, ease of entry has become a central feature in the assessment of the competitive significance of mergers. Antitrust enforcement has progressively made provision for both.

---

9. Timothy Muris and I explain the benefits of an economies defense; see Williamson, 1968b, 1977a; Muris, 1979. For a more cautious view of the benefits of an economies defense see Fisher and Lande, 1983.

10. It has been argued that "the economic background required for understanding antitrust issues seldom requires detailed mastery of economic refinements" (Areeda, 1967, p. 4). This means, presumably, that the standard economic models of firms and markets found in intermediate microtheory textbooks will suffice. I doubt it.

11. Blake and Jones, 1965, pp. 422, 427. The Supreme Court was evidently persuaded when it pronounced that "[p]ossible economies cannot be used as a defense to illegality," *Federal Trade Commission* v. *Proctor & Gamble Corp.*, 386 U.S. 568, 580 (1967), as though the illegalities in question were well defined, both then and forever.

The strategic behavior area is one in which legal scholars more recently have proposed highly circumscribed rules. Consider the following:

1. In general, if greater than competitive profits are to be made in an industry, entry should occur whether the entrant has to come in at both levels or not. I know of no theory of imperfections in the capital market which would lead suppliers of capital to avoid areas of higher return to seek areas of lower return. (Bork, 1969, pp. 139, 148)

2. [L]ong run possibilities must be disregarded because they are intrinsically speculative and indeterminate. No suitable administrative rules could be formulated to give them recognition. (Areeda and Turner, 1976, pp. 891, 897)

3. If there is any room in antitrust law for rules of per se legality, one should be created to encompass predatory conduct. The antitrust offense of predation should be forgotten. (Easterbrook, 1981b, pp. 336–37)

To be sure, market skeptics sometimes make bald claims of capital market imperfections of other defects without empirical support. Market enthusiasts sometimes respond with equally bald claims of capital market efficacy. Albeit understandable, such responses will not do. The issues to be addressed are (1) has there been a mistake in the use of competitive logic (e.g., a failure to trace out the ramifications of the contracting process in its entirety), or (2) has there been a mistake in assessing competitive efficacy.

As it turns out, transaction cost logic demonstrates that vertical integration can influence the cost of capital under carefully delimited circumstances (Williamson, 1975, 1977b), a consideration which is now admitted.[12] Moreover, numerous studies have since demonstrated that timing can have real cost-bearing, and therefore entry-deterring, consequences (see Spence, 1977; Dixit, 1980; Katz and Shapiro, 1986). Furthermore, while the economic analysis of strategic behavior has developed few operational rules, the purported irrationality of predatory pricing has been discredited (Kreps and Wilson, 1982; Milgrom and Roberts, 1982).

The upshot is that, although inflexible legal rules proposed by lawyers facilitate administrability by disregarding economies, differential capital costs and related costs of entry, long run possibilities and predatory conduct, and by "dichotomizing" transactions, the possibility of serving the needs of administrability under the aegis of more flexible legal process rather than legal rules warrants serious consideration. The needs of administrability would arguably be served by introducing new legal rules with the following introductory statement: "Temporarily, pending further economic analysis and deeper understanding of the economic *institutions and practices* in question, the legal rule for dealing with this class of cases will be. . . ." Successive refinements can thereafter be adopted. This more flexible approach is appropriate for antitrust administration when consensus is slow to form but successive theoretical refinements play a critical role in judicial enforcement.

---

12. Posner, 1979. Indeed, the merger guidelines now acknowledge this state of affairs (*U.S. Department of Justice Merger Guidelines*, 1982).

1.3. Adopting Refinements

Noneconomists frequently criticize economics because it works out of a rationality framework, but this is rarely the problem. Rationality analysis is really very elastic and can provide for any systematic feature. The main "problems" with the economic approach are that it sometimes postulates hypothetical ideals (e.g., costless compensation for injury), thereby making it nonoperational, or that it sometimes focuses too narrowly, thereby omitting or undervaluing important attributes.

Sociologists are frequent critics and often remark that the economic model of the worker focuses too narrowly on the intended or immediate effects of added incentives or controls to the neglect of unintended or secondary effects. Bureaucratic efforts to exercise control thus will often be deflected or defeated by "dysfunctional" responses by the groups at which they are directed (see March and Simon, 1958, chap. 2). A more complete analysis of the issues requires a sociological perspective in which secondary effects are observed and interpreted.

The fact that incentives and controls give rise to originally unintended consequences, however, does not imply that the economic approach is intrinsically unable to make allowance for sociological effects. To the contrary, rationality analysis not only permits but demands that all significant, predictable secondary consequences be *folded in,* thus making the theory more complete. Taking such secondary consequences into account from the outset will avoid remediable errors.

The same rationale applies to administrability considerations. Puzzles and tradeoffs frequently preoccupy economists to the neglect of administrability. They study issues that are interesting for their own sake, even if the "complexities" are poorly understood and well beyond the current capacity of the legal system. Economists, however, can and have dealt with issues of administrability where these needs are plainly salient. Moreover, improvements on legal rules can and have been realized in the process.

Peter Hutt's risk classification approach (1978, p. 558) to food safety is illustrative. Working from the premise that similar cases should receive similar treatment, Hutt argues that "similar risks should be treated similarly" (1978, p. 582). Hutt achieves simplification by employing three risk categories and measuring risk entirely with reference to the *probability of an unwanted outcome.* As discussed elsewhere, this simplification (1) assumes that the loss associated with an unwanted outcome is constant for all food items considered both within and across risk classifications; (2) ignores benefits, including health benefits associated with an item; and (3) assumes that all members of the consuming population are identical (Williamson, 1981c, p. 131). These are extreme simplifications and are frequently contradicted by the data. They are, moreover, unnecessary—since feasible administrable alternative *procedures,* as opposed to rules, for dealing with food risks are available that work more systematically out of an economic net benefit framework (Williamson, 1981c, pp. 139–47). These procedures—which I have referred to as the risk classification decision tree (Williamson, 1981c, pp. 142–50)—distinguish among different uses and users and examine the pertinent tradeoffs that apply to each. To be sure, the decision process is somewhat more complicated as a result. Excesses of simplification (rules as against procedures) frequently come, however, at a prohibitively high cost.

The approach to antitrust and economic regulation proposed herein recommends that administrability considerations be factored into the overall rationality analysis of the issues. The rules in force at each point in time would thus be required to pass an administrability test, but provision would be made to successively improve the rules upon refining the relevant theory and our understanding of complex phenomena.[13] Rationality and the needs of the legal process are thereby joined.

Donald Dewey's view of the role of economists in antitrust is broadly consonant:

> The important issues in the control of monopoly are 'economic' in the sense that judges and administrators are compelled to make decisions in the light of what they think the business world is 'really' like, and it is the task of economists through research and reflection to provide them with an *increasingly* accurate picture. (1959, p. i; emphasis added)

I would merely add that economists can and should incorporate administrability considerations within an extended rationality framework. Incorporation is already occurring and explains the dramatic changes in antitrust referred to above.[14]

2. Antitrust Filters

The purpose of a filter is to perform a sort between problematic and unproblematic cases. I argue that market power is the only true filter and that the four additional features introduced by Easterbrook are better regarded as relevant *factors* rather than as filters. The relevant market power test is a stringent one: market power should be present in sufficient degree to support strategic behavior. Merely to exceed the strategic behavior threshold is not, however, dispositive. Thus although all cases that fall below such a threshold would be exempted, those cases that are above threshold would thereafter be subject to an examination on the merits. The added factors to which Easterbrook refers are germane to such an assessment.

13. The recent paper by Michael Katz and Carl Shapiro illustrates complexities well beyond the competence of current antitrust (1986, pp. 835, 840).

14. That the 1982 merger guidelines (and successors thereto) differ from the 1968 version is at least partly because of the insistent press of economizing reasoning and a growing appreciation for the way the tradeoff calculus works. Had economists felt constrained by the purported limits of the legal process, these and related developments would not have occurred. Therefore, today one would not find mergers assessed with reference to ease of entry, economies of scale, managerial efficiencies, or related transaction cost features.

Thus assume that the structural factors that would support strategic behavior have been exceeded, on which account the behavior in question might possibly have strategic purpose and effect. The issue to be addressed is whether nonstrategic explanations *more plausibly* explain this behavior. Each of the factors to which Easterbrook refers are among those that would help to inform such a *comparative assessment on the merits.* But merely to satisfy any or even all of these four factors would not immunize a transaction, which is what a filter does, thereby vitiating the need for a comparative assessment.

That Easterbrook operates out of a nonstrategic antitrust tradition very possibly explains our differences on this. If market power is relevant only as it has a bearing on price, then strategic concerns can be dismissed and the only question is what has been the effect on price. I urge that this is too simple in circumstances where, to repeat, the strategic market power threshold has been crossed.

It is instructive to reexamine each of the Easterbrook factors (filters) with reference to this distraction.

2.1. Incentive Logic

As Ronald Coase has observed, it is often easy and was once common to ascribe anticompetitive purpose to virtually all forms of unfamiliar or nonstandard business behavior (1972). The older and now discredited "leverage theory" of tie-ins is one illustration (Posner, 1979). Those that subscribed to this theory had simply failed to assess the contracting process in its entirety.

As it turns out, however, the intuition that informed leverage theory was not totally mistaken. The problem was that this intuition was applied too broadly and should have been reserved for circumstances of a strategic kind (Kaplow, 1985). The same applies to other issues in which mistaken incentive logic is claimed.

2.1.1. *Myopic logic*

Predatory pricing complaints that implicate customers in predation sometimes fail because of myopic reasoning. As Easterbrook observes:

> No predatory strategy can work without the [unwitting] cooperation of consumers, who must desert the victim and buy from the predator even though that causes them to pay a monopoly price later on. If consumers are rational, they will not become instruments of their own harm. They will, instead, buoy up the intended victim with long term contracts. (1981a, pp. 415, 418–19)

The relevant logic test is whether customers are too small individually to influence competitive outcomes and thus will continuously accept the best immediate terms offered heedless of the future, or whether customers are large enough to recognize that they have a stake in influencing the quality of competitive outcomes. Claims of predation that implicate large consumers in their own demise fail the test of incentive logic and should be dismissed for this reason. Firms do not rationally shoot themselves in the foot (Easterbrook, 1984, p. 25).

The above argument is a variant of one made earlier by Richard Posner. Referring to *United Shoe*'s restrictive leasing practices, Posner argued that "the customers of United would be unlikely to participate in a campaign to strengthen United's monopoly position without insisting on being compensated for the loss of alternative, and less costly (because competitive) sources of supply" (1976, p. 203). Referring to many, rather than one or a few customers, the Posner statement is stronger than the Easterbrook statement, but even the Easterbrook version is overstated.

As Philippe Aghion and Patrick Bolton have recently shown, one can devise contracts with cancellation penalties that deter but do not completely block new entry (Aghion and Bolton, 1987). In effect, the incumbent seller and the single customer form a coalition, the effect of which is to extract some of the rent that an entrant with a superior low cost technology could otherwise earn upon entry.

To be sure, the model is highly "stylized" and makes no allowance for the fact that the law in the United States maintains that the "central objective behind the system of contract remedies is compensatory, not punitive."[15] Thus a liquidated damages clause is enforceable only if it is "reasonable in the light of the anticipated or actual harm caused by the breach, the difficulties of proof of loss, and the inconvenience or nonfeasibility of otherwise obtaining an adequate remedy. A term fixing unreasonably large damages is void as a penalty."[16] Consequently, the application of the Aghion-Bolton model would be restricted in any jurisdiction that limits liquidated damages.[17] As a result, one must know the context to reach an informed result. Nevertheless, Aghion and Bolton demonstrate that the normal or presumed opposition of interests between single buyer and single seller does not preclude bargaining whereby both can gain at the expense of potential lower cost entrants.

2.1.2. Summary judgment

Assume that the strategic threshold has been crossed and that, as in *Matsushita*,[18] a motion for summary judgment has been made. Since summary judgments are to be assessed with reference to a theory of the case congenial to the plaintiff, it would be a gross misuse of the incentive logic argument to dismiss such a motion because a "more plausible" explanation of a nonstrategic kind has been asserted.

15. *Restatement (Second) of Contracts* § 356 comment a (1979).

16. *U.C.C. § 2-718(1)*.

17. Charges of irrationality have been lodged against imposing lawful limits on liquidated damages, since parties to a contract are best qualified to determine what contractual provisions meet their contractual needs. It is now appropriate to entertain the possibility that the law on liquidated damages is (at least partly) designed to deter strategic abuses of the contracting process.

Contrived cancellation of contract is another reason why the law might place limits on penalty clauses. See Clarkson, Miller, and Muris, 1978; Williamson, 1985b.

18. *Matsushita Elec. Indus. Co. v. Zenith Radio Corp.*, 475 U.S. 574 (1986).

Not only would such a dismissal run contrary to the spirit of a summary judgment proceeding, but it is rare that the differences between two plausible scenarios will be so large and transparent that an easy choice between them can be made without conducting a careful comparative examination of the merits. I return to these issues in Section 3.2 below.

2.2.   Uniformity of Practices

Easterbrook advises that complaints about vertical market restrictions should be dismissed without a review on the merits unless the practice is adopted uniformly. This criterion has merit, and others previously suggested a similar criterion.[19] Easterbrook, however, goes beyond earlier arguments and ascribes added power to this filter by expressing it in an extreme way: A practice is unobjectionable unless *everyone* is implicated. Such a "uniform-practice filter is exceptionally powerful. It screens out almost all challenges to vertical practices" (1984, p. 30).

Although Easterbrook correctly describes the effect of a uniform practice filter, the more pertinent issue is whether adverse anticompetitive consequences may exist in the absence of uniformity. If a dominant firm or all the leading firms in an industry erect strategic entry impediments, the practice should be subject to antitrust complaints even if certain small rivals on the fringe do not practice. Also, one may need to distinguish between niche markets serviced by small firms and main markets serviced by dominant firms. If the practice in question effectively impedes entry into the main market, then a problematic (mixed case) condition is arguably posed. Filtering these cases out because of an absence of strict uniformity produces arbitrary resolution of such cases.

More generally, although cases that fall below the threshold for strategic market power might be regarded as more troublesome if uniform practices are observed, the failure of strict uniformity does not immunize behavior that falls within the strategic market power to subset. Nonuniformity is not therefore a filter but is merely a factor to be assessed comparatively in these circumstances.[20]

2.3.   Output Changes

Easterbrook contends that "[i]f arrangements are anticompetitive, the output and market share of those using them must fall" (1984, p. 31). He therefore advises that "we . . . look at what happens when the manufacturer adopts the

19. The fact that the contractual restraints employed by Schwinn were not used by other bicycle manufacturers relieved concern of anticompetitive effect (Williamson, 1979a).

20. The key arguments advanced by the Government in *Schwinn* and a critique thereof appear in Williamson, 1979a, pp. 980–85. The principle issue in *Schwinn* was "whether Schwinn, by itself or in conjunction with other large bicycle manufacturers, introduced vertical restraints that placed customers or rivals at strategic disadvantage" (pp. 980–81).

challenged practice. . . . If the manufacturer's sales rise, the practice confers benefits exceeding its costs" (1984, p. 31). However, inasmuch as price predation and other forms of strategic behavior entail contingent output expansion (Williamson, 1977b, pp. 292–95), Easterbrook's criterion is unhelpful within the market power subset to which predation is plausibly ascribed.

Easterbrook's permissive interpretation of contingent output increases is not unrelated to his earlier advice that the "antitrust offense of predation should be forgotten" (1986b, p. 337). However, others may disagree[21] and defendants may decide to pick and choose defenses: If one defense against predation is that the output of the dominant firm has remained unchanged or been reduced in the post-entry period (Williamson, 1977b, pp. 297–300), and if a second defense is that the output of the dominant firm has risen (Easterbrook, 1981b, p. 336), then anything goes. Lacking more substantial support, the proposed output filter fails to discriminate among problematic practices.

Perhaps out of recognition that problematic practices require a longer period for assessment, Easterbrook proposes judging challenged practices in terms of survival in the following manner: If a firm or group of firms have employed some arrangement continuously for five years and have not substantially lost market position, a challenge to the practice should be dismissed (1984, p. 33). Easterbrook does not provide the basis, however, for resolving two-sided practices uniformly in favor of an efficiency hypothesis. Moreover, his rule introduces strategic incentives to continue objectionable or problematic practices even after expiration of entry-deterring effects, because practices otherwise subject to challenge will be dismissed by continuing them beyond the five-year test interval (supported, perhaps, by price reductions in the later part of the test period).

2.4. Plaintiff Identity

Easterbrook's last filter focuses on plaintiff identity and is based on the following dichotomy: If a practice is collusive then rivals will benefit and will not complain; if instead a practice is competitive, complaints by rivals should be dismissed. Easterbrook mainly applies this filter to mergers, but a variation on the filter is used to assess predatory pricing.

---

21. Whereas economists who study strategic behavior frequently urge that "the nub of the problem . . . [is] the intertemporal aspect of the situation" (referring to nature of strategic decisions) the advice of legal scholars in the area of strategic behavior appeals to static price theory (Baumol, 1979, pp. 1, 3). Moreover, the rules so derived are often defended on grounds that more complex treatments of the issues are "nonadministrable."

As I have argued elsewhere, addressing strategic issues in a nonstrategic way does not reliably yield an informed antitrust assessment (Williamson, 1977b). Janusz Ordover and Garth Saloner concur. They observe that the Areeda–Turner marginal cost pricing test for predatory pricing is "based on static considerations . . . [which] beg the question of how anticompetitive conduct is to be handled in a strategic context" (1987, pp. 64–65).

2.4.1. Mergers

In considering mergers Easterbrook states that "[t]he identity of the plaintiff is all the court needs to know. . . . [Antitrust suits brought] by a business rival against a merger or joint venture should be dismissed" (1984, p. 36). Consumer-originated suits aside, the antitrust enforcement agencies would thereby be awarded exclusive control (sometimes referred to as a monopoly) over suits involving either mergers or joint ventures.

Although I am likewise dismayed by the protectionist uses of private suits and believe such suits should be regarded with grave skepticism, the antitrust dichotomy from which Easterbrook works is too simplistic. In addition to Type A (collusion enhancing) and Type B (efficiency enhancing) mergers, the possibility of strategic effects (Type C) also exists.

There are at least two kinds of mergers with strategic purposes. First, the merger of two adjacent firms in competitive space will avert head-to-head competition (Williamson, 1977a, pp. 735–36; Campbell, 1986). Second, merged firms are better able to focus replies to new entry and effect deterrence than if the two firms remained independent.

Ideally, the government should spot and challenge mergers that pose such strategic concerns, since they would exceed the mergers guidelines limits that are set strictly with reference to collusion concerns (Werden, 1986, pp. 228–29). It might therefore be argued that no useful purposes are served by preserving private suits to challenge Type C mergers.

Suppose, however, that defects are present in the government's decision process. Initially, the government could fail to discover relevant competitive features, because the government is less familiar with the relevant spatial features of markets than rivals. However, inasmuch as Easterbrook counsels that objections raised by rivals under Type A/Type B reasoning be regarded as Type B evidence (the merger must have efficiency properties if rivals complain), convincing the government that it has erred in its assessment presents real difficulties. Thus, better that opposed rivals praise a merger than express reservations!

Second, principled behavior within the antitrust enforcement agencies notwithstanding, antitrust "deals and understandings" are nevertheless made[22] and become more likely in a regime where the government's decisions on a merger are final. Absent a legal forum in which errors of the government are subsequently displayed, the "political antitruster" is secure against review and reversal.

---

22. Recall that Attorney General Herbert Brownell signed the 1954 consent decree between AT&T and the government—which is consistent both with the proposition that the Antitrust Division takes principled stands and with the proposition that politics and antitrust mix. Judge Harold Greene discusses some of the politics of this case in his opinion in *United States* v. *American Tel. & Tel. Co.,* 552 F. Supp. 131, 136–38 (D.D.C. 1982) *aff'd sub nom. Maryland* v. *United States,* 460 U.S. 1001 (1983). Congress passed the Tunney Act "to expose to public scrutiny and to a judicial public interest determination the settlements negotiated between the Department of Justice and the various antitrust defendants" (p. 145).

2.4.2. Predation

Easterbrook argues for dismissal of "predatory pricing suits brought by firms that have not left the market" (1984, pp. 36–37). In addition, he introduces a second dichotomous choice model to support his recommendation.

Thus consider a two-period model (the Easterbrook system) in which purportedly predatory practices undertaken in period one are judged by their effect in period two. The dichotomy for assessing a practice is as follows: a practice is judged to be a predatory success if the rivals at which it was directed expire; if the rival firms survive, however, the predatory effort is judged a failure. Since surviving firms "will collect the same price in period two as the aggressor" (Easterbrook, 1984, p. 37), suits by surviving plaintiffs should be dismissed.

This convenient dichotomy is based on the assumption that predation is designed to "kill a rival" (Bork, 1978, p. 149). This form of predation is extreme, however, and overlooks the possibility that discipline rather than destruction motivates some (perhaps many) aggressive competitive moves.[23] If punitive behavior carries signals to the target and other firms in future periods, in other geographic areas, and in other lines of commerce, then the dichotomous kill/survival model advocated by Easterbrook of predation oversimplifies.

Easterbrook and others can respond with some justification that our understanding of gaming responses, replies, reputation effects and the like is very imperfect. Considerable progress has nevertheless been made during the past decade in addressing precisely these issues,[24] and more is in prospect. If

23. Ordover and Saloner distinguish three ways in which a firm's conduct produces anticompetitive effects: (1) it can deter potential rivals; (2) it can disadvantage or discipline actual rivals without necessarily causing exit; and (3) it can destroy (cause a rival to exit) (1987). Easterbrook considers only the last effect.

24. One of the most widely cited studies on predation is that of Kohler (1971). He employs a dichotomy that distinguishes between Type 1 predation when "the objective of the predator is to *eliminate* a competitor" and Type 2 when the objective is to merge with or induce a competitor to collude (p. 106). Type 3 is ignored. Type 3 refers to a situation in which the purpose is to discipline a rival and transmit signals to this and other firms in future periods, in other geographic areas, and in other lines of commerce. For example, Paul Milgrom and John Roberts argue as follows:

> [P]redation emerges as a rational, profit maximizing strategy . . . not because it is directly profitable to eliminate the particular rival in question, but rather because it may deter future potential rivals. The mechanism by which this deterrent effect comes about is, by practicing predation the firm establishes a *reputation* as a predator. (1982, p. 281; emphasis added)

Gregory Werden nevertheless characterizes the Milgrom and Roberts article as one that demonstrates "that predation can be rational . . . only under special conditions" and goes on to observe that "more recent commentary has argued that predation is sufficiently rare and the potential adverse effects of trying to prevent or punish it sufficiently great that predation should be per se legal" (1986, pp. 229–30). The authorities, however, on which Werden relies (Bork and Easterbrook) wrote *before* Milgrom and Roberts and do not address the reputation rationality issues with which Milgrom and Roberts are concerned.

the world of antitrust is populated in part by Type C (strategic mixed or complex) cases, it is folly to pretend otherwise.

This is not to say, however, that the law should attempt expressly to evaluate Type C predation *at this time*.[25] The administrability concerns expressed by Breyer and Bok may temporarily require addressing all predation cases in a simplistic way. But as our understanding of predation increases, better classification schemes should evolve. In awaiting these developments, claims of predation are appropriately regarded with grave skepticism (Williamson, 1985b, pp. 378–82).

Overall, the five-filter approach proposed by Easterbrook possesses rather dubious properties. Although the first filter—market power—clearly survives, that is what antitrust has been working from all along. Each of the other four filters that Easterbrook introduces is more appropriately regarded as a factor to be taken into account in assessing the comparative plausibility of those antitrust complaints that fall within the strategic market power subset. But neither individually nor collectively do these four added factors exempt a case that poses genuine strategic concerns from being examined on the merits.

My reservations with Easterbrook's filters notwithstanding, I nonetheless am sympathetic to his main purpose. That is, to develop better criteria to distinguish good and bad cases. To be sure, this can never be done perfectly. Every effort to sort will carry two errors: "false positives," that is, cases that are exempted but which are problematic and should go forward; and "false negatives," that is, cases that are prosecuted but should have been exempted. Each type of error carries a cost. Thus, the object is to construct the filters so that expected social costs are minimized.[26]

It is possible, especially during this period of vigorous international competition, that the costs of false positives are very low in relation to false negatives. This is plainly Easterbrook's position when he argues that "errors on the side of excusing questionable practices are preferable," partly because "the economic system corrects monopoly more readily than it corrects judicial errors" and partly because "in many cases the costs of monopoly wrongly permitted are small, while the costs of competition wrongly condemned are large" (1984, p. 15). Economies as an antitrust defense excepted (see n. 4), no one has provided a demonstration that the cost differences are as Easterbrook indicates. Easterbrook has an undischarged burden of proof that the cost of false positives in the market power region where strategic behavior is implicated is similarly low.

In the meantime, antitrust enforcement agencies and courts must decide the cases as they arise. Although appealing to "hard-edged" legal rules relieves

25. The most extensive, advanced, and ambitious effort to evaluate and provide enforcement criteria to address anticompetitive exclusionary behavior is that of Thomas Krattenmaker and Steven Salop (1986). However, just as Easterbrook's filter scheme can benefit from academic critique, I would urge that the same is true for the Krattenmaker and Salop effort. If their criteria emerge from such a critique unscathed, then we are in better shape than I indicate. Be that as it may, the Krattenmaker and Salop analysis plainly advances the dialogue.

26. Cost assessment should include enforcement costs, a point made forcefully by Easterbrook (1981a, pp. 417, 425–27).

strains on the enforcement process, today's false confidence is tomorrow's precedent and becomes the basis for repeated error. Complex cases that are imperfectly understood are better decided in a more modest and provisional way. Working out of a legal process approach which invokes temporary constraints but anticipates evolutionary refinements is therefore proposed. The legal rule approach resolves too many of these issues prematurely (Rey and Tirole, 1986, pp. 921, 937).

3.   Strategic Behavior

Behavior by one firm that influences the choice set of another may be said to have a strategic aspect. Such behavior is not by itself objectionable. It is commonly the unavoidable consequence whenever the number of rivals is few and the condition of entry is difficult. Behavior, however, that is focused and contingent is often highly problematic. Some egregious forms of strategic behavior possess no redeeming social purpose (see Ordover and Saloner, 1987).

Much of the recent antitrust literature and court opinions are intended to delimit strategic behavior that is considered to be unlawful. Concern over strategic behavior has been progressively narrowed by (1) exempting all strategic behavior except strategic pricing from antitrust scrutiny; (2) restricting attention within the strategic pricing subset to that which qualifies as predatory; and (3) defining predatory pricing as that which would assuredly "kill" an established rival if continued. It is easy to conclude from this exercise[27] that strategic behavior poses few, if any, relevant antitrust concerns, since pricing to kill established rivals borders on irrationality.

Claims of strategic behavior thus must be contrived or based on mistaken incentive logic (e.g., failures to assess the underlying contracting process in its entirety) and are properly exempt from antitrust concern. Exempting strategic behavior from antitrust concern for such reasons is different, however, from delimiting antitrust enforcement because the legal process inadequately assesses relevant antitrust issues. Whereas the absence of antitrust concern is settled once-and-for-all by the former, the latter does not contemplate such

27. Gregory Werden's recent piece (1986) on private antitrust suits is illustrative. He begins with reference to incipient predatory behavior but thereafter focuses almost entirely on predatory pricing (p. 222). His statement, for example, that "[m]ost observers agree that predation is unlikely under any set of circumstances" is supported almost exclusively by references to predatory pricing (p. 230). His references to "predation cases" and the claim that "collusion is concealable while predation is not" has a narrow (overt pricing) focus (pp. 230, 232).

Similarly the amicus brief filed by the government in *Monfort* supports its arguments that rivals should be denied standing in merger cases entirely by references to predatory pricing as though reference to predatory pricing exhausted the concerns (Brief for *United States and the Federal Trade Commission as Amici Curiae Supporting Petitioners*, at 21–25, *Cargill, Inc.* v. *Monfort of Colo., Inc.*, 107 S. Ct. 484 (1986) (No. 85–473).

Although Robert Bork discusses a variety of possibly predatory practices, he focuses primarily on predatory pricing. Others cite Bork as an authority for the proposition that predatory pricing is designed to "kill" a rival (1978, pp. 149–55).

finality. To the contrary, as better economic models progressively evolve and their ramifications are displayed, behavior once exempted because of legal process concerns subsequently may be included in the antitrust enforcement scheme. Periodic reassessment that takes into account growing knowledge of and experience with specific strategic phenomena is thus characteristic of the legal process approach to strategic behavior. If and when the expected net benefits of antitrust scrutiny of strategic behavior switch from negative to positive (or the reverse), the ambit of antitrust must be redefined accordingly.

Dispositive pronouncements of a once-and-for-all kind are thus supplanted by evolutionary assessments of a state-of-the-art kind. As a result, the potential scope of strategic behavior is much wider than is admitted by the strategic behavior/strategic pricing/predatory pricing/predatory "kill-the-rival" pricing sequences referred to above.

Lest antitrust interest in strategic behavior potentially warranting future enforcement be inadvertently foreclosed, a broad statement of the scope of strategic behavior is arguably warranted. Such a broad statement of scope is set out below. Note, however, that I do not claim that my classification of strategic behavior is exhaustive or best; others have visited this territory before (see Salop, 1981; Spence, 1981; Kreps and Spence, 1985; Campbell, 1986; Krattenmaker and Salop, 1986; Ordover and Saloner, 1987).

The distinction between strategic and operating decisions is usefully made in studying firm behavior. Strategic decisions refer to overall product development, marketing, and investment plans, while operating decisions concern implementation. In the context of W. Ross Ashby's description (1960) of ultrastable systems, the higher frequency (or short-run) dynamics are associated with the operating parts, and the lower frequency (or long-run) dynamics are associated with the strategic system (Simon, 1962a).

All decisions with significant long-term importance carry strategic potential. The following list identifies some of the more important of these:

1. pricing
   a. final product
   b. intermediate product (squeeze)
2. product development
   a. research and development
   b. introduction
3. marketing
   a. advertising
   b. other promotion
   c. testing
4. investment
   a. plant location
   b. integration
   c. asset attributes (kind and amount)
5. government
   a. standards (product and environment)
   b. contracting

    c. trade policy
    d. litigation
6. other
    a. wages
    b. taxes

Strategic behavior can either be preemptive or contingent. Focused and contingent strategic behavior is especially troublesome (Williamson, 1977b; Baumol, 1979), but that does not mean that preemptive moves pose no problems. Pricing and marketing are the areas where contingent actions (i.e., focused, responsive behavior designed to defeat or discipline a rival; after such defeat the practice in question will be discontinued) are especially likely. Unsurprisingly, most strategic behavior complaints are lodged in these two areas.

Specific examples of strategic behavior that is problematic—not all of which, however, are necessarily objectionable (considering our current limited understanding)—include

1. predatory pricing (which Kohler ascribes to American Tobacco in 1908 even under his narrow criteria) (1971, p. 114; see also Ordover and Saloner, 1987, pp. 14–15);
2. price squeeze (which was part of the *Alcoa* complaint and has more recently been imputed to Kaiser Aluminum)[28]
3. dumping (see Viner, 1923);
4. contrived patent licensing;
5. selective unbundling of services;
6. efforts to confuse test marketing by rivals (as alleged in *Purex* v. *Proctor & Gamble*);[29]
7. inducing the government to write contract specification to favor particular suppliers (which has occurred repeatedly with computer and communication equipment);
8. using high and uniform wages to deter rivalry by labor intensive firms (as alleged in the *Pennington* case);
9. vertical integration with capital market deterring effects (as in color film processing);
10. the strategic preemption of a critical resource (a concern of the USFL regarding access to TV networks vis-a-vis the NFL);

---

28. *Columbia Metal Culvert* v. *Kaiser Aluminum & Chem. Corp.*, 579 F.2d 20 (3d Cir.), *cert. denied*, 439 U.S. 876 (1978). Note that the economic logic of this case has been disputed by John Wiley, Jr. (1986). Wiley argues that Kaiser purportedly "applied a classical price squeeze to pressure Columbia into *an exclusive dealing arrangement*" (p. 1010, emphasis added). The Wiley position, however, is mistaken. Kaiser applied a price squeeze when Columbia refused to sell out to Kaiser. The merger of Columbia and Kaiser would facilitate uncontested aluminum culvert fabrication by Kaiser. The success of Kaiser's squeeze required (1) that other suppliers of aluminum culvert coil (of which Kaiser was the largest) follow Kaiser's pricing lead, and (2) that Columbia would be unable to match the low bids of the rival fabricator that Kaiser created and supported to contest the Columbia market.

29. 419 F. Supp. 931 (N.D. Cal. 1976).

11. using the regulatory process to defeat entry (as in the repeated pleas by AT&T to protect "system integrity" against foreign attachments);

12. use of local government controls—inspection, local content and other requirements, certification, and the like—to favor incumbents (as is repeatedly claimed by those attempting to sell into Japanese markets); and

13. the creation of closed contracting networks and hubs that resist invasion (as discussed by Levine (1987) in connection with airline deregulation).

I have urged elsewhere in my discussions of strategic and predatory behavior that severe structural preconditions must be satisfied before a potential antitrust concern is seriously posed. High concentration coupled with high barriers to entry are needed (Williamson, 1977b, pp. 292–93). Paul Joskow and Alvin Klevorick in one analysis (1979) and Janucz Ordover and Robert Willig in another analysis (1985) agree and propose a "two tier test" for predation. Recall that Easterbrook's first filter is a structural one (i.e., market structure). Campbell also states that submarkets must be defined with care in discussing spatial competition (1986). Assuming that adequate provision is made for Campbell's point, the subset of industries where problematic strategic behavior is most apt to be located includes the following: (1) the sitting monopolist/duopolist situation; (2) regulated monopolies; (3) dominant firm industries; and (4) collusive oligopolies (especially those William Fellner referred to as "Case 3 oligopoly" (1949), where an outside agency (e.g., a union) enforces collective action).[30]

4. Recent Antitrust Suits

This part examines three recent antitrust suits. The first involves a private suit challenging the acquisition of KitchenAid by the Whirlpool Corporation.[31] Here I illustrate my concern with proposals to exclude rivals from bringing suit by evaluating the FTC's earlier disposition of this merger. The second case is *Matsushita*,[32] where I question the economic analysis used by the majority on the Supreme Court. The last case is *Monfort*,[33] where I examine

30. Firms outside this group still may take strategic actions that adversely affect specific rivals. But the added question must be asked as to whether firms outside the group can recoup. "Mistaken predation" is that for which expected recoupment cannot be projected *ex ante*. Note that mere failure to recoup *ex post* does not demonstrate that predatory designs were mistaken *ex ante*. Easterbrook's view that only *ex post* successful predation is unlawful is a further illustration of "overdelimiting" the relevant set (Easterbrook, 1984, pp. 32–33 [source in which Easterbrook makes mentioned argument]).

31. *White Consol. Indus.* v. *Whirlpool Corp.*, 612 F. Supp. 1009 (N.D. Ohio 1985). I served as an economic consultant to and expert witness for White Consolidated Industries in its challenge to this merger.

32. *Matsushita Elec. Indus. Co.* v. *Zenith Radio Corp.*, 475 U.S. 574 (1986).

33. *Cargill, Inc.* v. *Monfort of Colo., Inc.*, 107 S. Ct. 484 (1986).

the amicus brief by the government asking that rivals be precluded from challenging mergers.

4.1. Whirlpool–KitchenAid

Whirlpool's acquisition of KitchenAid is of interest because it demonstrates (1) the propensity to classify mergers as Type A (collusion enhancing) or Type B (cost reducing) to the exclusion of Type C (strategic); (2) the readiness with which the FTC accepts cosmetic divestitures as curative; (3) the propensity of the courts to dismiss strategic concerns as "speculative"; and (4) the bases upon which economies are claimed. I consider each of these seriatim.

4.1.1. The naive dichotomy

A complaint by rivals that a merger will have anticompetitive effects should be regarded with suspicion. Such complaints often reflect a concern not with competition (a process) but with competitors (themselves). If a merger has market power effects to which price increases are ascribed (a Type A merger), then rivals will benefit. Therefore, private complaints will not appear in a Type A merger. If the merger is the source of prospective cost savings with attendant price reductions (a Type B merger), then the public stands to benefit. Private suits merely serve protectionist purposes in Type B circumstances.

This convenient dichotomy is sometimes used as the basis for adjudicatory bodies to disallow merger complaints brought by rivals. It ignores, however, a third possibility—that is, that the price effects could be localized rather than spread across all market segments and that merged firms could strategically occupy market niches, resist intrusion, and discipline rivals more effectively than if they were to remain independent. The omission of relevant alternatives is an old antitrust gambit (see nn. 19 and 20), but antitrust enforcement is the poorer when relevant Type C alternatives are suppressed or ignored.

Ronald Coase took exception with pre-1970 antitrust enforcement because it was informed by an excessively narrow conception of the economic process. "Applied price theory" was used in the 1960s to ascribe monopoly purpose to many beneficial nonstandard practices (Coase, 1972). This same framework is now employed to exclude the Type C alternative, because strategic behavior has no place within the applied price theory tradition or at least within the "die-hard Chicagoan" variant thereof.[34]

Aware that the FTC was working out of a Type A/Type B merger calculus, White Consolidated Industries (which was a "white goods" rival to Whirlpool and more distant rival in quality space to KitchenAid) nevertheless asked the Commission to enjoin the acquisition of KitchenAid by Whirlpool. White Consolidated propounded the following reasons for enjoining the acquisition:

---

34. The term "die-hard Chicagoan" originates with Richard Posner (1975a). He uses the term to characterize those who in effect reduce strategic behavior to the null set.

1. The "curative" divestiture whereby Whirlpool had purportedly disposed of the dishwasher business of KitchenAid (which is where the main competitive overlap was concentrated) was cosmetic.

2. KitchenAid occupied a high price/quality niche in the dishwasher market and displayed an interest (as revealed in its planning documents) in expanding its market presence. Whirlpool occupied a middle price/quality dishwasher position region. The merger of KitchenAid and Whirlpool not only removed the prospective head-to-head competition, but a combined Whirlpool–KitchenAid would be better able to resist encroachments into the upper end of the market by other firms (such as White) than if Whirlpool and KitchenAid were independent.

3. Redeeming economies did not justify the merger.

4.1.2. Curative divestiture

The main competitive overlap between Whirlpool and KitchenAid was in the dishwasher business where market shares (even without reference to market niches) exceeded the merger guidelines. Whirlpool proposed to rectify this problem by selling the KitchenAid dishwasher plant to Emersion Electric. The contract whereby curative divestitute was to be accomplished provided that:

1. Emerson would manufacture KitchenAid dishwashers for sale by Whirlpool under the KitchenAid name and could produce and sell additional dishwashers only under design restrictions and severe marketing constraints.

2. Whirlpool was in a position to preempt production from the Emerson plant.

3. The Emerson contract was, in effect, a supply agreement that guaranteed to Emerson a twenty percent after tax rate of return on invested capital. Whirlpool could terminate the contract at the end of five years by buying the plant back from Emerson for the unexpired portion of Emerson's original investment. During the supply interval, capital enhancement could only be done with Whirlpool's consent. Emerson agreed to annual audits by Whirlpool of fixed and variable costs.

The Whirlpool–Emerson transaction is not simple. The transaction joins a banking function (Emerson buys the dishwasher plant) with rate of return regulation (Emerson receives a guaranteed rate of return but is subject to investment and audit restraints). The obvious purpose of the sale was to sanitize a merger while leaving Whirlpool in effective control of critical assets.

The FTC glossed over the substance of the sale in its initial review of the merger. Moreover, even after these contractual features were expressly called to the Commission's attention, the merger was approved by the FTC with the contractual features in place.

White Consolidated thereafter brought suit in federal district court to enjoin the merger.[35] The court examined the conditions of the supply agreement and found them "sufficiently inhibitive of Emerson's ability to compete in

---

35. *White Consol. Indus.*, 612 F. Supp. at 1009.

the market that Emerson will not act as a post-transaction check on Whirlpool and will not in any way make up for the loss of KitchenAid" (p. 1029). Specifically, the court held that the supply agreement would "so hinder Emerson that Whirlpool will effectively control Emerson's level of production" (p. 1029). The court therefore granted a preliminary injunction against the acquisition but gave Whirlpool the options of amending the merger agreement to remove the objectionable contracting features. Whirlpool promptly removed the objectionable features and the preliminary injunction was vacated.

I submit that a better, or at least more informed, antitrust result would not have occurred if the FTC's decision regarding this merger had been final. This should give pause to those who would prohibit private antitrust suits. The option to ask for court-ordered relief not only permits challenge to defective decisions by the antitrust enforcement agencies and possible correction, but places the enforcement agencies under greater pressure to reach decisions on the merits in the first place.

4.1.3. *Strategic concerns*

Whether or not this is a Type C merger in which the head-to-head competition of the merging firms had strategic significance depends on whether the upper end of the dishwasher market constituted a meaningful submarket. This is a difficult question and was never determined. Strategic considerations become important if one assumes that spatial considerations apply and that this is a meaningful submarket.

Although it is common to argue that strategic abuses can be dealt with directly if and when they occur (Werden, 1986, p. 232), the fact remains that our capacity to evaluate strategic abuses is very primitive. Consequently, earlier advice that the merger statutes be viewed to foreclose strategic hazards warrants renewed consideration. The merger guidelines do not presently contemplate such uses (Werden, 1986, pp. 226–29).

4.1.4. *Economies*

Whirlpool's keen interest in this acquisition turned on the value that it placed in the KitchenAid brand name. Possibly this was because Whirlpool could realize greater *real* economic value than KitchenAid with the KitchenAid name. The name connoted high quality and would allow Whirlpool to sell a broader line of high quality goods in larger volumes. But possibly the value realization that Whirlpool had in mind was more problematic: Whirlpool planned to attach the KitchenAid name to Whirlpool appliances after making only cosmetic adjustments.

Carl Shapiro's treatment of "milking a reputation" in selling products to consumers who initially overestimate quality is pertinent. The optimal strategy in "milking a reputation" entails starting with a high price and progressively reducing it until "the price and quantity revert to the same levels that would prevail under perfect information and remain there indefinitely."[36]

Although many Whirlpool planning documents supported the cosmetic hypothesis, the defendant understandably presented the real value hypothesis to the FTC and the court. A new marketing concept was introduced for this purpose, whereby value was ascribed to "white goods–brand name."[37] The court did not rule on either of these possibilities. However, when considering a conflict between expressed intention, as disclosed in planning documents, against the hypothetical benefits of a novel marketing theory, there is much to be said for the former. The FTC was nonetheless impressed by the latter.

4.2. Matsushita

The *Matsushita* case dragged on for over a dozen years. Although a complex case, the core economic theory espoused by the plaintiff apparently was that Japanese television manufacturers engaged in collusion and dumping.[38] The Japanese firms had a protected home market and sold abroad on terms that were held to be predatory. The general theory appears to have been that set out many years ago by Jacob Viner: "once monopoly control has been achieved in the domestic market, it may pay, if domestic orders do not fully occupy the productive facilities, to bid for orders in other markets at prices lower than those exacted at home" (1923, p. 94). There are several possibilities:

> A producer may engage in export dumping primarily with a view to main-taining full production during a period of depression in the domestic market, but he may at the same time deliberately manage his dumping so that it will inflict as much injury as possible upon his foreign competitors. Moreover, the predatory dumper *may not expect that he will succeed in wholly eliminating* the competitors against whom he is dumping, but he may be content if his dumping so weakens them that they will thereafter refrain from contesting his prices or from extending their activities into his special markets. (Viner, 1923, p. 122; emphasis in original)

The study of strategic behavior has since been elaborated to include the learning curve benefits of cumulative production (Spence, 1977), the attributes of investment (Dixit, 1980), techniques for raising rivals' costs (Salop and Scheffman, 1983), strategic reputation effects (Kreps and Wilson, 1982; Milgrom and Roberts, 1982), and even international strategic features (Ordover

36. Shapiro, 1983. If Whirlpool could realize gains from strategically devaluing the Kitchen-Aid brand name, one might ask why KitchenAid could not have pursued a similar strategy (e.g., by acquiring Whirlpool or White or simply procuring inferior products and attaching its brand name). Asymmetries between Whirlpool and KitchenAid—in terms of strategic competence, knowledge of the market, and preexisting but imperfectly transferable organizational competence (including management team features) generally—arguably existed and favored the Whirlpool initiative.

37. Benjamin Klein introduced the concept and argued its antitrust relevance to the FTC and district court.

38. In re *Japanese Electronic Products,* 723 F.2d 238, 251 (3d Cir. 1983), rev'd and remanded sub nom. *Matsushita Elec. Indus. Co.* v. *Zenith Ratio Corp.,* 475 U.S. 574 (1986).

and Willig, 1985). However, the basic argument is the one stated by Viner. The plausibility of such an argument was pertinent in deciding *Matsushita.*

The Supreme Court, however, did not evaluate the plausibility of the case by assessing the plaintiff's theory.[39] Rather, the Court examined the plausibility of the defendant's case. In effect, the Court embraced the Easterbrook scenario, which is as follows:

> The plaintiffs maintain that for the last fifteen years or more at least ten Japanese manufacturers have sold TV sets at less than cost in order to drive United States firms out of business. Such conduct cannot possibly produce profits by harming competition, however. If the Japanese firms drive some United States firms out of business they could not recoup. Fifteen years of losses could be made up only by very high prices for the indefinite future. (The losses are investments, which must be recovered with compound interest.) If the defendants should try to raise prices to such a level, they would attract new competition. There are no barriers into electronics, as the proliferation of computer and audio firms shows. (Easterbrook, 1984, pp. 26–27)

The strategic model on which Easterbrook relies for his assessment is not expressly stated. He ascribes very severe purposes (drive rivals out) rather than more limited ones (discipline). Recoupment is examined not in *ex ante* respects, but only in *ex post* terms. He infers conditions about entry into television manufacturing and marketing from the "proliferation of computer and audio firms." He questions the force of plaintiffs' case and suggests that "we are left with the more plausible inference that the Japanese firms ... were just engaged in hard competition" (1984, p. 27). However, others may ask for the examination of alternative models and for a more complete parameterization.

Note that admissible evidence must be construed in the light most favorable to the non-movant in motions for summary judgment. Therefore, evidence should be viewed most favorable to respondent (the United States firms).[40] The

39. Perhaps this is too strong. The Court states that "the conduct in question consists largely of (i) pricing at levels that succeeded in taking business away from [U.S. firms], and (ii) arrangements that may have limited [Japanese firms'] ability to compete with each other...." *Matsushita Elec. Indus. Co.* v. *Zenith Radio Corp.,* 475 U.S. 574, 597 (1986). This analysis is consonant with the Viner dumping/predation scenario. But rather than assess whether dumping/predation was present, the Court asserts: "This conduct suggests either that [Japanese firms] behaved competitively, or that [Japanese firms] conspired to *raise* prices" (p. 597, emphasis in original). The Court is evidently taken with Type A/Type B thinking. In any event, no serious examination of the Viner scenario is anywhere attempted.

40. The plaintiff is constrained to (1) choose his theory of the cases from an admissible subset, and (2) demonstrate that the data on which he relies support the complaint. Therefore, discredited theories, such as old style "leverage theory," cannot be invoked. However, inasmuch as dumping has not similarly been discredited, only the data can warrant the dismissal of such a complaint.

Moreover, simply because dumping was unsuccessful does not prove that it was never tried or that no injury occurred. Thus attempted dumping may be defeated because it was misconceived from the outset; that is, the requisite preconditions were not satisfied. Since mistaken predation will be rare or at least not repeated, and since claims of predation are easy to register and hard to evaluate, all predation claims that fail the structural test for preconditions might be disallowed

majority in *Matsushita,* however, selectively processed the evidence through a lens unfavorable to the United States firms. Unsurprisingly, it found that the conspiracy was "implausible" because the Japanese firms had "no motive to enter into the alleged conspiracy."[41]

Although "no motive" is surely too strong, I likewise view the claims by the United States firms in this case with grave reservations (partially because I, like many other economists, have grave doubts about the efficacy of conspiracy (Williamson, 1975, pp. 238–47, 1985b, pp. 277–79); but the ability to support conspiracy may differ between Japanese and domestic firms, some of which differences are manifest in the record). If settled legal doctrine is to be respected, the minority opinion in *Matsushita* adheres more closely to the circumspect standards that one expects in summary judgment proceedings.[42]

4.3. Monfort

The Supreme Court rejected claims alleging injury to competition brought by Monfort. Monfort opposed the merger of the second and third largest beef packing and fabricating firms in the United States (which, when combined would occupy a twenty-one percent market share).[43] Monfort's arguments in opposition to the merger have a strongly protectionist character.[44]

My concern with this case is not with the Supreme Court opinion, but with the amicus brief filed by the Justice Department and the FTC. The brief argues that:

> Where a plaintiff challenges an acquisition on the ground that it creates a possibility of *future* predatory pricing, he does not allege a "real and immediate threat" of antitrust injury to himself unless, at a minimum, he alleges that the defendant will dominate the post-acquisition market. . . . Excel's post-acquisition share of the market would have been less than 21%, which would not even make it the largest firm in the market.
>
> While the foregoing considerations are sufficient to decide the case, there are important reasons why the Court should take the further step of ruling

---

(Williamson, 1985b, p. 382). I nevertheless understand that other students of predation could argue for punishment of all forms of *egregious* predation, mistaken predation included. Firms really do make significant strategic errors (witness Ford Motor Co. in the 1920s and General Motors in the 1980s). Mistaken predation is not exempt (Williamson, 1985b, p. 111).

The more troublesome case occurs where the requisite preconditions are satisfied, yet focused strategic behavior fails because of unanticipated developments (changes in demand, defections from the agreement, etc.). The Easterbrook 20/20 hindsight test would excuse all predation efforts that fail. Real damages and unambiguous intent notwithstanding, muggers whose victims survive go free.

41. *Matsushita,* 475 U.S. at 595.

42. The dissenting opinion was written by Justice White, who at one juncture observes that "[i]f the court intends to give every judge hearing a motion for summary judgment in an antitrust case the job of determining if the evidence makes the inference of conspiracy *more probable* or not, it is overturning settled law" (*Matsushita,* 475 U.S. at 572).

43. *Cargill, Inc.* v. *Monfort of Colo., Inc.,* 107 S. Ct. 484 (1986).

44. The case illustrates some of the speculative hazards that unavoidably appear if strategic behavior complaints are presented at a hearing.

that an allegation of threatened future predatory pricing is never sufficient to give a competitor standing to challenge an acquisition. Injunctive actions brought by competitors on a "predatory pricing" theory will often stifle pre-competitive acquisitions, and they are likely to do so before the matter can reach this Court; such anticipatory lawsuits are not necessary to combat predatory behavior, which can be remedied if and when it actually occurs. In light of (1) a competitor's strong incentive to seek to scuttle a procompetitive acquisition and the high risk that a court challenge will do so, (2) the remoteness of the possibility that an acquisition will lead to predatory pricing, and (3) the ability of any competitor later faced with actual predatory pricing to invoke the prohibitions of the Sherman Act, the purposes of the antitrust laws would be best served by denying competitors standing to challenge acquisition on the basis of predatory pricing theories.[45]

The brief further urges that:

> [A]n antitrust complaint that can withstand a motion to dismiss is often not hard to frame, and the mere pendency of lawsuits will often be fatal to future procompetitive acquisitions before they can reach this Court. Allowing competitors' suits to proceed on a predatory pricing theory thus invites competitor that will frustrate procompetitive acquisitions and "chill the very conduct the antitrust laws are designed to protect."[46]

Although the amicus brief raises legitimate issues, it is overreaching in the following respects: (1) the efficacy of section 2 challenges to predatory pricing is seriously to be doubted; (2) giving the government a monopoly over merger cases invites careless disposition; and (3) strategic behavior spans a much wider class of events that is comprehended by predatory pricing.

That the Supreme Court declined the invitation to prohibit private suits at this time, albeit on different grounds than those stated here,[47] is encouraging. A symmetrical assessment of all of the effects, including those to which I refer above, is needed before the result requested by the government is warranted.

5. Concluding Remarks

Delimiting antitrust is a commendable objective, but delimitation can be taken to excess. Dichotomous reasoning—by artificially classifying mergers or predation as Type A/Type B—is too simple. Efforts to derogate strategic behavior have likewise been overdone. Moreover, legal rules proclaimed in the name of administrability can come at an unacceptably high price:

> To insist that we understand matters on which we are truly ignorant can only lead to erratic, controverted decisions and to opinions which lack the reasoned logic on which respect for law depends. Dismissed with quick assertions, these

45. *Cargill, Inc.* v. *Monfort of Colo., Inc.,* 107 S.Ct. 484 (1986) (No. 85–473), at 10.
46. Ibid., 22.
47. The Court observes that "[i]t would be novel indeed for a court to deny standing to a party seeking an injunction against threatened injury merely because such injuries rarely occur" (*Monfort,* 107 S. Ct. at 495).

troublesome questions may fail to evoke the continued inquiry which they deserve, so that mistaken notions may persist, entombed in the law, beyond the day when fresher doctrines could lay them suitably to rest. (Bok, 1960, p. 228)

Antitrust in the 1960s was overconfident and even shrill.[48] This has fortunately be redressed. To go further by "balancing" the excesses of monopoly reasoning in that era with excesses of competitive reasoning today does not, however, produce a better result.

The approach to antitrust enforcement proposed herein (1) regards economizing as the main case, (2) takes strategic behavior in all of its forms seriously, and, provided that due allowance has been made for the operational infirmities of the enforcement process, (3) expressly introduces strategic exceptions to the main case provided that (a) the requisite structural preconditions have been satisfied and (b) the supporting strategic logic withstands scrutiny. The inhospitality excesses of the 1960s are avoided by treating economizing as the main case. Die-hard Chicagoan excesses are similarly avoided by insisting that strategic hazards of subtle and even poorly understood kinds be admitted, added complexities notwithstanding, rather than being arbitrarily dismissed through the use of artificial dichotomies or otherwise.

The limitations of the flexible legal process method are nonetheless real and need to be respected. Provision for these are made by insisting that hypothetical gains await operationalization. Lags between the development of new theory and efforts to adopt these refinements into the enforcement process therefore occur routinely. But while antitrust enforcement works out yesterday's theory, this is done with a keen eye to recent and prospective developments.

Those with a strong predilection for certitude or those who believe that the state of yesterday's theory is fully adequate will find this evolutionary recipe unacceptable. Let them reflect, however, on what would have happened had antitrust enforcement been frozen in the 1960s mold. And let them further reflect on the robust state of industrial organization.

Thus, whereas industrial organization was thought to have languished as recently as 1972,[49] today's verdict is that industrial organization is alive and well and is the queen of applied microeconomics. Antitrust enforcement has been and will continue to be the beneficiary.

48. Justice Potter Stewart, in a dissenting opinion in 1966, expressed his frustration as follows: the "sole consistency that I can find . . . in [merger] litigation under Section 7 [is that] the Government always wins." *United States* v. *Von's Grocery Co.*, 384 U.S. 270, 301 (1966) (Stewart, J., dissenting).

49. Victor Fuchs asked in his foreword to a recent National Bureau of Economic Research publication "whither industrial organization?" to which he responded that "all is not well in this once flourishing field" (1972, p. xv).

12

Strategizing, Economizing, and Economic Organization

Business strategy is a complex subject. It not only spans the functional areas in business—marketing, finance, manufacturing, international business, etc.—but it is genuinely interdisciplinary—involving, as it does, economics, politics, organization theory, and aspects of the law. Business strategy has become increasingly important with the growth of the multinational enterprise and of international trade and competition.

Although several different approaches to the substantive aspects of business strategy can be distinguished, the main contestants cluster under two general headings: strategizing and economizing. The first of these appeals to a power perspective; the second is principally concerned with efficiency. Both of these orientations are pertinent to the study of business strategy, but power approaches have played a role in the recent business strategy literature that belies its relative importance.

Partly that may be because the analysis of efficiency is believed to have reached such an advanced state of development that further work of this kind is not needed. Economizing is important, but we know all about that. What we don't understand, and need to study, goes the argument, is strategizing. Not only is strategizing where many of the novel practices and new issues are said to reside, but the pressing realities of foreign competition are first and foremost of a strategizing kind.

I take exception with arguments of both kinds. Thus, although it is true that efficiency analysis of the firm-as-production function genre has reached a high state of refinement, that does not exhaust all that is relevant to the assessment of efficiency. Efficiency analysis properly encompasses governance costs as well as production costs, and the analysis of comparative economic organization (governance) is still in early stages of development.

I furthermore aver that, as between economizing and strategizing, economizing is much the more fundamental. That is because strategizing is relevant principally to firms that possess market power—which are a small fraction of the total (ephemeral market advantages ignored). More importantly, I maintain that a strategizing effort will rarely prevail if a program is burdened by significant cost excesses in production, distribution, or organization. All the clever ploys and positioning, aye, all the king's horses and all the king's men, will rarely save a project that is seriously flawed in first-order economizing respects.

Accordingly, I advance the argument that economizing is more fundamental than strategizing—or, put differently, that *economy is the best strategy*. That is the central and unchanging message of the transaction cost economics perspective. Among other things, emphasis on economizing restores manufacturing and merchandising to a place of importance within the business firm and on the academic research agenda.[1]

To be sure, economizing and strategizing are not mutually exclusive. Strategic ploys are sometimes used to disguise economizing weaknesses. (Lee Iacocca has tried this.) More often, strategic ploys can be used to promote economizing outcomes. Pricing with reference to learning curve costs is an illustration. "Technostructure" (Galbraith, 1967) and related theories of the firm that hold that the imperatives of strategic planning carry the day have turned out, however, to be unserviceable. The beguiling language of strategizing—warfare, credible threats, and the like—notwithstanding, students of economic organization are better advised to focus on more mundane issues of an economizing kind—of which harmonizing, credible commitments, adaptation, and discriminating alignments are examples. Here as elsewhere, the need is to get and keep the priorities straight.

This chapter is organized in four parts.[2] The first section sketches what I take to be the principal efficiency approaches to strategy and sets out the rudiments of the transaction cost economics approach. Applications of transaction cost economics to the governance of contractual relations are treated in the next section. An economizing interpretation of the Japanese corporation is advanced in the third section. Concluding remarks follow.

1. Economizing, General

The leading efficiency approaches to business strategy are the resource-based and the dynamic capabilities approach. These two approaches have been

---

1. This is broadly consonant with the Hayes and Wheelwright perspective:

> The notion that manufacturing can be a competitive weapon, rather than just a collection of rather ponderous resources and constraints, is not new, although its practice is not very widespread. Even in many well-managed firms, manufacturing plays an essentially neutral role, reflecting the view that marketing, sales and R and D provide better bases for achieving a competitive advantage. (1984, p. 27)

But the argument extends beyond manufacturing to core businesses of every kind. Thus Sears is reported "finally [to be] focusing on [its] biggest problem. Its costs are among the highest in retailing" (Schwadel, 1990, p. B1).

2. The Conference version of this chapter, which is published in Rumelt, Schendel and Teece (1992), includes a section on organization form and its relation to the modern corporation.

developing very rapidly[3] and, as described by Mahoney and Pandian (1990), blend into each other. Penrose's early work on the growth of the firm (1959) and more recent work by Barney (1991), Montgomery and Wernerfelt (1988), Ouchi (1981), Peteraf (1990), Teece (1982a), Wernerfelt (1984), and others have been especially influential to the resource-based perspective. The dynamic capabilities approach takes its inspiration from Schumpeter (1942) and has been successively elaborated by Dosi (1982), Nelson and Winter (1982), Prahalad and Hamel (1990), Rumelt (1984), Teece (1986), Winter (1987), and others.

It is not obvious to me how these two literatures will play out—either individually or in combination. Plainly, they deal with core issues. Possibly they will be joined. As matters stand presently, these two literatures offer general frameworks and provoke insights to which added structure is needed.

As I have discussed elsewhere (Williamson, 1975, 1985b), transaction cost economics is inspired by the work of Commons (1934), Coase (1937), Barnard (1938), Hayek (1945), Simon (1947; 1962a), Chandler (1962), and Arrow (1962a, 1969). Whether this approach can help to explicate the strategic issues that the resource based and dynamic capabilities approaches have raised remains to be seen. Be that as it may, my treatment of efficiency is predominantly informed by the transaction cost economics perspective.[4]

That has both advantages and disadvantages. On the one hand, the efficiency approach to business strategy is sorely in need of a well-focused perspective. On the other hand, business strategy has a broad mandate. A narrow lens cannot be expected to inform all of the relevant strategy issues. I submit, however, that transaction cost economics illuminates a wide range of issues of an economizing kind. If, as I argued at the outset, economy is the best strategy, then this view deserves to be heard.

1.1. First-Order Economizing

Although the need to get priorities straight is unarguably important, first-order economizing—effective adaptation and the elimination of waste—has been neglected. The adaptation argument is developed in earlier chapters. Waste is considered here.

Bureaucracy and waste are irrelevant if firms can be assumed continuously to be operating on production functions and maximizing profits. Alas, that is an egregious oversimplification.[5] As Hayek remarked,

3. The recent Mahoney and Pandian (1990) review lists over 100 books and articles of these kinds.

4. Pertinent contributions include Williamson (1975; 1985b; 1991), Klein, Crawford, and Alchian (1978), Alchian (1984), Teece (1982a; 1986), Grossman and Hart (1986), and Masten, Meehan, and Snyder (1991).

5. To be sure, the literature on X-efficiency is concerned with many of the salient issues. That literature, however, has never developed a positive research agenda. It operates at a very high level of generality and has never identified the appropriate unit of analysis. Among other

the task of keeping cost from rising requires constant struggle, absorbing a great part of the energy of the manager. How easy it is for an inefficient manager to dissipate the differentials on which profitability rests, and that it is possible, with the same technical facilities, to produce at a great variety of costs, are among the commonplaces of business experience which do not seem to be equally familiar in the study of the economist. (1945, p. 523)

Relatedly, Frank Knight expressed concern over the neglect of waste:

men in general, and within limits, wish to behave economically, to make their activities and their organization "efficient" rather than wasteful. This fact does deserve the utmost emphasis; and an adequate definition of the science of economics . . . might well make it explicit that the main relevance of the discussion is found in its relation to social policy, assumed to be directed toward the end indicated, of increasing economic efficiency, of reducing waste. (1941, p. 252)

Or recall Oskar Lange's argument that *"the real danger of socialism is that of the bureaucratization of economic life,* and not the impossibility of coping with the problem of allocation of resources" (1938, p. 109; emphasis in original). Inasmuch, however, as Lange believed that this argument belonged "in the field of sociology" he concluded that it "must be dispensed with here" (1938, p. 109).

One way of interpreting waste, bureaucracy, slack, and the like is that these are sources of managerial utility (Williamson, 1964). I want here, however, to argue a different position: these cost excesses contribute negligibly to utility but are principally due to inferior organization and maladapted operations. That the profits differ in two firms in the same industry using the same technology selling to the same customers is not because the managers in the one are working harder than managers in the other. Instead, managers in the two firms are working equally hard but one is working smarter—better organization form; better internal incentives and controls; better alignment of the contractual (interfirm and intrafirm) interfaces.

The differences between first- and second-order economizing can be illustrated with a simple partial equilibrium welfare economics setup. Thus consider an industry that is selling product q_1 at a price p_1 and is just covering its average, but bloated, costs, which are given by $c_0 + b$—where c_0 is the minimum average costs at which product q_1 can be supplied and b represents the bloat (excess bureaucratic costs or waste). Suppose now that the bloat is removed by a reorganization that eliminates unneeded bureaucrats and wasteful bureaucratic practices. But suppose that the price remains at p_1. Substantial social gain nonetheless results from waste elimination—the cost savings being measured by the rectangle $W = bq_1$ (where W denote waste) in Figure 12.1. Assume now that price is reduced to the new level of costs, whence $p_2 = c_0$.

things, issues of remediable and irremediable X-inefficiency are never faced. Irremediable flaws—that is, those that cannot be remedied with net gains (Coase, 1964)—are operationally irrelevant.

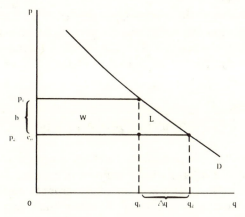

Figure 12.1. Efficiency losses.

Added allocative efficiency benefits—given by $L = \frac{1}{2}b\Delta_q$ (where $\Delta_q = q_2 - q_1$ and L denotes deadweight loss)—thereby result. Albeit important, this price induced (second order) efficiency gain is small in relation to the first order efficiency gain (from waste elimination). Indeed, the ratio of W to L, which is given by $2q_1/\Delta_q$, can easily be of the order of 10 : 1.

The message here is plain: the principal action is in the first order efficiency rectangles (the base and height of which are q_1 and b, respectively) rather than in the second order efficiency triangles (the base and height of which are Δ_q and b, respectively). What may have been obvious to Knight and was intuited by Lange, however, did not carry the day: economists have mainly assumed the problem of waste away and have concentrated attention on the triangles. Little wonder that the welfare consequences of monopoly, which focus on second order price distortions, are held to be negligible (Harberger, 1954).

1.2. Transaction Cost Economics

The main hypothesis out of which transaction cost economics works is this: *align transactions, which differ in their attributes, with governance structures, which differ in their costs and competencies, in a discriminating (mainly, transaction cost economizing) way.* This economizing orientation notwithstanding, transaction cost economics does not assert, much less insist, that economic organization is relentlessly taut.[6] To the contrary, if economic organization is formidably complex, which it is, and if economic agents are subject to very real cognitive limits, which they are, then failures of alignment will occur routinely. Excesses of waste, bureaucracy, slack, and the like are mainly explained, I submit, by failures of alignment. The reason why transaction cost

---

6. One informed student of economic organization has remarked that Alfred P. Sloan, Jr. was relentlessly given to profit maximization. Sloan was also an organizational genius. He is perhaps the exception who proves the rule.

economics is pertinent to the study of business strategy is precisely because first-order economizing alignments are not always obvious and/or sometimes are at variance with managerial preferences.[7] It is therefore important to examine the microanalytics of organization and explicate which alignments go where and why.

2.   Comparative Contracting

It is not only possible but customary to study the modern corporation by examining alternative forms of administrative organization. This entails making comparisons *within* a generic form of governance—namely, hierarchy. Transaction cost economics maintains, however, that comparisons *between* alternative generic modes—markets, hybrids, and hierarchies—are at least as important, if not more so. Many of the errors of myopic strategic reasoning can be avoided by approaching the problem of economic organization as one of incomplete contracting in its entirety. As discussed above, parties to an incomplete contract are assumed to behave perceptively with respect to present and prospective benefits and hazards, whence they decide *simultaneously* on (1) the technology to be employed, (2) the price under which a good or service will be transferred, and (3) the governance structure within which a transaction is located.

As set out below, transactions cost economics is pertinent to questions of the following kinds:

1. When can forward integration into distribution be used to deter entry and when will such efforts predictably fail? (The attempt by American Sugar Company to drive out its competitors by buying into wholesale and retail distribution predictably ended as a miserable failure.)
2. When does lateral integration offer added value and when does it represent a misuse of corporate resources? (The acquisition of Reliance Electric by the Exxon Corporation was arguably of the latter kind and could have been so identified at the outset.)
3. Why is the acquisition of one firm by another always attended by the loss of incentive intensity? (The incentive failures of Series E and Series H stock issues by General Motors (following the acquisition by GM of EDS and Hughes Electronics, respectively) were the predictable consequences of the "impossibility of selective intervention.")
4. What additional factors need to be considered when contracting under a weak property rights regime? (Both marketing channel and technology transfer decisions are pertinent.)
5. Is there an efficient choice of debt and equity, and how does this relate to the use of leveraged buyouts and management buyouts?

7. The waste consequences of managerial preferences—say, in favor of vertical integration—are assumed greatly to exceed the managerial utility gains (to which salary or other reductions in the managerial compensation package could be ascribed).

6. Should membership on the board of directors be shared among interested stakeholders or should it be concentrated on a particular group?
7. What types of businesses are well-suited for the partnership form, and what happens if a mismatch occurs? (The decision of Booz-Allen to go public is an example of a mismatch that was subsequently reversed.)
8. Given the intertemporal propensities of bureaucratic forms of organization to ratify and renew earlier decisions, what counterbiasing checks should be made? (The obvious check is to require all new projects to cross a very high threshold for approval.)

Applications of transaction cost economics to intermediate product markets and to finance were developed in earlier chapters (especially Chapters 3, 4, and 7). Applications to stakeholder participation on the board of directors are sketched here.

Worker participation can take many forms and many of these are productive (Levine, 1990). Participation can yield both direct (private) benefits and indirect (social) benefits. Above some threshold level, added participation usually comes at a cost. The nature of these costs and benefits varies with the task, the group, and the context.

My concern here is strictly with participation on the board of directors and I address this matter entirely with respect to the composition of one-tier boards. The modern manufacturing corporation is considered first. The organization of professional firms follows.

Stakeholder approaches to corporate governance in the modern manufacturing corporation take a variety of forms. One variant of "interest group management" would award seats on the boards of directors to "one-third representatives elected by employees, one-third consumer representatives, one-third delegates of federal, state, and local governments" (Dahl, 1970, p. 20). The view is that it is ungenerous, antidemocratic, and antiproductive to deny workers, consumers, the public, and other interested stakeholders from representation on the board of directors.

Transaction cost economics aspires to assess the contractual relation between each constituency and the enterprise symmetrically. The general argument is that each input will contract with the enterprise in a discriminating way. Specifically, inputs that are exposed to contractual hazards will either devise a contractual safeguard or the input will demand and receive a risk premium. Assuming that corporate governance matters, in that awarding corporate control to the wrong constituencies introduces added risk—which in turn will be reflected in the costs of organization, the first and simplest lesson of transaction cost economics is that corporate governance should be reserved for those who supply or finance specialized assets to the firm. Large numbers of nonspecific groups with which the firm has contracts are thus eliminated from potential stakeholder status immediately.

Among those who qualify as stakeholders in asset specificity terms, the key issue is how best to secure that stake. The possibility of using the board of directors as a security instrument for some or all of these constituencies warrants consideration. There are several options: (1) mixed boards, in which all constituencies that make specific investments are awarded a prorata stake; (2) specialized boards, whereby the contractual relation with all types of stakeholders but one is perfected at the contractual interface, the board being awarded to the stakeholder whose contractual relation to the firm is most difficult to perfect (and thus has the status of a residual claimant); and (3) specialized boards in which one stakeholder group is dominant but where provision for others is made by awarding them observer status, thereby to permit their specialized advice and/or to satisfy their informational needs.

These issues are discussed elsewhere (Williamson, 1985b, chap. 12, 1988b). Suffice it to observe here that constituencies that have a well-defined contractual relation to the firm will benefit by tuning up the contractual interface in a well-defined way. Not only is the board of directors a diffuse and cumbersome, rather than a well-defined instrument, but such protective powers as it possesses are compromised by inviting broad participation on the board. Residual claimant status is at best risky and is made all the more so if the claims of many constituencies are subject to *ex post* bargaining at the board level. In effect, broad participation on the board invites two bites at the apple (get your full entitlement at the contractual interface; get more in the distribution of the residual). Confronted with added risk, those who are the "natural" residual claimants in the nexus of contracts will adjust the terms under which they will contract adversely. If, as is typically the case in manufacturing (declining industries being a possible exception), equity is the natural residual claimant, the cost of equity would increase if the interest group management model of the board (or some variant thereof) were to be adopted.

The contrast between boards of directors in manufacturing firms and professional firms (law firms, accounting firms, and the like) is striking. The boards of directors in professional firms are entirely made up of the employees (managing partners). Why the difference?

Two things are very different. First, the physical assets in these professional firms are very generic and redeployable—hence can be leased or financed by debt. Outside equity is unneeded—indeed, is contraindicated, since to use equity finance for such assets is to incur costs without benefits. Having financed these assets with debt (or by the membership), the assets at risk, for which added protection is needed, are the human assets and the reputation of the firm. Control and residual claimancy is appropriately assigned to the key employees who have a stake in developing and preserving the value of these assets. Hansmann agrees and observes that

> The only important industries in the United States in which worker-owned firms are clearly the dominant form of organization are the service industries, such as law, accounting, investment banking, and management consulting, where partnership and professional corporations (that is, corporations in which shareholding is confined to professionals practicing in the firm) are the typical form of practice. (1986, p. 54)

Interestingly, the transaction cost logic of economic organization not only supports this general result, but furthermore helps to explain organizational differences within the partnership form. Thus Gilson and Mnookin (1985) examine compensation practices in law firms—the leading payment alternatives being equal shares to senior partners vs. a marginal productivity payment scheme—and advance a rationale in which differential transaction-specific values (between clients, lawyers, and law firms) figure prominently. *Ceteris paribus,* sharing arrangements among partners are favored, which is to say that high-powered incentives are disfavored, as the relation between clients and law firms deepens.

The central message of this chapter and of this book is that there is a logic to economic organization that (1) turns on a few key transaction cost economizing principles, (2) deals with comparative economic organization at a microanalytic level, (3) has wide application, (4) can be adapted to address anomalies (weak property rights; professional firms), (5) can be communicated to and explicated for managers, and (6) violations of which are the source of avoidable costs (competitive *dis*advantages). Although transaction cost economizing does not exhaust all that is germane to business strategy, it fundamentally implicates and gives predictive content to the proposition that "economy is the best strategy."

3. The Japanese Corporation

One reason for extending the argument to consider the Japanese corporation is because it is impossible to discuss the matter of business strategy long without the issue of Japanese economic organization surfacing, if not dominating, the conversation. My main reason, however, is that I argue that the Japanese firm is distinguished not merely by different attributes but by a *syndrome* of attributes. This last pushes the analyst to consider systems considerations that do not arise when contractual relations are examined one at a time.

A variety of explanations have been advanced to explain why Japanese firms have been so successful in international competition. One of the leading explanations is that the Japanese employment relation (lifetime employment; seniority promotions) is different. Another is that Japanese industry has been the beneficiary of planning and targeting by the Ministry of International Trade and Industry. Relatedly, Japanese firms engaged in sharp, possibly predatory, business practices in which the home market is protected (and organized as a cartel) while foreign markets are subject to dumping. Cultural differences, including legal differences, purportedly contribute to the differential success. Also, extensive subcontracting is believed to be a contributing factor; Japanese banking, finance, and control are different; and the Japanese have been unusually clever in hiring the marketing expertise and subverting the political process in foreign countries to promote their economic interests.

There plainly is no lack of explanatory factors. The more favored explanations, at least in the popular press, are of a strategizing kind. I submit, however, that the Japanese have long been aware that economy is the best strategy. The main explanation for their success is that first-order economizing has been assiduously pursued.

My arguments rely in significant degree on the recent survey and assessment of the Japanese firm by Aoki (1990). The basic argument (which I believe is consistent with, but is nevertheless different from Aoki) is this: (1) three key factors—employment, subcontracting, and banking—are fundamentally responsible for the success of the Japanese firm; (2) the efficacy of each of these rests on distinctive institutional supports; and (3) the three key factors bear a complementary relation to each other.

3.1. The Employment Relation

As Aoki puts it, the "mystifying notion of 'lifetime' employment and the 'seniority' system tells only half of the truth," and even that fraction has been declining in later years (1990, p. 12). Not only does the Japanese firm use rank hierarchy as an incentive system, but "The existence of a credible threat of discharge when the employee does not meet the criteria for continual promotion" buttresses the rank hierarchy (Aoki, 1990, p. 12).[8]

What I would like to emphasize here is that the administration of rank hierarchies in the Japanese firm relies on two crucial *institutional* supports. The first of these is the elevation of the personnel department within the firm. The second is the enterprise union.

The personnel department administers the rank hierarchy in the Japanese firm in a much more comprehensive, career-oriented manner than is attempted by the usual U.S. corporation. Added confidence is infused in the rank hierarchy by transforming the relation between superiors and subordinates. As compared with most U.S. firms, immediate superiors in Japanese firms have much less control over the destiny of subordinates. If the career tracks of both superiors and subordinates are administered "on the merits" by the same personnel department, then endemic problems of corporate politicking are arguably relieved.

To be sure, there are trade-offs between current, local knowledge (where immediate superiors have the advantage, and overall career performance (where the personnel department has the advantage). Conceivably, however, the allocation and professionalization of the personnel department in the Japanese firm has had effects not unlike those that Chandler ascribed to the M-form structure: managers at every level relate to their jobs in a more objective way (Chandler, 1962, pp. 382–83; 1977, p. 460). If so, the Japanese personnel department is an organizational innovation of real importance.

Additionally, as compared with a craft or industry union in the U.S., the enterprise union in the Japanese firm both relates to the purposes and needs of the firm in a more nuanced way and serves as a more effective check on and voice with respect to the integrity of the personnel department. Being an enterprise union, its purposes are more narrowly focused on the economic needs of the enterprise and its workers. The more general political purposes

---

8. Note that Aoki expressly takes exception with the prevailing U.S. view that Japanese wages are tied more closely to seniority than are U.S. wages. Contrast Blinder (1990, p. 21) with Aoki (1988, chap. 3).

to which industry unions relate are therefore less apt to intrude; and the needs of distant firms and workers, which are often very different, do not need to be factored in. To be sure, there is always a hazard that local union leadership will be bought off or will be ineffectual. Here as elsewhere, credible checks against opportunism (Williamson, 1983) are not only vital but will frequently be in the long-term interests of workers and firms alike (indeed, union integrity is one manifestation of "enlightened management"—which is too often an empty slogan under U.S. personnel administration).

Taken together, the deepening and more effective deployment of firm-specific human capital is promoted by these twin institutional supports for the employment relation.

3.2.   Subcontracting

Large Japanese manufacturing firms are much less integrated than their U.S. counterparts. In terms of the intermediate product market schema described earlier, Japanese manufacturers rely much more extensively on hybrid contracting. In effect, the locus $X(k)$ in Figure 4.1 of Chapter 4 is lower among Japanese than among U.S. firms—whence the value $\bar{k}_2$ is pushed to the right and a larger amount of activity that would be organized under hierarchy in the U.S. is organized under the hybrid mode in Japan.

The contracting mystique is that the Japanese have a greater propensity to cooperate (Aoki, 1988, chap. 8). Ethnic homogeneity and long experience with the sharing of water rights are believed to be contributing factors. As with the employment relation, however, investments in specialized assets for which bilateral adaptability is needed will be promoted by crafting supporting governance structures and providing added safeguards.

Again, contracting mystique gives way to the logic of economic organization. At a very general level, Japanese and U.S. procurement practices are alike. Thus, strategic investments and those of a highly specific kind are undertaken by the prime contractor. Vertical integration is used for these. At the other end of the spectrum are generic items. Classical market procurement is observed for these. The question, however, is what supports the broader band of hybrid contracting.

Asanuma (1989) develops a seven-part scale to characterize outside contracting and uses four measures of relation-specific skills to describe Japanese buyer–supplier relations. As Asanuma observes and interprets Japanese contracting practices, contracts vary systematically with (1) the nature of the part to be supplied, (2) the history of the contractual relation, (3) the maturity of the industry, and (4) supplier ratings on each of the relation-specific skills. An economizing orientation informs the entire procurement exercise (Asanuma, 1989, p. 29). This is done, moreover, in a highly individuated way: "core plants in the electric machinery industry purchase both [generic] parts . . . and [specialized] parts" from the same supplier but contract differently for parts of each kind (Asanuma, 1989, p. 13).

Suppliers are graded A through D. Suppliers of grades A and B are cultivated, grade D suppliers are eliminated, and grade C suppliers are used to buffer variations in demand (Asanuma, 1989, pp. 17–18). Even grade A and B suppliers are subject to competition at contract renewal intervals (the period of which varies with the nature of the part in question) (Asanuma, 1989, pp. 4, 8). Relations of trust notwithstanding, bilateral monopoly conditions are avoided: "Whenever feasible, [core firms] endeavor to correct the situation by developing alternative qualified sources" (Asanuma, 1989, p. 26).

There is nothing romantic or soft-headed about Japanese contracting practices. What seems to distinguish these practices is that they have been raised to a higher level of refinement than are observed elsewhere. Partly that may reflect the Japanese understanding that vertical integration is the organization form of last resort. As discussed below, systems considerations are pertinent to both the attractions and successes of Japanese subcontracting.

3.3.   Banking

Individual banks in Japan are permitted to hold stocks in nonfinancial companies up to a maximum of 5 percent. But combinations of banks can own more, and do: "Financial institutions as a whole (including insurance companies) own about 40 percent of the total stock outstanding of listed companies" (Aoki, 1990, p. 14). What is additionally interesting, moreover, is that banks behave collectively: one "main bank" is assigned to each company. Aoki describes the relation as follows:

> The main bank plays the role of manager of a loan consortium when a group of banks extends major long-term credit to the company, and it is responsible for closely monitoring the business affairs of the company. If the company suffers a business crisis, the main bank assumes major responsibility for various rescue operations, which include the rescheduling of loan payments, emergency loans, advice for the liquidation of some assets, the facilitation of business opportunities, the supply of management resources, and finally reorganization, to secure the claims of the consortium (Sheard, 1989). In the normal course of events, however, the main bank exercises explicit control neither in the selection of management nor in corporate policy making. (1990, p. 14)

One of the interesting questions is whether the main bank will refuse to discharge its responsibilities during a business crisis. I submit that this is an example of collective organization where reputation effects can be expected to operate with usual reliability. Failure by a main bank to discharge its assigned function virtually guarantees that it will be punished by others in the banking group of which it is a member. Furthermore, other groups will observe and record this behavior, regard it as an unacceptable breach, and will themselves refuse membership. The would-be defector is thus faced with massive reputation effect penalties.

Another interesting feature of this bank ownership system is that the managements of Japanese firms are insulated from takeover raids through the open market (Aoki, 1990, p. 14). Management displacement, if it occurs, is orchestrated by the main bank (Aoki, 1990, p. 15).

3.4. System Effects

Each of these Japanese practices is interesting in its own right. Moreover, some can be and have been imitated by U.S. corporations—who now, for example, are much more aware of the potential cost-saving merits of hybrid contracting.

What I want to emphasize here, however, is that these three practices are linked. In particular, the efficacy of Japanese employment practices is supported both by extensive subcontracting and by banking control.

As previously remarked, transaction cost economics maintains that all long-term contracts are unavoidably incomplete and pose contractual hazards. Lifetime employment is an especially long-term contract. Hazards of four kinds are posed.

For one thing, firms that assume this obligation are potentially subject to severe strain if they are beset by economic adversity—due, say, to periodic drops in demand. Secondly, workers in core firms may treat the job as a sinecure and shirk their duties. Third, the workers who specialize their productive talents to the needs of a particular firm may find that the agreement is breached—possibly through takeover. Finally, not all workers in the firm may bear the same important relation to the enterprise, yet demands for equalitarian treatment are hard to resist. Accordingly, life-time guarantees are awarded to all. I will hereafter refer to these as adversity, shirking, breach, and equalitarianism.

I contend that the institutional matrix within which core firms operate relieve these hazards. For one thing, the Japanese personnel office in combination with enterprise unions significantly relieve shirking and help to relieve equalitarianism. If subcontractors are less constrained in life-time employment respects than core firms, then extensive subcontracting helps to relieve adversity. But there are added benefits. Extensive subcontracting simplifies the personnel administration and enterprise union operations in the prime contractor by homogenizing the work force. There being less variety, the task of personnel administration, which is incredibly ambitious, is significantly reduced in scope. Also, wage disparities within the membership of the enterprise union are reduced. In effect, variety is removed to the subcontractors (each of which is relatively homogeneous), which relieves equalitarianism. The system as a whole supports variety, but each of the parts is relatively homogeneous. But for this simplification, the Japanese employment system would experience much greater strain.[9]

9. As Aoki observes, "the differentiation of employment status with a single firm is not easy to administer from the industrial relations point of view. Also, under the institution of enterprise-based unions organized on the union-shop principle, it may become difficult for the union to represent the divergent interests of different groups of employees fairly." These considerations encourage firms to "spin off or subcontract those activities which require qualitatively different working conditions." A "relatively undifferentiated employment structure" results (Aoki, 1984, pp. 27–29).

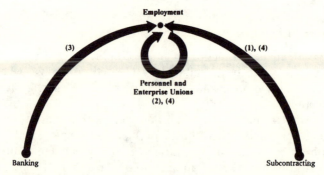

Figure 12.2. Supports for life-time employment: (1) Adversity; (2) Shirking; (3) Breach; (4) Equalitarianism.

Hazards of breach that arise because incumbent managements have been displaced by new owners (takeover) ar arguably reduced by the Japanese main bank ownership scheme. To be sure, the so-called breach of trust that Shleiffer and Summers (1988) have ascribed to takeover are, I think, exaggerated (Williamson, 1988b). To the extent, however, that life-time employment arrangements are in place, this hazard is greater and added protection is warranted.

The upshot is that the hazards associated with life-time employment are mitigated by the combined forces shown in Figure 12.2. More generally, the set of connections that join the Japanese employment relation, banking, and subcontracting go beyond those shown in Figure 12.2 to encompass the wider set of forces shown in Figure 12.3. Arguably, this network of relations has value-infusing consequences—which is to say that the whole is larger than (and more difficult to replicate) than the sum of the parts.[10]

4.   Conclusions

Peter Drucker wrote an important book on *The Concept of the Corporation* in 1946. That book had significant ramifications for an understanding of the headquarters unit in a multibusiness firm. Alfred Chandler's *Strategy and Structure* was published in 1962 and Alfred P. Sloan's *My Years with General Motors* in 1964. Both of these significantly advanced our knowledge of the purposes served by the headquarters unit of a multibusiness firm. My own understanding of and approach to the modern corporation and the purposes served by organization form was massively influenced by Chandler.

The elemental foundations for the approach to business strategy proposed here goes back, however, to a much earlier contribution: Ronald Coase's

---

10. Japanese economic organization continues, however, to evolve. The role of banks has been less significant since 1984–85 than it had been previously. The possibility that the interpretation of the Japanese corporation set out here will be obsolete and mainly of historical interest cannot be dismissed (Emmett, 1991, pp. 36–40).

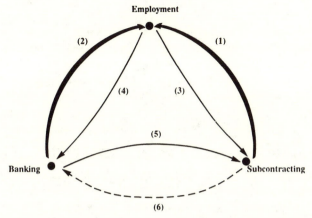

Figure 12.3. Japanese corporate connectedness. ➤ denotes strong support; → denotes support; ⟶➤ denotes weaker support. (1) Greater homogeneity; (2) greater contract stability; (3) feedback stability; (4) reliably responsive to adversity; (5) financial planning (convergent expectations); (6) no surprises.

prescient article on "The Nature of the Firm" (1937) together with the related literature that I refer to in the first section is where I suggest that the study of business strategy should begin. The proposition that economy is the best strategy needs to be related to those foundations.

What is missing in business strategy, but is desperately needed, is a core theory. To be sure, game theory provides the requisite needs for the strategizing branch of strategy. But strategizing is pertinent for only a small subset of transactions, whereas economizing is relevant for all. A core theory to anchor economizing is the pressing need.

My argument is that the microanalytic, comparative institutional, economizing orientation of transaction cost economics deals with many of the key issues with which business strategy is or should be concerned. With effort, moreover, extensions and refinements can be made which extend the reach, sharpen the analysis, and make the approach even more germane. As I have observed in Chapters 2 and 6, the 1990s is the decade when the new science of organization will come of age. The economizing approach to strategy should both contribute to and be the beneficiary of these developments.

13

The Institutions and Governance of Economic Development and Reform

Complex economic organization in general, and such ambitious undertakings as economic development and reform in particular, are usefully informed from several perspectives. The New Institutional Economics (NIE) has recently been invited to speak to the issues of development and reform. What does the NIE have to offer?

The first and most candid response is that the NIE provides few answers. Partly, however, that is because the NIE is still young and has only recently entered the development arena. As discussed later (see especially Sections 5 and 6), recent efforts to apply the NIE to privatization and to development and reform have made real headway, and more is expected. At best, however, the NIE is but one useful perspective among many.

As it turns out, the NIE offers not one but several (related) perspectives. The main divide is between the institutional environment approach, which is more a macroperspective and is concerned with the political and legal rules of the game, and the institutions of governance, which is more a microperspective and deals with firm and market modes of contract and organization. Of these two, the former is arguably the more pertinent to economic development and reform. I nevertheless work predominantly from the governance perspective; that is, I adopt a bottom–up, rather than a top–down, approach to economic organization. The following three propositions inform the exercise:

1. Institutions are important and are susceptible to analysis.
2. The action resides in the details.
3. Positive analysis (with an emphasis on private ordering and de facto organization), rather than normative analysis (court ordering and de jure organization) is where the NIE focuses its attention.

I begin by examining the way in which the study of economic development and economic reform has moved in the direction of institutional economics. Then in Section 2, I set out the general NIE framework. The pertinence of each of these three propositions to development and reform is sketched in

322

Sections 3 through 5. Applications to *The East Asian Miracle* and to privatization in telecommunications are developed in Section 6, with my concluding remarks following.

1. Economic Development and Reform: A Preview

An evaluation of the huge postwar literature that deals with economic development and reform is beyond the scope of this chapter. Figure 13.1, however, sketches what I see to be the salient moves that have brought us to the point that institutional economics has been invited to enter the arena.

As Figure 13.1 shows, the main divide is between macro and micro approaches to development and reform. Because institutional economics is mainly concerned with microanalytic matters, it is our principal interest. I should note, however, that there would be much less incentive to turn to the micro side had the macro approach been more successful.

Indeed, although the study of economic development and that of industrial organization (IO) are quite distinct, they also have striking similarities. As we shall show, the study of governance is pertinent to both. What I want to emphasize here is that both development economics and IO have undergone

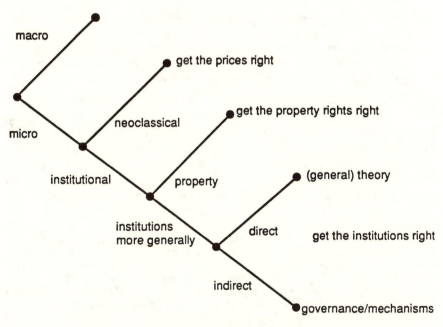

Figure 13.1. The economic development progression

a similar three-stage progression.[1] Stage I is the relatively aggregative or macro approach (the Harvard tradition). The neoclassical approach (the Chicago tradition) is conspicuous in Stage II, and the New Institutional Economics does not appear until Stage III. Because it is primitive and still growing, the NIE is used only as a last resort. Finally, the stages are overlapping, so the appearance of a new stage does not annihilate its predecessors.

An extreme version of the macro approach is referred to by Deepak Lal as the "Dirigiste Dogma." This prescription calls for governments to chart and implement "a 'strategy' for rapid and equitable growth which attaches prime importance to macro-economic accounting aggregates such as savings, the balance of payments, and the relative balance between broadly defined 'sectors' such as 'industry' and 'agriculture'" (Lal, 1983, p. 5). But this was a disappointing prescription,[2] and the pendulum swung in the opposite direction. Many concluded that "the most important advice that economists can . . . offer is that of . . . [the] so-called Price Mechanist: 'Get the prices right'" (Lal, 1983, p. 107). Although the elimination of tariffs, quotas, and subsidies—more generally, making markets work—has much to recommend it, this too is overly simple and poorly suited to the needs of reforming (as against developing) economies. "Getting the property rights right" seemed to be more responsive to the pressing needs for reform in Eastern Europe and the former Soviet Union.

Privatization thus became the new prescription, but as Roman Frydman and Andrzej Rapacynski concluded,

> [T]he meaning of "privatization" in Eastern Europe has turned out to be complex and ambiguous. Instead of the clarification of property rights and the introduction of incentives characteristic of a capitalist society, the privatization process has so far often led to a maze of complicated economic and legal relations that may even impede a speedy transition to a system in which the rights of capital are clearly delineated and protected. (1993, p. 13)

One problem is that conflicts broke out "between the interests of insiders, intent on retaining authority over their enterprises, and the right of outside investors to acquire control" (Frydman and Rapacynski, 1993, p. 13). But the deeper problem is that getting the property rights right is too narrow a conception of institutional economics. The more general need is to "get the institutions right," of which property is only one part.[3] But what does this mean? In their 1991 and 1993 Nobel Prize lectures, both Ronald Coase and

---

1. For a discussion of this progression in antitrust, see Williamson, 1985b, chap. 14.

2. Disappointments with the Balcerowicz program in Poland—which made "macroeconomic measures such as credit restrictions, wage restraints, and reductions of subsidies" the centerpiece of reform—illustrate the limits of the standard prescription (Rausser, 1992, p. 322).

3. Not only is the definition of property rights sometimes costly (consider the difficult problems of defining intellectual property rights), but also court ordering can be a costly way to proceed. A comparative contractual approach—according to which court ordering is often (but selectively) supplanted by private ordering for purposes of governing contractual relations (Macneil, 1974, 1978; Williamson, 1979b, 1991a)—rather than a pure property rights approach, therefore has a great deal to recommend it.

Douglass North spoke frankly to the issues. Coase observed:

> The value of including ... institutional factors in the corpus of mainstream economics is made clear by recent events in Eastern Europe. These ex-communist countries are advised to move to a market economy, and their leaders wish to do so, but without the appropriate institutions no market economy of any significance is possible. If we knew more about our own economy, we would be in a better position to advise them. (1992, p. 714)

And North remarked that "polities significantly shape economic performance because they define and enforce the economic rules. Therefore an essential part of development policy is the creation of polities that will create and enforce efficient property rights. However, we know very little about how to create such polities" (1994, p. 366).

As shown by the last node in Figure 13.1, the idea of getting the institutions right can be viewed as an exercise in (general) theory or an exercise in governance/mechanisms. The former tends to be more ambitious and normative, and the latter is more partial and positive. Gordon Rausser and Leo Simon's prescription illustrates the first of these, in which they attempt

> a general conceptual framework that provides an overview of the entire transition process, viewing it through a wide-angled lens. An ideal formulation would provide an exhaustive, conceptual classification of the decisions that have to be made, the players that will have to make them, the institutional structures within which decision making will take place and a set of performance criteria against which the process can be evaluated. A particularly important requirement of the ideal formulation is that it be "logically complete," in the sense of specifying an explicit decision-making process for dealing with "residual contingencies" not dealt with elsewhere in the formulation. (1992, p. 270)

The transaction cost economies approach to economic organization looks to partial mechanisms, however, and works from variations on a few key, recurring themes. Indeed, recalling Elster's advice, such a strategy applies more generally: "Explanations in the social sciences should be organized around (partial) *mechanisms* rather than (general) *theories*" (Elster, 1994, p. 75; emphasis in original). The bottom–up approach to the study of development and reform to which I referred at the outset is consonant with this more modest (but more operational) mechanisms treatment of the issues.

2.   The New Institutional Economics

As indicated, the NIE actually took shape in two complementary parts. One of these parts deals predominantly with background conditions, and the second branch deals with the mechanisms of governance. The two-part definition proposed by Lance Davis and Douglass North (1971, p. 5–6) distinguishes between the institutional environment and the institutional arrangements. The first of these describes the rules of the game. The second is what I refer to as the institutions of governance, is what transaction cost economics has been

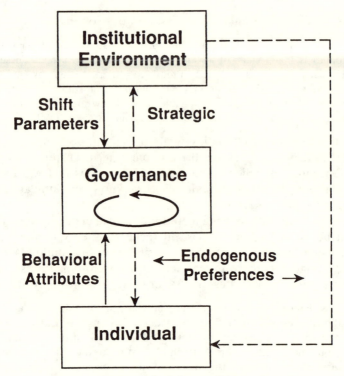

Figure 13.2. A layer schema.

predominantly concerned with, and describes the bottom–up approach to economic organization.

As it turns out, a third level—the level of the individual—also is pertinent. The schema set out in Chapter 9, and reproduced as Figure 13.2, shows how these three levels—the individual, the governance structures, and the institutional environment—relate to one another.[4] The main effects are shown by the solid arrows, and the feedback effects are the broken arrows.

2.1. Individuals

The pressing need is to describe individuals in workably realistic terms. Herbert Simon's views bear repeating: "Nothing is more fundamental in setting our research agenda and informing our research methods than our view of the nature of the human beings whose behavior we are studying. It makes a difference, a very large difference, to our research strategy; but it also makes a difference for the proper design of political institutions" (1985, p. 303). Transaction cost economics expressly adopts the proposition that human cog-

---

4. The remainder of this subsection is taken from Williamson, 1985b.

nition is subject to bounded rationality, but differs from Simon's interpretation of self-interest seeking as "frailties of motive and reason" (1985, p. 303). Transaction cost economics defines these frailties instead as opportunism, to include self-interest seeking with guile. The ramifications of these alternative prescriptions for the study of economic organization are developed in Section 5.

2.2. Governance

Transaction cost economics and this chapter are principally concerned with governance. As it relates to the three propositions offered at the outset, the argument is developed in the following sections. By way of overview, however, I suggest this:

1. Transaction cost economics is an interdisciplinary undertaking in which law, economics, and organization are joined. Law and the judiciary are reflected in the constraints that originate in the institutional environment, which define the rules of the game. Organization theory is implicated through the behavioral assumptions and by the arrow in the governance box that turns back on itself. This latter reflects the proposition that "organizations have a life of their own," that is, that organizations undergo intertemporal transformations that must be identified and factored into the analysis. Economics provides the core logic, in that the analysis works out of the "rational spirit" to which Kenneth Arrow refers (1974, p. 17). The object is to examine "incomplete contracts in their entirety."

2. Transaction cost economics is an exercise in comparative institutional analysis, in which the efficacy of alternative modes of organization—markets, hybrids, hierarchies, public bureaus—are examined in relation to and aligned with the attributes of transactions.

3. Of special importance in this connection is that the central problem of economic organization is one of adaptation, of which two kinds can be distinguished: autonomous adaptation accomplished through the market in response to price signals (Hayek, 1945) and cooperative adaptation accomplished within the firm with the support of fiat (Barnard, 1938).[5] A high-performance system aligns transactions with governance structures in relation to their adaptive needs. Both investment and contracting are implicated.

2.3. Institutional Environment

It almost goes without saying that the institutional environment (the rules of the game) is vital to the study of economic organization. But there is also a

---

5. Although North points out that "we do not know how to create adaptive efficiency in the short run" (1994, p. 367), we know more about governance than we do about the institutional environment. It also is noteworthy that the logic and empirical analysis of the governance branch are much more advanced than are the logic and empirical analysis of the institutional environment branch (Matthews, 1986).

concern that too much weight will be assigned to the institutional environment, as opposed to the institutions of governance. The exaggerated weight that is placed on court ordering (as provided by the institutions of the state) in relation to private ordering (as crafted by the immediate parties to and affiliates of a transaction) is one example, and the propensity to emphasize de jure constitutional arrangements, as compared with de facto governance, is another.

3. Institutions Matter

The NIE maintains that (1) institutions matter and (2) institutions are susceptible to analysis (Matthews, 1986, p. 903). But whereas the former is easy to assert, convincing demonstrations of the latter have been elusive. Partly because of this elusiveness, but also because neoclassical economics appeared to be successful in working from noninstitutional or preinstitutional setups, economics for a long time proceeded "as if" institutions could be ignored. That has changed.

3.1. Firm and Market Organization

Neoclassical economics describes the firm as a production function. Albeit a useful construction for purposes of studying price and output, that approach led to contrived or mistaken interpretations of nonstandard and unfamiliar forms of contracting and organization. As described in Chapter 11, the prevailing tendency was to invoke monopoly to explain puzzling (nonstandard and unfamiliar) business practices.

That propensity (and the mistaken public-policy ramifications of it) was overcome only as a rival conception of the firm (the firm as governance structure) progressively took shape, with the latter an organizational rather than a technological construction. As David Kreps explained, "The [neoclassical] firm is like individual agents in textbook economics. . . . Agents have utility functions, firms have a profit motive; agents have consumption sets, firms have production possibility sets. But in transaction-cost economics, firms are more like markets—both are arenas within which the individual can transact" (1990a, p. 96). Without pre-existing market power, the presumption is that nonstandard and unfamiliar business/contracting practices have the purpose and effect of economizing on transaction costs.

More than a presumption, however, was needed. What is the logic of organization that informs this perspective? What are the refutable implications? Do the data line up? This is the transaction cost economics project as it was successively developed over the past twenty-five years. Without the demonstration that institutions are susceptible to analysis, the proposition that institutions matter would still be ignored.

3.2. Development and Reform

What transpired in the field of industrial organization has parallels in the fields of comparative economic systems and development. Although the latter two fields conceded the importance of organization and institutions only recently, the key issues were identified by Oskar Lange over fifty years ago, when he noted that *"the real danger of socialism is that of a bureaucratization of economic life,* and not the impossibility of coping with the problem of allocation of resources" (1938, p. 109, emphasis in original). Inasmuch, however, as the study of bureaucracy was beyond the reach of economics ("belonging" instead to sociology), Lange was content to dismiss the argument with an unproven claim that the bureaucratic problems of capitalism were even more severe. The "socialist controversy" thus reverted to an abstract assessment of the allocative efficiency properties of the socialist system, whereupon it was generally agreed that Lange and Lerner had prevailed in their dispute with Hayek and von Mises on the efficacy of socialism (Schumpeter, 1942, pp. 167, 172; Bergson, 1948, pp. 424, 435). Subsequent work on comparative economic systems held that its "preinstitutional" character was a virtue (Koopmans, 1977, pp. 264–65).

I submit, however, that the former Soviet Union was overcome not by failures of activity analysis but by the cumulative burdens of bureaucracy. The consensus in the field of comparative economic systems to eschew institutions and ex post governance in favor of technology and ex ante incentive alignment thus turned out to be fateful. Secondary effects (of a marginal analysis kind) were emphasized to the neglect of primary effects (of a discrete structural kind), and as a consequence, the salient differences between capitalism and socialism in bureaucratic respects were obscured.[6]

The NIE is predominantly an exercise in discrete structural analysis in which alternative modes of organization—markets, hybrids, hierarchies, bureaus—are described as syndromes of related attributes (Williamson, 1991a; Aoki, 1994; Milgrom and Roberts, 1994). The exercise, which was developed mainly with reference to the traditional concerns of industrial organization, is relevant also to an understanding of the bureaucratic and incentive differences among comparative economic systems.

4. The Microanalytics

The New Institutional Economics demonstrates that institutions are susceptible to analysis by focusing on the microanalytics of contract and organization.

---

6. Herbert Simon's remarks are pertinent: "As economics expands beyond its central core of price theory ... in which equilibrium at the margin plays a central role, [we observe a shift] to a much more qualitative analysis, in which discrete structural alternatives are compared" (1978, p. 6).

4.1.   Firm and Market Organization

The microanalytics of firm and market organization are developed in three
parts: (1) The transaction is made the basic unit of analysis and is dimensionalized; (2) the attributes that describe and distinguish alternative modes of
governance are set out; and (3) transactions and governance structures are
aligned in relation to a transaction cost–economizing purpose. Problems with
markets arise as bilateral dependencies, and the need for cooperative adaptations, build up. Markets give way to hybrids, which in turn give way to hierarchies (which is the organization form of last resort) as asset specificity
($k > 0$) and the needs for cooperative adaptation build up.

4.2.   Development and Reform

The lessons of firm and market organization carry over to the study of development and reform. Thus in response to the question of how one should describe
a high-performance economy, the answer in regard to transaction cost economics is that the nature and level of investment and the characteristics of contracting are crucial. Moreover, differences among nation-states in terms of
investment and contracting can be predicted.

4.2.1.   Investment

As indicated, asset specificity is the transaction attribute that is most determinative of economic organization in the intermediate product markets (make or
buy), capital markets (debt or equity), labor markets (differential governance
supports), regulation or deregulation (which has ramifications for privatization), and the like. Transactions that cause especially severe contractual
hazards, because of bilateral dependency, either are afforded added safeguards (of which unified ownership of the two trading stages is one possibility) or are reformed (by shifting from a specific to a more generic technology).

Similar reasoning carries over to the level of the economy, although here
an added source of investment hazard appears: The state may be the source
of investment uncertainty.

Consider the hazard of "takings," in which a taking may be defined as
"constitutional law's expression for any sort of publicly inflicted private injury
for which the constitution requires payment of compensation" (Michelman,
1967, p. 1165). The question is how this provision, which is not self-enforcing,
is to be implemented.

Among the principled ways to implement the constitution is to appeal to
political theory, of which John Rawls's treatment of "justice as fairness" is a

candidate (Michelman, 1967, pp. 1218–24). As it turns out, this is a vague prescription and not easy to operationalize. A second way is to approach the issues in a bottom–up manner. Given the administrative costs of paying compensation, on the one hand, and the disincentives (for future investment) that arise if injuries are not compensated, on the other, what are the attributes of the transaction that are responsible for high costs of both kinds?

This is an exercise to which transaction cost economics easily relates. Not only are (1) the administrative costs of paying compensation a type of transaction cost, but (2) the "demoralization costs" to which Michelman refers depend very much on the characteristics of the assets. Also, (3) the farsighted approach to investment and (4) the idea of "security of expectations" to which Michelman appeals are very much in the spirit of credible commitments.

Michelman joins these several concepts. He argues that if administrative costs are great, because it is very costly to establish who was adversely affected and in what degree, and if neither those who bear the loss nor interested observers change the amount (K) or the composition (k) of future investments, then it will be inefficient to compensate, for administrative costs would be incurred for which there would be little offsetting benefit. If, however, the failure to pay compensation to losers "demoralizes" investors (both those who bear the losses and interested observers), with the result that the amount and kind of future investment are moved to safer (but less productive) uses, then compensation, despite the administrative costs, may yield net social gains.

Critical to an assessment of demoralization is whether the loss is perceived to be strategic rather than adventitious. Investors who perceive themselves to be strategically expropriated will view the government as malevolent. Note, moreover, that assets can be devalued not merely by seizure but also by a variety of control mechanisms, including taxation, input controls, operating requirements, price, output, and effluent controls, reporting requirements, rate of return limitations, and other bureaucratic and oversight practices.

Investors who realize that they are disadvantaged in relation to other, more favored members of the society can and will adapt in a variety of ways. Thus more durable assets will be replaced by less durable; nonmobile assets will be replaced by more mobile; conspicuous assets will give way to those that can be sequestered; and assets may flee by relocating in more secure jurisdictions. More generally, nonredeployable investments $(k > 0)$ that would be made if expectations were secure will give way to nonredeployable assets and by capital flight and asset concealment. Productivity will be lost as a result.

Michelman offered a series of criteria by which to assess how administrative costs in relation to demoralization costs net out (1967, pp. 1217–18, 1223). Perceived opportunism on the part of the government is a recurrent theme. For my purposes here, the basic point is this: Rather than focusing mainly or exclusively on the de jure constitution (top–down), the quality of a compensation regime is to be inferred principally from a de facto, bottom–up examination of the mechanisms.

4.2.2. Contracting

The economywide concept that corresponds to governance is that of the distribution of transactions. Thus consider the three-part division of governance as among spot-market trading, long-term contracting, and hierarchy. Both spot-market and hierarchical transactions need little support from the judiciary, because disappointed spot-market traders can easily limit their exposure and can seek relief by terminating and turning to other traders and because internal organization is its own court of ultimate appeal. Accordingly, the transactions in the middle range are the most difficult to "stabilize."

To be sure, parties to such middle-range transactions can provide a variety of private-ordering supports. When, however, push comes to shove, middle-range transactions will benefit if they can be appealed to a principled authority. It is here that Karl Llewellyn's concept of contract as a framework that is, as "a rough indication around which such relations vary, an occasional guide in cases of doubt, and a norm of ultimate appeal when the relations cease in fact to work," is most relevant (1931, pp. 736–37). Unless the ultimate appeal works in an informed and uncorrupted manner, however, transactions in the middle range will be in jeopardy, which will lead to a reorganization of transactions (which will be attended by a change in the degree of asset specificity (Riordan and Williamson, 1985)), in that transactions in the middle range will be moved toward one or the other pole.

The result will be that the quality of a judiciary can be inferred by indirection: A high-performance economy (expressed in governance terms) can support more transactions in the middle range than can an economy in which the judiciary is problematic. Put differently, the distribution of transactions in a low-performance economy is more bimodal (because there are more spot-market and hierarchical transactions and fewer in the middle range).

4.2.3. Discriminating alignments

Discriminating alignments appear not only at the level of transactions but also at the level of nation-states. The argument, with reference to the nation-states, is this: Nation-states that pose severe investment hazards support lower levels of specialized, durable investments (low k and low K) than do more credible investment regimes, and nation-states with problematic judiciaries are similarly disadvantaged. This shows up in, among other places, the nature of the technology.

Specifically, regimes that offer weak supports for investment and contracting rarely are able to provide strong supports for intellectual property rights. Industries that benefit from specialized, durable investments and/or are described as high-technology industries thus "flee" from regimes with great investment and contractual insecurities, in favor of safer havens.[7]

5.   Private Ordering

Compared with neoclassical economics, in which court ordering is presumed to be efficacious, transaction cost economics places much greater weight on private ordering. Issues of credible commitment and remediableness arise in conjunction with the latter.

5.1.   Firm and Market Organization

The legal centralism tradition presumes that efficacious rules of law regarding contract disputes are in place and are applied by the courts in an informed, sophisticated, and low-cost way. Those assumptions are convenient, but they suppress rather than encourage the study of institutions.

Clyde Summer's distinction between "black letter law," on the one hand, and a more circumstantial approach to law, on the other, is pertinent. "The epitome of abstraction is the *Restatement*, which illustrates its black letter rules by transactions suspended in midair, creating the illusion that contract rules can be stated without reference to surrounding circumstances and are therefore generally applicable to all contractual transactions" (Summers, 1969, p. 566). Such a conception does not and cannot provide a "framework for integrating rules and principles applicable to all contractual transactions" (Summers, 1969, p. 566). A broader conception of contract, which emphasizes the affirmative purposes of the law and effective governance relations, is needed if that is to be realized. The concepts of private ordering (Chapters 3 and 6), credible commitment (Chapter 5), and remediableness (Chapter 8) are especially crucial.

5.2.   Development and Reform

Much of the transaction cost reasoning that was developed in conjunction with the microanalytics of economic organization carries over to the study of development and reform.

5.2.1.   De facto property rights

The distinction between legal centralism and private ordering helps clarify the differences between de jure and de facto property rights. The conceptual

---

7. As discussed in Section 5.2.1, the de facto property rights that work well in a less-developed economy (such as China) may need to add de jure supports if a move into high technology is to succeed.

hazard in both cases is to assign too much weight to the formal features (court ordering and de jure legal rights) at the expense of the unremarked and more subtle real features (private ordering and de facto economic rights). The issues are nicely expressed in the puzzle of Chinese economic reform. As Gabriella Montignola, Yingyi Qian, and Barry Weingast explained,

> The remarkable success of China's economic reforms—fostering economic growth averaging nine percent per year over the past fifteen years—seems to defy conventional wisdom. Consider:
>
> • Economic reform appears to have been successfully pursued without any political reform.
> • The Central Government seems to retain considerable political discretion, including the ability to reverse suddenly the reform process or to impose onerous exactions on successful enterprises.
> • Finally, there has been little attempt to provide the central feature of private markets, a system of secure private property rights. Nor has an attempt been made to develop a commercial law (e.g., property and contract law) or an independent court system for adjudication.
>
> Each of these factors appears to bode ill for economic reform. Without political reform, economic returns remain at the mercy of politics. Political discretion, in turn, implies that there are no impediments to the government reversing the reforms. Leadership turnover, for example, might induce the new government to reverse the reforms, possibly confiscating considerable wealth and punishing those who were successful under the new system. Alternatively, problems may occur during unexpectedly hard times. With severe budget problems and a population clamoring for "solutions, now," the immediate need for revenue produces powerful pressure for a partial or wholesale reversal of the reforms. (1993, pp. 1–2)

Montignola and her colleagues responded to this puzzle by arguing, in effect, that the hazards are more apparent than real. What China has done is adopt a series of decentralizing reforms, the effect of which has been to introduce *de facto federalism* into China.

Consider in this connection a 2×2 matrix in which de jure federalism can be either present or absent and de facto federalism can be either present or absent. The usual assumption is that de jure and de facto go together, but Montignola and her colleagues introduced the possibility that they need not correspond. Figure 13.3 shows the four possibilities.

Cell II, in which de jure federalism is absent but de facto decentralization is extensive, is what Montignola and her associates are referring to in explaining the unusual success of a Chinese economy in which formal legal property rights protections are lacking. But although they make an interesting case for de facto federalism and the effective safeguards that it provides, I would nevertheless offer two caveats: (1) There is a chronic problem of ex post rationalization in explaining successes in de facto terms[8] and (2) with

---

8. The obvious remedy is to demonstrate that the details of Chinese economic organization line up with the argument, which is what Montignola and his colleagues (1993) do.

		\multicolumn{2}{c}{de jure federalism}
		present	**absent**
de facto federalism	**present**	I federalism "ideal"	II neglected alternative: "chinese federalism"
	absent	III bogus federalism	IV highly centralized, in theory and practice

Figure 13.3. Forms of federalism.

weak de jure property rights, I predict that China will be unable to support highly specific investments in leading-edge technologies. This latter problem will offer a challenge to Chinese economic organization in the future.

5.2.2. Credible commitments

Weingast addressed the correspondences between political and economic organization:

> In important respects, the logic of political institutions parallels that of economic institutions. To borrow Williamson's phrase, the political institutions of society create a "governance structure" that at once allows the society to deal with on-going problems as they arise and yet provides a degree of durability to economic and political rights. Importantly, these help limit the ability of the state to act opportunistically. (1993, p. 288)

A farsighted state thus recognizes that organization matters and that it can take actions that inspire confidence in both contracting and investment respects. Because, however, politics is different, credible commitments may fail to materialize by reason of ignorance, front-loading, or looting.

The ignorance argument is that long-run efficiency reasoning does not come easily to politicians who are more familiar and comfortable with power reasoning. Not only does ready recourse to political favors/power/discretion place those who have already invested at hazard, but those who are contemplating investment will think again. The paradox is that fewer degrees of freedom (rules) can have advantages over more (discretion) if added credible commitments obtain in this way (Kydland and Prescott, 1977). That is not an intuitively obvious result.[9]

The front-loading to which I refer is due to the weakness of political property rights. Thus even if the parties have the capacity to look ahead and factor future consequences back into present policy choices, the political process will pose hazards of its own. If current politicians cannot bind their successors, then they will prefer projects that are front-end loaded, *ceteris paribus* (Moe, 1990a, 1990b).

Looting is explained similarly. Thus although a bigger pie is always better than a smaller pie, *ceteris paribus,* the *cetera* may not be *paria.* If politicians with short horizons can seize assets or otherwise reward favored constituencies now, and if a big (and certain) piece of a small pie is perceived to be better than a smaller (and uncertain) piece of a bigger but deferred pie, then credibility may get short shrift.

In regard to these disabilities, what should we do? The argument throughout is that the action resides in the mechanisms of governance, specifically, find mechanisms that communicate credible commitments.

Although there is growing agreement that credible commitments are the key (Shepsle, 1992; North, 1994), the need is to get beyond the agreement stage and into the specifics. Otherwise, credible commitments will acquire the "well-deserved bad name" that Stanley Fischer (1977, p. 322, n. 5) once gave to transaction costs.

The problem with transaction costs in the early 1970s is that the concept was too elastic: Anything could be explained by invoking suitable transaction costs after the fact. This tautology was overcome by moving the analysis of transaction costs from (vague) generalities to the microanalytic particulars of transactions and governance: Transactions were dimensionalized; the Fundamental Transformation was explicated; the discrete structural attributes of governance were displayed; and so forth.

The concept of credible commitments (as employed at the level of the institutional environment, as opposed to the level of governance) in the 1990s is similar: Because there are so many degrees of freedom, any outcome can be rationalized in credible commitment terms after the fact. The parallel prescription, to overcome this tautological status, is similarly to engage the relevant microanalytics, in this instance at the level of the mechanisms of the polity. Although this is an ambitious prescription, it is nonetheless beginning to take shape (Soskice, Bates, and Epstein, 1992).

5.2.3. Remediableness

As discussed in Chapter 8, it was once customary, and is a continuing hazard, to regard the "government as a benevolent guardian, hampered only by igno-

9. "Soviet Economic Development," *International Herald Tribune,* June 5, 1990, p. 5.

rance of proper economic policy as it seeks disinterestedly to maximize a Benthamite social welfare function" (Krueger, 1990, p. 172). But this has begun to change (Stiglitz, 1989, pp. 38–39) and will change all the more as the standard of remediableness takes hold. The relevant comparisons are always and everywhere among alternative feasible modes of economic and political organization—which is to say that hypothetical ideals (governments as benevolent guardians) do not qualify.

6.   Some Applications

In what degree does the literature on economic development and reform support a bottom–up institutional economics approach that emphasizes investment, contracting, and the mechanisms of credible commitment? The short answer is "not much," which is not surprising. After all, little of this literature was written from an institutional economics perspective. It suffices for my purposes here to establish that there are hints in the literature for which institutional economics provides a useful lens.

The study of Chinese de facto federalism (Montignola et al., 1993) is one example, and the mistaken views of Gorbachev on credible commitments is another. I discuss here two further applications: the "East Asian Miracle" and the recent five-nation study of the privatization of telecommunications (Levy and Spiller, 1994).

6.1.   East Asia

My remarks here are concerned with the recent World Bank Policy Research Report, *The East Asian Miracle.* I begin with three observations: The report is an informative, thoughtful, and cautious treatment of the issues; it relies hardly at all on institutional economics reasoning; and yet institutional economics is relevant to some of the more interesting phenomena and practices that are addressed.

The report interprets the East Asian growth experience through neoclassical, revisionist, and market-friendly lenses (pp. 82–86). The neoclassical view is to allocate resources through markets in the context of macrostability and limited inflation. The revisionist view "sees market failures as pervasive and a justification for governments to lead the market in critical ways" (p. 83). The market-friendly view is that "the appropriate role of government . . . is to ensure adequate investments in people, provision of a competitive climate for enterprise, openness to international trade, and stable macroeconomic management." It also recognizes both market failure and government failure (p. 84).

The institutional approach is closest to the market-friendly view, but it focuses on credible investment and credible contracting. It is also more expressly concerned with the attributes of human and physical assets.

Although we are told on p. 221 that "property rights . . . [is a] key element of the market-friendly institutional environment discussed in Chapter 4," it takes an extraordinarily perceptive eye to interpret Chapter 4 in that respect. And although we are also told the enforcement of contracts is important (p. 221), it is an almost subliminal message. Nowhere in the concluding discussion, the "Foundations of Rapid Growth—Getting the Fundamentals Right" (pp. 347–52), is there mention of either property or contracting. Rather, the "positive lessons" are listed: "Keep the macroeconomy stable; focus on early education; do not neglect agriculture; use banks to build a sound financial system; be open to foreign ideas and technology; and let prices reflect economic scarcity" (p. 367). Shift parameters from the institutional environment—culture, politics, and history—receive only limited treatment (p. vii).

An implicit reliance on institutional economics reasoning can nonetheless be inferred from the following:

I. Investment
  1. The fact that two-thirds of the growth of the eight East Asian economies is accounted for by high rates of investment in physical and human capital speaks to the importance of a credible investment condition (p. 8).
  2. The allocation of capital to "high-yielding investments" (p. 8) can be interpreted in asset specificity ($k > 0$) terms.
  3. Education is discussed mainly with reference to government support for education, especially at the primary and secondary levels (pp. 193–203), because there are reasons for concern about market failures (p. 197). The comparative failures of government are not, however, discussed symmetrically. Remediableness issues are not, therefore, addressed.
  4. Credibility. Except for one passing reference to credibility (p. 188), the concept of credible commitment is ignored. A variety of phenomena could, however, be interpreted as indirect indicators of confidence. For example, an economy that inspires confidence encourages more students to invest in education because they perceive that they will realize future gains. By contrast, in a predatory regime, disfavored secondary school students bypass education. Enrollment rates (p. 109) and mix can thus be interpreted in credibility terms. Investments by the government in durable, complementary assets also have credibility-signaling properties (pp. 16–17, 221–40, 366–67). Direct foreign investment is also a useful credibility signal, and information sharing with business (pp. 183–85) can likewise serve these purposes.

5. The hurdle rate for investment is an indirect measure of credibility. Hurdle rates are lower in those countries in which political hazards are perceived to be lower, or put differently, the security of expectations is better (p. 221), other things being equal.

II. Contracting

1. Repeated references to support for small and medium enterprises (pp. 161, 181, 223, 226) can be interpreted as support for contracting, although the report emphasizes credit and related supports rather than contract per se. More subcontracting should be observed in regimes in which contract laws and their enforcement are perceived to be credible.

2. The emphasis on restructuring the labor sector "to suppress radical activity . . . [and] to ensure political stability" as well as to promote company- or enterprise-based unions (pp. 164–65) can be interpreted as efforts to place confidence in labor contracting (Williamson, 1985b), pp. 255–56). This will encourage greater investments in durable and specific physical assets (K and k).[10]

3. The idea that workers should be encouraged to organize cooperatives (p. 165) is followed by the example of organizing taxis (p. 166). There is no mention of the limits of the cooperative form of organization as firms grow large and assets become more specific (Williamson, 1985b, pp. 265–68). (The latter is because contracting for equity capital will become problematic if the firm is organized as a cooperative, and debt capital is poorly suited to support firm-specific investments.) Taxis, as it turns out, are highly redeployable assets (k 5 0) and hence are much more easily organized as cooperatives.

III. Mechanisms

1. There are numerous references to mechanisms on pp. 168 to 185. Although many of these are macroeconomic references, others implicate the government and business in more microanalytic ways. These matters need to be described more fully in order to be adequately interpreted.

2. A complicating factor is that linkages sometimes work through "informal networks," as they do in Indonesia (p. 185).

3. The importance of qualified technocrats to run the bureaucracy and the suppression of lobbying (pp. 167–79) are important sources of credible commitment. Qualified bureaucrats with job security for whom reputation effects work well have a long-term productivity orientation very different from that of politicians.

4. Adaptation goes almost unmentioned, although the adaptability of labor gets a brief comment (p. 266).

10. For a discussion in the context of Western Europe, see Eichengreen, 1994.

Albeit very tentatively and preliminarily, I would argue that institutional economics helps interpret what is going on out there. It could be used to even greater advantage if further reports focused on more microanalytic phenomena, with special emphasis on the institutional supports for contracting and investment.

6.2. Telecommunications

The World Bank conference, "Regulation, Institutions and Commitment in Telecommunications: Five Country Studies with a Comparative Analysis" (Levy et al., 1993), is a more microanalytic undertaking and is a model of what I think needs to be done. The study deals with a well-defined purpose (telecommunications) in relation to which governments differ in their perceptions of and their abilities to communicate credible commitments. Issues of investments, contracting, and mechanisms are raised.

The summary paper, by Brian Levy and Pablo Spiller (1994), and the paper on British telecommunications (Spiller and Vogelsang, 1994) are especially illuminating. The latter observes that commitment is more difficult to provide in a parliamentary (as compared with a division of powers) democracy, because

> the party in power controls both Parliament and Government. Furthermore, and perhaps as a consequence, active judicial oversight over regulatory bodies has been traditionally lacking. Thus, UK governments and regulators cannot easily commit not to use administrative discretion to expropriate part of a regulated firm's specific assets via tight regulation. Even if courts rejected a particular regulatory interference the Government could undo the court order through new legislation or through following a slightly different procedure. (Spiller and Vogelsang, 1994, p. 1)

Given that the assets in question were durable and nonredeployable, it was vital that the United Kingdom develop mechanisms that inspire investment confidence. Partly this entailed the creation of pricing formulas (of the so-called price cap kind) to which both telecommunications companies and regulators could refer with confidence. More important was the creation of the "regulatory game" in which privatized public utilities were embedded. As Spiller and Vogelsang explained,

> Several features that characterize the regulatory process limit the extent of government's regulatory discretion: First, there is a very precise and complex process to amend the license against the wish of the company. Second, since the main regulatory features are enshrined in the license, major regulatory changes have to follow the specified license amendment process. Failure to follow that process could easily be contested in courts. Third, by requiring the agreement of several agencies the amendment process reduces the extent of regulatory discretion. Fourth, by delegating major regulatory powers to

the agency head rather than retaining these powers at the level of the Ministry, the latter's powers are limited. Finally, the initial use of price cap as the price-setting method limits both the current price-setting powers of the regulator, and because price-caps are part of the license, it limits the regulator's ability to drastically change the price-setting process. (1994, pp. 24–25)

I interpret these telecommunications studies as support for the following: (1) Credibility is vital to support the requisite nonredeployable investments; (2) the regulatory regime and the political context jointly determine credibility (or the lack thereof); and (3) the mechanisms of bureaucracy can and, at least in the United Kingdom, do operate in the service of stability/credibility. Without the creation of mechanisms that communicate confidence (if not full credibility), the privatization of telecommunications (and electricity, water, gas, and airports) in the United Kingdom would have been much more problematic. As David Newberry put it, "The main case for investment in public enterprise is that it is necessary to make up for the lack of private sector confidence in the future rules of the game" (1993, p. 3).

As shown in Figure 13.4, this last shows up as Nodes I and II. More central to the arguments of this chapter are that (1) Nodes III and IV work out of a de facto judicial tradition and (2) Node VI combines de jure and de facto judicial independence with a strong bureaucracy. Node VI can thus be thought of as an "ideal." It is nevertheless noteworthy that privatization can be made to work short of this ideal if it has the requisite de facto supports. Indeed, as between de jure judicial independence that is lacking in commitment

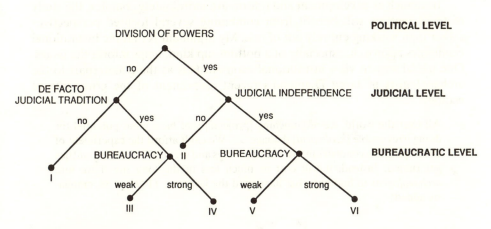

Figure 13.4. Interpreting Levy and Spiller (1994).

(Node II) and a de facto judicial tradition (Nodes III and IV), the latter has the advantage.

7. Concluding Remarks

Ronald Coase once remarked that "we have less to fear from institutionalists who are not theorists than from theorists who are not institutionalists" (Coase, 1964, p. 196), but not everyone would agree. I submit, however, that the following is (almost) uncontroversial: It is both possible and desirable to combine institutional economics with theory, and the time has come to do precisely that.

Many might nod in agreement but then return to business as usual. That will not suffice. If the World Bank, AID, OECD, and others are persuaded that institutions are important, then staffing changes are implied. Not only are institutional economists needed to do the archaeology of development and reform, but they should be expressly included at the planning stages and in the oversight process. Because this will "mess things up" for those with orthodox predilections, institutional economists will need the support of strong advocates.

Moving the NIE into the study of economic development and economic reform has so far proved to be difficult.[11] Taking institutions seriously is the first step. Working out the microanalytic logic of economic organization is the second. Explicating the mechanisms comes next. A successful project will feature variations on a few key themes, of which adaptation, private ordering, ex post governance, and credible commitments are prominent candidates.

Inasmuch as development and reform are inordinately complex, the study of these matters will benefit from combining several focused perspectives rather than working entirely out of one. My argument is that the institutional economics approach, especially of a bottom–up kind, helps inform the issues. One useful way to view institutional economists is as the counterpart to the archaeologists in Jared Diamond's recent assessment of the grim state of ecology:

> All over the world, we're launching [projects] that have great potential for doing irreversible [*ecological*] damage. . . . We can't afford the experiment of developing five countries in five different ways and seeing which four countries get ruined. Instead, it will cost us much less in the long run if we hire *archaeologists* to find out what happened the last time. (1994, p. 58, emphasis added)

---

11. Relevant institutionally informed works not referred to in the text that deal expressly with development include those by Robert Bates (1994); Elinor Ostrom, Larry Schroeder, and Susan Wynne (1993); and Mustapha Nabli and Jeffrey Nugent (1989). The works of Douglass North (1990) and Thraine Eggertsson (1990) are likewise pertinent. For an overview, see Eirik Furubotn and Rudolf Richter (1991, pp. 1–32).

Substituting *economic and political* for *ecological* and *institutional economists* for *archaeologists,* my prescription reads:

All over the world, we're launching [projects] that have great potential for doing irreversible *economic and political* damage.... We can't afford the experiment of developing five countries in five different ways and seeing which four countries get ruined. Instead, it will cost us much less in the long run if we hire *institutional economists* to find out what happened the last time.

V

CONTROVERSY AND
PERSPECTIVES

Transaction cost economics is not only different from orthodoxy, but in modest ways, it has also helped reshape orthodoxy. There is growing agreement, for example, that the business firm is usefully regarded as a governance structure (as well as a production function), that institutions matter and are susceptible to analysis, that nonstandard and unfamiliar business practices often serve economizing (rather than monopolizing) purposes, and that much of the action resides in the details (including the attributes of transactions and the mechanisms of governance).

Contrary to widespread complaints that orthodoxy is rigid and unyielding, it is my judgment and experience that orthodoxy is resistant yet susceptible to, rather than opposed to, reform. Because orthodoxy is both self-confident and aware of some of its limitations, it is often open to critique. Albeit gradually—almost imperceptibly (and certainly without conceding error)—orthodoxy redefines itself. Issues that were once declared to be outside the ambit are incorporated in a larger definition of the domain.

Transaction cost economics and the New Institutional Economics encountered their greatest resistance not from orthodoxy but from other movements with which it occupies "contested terrain." Rival forms of institutional economics are one example (Geoffrey Hodgson, 1988). Radical economics and transaction cost economics also interpret differently the purposes served by hierarchy (see Stephen Marglin, 1974, versus Williamson, 1980; and Samuel Bowles and Herbert Gintis, 1993, versus Williamson, 1993b). Also, as is evident from Chapter 9, the mainly complementary relation between transaction cost economics and organization theory is strained. And whereas evolutionary economics and transaction cost economics share many interests, they also share unresolved differences.

345

Law and economics similarly occupies much common ground with institutional economics/transaction cost economics.[1] But law and economics comes in different flavors. As it turns out, the relation between institutional economics and the Posnerian variant of law and economics is prickly.

Although there were hints, I was not aware of this relation until I received Richard Posner's paper, "The New Institutional Economics Meets Law and Economics" (1993a), which was given at the tenth annual conference on the New Institutional Economics. Shortly thereafter I read Posner's companion paper, "Ronald Coase and Methodology" (1993c), which is in the same spirit.

Ronald Coase takes sharp exception with the first of these papers in his "Coase on Posner on Coase" (1993), but he has declined to respond to the second. I think that both papers are off the mark.

My response to Posner's conference paper is contained in the conference volume (Williamson, 1993d), where I argue that Posner misunderstands and misconstrues much of what economics (including transaction cost economics) is all about and needlessly sets back the combined New Institutional Economics/law and economics agenda. I also offer a different perspective on the Coasian project in the Spring 1994 issue of the *Journal of Economic Perspectives* (pp. 201–4). Although I share some of Posner's puzzlement over Coase's views on methodology, that is not where the central contributions reside. On my reading, the essence of Coase turns on a subtle and powerful combination of four ideas:

1. Push the logic of zero transaction costs to the limit.
2. Study the world of positive transaction costs.
3. Because hypothetical forms of economic organization are operationally irrelevant and because all feasible forms of organization are flawed, assess alternative feasible forms in a comparative institutional way.
4. Because the action resides in the details, study the mechanisms of contract, contracting, and organization.

Of these four, the most important is "study the world of positive transaction costs," which is a message that Douglass North, the 1993 Nobel Prize winner, took to heart.

This book ends with an autobiographical chapter, "Transaction Cost Economics and the Evolving Science of Organization," which was written at the request of Arnold Heertje for his forthcoming book *Makers of Modern Economics II*. I feel privileged to have participated in the evolving science of organization, as both a student and a faculty member, for the past thirty-

---

1. The *Journal of Law, Economics, and Organization,* which published its first issue in Spring 1985 and is now into its eleventh volume, clearly views "law and economics" and "institutional economics" as complementary projects.

seven years, and I was naturally pleased to be asked to contribute to the Heertje volume. Although my intent was to "tell it like it was," I concede that I sometimes emphasized the affirmative and glossed over some of the setbacks. Be that as it may, I hope that verisimilitude will register with those who know firsthand of the events.

14

Transaction Cost Economics and the Evolving Science of Organization

Early accomplishments notwithstanding (Simon, 1947; Ashby, 1960; Arrow, 1963a), the science of organization to which Chester Barnard made perceptive but cautious reference in 1938 fell on hard times. Around 1970, many economists and most organization theory specialists regarded any suggestion of, much less any pretense to, a science of organization as a bad joke. That has changed dramatically over the past twenty-five years, to the degree that I predict that Barnard's aspirations will be realized by the turn of the century (Williamson, 1990a; 1993c).

The evolving science of organization can be variously described. I would define the parts of the enterprise with which I have been involved as (1) interdisciplinary (combining law, economics, and organization), (2) relentlessly comparative (organization forms are always examined in relation to alternative feasible forms), (3) microanalytic (the action resides in the details), (4) discrete structural (alternative forms of governance differ in kind, on which account it is impossible to replicate markets by hierarchies, or the reverse), and (5) preoccupied with economizing, principally with reference to organization rather than technology. Moreover, the enterprise is mainly concerned with the question "What's going on here?" rather than the imperative "This is the law here."[1]

I begin my story of this enterprise with some personal recollections, especially of my college education.[2] I then tell the story twice: first in a linear way, as though one thing "inevitably" led to the next, and then in a more contextual way in which some of the adventitious aspects of the enterprise become more apparent. The second and more expansive version divides my research and teaching into three periods: before 1970, during which time I was working mainly within an orthodox setup; the decade of the 1970s, which was a transition interval; and after 1980, by which time my shift into transaction cost economics was complete. I conclude with a discussion of the research agenda.

1. These methodological differences are discussed in Roy D'Andrade, 1986 and Donald McCloskey, 1986.
2. The original essay sketched my personal background before going to college.

1.   College

I had originally thought of becoming a lawyer, but I was attracted to math and science in high school and began talking instead of becoming an engineer. My mother declared that MIT was the place to go. With the advice of the physics teacher at the local college, it was decided that I would reach MIT through the combined plan program that MIT offered with Ripon College.

Ripon was a good place for me to start, and MIT deserved its strong reputation. The economics to which I was exposed at Ripon was dry and easy, however, and I was studying engineering and management at MIT. I enjoyed both, especially physical chemistry and thermodynamics in engineering and finance and new enterprise planning in management. One of the benefits of my engineering training is that it dealt with real problems and demanded disciplined answers. Perfect gas laws and frictionless systems may be the place to start, but the study of hypothetical ideals quickly gave way to the engineering realities of friction, resistance, turbulence, and the like.

By far the most important event in my intellectual development was my Ph.D. training at Carnegie-Mellon (then the Carnegie Institute of Technology). I did not, however, go there directly after getting my bachelor's degree but worked first as a project engineer for the U.S. government in Washington, D.C.; and I went to Stanford for two years before transferring to Carnegie. That interval was significant in four respects.

First and most important for me was to meet and marry Dolores. Second, I think it important to have firsthand experience with large bureaucracies in order to understand the problems of complex economic organization. I witnessed not only the workings of the government but also the behavior of the R&D function in many large firms. Third, because the Ph.D. program in business administration at Stanford was in poor shape when we arrived in 1958 (it has been dramatically reshaped since) and because I had the good fortune to have James Howell, who had just arrived at Stanford, as my mentor, I developed a new respect for and keen interest in economics. All these fascinating problems to which engineering skills could be brought to bear! My program underwent a vast transformation under Howell's instruction, and I found myself in the classrooms of Kenneth Arrow, Herman Chernoff, Bernard Haley, Emanuel Parzen, Melvin Reder, and Hirofumi Uzawa.

Finally, because of a shortage of offices, I shared an office in my second year at Stanford with Charles Bonini, a freshly minted Carnegie-Tech graduate who had just joined the Stanford faculty. After learning of my interests, Chuck convinced me that Carnegie was the natural place for me to go to complete my Ph.D. When the then dean, George Leland Bach, responded to my queries with two-page letters, I began to melt. I showed up at Carnegie in September 1960.

As I relate in Chapter 1, Carnegie was an incredible place at which to be a student. That was obvious to me in 1960 and has become even more evident to me since. The faculty at Carnegie was small but extraordinarily able, highly motivated, mainly accessible, and very serious about research. It was an infectious place.

Although my wife and I had originally assumed that I would teach in a small college, such as Ripon, my career aspirations had begun to change by the time I reached Carnegie. Research had begun to figure more prominently. I had been surprised when taking a graduate microtheory course from Melvin Reder at Stanford that many interesting problems were still open and some had scarcely been touched. I sketched what I thought was a new result for Reder, who identified a flaw in my reasoning but nevertheless commended me for the effort (which was high praise, since Reder was a severe taskmaster). And although the publication of Franco Modigliani's paper (1961) on the burden of the national debt precluded my working up the same argument, I was nonetheless gratified that my formulation of the problem was very close to Modigliani's.

That I had promising research instincts was confirmed by the organization theory and follow-on reading course that I took with James March, who declared that I was a natural-born experimental social psychologist. In other classes I did a wrinkle on one of Robert Solow's growth models and estimated a small simultaneous equations macromodel (into which political variables had been introduced) for econometrics. My first published paper was a short comment on Lorie Tarshis's (1961) treatment of the marginal efficiency function (Williamson, 1962). The paper that I prepared for Herbert Simon's course on mathematical social science, "Selling Expense as a Barrier to Entry," found its way (with revisions) into the pages of the February 1963 issue of the *Quarterly Journal of Economics.*

I worked mainly with the behavioral economics group at Carnegie, of which Herbert Simon was the towering figure. Bounded rationality seemed to me, then and since, as a useful way to go. James March's course in organization theory revealed that one did not need to think about organizations in classical (machine model) or fanciful (hyperrationality or nonrationality) terms but could address these matters in a behaviorally informed and scientific way. I learned about the behavioral theory of the firm from Richard Cyert—the famous Cyert and March (1963) book then being in the late stages of completion.

But while I was greatly attracted to behavioral economics, I was never entirely persuaded. Even granting that "satisficing" is more descriptively accurate than "maximizing," satisficing is also a cumbersome concept and is difficult to model. Furthermore, although the computer simulation of decision processes in which satisficing is featured is a productive way to address many issues, many of the problems for which computer simulation enjoys an advantage—such as the department store–pricing model, for which Cyert and March were able to predict both standard and sale prices to the penny—are not of general interest to economists. Thus although my dissertation had its origins in March's remark that "managers maximize slack," I addressed managerial discretion issues in terms of constrained utility maximization (in which measures of slack as well as profits were entered into the managerial utility function).

Not only did this seem to me to be the natural way to go—a variation, in some sense, on the revenue maximization model that William Baumol (1959) had devised earlier and to which I had been exposed as a student at Stanford—but the other strand of economics research at Carnegie made it easy to work out of a maximizing setup. Allan Meltzer was on my dissertation committee and encouraged that formulation. Also, I discussed the issues with Jack Muth, who emphasized the importance of thinking problems through "in their entirety" and of the need to avoid myopic formulations.

Methodological controversies between satisficing and maximizing are ones that I have usually avoided. Partly this is because I can see merit on both sides, but mainly it is because methodological controversies are rarely dispositive and are sometimes disparaging. Once you have stated your approach and I have stated mine, it is better if we both get on with our research. What added understandings are realized by each? What are the predictions? What do the data support?[3]

I am not, for example, unsympathetic to the idea that "information costs," if assiduously applied, can be made to cover virtually all the terrain to which bounded rationality applies. For that matter, I would encourage those who are put off by bounded rationality, yet recognize the cognitive limits of human actors, to develop information costs in a systematic and disciplined way. The problem, as I see it, is that most treatments of information costs tend to be selective and truncated. Bounded rationality is a more encompassing concept and is less apt to be applied in a piecemeal fashion. If, however, information costs are systematically brought to bear on all the relevant phenomena, especially including the unavoidable incompleteness of complex contracting, I have no complaints.

As I observed in Chapter 1, the research approach as I learned it at Carnegie was this: Have an active mind; be disciplined; and be interdisciplinary. To which there was an additional lesson: research problems that do not fit into orthodox boxes should be addressed on their own terms.

2.   The Linear Rendition

The story as related here is written "as if" one thing led to the next as surely as day follows the night. (To the degree to which there is a logic of organization and the enterprise described in this book contributes to that purpose, a "natural" progression does unfold.) The key moves entailed (1) identifying the requisite pieces, (2) explicating their properties, (3) ascertaining the relation among them, and (4) assembling a coherent whole. In fact, it was necessary to glimpse this last stage before work on the earlier stages could get under way.

Although my colleagues have remarked that this was a risky venture, I did not perceive it as such. First, consciously or not, I held a diversified

3. Nicholas Georgescu-Roegen advanced what I consider to be the most fellicitous standard for judging research: "The purpose of science in general is not prediction, but knowledge for its own sake," yet prediction is "the touchstone of scientific knowledge" (1971, p. 37).

portfolio of both orthodox and transaction cost economics projects during the earlier years. (This is not evident from the linear rendition, but it is obvious from the next three sections.) Second, although I knew that the problems of organization on which I was working were poorly structured, I also knew that they were important and believed that only an interdisciplinary treatment would be responsive to the needs. Carnegie gave me a leg up.

Having been encouraged from my training and experience as a youth to raise questions about the emperor's clothes, asking and attempting to answer the question "What's going on here?" came naturally. My engineering training at MIT was also pertinent. Engineers learn early of the need to go beyond hypotheticals and deal with real problems. Ronald Coase's counsel that the fiction of zero transaction costs was meant to be used as a "stepping stone on the way to an analysis of an economy with positive transaction costs" (1992, p. 717) and that all forms of organization are subject to failures, hence the need always and everywhere to do comparative institutional analysis (Coase, 1964), were ideas that I immediately embraced.

My work experience, before returning to graduate school, with large public and private bureaucracies reinforced those ideas. I could easily relate to the "inanities" of bureaucracy, could recognize unintended consequences, had experience with subgoal pursuit, and the like. It was also fortunate that I attended Stanford before going to Carnegie.

One reason was that the classical organization theory to which I was exposed to at Stanford simply did not connect, and I knew that there had to be something better. Second, getting an MBA degree exposed me to a variety of functional business specialties and case studies that provided a useful background for someone interested in the modern corporation. And third, I took my microeconomic theory courses with economics graduate students (the most famous being Menachem Yaari) and from economic theorists—Arrow, Reder, Haley, Uzawa—who were wholly absorbed, for classroom purposes, with neoclassical economics.

As I have already mentioned, the move to Carnegie was enormously exciting. Here was organization theory that was simultaneously disciplined and related to real phenomena. Here was the behavioral theory of the firm (Cyert and March) residing cheek by jowl with rational expectations (Muth). Here was bounded rationality featured by the world's leading organization theorist (Simon). Taken together with my background at Stanford, this was a rich mixture indeed. My dissertation on the economics of managerial discretion came together as a natural marriage of my Carnegie and Stanford training.

My appointment to the economics department at Berkeley also was important in several respects. First, economics at Berkeley was flourishing when the class of 1963—Peter Diamond, David Laidler, Daniel McFadden, Sidney Winter, and I—arrived. There was strength in the department in every direction, which added to my confidence. Second, I taught the undergraduate sequence in industrial organization, which got me into a field that was of obvious interest to me but in which I had never taken a course. Third, I had the opportunity to teach a graduate seminar in which the students and I went through the social choice and market failure literatures. The latter turned out to be especially important to transaction cost economics.

My move to the economics department at the University of Pennsylvania in 1965 also had salutary effects.[4] My teaching responsibilities were expanded to include graduate courses in both microeconomic theory and industrial organization, and Penn was also in a growth phase, having hired Jere Behrman, Edwin Burmeister, Edmund Phelps, Robert Pollak, Stephen Ross, Karl Shell, Paul Taubman, and Michael Wachter at our about the same time that I arrived.

I spent the academic year 1966/67 as special economic assistant to Donald Turner, the head of the Antitrust Division of the U.S. Department of Justice. That experience involved me with lawyers in a serious way and exposed me to a variety of antitrust problems on which I subsequently did research. It was a lively year. Potomac fever did not, however, strike, and I was pleased to return to Penn and reengage my teaching and research in the fall of 1967.

Being dissatisfied with the state of theory and policy on vertical integration, I organized a seminar dealing with this at Penn and the students and I worked our way assiduously through the literature. Sure enough, there were some gems, but mainly I was persuaded that the time was ripe to reformulate the problem. Coase's paper, "The Nature of the Firm" (1937), and Alfred Chandler's book, *Strategy and Structure* (1962), were obviously pertinent, but I did not yet see how to pull it off.

Then Julius Margolis was appointed to head the Fels Center of Government, and he organized a new Ph.D. program in public policy analysis. he asked me to teach the core course in organization theory, and I quickly agreed. That literature was also in very bad shape, and so I decided to include much of the market failure literature in the course. One of the important articles that we went through was Arrow's 1969 paper, "The Organization of Economic Activity," in which he argued that externalities were subsumed under market failures, which were in turn subsumed by a still more general concept, transaction costs. Given related developments in the postwar market failure literature, I saw the opportunity to pull Coase (1937) and Arrow (1969) together in my first transaction cost economics effort: "The Vertical Integration of Production: Market Failure Considerations" (Williamson, 1971b).

That was just the tip of the iceberg. It was obvious to me and my students that a few underlying regularities kept recurring throughout the market failure literature. I gave them the assignment (and took it myself) to ascertain what these were. What came to be known as the "organizational failures frame-

---

4. In November 1964 I was advised the Berkeley economics department thought my request for tenure was "premature." I related this to Dolores and we commiserated. She had made plans to go out with Beverly McFadden that night, however, and left for the evening after we got the children to bed. I played the "Tara Theme" on the piano, which seemed to capture the moment, before going to my desk, where I had a productive night of research. Evidently the end of the world was not at hand. Upon reflection, I was rather brash to ask to be considered for tenure at Berkeley after being an assistant professor for one year and four months. I was nonetheless gratified that my assistant professor cohort at Berkeley protested the tenure decision of the senior faculty when that decision was announced.

work" (Williamson, 1975) was the result. The *Markets and Hierarchies* enterprise was under way.

The argument is that markets and hierarchies are alternative instruments for organizing production and that the comparative strengths and weaknesses of these two must be examined together.[5] (By contrast, the comparative systems literature deals with either markets or hierarchies, which is a very different orientation.) Also, the variations on a theme to which Friedrich Hayek referred (1967, p. 50) were becoming evident as soon as problems of organization were recast in comparative contracting terms. In effect, vertical integration was the paradigm problem, in relation to which the organization of economic activity generally (labor, finance, franchising, corporate governance, regulation, etc.) could be examined in a similar way and with similar results. New lenses in which transaction cost economizing was featured were leading to entirely new interpretations of phenomena that were earlier believed to be without redeeming purpose (because they were thought to have monopoly purpose and effect).

But transaction cost economics cuts both ways. It can be applied to both excesses of competitive reasoning and excesses of monopoly reasoning (Matthews, 1986). The purported efficacy of franchise bidding for natural monopoly is an example of the former.

Richard Posner (1972) had taken a good argument—that franchise bidding could be used to supplant regulation for natural monopolies (first advanced by Harold Demsetz (1968b) and subsequently endorsed by George Stigler (1968))—to unreasonable extremes. Specifically, Posner contended that franchise bidding was a wholly efficacious way to deal with cable television. I had had some experience with that (having served on Mayor John Lindsay's New York City CATV Task Force) and knew that the issues were more complicated. My paper "Franchise Bidding for Natural Monopolies—In General and with Respect to CATV" (1976) was the result.

The condition of asset specificity, which had been featured in transaction cost economics from the outset, was of special importance to an assessment of when franchise bidding would work well and poorly. In addition, the behavioral assumptions of bounded rationality and opportunism, which relate to Carnegie and the sociology literatures, were clearly implicated.

Although the law was obviously relevant to what I was doing, in that it had a bearing on the employment relation and on externalities, its more general significance was not obvious to me until Victor Goldberg, who was also interested in the efficacy of regulation (1976b), suggested that I examine some of Ian Macneil's recent work on contract law (1974). Macneil's treatment of contract was much more expansive, nuanced, and interdisciplinary (mainly combining law and sociology) than I had seen previously. He described three

---

5. I presented a paper at a conference in the early 1970s in which I referred expressly to markets and hierarchies as alternative instruments for doing the very same task. Several members of the audience objected, and one denounced the enterprise. The issue, as he saw it, was markets *or* hierarchies, and any effort to deal with both was wrongheaded, misleading, and reprehensible. We have come a long way since.

different types of contract law—classical, neoclassical, and relational—and identified twelve different "concepts" for distinguishing among them. This invited a more general formulation in which law, economics, and organization were joined in the effort to assess the governance of contractual relations (Williamson, 1979b). Not only did the firm-as-production function give way to the firm-as-governance structure (in which the firm is understood mainly as an organizational rather than a technological entity), but three of the critical dimensions on which transactions differed—asset specificity, frequency, and uncertainty—were identified. This invited the study of economic organization with reference to the following objective: Align transactions, which differ in their attributes, with governance structures, which differ in their costs and competence, in a discriminating (mainly transaction cost–economizing) way. This has turned out to be a productive formulation.

It also invited me to think about the problems of stabilizing long-term contracts in a more complete way. That is, although the mechanisms that supported markets and hierarchies were clear to me, the mechanisms that supported long-term contracts were more elusive. My paper "Credible Commitments: Using Hostages to Support Exchange" (Chapter 5), which had its origins in puzzlement over the practice of petroleum exchanges among oil companies and which relates to earlier work on private ordering (Schelling, 1956; Galanter, 1981; Klein and Leffler, 1981; Telser, 1981), helped me get over that hurdle.

That in turn led to the "simple contractual schema," in which the contract is described as a triple in which price, asset specificity, and contractual safeguards all are determined simultaneously. And that framework invited still further applications, to such esoteric phenomena as company towns and to such controversial issues as corporate finance and corporate governance. I pulled many of these issues together in *The Economic Institutions of Capitalism* (1985b).

One of the missing pieces that had to be addressed in that book was the answer to the puzzle "Why can't a large firm do everything that a collection of small firms can do and more?" It is a variant of the limits-to-firm-size issue raised much earlier by Frank Knight (1965) and Ronald Coase (1937) and was a matter that Sanford Grossman, Oliver Hart, and I explored at length, but inconclusively, one evening over dinner. I invented the fiction of selective intervention—in which a large firm would replicate small firms for all activities save those for which the expected net gains from intervention could be projected—to examine this issue.

Selective intervention is an appealing concept but has a very troubling implication: If it could be implemented, then all economic activity would be organized in one large firm. Because this was contradicted by the data, the puzzle was to discover the reasons that selective intervention broke down. The discrete structural features that distinguish markets and hierarchies came more forcefully to the fore once the issues were phrased in those terms.

What had been gradually unfolding was the successive evolution of transaction cost economics from informal stages (Coase) into preformal (vertical integration) and semiformal (credible commitment) stages of analysis, and the time was becoming ripe to examine incomplete contracting in a fully formal way. That was accomplished by the paper by Sanford Grossman and Oliver Hart (1986), which has opened up a rich literature on formal modes of incomplete contracts. Although one could view this last stage as the final one in the evolving science of organization, my own sense is that conceptual and semiformal work will remain in a dialogue with fully formal work for a number of years to come.

Thus although full formalization is always the ultimate objective, premature formalization—sometimes operating under the guise of the "honest poverty" of mathematics—is a dubious undertaking. Premature formalization reflects impatience, perhaps even intolerance, with the question, "What's going on here?" Preformal analysis, by contrast, addresses complex problems in a "modest, slow, molecular, definitive" way,[6] which is why "almost any theory of organization that is addressed by game theory will do more for game theory than game theory will do for it" (Kreps, 1992, p. 1).

Mechanical applications of game theory (and other formal apparatus) to problems of comparative economic organization are therefore eschewed in favor of more institutionally informed applications. The need for a microanalytic logic of organization—in which the attributes of transactions, the attributes of alternative modes of governance, the underlying trade-offs, and the predicted alignments have been addressed—therefore becomes a game-theoretic antecedent.

This logic is in progress, but the unmet conceptual needs of the evolving science of organization are still very real. Thus although the fully formal modeling of incomplete contracts—by Grossman, Hart, Moore, Riordan, and others—represents a considerable intellectual achievement, puzzles remain. The need, for example, to discover and explicate the discrete structural features that distinguish alternative modes of governance became clearer to me after I had read Grossman and Hart (1986) and began offering a course at Berkeley entitled "The Economics of Institutions." The paper that eventually resulted, "Comparative Economic Organization: The Analysis of Discrete Structural Alternatives" (Chapter 4), can be viewed as an effort to implement Simon's (1978) distinction between discrete structural and marginal analysis. It advances the hypothesis that each generic mode of governance (market, hybrid, hierarchy, bureau, etc.) is supported by a distinctive form of contract law. As developed therein, "forbearance law," rather than the employment relation, is the form of contract law that most distinguishes hierarchy.

Beyond that, there is a pressing need to develop a theory of bureaucratic failure that approaches parity with the theory of market failure. Looking to the future, there is also a need to go beyond the idea of credible commitments to shape an "economics of integrity." Likewise, both "core competence," which is an elusive but important concept in the recent corporate capabilities literature (Wernerfelt, 1984; Eliasson, 1990; Teece, Pisano, and Shuen, 1990; Dosi

---

6. The quotation is from Peguy, source unknown.

and Marengo, 1993), and "real-time responsiveness" (Williamson, 1991a, Langlois, 1992), should be conceptualized more rigorously. The result is that real conceptual needs persist. I project headway of both conceptual and formal analytical kinds as the new science of organization progresses.

That there have been important interim accomplishments is nonetheless evident from Arrow's comparison of the New Institutional Economics with earlier work in organization theory (Simon) and institutional economics (Veblen, Commons, and Mitchell). What distinguishes the newer from the older work are "important specific analyses . . . answering new questions . . . [and supported by] nanoeconomic reasoning" (Arrow, 1987, p. 734).

These accomplishments have supported numerous applications, which should be made clear in the voluminous reference list at the end of this book. Although most of these applications are in the private sector, the recent World Bank project, "The Institutional Foundations of Utility Regulation: Research Results and Their Operational Implications" is a public-sector illustration. This study of the privatization of telecommunications in five nations breaks important new ground and would have been an unthinkable project ten years ago (see especially the summary by Brian Levy and Pablo Spiller, 1994).

I now turn to my nonlinear version of transaction cost economics and the incipient science of organization. Curious readers aside, others can turn to the conclusions.

3. Before 1970

In 1982 I attended a conference celebrating the fiftieth anniversary of the Adolph Berle and Gardiner Means book, *The Modern Corporation and Private Property,* at the Hoover Institute and was the discussant of an interesting paper by Eugene Fama and Michael Jensen (1983). At the conclusion of the session, Jensen turned to me with great excitement and asked, "Did you hear what George said?" I replied that I had but asked for clarification. George Stigler, I was told, had said "agency costs."

New ideas proliferate, and many of them are defective. It is therefore useful to have gatekeepers who insist that new ideas have value added. George Stigler usefully performed that role (and many others). It had been my experience, however, confirmed by my organization theory courses at Carnegie, that managerial discretion in large corporations was the rule, to which unremitting profit maximization (the absence of agency costs) was the exception.

That general orientation was featured in my dissertation, which was published under Ford Foundation auspices in 1964, and also in follow-up work (Williamson, 1963, 1967b, 1968a, 1970). Managerial discretion predates agency theory, both the more formal (Ross, 1973; Holmstrom, 1979) and less formal (Jensen and Meckling, 1976), and relates easily to public choice (Buchanan and Tullock, 1964), to regulation (Alchian and Kessel, 1962), to aspects of property rights (Alchian, 1961; Demsetz, 1967), and to the study of bureaucracy (Downs, 1967; Crozier, 1964) and permeates the study of organization more generally. By comparison with the behavioral theory of the firm, which emphasizes realism in process, managerial discretion emphasizes realism in motivation. It used, without expressly developing, both the two key behavioral assumptions on which transaction cost economics relies: bounded rationality and opportunism.

After completing the dissertation, my plan was to develop more fully the ramifications of this approach in intertemporal (Williamson, 1968c), regulatory (Williamson, 1971a), and contractual (Williamson, 1967a) respects and by performing empirical tests to assess the magnitudes of the distortions. As I got further into this project, however, it became clear that the issues could be approached by indirection and, in addition, that there were other approaches that could be used productively. Thus rather than emphasize the distortions that had their origins in managerial discretion, one could also ask what corrective measures could be taken to bring managerial discretion under more effective control. As discussed below, Alfred Chandler's book *Strategy and Structure* had a great impact on my later treatment of these issues. Also, although this, too, was to come later, a generalized economizing lens in which transaction costs were featured has turned out to be especially powerful.

My second book, *Corporate Control and Business Behavior* (1970), was also in the managerial discretion tradition. But things were moving fast. I had already begun to think of the managerial discretion hypothesis as an introduction to the "main case," namely, economizing on transaction costs, before that book had reached print. Transaction cost economics was to come later, however, and benefited from other work on which I was engaged in the 1960s. So let me back up.

After receiving my Ph.D. degree from Carnegie in 1963, I became an assistant professor in the economics department at the University of California, Berkeley. Given my nonstandard training at Carnegie, I did not fit into any of the orthodox fields of economics, but industrial organization (IO) came closest. Joe Bain was the senior person in the field at Berkeley. I taught the undergraduate IO sequence.

Bain was famous for his *Barriers to New Competition* (1956), and several of my earliest articles likewise dealt with barriers to entry. The first of these was "Selling Expense as a Barrier to Entry," and as I mentioned earlier, it was written for Simon's course on mathematical social science (Williamson, 1963). Rather than viewing barriers to entry as the simple by-product of promotional activity, the problem was formulated as one in which selling expense was set strategically, both with reference to its instrumental effect on demand and because it influenced the condition of entry. A later paper, "Wage Rates as a Barrier to Entry: The Pennington Case in Perspective" (Williamson, 1968c), which also included an empirical aspect, developed this approach further. As Steven Salop subsequently observed, these papers were the first in the strategic entry barriers literature, which Salop and others have developed much more fully in the context of raising rivals' costs (Salop and Scheffman, 1983). The papers by Michael Spence (1977) and Avinash Dixit (1980) were especially influential.

I also inherited a course at Berkeley, "Pricing of Public Services," when Julius Margolis left Berkeley for Stanford. That got me interested in applied welfare economics, led to my paper "Peak Load Pricing and Optimal Capacity Under Indivisibility Constraints" (Williamson, 1966), and was a forum in which to discuss "Social Choice: A Probabilistic Approach" (Williamson and Sargent, 1967). These were useful exercises for an assistant professor, and the peak-load paper has had a long half-life.

I left Berkeley in 1965 to accept an appointment at the University of Pennsylvania as a nontenured associate professor of economics. Penn was a very good place for me and gave me more latitude. I was teaching graduate microtheory, industrial organization, and specialized seminars on topics in applied welfare economics. I spent the year 1966/67 on leave in Washington, D.C., where I served as special economic assistant to the head of the Antitrust Division of the U.S. Department of Justice. I enjoyed working with Donald Turner and the lawyers that he assembled and I gained a much deeper appreciation for many of the issues with which antitrust enforcement was wrestling.

One of the major problems with antitrust enforcement at that time is that it approached nonstandard and unfamiliar business practices from an "inhospitality" point of view. Economies were perversely regarded as antisocial because smaller rivals were disadvantaged by them; contractual restraints, as in the franchising restrictions complained of in the *Schwinn* case, were held to be unnatural, unneeded, and unlawful; and barriers to entry were invented by imaginative antitrust lawyers and economists to suit their advocacy purposes.

Turner (1965) had correctly labeled the prevailing hostility to economies as bad law and bad economics, and my "Economies as an Antitrust Defense: The Welfare Trade-Offs" (Williamson, 1968b), which was prepared initially to advise Turner on the merits of a merger case under review in the Antitrust Division, helped demonstrate that the costs of current merger enforcement were unacceptably high. It took longer for an efficiency interpretation of contractual restraints in the *Schwinn* case to register, partly because the comparative contractual approach from which transaction cost economics works had not yet been devised. My Carnegie-based reasoning that customers could sometimes benefit from franchise restrictions was dismissed in favor of the "then prevailing thinking of the economics profession" (Posner, 1977, p. 3). The U.S. Supreme Court was thus advised (incorrectly) that contractual restrictions had no redemptive features and instead had anticompetitive purpose and effect. (See Williamson, 1979a, for a review of the issues and the subsequent reversal of *Schwinn* in the Supreme Court's 1977 decision on *GTE–Sylvania*.) It took the better part of a decade and the collective efforts of many scholars, many of them located at the University of Chicago, to turn antitrust enforcement around (Bork, 1978). William Baxter, who became head of the Antitrust Division under Ronald Reagan, also deserves much of the credit.

Antitrust is a subject to which I have recurrently returned (Williamson, 1987a), but it is not where my central interests reside. Understanding economic organization is my main project. The Chandler book to which I referred earlier and the comparative contractual approach to economic organization that I was beginning to get into in the late 1960s are more central.

Alfred Chandler's book *Strategy and Structure* (1962) is an important and influential contribution to the business history literature, as, for that matter, are all of his books. Indeed, in many ways, Chandler has redefined the area. In addition, however, to its relevance to business history, *Strategy and Structure* was important to me for another reason: It had a massive influence on my understanding of managerial discretion.

I had previously argued (as had others before me) that competition in the product market and competition in the capital market were important checks on managerial discretion. Chandler's book now opened up a new possibility: Rather than relying mainly or entirely on forces outside the firm to bring managerial discretion under control, the organizational structure of the firm could also be an instrument for checking managerial discretion.

This was a revolutionary concept, and I was reluctant to embrace it. Could it be that management was both the problem and the solution? This possibility certainly had to be entertained if, contrary to received microtheory, organization form mattered. The first step, which I had already taken, was to recognize that managerial discretion was problematic. The second step was to confront the latent lesson of Chandlerian business history: If organization form mattered, then organization form was a decision variable and could be made the object of theoretical and empirical analysis.

As described and explained by Chandler, the invention of the multidivisional form organization (by Alfred P. Sloan Jr., Donaldson Brown, Pierre du Pont, and others) served as a check on managerial discretion on the earlier unitary, or functional, form of organization. Compared with the unitary form, in which strategic and operating decisions were joined, the M-form structure worked out of a logic of organization in which operating and strategic decisions were separated (the logic being akin to that set out by W. Ross Ashby in his 1960 *Design for a Brain*). The resulting decentralized structure was one in which the top management (the general office, as Chandler described it) had been removed from operating involvements and had been made responsible for strategic decision making and resource allocation within the firm, and the operating parts were organized as a series of quasi-autonomous divisions, each of which could be held accountable for its own net receipts. Not only could projections of differential rates of return among the operating divisions be used to allocate resources internally, but also (compared with the more centralized, functional form) more effective oversight and control were realized. In many respects, the multidivisional enterprise took on the attributes of a miniature capital market. This led to the M-form hypothesis: The organization and operation of the enterprise along the lines of the M-form favor goal pursuit and least-cost behavior more nearly associated with the neoclassical profit maximization hypothesis than does the U-form organizational alternative. Because the hypothesis is comparative, unfailing profit maximization by the M-form is not implied.

The M-form hypothesis expressly asserts that organization form matters, an idea that contradicts orthodox microeconomic theory and was regarded by most of the organization theorists of that era as wrong or whimsical. Empirical work on the M-form hypothesis nevertheless began in the 1970s (the initial work in the United States was done by Armour and Teece (1978) and in the United Kingdom by Steer and Cable (1978)) and, with caveats (Ingham, 1992), has been corroborative.

The idea that organization form matters was a precursor to the more general propositions that institutions matter and are susceptible to analysis (Matthews, 1986). These last two are controversial ideas.

The proposition that institutions matter in economics (as distinguished, say, from sociology) is alien to the aspiration that economics could and should operate out of an "institution-free core."[7] The idea, moreover, that institutions are susceptible to analysis was belied by previous experience. The earlier institutional economics movement "failed in America" because it was preoccupied with methodology (Stigler, 1983, p. 170) and lacked operationality (Coase, 1984, p. 230). What, then, is the basis for Matthews's contention that institutions, around 1986, had become susceptible to analysis? As Matthews makes clear, transaction cost economics was implicated.

4. The 1970s

Late in the 1970s, sometime after the publication of *Markets and Hierarchies,* Michael Spence remarked that I appeared to reformulate in transaction cost economics terms each problem that came up. Having just completed a paper on predatory pricing (Williamson, 1977b) that examined predation in very orthodox terms, I protested that this was not the case, that I was an eclectic fellow and dealt with the phenomena on which I worked in whatever terms seemed most appropriate. The record through the 1960s, moreover, bears that out, as at that time my predilection had been to use orthodox techniques of constrained maximization, dynamic programming, Monte-Carlo simulations, nonlinear differential equations, and/or linear regression to suit the needs of the problem.[8] Many of the public-policy issues on which I had worked, moreover, employed the orthodox apparatus of partial equilibrium welfare economics.[9]

---

7. Vernon Smith originated the expression.

8. Examples of constrained maximization include my managerial utility function formulation (Williamson, 1963; 1964) and barriers to entry work (Williamson, 1963, 1968c); dynamic–stochastic programming was subsequently used to examine managerial behavior in an intertemporal, stochastic context (Williamson, 1968a); Monte-Carlo methods were used to study social choice in a probabilistic setup (Williamson and Sargent, 1967); nonlinear differential equations were used to study oligopoly (Williamson, 1965); and linear regression was used repeatedly.

9. The standard partial equilibrium welfare economics apparatus was used to study peak-load pricing (Williamson, 1966), economies as an antitrust defense (Williamson, 1968b, 1977a), externalities and insurance (Williamson, Olson, and Ralston, 1967; Williamson, 1970), and predation (Williamson, 1977b). Of these, I am disappointed only that the Williamson, Olson, and Ralston paper has not had more influence.

What Spence perceived and what I had not yet come to terms with is that the problems on which I now worked were increasingly ones of comparative economic organization in which discrete structural choices were offered and for which the orthodox apparatus was less well suited. An interdisciplinary approach to the study of economic organization—in which law, economics, and organization are joined—as opposed to an exclusive reliance on price theory is where my interests had been taking me. What had begun as a serious but part-time interest—to address and help solve the puzzles of economic organization—had progressively become an obsession. Because, however, the world of economic organization is so wonderfully varied and endlessly fascinating, I did not begrudge the monomania with which I had been stricken. Self-infliction is closer to the mark.

The problem that got me into these issues was that of vertical integration. I had been aware of the issues for a long time, of course, but did not appreciate their significance until I was exposed to the "prevailing thinking" in antitrust. Being dissatisfied, I organized a seminar on vertical integration when I returned from the Antitrust Division to resume my teaching at Penn. The students and I worked our way methodically through the literature. Although some of it was illuminating (Coase, 1937; McKenzie, 1951; Stigler, 1951), much of it was confused, irrelevant, or wrongheaded. To realize that the literature was not grappling with the principal issues was one thing; to do something about it was another. I did not have a better formulation.

Then a lucky thing happened. Julius Margolis came from Stanford to Penn to head the Fels Center of State and Local Government and to organize a Ph.D. program in public policy. Julie asked if I would teach the organization theory course in the core sequence of that program. Since I had always been interested in organization theory and believed that a richer joinder of economics and organization theory would be useful, I agreed.

Organization theory, in my experience, is a difficult subject to teach. The literature is incredibly diffuse, with specialists from sociology, political science, social psychology, computer science, and economics all having something to say. I emphasized mainly the economics and sociology literatures.

The market failure literature was prominently featured, including Coase's famous 1937 and 1960 papers ("The Nature of the Firm" and "The Problem of Social Cost") and the more recent and more general treatment by Arrow, "The Organization of Economic Activity" (1969). But since this was not an economics class but an organization theory class, the students and I were also examining the issues from a behavioral point of view. Each time we encountered a "failure," we would ask, "What are the key underlying factors without which the failure would vanish?" Although technology (e.g., nonseparabilities) and problems of pricing (e.g., public goods) posed obvious problems, the real difficulties could invariably be traced to the behavioral attributes of human actors.

So I asked the students on Thursday to work out the underlying regularities over the weekend, and I also did this assignment myself. What has since been described as the "organizational failures framework" (Williamson, 1975, pp. 39–40) began to take shape. The relevant factors clustered under two headings: human factors (bounded rationality and opportunism) and transactional factors (uncertainty and small numbers) (Williamson, 1973). Vertical integration was the natural first problem to which an early version of the argument was applied (Williamson, 1971b).

That was the issue with which Coase had been concerned in his 1937 article. One of the key ideas in Coase is that markets and hierarchies are *alternative* instruments for accomplishing the same, rather than different, economic purposes: "It is clear that these are alternative methods for coordinating production" (Coase, 1991b, p. 19). That contradicted prevailing economic thinking, which regarded the firm as a technological entity (production function) and relied on the market (price mechanism) to effect coordination. A second idea is that differential transaction costs were principally responsible for choosing one mode of organization rather than another. That was even more revolutionary. Not only was transaction cost an alien concept within the orthodox setup, but it was hard to give it operational content. Coase's argument, for example, that the most obvious reason that it was costly to use the market was that "of discovering what the relevant prices are" (1991b, p. 21) does not withstand comparative institutional scrutiny. However, he is greatly to be credited with posing two fundamental puzzles with which economics must come to terms. First, if markets are a marvel, why do we take transactions out of markets and organize them internally? Second, and symmetrically, if internal organization is such a powerful organizing instrument, why is not all production carried on in one big firm?

These are discomfiting observations and difficult questions. Although neoclassical economics made note of these matters, the issues were mainly ignored for most of the next thirty-five years. In the interim, vertical integration was mainly explained in technological (Bain, 1968), successive marginalization (McKenzie, 1951), life cycle (Stigler, 1951), or monopolization terms.

My article "The Vertical Integration of Production: Market Failure Considerations" focused on the firm and those parts of the market failure literature that were most pertinent to the study of intermediate product markets. This twin focus was useful. One of the problems with the market failure literature was that its broad sweep—to include public goods, externalities (within and between commercial and household sectors), nonprofit organization, and the like—often made it difficult to discover the underlying regularities. I was concerned only with purported failures in intermediate product markets. Also, firms operating in intermediate product markets could ordinarily be presumed to be knowledgeable about the transactions in which they were engaged. Neither differential cognitive competence (which arises with contracts between firms and households) nor differential risk aversion[10] (which is more relevant to contracting for labor) is at issue. That cleared the deck for a "main-case" hypothesis that had hitherto been neglected: Economic organization has the main purpose and effect of economizing on transaction costs.

---

10. Differential risk aversion in the 1970s replaced monopolization as the neoclasical explanation for nonstandard and unfamiliar contracting practices.

The orthodox firm-as-production function described the firm as a technology to which a profit maximization purpose was ascribed. That is a straightforward construction and is especially useful for doing comparative statics, studying strategic interaction between firms (Tirole, 1988), and aggregating up from firm-level to industry-level effects. It is less useful, however, for understanding complex contractual practices, of which vertical integration, reciprocal trading, and franchise restraints are examples. Without a technological rationale, such nonstandard and unfamiliar business practices were commonly presumed to have monopoly purpose and effect.

By contrast, the firm-as-governance structure approach adopts an efficient contracting/comparative organizational orientation. Rather than presume that nonstandard practices serve monopoly purposes, it holds that the main purpose (which is not to say the only purpose) of economic organization is to infuse integrity into contractual relations. Because this is a very different orientation, transaction cost economics took a while to take hold.[11]

The precontractual view of vertical integration was that without any special "physical or technical aspects"—the standard example being that of a blast furnace and a rolling mill, in which integration purportedly avoided the need to reheat the ingots and hence realized thermal economies (Bain, 1968, p. 381)—vertical integration was deeply problematic and probably anticompetitive. In fact, however, the thermal economies on which Bain relied to supply an affirmative rationale for vertical integration did not withstand comparative institutional scrutiny.

The interesting comparative problems of managing transactions across successive stages of production show up when bilateral dependency conditions appear. Although that was held to be a rare event, bilateral dependency is a much more widespread condition than the usual examination of the technology reveals. The reason is that what begins as a large numbers supply condition frequently is transformed into a small numbers exchange relation during the contract's execution and at the contract's renewal intervals. That had been missed by the "prevailing thinking," which sighted organization in favor of technology, did not view the contracting process in its entirety, and led to public-policy mistakes.

Examining the issues of economic organization from a comparative contractual point of view requires that the behavioral attributes of human actors and the microanalytic attributes of transactions and of organization be described. Of special importance are the behavioral assumptions, since the interesting problems of comparative economic organization vanish if either hyperrationality or faithful stewardship is ascribed to economic actors. That was obvious to me and my class from our examination of the market failure literature, and the same considerations also reappear when assessing the failures of

11. Take a hold, however, it eventually did (Tirole, 1988, chap. 2; Kreps, 1990a; Milgrom and Roberts, 1992). Oliver Hart endorsed (and has greatly contributed to) the comparative contractual approach to economic organization and observed that the neoclassical theory of the firm "begs the question of what a firm is" (Hart, 1990, p. 155). See Simon, 1991, for a more skeptical view of the transaction cost economics enterprise. Stigler, 1988 and 1992, is also pertinent.

nonmarket organization. Simon's insistence that "nothing is more fundamental in setting our research agenda and informing our research methods than our view of the nature of the human beings whose behavior we are studying" (Simon, 1985, p. 303) is exactly right. Were it not that (1) all complex contracts are unavoidably incomplete, by reason of *bounded rationality,* and (2) autonomous parties to a bilateral exchange cannot be relied on to close gaps, correct errors, repair omissions, eschew strategizing, and so on, by reason of *opportunism,* the interesting problems of comparison economic organization would evaporate.

My 1971 paper on vertical integration examined three alternative modes of procurement: long-term contracting, recurrent short-term contracting, and internal organization. Because the first of these presented severe contractual incompleteness problems and because I was originally skeptical that the requisite supports for long-term incomplete contracts could be provided, the main emphasis was on a comparison of recurrent short-term contracts with vertical integration. I observed in this connection that even though short-term contracts relieved (but did not eliminate) the burdens of incompleteness created by long-term contracts, problems could arise

> if either (1) efficient supply requires investment in special-purpose, long-life equipment, or (2) the winners of the original contract acquire a cost advantage, say by reason of "first-mover" advantages (such as unique location or learning, including the acquisition of undisclosed or proprietary technical and managerial procedures and task-specific labor skills). (Williamson, 1971b, p. 116)

The latter effect is now recognized as the Fundamental Transformation and gives rise to the bilateral dependency condition described earlier. Asset specificity—which was mentioned but hardly developed by Alfred Marshall (1948, p. 626), Jacob Marschak (1968, p. 14), and Michael Polanyi (1962, pp. 52–53)—turns out to have pervasive organizational ramifications (Williamson, 1971b, 1975, 1983; Klein, Crawford, and Alchian, 1978).

The governance structure approach to economic organization not only postulates different drivers (economizing as opposed to monopolizing), but it is also more microanalytic than the neoclassical setup (both with reference to the attributes of transactions and organization) and relies more on discrete structural (rather than marginal) analysis. Understandably, it met with early skepticism. I recall, however, telling Dan McFadden in the spring of 1971 that I felt that I was the first person in the world to understand vertical integration. Dan was intrigued (or perhaps polite), and I interpreted his response favorably. I sensed, moreover, that the approach could be used to address other phenomena.

As it turns out, any issue that can be expressed directly or indirectly as a contracting problem can be examined to advantage in transaction cost–economizing terms. A huge number of phenomena—including vertical integration, vertical market restrictions, franchising, regulation and deregulation, labor market organization, the organization of work, corporate finance and corporate governance, family firms, multinational firms, and the economics of trust—qualify. The fact that certain regularities keep recurring is responsive to Milton Friedman's observation that "a fundamental hypothesis in science is that appearances are deceptive and that there is a way of looking at or interpreting or organizing the evidence that will reveal superficially disconnected and diverse phenomena to be manifestations of a more fundamental and relatively simple structure" (1953, p. 33).

The first variant that I examined was labor market organization. The idea that labor could acquire firm-specific attributes had already surfaced in my examination of vertical integration, and Gary Becker (1962) had made prominent use of human asset specificity in his work on labor economics. What I had in mind, however, was different. Might the contractual integrity of labor markets be studied along the same lines as the contractual integrity of intermediate product markets?

Because I had much less knowledge of the labor market literature, some parts of which were very neoclassical (emphasizing marginal productivity and monopsony power) and other parts were very institutional (the industrial relations literature), I needed an entrée. That occurred when I came across a reference to the recent book by Peter Doeringer and Michael Piore, *Internal Labor Markets* (1971). It sounded relevant, and I immediately went to the library. I had two concerns as I removed the book from the shelf: (1) The book would not deal with the issues of labor contracting in sufficient detail, and (2) the book would deal in detail with the relevant issues, and the authors would have already interpreted them in transaction cost economics terms. As it turned out, the book raised many of the pertinent issues, but there was still room for further interpretation.

I was discussing the issues of labor organization with Jeffrey Harris, an outstanding graduate student at the University of Pennsylvania. He in turn discussed them with his wife, who was a labor lawyer. She indicated that the labor law literature—as developed by Harry Schulman (at Yale), Archibald Cox (at Harvard), Justice William Douglas (on the Supreme Court), and Arthur Goldberg (when he had been a labor lawyer)—was germane to my topic. Sure enough, that literature was also struggling with issues of efficient governance. Because we had a better framework, however, we were able to deal with these matters more completely. Harris and I were later joined by Michael Wachter and wrote the paper "Understanding the Employment Relation: The Analysis of Idiosyncratic Exchange" (Williamson, Wachter, and Harris, 1975). Similar ideas were advanced independently by Arthur Okun (1981), and Wachter has since developed the approach more fully in both the labor economics and the labor law literatures. One of the benefits of that exercise for me was that I was becoming aware that there were many more complementarities between transaction cost economics and the law than I had hitherto imagined. And although I was disappointed when Clyde Summers, another labor lawyer on whom we had relied, did not at first consent to those complementarities, I was gratified when he later changed his mind.

I was also coming to appreciate that transaction cost economics could both learn from and contribute to the business history literature. To be sure, that was evident from my earlier exposure to Chandler. Lisa Moses, one of my students, called my attention to John Buttrick's interesting treatment (1952) of "inside contracting" in New England manufacturing in the late 1800s. Inside contracting was an interesting organizational form, whose comparative strengths and weaknesses could be usefully examined in transaction cost economics terms.

More generally, there appeared to be many related contractual phenomena out there, and I was keen to pull them together. Given my interests in antitrust and my sense that public policy was poorly served by the prevailing approach to nonstandard and unfamiliar business practices, I also saw this as an opportunity to bring together comparative institutional analysis and public policy.

The Brookings Institution had a long-standing interest in antitrust, and the director of research at Brookings, Joseph Peckman, had been a former teacher of mine at MIT. Brookings agreed to buy some of my teaching time, and so I began to write what was to become *Markets and Hierarchies: Analysis and Antitrust Implications.* (The original title, when the project started, was *Aspects of Monopoly Theory and Policy.*) The early chapters of *Markets and Hierarchies* traced the antecedents and constructed the organizational failures framework. Applications were thereafter made to peer group organization, the employment relation, and vertical integration (including inside contracting). Antitrust applications included vertical integration, conglomerate organization, technical and organization innovation, dominant firms, and oligopoly.

Markets and Hierarchies was an enormously difficult book to write, and it placed severe burdens on its readers, asking them to examine problems through unfamiliar lenses and exposing them to unfamiliar terms (such as *bounded rationality, opportunism,* and *information impactedness*). I was not surprised when Brookings, which had rights of first refusal, advised me to take the manuscript elsewhere. I then approached the Free Press, which expressed an interest. The book was published in 1975.

The Free Press did not project great success for the book and had no plans to reprint it when the initial production run was exhausted. But partly because of a favorable review of the book by William Ouchi (1977), who declared that this was the most important book on economic organization since Berle and Means (1932), and partly because there was growing interest in more microanalytic modes of analysis (Alchian and Demsetz, 1972; Arrow, 1974; Bell Journal Symposium, 1975; Jensen and Meckling, 1976), readership of the book grew. I was convinced that the book would succeed when in 1977 I found myself seated behind a student at the Stanford Business School where we were both attending a seminar by Herbert Simon: She and others in her class had photocopied the entire book.

Faced with a backlog, the Free Press reprinted the book and eventually brought out a paperback edition. Indeed, I was advised by a young Norwegian economist (at a conference in Toulouse in January 1992) that the five most cited books in the Social Science Citations Index in 1990 were Marx's *Kapital,* followed by *Markets and Hierarchies, The Economic Institutions of Capitalism* Keynes's *General Theory,* and Smith's *Wealth of Nations,* in descending order.

To be sure, that will not last. It is nevertheless gratifying that a book for which such limited prospects were predicted should have had this impact.

Markets and Hierarchies was an entering wedge rather than the final word on transaction cost economics. Among the issues awaiting analysis was that of franchise bidding for natural monopoly. Along with many others, I was persuaded that all forms of organization are subject to failure (Coase, 1964). The regulation (or not) of natural monopolies was an obvious candidate to be examined from the perspective of comparative economic organization.

Harold Demsetz had adopted a farsighted contracting approach to natural monopoly in his imaginative article "Why Regulate Public Utilities?" (1968b). His basic argument was that ex post monopoly problems could be "solved" through ex ante bidding for the right to serve the market, with the award criterion being to offer to supply cheaply (Demsetz, 1968b). This idea was subsequently endorsed by Stigler (1968), and Peckman and I appealed to those ideas when we served on Mayor John Lindsay's CATV task force in 1969/70. I nevertheless perceived problems with recurrent bidding in the CATV context and became all the more concerned with these after reading Posner's sanguine treatment of franchise bidding in his paper "The Appropriate Scope of Regulation in the Cable Television Industry" (1972). With the markets and hierarchies apparatus in place, I decided to address these issues in my paper "Franchise Bidding for Natural Monopoly—in General and with Respect to CATV" (Williamson, 1976).

This paper examined franchise bidding and regulation in a side-by-side way and made express provision for the attributes of the transaction. Thus although Demsetz had raised the possibility that the characteristics of the assets and market uncertainties might influence the efficacy of franchise bidding, he had set these aside, for purposes of the analysis, and he concluded on an optimistic note that franchise bidding compared favorably with regulation quite generally. Posner genially declared that the mechanics of franchise bidding for CATV were efficacious.

My examination of the issues revealed that the use of franchise bidding was much more problematic. To be sure, there were circumstances in which it would work well, namely, those in which the principal assets were generic and the technology was mature. Obvious candidates for deregulation, under my formulation, were trucking, local service airlines, and postal delivery (Williamson, 1976, pp. 102–3). Deregulation/franchise bidding was not, however, a panacea: Goods or services that required investments in special-purpose durable assets and whose market and technological uncertainties were great created much greater difficulties. Like it or not, franchise bidding in these latter circumstances needed to be supported by an elaborate administrative apparatus. In that event, franchise bidding took on many of the properties of, and was not obviously superior to, rate-of-return regulation (Laffont and Tirole, 1993, chap. 8). As it turns out, moreover, the approach has general relevance to the matter of privatization, when it can be expected to work both well (as in many local services; Donahue, 1989, chap. 7) and poorly (as in prisons; Donahue, 1989, chap. 8).

My abstract (comparative contractual) assessment of franchise bidding for CATV was supported, moreover, by a detailed case study in which virtually all the contracting problems that were turned up in the abstract analysis of franchising versus regulation actually materialized in practice. As Peter Bauer and Alan Walters remind us, "the complexity, instability, and local variation of many economic phenomena ... require that the inquiry must often be supplemented by extensive observations, and also that the inquiry must often extend beyond statistical information to include direct observation and use of primary sources" (1975, p. 12). The microanalytics matter.

Although I continued to work in both the older neoclassical and the newer transactional domains over the next several years, I was progressively moving the mix in favor of the latter. Victor Goldberg, who was also interested in some of the same regulatory issues as I was (Goldberg, 1976a), called my attention to Ian Macneil's paper "Many Futures of Contracts" (1974). Contrary to much of the legal scholarship and to almost all of economics, Macneil argued that it was naive to proceed as if there were only one, single, all-purpose law of contract. What we had instead were several.

I was intrigued by Macneil's examination of how the objective needs of contracts varied and how contract law responded to these. I was also led further into an examination of the legal literature on contracts, both backward, into earlier formulations by Karl Llewellyn (1931) and Stewart Macaulay (1963), as well as into the later formulations, especially those by Macneil (1978) and Marc Galanter (1981). There were clearly many complementarities between transaction cost economics and the new contract law. Both also shared the property that they were working out of, but deviating from, the main traditions (in economics and law, respectively).

The ideal transaction in both law and economics was the discrete transaction paradigm—"sharp in by clear agreement; sharp out by clear performance" (Macneil, 1974, p. 738)—in which the identity of the parties did not matter. That was a building block for Macneil, and it was also a building block for me. But whereas most of law and economics worked wholly within this discrete transaction domain, some contract law specialists and some economists were becoming more interested in phenomena in which continuity between unchanging parties to a contract was the source of productive value. Identity, for these transactions, plainly mattered. In addition to Goldberg and myself, others who were persuaded of the need to study bilateral dependency relations more carefully included Benjamin Klein, Robert Crawford, and Armen Alchian (1978), Yoram Ben-Porath (1980), and Charles Goetz and Robert Scott (1981).

I spent the academic year (1977/78) as a fellow at the Center for Advanced Study in the Behavioral Sciences. It was the first year that I had no regular duties whatsoever, and I found it a mixed experience. Although I enjoy research, I also get a lot out of teaching. Partly this is because my research does not always go smoothly (the above does not reflect all the wrong turns and blind alleys), and so it is gratifying to have a background demand, like teaching, to relieve the anxieties. Furthermore, it is a challenge to present new ideas, and being around young people is refreshing: Ideas matter, and good students are an intellectual stimulus.

The project that I intended to complete at the center was a general treatment of the organization of work. I had already completed a paper on comparative work organization that examined Stephen Marglin's provocative argument that because the hierarchical organization of work lacked a neoclassical efficiency justification, work organization should be understood as an effort by bosses to exploit workers (Marglin, 1974). My examination of alternative work modes disclosed numerous efficiency effects—albeit of a transaction cost, rather than neoclassical production function, kind. Because, however, Marglin had used only neoclassical lenses, the possibility that there were transaction cost differences among modes had been suppressed.

My intention during 1977/78 was to generalize the argument from the production line setting in which Marglin had developed it to include the organization of work quite generally (including the organization of law firms). I should have known that this required greater knowledge of institutional details than I had at my command, but that did not become apparent until I was several frustrating months into the project. Ronald Gilson and Robert Mnookin, who are lawyers, have since examined law firm organization (Gilson and Mnookin, 1985; Gilson, 1989) in the relevant microanalytic terms.

To be sure, I had other things going on, including the aforementioned predatory-pricing paper (Williamson, 1977a). The most important project that I began at the center, however, was my paper "Transaction Cost Economics: The Governance of Contractual Relations" (1979b). It was the first time that I raised the possibility in print that a new form of economics—namely, transaction cost economics—was taking shape. That paper makes clear that the integrity of trading relations—Do buyers get what they want on cost-effective terms? Are suppliers satisfied that their specialized investments are adequately protected?—is crucial, which is very different from the production function/monopoly purpose setup. The correspondence between the transaction cost/governance approach and Macneil's contract law regimes are also developed in that paper. More important, the dimensionalization of transactions was expressly confronted.

Although John R. Commons (1934) had proposed that the transaction be made the basic unit of analysis, that is merely the first step. The question that then needed to be asked and answered is what the critical dimensions are on which transactions differ. Because the number of possible dimensions is limited only by imagination, a focus was needed. This was accomplished by concentrating on those dimensions that appear to be most responsible for comparative transaction cost consequences.

My 1979 paper proposes that asset specificity, uncertainty, and frequency are the critical dimensions. The discriminating alignment hypothesis is then applied: Align transactions, which differ in their attributes, with alternative governance structures, which differ in cost and competence, so as to realize a transaction cost economizing result. Not only do the key trade-offs become more transparent, but the broad reach of transaction cost reasoning also is suggested.

5. After 1980

The first paper of mine published in the 1980s was "The Organization of Work," which has been very controversial. It is the paper I referred to earlier in which I take exception with Marglin's neoclassical conception of efficiency. I had prepared the paper for my students and used it in my classes but had never submitted it for publication. When Richard Day and Sidney Winter organized the *Journal of Economic Behavior and Organization* and asked me to serve on its editorial board, they also asked me to submit a paper. I mentioned that I had this "irremediably flawed" paper on Marglin, and they expressed interest. It appeared as the lead article in their first issue.

The paper was irremediably flawed because it was not possible to deal with all the relevant issues in a definitive and uncontroversial manner. If the paper did succeed, it was because it made a plausible case that a large number of previously neglected economizing factors were responsible for work organization and that these could be examined in a systematic and reasonably objective way. Although the list of performance features, the description of work modes, my assessments of each, my weighting and aggregation procedures, and so forth all could be disputed, it was nevertheless clear that technology was not determinative of work organization and that neoclassical economic theory did not exhaust the reach of efficiency reasoning.

Less controversial were two overviews that I had under way—one to appear in the *Journal of Economic Literature* (1981c) and the other in the *American Journal of Sociology* (1981a). The first of these, "The Modern Corporation: Origins, Evolution, Attributes," made the case that organization form (1) matters, (2) is susceptible to analysis, and (3) has public-policy consequences (Williamson, 1981a). The second was an effort to show that transaction cost economics was both informed by and helped inform organization theory (Williamson, 1981c). The intended readers were sociologists, and the article contributed to a growing dialogue between economics and sociology in the organization theory arena.

More important than either of these was my article "Credible Commitments: Using Hostages to Support Exchange," which is reprinted here as Chapter 5. As it turns out, credible commitment arguments that were first developed at the level of governance have found widespread application at the level of the institutional environment, especially in relation to the hazards of expropriation in public utilities (Levy and Spiller, 1994) and de facto federalism (Weingast, 1995).

As commented earlier, the transaction cost approach to economic organization has progressively developed from its informal stages (Coase, 1937) through preformal and semiformal stages into fully formal analysis. The path-breaking paper by Sanford Grossman and Oliver Hart (1986), in which the incomplete contracting process was first modeled in a fully rigorous way, has been followed by a large and growing literature on incomplete contracting. Among the more important articles are the generalizations developed by Hart and John Moore (1990), "Contracts as a Barrier to Entry" (Aghion and Bolton, 1987), applications to financial contracting (Aghion and Bolton, 1992), and "What Is Vertical Integration?" (Riordan, 1990).[12]

Attempts, moreover, to restore comprehensive contracting—by arguing that a sequence of short-term contracts can implement completeness (Fudenberg, Holmstrom, and Milgrom, 1990; Milgrom and Roberts, 1990a)—actually rely on very special constructions (Kreps, 1990a, p. 760; Chapter 6). Because implausible assumptions are needed to support the argument that the incompleteness of long-term contracts is remedied by reverting to a series of short-term complete contracts, these papers effectively prove the opposite: All complex contracts are incomplete. Confronting that reality means that the issues of incomplete contracting need to be faced head-on (Hart, 1990).

Because transaction cost economics has generated a large number of refutable implications, it invites empirical testing, in contrast with much of the earlier organization theory literature, which had few implications of interest to economists and generated little empirical research. I am always puzzled, therefore, by claims that transaction cost economics is remiss in empirical respects (Simon, 1991). As I see it, transaction cost economics is an empirical success story, as there are around two hundred empirical studies (for an overview, see Joskow, 1988, 1991; Klein and Shelanski, 1995; and Masten, 1995) and more are in progress.

Two dissertations that were completed in the early 1980s were instrumental in getting this empirical work started. The first was by Thomas Palay and examined freight contracts between manufacturers and railroads. Although I thought that this was a good project, I did not expect that transaction cost economics would have much application, because all the interesting variety would be squeezed out by regulation. Palay nevertheless persevered. The action, I should have known, resided in the details. Palay not only discovered that there was contractual variety but also showed that observed practices were consonant with transaction cost economizing principles (Palay, 1981).

Scott Masten's dissertation dealt with the theory and practice of vertical integration. His empirical analysis of make-or-buy decisions in the aerospace industry likewise found that contractual practice tracked transaction cost reasoning (Masten, 1984). Empirical transaction cost economics has since become a growth area.

Those who have pioneered this empirical work deserve enormous credit. Unable to work from census reports and data tapes—because these do not record the relevant observations and/or are too aggregative—empirical trans-

---

12. Also see the survey papers by Hart and Bengt Holmstrom (1987) and by Holmstrom and Jean Tirole (1989). Although it is a difficult arena, the study of "incomplete contracting in its entirety" has become a productive line for new research.

action cost economics has had to develop primary, microanalytic data. The cost, however, is more than repaid by the analytical benefits. As Thomas Kuhn remarked, a new science collects its own, rather than working from existing, data (1962).

To be sure, transaction cost economics (like everything else) needs more and better empirical research. If, however, "this empirical work is in much better shape than much of the empirical work in industrial organization generally" (Joskow, 1991, p. 81), then we should celebrate its accomplishments. To repeat, empirical transaction cost economics is a success story.

Perhaps because they are keenly aware of the limitations of orthodox theory, many economic theorists have been permissive about the new institutional economics, and some have been very generous in relating to it, for example, Kenneth Arrow (1987), Oliver Hart (1990), Bengt Holmstrom and Jean Tirole (1989, 1991), and David Kreps (1990b, 1992). As indicated, moreover, empirical work in transaction cost economics has flourished. This in turn has helped promote a more productive dialogue between transaction cost economics and sociology. What was once an acerbic relation (Perrow, 1981; Williamson and Ouchi, 1981) has been replaced by a much more productive dialogue in which each has benefited from, without capitulating to, the other (Zald, 1987; Lindenberg, 1992; Scott 1992).

6.   Ruminations and Projections[13]

The study of transactions cost economics urges students of economic organization to discover and explicate the properties of discrete structural organizational alternatives (markets, hybrids, and hierarchies, to which bureaus are a recent addition). It further maintains that each candidate theory of economic organization should name its "main case," with economizing on transaction costs being the main case from which transaction cost economics works. Such a combination of discrete structural and main-case analysis might be judged to be primitive, and in many ways it is. The object of main-case analysis, after all, is to identify the jugular. As noted earlier, it makes contact with and helps illuminate a large and growing number of subtle issues that were missed or misconstrued by earlier formulations.

My reasons for believing that the prospects for a science of organization are excellent are these: (1) The economics of organization has witnessed exponential progress over the past twenty-five years; (2) many talented scholars are currently working on this project; and (3) the need for such a science is real and growing. Thus although some may judge financial economics to be a bigger success story (Varian, 1993) than the economics of organization, I consider the latter to be a huge success nonetheless. This is especially evident

---

13. Section 6 of the original autobiographical sketch deals with the way in which conferences, journals, and visiting appointments figured into the exercise. Space considerations explain its deletion here.

in the journals and the economics of organization is beginning to make its presence felt in the textbooks as well (Kreps, 1990b, chap. 20; Eaton and Eaton, 1991; Milgrom and Roberts, 1992). The extraordinary young talent that is involved in this adventure is evident in this chapter and the References.

The need for a more adequate theory of organizations and institutions is massive. Industrial organization and applications to public policy (antitrust and regulation) have already been discussed. But labor economics (Wachter and Cohen, 1988), comparative systems (Sacks, 1983; Kornai, 1992; Bowles and Gintis, 1993), corporate strategy (Teece, 1986; Mahoney and Pandian, 1992; Muris, Scheffman, and Spiller, 1992), marketing (Anderson and Schmitt-lein, 1984; Heide and John, 1988), game theory (Kreps, 1992), health economics (Robinson, 1992, 1993a, 1993b), economic development (Nabli and Nugent, 1988; Ellickson, 1993) and economic reform (Levy and Spiller, 1994), international trade (Keohane, 1984; Yarborough and Yarborough, 1987; Hennart, 1990), family firms (Pollak, 1985), organization theory (Davis and Powell, 1992; Lindenberg, 1992), and economic history (North, 1991; Greif, 1991; Eggertsson, 1990) all are prospective beneficiaries. If we only had a better theory of organization and institutions, the agonies—false starts, mistakes, conundrums—of economic reform in Eastern Europe and the former Soviet Union would be much relieved. Indeed, it is my belief that prices will largely take care of themselves once the reformers focus on and get the institutions right. (The tendency to neglect institutions in favor of the pricing instruments that economists know best is understandable, but that was more excusable for Oskar Lange (1938) than it is today.)

A deep curiosity in "What's going on out there?" is a great help to—perhaps even an essential requisite for—good institutional research. The first move is to entertain the idea that institutions matter, whereupon the challenge is to demonstrate that institutions are susceptible to analysis. A logic of organization that yields refutable implications and invites empirical testing is needed. The study of incomplete contracting—with emphasis on the microanalytics of transactions, governance structures, and the mechanisms that relate thereto—is one way to implement this program. That project and related work have been progressively taking shape, to the degree that I anticipate that the science of organization to which Barnard referred in 1938 will be realized by this generation of scholars.

Glossary

N.B.: *Italicized terms are defined elsewhere in the glossary.*

Asset specificity   A specialized investment that cannot be redeployed to alternative uses or by alternative users except at a loss of productive value. Asset specificity can take several forms, of which human, physical, site, and dedicated assets are the most common. Specific assets give rise to *bilateral dependency,* which complicates contractual relations. Accordingly, such investments would never be made except to contribute to prospective reductions in production costs or additions to revenue.

Bilateral dependency   An ongoing dependency relation obtains between a buyer and a supplier when one or both have made durable specialized investments in support of the other. Although sometimes this condition exists from the outset (the familiar bilateral monopoly condition), often it evolves during an ongoing contractual relation. Bilateral dependency, in which one or both parties specialize for the other, is a much more widespread condition than preexisting bilateral monopoly. Such dependency poses contractual hazards in the face of *incomplete contracting* and *opportunism,* in response to which contractual safeguards are commonly provided.

Bounded rationality   This refers to behavior that is intendedly rational but only limitedly so; it is a condition of limited cognitive competence to receive, store, retrieve, and process information. All complex contracts are unavoidably incomplete because of bounds on rationality.

Bureaucracy   The support staff that is responsible for developing plans, collecting and processing information, operationalizing and implementing executive decisions, auditing performance, and, more generally, providing direction to the operating parts of a hierarchical enterprise. Bureaucracy is attended by low-powered incentives (due to the impossibility of *selective intervention*) and is given to subgoal pursuit (which is a manifestation of *opportunism*).

Contract   An agreement between a buyer and a supplier in which the terms of exchange are defined by a triple: price, *asset specificity,* and *safeguards.* (This assumes that quantity, quality, and duration all are specified.)

Credible commitment   A contract in which a promisee is reliably compensated should the promisor prematurely terminate or otherwise alter the agreement. This should be contrasted with noncredible commitments, which are empty promises, and semicredible commitments, in which there is a residual hazard. Credible commitments are pertinent to contracts in which one or both parties invest in specific assets.

Discriminating alignment   The assignment of least-cost *governance structures* to manage *transactions*.

Governance structure   The institutional matrix in which the integrity of a transaction is decided. In the commercial sector, three discrete structural governance alternatives are commonly recognized: classical *market, hybrid* contracting, and *hierarchy.*

Hierarchy   Transactions that are placed under unified ownership (buyer and supplier are in the same enterprise) and subject to administrative controls (an authority relation, to include fiat) are managed by hierarchy. The contract law of hierarchy is that of forebearance, according to which internal organization is its own court of ultimate appeal.

Hybrid   Long-term contractual relations that preserve autonomy but provide added transaction-specific *safeguards,* compared with the *market.*

Incentive intensity   A measure of the degree to which a party reliably appropriates the net receipts (which could be negative) associated with its efforts and decisions. High-powered incentives will obtain if a party has a clear entitlement to and can establish the magnitude of its net receipts easily. Lower-powered incentives will obtain if the net receipts are pooled and/or if the magnitude is difficult to ascertain.

Incomplete contracting   Contracts are effectively incomplete if (1) not all the relevant future contingencies can be imagined, (2) the details of some of the future contingencies are obscure, (3) a common understanding of the nature of the future contingencies cannot be reached, (4) a common and complete understanding of the appropriate adaptations to future contingencies cannot be reached, (5) the parties are unable to agree on what contingent event has materialized, (6) the parties are unable to agree on whether actual adaptations to realized contingencies correspond to those specified in the contract, and (7) even though both the parties may be fully apprised of the realized contingency and the actual adaptations that have been made, third parties (e.g., the courts) may be fully apprised of neither, in which event costly haggling between bilaterally dependent parties may ensue.

Institutional arrangement   The contractual relation or governance structure between economic entities that defines the way in which they cooperate and/or compete.

Institutional environment   The rules of the game that define the context in which economic activity takes place. The political, social, and legal ground rules establish the basis for production, exchange, and distribution.

Market   The arena in which autonomous parties engage in exchange. Markets can either be thick or thin. Classical markets are thick, in which case there are large numbers of buyers and sellers on each side of the transaction and identity is not important, because each can go its own way at negligible cost to the other. Thin markets are characterized by fewness, which is mainly due to asset specificity. *Hybrid* contracts and *hierarchy* emerge as *asset specificity* builds up and identity matters.

Opportunism   Self-interest seeking with guile, to include calculated efforts to mislead, deceive, obfuscate, and otherwise confuse. Opportunism should be distinguished from simple self-interest seeking, accordance to which individuals play a game with fixed rules that they reliably obey.

Private ordering   The self-created mechanisms to accomplish adaptive, sequential decision making between autonomous parties to a contract, including information disclosure, dispute settlement, and distributional mechanisms to deal with gaps, errors, omissions, and inequities. (Court ordering, however, is normally available for purposes of ultimate appeal.)

Remediable   A condition is held to be remediable if a superior feasible alternative can be described and implemented with net gains.

Safeguard   The added security features, if any, that are introduced into a contract in order to reduce hazards (due mainly to asset specificity) and to create confidence. Safeguards can take the form of penalties, a reduction in *incentive intensity,* and/ or more fully developed *private-ordering* apparatus to deal with contingencies.

Selective intervention   This would obtain if bureaucratic intervention between the semiautonomous parts of a hierarchical enterprise occurred only but always when there is a prospect of expected net gain. Because promises to intervene selectively lack credibility, selective intervention is impossible. If it were otherwise, everything would be organized in one large firm. Because, however, selective intervention is impossible, hierarchies are unable to replicate market incentives.

Transaction   The microanalytic unit of analysis in transaction cost economics. A transaction occurs when a good or service is transferred across a technologically separable interface. Transactions are mediated by governance structures *(markets, hybrids, hierarchies)*.

Transaction cost   The ex ante costs of drafting, negotiating, and *safeguarding* an agreement and, more especially, the ex post costs of maladaptation and adjustment that arise when contract execution is misaligned as a result of gaps, errors, omissions, and unanticipated disturbances; the costs of running the economic system

Weak form selection   Selection from among the better of the feasible alternatives, as contrasted with selection of the best from among all possible, to include hypothetical alternatives. In a relative sense, the fitter survive, but these may not be the fittest in any absolute sense.

References

Adelman, M. A. 1961. "The Antimerger Act, 1950–1960." *American Economic Review* 51 (May): 236–44.

Aghion, Phillipe, and Patrick Bolton. 1987. "Contracts as a Barrier to Entry." *American Economic Review* 77 (June): 388–402.

——. 1992. "An Incomplete Contracts Approach to Financial Contracting." Review of Economic Studies 59 (July): 473–94.

Aghion, Phillipe, and Jean Tirole, 1994. "Formal and Real Authority in Organizations." Unpublished manuscript, Institut d'Economie Industrielle.

Akerlof, George A. 1970. "The Market for 'Lemons': Qualitative Uncertainty and the Market Mechanism." *Quarterly Journal of Economics* 84 (August): 488–500.

Alchian, Armen. 1950. "Uncertainty, Evolution and Economic Theory." *Journal of Political Economy* 58 (June): 211–21.

——. 1961. *Some Economics of Property.* RAND D-2316. Santa Monica, CA: RAND Corporation.

——. 1965. "The Basis of Some Recent Advances in the Theory of Management of the Firm." *Journal of Industrial Economics* 14 (December): 30–41.

——. 1984. "Specificity, Specialization, and Coalitions." *Journal of Institutions and Theoretical Economics* 140 (March): 34–49.

——, and H. Demsetz. 1972. "Production, Information Costs, and Economic Organization." *American Economic Review* 62 (December): 777–95.

——, and Rubin Kessel. 1962. "Competition, Monopoly, and the Pursuit of Pecuniary Gain." In *Aspects of Labor Economics.* Princeton, NJ: Princeton University Press, pp. 140–65.

——, and Susan Woodward. 1987. "Reflections on the Theory of the Firm." *Journal of Institutional and Theoretical Economics* 143 (March): 110–36.

Anderson, Erin. 1985. "Implications of Transaction Cost Analysis for the Management of Distribution Channels." In R. E. Spekman, ed., *Proceedings: A Strategic Approach to Business Marketing.* Chicago: American Marketing Association, pp. 160–68.

——, and David Schmittlein. 1984. "Integration of the Sales Force: An Empirical Examination." *RAND Journal of Economics* 15 (Autumn): 385–95.

Aoki, Masahiko. 1983. "Managerialism Revisited in the Light of Bargaining–Gain Theory." *International Journal of Industrial Organization* 1: 1–21.

——. 1984. *The Economic Analysis of the Japanese Firm.* New York: North-Holland.

——. 1988. *Information, Incentives, and Bargaining in the Japanese Economy.* Cambridge: Cambridge University Press.

381

————. 1990. "Toward an Economic Model of the Japanese Firm." *Journal of Economic Literature* 28 (March): 1–27.

————. 1992. "The Japanese Firm as a System of Attributes: A Survey and Research Agenda." Unpublished manuscript, Stanford University.

————. 1994. "The Japanese Firm as a System of Attributes: A Survey and Research Agenda." In Masahiko Aoki and Ronald Dore, eds., *The Japanese Firm*. Oxford: Oxford University Press, pp. 12–40.

————, Bo Gustafsson, and Oliver Williamson. 1989. *The Firm as a Nexus of Treaties*. London: Sage.

Areeda, Philip. 1967. *Antitrust Analysis*. Boston: Little, Brown.

Areeda, Philip, and D. F. Turner. 1976. "Scherer on Predatory Pricing: A Reply." *Harvard Law Review* 89: 891–97, 139, 148.

Armour, Henry, and David Teece. 1978. "Organizational Structure and Economic Performance." *Bell Journal of Economics* 9: 106–22.

Arrow, Kenneth J. 1951. *Social Choice and Individual Values*. New York: Wiley.

————. 1962. "Economic Welfare and the Allocation of Resources of Invention." In National Bureau of Economic Research, ed., *The Rate and Direction of Inventive Activity: Economic and Social Factors*. Princeton, NJ: Princeton University Press, pp. 609–25.

————. 1963a. "Control in Large Organization." *Management Science* 10 (September): 397–408.

————. 1963b. "Uncertainty and the Welfare Economics of Medical Care." *American Economic Review* 53 (December): 941–73.

————. 1969. "The Organization of Economic Activity: Issues Pertinent to the Choice of Market Versus Nonmarket Allocation." In *The Analysis and Evaluation of Public Expenditure: The PPB System*. Vol. 1. U.S. Joint Economic Committee, 91st Cong., 1st sess. Washington, DC: U.S. Government Printing Office, pp. 59–73.

————. 1971. *Essays in the Theory of Risk-Bearing*. Chicago: Markham.

————. 1974. *The Limits of Organization*. New York: Norton.

————. 1983. *Collected Papers of Kenneth J. Arrow*. Vol. 2: General Equilibrium. Cambridge, MA: Harvard University Press.

————. 1985a. "The Economics of Agency." In John Pratt and Richard Zeckhauser, eds., *Principals and Agents*. Cambridge, MA: Harvard University Press, pp. 37–51.

————. 1985b. "Informational Structure of the Firm." *American Economic Review* 75: 303–7.

————. 1987. "Reflections on the Essays." In George Feiwel, ed., *Arrow and the Foundations of the Theory of Economic Policy*. New York: New York University Press, pp. 727–34.

Arthur, Brian. 1989. "Competing Technologies, Increasing Returns, and Lock-in by Historical Events." *Economic Journal* 99 (March): 116–31.

————. 1990. "Positive Feedbacks in the Economy." *Scientific American,* February, pp. 92–99.

Asanuma, B. 1989. "Manufacturer–Supplier Relationships in Japan and the Concept of Relationship-Specific Skill." *Journal of Japanese and International Economies* 3 (1): 1–30.

Ashby, W. Ross. 1960. *Design for a Brain*. New York: Wiley.

Aumann, Robert. 1985. "What Is Game Theory Trying to Accomplish?" In Kenneth Arrow and Seppo Hankapohja, eds., *Frontiers of Economics*. Oxford: Basil Blackwell, pp. 28–78.

Axelrod, Robert. 1984. *The Evolution of Cooperation.* New York: Basic Books.

Azariadis, C., and J. Stiglitz. 1983. "Implicit Contracts and Fixed Price Equilibria." *Quarterly Journal of Economics* 94: 1–22.

Baiman, Stanley. 1982. "Agency Research in Managerial Accounting: A Survey." *Journal of Accounting Literature* 1: 154–213.

Bain, Joe. 1956. *Barriers to New Competition.* Cambridge, MA: Harvard University Press.

———. 1958. *Industrial Organization.* New York: Wiley.

———. 1968. *Industrial Organization.* 2nd ed. New York: Wiley.

Banfield, E. C. 1958. *The Moral Basis of a Backward Society.* New York: Free Press.

Barnard, Chester. 1938. *The Functions of the Executive.* Cambridge, MA: Harvard University Press.

Barnett, W., and G. Carroll. 1993. "How Institutional Constraints Affected the Organization of the Early American Telephone Industry." *Journal of Law, Economics, and Organization* 9 (April): 98–126.

Barney, J. 1991. "Firm Resources and Sustained Competitive Advantage." *Journal of Management* 17: 19–120.

Barney, Jay, and William Ouchi. 1986. *Organizational Economics.* San Francisco: Jossey-Bass.

Baron, J., and M. Hannan. 1992. "The Impact of Economics on Contemporary Sociology." Unpublished manuscript.

Barry Wright Corp. v. *ITT Grinnell Corp.* 724 F.2d 227, 234 (1st Cir. 1983).

Barzel, Yoram. 1982. "Measurement Cost and the Organization of Markets." *Journal of Law and Economics* 25 (April): 27–48.

Bates, Robert. 1994. "Social Dilemmas and Rational Individuals: An Essay on the New Individualism." Unpublished manuscript.

Bauer, P. T., and A. A. Walters. 1975. "The State of Economics." *Journal of Law and Economics* 18 (April): 1–24.

Baumol, William. 1959. *Business Behavior, Value and Growth.* New York: Macmillan.

———. 1979. "Quasi-Permanence of Price Reductions: A Policy for Prevention of Predatory Pricing." *Yale Law Journal* 89 (November): 1–26.

Becker, Gary. 1962. "Investment in Human Capital: Effects on Earnings." *Journal of Political Economy* 70 (October): 9–49.

———. 1976. *The Economic Approach to Human Behavior.* Chicago: University of Chicago Press.

———. 1983. "A Theory of Competition Among Pressure Groups for Political Influence." *Quarterly Journal of Economics* 98 (August): 371–400.

———. 1991. "Habits, Addictions, and Traditions." Unpublished manuscript.

Ben-Porath, Yoram. 1980. "The F-Connection: Families, Friends, and Firms and the Organization of Exchange." *Population and Development Review* 6 (March): 1–30.

Berglof, Eric. 1989. "Capital Structure as a Mechanism of Control." In Masahiko Aoki, Bo Gustafsson, and Oliver Williamson, eds., *The Firm as a Nexus of Treaties.* London: Sage, chap. 11.

Bergson, Abram. 1948. "Socialist Economics." In Howard Ellis, ed, *Survey of Contemporary Economies.* Philadelphia: Blakiston, pp. 430–58.

Berle, Adolph A., and Gardner C. Means Jr. 1932. *The Modern Corporation and Private Property.* New York: Macmillan.

Berman, Harold. 1983. *Law and Revolution.* Cambridge, MA: Harvard University Press.

Bernstein, Lisa. 1990. "The Choice Between Public and Private Law." Discussion Paper no. 70. Program in Law and Economics, Harvard Law School.

Bernstein, Marver. 1955. *Regulating Business by Independent Regulatory Commission.* Princeton, NJ: Princeton University Press.

Bewley, T. 1986. "A Theory of Layoffs, Strikes and Wage Determination." Unpublished research proposal, Cowles Foundation.

Blake, Harlan M. 1973. "Conglomerate Mergers and the Antitrust Laws." *Columbia Law Review* 73 (March): 555–92.

Blake, Harlan, and William Jones. 1965. "Towards a Three-Dimensional Antitrust Policy." *Columbia Law Review* 65: 422–27.

Blinder, Alan. 1990. "There Are Capitalists, Then There Are the Japanese." *Business Week,* October 8, p. 21.

Bok, Derek. 1960. "Section 7 of the Clayton Act and the Merging Law and Economics." *Harvard Law Review* 74 (December): 226–355.

Bonin, John, and Louis Putterman. 1987. *Economics of Cooperation and Labor Managed Economies.* Cambridge: Cambridge University Press.

Bork, R. H. 1969. "Vertical Integration and Competitive Processes." In J. Fred Weston and S. Peltzman, eds., *Public Policy Towards Mergers.* Pacific Palisades, CA: Goodyear, pp. 139–49.

———. 1978. *The Antitrust Paradox.* New York: Basic Books.

———. 1985. "The Rule of the Courts in Applying Economics." *Antitrust Law Journal* 54: 21–25.

Boulding, K. E. 1966. "The Economics of Knowledge and the Knowledge of Economics." *American Economic Review* 58 (May): 1–13.

Bowles, S., and Gintis, H. 1986. *Democracy and Capitalism.* New York: Basic Books.

———. 1993. "The Revenge of Homo Economicus: Contested Exchange and the Revival of Political Economy." *Journal of Economic Perspectives* 7 (Winter): 83–102.

Bradach, Jeffrey, and Robert Eccles. 1989. "Price, Authority, and Trust." *American Review of Sociology* 15: 97–118.

Brennan, Geoffrey, and James Buchanan. 1985. *The Reason of Rules.* Cambridge: Cambridge University Press.

Bridgeman, Percy. 1955. *Reflections of a Physicist* 2nd ed. New York: Philosophical Library.

Brockman, Rosser H. 1980. "Commercial Contract Law in the Late Nineteenth Century Taiwan." In Jerome Alou Cohen et al., eds., *Essays on China's Legal Tradition.* Princeton, NJ: Princeton University Press, 1980, pp. 76–136.

Bromley, Daniel. 1989. *Economic Interests and Institutions.* New York: Basil Blackwell.

Brown, Donaldson. 1924. "Pricing Policy in Relation to Financial Control." *Management and Administration* 1 (February): 195–258.

Buchanan, James. 1975. "A Contractarian Paradigm for Applying Economic Theory." *American Economic Review* 65 (May): 225–30.

———, and Gordon Tullock. 1964. *The Calculus of Consent.* Ann Arbor: University of Michigan Press.

Buttrick, J. 1952. "The Inside Contracting System." *Journal of Economic History* 12 (Summer): 205–21.

Buxbaum, Richard M. 1985. "Modification and Adaptation of Contracts: American Legal Developments." *Studies in Transnational Economic Law* 3: 31–54.

Calabresi, Guido. 1961. "Some Thoughts on Risk Distribution and the Law of Torts." *Yale Law Journal* 70: 499–535.

Campbell, Thomas. 1986. "Spatial Predation and Competition in Antitrust." Working Paper no. 27. Presented at 1986 Law and Economics Program, Stanford University.

Cargill, Inc., v. *Monfort of Colo., Inc.* 1986. 107 S. Ct. 484.

Carroll, G., and J. R. Harrison. 1992. "Chance and Rationality in Organizational Evolution." Unpublished manuscript.

Caves, R., and R. Bradburg. 1988. "The Empirical Determinants of Vertical Integration." *Journal of Economic Behavior and Organization* 9: 265–80.

Chandler, Alfred D., Jr. 1962. *Strategy and Structure.* Cambridge, MA: MIT Press.

———. 1977. *The Visible Hand: The Managerial Revolution in American Business.* Cambridge, MA: Harvard University Press.

"Chrysler and Mitsubishi Motors." 1991. *The Economist,* April 20, p. 71.

Chubb, John, and Terry Moe. 1990. *Schools, Politics, and Markets.* Washington, DC: Brookings Institution.

Clarkson, Kenneth W., Roger L. Miller, and Timothy J. Muris. 1978. "Liquidated Damages v. Penalties." *Wisconsin Law Review* 54: 351–90.

Clausewitz, Karl von. 1980. *Vom Kriege.* 19th ed. (Originally published in 1832). Bonn: Dremmler.

Coase, Ronald H. 1937. "The Nature of the Firm." *Economica N.S.* 4: 386–405. Reprinted in Oliver E. Williamson and Sidney Winter, eds., 1991. *The Nature of the Firm: Origins, Evolution, Development.* New York: Oxford University Press, pp. 18–33.

———. 1959. "The Federal Communications Commission." *Journal of Law and Economics* 2 (October): 1–40.

———. 1960. "The Problem of Social Costs." *Journal of Law and Economics* 3 (October): 1–44.

———. 1964. "The Regulated Industries: Discussion." *American Economic Review* 54 (May): 194–97.

———. 1972. "Industrial Organization: A Proposal for Research." In V. R. Fuchs, ed., *Policy Issues and Research Opportunities in Industrial Organization.* New York: National Bureau of Economic Research, pp. 59–73.

———. 1978. "Economics and Contiguous Disciplines." *Journal of Legal Studies* 7: 201–11.

———. 1984. "The New Institutional Economics." *Journal of Institutional and Theoretical Economics* 140 (March): 229–31.

———. 1988a. *The Firm, the Market, and the Law.* Chicago: University of Chicago Press.

———. 1988b. "The Nature of the Firm: Influence." *Journal of Law, Economics, and Organization* 4 (Spring): 33–47.

———. 1988c. "The Nature of the Firm: Meaning." *Journal of Law, Economics, and Organization* 4 (Spring): 19–32.

———. 1988d. "The Nature of the Firm: Origins." *Journal of Law, Economics, and Organization* 4 (Spring): 1–18.

———. 1991a. "The Institutional Structure of Production." 1991 Alfred Nobel Memorial Prize Lecture in Economic Sciences.

———. 1991b. "The Nature of the Firm: Origin, Meaning, Influence." In Oliver Williamson and Sidney Winter, eds., *The Nature of the Firm: Origin, Evolution, Development.* New York: Oxford University Press.

———. 1992. "The Institutional Structure of Production." *American Economic Review* 82 (September): 713–19.

———. 1993. "Coase on Posner on Coase." *Journal of Institutional and Theoretical Economics* 149 (March): 96–98.

————, and Ronald Fowler. 1935. "Bacon Production and the Pig Cycle in Great Britain." *Economica* 2: 142–67.

Cole, A. H. 1968. "The Entrepreneur: Introductory Remarks." *American Economic Review* 63 (May): 60–63.

Coleman, James. 1982. *The Asymmetric Society*. Syracuse, NY: Syracuse University Press.

————. 1990. *The Foundations of Social Theory*. Cambridge, MA: Harvard University Press.

Colman, R. 1981. "Overview of Leveraged Buyouts." In S. Lee and R. Colman, eds., *Handbook of Mergers, Acquisitions and Buyouts*. Englewood Cliffs, NJ: Prentice-Hall, pp. 530–46.

Columbia Metal Culvert v. *Kaiser Aluminum & Chem. Corp.* 1978. 579 F.2d 20 (3d Cir.), cert. denied, 439 U.S. 876.

Commons, John R. 1924. *Legal Foundations of Capitalism*. New York: Macmillan.

————. 1925. "Law and Economics." *Yale Law Journal* 34: 371–82.

————. 1932. "The Problem of Correlating Law, Economics and Ethics." *Wisconsin Law Review* 8: 3–26.

————. 1934. *Institutional Economics*. Madison: University of Wisconsin Press.

Continental T. V. Inc. et al. v. *GTE Sylvania Inc.,* 433 U.S. 36 (1977).

Contractor, Farok. 1981. "The Role of Licensing in International Strategy." *Columbia Journal of World Business,* Winter, pp. 73–83.

Cooter, Robert. 1992. "Organization as Property." In Christopher Clague and Gordon C. Rausser, eds., *The Emergence of Market Economies in Eastern Europe*. Cambridge, MA: Basil Blackwell, pp. 77–97.

Coughlin, R. 1992. "Interdisciplinary Nature of Socio-Economics." Unpublished manuscript.

Cowan, Alison. 1987. "When a Leveraged Buyout Fails." *New York Times,* November 10, sec. 3, pp. 1, 8.

Cox, Archibald. 1958. "The Legal Nature of Collective Bargaining Agreements." *Michigan Law Review* 57 (November): 1–36.

Crocker, K., and K. Reynolds. 1993. "The Efficiency of Incomplete Contracts: An Empirical Analysis of Air Force Engine Procurement." *RAND Journal of Economics* 24 (Spring): 126–46.

Crozier, M. 1964. *The Bureaucratic Phenomenon*. Chicago: University of Chicago Press.

Cyert, Richard M., and James G. March. 1963. *A Behavioral Theory of the Firm*. Englewood Cliffs, NJ: Prentice-Hall.

Dahl, R. R. 1970. "Power to the Workers?" *New York Review of Books,* November 19, pp. 20–24.

D'Andrade, Roy. 1986. "Three Scientific World Views and the Covering Law Model." In Donald W. Fiske and Richard A. Schweder, eds., *Metatheory in Social Science: Pluralisms and Subjectivities*. Chicago: University of Chicago Press.

Dasgupta, Partha. 1988. "Trust as a Commodity." In Diego Gambetta, ed., *Trust: Making and Breaking Cooperative Relations*. Oxford: Basil Blackwell, pp. 49–72.

David, Paul. 1985. "Clio in the Economics of QWERTY." *American Economic Review* 75 (May): 332–37.

————. 1986. "Understanding the Economics of QWERTY: The Necessity of History." In W. N. Parker, ed., *Economic History and the Modern Economist*. New York: Basil Blackwell, pp. 30–40.

————. 1992. "Heroes, Herds, and Hysteresis in Technological History." *Industrial and Corporate Change* 1: 129–80.

Davis, G. F., and W. W. Powell. 1992. "Organization–Environment Relations." In M. Dunnette, ed., *Handbook of Industrial and Organizational Psychology.* Vol. 3. New York: Consulting Psychologists Press, pp. 315–75.

Davis, Lance E., and Douglas C. North. 1971. *Institutional Change and American Economic Growth.* Cambridge: Cambridge University Press.

Dawkins, Richard. 1976. *The Selfish Gene.* New York: Oxford University Press.

Debreu, Gerhard. 1959. *Theory of Value.* New York: Wiley.

Demsetz, Harold. 1967. "Toward a Theory of Property Rights." *American Economic Review* 57 (May): 347–59.

———. 1968a. "The Cost of Transacting." *Quarterly Journal of Economics* 82 (February): 33–53.

———. 1968b. "Why Regulate Utilities?" *Journal of Law and Economics* 11 (April): 55–66.

———. 1969. "Information and Efficiency: Another Viewpoint." *Journal of Law and Economics* 12 (April): 1–22.

———. 1988. "The Theory of the Firm Revisited." *Journal of Law, Economics, and Organization* 4: 141–62.

Dewatripont, Mathias, and G. Ronald. 1992. "Economic Reform and Dynamic Political Constraints." *Review of Economic Studies* 59 (October): 703–30.

Dewey, D. J. 1959. *Monopoly in Economics and Law.* Chicago: Rand McNally.

Diamond, Jared. 1994. "Ecological Collapses of Ancient Civilizations: The Golden Age That Never Was." *Bulletin of the American Academy of Arts and Sciences* 47 (February): 37–59.

Diamond, Peter A., and Eric Maskin. 1979. "An Equilibrium Analysis of Search and Breach of Contract." *Bell Journal of Economics* 10 (Spring): 282–316.

DiMaggio, P., and W. Powell. 1991. "Introduction." In Walter Powell and Paul DiMaggio, eds., *The New Institutionalism in Organizational Analysis.* Chicago: University of Chicago Press, pp. 1–38.

Director, Aaron, and Levi Edward. 1956. "Law and the Future: Trade Regulation." *Northwestern University Law Review* 10: 281–317.

Dixit, Avinach. 1979. "A Model of Duopoly Suggesting a Theory of Entry Barriers." *Bell Journal of Economics* 10 (Spring): 20–32.

———. 1980. "The Role of Investment in Entry Deterrence." *Economic Journal* 90 (March): 95–106.

———. 1982. "Recent Developments in Oligopoly Theory." *American Economic Review Proceedings* 72 (May): 12–17.

Dodd, E. Merrick. 1932. "For Whom Are Corporate Managers Trustees?" *Harvard Law Review* 45 (June): 1145–63.

Doeringer, P., and M. Piore. 1971. *Internal Labor Markets and Manpower Analysis.* Lexington, MA: Heath.

Donahue, John. 1989. *The Privatization Decision.* New York: Basic Books.

———, and Ian Ayres. 1987. "Posner's Symphony No. 3: Thinking About the Unthinkable." *Stanford Law Review* 39 (February): 791–812.

Donaldson, Gordon. 1981. *Corporate Debt Capacity.* Boston: Harvard Business School Press.

Dore, Ronald. 1983. "Goodwill and the Spirit of Market Capitalism." *British Journal of Sociology* 34 (December): 459–82.

Dosi, G. 1982. "Technological Paradigms and Technological Trajectories." *Research Policy* 11: 147–62.

———, and Luigi Marengo. 1993. "Some Elements of an Evolutionary Theory of

Organizational Competencies." In R. W. England, ed., *Evolutionary Concepts in Contemporary Economics.* Ann Arbor: University of Michigan Press, pp. 87–103.

Dow, Gregory. 1987. "The Function of Authority in Transaction Cost Economics." *Journal of Economic Behavior and Organization* 8 (March): 13–38.

———. 1993. "Why Capital Hires Labor: A Bargaining Perspective." *American Economic Review* 83 (March): 118–34.

Downs, Anthony. 1957. *An Economic Theory of Democracy.* New York: Harper & Row.

Drucker, Peter F. 1946. *The Concept of the Corporation.* New York: John Day.

Duesenberry, James. 1960. "An Economic Analysis of Fertility: Comment." In *Demographic and Economic Change in Developed Countries.* National Bureau of Economic Research. Princeton, NJ: Princeton University Press.

Dunn, John. 1988. "Trust and Political Agency." In Diego Gambetta, ed., *Trust: Making and Breaking Cooperative Relations.* Oxford: Basil Blackwell, pp. 73–93.

Easterbrook, Frank. 1981a. "Comments on An Economic Definition of Product Innovation." In S. Salop, ed., *Strategy, Predation, and Antitrust Analysis.* Federal Trade Commission Report. Washington, DC: U.S. Government Printing Office, pp. 415, 418–19.

———. 1981b. "Predatory Strategies and Counterstrategies." *University of Chicago Law Review,* 48: 263, 336–37.

———. 1984. "The Limits of Antitrust." *Texas Law Review* 63 (August): 1–40.

———, and Daniel Fischel. 1986. "Close Corporations and Agency Costs." *Stanford Law Review* 38 (January): 271–301.

Eaton, B. C., and D. F. Eaton. 1991. *Microeconomics.* 2nd ed. New York: Freeman.

Eaton, B. Curtis, and Richard G. Lipsey. 1981. "Capital Commitment, and Entry Equilibrium." *Bell Journal of Economics* 12 (Autumn): 593–604.

Eccles, Robert. 1981. "The Quasifirm in the Construction Industry." *Journal of Economic Behavior and Organization* 2 (December): 335–58.

Edgeworth, F. Y. 1881. *Mathematical Physics.* London: Kegan Paul. Reprinted New York: Kelley and Millman, 1954.

Eggertsson, Thraine. 1990. *Economic Behavior and Institutions.* Cambridge: Cambridge University Press.

Ehrlich, Eugen. 1936. *Fundamental Principles of the Sociology of Law.* Cambridge, MA: Harvard University Press.

Eichengreen, Barry. 1994. "Institutions and Economic Growth: Europe After World War II." Unpublished manuscript, University of California, Berkeley.

Eliasson, Gunnar. 1990. "The Firm as a Competent Team." *Journal of Economic Behavior and Organization* 13: 275–98.

Ellickson, Robert. 1993. "Property in Land," *Yale Law Journal* 102 (April): 1315–400.

Elster, J. 1983. *Explaining Technical Change.* Cambridge: Cambridge University Press.

———. 1993. "Comments on Oliver Williamson." Unpublished manuscript. Remarks prepared for the Venice Summer School.

———. 1994. "Arguing and Bargaining in Two Constituent Assemblies." Unpublished manuscript. Remarks given at the University of California, Berkeley.

Emerson, Richard. 1962. "Power-Dependence Relations." *American Sociological Review* 27 (February): 31–40.

Emmett, William. 1991. "International Finance: Gamblers, Masters, and Slaves." *The Economist,* April 27, pp. 5–52.

Encaoua, D., P. Geroski, and A. Jacquemin. 1986. "Strategic Competition and the Persistence of Dominant Firms: A Survey." In Joseph Stiglitz and G. Frank Mathewson, eds., *New Developments in the Analysis of Market Structure.* Cambridge, MA: MIT Press, pp. 55–86.

Fama, Eugene F. 1980. "Agency Problems and the Theory of the Firm." *Journal of Political Economy* 88: 288–307.

———. 1985. "Organization Forms and Investment Decisions." *Journal of Financial Economics* 14: 101–19.

———, and Michael C. Jensen. 1983. "Separation of Ownership and Control." *Journal of Law and Economics* 26 (June): 301–26.

Fama, Eugene F., and Michael D. Jensen. 1983. "Separation of Ownership and Control," *Journal of Law and Economics* 26 (June): 301–26.

Farnsworth, Edward Allan. 1968. "Disputes over Omissions in Contracts." *Columbia Law Review* 68 (May): 860–91.

Federal Trade Commission v. *Exxon et al.,* Docket no. 8934 (1963).

Federal Trade Commission v. *Morton Salt Co.,* 334 U.S. 37 (1948).

Federal Trade Commission v. *Procter & Gamble Corp.,* 386 U.S. 586 (1967).

Tellner, William. 1949. *Competition Among the Few.* New York: Knopf.

Ferejohn, John. 1990. "Rationality and Interpretation: Parliamentary Elections in Early Stuart England." Working Paper no. 44. Center for Law and Economic Studies, Columbia University Law School.

Fischer, Stanley. 1977. "Long-Term Contracting, Sticky Prices, and Monetary Policy: Comment." *Journal of Monetary Economics* 3: 317–24.

Fisher, Alan, and Robert Lande. 1983. "Efficiency Considerations in Merger Enforcement." *California Law Review* 71 (December): 1580–1696.

Foremost Dairies, Inc., 60 F.T.C., 944, 1084 (1962).

Francis, Arthur, Jeremy Turk, and Paul Willman, eds. 1983. *Power, Efficiency, and Institutions.* London. Heinemann Educational Books, Ltd.

Frank, R. 1992. "Melding Sociology and Economics." *Journal of Economic Literature* 30 (March): 147–70.

Frech, Theodore. 1987. "Comments on Antitrust Issues." *Health Economic Health Services Research* 7: 263–75.

Friedland, R., and R. Alford. 1991. "Bringing Society Back In: Symbols, Practices, and Institutional Contradictions." In Walter Powell and Paul DiMaggio, eds., *The New Institutionalism in Organizational Analysis.* Chicago: University of Chicago Press, pp. 232–66.

Friedman, L. M. 1965. *Contract Law in America.* Madison: University of Wisconsin Press.

Friedman, Milton. 1953. *Essays in Positive Economics.* Chicago: University of Chicago Press.

———. 1962. *Capitalism and Freedom.* Chicago: University of Chicago Press.

Frydman, Roman, and Andryej Rapacynski. 1993. "Privatization in Eastern Europe." *Finance and Development,* June, pp. 10–13.

Fuchs, Victor, ed. 1972. *Policy Issues and Research Opportunities in Industrial Organization.* New York: Columbia University Press.

Fudenberg, Drew, Bengt Holmstrom, and Paul Milgrom. 1990. "Short-Term Contracts and Long-Term Agency Relationships." *Journal of Economic Theory* 51 (June): 1–31.

———. 1963. "Collective Bargaining and the Arbitrator." *Wisconsin Law Review,* January, pp. 3–46.

————. 1978. "The Forms and Limits of Adjudication." *Harvard Law Review* 92: 353–409.

————. 1981. "Human Interaction and the Law." In Kenneth I. Winston, ed., *The Principles of Social Order: Selected Essays of Lon L. Fuller.* Durham, NC: Duke University Press, pp. 212–46.

Furubotn, E., and S. Pejovich. 1974. *The Economics of Property Rights.* Cambridge, MA: Ballinger.

————, and Rudolf Richter. 1991. "The New Institutional Economics: An Assessment." In E. Furobton and R. Richter, eds., *The New Institutional Economics.* College Station, TX: Texas A&M University Press, pp. 1–32.

Galanter, Marc. 1981. "Justice in Many Rooms: Courts, Private Ordering, and Indigenous Law." *Journal of Legal Pluralism* 19: 1–47.

Galbraith, J. K. 1967. *The New Industrial State.* Boston: Houghton-Mifflin.

Gambetta, Diego. 1988. "Can We Trust Trust?" In Diego Gambetta, ed., *Trust: Making and Breaking Cooperative Relations.* Oxford: Basil Blackwell, pp. 213–37.

Gatignon, H., and E. Anderson. (1986). "The Multinational Corporation's Degree of Control over Foreign Subsidiaries: An Empirical Test of a Transaction Cost Explanation." Unpublished manuscript.

Gauss, Christian. 1952. "Introduction" to Niccolò Machiavelli, *The Prince.* New York: New American Library, pp. 7–32.

Georgescu-Roegen, N. 1971. *The Entropy Law and Economic Process.* Cambridge, MA: Harvard University Press.

Gerlach, Michael. 1987. "Business Alliances and the Strategy of the Japanese Firm." *California Management Review* 30 (Fall): 126–42.

————. 1992. *Alliance Capitalism.* Berkeley and Los Angeles: University of California Press.

Gilson, Ronald. 1984. "Value Creation by Business Lawyers: Legal Skills and Asset Pricing." *Yale Law Journal* 94: 239–306.

————. 1986. *The Law and Finance of Corporate Acquisitions.* Mineola, NY: Foundation Press.

————. 1989. "Coming of Age in a Corporate Law Firm: The Economics of Associate Career Patterns." *Stanford Law Review* 41 (February): 567–95.

————, and Robert Mnookin. 1985. "Sharing Among the Human Capitalists: An Economic Inquiry into the Corporate Law Firm and How Partners Split Profits." *Stanford Law Review* 37 (January): 313–97.

Goetz, Charles, and Robert Scott. 1981. "Principles of Relational Contracts." *Virginia Law Review* 67: 1089–1151.

Goldberg, Jeffrey. 1982. "A Theoretical and Econometric Analysis of Franchising." Draft, doctoral dissertation, University of Pennsylvania.

Goldberg, Victor. 1976a. "Regulation and Administered Contracts." *Bell Journal of Economics* 7 (Autumn): 426–52.

————. 1976b. "Toward an Expanded Economic Theory of Contract." *Journal of Economics Issues* 10 (March): 45–61.

————. 1990. "Aversion to Risk Aversion in the New Institutional Economics." *Journal of Institutional and Theoretical Economics* 146 (March): 216–22.

————, and John E. Erickson. 1982. "Long-Term Contracts for Petroleum Coke." Department of Economics Working Paper Series no. 206, University of California, Davis, September.

Gould, Stephen Jay. 1987. *An Urchin in the Storm.* New York: Norton.

Gouldner, A. W. 1954. *Industrial Bureaucracy.* Glencoe, IL: Free Press.

Gower, E. C. B. 1969. *Principles of Modern Company Law.* London: Stevens & Sons.

Granovetter, Mark. 1985. "Economic Action and Social Structure: The Problem of Embeddedness." *American Journal of Sociology* 91 (November): 481–501.

———. 1988. "The Sociological and Economic Approaches to Labor Market Analysis." In George Farkas and Paula England, eds., *Industries, Firms, and Jobs.* New York: Plenum, pp. 187–218.

———. 1990. "The Old and the New Economic Sociology: A History and an Agenda." In Roger Friedland and A. F. Robertson, eds., *Beyond the Marketplace.* New York: Aldine.

———. 1992. "Economic Institutions of Social Construction: A Framework for Analysis." *Acta Sociologica* 35: 3–11.

Greenwald, Bruce, and Joseph Stiglitz. 1989. "Information, Finance, and Markets." Unpublished manuscript.

Greif, Avner. 1991. "The Organization of Long-Distance Trade: Reputations and Coalitions in the Geniza Documents and Genoa During the Eleventh and Twelfth Century." *Journal of Economic History* 51 (June): 459–62.

Grossekettler, H. 1989. "On Designing and Economic Order: The Contributions of the Freiburg School." In Donald Walker, ed., *Perspectives on the History of Economic Thought.* Vol. 2. Aldershot: Edward Elgar, pp. 38–84.

Grossman, Sanford, and Oliver Hart. 1982. "Corporate Financial Structure and Managerial Incentives." In John J. McCall, ed., *The Economics of Information.* Chicago: University of Chicago Press, pp. 107–40.

———. 1986. "The Costs and Benefits of Ownership: A Theory of Vertical and Lateral Integration." *Journal of Political Economy* 94 (August): 691–719.

Hadfield, Gillian. 1990."Problematic Relations: Franchising and the Law of Incomplete Contracts." *Stanford Law Review* 42: 927–92.

———. 1991. "Bargaining, Asymmetric Information and the Determination of Contract Duration." Unpublished manuscript, University of California, Berkeley.

Hamilton, Gray, and Nicole Biggart. 1988. "Market, Culture, and Authority." *American Journal of Sociology* (supplement) 94: S52–S94.

Hansmann, H. 1986. "A General Theory of Ownership." Unpublished manuscript.

———. 1988. "The Ownership of the Firm." *Journal of Law, Economics, and Organization* 4 (Fall): 267–303.

Harberger, Arnold. 1954. "Monopoly and Resource Allocation." *American Economic Review* 44 (May): 77–87.

———. 1971. "Three Basic Postulates for Applied Welfare Economics: An Interpretative Essay." *Journal of Economic Literature* 2 (September): 785–97.

Hardin, Russell. 1991. "Trusting Persons, Trusting Institutions." In Richard J. Zeckhauser, ed., *Strategy and Choice.* Cambridge, MA: MIT Press, pp. 187–209.

———. 1992. "Comments on Shepsle: Discretion, Institutions, and the Problem of Government Commitment." In Pierre Bourdrieu and James Coleman, eds., *Social Theory for a Changing Society.* Boulder, CO: Westview Press, pp. 265–66.

Hart, H. L. A. 1961. *The Concept of Law.* Oxford: Oxford University Press.

Hart, Oliver. 1988. "Incomplete Contracts and the Theory of the Firm." *Journal of Law Economics, and Organization* 4 (Spring): 119–39.

———. 1990. "An Economist's Perspective on the Theory of the Firm." In Oliver Williamson, ed., *Organization Theory.* New York: Oxford University Press, pp. 154–71.

———, and Bengt Holmstrom. 1987 "The Theory of Contracts." In T. Bewley, ed.,

Advances in Economic Theory. Cambridge: Cambridge University Press, pp. 305–29.

——, and John Moore. 1990. "Property Rights and the Nature of the Firm." *Journal of Political Economy* 98 (December): 691–719.

——, and Jean Tirole. 1990. "Vertical Integration and Market Foreclosure." In Martin Neil Baily and Clifford Winston, eds., *Brookings Papers on Economic Activity: Microeconomics.* Washington, DC: Brookings Institution, pp. 205–76.

Hayek, Friedrich. 1945. "The Use of Knowledge in Society." *American Economic Review* 35 (September): 519–30.

——. 1955. *The Counterrevolution of Science.* New York: Free Press.

——. 1967. *Studies in Philosophy, Politics, and Economics.* London: Routledge & Kegan Paul.

Hayes, R. H., and Steven Wheelwright. 1984. *Restoring Our Competitive Edge: Competing Through Manufacturing.* New York: Wiley.

Hearings Before the Subcommittee on Antitrust and Monopolies of the Senate Commission on the Judiciary. 1978. 95th Cong., 1st sess., p. 65 (testimony of John H. Shenefield).

Hechter, Michael. 1987. *Principles of Group Solidarity.* Berkeley and Los Angeles: University of California Press.

Heide, Jan, and George John. 1988. "The Role of Dependence Balancing in Safeguarding Transaction-Specific Assets in Conventional Channels." *Journal of Marketing* 52 (January): 20–35.

Helfat, Constance, and David Teece. 1987. "Vertical Integration and Risk Reduction." *Journal of Law, Economics, and Organization* 3 (Spring): 47–68.

Helper, Susan, and David Levine. 1992. "Long-Term Supplier Relations and Product–Market Structure." *Journal of Law, Economics, and Organization* 8 (October): 561–81.

Hennart, Jean-François. 1989. "The Transaction Costs Rationale of Countertrade." *Journal of Law, Economics, and Organization* 5 (Spring): 127–53.

Hinds, Manuel. 1990. "Issues in the Introduction of Market Forces in Eastern European Socialist Economies." *World Bank Report* no. IDP-0057.

Hirschman, Albert O. 1970. *Exit, Voice and Loyalty.* Cambridge, MA: Harvard University Press.

——. 1982. "Rival Interpretations of Market Society: Civilizing, Destructive, or Feeble?" *Journal of Economic Literature* 20 (December): 1463–84.

Hobbes, Thomas. 1928. *Leviathan, or the Matter, Forme, and Power of Commonwealth Ecclesiastical and Civil.* Oxford: Basil Blackwell.

Hodgson, Geoffrey. 1988. *Economics and Institutions.* Cambridge: Polity Press.

Holmstrom, Bengt. 1979. "Moral Hazard and Observability." *Bell Journal of Economics* 10 (Spring): 74–91.

——. 1989. "Agency Costs and Innovation." *Journal of Economic Behavior and Organization* 12 (December): 305–27.

——. 1991a. "Multi-Task Princiipal–Agent Analysis." *Journal of Law, Economics, and Organization* 7 (special issue): 24–52.

——. 1991b. "Transfer Pricing and Organizational Form." *Journal of Law, Economics, and Organization* 7 (Fall): 201–28.

——, and Paul Milgrom. 1989. "Regulating Trade Among Agents." *Journal of Institutional and Theoretical Economics* 146 (March): 85–105.

Holmstrom, Bengt, and Paul Milgrom. 1991. "Multi-Task Principal-Agent Analysis." *Journal of Law, Economics, and Organization* 7 (special issue): 24–52.

————, and Jean Tirole. 1989. "The Theory of the Firm." In Richard Schmalensee and Robert Willig, eds., *Handbook of Industrial Organization.* New York: North-Holland, pp. 61–133.

Holmstrom, Bengt, and Jean Tirole. 1991. "Transfer Pricing and Organizational Form." *Journal of Law, Economics, and Organization* 7 (Fall): 201–28.

Homans, George. 1958. "Social Behavior as Exchange." *American Journal of Sociology* 62: 597–606.

Horvat, Branko. 1982. *The Political Economy of Socialism.* New York: M. E. Sharpe.

————. 1991. "Review of Janos Kornai, the Road to a Free Economy." *Journal of Economic Behavior and Organization* 15 (May): 408–10.

Hurwicz, Leonid. 1972. "On Informationally Decentralized Systems." In C. B. McGuire and R. Radner, eds., *Decision and Organization.* Amsterdam: North-Holland, pp. 297–336.

————. 1973. "The Design of Mechanisms for Resource Allocation." *American Economic Review* 63 (May): 1–30.

Hutchison, T. 1984. "Institutional Economics Old and New." *Journal of Institutional and Theoretical Economics* 140 (March): 20–29.

Hutt, Peter. 1978. "Unresolved Issues in the Conflict Between Industrial Freedom and Government Control of Food Safety." *Food Drug Cosmetics Law Journal* 33: 558.

Ingham, Hilary. 1992. "Organizational Structure and Firm Performance: An Intertemporal Perspective." *Journal of Economic Studies* 19: 19–35.

Iwanek, M. 1991. "Issues of Institutions, Transformations and Ownership Changes in Poland." *Journal of Institutional and Theoretical Economics* 147: 83–95.

Jensen, Michael. 1983. "Organization Theory and Methodology." *Accounting Review* 50 (April): 319–39.

————. 1986. "Agency Costs and Free Cash Flow, Corporate Finance, and Takeovers." *American Economic Review* 76: 323–29.

————, and William Meckling. 1976. "Theory of the Firm: Managerial Behavior, Agency Costs, and Capital Structure." *Journal of Financial Economics* 3 (October): 305–60.

————, and William Meckling. 1979. "Rights and Production Functions." *Journal of Business* 52 (October): 496–506.

————, and William Meckling. 1990. "Knowledge, Control, and Organizational Structure." *Journal of Law, Economics, and Organization* 4 (Spring): 95–118.

————, and Clifford Smith. 1985. "Stockholder, Managers, and Creditor Interests: Applications of Agency Theory." In Edward Altman and Marti Subramanyam, eds., *Recent Advances in Corporate Finance.* Homewood, Ill.: Irwin, pp. 93–132.

John, George, and Barton Weitz. 1988. "Forward Integration into Distribution." *Journal of Law, Economics, and Organization* 4 (Fall): 337–56.

Jorde, Thomas, and David Teece. 1988. "Innovation, Cooperation, and Antitrust." Unpublished manuscript.

Joskow, Paul. 1985. "Vertical Integration and Long-Term Contracts." *Journal of Law, Economics, and Organization* 1 (Spring): 33–80.

————. 1987. "Contract Duration and Relationship-Specific Investments." *American Economic Review* 77 (March): 168–85.

————. 1988. "Asset Specificity and the Structure of Vertical Relationships: Empirical Evidence." *Journal of Law, Economics, and Organization* 4 (Spring): 95–117.

————. 1991. "The Role of Transaction Cost Economics in Antitrust and Public Utility

Regulatory Policies." *Journal of Law, Economics, and Organization* 7 (special issue): 53–83.

———, and A. K. Klevorick. 1979. "A Framework for Analyzing Predatory Pricing Policy." *Yale Law Journal* 89 (December): 213–70.

———, and Richard Schmalensee. 1983. *Markets for Power.* Cambridge, MA: MIT Press.

Kaldor, Nicholas. 1934. "The Equilibrium of the Firm." *Economic Journal* 44 (March): 70–81.

Kaplow, Louis. 1985. "Extension of Monopoly Power Through Leverage." Program in Law and Economics, Discussion Paper no. 4, Harvard Law School.

Katz, Michael, and Carl Shapiro. 1986. "Technology Adoption in the Presence of Network Externalities." *Journal of Political Economy* 94 (August): 822–41.

Kaysen, Carl, and D. F. Turner. 1959. *Antitrust Policy.* Cambridge, MA: Harvard University Press.

Kenney, Roy, and Benjamin Klein. 1983. "The Economics of Block Booking." *Journal of Law and Economics* 26 (October): 497–540.

Keohane, Robert. 1984. *After Hegemony: Cooperation and Discord in the World Political Economy.* Princeton, NJ: Princeton University Press.

Kitch, Edmund W. 1983. "The Fire of Truth: A Remembrance of Law and Economics at Chicago, 1932–1970." *Journal of Law and Economics* 26: 163–70.

Klein, Benjamin. 1980. "Transaction Cost Determinants of 'Unfair' Contractual Arrangements." *American Economic Review* 70 (May): 356–62.

———. 1988. "Vertical Integration as Organizational Ownership." *Journal of Law, Economics, and Organization* 4, 199–213.

———, R. A. Crawford, and A. A. Alchian. 1978. "Vertical Integration, Appropriable Rents, and the Competitive Contracting Process." *Journal of Law and Economics* 21 (October): 297–326.

———, and Keith B. Leffler. 1981. "The Role of Market Forces in Assuring Contractual Performance." *Journal of Political Economy* 89 (August): 615–41.

Klein, Peter, and Howard Shelanski. 1995. "Empirical Work in Transaction Cost Economics." *Journal of Law, Economics, and Organization* 11 (October).

Knight, Frank H. 1941. "Review of Melville J. Herskovits' Economic Anthropology'." *Journal of Political Economy* 49 (April): 247–58.

———. 1965. *Risk, Uncertainty, and Profit.* New York: Harper & Row.

Knudsen, Christian. 1993. "Modelling Rationality, Institutions and Processes in Economic Theory." In Uslaki Maki, Bo Gustafsson, and Christian Knudsen, eds., *Rationality, Institutions, and Economic Methodology.* London: Routledge.

Koller, R. 1971. "The Myth of Predatory Pricing—An Empirical Study." *Antitrust Law & Economics Review* 4: 105.

Koopmans, Tjalling. 1957. *Three Essays on the State of Economic Science.* New York: McGraw-Hill.

———. 1977. "Concepts of Optimality and Their Uses." *American Economic Review* 67: 261–74.

Kornai, Janos. 1986. "The Hungarian Reform Process." *Journal of Economic Literature* 24 (December): 1687–1737.

———. 1990. "The Affinity Between Ownership Forms and Coordination Mechanisms: The Common Experience of Reform in Socialist Countries." *Journal of Economic Perspectives* 4 (Summer): 131–47.

———. 1992. "Bureaucracy and Market, Introduction to the Political Economy of Socialism." Unpublished lecture notes.

Krattenmaker, Thomas, and Steven Salop. 1986. "Anticompetitive Exclusion: Raising Rivals' Costs to Achieve Power over Price." *Yale Law Journal* 96: 209.

Kreps, David M. 1984. "Corporate Culture and Economic Theory." Unpublished manuscript, Graduate School of Business, Stanford University.

———. 1990a. "Corporate Culture and Economic Theory." In James Alt and Kenneth Shepsle, eds., *Perspectives on Positive Political Economy*. Cambridge: Cambridge University Press, pp. 90–143.

———. 1990b. *A Course in Microeconomic Theory*. Princeton, NJ: Princeton University Press.

———. 1990c. *Game Theory and Economic Modelling*. Oxford: Clarendon Press.

———. 1992. "(How) Can Game Theory Lead to a Unified Theory of Organization?" Unpublished manuscript.

———, and Michael Spence. 1985. "Modelling the Role of History in Industrial Organization and Competition." In George Feiwel, ed., *Issues in Contemporary Microeconomics and Welfare*. London: Macmillan, pp. 340–79.

———, and Robert Wilson. 1982. "Reputation and Imperfect Information." *Journal of Economic Theory* 27 (August): 253–79.

Krueger, Anne. 1990. "The Political Economy of Controls: American Sugar." In Maurice Scott and Deepak Lal, eds., *Public Policy and Economic Development: Essays in Honor of Ian Little*. Oxford: Clarendon Press, pp. 170–216.

Kuhn, Thomas S. 1962. *The Structure of Scientific Revolutions*. Chicago: University of Chicago Press.

———. 1970. *The Structure of Scientific Revolutions*. 2nd ed. Chicago: University of Chicago Press.

Kydland, Finn, and Edward Prescott. 1977. "Rules Rather Than Discretion: The Inconsistency of Optimal Plans." *Journal of Political Economy* 85 (June): 473–91.

Laffont, Jean-Jacques, and Jean Tirole. 1993. *A Theory of Incentives in Procurement and Regulation*. Cambridge, MA: MIT Press.

Lal, Deepak. 1985. *The Poverty of "Development Economics."* Cambridge, MA: Harvard University Press.

Landa, Janet T. 1981. "A Theory of the Ethnically Homogeneous Middleman Group: An Institutional Alternative to Contract Law." *Journal of Legal Studies* 10: 394–62.

Lange, Oskar. 1938. "On the Theory of Economic Socialism." In Benjamin Lippincott, ed., *On the Economic Theory of Socialism*. Minneapolis: University of Minnesota Press, pp. 55–143.

Lardner, James. 1993. "The Whistle-Blower—Part II." *The New Yorker,* July 12, pp. 39–58.

Levine, David. 1987. "Airline Competition in Deregulated Markets: Theory, Firm Strategy, and Public Policy." *Yale Journal on Regulation* 4: 393–434.

———. 1990. "Employee Involvement Efforts." Unpublished manuscript.

Levy, Brian, Hadi Selahi Esfahani, Ahmed Galal, Ingo Vogelsang, Cezley I. Sampson, and Pablo T. Spiller. 1993. *Regulation, Institutions, and Commitment in Telecommunications*. Washington, DC: World Bank Conference.

Levy, Brian, and Pablo Spiller. 1993. "Regulation, Institutions, and Commitment in Telecommunications: A Comparative Analysis of Five Country Studies." Unpublished manuscript.

———. 1994. "The Institutional Foundations of Regulatory Commitment." *Journal of Law, Economics, and Organization* 9 (Fall): 201–46.

Lewis, Tracy. 1983. "Preemption, Divestiture, and Forward Contracting in a Market

Dominated by a Single Firm." *American Economic Review* 73 (December): 1092–1101.

Liebeler, W. C. 1978. "Market Power and Competitive Superiority in Concentrated Industries." *UCLA Law Review* 25 (August): 1231–1300.

Liebowitz, Stanley J., and Stephen Margolis. 1990. "The Fable of the Keys." *Journal of Law and Economics* 33 (April): 1–26.

———. 1995. "Path Dependency, Lock-in, and History." *Journal of Law, Economics, and Organization* 11 (Spring): 205–26.

Light, Ivan. 1972. *Ethnic Enterprise in America: Business and Welfare Among Chinese, Japanese, and Blacks.* Berkeley and Los Angeles: University of California Press.

Lilien, G. L. 1979. "Advisor 2: Modelling the Market Mix Decision for Industrial Products." *Management Science* 25: 191–204.

Lincoln, J. 1990. "Japanese Organization and Organization Theory." *Research in Organizational Behavior* 12, 255–94.

Lindenberg, Siegwart. 1990. "Homo Socio-Economicus: The Emergence of a General Model of Man in the Social Sciences." *Journal of Institutional and Theoretical Economics* 146: 727–48.

———. 1992. "An Extended Theory of Institutions and Contractual Discipline." *Journal of Institutional and Theoretical Economics* 148 (March): 125–54.

Litwack, John. 1991. "Discretionary Behavior and Soviet Economic Reform." *Soviet Studies* 43: 255–79.

Llewellyn, Karl N. 1931. "What Price Contract? An Essay in perspective." *Yale Law Journal* 40 (May): 704–51.

Long, Michael, and Ileen Malitz. 1985. "Investment Patterns and Financial Leverage." In B. Friedman, ed., *Corporate Capital Structures in the United States.* Chicago: University of Chicago Press, pp. 325–48.

Lowenstein, Louis. 1985. "Management Buyouts." *Columbia Law Review* 85 (May): 730–84.

Macaulay, Stewart. 1963. "Non-Contractual Relations in Business." *American Sociological Review* 28: 55–70.

Machiavelli, Niccolò. 1952. *The Prince.* New York: New American Library.

Macneil, Ian R. 1974. "The Many Futures of Contracts." *Southern California Law Review* 47 (May): 691–816.

———. 1978. "Contracts: Adjustments of Long-Term Economic Relations Under Classical, Neoclassical, and Relational Contract Law." *Northwestern University Law Review* 72: 854–906.

Mahoney, Joseph, and J. R. Pandian. 1992. "The Resource-Based View Within the Conversation of Strategic Management." *Strategic Management Journal* 13: 363–80.

Maki, Uslaki. 1993. "Economics with Institutions: Agenda for Methodological Inquiry." In Uslaki Maki, Bo Gustafsson, and Christian Knudsen, eds., *Rationality, Institutions, and Economic Methodology.* London: Routledge, pp. 3–44.

Malmgren, H. 1961. "Information, Expectations and the Theory of the Firm." *Quarterly Journal of Economics* 75 (August): 399–421.

Manne, Henry. 1967. "Our Two Corporation Systems: Law and Economics." *University of Virginia Law Review* 53: 259–85.

March, James G. 1966. "The Power of Power." In David Easton, ed., *Varieties of Political Theory.* Englewood Cliffs, NJ: Prentice-Hall, pp. 39–70.

———. 1973. "Model Bias in Social Action." *Review of Educational Research* 42: 413–29.

————. 1988. *Decisions and Organizations.* Oxford: Basil Blackwell.

————, and Johan Olsen. 1989. *Rediscovering Institutions: The Organizational Basis of Politics.* New York: Free Press.

————, and Herbert A. Simon. 1958. *Organizations.* New York: Wiley.

Marglin, Stephen A. 1974. "What Do Bosses Do? The Origins and Functions of Hierarchy in Capitalist Production." *Review of Radical Political Economic* 6: 33–60.

Mariotti, S., and G. Cainara. 1986. "The Evolution of Transaction Governance in the Textile-Clothing Industry." *Journal of Economic Behavior and Organization* 7 (September): 351–74.

Marris, Robin. 1964. *The Economic Theory of Managerial Capitalism.* New York: Free Press.

Marshak, Jacob. 1968. "Economics of Inquiring, Communicating, Deciding." *American Economic Review* 58 (May): 1–18.

Marshall, Alfred. 1932. *Industry and Trade.* London: Macmillan.

————. 1948. *Principles of Economics.* 8th ed. New York: Macmillan.

Mason, Edward S. 1958. "The Apologetics of Managerialism." *Journal of Business* 31: 1–11.

————. 1959. "Preface" to C. Kaysen and D. Turner, *Antitrust Policy.* Cambridge, MA: Harvard University Press, pp. xi–xxiii.

Mason, L. 1984. *Structuring and Financial Management Buyouts.* San Diego, CA: Buyout Publications.

Masten, Scott. 1982. "Transaction Costs, Institutional Choice, and the Theory of the Firm." Ph.D. diss., University of Pennsylvania.

————. 1984. "The Organization of Production: Evidence from the Aerospace Industry." *Journal of Law and Economics* 27 (October): 403–18.

————. 1988. "A Legal Basis for the Firm." *Journal of Law, Economics, and Organization* 4 (Spring): 181–98.

————. 1993. "Transaction Costs, Mistakes, and Performance: Assessing the Importance of Governance." *Management and Decision Economics* 14 (January–February): 80–96.

————, and Keith Crocker. 1985. "Efficient Adaptation in Long-Term Contracts: Take or Pay Provisions for Natural Gas." *American Economic Review* 75 (December): 1085–96.

————, James Meehan Jr., and Edward Snyder. 1991. "The Costs of Organization." *Journal of Law, Economics, and Organization* 7 (Spring): 1–22.

Matsushita Elec. Indus. Co. v. *Zenith Radio Corp.* 1986. 475 U.S. 574.

Matthews, R. C. O. 1986. "The Economics of Institutions and the Sources of Economic Growth." *Economic Journal* 96 (December): 903–18.

McCain, Roger. 1977. "On the Optimal Financial Environment for Worker Cooperatives." *Zeitschrift für Nationalökonomie* 37: 355–84.

McCloskey, Donald. 1986. "The Postmodern Rhetoric of Sociology." *Contemporary Sociology* 15: 815–18.

McCullough, David. 1992. *Truman.* New York: Simon & Schuster.

McGuire, P., M. Granovetter, and M. Schwartz. 1992. "The Social Construction of Industry." Book prospectus.

McKenzie, L. 1951. "Ideal Output and the Interdependence of Firms." *Economic Journal* 61 (December): 785–803.

Meade, J. E. 1971. *The Controlled Economy.* London: Allen & Unwin.

Menger, Karl. 1963. *Problems in Economics and Sociology.* Translated by Francis J. Nock. Urbana: University of Illinois Press.

Merton, Robert. 1936. "The Unanticipated Consequences of Purposive Social Action."
    American Sociological Review 1: 894–904.
———. 1957. *Social Theory and Social Structure.* Glencoe, IL: Free Press.
Michelman, Frank. 1967. "Property, Utility and Fairness: Comments on the Ethical
    Foundations of 'Just Compensation' Law." *Harvard Law Review* 80 (April):
    1165–1257.
———. 1979. "A Comment on Some Uses and Abuses of Economics in Law." *University of Chicago Law Review* 46, 307–15.
Michels, Robert. 1962. *Political Parties.* Glencoe, IL: Free Press.
Miles, R., and C. Snow. 1992. "Causes of Failure in Network Organizations." *California Management Review* 34 (Summer): 53–72.
Milgrom, Paul, Douglass North, and Barry Weingast. 1990. "The Role of Institutions
    in the Revival of Trade." *Economics and Politics* 2 (March): 1–23.
Milgrom, Paul, and John Roberts. 1982. "Predation, Reputation, and Entry Deterrence." *Journal of Economic Theory* 27 (August): 280–312.
———. 1988. "An Economic Approach to Influence Activities in Organizations."
    American Journal of Sociology (supplement) 94: S154–S179.
———. 1990a. "Bargaining Costs, Influence Costs, and the Organization of Economic
    Activity." In James Alt and Kenneth Shepsle, eds., *Perspectives on Positive
    Political Economy.* Cambridge: Cambridge University Press, pp. 57–89.
———. 1990b. "The Economics of Modern Manufacturing: Technology, Strategy, and
    Organization." *American Economic Review* 80: 511–28.
———. 1992. *Economics, Organization, and Management.* Englewood Cliffs, NJ: Prentice-Hall.
———. 1994. "Continuous Adjustment and Fundamental Change in Business Strategy
    and Organization." Unpublished manuscript.
Mnookin, Robert H., and Lewis Kornhauser. 1979. "Bargaining in the Shadow of the
    Law: The Case of Divorce." *Yale Law Journal* 88 (March): 950–97.
Modiglilani, Franco. 1961. "Long-Run Implications of Alternative Fiscal Policies and
    the Burden of the National Debt." *Economic Journal* 71 (December): 730–55.
———, and Merton H. Miller. 1958. "The Cost of Capital, Corporation Finance, and
    the Theory of Investment." *American Economic Review* 48 (June): 261–97.
Moe, Terry. 1990a. "Political Institutions: The Neglected Side of the Story." *Journal
    of Law, Economics, and Organization* (special issues) 6: 213–53.
———. 1990b. "The Politics of Structural Choice: Toward a Theory of Public Bureaucracy." In Oliver Williamson, ed., *Organization Theory.* New York: Oxford
    University Press, pp. 116–53.
———, and Michael Caldwell. 1994. "The Institutional Foundations of Democratic
    Government: A Comparison of Presidential and Parliamentary Systems." *Journal of Institutional and Theoretical Economics* 150 (March): 171–95.
Mokyr, Joel. 1990. *The Lever of Riches.* New York: Oxford University Press.
Monteverde, Kirk, and David Teece. 1982. "Supplier Switching Costs and Vertical
    Integration in the Automobile Industry." *Bell Journal of Economics* 13
    (Spring): 206–13.
Montgomery, C., and B. Wernerfelt. 1988. "Diversification, Picardian Rents, and
    Tobin's q." *RAND Journal of Economics* 19: 623–32.
Montias, Michael. 1976. *The Structure of Economic Systems.* New Haven, CT: Yale
    University Press.
Montignola, Gabriella, Yingyi Qian, and Barry Weingast. 1993. "Federalism, Chinese
    Style." Unpublished manuscript.

Morris, Charles. 1980. *The Cost of Good Intentions.* New York: Norton.

Mulherin, J. H. 1986. "Complexity in Long Term Contracts: An Analysis of Natural Gas Contractual Provisions." *Journal of Law, Economics, and Organization* 2: 105–18.

Muris, Timothy J. 1979. "The Efficiency Defense Under Section 7 of the Clayton Act." *Case Western Reserve Law Review* 30 (Fall): 381–432.

———, David Scheffman, and Pablo Spiller. 1992. "Strategy and Transaction Costs in the Carbonated Soft Drink Industry." *Journal of Economics and Management Strategy* 1 (Spring): 83–129.

Myers, Stuart. 1977. "Determinants of Corporate Borrowing." *Journal of Financial Economics* 5: 147–75.

———. 1985. "Comment on Investment Patterns and Financial Leverage." In Benjamin Friedman, ed., *Corporate Capital Structures in the United States.* Chicago: University of Chicago Press, pp. 348–51.

Nabli, Mustapha, and Jeffrey Nugent. 1989. *The New Institutional Economics and Development.* New York: North-Holland.

Nelson, Richard R. 1961. "Uncertainty, Learning, and the Economics of Parallel R&D." *Review of Economics and Statistics* 43: 351–64.

———, and S. G. Winter. 1982. *An Evolutionary Theory of Economic Change.* Cambridge, MA: Harvard University Press.

Newberry, David. 1993. "Restructuring and Privatizing Electric Utilities in Eastern Europe." Institute for Policy Research Paper 66. Washington, D.C.

Newell, A., and H. Simon. 1972. *Human Problem Solving.* Englewood Cliffs, NJ: Prentice-Hall.

Newman, Barry. 1989. "Poland's Farmers Put the Screws to Leaders by Holding Back Crops." *Wall Street Journal,* October 25, pp. A1, A10.

North, Douglass. 1981. *Structure and Change in Economic History.* New York: Norton.

———. 1984. "Transaction Costs, Institutions, and Economic History." *Journal of Institutional and Theoretical Economics* 140 (March): 7–17.

———. 1986. "The New Institutional Economics." *Journal of Theoretical and Institutional Economics* 142: 230–37.

———. 1990. *Institutions, Institutional Change, and Economic Performance.* Cambridge: Cambridge University Press.

———. 1991. "Institutions." *Journal of Economic Perspectives* 5 (Winter): 97–112.

———. 1994. "Economic Performance Through Time." *American Economic Review* 84 (June): 359–68.

———, and Barry Weingast. 1989. "Constitutions and Commitment: The Evolution of Institutions Governing Public Choice in 17th Century England." *Journal of Economic History* 49 (December): 803–32.

Nozick, Robert. 1974. *Anarchy, State, and Utopia.* New York: Basic Books.

———. 1988. *An Examined Life.* New York: Simon & Schuster.

Nuti, D. M. 1989. "Feasible Financial Innovation Under Market Socialism." *Journal of Comparative Economics* 1: 85–104.

Okun, A. 1981. *Prices and Quantities: A Macroeconomic Analysis.* Washington, DC: Brookings Institution.

Olson, Mancur, Jr. 1965. *The Logic of Collective Action.* Cambridge, MA: Harvard University Press.

———. 1992. "The Hidden Path to a Successful Economy." In Christopher Clague and Gordon C. Rausser, eds., *The Emergence of Market Economies in Eastern Europe.* Cambridge, MA: Basil Blackwell, pp. 55–76.

Orbell, John, and Robyn Dawes. 1991. "A 'Cognitive Miser' Theory of Cooperators' Advantage." *American Political Science Review* 85 (June): 515–28.

Ordover, J. A., and G. Saloner. 1987. *Predation, Monopolization, and Antitrust.* C. V. Starr Center for Applied Economics, New York University.

Ordover, J. A., and R. D. Willig. 1981. "An Economic Definition of Predatory Product Innovation." In S. Salop, ed., *Strategic Views of Predation.* Washington, DC: Federal Trade Commission, pp. 301–96.

———. 1985. "Perspective on Mergers and World Competition." Economic Research Report no. 85-11, New York University.

Ostrom, Elinor, Larry Shroeder, and Susan Wynne. 1993. *Institutional Incentives and Sustainable Development.* Boulder, CO: Westview Press.

Ouchi, William G. 1977. "Review of Markets and Hierarchies." *Administrative Science Quarterly* 22 (September): 541–44.

———. 1980. "Markets, Bureaucracies, and Clans." *Administrative Science Quarterly* 25 (March): 120–42.

———. 1981. *Theory Z.* Reading, MA: Addison-Wesley.

Palay, Thomas. 1981. "The Governance of Rail-Freight Contracts: A Comparative Institutional Approach." Ph.D. diss., University of Pennsylvania.

———. 1984. "Comparative Institutional Economics: The Governance of Rail Freight Contracting." *Journal of Legal Studies* 13 (June): 265–88.

———. 1985. "Avoiding Regulatory Constraints: The Use of Informal Contracts." *Journal of Law, Economics, and Organization* 1 (Spring): 155–75.

Parsons, T., and N. Smelser. 1956. *Economy and Society.* New York: Free Press.

Passell, Peter. 1994. "F.C.C. 'Pioneer' Policy Under Attack." *New York Times,* January 31, p. C1.

Pelikan, Pavel. 1989. "Evolution, Economic Competence, and the Market for Corporate Control." *Journal of Economic Behavior and Organization* 12 (December): 279–304.

Penrose, Edith. 1959. *The Theory of Growth of the Firm.* New York: Wiley.

Perrow, Charles. 1981. "The Markets and Hierarchies Program of Research: Comment." In A. H. Van de Ven and W. F. Joyce, eds., *Perspectives on Organizing, Design, and Behavior.* New York: Wiley, pp. 370–76.

———. 1986. *Complex Organizations.* 3rd ed. New York: Random House.

———. 1992. "Review of the New Competition." *Administrative Science Quarterly* 37 (March): 162–66.

Perry, Martin. 1989. "Vertical Integration." In Richard Schmalensee and Robert Willig, ed., *Handbook of Industrial Organization.* Amsterdam: North-Holland, pp. 183–255.

Peteraf, M. A. 1990. "The Cornerstone of Competitive Advantage: A Resource-Based View." Discussion Paper no. 90-29. Kellogg Graduate School of Management, Northwestern University.

Pfeffer, Jeffrey. 1981. *Power in Organizations.* Marshfield, MA: Pitman.

———, and Gerald Salancik. 1978. *The External Control of Organizations.* New York: Harper & Row.

Polanyi, Michael. 1962. *Personal Knowledge: Towards a Post-Critical Philosophy.* New York: Harper & Row.

Polinsky, M. 1974. "Economic Analysis as a Potential Defective Product: A Buyer's Guide to Posner's *Economic Analysis of Law.*" *Harvard Law Review* 87: 1655–81.

Pollak, R. 1985. "A Transaction Cost Approach to Families and Households." *Journal of Economic Literature* 23: 581–608.

Posner, Richard A. 1969a. "Natural Monopoly and Its Regulation." *Stanford Law Review* 21 (February): 548–643.

———. 1969b. "Oligopoly and the Antitrust Laws: A Suggested Approach." *Stanford Law Review* 21 (June): 1562–1606.

———. 1972. "The Appropriate Scope of Regulation in the Cable Television Industry." *Bell Journal of Economics and Management Science* 3 (Spring): 98–129.

———. 1975a. "Antitrust Policy and the Supreme Court: An Analysis of the Restricted Distribution, Horizontal Merger and Potential Competition Decisions." *Columbia Law Review* 75: 282–313.

———. 1975b. "The Social Costs of Monopoly and Regulation." *Journal of Political Economy* 83 (August): 807–27.

———. 1976. *Antitrust Law*. Chicago: University of Chicago Press.

———. 1977. *Economic Analysis of Law*. Boston: Little, Brown.

———. 1979. "The Chicago School of Antitrust Analysis." *University of Pennsylvania Law Review* 127 (April): 925–48.

———. 1993a. "The New Institutional Economics Meets Law and Economics." *Journal of Institutional and Theoretical Economics* 149 (March): 73–87.

———. 1993b. "Reply to Coase and Williamson." *Journal of Institutional and Theoretical Economics* 149 (March): 119–21.

———. 1993c. "Ronald Coase and Methodology." *Journal of Economic Perspectives* 7: 195–210.

Prahalad, C. K., and G. Hamel. 1990. "The Core Competence of the Corporation." *Harvard Business Review* 68: 79–91.

President's Task Force Report on Productivity and Competition. 1969. Reprinted in Commerce Clearing House, *Trade Regulation Reporter* 419 (June): 39.

Purex v. *Procter & Gamble,* 419 F. Supp. 931 (N.D. Cal. 1976).

Putterman, Louis. 1984. "On Some Recent Explanations of Why Capital Hires Labor." *Economic Inquiry* 22: 171–87.

Radner, Roy. 1968. "Competitive Equilibrium Under Uncertainty." *Econometrica* 36 (January): 31–58.

Rausser, Gordon. 1992. "Lessons for Emerging Market Economies in Eastern Europe." In Christopher Clague and Gordon C. Rausser, eds., *The Emergence of Market Economies in Eastern Europe*. Cambridge, MA: Basil Blackwell, pp. 311–32.

———, and Leo Simon. 1992. "The Political Economy of Transition in Eastern Europe." In Christopher Clague and Gordon C. Rausser, eds., *The Emergence of Market Economies in Eastern Europe*. Cambridge, MA: Basil Blackwell, pp. 245–70.

Raz, Joseph. 1986. *The Morality of Freedom*. Oxford: Clarendon Press.

Rey, P., and Jean Tirole. 1986. "The Logic of Vertical Restraints." *American Economic Review* 76: 921, 937.

Richter, Rudolf. 1990. "A Socialist Market Economy—Can It Work?" Unpublished manuscript.

Riker, William J. 1964. *Federalism*. Boston: Little Brown.

Riley, John G. 1979a. "Informational Equilibrium." *Econometrica* 47 (March): 331–53.

———. 1979b. "Noncooperative Equilibrium and Market Signaling." *American Economic Review* 69 (May): 303–7.

Riordan, Michael. 1990. "What Is Vertical Integration?" In Masahiko Aoki, Bo Gustafsson, and Oliver Williamson, eds., *The Firm as a Nexus of Treaties*. London: Sage.

———, and Oliver Williamson. 1985. "Asset Specificity and Economic Organization." *International Journal of Industrial Organization* 3: 365–78.

Robbins, Lionel, ed. 1933. *The Common Sense of Political Economy, and Selected Papers on Economic Theory*, by Philip Wicksteed. London: Routledge and Sons.

Robertson, Dennis. 1976. "What Does the Economist Economize?" In *Economic Commentaries*. London: Staples Press, pp. 147–54.

Robinson, E. A. G. 1934. "The Problem of Management and the Size of Firms." *Economic Journal* 44 (June): 240–54.

Robinson, James. 1992. "A New Institutional Economics of Health Care." Unpublished manuscript.

———. 1993a. "Alternative Institutional Frameworks for Health Care Market Reform." Unpublished manuscript, University of California, Berkeley.

———. 1993b. "Who Shall Manage the Managed Care Organizations?" Unpublished manuscript.

Romano, R. 1985. "Law as a Product: Some Pieces of the Incorporation Puzzle." *Journal of Law, Economics, and Organization* 3: 365–68.

———. 1986. "The State Competition Debate in Corporate Law." Unpublished manuscript.

Rosen, Sherwin. 1988. "Transaction Costs and Internal Labor Markets." *Journal of Law, Economics, and Organization* 4 (Spring): 49–64.

Ross, Stephen. 1973. "The Economic Theory of Agency: The Principal's Problem." *American Economics Review* 63: 134–39.

———. 1977. "The Determinants of Financial Structure: The Incentive Signaling Approach." *Bell Journal of Economics* 8 (Spring): 23–40.

———. 1987. "The Interrelations of Finance and Economics: Theoretical Perspectives." *American Economic Review* 77 (May): 29–34.

Rothschild, Michael, and Joseph Stiglitz. 1976. "Equilibrium in Competitive Insurance Markets." *Quarterly Journal of Economics* 80 (November): 629–50.

Rumelt, Richard. 1984. "Towards a Strategic Theory of the Firm." In R. Lamb, ed., *Competitive Strategy Management*. Englewood Cliffs, NJ: Prentice-Hall, pp. 556–70.

———. 1987. "Theory, Strategy, and Entrepreneurship." In David Teece, ed., *The Competitive Challenge*. New York: Harper & Row, pp. 137–58.

Rumelt, R., D. Schendel, and D. Teece, eds. 1992. *Fundamental Issues in Strategy*. Boston: Harvard Business School Press.

Sacks, Stephen. 1983. *Self-Management and Efficiency*. London: Allen & Unwin.

Salop, S. 1981. "Introduction to Strategy, Predation, and Antitrust Analysis." *Strategy, Predation, and Antitrust Analysis*. 1 (S. Salop ed.). Federal Trade Commission Report. Washington, DC: U.S. Government Printing Office, pp. 1–23.

———, and D. Scheffman. 1983. "Raising Rival's Costs." *American Economic Review* 73 (May): 267–71.

Samuelson, Paul A. 1947. *Foundations of Economic Analysis*. Cambridge, MA: Harvard University Press.

Schelling, Thomas C. 1956. "An Essay on Bargaining." *American Economic Review* 46 (June): 281–306.

———. 1978. *Micromotives and Macrobehavior*. New York: Norton.

Scherer, F. M. 1970. *Industrial Market Structure and Economic Performance*. Chicago: Rand McNally.

————. 1980. *Industrial Market Structure and Economic Performance.* Chicago: Rand McNally.

Schmalensee, R. 1981. "Economies of Scale and Barriers to Entry." *Journal of Political Economy* 89 (December): 1228–38.

———— and Robert Willig, eds. 1989. Vol. 1: *Handbook of Industrial Organization.* 2 vols. Amsterdam: North Holland.

Schmid, Allan. 1972. "Analytical Institutional Economics." *American Journal of Agricultural Economics* 54: 893–901.

Schotter, Andrew. 1981. *The Economic Theory of Social Institutions.* Cambridge: Cambridge University Press.

Schumpeter, Joseph A. 1942. *Capitalism, Socialism, and Democracy.* New York: Harper & Row.

————. 1947. "The Creative Response in Economic History." *Journal of Economic History* 7 (November): 149–59.

————. 1989. *Essays of Entrepreneurs, Innovations, Business Cycles, and the Evolution of Capitalism.* New Brunswick, NJ: Transaction Publishers.

Schwadel, Francine. 1990. "Sear's Brennan Faces Facts About Costs." *Wall Street Journal,* August 10, p. B1.

Scott, W. Richard. 1987. *Organizations.* 2nd ed. Englewood Cliffs, NJ: Prentice-Hall.

————. 1992. "Institutions and Organizations: Toward a Theoretical Synthesis." Unpublished manuscript.

Selznick, Philip. 1949. *TVA and the Grass Roots.* Berkeley and Los Angeles: University of California Press.

————. 1957. *Leadership in Administration.* New York: Harper & Row.

————. 1969. *Law, Society, and Industrial Justice.* New York: Russell Sage Foundation.

Shapiro, Carl. 1982. "Consumer Information, Product Quality, and Seller Reputation." *Bell Journal of Economics* 13 (Spring): 20–35.

————. 1983. "Optimal Pricing of Experience Goods." *Bell Journal of Economics & Management Science* 14: 497, 504.

————. 1989. "The Theory of Business Strategy." *Rand Journal of Economics* 20 (Spring): 125–37.

Shapiro, Susan. 1987. "The Social Control of Impersonal Trust." *American Journal of Sociology* 93 (November): 623–58.

Shavell, Steven. 1980. "Damage Measures for Breach of Contract." *Bell Journal of Economics* 11 (Autumn): 446–90.

Sheard, Paul. 1989. "The Main Bank System and Corporate Monitoring in Japan." *Journal of Economic Behavior and Organization* 11 (May): 399–422.

————. 1993. "Transfer Pricing." Ph.D. diss., University of California, Berkeley.

Shenefield, John H. 1978. Hearings Before the Subcommittee on Antitrust and Monopolies of the Senate Committee on the Judiciary, 96th Cong., 1st sess. p. 65 (testimony).

Shepard, A. 1986. "Licensing to Enhance Demand for New Technologies." Unpublished manuscript, Yale University.

Shepsle, Kenneth. 1992. "Discretion, Institutions, and the Problem of Government Commitment." In Pierre Boudrieu and James Coleman, eds., *Social Theory in a Chanaging Society.* Boulder, CO: Westview Press, pp. 250–65.

Shirley, Mary, and Ahmad Galal. 1994. "The Changing Role of the State: Strategies for Reforming Public Enterprises." World Bank Conference, Washington, D.C.

Shleifer, Andrei, and Lawrence Summers. 1988. "Breach of Trust in Hostile Takeovers." In Alan Auerbach, ed., *Corporate Takeovers: Causes and Consequences.* Chicago: University of Chicago Press, pp. 33–56.

———. 1990. "The Takeover Wave of the 1990s." Unpublished manuscript.

Simon, Herbert. 1947. *Administrative Behavior.* New York: Macmillan.

———. 1951. "A Formal Theory of the Employment Relation." *Econometrica* 19 (July): 293–305.

———. 1955. "A Behavioral Model of Rational Choice." *Quarterly Journal of Economics,* 69 (February): 99–118.

———. 1957a. *Administrative Behavior.* 2nd ed. New York: Macmillan.

———. 1957b. *Models of Man.* New York: Wiley.

———. 1959. "Theories of Decision Making in Economics and Behavioral Science." *American Economic Review* 49 (June): 253–58.

———. 1961. *Administrative Behavior.* 2nd ed. New York: Macmillan.

———. 1962a. "The Architecture of Complexity." *Proceedings of the American Philosophical Society* 106 (December): 467–82.

———. 1962b. "New Developments in the Theory of the Firm." *American Economic Review 52 (March): 1–15.*

———. 1972. "Theories of Bounded Rationality." In C. B. McGuire and R. Radner, eds., *Decision and Organization.* New York: American Elsevier, pp. 161—76.

———. 1978. "Rationality as Process and as Product of Thought." *American Economic Review* 68 (May): 1–16.

———. 1983. *Reason in Human Affairs.* Stanford, CA: Stanford University Press.

———. 1984. "On the Behavioral and Rational Foundations of Economic Dynamics." *Journal of Economic Behavior and Organization* 5 (March): 35–56.

———. 1985. "Human Nature in Politics: The Dialogue of Psychology with Political Science." *American Political Science Review* 79: 293–304.

———. 1991. "Organizations and Markets." *Journal of Economic Perspectives* 5 (Spring): 25–44.

Sloan, A. P., Jr. 1964. *My Years with General Motors.* New York: McFadden.

Smith, Adam. 1922. *The Wealth of Nations.* London: J. M. Dent & Sons.

Smith, V. 1974. "Economic Theory and Its Discontents." *American Economic Review* 64 (May): 320–22.

Solow, R. 1985. "Economic History and Economics." *American Economic Review* 75: 328–31.

Soskice, David, Robert Bates, and David Epstein. 1992. "Ambition and Constraint: The Stabilizing Role of Institutions." *Journal of Law, Economics, and Organization* 8 (October): 547–60.

"Soviet Economic Developments." 1990. *International Herald Tribune,* June 5, p. 5.

Spence, A. M. 1977. "Entry, Investment and Oligopolistic Pricing." *Bell Journal of Economics* 8 (Autumn): 534–44.

———. 1981. "Competition, Entry, and Antitrust Policy." In S. Salop, ed., *Strategy, Predation, and Antitrust Analysis.* Federal Trade Commission Report. Washington, DC: U.S. Government Printing Office.

Spiller, Pablo. 1985. "On Vertical Mergers." *Journal of Law, Economics, and Organization* 1 (Fall): 285–312.

———, and Ingo Vogelsang. 1994. "Regulations, Institutions, and Commitment in the British Telecommunications Sector." Policy Research Working Paper No. 1241. Washington, DC: World Bank.

Steer, P. S., and John Cable. 1978. "Internal Organization and Profit: An Empirical Analysis of Large U.K. Companies." *Journal of Industrial Economics,* February, pp. 13–30.

Steffens, Joseph Lincoln. 1931. *The Autobiography of Lincoln Steffens.* New York: Harcourt, Brace.

Stigler, G. J. 1951. "The Division of Labor Is Limited by the Extent of the Market." *Journal of Political Economy* 59 (June): 185–93.

———. 1955. "Mergers and Preventive Antitrust Policy." *University of Pennsylvania Law Review* 104: 176–85.

———. 1961. "The Economics of Information." *Journal of Political Economy* 69 (June): 213–25.

———. 1964a. "Public Regulation and the Security Markets." *Journal of Business* 37 (March): 117–32.

———. 1964b. "A Theory of Oligopoly." *Journal of Political Economy* 22 (February): 44–61.

———. 1966. *Theory of Price.* New York: Macmillan.

———. 1968. *The Organization of Industry.* Homewood, IL: Irwin.

———. 1969. "Incentives and Risk Sharing in Sharecropping." *Review of Ecocnomic Studies* 41 (June): 219–57.

———. 1971. "The Theory of Economic Regulation." *Bell Journal of Economics* 2 (Spring): 3–21.

———. 1982. "The Economists and the Monopoly Problem." *American Economic Review* 72 (May): 1–11.

———. 1983. Comments in Edmund W. Kitch, ed., "The Fire of Truth: A Remembrance of Law and Economics at Chicago, 1932–1970." *Journal of Law and Economics* 26 (April): 163–234.

———. 1988. "Palgrave's Dictionary of Economics." *Journal of Economic Literature* 26 (December): 1729–36.

———. 1992. "Law or Economics?" *Journal of Law and Economics* 35 (October): 455–68.

Stiglitz, Joseph. 1974. "Incentives and Risk Sharing in Sharecropping." *Review of Economic Studies* 41 (June): 219–57.

———. 1989. "On the Economic Role of the State." In Arnold Heertje, ed., *The Economic Role of the State.* Oxford: Basil Blackwell, pp. 11–85.

Stocking, George W., and Willard F. Mueller. 1957. "Business Reciprocity and the Size of Firms." *Journal of Business* 30 (April): 73–95.

Stuckey, John. 1983. *Vertical Integration and Joint Ventures in the Aluminum Industry.* Cambridge, MA: Harvard University Press.

Summers, Clyde. 1969. "Collective Agreements and the Law of Contracts." *Yale Law Journal* 78 (March): 537–75.

———. 1982. "Codetermination in the United States: A Projection of Problems and Potentials." *Journal of Comparative Corporate Law and Security Regulation* 14: 155–83.

Sundaram, A., and J. S. Black. 1992. "The Environment and Internal Organization of Multinational Enterprise." *Academy of Management Review* 17 (October): 729–57.

Swedberg, Richard. 1987. "Economic Sociology: Past and Present." *Current Sociology* 35: 1–221.

———. 1990. *Economics and Sociology: On Redefining Their Boundaries.* Princeton, NJ: Princeton University Press.

———. 1991. "Major Traditions of Economic Sociology." *Annual Review of Sociology* 17: 251–76.

Tarshis, Lorie. 1961. "The Elasticity of the Marginal Efficiency Function." *American Economic Review* 51 (December): 958–85.

Teece, David J. 1977. "Technology Transfer by Multinational Firms." *Economic Journal* 87 (June): 242–61.

———. 1980. "Economies of Scope and the Scope of the Enterprise." *Journal of Economic Behavior and Organization* 1 (September): 223–45.

———. 1982a. "Towards an Economic Theory of the Multiproduct Firm." *Journal of Economic Behavior and Organization* 3 (March): 39–64.

———. 1982b. "A Transaction Cost Theory of the Multinational Enterprise." Unpublished manuscript.

———. 1986. "Profiting from Technological Innovation." *Research Policy* 15 (December): 285–305.

———. 1988. "Technological Change and the Nature of the Firm." In G. Dosi et al., *Technological Change and Economic Theory.* London: Pintner, pp. 256–81.

———, G. Pisano, and A. Shuen. 1990. "Firm Capabilities, Resources, and the Concept of Strategy." Unpublished manuscript, University of California, Berkeley.

———, Richard Rumelt, Giovanni Dosi, and Sidney Winter. 1992. "Understanding Corporate Coherence: Theory and Evidence." CCC Working Paper no. 92-6, University of California, Berkeley.

Telser, L. 1981. "A Theory of Self-Enforcing Agreements." *Journal of Business* 53 (February): 27–44.

Thomas, Craig. 1991. "Public Trust in Organizations and Institutions: A Sociological Perspective." Institute of Governmental Studies, University of California, Berkeley.

Tirole, Jean. 1986. "Hierarchies and Bureaucracy: On the Role of Collusion in Organizations." *Journal of Law, Economics, and Organization* 2 (Fall): 181–214.

———. 1988. *The Theory of Industrial Organization.* Cambridge, MA: MIT Press.

Topkis, Donald. 1978. "Maximizing a Submodular Function on a Lattice." *Operations Research* 26 (March–April): 305–21.

Turner, D. F. 1962. "The Definition of Agreement Under the Sherman Act: Conscious Parallelism and Refusals to Deal." *Harvard Law Review* 75 (February): 655–706.

———. 1965. "Conglomerate Mergers and Section 7 of the Clayton Act." *Harvard Law Review* 78 (May): 1313–95.

U.S. Department of Justice. 1982. *Merger Guidelines—1968.* Commerce Clearing House, *Trade Regulation Reports,* July 9.

United States v. *American Tel. & Tel. Co.,* 552 F. Supp. 131, 136–38 (D.D.C. 1982) aff'd sub nom. *Maryland* v. *United States,* 460 U.S. 1001 (1983).

United States v. *Arnold Schwinn & Co.,* 388 U.S. 365 (1967).

United States v. *Loew's Inc.,* 371 U.S. 38 (1962).

United States v. *Von's Grocery Co.,* 384 U.S. 270, 301 (1966) (Stewart, J., dissenting).

Van de Ven, A. 1993. "The Institutional Theory of John R. Commons: A Review and Commentary." *Academy of Management Review* 18 (January): 139–52.

———, and William Joyce, eds. 1981. *Organization Design.* New York: John Wiley.

Varian, Hal. 1993. "A Portfolio of Nobel Laureates: Markowitz, Miller, and Sharpe." *Journal of Economic Perspectives* 7 (Winter): 159–69.

Viner, J. 1923. *Dumping: A Problem of International Trade.* Chicago: University of Chicago Press.

von Clausewitz, Karl. 1873. *On War.* London: N. Trubner & Co.

von Neumann, J., and O. Morgenstern. 1953. *Theory of Games and Economic Behavior.* Princeton, NJ: Princeton University Press.

Wachter, Michael, and George Cohen. 1988. "The Law and Economics of Collective Bargaining." *University of Pennsylvania Law Review* 136 (May): 1349–1417.

————, and Oliver E. Williamson. 1978. "Obligational Markets and the Mechanics of Inflation." *Bell Journal of Economics* 9 (Autumn): 549–71.

Waldrop, M. M. 1992. *Complexity.* New York: Simon & Schuster.

Wallner, Nicholas. 1980. "Leveraged Buyouts: A Review of the State of the Art, Part II." *Mergers and Acquisitions,* Winter, pp. 16–26.

————, and J. Terrence Greve. 1983. *Leveraged Buyouts: A Review of the State of the Art (revised).* San Diego: Buyout Publications.

Ward, Benjamin N. 1967. *The Socialist Economy: A Study of Organizational Alternatives.* New York: Random House.

Weakliem, D. 1987. "Explaining the Outcomes of Collective Bargaining: Transaction Cost and Power Approaches." Unpublished manuscript, University of Wisconsin, Madison.

Weick, Karl E. 1969. *The Social Psychology of Organizing.* Reading, MA: Addison-Wesley.

————. 1977. "Re-Punctuating the Problem." In Paul S. Goodman and Johannes M. Penning, eds., *New Perspectives on Organizational Effectiveness.* San Francisco: Jossey-Bass, pp. 193–225.

Weingast, Barry. 1993. "Constitutions as Governance Structures." *Journal of Institutional and Theoretical Economics* 149 (March): 286–311.

————, and William Marshall. 1988. "The Industrial Organization of Congress; or, Why Legislatures, Like Firms, Are Not Organized as Markets." *Journal of Political Economy* 96 (February): 132–63.

Weitzman, M. 1984. *The Share Economy.* Cambridge, MA: Harvard University Press.

Weizsäcker, C. C. von. 1980. *Barriers to Entry.* New York: Springer-Verlag.

————. 1984. "The Costs of Substitution." *Econometrica* 52 (September): 1085–1116.

Werden, Gregory. 1986. "Challenges to Horizontal Mergers by Competitors Under Section 7 of the Clayton Act." *American Business Law Journal* 24: 213, 228–29.

Wernerfelt, B. 1984. "A Resource-Based View of the Firm." *Strategic Management Journal* 5: 171–80.

White Consol. Indus. v. *Whirlpool Corp.* 1985. 612 F. Suppl. 1009 N.D. Ohio.

Wiggis, Steven. 1990. "The Comparative Advantage of Long Term Contracts and Firms." *Journal of Law, Economics, and Organization* 6 (Spring): 155–70.

Williams, Bernard. 1988. "Formal Structure and Social Reality." In Diego Gambetta, ed., *Trust: Making and Breaking Cooperative Relations.* Oxford: Basil Blackwell, pp. 3–13.

Williamson, Oliver E. 1962. "The Elasticity of the Marginal Efficiency Function: Comment." *American Economic Review* 52 (December): 1099–1103.

————. 1963. "Selling Expense as a Barrier to Entry." *Quarterly Journal of Economics* 77: 112–28.

————. 1964. *The Economics of Discretionary Behavior: Managerial Objectives in a Theory of the Firm.* Englewood Cliffs, NJ: Prentice-Hall.

————. 1965. "A Dynamic Theory of Interfirm Behavior." *Quarterly Journal of Economics* 74 (November): 579–607.

————. 1966. "Peak Load Pricing and Optimal Capacity Under Indivisibility Constraints." *American Economic Review* 56 (September): 810–27.

————. 1967a. The Economics of Defense Contracting: Incentives and Performance." In *Issues in Defense Economics.* New York: National Bureau of Economic Research, pp. 271–56.

————. 1967b. "Hierarchical Control and Optimum Firm Size." *Journal of Political Economy* 75 (April): 123–38.

———. 1968b. "Economies as an Antitrust Defense: The Welfare Tradeoffs." *American Economic Review* 58 (March): 18–35.

———. 1968a. "A Dynamic Stochastic Theory of Managerial Behavior." In Almarin Phillips and Oliver Williamson, eds., *Prices: Issues in Theory, Practice, and Public Policy.* Philadelphia: University of Pennsylvania Press.

———. 1968c. "Wage Rates as a Barrier to Entry: The Pennington Case in Perspective." *Quarterly Journal of Economics* 82 (February): 85–116.

———. 1970. *Corporate Control and Business Behavior.* Englewood Cliffs, NJ: Prentice-Hall.

———. 1971a. "Administrative Controls and Regulatory Behavior." In Harry Trebing, ed., *Essays in Public Utility Pricing and Regulation.* East Lansing: Michigan State University Press, pp. 411–38.

———. 1971b. "The Vertical Integration of Production: Market Failure Considerations." *American Economic Review* 61 (May): 112–23.

———. 1973. "Markets and Hierarchies: Some Elementary Considerations." *American Economic Review* 63 (May): 316–25.

———. 1974. "Patent and Antitrust Law: Book Review." *Yale Law Journal* 83 (January): 647–61.

———. 1975. *Markets and Hierarchies: Analysis and Antitrust Implications.* New York: Free Press.

———. 1976. "Franchise Bidding for Natural Monopolies—In General and with Respect to CATV." *Bell Journal of Economics* 7 (Spring): 73–104.

———. 1977a. "Economies as an Antitrust Defense Revisited." *University of Pennsylvania Law Review* 125: 699.

———. 1977b. "Predatory Pricing: A Strategic and Welfare Analysis." *Yale Law Journal* 87 (December): 284–340.

———. 1979a. "Assessing Vertical Market Restrictions." *University of Pennsylvania Review* 127 (April): 953–93.

———. 1979b. "Transaction Cost Economics: The Governance of Contractual Relations." *Journal of Law and Economics* 22 (October): 233–61.

———. 1980. "The Organization of Work." *Journal of Economic Behavior and Organization* 1 (March): 5–38.

———. 1981a. "The Economics of Organization: The Transaction Cost Approach." *American Journal of Sociology* 87 (November): 548–77.

———. 1981b. "The Modern Corporation: Origins, Evolution, Attributes." *Journal of Economic Literature* 19 (December): 1537–68.

———. 1981c. "Saccharin: An Economist's View." In R. Crandall and L. Lave, eds., *The Scientific Basis of Health and Safety Regulation* Washington, DC: Brookings Institution, pp. 131–51.

———. 1982a. "Antitrust Enforcement: Where It Has Been; Where It Is Going." In John Craven, ed., *Industrial Organization, Antitrust, and Public Policy.* Boston: Kluwer-Nijhoff, pp. 41–68.

———. 1982b. "Mitigating Contractual Hazards: Using Hostages to Support Exchange." Discussion Paper no. 126, Center for the Study of Organizational Innovation, University of Pennsylvania, April.

———. 1983. "Credible Commitments: Using Hostages to Support Exchange." *American Economic Review* 73 (September): 519–40.

———. 1985a. "Assessing Contract." *Journal of Law, Economics, and Organization* 1 (Spring): 177–208.

———. 1985b. *The Economic Institutions of Capitalism.* New York: Free Press.

———. 1986a. *Economic Organization*. New York: New York University Press.

———. 1986b. "A Microanalytic Assessment of 'the Share Economy'." *Yale Law Journal* 95: 627–37.

———. 1987a. *Antitrust Economics*. New York: Basil Blackwell.

———. 1987b. "Transaction Cost Economics: The Comparative Contracting Perspective." *Journal of Economic Behavior and Organization* 8 (December): 617–26.

———. 1988a. "Breach of Trust in Hostile Takeovers: Comment." In Alan Auerbach, ed., *Corporate Takeovers: Causes and Consequences*. Chicago: University of Chicago Press, pp. 61–67.

———. 1988b. "Corporate Finance and Corporate Governance." *Journal of Finance* 43 (July): 567–91.

———. 1988c. "The Economics and Sociology of Organization: Promoting a Dialogue." In George Farkas and Paula England, eds., *Industries, Firms, and Jobs*. New York: Plenum, pp. 159–85.

———. 1988d. "The Logic of Economic Organization." *Journal of Law, Economics, and Organization* 4 (Spring): 65–93.

———. 1989a. "The Firm as a Nexus of Treaties: An Introduction." In Masahiko Aoki, Bo Gustafsson, and Oliver Williamson, eds., *The Firm as a Nexus of Treaties*. London: Sage, pp. 1–25.

———. 1989c. "Tansaction Cost Economics." In Richard Schmalensee and Robert Willig, eds., *Handbook of Industrial Organization*. Amsterdam: North-Holland, pp. 135–82.

———. 1989b. "International Economic Organization." In Oliver E. Williamson, Sven-Erik Sjostrand, and Jan Johanson, eds., *Perspectives on the Economics of Organization*. Lund: Lund University Press, pp. 7–48.

———. 1990a. "Chester Barnard and the Incipient Science of Organization." In Oliver E. Williamson, ed., *Organization Theory: From Chester Barnard to the Present and Beyond*. New York: Oxford University Press, pp. 172–206.

———. 1990b. "A Comparison of Alternative Approaches to Economic Organization." *Journal of Institutional and Theoretical Economics* 146 (March): 61–71.

———. 1990c. "Markets, Hierarchies, and the Modern Corporation: An Unfolding Perspective." Unpublished manuscript.

———. 1991a. "Comparative Economic Organization: The Analysis of Discrete Structural Alternatives." *Administrative Science Quarterly* 36 (June): 269–96.

———. 1991b. "Economic Institutions: Spontaneous and Intentional Governance." *Journal of Law, Economics, and Organization* 7 (special issue): 159–87.

———. 1991c. "Strategizing, Economizing, and Economic Organization." *Strategic Management Journal* 12: 75–94.

———. 1993a. "Calculativeness, Trust, and Economic Organization." *Journal of Law and Economics* 36 (April): 453–86.

———. 1993b. "Contested Exchange Versus the Governance of Contractual Relations." *Journal of Economic Perspectives* 7 (Winter): 103–8.

———. 1993c. "The Evolving Science of Organization." *Journal of Institutional and Theoretical Economics* 189 (March): 36–63.

———. 1993d. "Transaction Cost Economics Meets Posnerian Law and Economics." *Journal of Institutional and Theoretical Economics* 189 (March): 99–118.

———. 1993e. "Transaction Cost Economics and Organization Theory." *Institutional and Corporate Change* 2: 107–56.

———. 1994a. "Evaluating Coase." *Journal of Economic Perspectives* 8 (Spring): 201–4.

———. 1994b. "The Politics and Economics of Redistribution and Inefficiency." Unpublished manuscript.

———, and Scott E. Masten, eds. 1995. *Transaction Cost Economics.* Aldershot, Eng.: Edward Elgar.

———, Douglas Olson, and August Ralston. 1967. "Externalities, Insurance, and Disability Analysis." *Economica* 34 (August): 235–53.

———, and William G. Ouchi. 1981. "The Markets and Hierarchies Program of Research: Origins, Implications, Prospects." In William Joyce and Andrew Van de Ven, eds., *Organizational Design.* New York: John Wiley, pp. 347–70.

———, and Thomas Sargent. 1967. "Social Choice: A Probabilistic Approach." *Economic Journal* 27 (December): 797–813.

———, Michael Wachter, and Jeffrey Harris. 1975. "Understanding the Employment Relation." *Bell Journal of Economics* 6 (Spring): 250–78.

———, and Sidney Winter. 1993. *The Nature of the Firm.* New York: Oxford University Press.

Wilson, James Q. 1989. *Bureaucracy.* New York: Basic Books.

Winiecki, Jan. 1990. "Why Economic Reforms Fail in the Soviet System." *Economic Inquiry* 28 (April): 195–221.

Winter, S. 1987. "Knowledgeg and Competence as Strategic Assets." In D. Teece, ed., *The Competitive Challenge.* New York: Harper & Row, pp. 159–84.

World Bank Policy Research Report. 1993. *The East Asian Miracle.* New York: Oxford University Press.

Yarborough, Beth, and Robert Yarborough. 1987. "Institutions for the Governance of Opportunism in International Trade." *Journal of Law, Economics, and Organization* 3 (Spring): 129–39.

Zald, Mayer. 1987. "Review Essay: The New Institutional Economics." *American Journal of Sociology* 93 (November): 701–8.

Zucker, Lynne. 1986. "Production of Trust: Institutional Sources of Economic Structure, 1840–1920." *Research in Organizational Behavior* 6: 53–111.

Index